LAWRENCE HENRY GIPSON

AUTHOR

JARED INGERSOLL: A STUDY OF AMERICAN LOYALISM IN RELATION TO BRITISH COLONIAL GOVERNMENT

STUDIES IN CONNECTICUT COLONIAL TAXATION

THE MORAVIAN INDIAN MISSION ON WHITE RIVER

LEWIS EVANS

THE COMING OF THE REVOLUTION, 1763–1775

THE BRITISH EMPIRE BEFORE THE AMERICAN REVOLUTION

THE BRITISH EMPIRE
BEFORE THE AMERICAN REVOLUTION

VOLUME XIII

THE TRIUMPHANT EMPIRE:
THE EMPIRE BEYOND THE STORM,

1770–1776

THE
TRIUMPHANT EMPIRE:

PART I: THE EMPIRE BEYOND
THE STORM, 1770–1776

PART II: A SUMMARY OF THE SERIES

PART III: HISTORIOGRAPHY

BY

LAWRENCE HENRY GIPSON

MCMLXVII
ALFRED A. KNOPF
NEW YORK

L. C. catalog card number: 58–9670

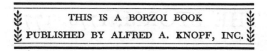

THIS IS A BORZOI BOOK
PUBLISHED BY ALFRED A. KNOPF, INC.

FIRST EDITION

To JERE KNIGHT—*widow of British-American author Eric Knight—for her invaluable contribution to this series over the past nine years.*

Preface

S INCE the formulation in 1924 of the original plan for launching this series on "The British Empire before the American Revolution," there have been certain inevitable changes in its broad outline—all of which, I trust, have enhanced the usefulness of the volumes. It is now necessary to make a further change. As the material encompassed in the present work makes a substantial volume in itself, I have felt it advisable to issue the announced bibliographical guide separately. This plan offers certain distinct advantages to students engaged in research that falls within the chronological limits of the series; for it will permit them to make handy use of the bibliography as a self-contained reference resource, either in connection with the series or in studying the period in general.

The growth of the British Empire over the centuries, its rise in the nineteenth century to its apogee, and its gradual decline constitute an epoch in world history that contains all the drama of a great epic—one divided into two parts by some historians. This series has, of course, been concerned only with the limited period of the eighteenth century that led to a declaration of independence by the Thirteen older North American Colonies, a period which also witnessed the planting of the seeds of the great British expansion that flowered in the next century. For at the very time the more mature North American colonies were in the act of breaking the bonds that had held them to the mother country, in other parts of the world conditions were gradually becoming favourable for the absorption within the Empire of additional lands and peoples. However, in the 1770's except for the initial steps taken by the government of Great Britain to gain indirect control over the activities of the United East India Company and to lay down claims to the Falkland Islands, there is little to record in the nature of British political or geographical expansion. But in 1788 the penal colony of New South Wales was established on the rim of the continental island of Australia as an outcome of Captain Cook's voyages of discovery which had begun twenty years earlier and which led ultimately to British territorial claims to all of Australia, Tasmania, and New Zealand. Then in 1803 the Dutch Cape Colony on the southern tip of Africa was added to the Empire by the Treaty of Amiens with Napoleon. Other acquisitions of territory followed to round out what has been called by some scholars the Second British Empire, as distinguished from the First or Old British Empire that was disrupted by the War for American Independence. Today the British Commonwealth of Nations replaces the Empire.

In 1776 the British dependencies—exclusive of the rebellious Thirteen Colonies—were the Kingdom of Ireland, the Crown possessions of Gibraltar and Minorca, those parts of India that had submitted to the British raj, the slaving and trading posts and the forts on the western coast of Africa, and certain islands in the Caribbean Sea, together with the British sphere of influence in Central America along what was called the Mosquito Shore and, to the north, in the logwood area of what is now British Honduras; in addition there were the Bahamas, the Bermudas, the island of Newfoundland, and in North America the Provinces of Nova Scotia and Quebec and the trading posts of the Hudson's Bay Company in the north as well as the two weak Provinces of East Florida and West Florida far southward. It is these dependencies which will be examined in Part I of this volume, beginning very properly with the Kingdom of Ireland and ending with the Province of Quebec. It is to be hoped that these chapters, used in conjunction with Volumes XI and XII, will help to throw light on certain fundamental aspects of the Old British Empire—among others, its strength and its weakness—as it met the challenge raised by the coming of the American Revolution.

Part II presents a summary of the entire series with an analysis of the more significant trends within the Empire between the years 1748 to 1776, and a special final note covering recent literature dealing with the American Revolution.

Part III is devoted to a series of historiographical sketches. Because of restrictions of time and space it has been necessary to limit the number of writers covered to those whose works seem to have been particularly influential in shaping the interpretation of events within the period under review.

The gathering of materials for this volume has taken me to many places over a period of years. In London I was able to draw upon the vast resources of the Public Record Office, the British Museum, and the archives in what had been the headquarters of the United

East India Company and is now the Commonwealth Relations build-
ing. Other depositories have yielded material in abundance; the
principal ones may be briefly listed. These were the Sheffield Public
Libraries, housing Burke and Rockingham papers; the National
Library and the Trinity College Library at Dublin in the republic of
Eire; the Public Record Office of Northern Ireland at Belfast; the
Public Record Office and Archives at Spanish Town, Jamaica, and
also the Jamaica Institute at Kingston; the Bermuda Archives at
Hamilton; the St. Augustine Historical Society with its useful transcripts; the Memorial University at St. John's, Newfoundland (where
in the vault of the President's office rests a large number of volumes
of transcripts relating to the island); the Archives of Nova Scotia at
Halifax, the Canadian Archives at Ottawa, and the Manuscript Division of the Library of Congress (each of the last three repositories
houses large collections of transcripts as well as original documents).
Other libraries and resources have been drawn upon, especially for
the summary and the historiography, but the full list of research
facilities that have been available to me must be reserved for the
bibliographical work I now have in hand.

For the convenience of the reader, the Index for this volume has
been divided into two sections. The General Index contains data to
be found in the nine chapters of text and the summary of the series.
The Historiographical Index contains references to the material contained in the historiographical essays. Due to the historiographical
nature of the section entitled "Note: Recent Literature on the Causes
of the American Revolution" references to the material there are to
be found in the Historiographical Index rather than in the General
Index.

Before closing, I should not fail to mention my indebtedness to
the Lehigh University Library, which for many years has provided
a centre for this project. Moreover, although the Lehigh Library has
in microprint the *Journals of the House of Commons*, acknowledge-
ment must again be made to Beaver College in Jenkintown, Pennsylvania, for the loan over an extended period of time of a number of
the published volumes. Both the Rockefeller Foundation and Lehigh University have given generous support to this project.

As was true in the preparation of other volumes of this series,
Mrs. Jere Knight as my research and editorial associate has lavished
attention on this volume. She was assisted by Mr. Neal Neamand
and Mr. Lyle Rosenberger, graduate students at Lehigh University,

and also Mrs. Janet Rosenberger. In addition to their other exacting
duties, Mr. Neamand assumed responsibility for the Index and Mr.
Rosenberger made the map of the British Empire as it was in 1776.
Nor must I forget to mention my obligation to Professor John H.
Cary of the Lehigh University Department of History, who read
over the typescript and made numerous helpful suggestions, and to
Mrs. Evelyn J. Evans, my secretary, for the care she has exercised in
typing the manuscript.

                                        Lawrence Henry Gipson

The Library
Lehigh University
Bethlehem, Pennsylvania
February 22, 1966

Contents

PART I

CHAPTER I

IRELAND AND THE AMERICAN REBELLION

Chapter II

MEDITERRANEAN OUTPOSTS

Gibraltar

Minorca

CHAPTER III

INDIA AND THE UNITED EAST INDIA
COMPANY, 1772–1775

CHAPTER IV

THE WEST AFRICAN TRADING POSTS
AND SLAVERY

Chapter V

THE EMPIRE ON THE FRINGE OF THE STORM:
THE BRITISH WEST INDIES

CHAPTER VI

THE EMPIRE ON THE FRINGE OF THE STORM:
THE BERMUDAS

CHAPTER VII

THE EMPIRE ON THE FRINGE OF THE STORM:

EAST FLORIDA

CHAPTER VIII

THE EMPIRE ON THE FRINGE OF THE STORM:
WEST FLORIDA

CHAPTER IX

THE EMPIRE ON THE FRINGE OF THE STORM: NEWFOUNDLAND AND LABRADOR

CHAPTER X

THE EMPIRE ON THE FRINGE OF THE STORM:
NOVA SCOTIA

CHAPTER XI

THE EMPIRE ON THE FRINGE OF THE STORM:
THE PROVINCE OF QUEBEC

PART II

SUMMARY OF THE SERIES

PART III: HISTORIOGRAPHICAL
SKETCHES RELATING TO THE HISTORY
OF THE BRITISH EMPIRE, 1748–1776

BRITISH HISTORIANS

CANADIAN HISTORIANS

AMERICAN HISTORIANS

MAPS

Chronology*

Pre-1761

1495 Passage of Poynings' Law by the Irish Parliament.

1696 Parliament asserts its supremacy over the colonies.

1698 Parliament asserts its right to control the conditions of trade with India and the Far East.

1704 Passage of the Sacramental Test Act by the Irish Parliament.

1709 Formation of the United Company of Merchants Trading to the East Indies.

1713 Treaty of Utrecht.

1718 Spanish rejection of the British offer to return Gibraltar.

1719 Indemnity acts passed by the British Parliament ease the position of Protestant dissenters in Ireland.

1750 The Act of 1750 (23 George II, c.31) establishing the Company of Merchants Trading to Africa as a regulated company.

1754 Moravian missionaries arrive in Jamaica to establish a mission for slaves.

1755 Appearance of Charles O'Conor's pamphlet on Irish agricultural conditions in the peak year of the Irish enclosure movement.

1756 In the Mediterranean, Spain rejects an alliance with Britain as the French capture Minorca.

1757 Appearance of Edward Sexton Pery's pamphlet surveying Irish conditions.

1759 Publication of Adam Smith's *Theory of Moral Sentiments* containing anti-slavery opinions.

1760 The Koromantyn slave uprisings in Jamaica.

---

* It should be noted that this chronology lists certain important background events of both the years preceding and those following the period chiefly covered by this volume (1770–1776). The arbitrary choice of the year 1761 for a more detailed listing is made as an aid to the student in following the thread of the intricate developments. The events within the Thirteen North American Colonies during these years are not included, but may be found in earlier volumes of the series.

1761

April   1   Henry Ellis commissioned Governor of Nova Scotia.
May   19   Thomas Graves commissioned Governor of Newfoundland succeeding James Webb.
            Labrador annexed to Newfoundland by order of the King in Council.
Oct.   22   The initial legislation of the Bermuda Assembly for controlling slave insurrections.
Dec.   7   Martial law is declared in the Bermudas because of the continuing difficulties regarding slave uprisings.

1762

Jan.   20   William Henry Lyttelton assumes his post as Governor of Jamaica.
June   27   The French invade Newfoundland and capture St. John's.
Sept. 18   Surrender of the French forces at St. John's, Newfoundland.

1763

            Uprisings in Tyrone, Londonderry, and Fermanagh Counties and riots of the "Oak Boys" and "Whiteboys" in Ireland.
Feb.   10   Peace of Paris between Great Britain, France, and Spain.
Oct.   5   Montagu Wilmot commissioned Governor of Nova Scotia.
Oct.   8   Proclamation of 1763.
Nov.   21   James Murray commissioned Governor in Chief of Quebec.

1764

            Adoption of a temporary act in Jamaica for suppressing slave rebellions.
June   18   Hugh Palliser takes up his duties as Governor of Newfoundland.
July   The Board of Trade's comprehensive plan for regulating the Indian fur trade.

Aug.   9   George James Bruere begins his administration as the Governor of the Bermudas.

1765

Granville Sharp begins his crusade against slavery.

The Divesting Act (5 George III, c.44) places the Senegal forts and factories under the Crown.

March 22   The Stamp Act (5 George III, c.12) passed to raise a revenue in North America.

Aug.   16   Defeat of the Vizier of Oudh and signing of the peace treaty with Clive.

Oct.&Nov.   Nova Scotia's reactions to the Stamp Act.

Nov.   1   Creation of the Province of Senegambia by order in Council.

Nov.   11   Charles O'Hara commissioned Governor of Senegambia.

1766

Beginning of speculation in East India Company stock.

March 28   Michael Francklin begins his administration as Lieutenant Governor of Nova Scotia.

April   7   Guy Carleton commissioned Lieutenant Governor of Quebec.

April   14   Attorney General Charles Yorke's plan for the government of the Province of Quebec.

June   2   Robert Hope Elletson begins his administration as Lieutenant Governor of Jamaica.

June   18   An order in Council grants 20,000 acres in East Florida for Dr. Andrew Turnbull's Greek settlement.

Aug.   1   Governor Palliser's proclamation restricting fishing activities off the Labrador coast.

Sept.   21   Major Rogers takes command at Fort Michilimackinac and begins to revise Indian trade regulations.

Oct.   Jamaica slave uprisings in St. Elizabeth Parish.

Oct.   9   Lieutenant Governor Carleton's action to gain control over the Council in Quebec.

Nov.   The opening session of the newly established Assembly of West Florida.

Nov.   22   Representation of the West Florida Assembly to the Board of Trade.

1767

Jan.	9	Montforte Browne becomes Lieutenant Governor of West Florida.
May	17	Harry Verelst is confirmed as Governor of Bengal.
June	29	The King's approval of a bill regulating the dividends of joint stock companies advances parliamentary control over East India Company affairs.
July	2	Adoption by Parliament of legislation pertaining to the revenues of the East India Company.
Aug.	19	George Townshend, 4th Viscount Townshend, is appointed Lord-Lieutenant of Ireland.
Oct.	14	Viscount Townshend brings to Ireland instructions to do away with the Undertaker system.

1768

		The Irish House of Commons is reformed by the passage of the Octennial Act.
Feb.		Nova Scotia's reaction to the Massachusetts Bay House of Representatives circular letter.
April	12	Guy Carleton is commissioned Governor of Quebec.
June–Aug.		Arrival of the Greek immigrants at New Smyrna, East Florida.
Aug.	19	The mutiny at New Smyrna.
Sept.	10	Lord William Campbell takes up his duties as Governor of Nova Scotia.
Sept.	28	Plan of the Advocate and Solicitor Generals for the ecclesiastical affairs of Quebec.

1769

		Parliament passes an act to continue payment by the East India Company of a yearly sum in return for preservation of its territorial acquisitions and revenues in India.
		Prince Edward Island (Isle St. Jean) becomes a separate Province.
April	7	John Byron commissioned Governor of Newfoundland.

May   26   East India Company stock panic.

June   The East India Company seeks to effect reforms in India by
            sending a committee of supervisors.

Dec.   4   The Privy Council disallows a West Florida act establishing
            a government unit west of Mobile.

Dec.   26   Lieutenant Governor Elias Durnford becomes acting Gover-
            nor of West Florida.

1770

The great famine in India.

Feb.   1   "An Ordinance for the More Effective Administration of Jus-
            tice . . ." adopted by the Governor and Council of Quebec.

March 20   Prorogation of the Irish Parliament in an effort to break the
            Undertaker system.

Aug.   10   Peter Chester assumes his duties as Governor of West Florida.

1771

Jan.   5   The Bermuda Governor's proclamation for putting down
            marooning and wrecking.

June   6   Hector Theophilus Cramahé is commissioned Lieutenant
            Governor of Quebec.

1772

British troops transferred from the Bermudas to East Florida.

Riots of the "Steelboys" in northern Ireland.

April 13   Warren Hastings takes office as Governor of Bengal.

May   5   The House of Commons debates on the management of the
            African trade.

May   26–   Reports of committees of the House of Commons on the East
June   18   India Company.

June   22   Chief Justice Lord Mansfield's decision sets a precedent in
            the movement for the abolition of slavery within the Brit-
            ish Empire.

Oct.   29   Simon Harcourt, 1st Earl of Harcourt, is appointed Lord
            Lieutenant of Ireland.

Dec.   Parliamentary act forbids the East India Company from sending a supervisory commission to India.

Dec.   6 Solicitor General Wedderburne's report on Quebec.

1773

Jan.   22 Advocate General Sir Charles Marriott's report on Quebec.

May 10 Passage of the Tea Act.

June 21 Passage of the Regulating Act to better regulate the affairs of the East India Company.

Warren Hastings becomes Governor General of India.

July   1 Passage of the Loan Act for relief of East India Company finances.

Sept. 7 The East India Company makes territorial adjustments in India by the Treaty of Benares.

Oct. 15 Francis Legge begins his administration as Governor of Nova Scotia.

Nov. 26 Defeat in the Irish House of Commons of the Absentee Tax Bill.

Nov. 29 Petition of the English-speaking settlers of Canada to the Lieutenant Governor and Council for a general assembly.

1774

March 1 Patrick Tonyn takes up his duties as Governor of East Florida.

April   The war against the Rohillas in northern India.

June   3 Attorney General Edward Thurlow's report on Quebec.

June 22 Passage of the Quebec Act.

Passage of the Quebec Revenue Act.

Summer Hudson's Bay Company explorer Samuel Hearne proves the theory of a Northwest Passage.

Oct. 20 The Association of the First Continental Congress cuts off all commerce with the British West Indies as well as with Great Britain and Ireland.

Dec.   5 Guy Carleton's second commission as Governor of Quebec.

Dec. 23 The Jamaica Assembly's petition to the King professing loyalty to the Crown, asserting the rights of British subjects, and expressing sympathy for the American position.

1775

Irish linen trade heavily damaged by the embargo by the Thirteen North American Colonies.

Feb.   2   West Indies absentee planters and traders to the islands petition the House of Commons concerning the Continental Congress Association.

March 9   The Board of Trade disallows legislation of the Jamaica Assembly for the restrictions on the slave trade.

March 30 Passage of the New England Restraining Act.

April 13   Passage of the bill restraining the trade of the colonies south of New England.

May   25   Passage of An Act for the Encouragement of the Fisheries restricts New England fishermen in the cod fisheries.

June   21   Presentment of the grand jury of East Florida concerning a general assembly in the colony.

June   24   Appeal of the Nova Scotia Assembly for reconciliation between Great Britain and the Thirteen Colonies.

July   11   Col. Henry Tucker of the Bermudas addresses the Continental Congress on the effect of the Association on the islands.

Aug.   14   The Tucker raid on the King's powder magazine at St. George in the Bermudas.

Oct.   10   The Irish Parliament's declaration of allegiance to the King.

Nov.   22   Resolves of the Continental Congress to permit the export of provisions to the Bermudas.

Nov.   27   The decision of Parliament to transfer 4,000 regular troops from Ireland to the American colonies.

Dec.   22   The Jamaican Assembly and Council frame loyal addresses to the King.

Dec.   30   Failure of American forces to storm Quebec.

Post-1776

1777   Collapse of the Greek colony at New Smyrna, East Florida.

1778   An act of the Irish Parliament permitting loyal Roman Catholics to acquire land on the same basis as Protestants.
        The invasion of West Florida by a force of patriots.

1779   Formation of the North West Company by Montreal merchants.
        Spain begins the siege of Gibraltar.

1781   The conquest of West Florida by Governor Gálvez of Spanish Louisiana.
       Passage of the India Amending Act.
       Establishment of an Assembly for East Florida.
1782   The British lose Minorca to a combined French-Spanish force.
       Repeal of Poynings' Law.
1783   Ireland granted legislative and judicial independence by act of Parliament.
       The Treaty of Paris between Great Britain, France, Spain, and the United States.
1784   New Brunswick becomes a separate Province.
       Passage of Pitt's India Act.
1788   Impeachment of Warren Hastings by the House of Commons.
1791   Passage of the Constitutional Act for Canada.
1793   Catholic Relief Act.
1795   Warren Hastings acquitted of all charges.
1797   Minorca recaptured by Britain.
1798   Rebellion of the United Irishmen.
1801   Political union of Ireland with Great Britain.
1802   Peace of Amiens.
1807   Abolition of the slave trade within the British Empire.
1813   The East India Company loses its monopoly of the Indian trade by the terms of the Charter Act.
1817   Newfoundland gets its first resident Governor.
1825   The first Council appointed for Newfoundland.
1832   The first Assembly called in Newfoundland.
1833   Slavery abolished within the British Empire.
       Passage of the Government of India Act.
1837   Revolts in Canada.
1840   Passage of an Act of Union for the Provinces of Canada.
1858   Passage of the Act for the Better Government of India.
1861   The East India Company stripped of power by the Indian Councils Act.

THE BRITISH EMPIRE
BEFORE THE AMERICAN REVOLUTION

VOLUME XIII

THE TRIUMPHANT EMPIRE

PART I

THE EMPIRE BEYOND THE STORM, 1770–1776

CHAPTER I

Ireland and the American Rebellion

O F ALL the parts of the Empire that did not revolt in 1775, perhaps the closest in sympathy with the revolutionary movement in North America was Ireland. Emigration from northern Ireland to the middle colonies took place on a large scale in the eighteenth century. In 1718 over 1,200 people left during the summer months. For years after the famines of 1740 and 1741 the annual emigration was at least 12,000 and in 1773 from Belfast alone it was 4,000.[1] Unlike the movement to Newfoundland of Irishmen, the majority of whom were native Roman Catholics,[2] most of those who went to the Thirteen older Colonies were Ulster Scot Presbyterians. As a group these emigrants were deeply dissatisfied with the British government, were literate, helped to promote the Revolution, and formed a chain of connection with those of their religious persuasion who remained in Ireland. It is therefore not surprising that American complaints against British policies in the 1760's and 1770's were freely aired in the Irish press, with such a paper as the *Public Register or Freeman's Journal* (consistently referred to as *The Freeman's Journal*) giving especial emphasis to the growing alienation of Americans from the government of Great Britain.[3]

---

[1] W. T. Latimer: "Ulster Emigration to America," *Journal of the Proceedings of the Royal Society of Antiquarians of Ireland*, XXXII, Part 4, pp. 388–93; Arthur Young: *A Tour in Ireland* . . . (2nd edn., 2 vols., London, 1780), I, 164; W. E. H. Lecky: *A History of Ireland in the Eighteenth Century* (new edn., 5 vols., London, 1892), I, 247, cited hereafter as Lecky's *History of Ireland*.

[2] For the Irish in Newfoundland see R. G. Lounsbury: *The British at Newfoundland, 1634–1763* (New Haven, 1934), pp. 300–4.

[3] See Michael Kraus: "America and the Irish Revolutionary Movement in the Eighteenth Century," in *The Era of the American Revolution, Studies Inscribed to Evarts Boutell Green* (ed. R. B. Morris, New York, 1939), pp. 332–48.

However, the internal situation in Ireland is what must primarily concern us at this point in the history of the Old British Empire. As conditions in the dependent kingdom in the middle of the eighteenth century have already been considered at some length,[4] we must turn now to later developments.

In 1757 a pamphlet of more than usual interest appeared in London. It was entitled *Letters from an Armenian in Ireland to his Friends in Trebisond, &c. (Translated in the year 1756)*. The pamphlet was, in fact, a tract from the pen of an Anglo-Irishman, Edmund Sexton Pery, who had a distinguished and highly honourable career in public life as a member of the House of Commons of Ireland. In 1771 he was elected its Speaker, a post he held for many years. For his services he was finally given a pension by George III and raised to the Irish peerage as Viscount Pery of Newtown-Pery, Limerick. The pamphlet is important as a survey of conditions in Ireland at the end of the 1750's.[5] Although critical in essence, it was restrained in tone and adhered closely to incontrovertible facts. Among the many criticisms voiced in it was the complaint that while the King of England was also King of Ireland, and a voyage from England took only eight hours to the port of Dublin, the people of Ireland never saw their sovereign. Yet the royal palace in Dublin was much "grander than St. James's in London." Instead, the King was always represented by a Lord Lieutenant whose handsome salary permitted him to live with even more magnificence than did his royal master in London. For example, when the Lord Lieutenant went to Parliament the streets were enclosed and filled with armed troops—a sight seldom or never seen in London when the King proceeded to Parliament.

Pery's pamphlet continued with a picture of how Ireland was administered. To manage the Irish Parliament, the Lord Lieutenant brought with him a Secretary, whose position was one of great influence in government, especially in the Irish House of Commons where he held a seat. Moreover, most of the other great appointments, such as those to the bishoprics in the Church of Ireland and to profitable Court offices, went to Englishmen. The Parliament consisted of a House of Lords and a House of Commons. The House

---

[4] See Volume I, Revised, of this series, Chap. 8, "Native Hibernians and Transplanted Britons," and Chap. 9, "The Dependent Kingdom"; for a map of Ireland in the eighteenth century see *ibid.*, facing p. 186.

[5] A copy of the Pery pamphlet is available in the Huntington Library, San Marino, Calif.

of Lords, with its hereditary nobility and its bishops, unlike its English counterpart contained lay peers who were not men of liberal education or of assiduity, with the result that the chief business in that House devolved upon the bishops. These prelates, by reason of their training and interests were likely to take positions on public matters consonant with the views of the Court. As to the House of Commons, with its membership of three hundred, the writer stated that its chief role lay in exercising the power to determine the nature of the taxes, a power that gave it an importance beyond that of the upper House. Yet the individual members of the House of Lords with their large landed interests and local influence were able to a great extent to determine who would sit in the House of Commons. In order to stand high at Court, the peers were accustomed "to cajole the people" to vote for their friends or for men who shared their views, a practice that, together with the seating of pensioners and placemen, minimized the independence of the House of Commons.[6] Moreover, as general elections were held only after the dissolution of a Parliament by the King, or upon his death, a member of the Commons usually held his seat until such an event took place.

Standing behind the Lord Lieutenant was the Privy Council of Ireland, all of whose members were nominated and removed by the Crown. The Irish Privy Council's function of advising the Lord Lieutenant on affairs of state was especially important in all matters of legislation. A bill when passed by the two Houses of Parliament was sent to the Lord Lieutenant for transmittal to England for royal approval. The Lord Lieutenant, as a necessary preliminary, submitted it first to the Privy Council in order that this body should determine "whether it should be altered, or sent to the King, or destroyed." Commenting on this procedure, Pery observed: "Tho' this be called a free Kingdom, I do not find that the Lords and Commons endeavour to restrain this Council, and to open an Inter-

---

[6] Pery, it appears, rather underrated the power of the peerage to determine the membership of the House of Commons. It was stated that, in the latter part of the eighteenth century, out of a membership of 300 only 66 members sat for counties and 200 were returned from 100 small boroughs; that in 1783 but 72 members were returned by free elections and that 53 peers nominated 124 members and were able to influence the election of other members. Among the peers who had the greatest control of seats was Lord Shannon who filled 16, the Ponsonby family which filled 14, Lord Hillsborough who filled 9, and the Duke of Leinster who filled 7. See *The Irish Parliament, 1775. From an Official and Contemporary Manuscript* (ed. William Hunt, London, Dublin, etc., 1907), Introduction, p. viii, cited hereafter as William Hunt: *op. cit.* See also Lecky's: *History of Ireland,* I, 195.

course with the King; yet the Effects of this Power in the Council are very grievous at this Day."

Pery's last statement calls for explanation. Parliament's complacent attitude toward the exercise of great and even decisive power over legislation by the Irish Privy Council stemmed not only from the accepted restrictions on Irish legislation during the past 182 years—that is, since the passing of "Poynings' Law" [7]—but from the fact that the two Houses of Parliament did not represent the vital interests of the majority of the people of Ireland. Most of them were Roman Catholics who could neither sit in Parliament, vote for members of the House of Commons, hold any public office, nor yet engage in law practice, possess arms, or even secure a lease of land

---

[7] Reference is here made to the famous ordinance of Drogheda passed by the Irish Parliament in 1495 during the reign of Henry VII, usually called "Poynings' Law" (10 Henry VII, c. 4) for Sir Edward Poynings, the King's deputy in Ireland at that time. By this ordinance the Irish Parliament acknowledged that it could pass no legislation unless it had been previously approved by the King and his Privy Council in England. See R. D. Edwards and T. W. Moody: "The History of Poynings' Law, Part I," *Irish Historical Studies*, II, 414–24. Another feature of Poynings' Law (10 Henry VII, c. 22) provided that all statutes of the English Parliament passed before 1495 were in force in Ireland and all subsequent statutes likewise applied there if this country were named in the act. For these statutes see *Statutes at Large, Passed . . . in Ireland: from . . . 1310 . . .* (13 vols.+, Dublin, 1786+) I, 44 and 56 (cited hereafter as *Irish Statutes*) and *Irish Historical Documents* (eds. Edmund Curtis and R. B. McDowell, London, 1943), pp. 83–7. See also [R. French]: *The Constitution of Ireland and Poynings' Law Explained* (Dublin, 1770); for the relation of "Calvin's Case" to Poynings' Law see Sir Edward Coke: *Reports* (1600–1615), Part VII, folio 17. The *Post-Nati* or "Calvin's Case" was of course concerned with the applicability of English law to the people of Scotland. For a treatment of Poynings' Law, and Calvin's Case, see J. T. Ball: *Historical Review of the Legislative Systems Operative in Ireland . . . 1172–1800* (new edn., London & Dublin, 1889), pp. 14–15, 20–3, 38–9 and *passim*. See also Edward and Annie G. Porritt: *The Unreformed House of Commons . . .* (2 vols., Cambridge, 1903), II, Chap. 54, "Poynings' Law."

Although William Molyneux, a highly esteemed member of the Irish Parliament for Dublin University, challenged the binding authority of the English Parliament in his powerful treatise *The Case of Ireland's being bound by Acts of Parliament in England Stated* (Dublin, 1698), the legislative supremacy of the British Parliament continued to go undisputed by the Irish Parliament and was even reiterated, somewhat superfluously, by the Declaratory Act of 1719 (6 Geo. I, c. 5). However, the Molyneux treatise was not without subsequent influence not only in Ireland but also upon American patriot leaders such as Benjamin Franklin; for it was Molyneux who declared (p. 48) that "the liberties of Englishmen are founded on the universal law of nature that ought to prevail throughout the whole world, of being governed only by laws to which consent is given by representatives in Parliament. . . . Are we to be denied this birthright of every English subject, by having laws imposed on us, when we are neither personally nor representatively present?" See footnote 91 to follow and J. T. Ball: *op. cit.*, p. 60. Poynings' Law and the Declaratory Act of 1719 remained intact until repealed in 1782, but in the course of time the procedure governing their application was modified.

for longer than thirty-one years. They also laboured under other grievous restrictions which formed a penal code that kept them thoroughly subordinated to the Protestant minority.[8]

Although as a group the native Roman Catholics were fairly subdued and voiced no demands for political rights, their presence in overwhelming numbers could not be ignored by the minority that held power, which also could not overlook the large concentration of Scottish Presbyterians, particularly in northern Ireland. They too were subject to the disabilities of the Sacramental Test Act of 1704 passed by the Irish Parliament.[9] This act required those holding public office to take communion according to the rites of the (Anglican) Church of Ireland. The passing of indemnity acts beginning in 1719 somewhat eased the position of Protestant dissenters; [10] nevertheless, they were obliged to wait for full relief until the repeal of the 1704 statute during the course of the War for American Independence.[11]

Beyond the inequity of the monopoly of political power by a minority supported by the government of Great Britain, the Irish nation could also complain of economic exploitation. Most of the lands of Ireland, through the process of confiscation and other methods, had during the past two centuries come into the possession of a comparatively small number of great landowners. With the leasing of these lands from the original owners and subsequent subleasing, and with each successive lessee demanding a profit, the lot of the great mass of actual cultivators of the soil was an unhappy one, to say the least. Vast numbers of them were cottiers who had a verbal understanding with the lessor but no actual lease. The cottier might be granted the use of about an acre of ground for a garden and pasturage for a cow or two but, since he had no money, he worked out his rent at a specified sum allowed for his labour.[12] Pery affirmed

---

[8] For a list of English and Irish statutes in force in 1757 that were directed against Irish Roman Catholics see Vol. I, Revised, of this series, pp. 219–20. For a discussion of the relationship between the Catholics and Protestants, based on contemporary writings, see R. B. McDowell: *Irish Public Opinion, 1750–1800, Studies in Irish History* (London, 1944), pp. 10–16.

[9] 2 Anne, c. 6, Sec. 1618, *Irish Statutes*, IV, 22–5; see also J. C. Beckett: *Protestant Dissent in Ireland, 1687–1780, Studies in Irish History* (London, 1948) Chap. 4, "The Imposition of the Sacramental Test."

[10] For a list of indemnity acts passed by the Irish Parliament between 1719 and 1778, twenty-four in all, see *ibid.*, pp. 81–2.

[11] For the repeal of the Sacramental Test see *ibid.*, pp. 82n and 103; for the repeal statute see 19 and 20 Geo. III, c. 6 (Irish).

[12] The most reliable contemporary authority on agricultural conditions in Ireland

that two thirds of the cottiers had scarcely sufficient food to support their toil, and as to their habitations these would "not defend from Rain the Straw on which they Repose." [13] However, in turning to the situation in northern Ireland he presented a much brighter picture. For "the Poverty of the Land induced Industry and Arts, and the Cultivation of these Arts, makes the People of easier Condition and of larger Spirit; it supplies them money, and money enables them to purchase Lands from the Lords, who by extravagance, become Needy. . . . This has produced an Independence there unrivalled by any other Part of the Island."

Why was most of the native Irish agricultural population living under such deplorable conditions? No better answer seems to have arisen at this period than that given in 1755 by the well-to-do Catholic antiquary and bibliophile, Charles O'Conor, of Kilmactrany, County Sligo. In *The Case of the Roman Catholics of Ireland, wherein the principles and conduct of that body are fully explained and vindicated,* published in Dublin anonymously but written by O'Conor, he stated that not only was no encouragement given to an enterprising Catholic tenant who worked the land to improve it, but he was positively discouraged from such enterprise. The lease of the land, he pointed out, was of short duration; and should the one who enjoyed it make improvements, at the expiration of his lease the lessor would be sure to demand a higher rent which if refused would result in eviction. O'Conor, writing as though he were a liberal-minded Protestant, argued that if it were deemed dangerous to entrust "Papists" with large tracts of land, what should prevent "their admission into smaller holdings of one or two hundred acres,

---

in the 1770's is Arthur Young, who travelled in Ireland in 1776, 1777, and 1778, taking careful notes. He estimated that the combined rental of potato land and pasturage per year averaged £3.5.1. An acre of land, he determined, would produce an average of eighty-two barrels of potatoes, as compared to fifty-two barrels in England—the selling price per barrel in each case four shillings and ninepence—or a total of £16.12.6. from an acre in Ireland. He found that while the cottier who operated on these rental terms was well removed from starvation, there were many others from whom greater exactions were made. See Arthur Young: *op. cit.*, II, 109-11. The student will notice, in referring to Young's work, that in his section on the "Labouring Poor" he speaks of the "cottar system . . . which much resembles that of Scotland" (II, 109) and then continues to use the expression "cottar," whereas it should properly be "cottier" for the Irish and "cottar" for the Scots.

[13] That at the time of writing Pery was not exaggerating the deplorable condition of the native cultivators of the soil is indicated by a traveller's description of a typical cultivator's home toward the end of the century. The hovel was some six to seven feet high, with a floor of soil, a bundle of furze for a door, and a "pig as a 'parlour boarder.' . . . 'Their wretchedness and misery is only equalled by their extreme ignorance and brutal savagery'" (quoted by R. B. McDowell: *op. cit.*, p. 33).

upon the same footing with all other his Majesty's loyal subjects?" In arguing for this concession he emphasized the great benefits that Ireland would receive from it. "The work of inclosing, planting, reclaiming [waste lands], and building (the benefits of which are distant), cannot be the proper employment of people who by law have but a transitory interest." In ending his essay he pleaded: "Give your Papists a power over moderate parcels of land, such as is common to all our ecclesiastical conformists, or even to all other dissenters, and the cure is effected. Let them create, as it were, a new country, in addition to the old, by the like power over our pestiferous wastes; and your island from the most sickly gets the most florid face in our western world." [14] Although this pamphlet with its enlightened point of view was widely circulated and at the time favourably impressed both the Lord Lieutenant of Ireland and the Primate, no steps were taken to relieve the lot of the native tenants.[15]

In addition to the grievance of high and insecure rentals of land was that of the forced payment of the tithe levied for the support of clergymen of the established Church of Ireland. This was exacted not only from members of this communion but from all other occupiers of arable land, despite the fact that either as Catholic or Presbyterian they derived no possible benefit from this levy and also that the clergyman was frequently a non-resident. Yet the anger of the peasantry was not usually directed against the clergyman who was to receive the tithe (modest enough as fixed by custom) but against his deputy, the tithe-proctor, who levied directly upon the people of the parish and frequently bore unfairly upon them to his own enrichment. Added to these grievances was another, something that the high profits of the export provision trade of southern Ireland encouraged. This was the enclosing of common lands in order to expand cattle pasturage for the benefit of the proprietors of neighbouring lands.

Out of this enclosure movement arose the great riots of the so-called "Whiteboys," who in the 1760's and 1770's, disguised in white, went about southern Ireland in great bands committing terroristic acts at night.[16] These disturbances began in County Tipperary

---

[14] See *Historical Manuscripts Commission, Eighth Report, Appendix, Part I* (Sec. 2), 445b–7b.

[15] *Ibid.*

[16] For the part played by the Rev. Nicholas Sheeby in fomenting the riots see Volume I in this series, pp. 224–5.

within the Province of Munster, where the rioters levelled enclosures put up around the common land and thereby temporarily acquired the name of "Levellers." The Whiteboys next turned their attention to the tithe-proctors and thereafter to those who had advanced the price of land rentals or who had secured land from the former occupier by outbidding him.[17] The houses of the people whose actions they resented were burned and, according to Arthur Young, those who were considered most obnoxious they took "out of their beds, carrying them naked in winter, on horse-back, for some distance, and burying them up to their chin in a hole filled with briars, not forgetting to cut off one of their ears." [18] In the course of these activities they also terrorized some who had never given offence, by levying sums of money upon them to support the cause or simply plundering them. At one point the Catholic inhabitants of the market town of Ballyragget in County Kilkenny became so aroused at the lawless conduct of the Whiteboys that they took up arms in resistance to an attack and killed a number of rioters.[19] Although stern measures were taken against them, the Whiteboys continued their activities in protest against the abuses of the poor in southern Ireland well into the period of the American War.

The heart of the difficulty was the rise in rentals due to increases in the value of land. In some parts of Ireland, it was calculated, rentals of land were four times as high in 1773 as they had been thirty years earlier; in other parts they had trebled and in still others

---

[17] Hand in hand with the evil of subdividing the land in southern Ireland into small parcels scarcely sufficient to maintain a cottier and his family went the practice by proprietors of great estates of converting their arable land into pasture. The reduction of the quantity of land available for cultivation heightened the competition for each parcel that came up for rental. In 1727 the Irish Parliament recognized the hardship that this placed upon the poor. "An Act . . . for promoting Husbandry in this Kingdom," provided that since "several persons in this kingdom keep great quantities of land under stock, to the great discouragement of tillage, and manifest prejudice to the poor of this kingdom," five acres out of every hundred acres capable of cultivation should after November 1729 be tilled, plowed, and sowed to crops, under penalty of forty shillings for each such acre not converted into arable land. See 1 Geo. II, c. 10, *Irish Statutes*, V, 226–8. But this humane law was apparently never enforced. In a list of laws concerning tillage sent to London by the Irish Privy Council on April 16, 1774, 1 Geo. II, c. 10 (Irish) was listed with the following comment: "This law, though a perpetual one, has never been observed nor attended to in a single instance" (as quoted in Lecky's *History of Ireland*, II, 2n).

[18] Arthur Young: *op. cit.*, I, 82–3.

[19] *Ibid.*, I, 84. Young, who made his notes on this episode in 1776, indicated that some twenty of the Whiteboys had already been apprehended and executed for their crimes and that the gaols of Counties Kilkenny, Carlow, Tipperary, and Queen's "have many in them whose trials are put off till next assizes."

had doubled.[20] An index of the presence of wealth in any country is its ability to increase consumption of imports, especially of luxury items. A calculation demonstrated that the annual value of exports from England to Ireland during a twenty-five-year period before 1748 averaged but £657,972, while from 1748 to 1773 the annual value of these exports averaged £1,482,513.[21] Between Christmas 1772 and Christmas 1773, the value of English exports to Ireland was £1,918,802, an amount almost equal to the value of English exports to all North America during the same period, which stood at £1,981,544.[22] But little of this prosperity reached the oppressed tenant agrarian population. Even among the industrious labouring poor in Ulster there was bitter dissatisfaction.

When an attempt was made in 1763 to advance the tithes in the Ulster County of Armagh to the legal limits, it provoked resistance. This uprising, for such it became, spread to Counties Tyrone, Londonderry, and Fermanagh.[23] The clergy and the tenants each had a case. It would appear that with the general advance in prices the clergy, whose salaries had remained constant for thirty-six years, were much poorer than they had been at the time their stipends were established.[24] The movement to resist tithes was combined with a rising opposition to the requirement that roads should be kept in good repair. Every herdsman, shepherd, labourer, and householder was required to give six days' labour each year under supervision of a roadmaster, or pay a fine of a shilling a day.[25] This

[20] *Ibid.,* II, 332.   [21] *Ibid.*

[22] *Ibid.,* II, 334.

[23] The disturbances began, according to the Earl of Charlemont (then Viscount Caulfield), when Dr. Clarke, the rector of the parish of Clonfeikle in County Armagh, was induced by his agent to attempt to raise the income from tithes due to him from £900 to the legal limit of £1,300. See Charlemont's "Memoirs," in *Manuscripts and Correspondence of James, First Earl of Charlemont, I, Historical Manuscripts Commission, Twelfth Report, Appendix,* Part X, 21-2, 137-8. Volume II of the Charlemont Manuscripts appears as *Historical Manuscript Commission, Thirteenth Report, Appendix,* Part VIII. Thus the Charlemont Papers will be cited hereafter as *Charlemont Mss.,* I or II.

[24] A member of the Irish House of Commons representing the city of Londonderry pointed out in a speech delivered in the House on October 28, 1763, that the salary of a curate, which had been generally fixed at £40 a year thirty-six years before, was in purchasing power equal to only half that amount in 1763. See [James Caldwell]: *Debates Relative to the Affairs of Ireland In the Years 1763 and 1764* . . . (2 vols., London, 1766), I, 68-9. An act passed by the Irish Parliament in 1727 (amending an earlier act for the better maintenance of curates within the Church of Ireland) provided that a curate should receive a stipend of not over £50 or less than £10. See *Irish Statutes,* V, 291-4.

[25] See the act of 1727 (1 Geo. II, c. 13) for "Amending The Highways and Roads in this Kingdom; and for the Application of Six Days Labour," *ibid.,* V, 239-49.

was a reasonable enough requirement in theory but in practice it seems to have been frequently unfair and often oppressive. The determination as to which roads should be built or repaired rested largely in the hands of great landowners who composed the grand juries of counties and who made their presentments respecting the roads to the judges of the assizes.[26] Many roads, according to the Earl of Charlemont, were constructed "merely for the emolument and convenience of particular persons, and by no means with any view to the advantage of the community" and some even "seem to go out of their way in search of mountains. . . ."[27] Called "Oakboys" (or "Hearts of Oak Boys") for the branch of the oak tree worn in their hats, the rioters for a time carried everything before them. Roving about in bands of four or five hundred, they set up gallows before the homes of the clergy and those members of the laity who had aroused their anger and compelled them to swear, in the case of the clergy, not to levy more than a portion of the tithes, and, in the case of those exercising political power as grand jurymen, not to assess the county at a rate more than they (the rioters) had fixed. But under the leadership of Viscount Caulfield (soon to be made the Earl of Charlemont)[28]—he was lieutenant of County Armagh, where his chief estate was located—order was restored. Many of the insurgents were placed in gaol and some of them ultimately executed on the charge of high treason.[29]

In other parts of northern Ireland in the early 1770's the "Hearts

---

[26] *Ibid.*

[27] *Charlemont Mss.*, I, 138.

[28] For additional light on Charlemont, an independent nobleman who sought reforms in administration and was an ardent supporter of the popular cause, see Francis Hardy: *Memoirs . . . of James Caulfield, Earl of Charlemont* 2nd edn., 2 vols., London, 1812); see also *Memoirs . . . of the Rt. Hon. Henry Grattan. by his son Henry Grattan* (5 vols., London, 1839–46), III, 197, and Warden Flood: *Memoirs of the Life and Correspondence of the Right Hon. Henry Flood, M.P.* (Dublin & London, 1838).

[29] *Charlemont Mss.*, I, 139–42. It is of interest to note that Dr. Charles Lucas, a member of the Irish House of Commons and an ardent Protestant, formerly a Dublin apothecary, took the position in a speech delivered in the House on October 13, 1763, that the Catholic Whiteboys of southern Ireland were treated with more leniency than were the Presbyterian Oakboys of Ulster. "It seemed," he asserted, "very extraordinary . . . that the indictments in the North were all laid for high Treason, and those in the South only for a Riot, and a Breach of the Peace." In reply, Solicitor General John Gore denied that any partiality had been shown to the leaders of the insurgents in the south and stated that in many cases the indictments had been for high treason and that several of the accused had been executed according to the statute relating to this crime. At the same time he admitted that there had been lenity on the part of the judges toward those in the south "when Reason and Humanity required it. . . ." See [James Caldwell]: *op. cit.*, I, 47–9. See also H. B. C. Pollard: *The Secret Societies of Ireland* (London, 1922).

of Steel" or "Steelboys" movement took hold. It seems to have begun
in County Antrim on the estate of the Marquess of Donegal, a well-
known absentee landowner,[30] who demanded great increases in
rentals and when these were refused by the tenants leased the land
to others who proceeded to turn them into pasturage. Other great
landowners in County Down and in other nearby Ulster Counties
followed Donegal's example. In the course of the violence that broke
out, cattle pastures on the heretofore arable lands were destroyed, as
were buildings and fields of grain; the homes of those who were
obnoxious to the rioters were also attacked. When one of the rioters
was placed in gaol at Belfast, thousands of people concentrated
upon the town and effected his liberation; other rioters when
brought to trial were acquitted by juries despite the accusations that
they were "guilty of various Treasons and Felonies." At the point
where it seemed to the members of the Irish Parliament that the
movement had begun to assume the proportions of an insurrection
and to have objectives that went far beyond the original grievances
—such as the abolition or reduction of tithes "to what value they
think proper and also to lower and bring down the old rents that
have been of many years standing to what they shall be pleased to
think reasonable"—large numbers of soldiers were brought into the
disaffected areas. Further, in view of the jurymen's manifest fear
that they would suffer vengeance at the hands of their neighbours
should they vote for convictions and their consequent unwillingness
to bring in verdicts of guilty, the House of Commons on December
20, 1771, passed a series of resolves. After summarizing what had
taken place in northern Ireland, these resolves recommended two
measures that would presumably put a check on the uprising. One
was for an act of the Irish Parliament to provide that "all Persons
indicted for offences of such a nature as said Hearts of Steel have
been guilty of, shall for a limited time be tried by juries of some
other county or counties, in such cases where the Grand Jury finding
Bills of Indictment shall require the same." [31] The other measure
would provide that "if the damages such as suffered . . . were

---

[30] According to figures compiled by Arthur Young on the annual value of rentals of
various absentees residing in England, Donegal in the 1770's was drawing £31,000,
the highest amount of any absentee. See *Tour in Ireland*, II, 191. In an "Estimate of
the Rentals of Irish Absentee Proprietors," the value of Donegal's rentals was placed
in 1773 at £18,000. This estimate, made by or for the Marquess of Rockingham, is
among the Wentworth-Woodhouse Papers, R. 3:166, in the Sheffield Central Library.

[31] As previously noted, the grand juries of the counties in Ireland were made up of
large landowners.

levied upon the County or a Barony or Parish of it, this would greatly aid in restoring and preserving peace in said County, Barony or Parish." [32] Two days later a committee was appointed to draft an appropriate bill which in due course was adopted by Parliament.[33] By convicting and executing some of the leaders of the Hearts of Steel, and holding the localities where injury was sustained responsible for property damage, quiet was at length restored—but to Ireland's great and permanent loss. For as a result large numbers of embittered Protestant tenants left Ulster to begin life anew in the American colonies.[34]

In view of the virtual life tenure of members of the Irish House of

---

[32] The resolves were twelve in number. See *The Journals of the House of Commons . . . of Ireland* (20 vols., Dublin, 1796–1800), VIII, 466–9, cited hereafter as *Irish House of Commons Journals.*

[33] The statute carried the title: "An Act for the more effectual punishing wicked and disorderly Persons, who have committed or shall commit Violences, and do Injuries to the Persons or Properties of any of his Majesty's Subjects in the Counties of Antrim, Down, Armagh, City and County of Londonderry, and County of Tyrone. . . ." The act was very unpopular and on October 12, 1773, leave was given in the House of Commons to bring in a bill to repeal it, which was done. On October 29, when the head of a bill for this purpose came before the House it was ordered, "That the Marquis of Kildare do attend his Excellency, the Lord Lieutenant, with said Head of a Bill, and desire the same may be transmitted into Great-Britain in due Form" (*ibid.*, IX, 11 and 19).

[34] For Arthur Young's argument that the rise of rentals was the chief cause of the migration from Ireland to the New World see his *Tour in Ireland,* II, 131. However, W. E. H. Lecky (*History of Ireland,* II, 47–8) arrived at the conclusion that the great migration was primarily due to the falling off of the export of linen. A committee of the British House of Commons which held hearings in 1773 provides evidence (in its *Report* published that year) of the crisis in the Irish linen industry. Robert Stephenson, inspector to the Trustees of the Linen Manufacturers of Ireland, presented figures which indicated that while there was an increase in linen exports up to March, 1771, by March of the following year the exports of linen cloth and yarn had decreased in value by £350,000; that up to the time of his testimony in 1773 the "great increased Stock of Irish Linen unsold . . . has put almost an entire Stop to the Currency of Trade in the Country . . . not less than One full Third of the Inhabitants employed in the Manufacture are turned totally idle, having no other Trade. . . ; such of them as have Money enough to pay their Passage are getting away to America." George Carleton of Dublin, a long-time merchant in linen, confirmed Stephenson's testimony; he stated that during the winter of 1772–3 one half of the looms of Ireland were idle with "great Number[s] of Weavers and others . . . emigrating with their Families to America. . . ." Others also involved in the trade testified to the relation of unemployment in the linen trade to the departure of large groups to America. See *Report from the Committee Appointed to Enquire into the Present State of the Linen Trade in Great Britain and Ireland* (London, 1773), pp. 18, 23–4, 26, together with the valuable Appendix containing various statistics relating to linen trade.

It seems clear that the Ulster Scots emigrated to the colonies for a variety of reasons. See Volume I, Revised, of this series, pp. 226–30; for a fuller account see W. F. Adams: *Ireland and Irish Emigration to the New World, Yale Historical Publications Miscellany,* XXIII (New Haven & London, 1932); also K. H. Connell: *The Population of Ireland, 1750–1845* (Oxford, 1950). For studies of the economic problems facing Ireland see George O'Brien: *The Economic History of Ireland in the Eighteenth Century* (Dublin & London, 1918), and Alice E. Murray: *History of the*

Commons once elected, the House was in no true sense a representative body. As Dr. Charles Lucas pointed out in a speech delivered in the House on October 13, 1763, when a member had been elected to a seat he had "nothing either to hope or to fear from his Constituents; but from a Minister his Expectations may reasonably be great; he will be tempted to oppose the Measures of a good Minister, merely, that he may be bought into his Service, and to sell himself into the Service of a bad Minister for the same Advantage; the Minister also may afford to bid high, when he buys for Life. . . ." Lucas further stated that "this iniquitous Compact" would not take place if Parliament lasted only one year, as was the case at an early period, or even three years, as provided by a later regulation.[35] Indeed, from the time Lucas himself entered Parliament in 1761 as a member from Dublin, he continued to press for a bill to shorten the duration of Parliament.[36] But he was not the only Irish leader who sought this salutary reform; Henry Flood,[37] even more prominent among the opposition in the House of Commons, and the Earl of Charlemont in the House of Lords, both bent their efforts in that direction while also seeking other reforms. For example, they sought to do away with the granting of pensions to those who had no just claim on the public funds, in order to secure a greater degree of independence for the Irish Parliament in line with the principles urged by the influential William Molyneux,[38] and to create a constitutional militia. These injustices, they felt, would be greatly lessened

---

Commercial and Financial Relations between England and Ireland . . . (new edn., London, 1907). For a challenge to the traditional assumption that Ireland's depressed economic position was a result of English mercantilism see F. G. James: "Irish Colonial Trade in the Eighteenth Century," *William and Mary Quarterly*, 3rd ser., XX, 574–84.

[35] [James Caldwell]: *op. cit.*, I, 40–1.

[36] When writing of the Octennial Act in his "Memoirs," the Earl of Charlemont paid tribute to Dr. Lucas "who in every session from his first sitting in parliament had, with a manly and unwearied perseverance, renewed his endeavours towards the attainment of this great point, and whose conduct, influence, and writings had raised a spirit in the people without which all our labours would have been fruitless" (*Charlemont Mss.*, I, 24). See also W. E. H. Lecky's picture of Lucas in *Leaders of Public Opinion in Ireland* (2 vols., London, 1912), I, 41–2, cited hereafter as Lecky's *Leaders*, and R. B. McDowell's view of the influence of Lucas's writings in his *Irish Public Opinion*, pp. 17–18, 25–6.

[37] For Flood's part in furthering the Octennial Act see Warden Flood: *op. cit.*, p. 76; see also Lecky's *Leaders*, I, 41–4.

[38] *Case of Ireland's being bound by Acts of Parliament in England* (Dublin, 1698), a work that—together with Jonathan Swift's *Drapier's Letters* (London, 1724, & Oxford, 1941)—had the strongest influence on the Irish reform and patriot movement. For contemporary Irish pamphleteers and other influential writings after 1750, see R. B. McDowell: *op. cit.*, Chap. 1.

if not completely removed by frequent elections which could bring public opinion to bear on the affairs of state.

Moreover, there was the example of England to encourage the reformers; for, at an earlier period in its history, the English Parliament—as was still true of the Irish—was summoned by the writ of a particular King; its duration therefore depended upon his pleasure or upon the lapse of the writ with his death. But in 1694, in the reign of William and Mary, the Triennial Act (6 William and Mary, c. 2) had been passed; this act provided not only that a new Parliament must be called within three years after the dissolution of its predecessor, but that the life of the Parliament elected should last no longer than three years. Then, in 1715, came the Septennial Act (1 George I, c. 38) which extended the duration of the British Parliament to seven years unless earlier dissolved by the King—an act that is still in force. As a result of the constant agitation in Ireland for frequent elections, and the pressure of county grand juries who introduced this necessary reform in their presentments, the Pitt-Grafton Ministry came to the decision that a bill to this effect should be looked upon with favour. Thus when on August 12, 1767, George, Viscount Townshend, the brother of Charles Townshend, was appointed Lord Lieutenant of Ireland,[39] he was authorized (among other things) to approve a limitation on the life of Parliament in that kingdom.

Such an alteration in the constitution of Ireland was by no means favoured by the majority of the Irish House of Commons. Session after session a septennial act had been presented to Parliament but, in the words of the Earl of Charlemont, "rejected in the commons, stifled in the council, or refused in England by the strength of a great and interested majority, by the efforts of those leaders at whose unnatural influence it aimed a great and deadly blow. . . ."[40] But under the opposition leadership of Flood, the agitation for shorter Parliaments had become a national issue of such proportions that by 1767 the House of Commons felt impelled to pass a bill limiting the duration of Parliament to eight years.[41]

---

[39] See *Acts of the Privy Council, Col. Ser., 1766–1783*, p. 741. Townshend followed the Earl of Bristol, who was preceded by the Marquess of Hertford in that high office.

[40] *Charlemont Mss.*, I, 25. In the general election held in Ireland upon the accession of George III, nearly all the candidates for seats in the House of Commons had been obliged to pledge themselves to vote for a septennial bill. See Lord Edmond Fitzmaurice: *Life of William, Earl of Shelburne* . . . (3 vols., London, 1875–6), II, 92.

[41] An octennial, rather than a septennial, bill was decided upon since the Irish

The Irish Privy Council, although opposed to the Octennial Bill, at length certified it in 1768 and duly transmitted it to the Privy Council in London confident that it would not be returned as approved by that body. In this expectation the members were mistaken; the bill was returned for adoption with an additional clause appended to provide both for the dissolution of the present Parliament and for a new election. These were the terms under which it was brought back to the Irish House of Commons for action. "Detesting the measure with all their hearts, and sensible that in passing it they voted against all their darling interests," wrote Charlemont, "they saw in the exultation of the people the imminent danger of rejection. . . , and were forced by their fears into an apparently heroic act of self-denial. . . ." As for the Irish House of Lords, this body passed the amended bill with unprecedented speed, giving it three readings in one day "as a distinguishing mark of the approbation of this house of that bill, and yet making clear it was not to be drawn into precedent." [42] The passage of the Octennial Act in 1768 may justly be regarded as a great triumph of public opinion in Ireland—one that was to lead in the years to come to other successes on the part of those who sought to give the kingdom a more independent position in its relations with the government of Great Britain.

When Townshend arrived in Ireland on October 14, 1767, his mission included doing away with the so-called "Undertaker" system of government,[43] whereby a few great landowners and controllers of boroughs kept Parliament in line by the use of the patronage at the disposal of the Crown. This system had been possible since it had been the practice of the Lord Lieutenants who preceded Townshend to spend much of their time in England, leaving the business of carrying on the government during their prolonged absences to a small number of powerful men who were commissioned Lord Jus-

---

Parliament met every other year, whereas the Parliament of Great Britain was obliged to meet each year in order to approve an annual mutiny act, in line with the first Mutiny Act passed in 1688 which stipulated that supplies for the support of the armed forces should be for one year only. See 1 Wm. and Mary, c. 5, c. 20, c. 31. The illegality of keeping a standing army in England in time of peace without the consent of Parliament was set forth in the Bill of Rights.

[42] *Charlemont Mss.*, I, 26–7. The act is cited as 7 Geo. III, c. 3, and carries the simple title: "An Act for Limiting the Duration of Parliaments"; see *Irish Statutes*, IX, 504.

[43] For the attempt in the 1750's to do away with the Undertakers see Volume I, Revised, 234–8, of this series. The leading Undertakers during the period under consideration were Henry Boyle, 2nd Earl of Shannon, William Robert Fitzgerald, Duke of Leinster, and John Ponsonby.

tices.[44] It would appear that the growing spirit of independence and self-assertiveness in the American colonies had made the British Ministry apprehensive that Ireland would follow a similar trend unless steps were taken to bind the country more closely to Great Britain. Townshend was therefore called upon to reside in Ireland and to take over the direction of all public matters, including that of patronage. The most powerful of the Undertakers was John Ponsonby, first commissioner on the revenue board, long-time member of the Privy Council, Speaker of the House of Commons, brother of the Earl of Bessborough, and—by marriage to Elizabeth, daughter of the Duke of Devonshire—a great landowner with considerable influence both in England and Ireland. At the beginning of Townshend's administration relations between the two men seemed to be fairly friendly, but this was obviously on the surface.[45] Open hostility was not long in developing when the Lord Lieutenant attempted, as was expected of him, to build up a support in Parliament independent of the Undertakers—something that proved to be a most complicated and, in the end, expensive business.[46]

By the beginning of 1769, all intercourse of an informal nature between the Lord Lieutenant and Ponsonby—and similarly Lord Shannon, another Undertaker—had ceased.[47] Townshend was at

---

[44] See J. L. McCracken: "The Irish Viceroyalty, 1760–73," in *Essays in British and Irish History in Honour of James Eadis Todd* (eds. H. A. Cronne, T. W. Moody, and D. B. Quinn, London, 1949), pp. 152–68.

[45] On November 21, 1767, Townshend wrote to the Earl of Bessborough in England asking him to come to Ireland "in order to conciliate matters." Bessborough replied on December 3 that he had already been disposed to go, had Townshend previously expressed a desire to have him there, and that he had so indicated. "*The only good* that could have been attained by my going there," he wrote, "would have been, to bring about (as a mediation between your Ex. and my relations and friends there) a firm, cordial, and right understanding . . . that you and my relation (my Brother) might serve each other reciprocally. . . ." (Townshend Papers, National Library, Dublin, papers that throw a great deal of light on the Townshend administration in Ireland).

[46] See, for example, the letter George Lill wrote to Townshend from Carlow on April 3, 1768, while "busy with assizes, elections, and canvassing," in which Lill offers many suggestions not only for his own advancement but also for that of others by various exchanges of offices. Townshend Papers, *loc. cit.*

[47] Townshend, writing on February 8, 1769, to Sir George Macartney who had just become Chief Secretary for Ireland, declared: "I have no communication with those Powerful Men whose weight in this Kingdom has enabled them to defeat y⁰ measures of the Crown. . . ." (Macartney Letter Books, 1, Public Record Office of Northern Ireland, Belfast). Macartney was a man of great ability and cultivation. Born in County Antrim, he was educated at Trinity College, Dublin, and then travelled extensively. Sent by the British government to Russia to conclude a commercial treaty, he was highly successful, but declined the offer of an ambassadorship to St. Petersburg. Although elected to the British House of Commons as a member for

this juncture fortunate to have had the support of a Secretary of the calibre of Sir George (later Earl) Macartney, a high-minded man devoted to the service of the King, whose standing remained high in both Ireland and England throughout his long public career. He was the chief confidant of the Lord Lieutenant, and his papers disclose many details of the efforts to break the hold of the Under-takers—those men who had wielded so much power heretofore by creating or increasing the salaries of office-holders and by doling out £116,000 every two years "in Jobbs," which, according to Town-shend, gave them "a weight greatly superior to the anticipated & mortgaged Patronage of a Chief Governour. . . ." [48] With Ponsonby holding the position of first commissioner of the revenue board and Speaker of the House of Commons, the Undertakers in the spring of 1769 claimed they would have a majority of forty in the lower House in the next session of Parliament.[49] When Parliament met in its first Octennial Session on October 17, 1769, the continued power of the Undertakers, supported by the independent members, was demonstrated. A money bill, which had originated in the Irish Privy Council and had been sent to England for approval, was submitted to the House of Commons on the 21st of November and was there-upon rejected in a division by 94 to 71, "because it had not taken rise in that house." [50] To the administration in Ireland, this statement

Cockermouth, he resigned this seat upon his appointment as Chief Secretary of Ireland in order to enter the Irish House of Commons as a member for Antrim. For later events in Macartney's exemplary public career see Sir John Barrow: *Some Account of the Public Life of Earl Macartney* (2 vols., London, 1807).

[48] Townshend to Macartney, February 8, 1769, Macartney Letter Books, 1, *loc. cit.* It is clear that Townshend investigated deeply the Undertakers' practices of granting pensions and places. Among the Townshend Papers in the British Museum is a most revealing one that carries the title: "Remarks on the Extraordinary Pensions as they appear by yᵉ Civil Establishment, 1768"; in this document twenty-nine pensions are commented upon. Another document, "Observations on yᵉ Civil Establishment," of the same year is of equal interest. For example, on the office of Chancellor of the Exchequer held by William Gerard Hamilton in 1763 and 1764 it gives the following comment: "£1200 salary, besides seal £700. A Damn'd job. A great discouragement to yᵉ Country & impediment to yᵉ King's service." On the office of Lord Treasurer, held by the Duke of Devonshire at an annual stipend of £365, the comment reads: "A poor thing, unworthy of a great family, not worth keeping." For these documents see Townshend Papers, Vol. 6, B. M., Add. Mss., 38497:25–8 and 29.

[49] Townshend to Macartney, February 8, 1769, Macartney Letter Books, 1, *loc. cit.* Writing to Macartney on May 18 Townshend sent him the somewhat more optimistic report that out of some 300 members the government would probably have 117 supporters as against 104 in open opposition, 84 who were doubtful, and 4 who were involved in double returns. *Ibid.*

[50] *Charlemont Mss.,* I, 28; the King to the Duke of Grafton, November 29, 1769, *Correspondence of King George the Third* (ed. Sir John Fortescue, 6 vols., London, 1927–8), II, 60.

struck at the binding power of Poynings' Law and the traditional procedures connected with the finances of the kingdom. But, having taken this step, the Irish Parliament now proceeded readily to vote supplies, and to accede to the desires of the British government to augment the army in Ireland by raising it from 12,000 to 15,235 men.[51] Once this was accomplished, Townshend felt it incumbent upon him to vindicate the binding power of Poynings' Law and in so doing to rebuke Parliament for its earlier conduct. On December 26 he summoned the members of the House of Commons to the House of Lords and there not only protested the basis of their action for refusing the first money bill but demanded that the protest be entered upon the journals of the two Houses. The House of Commons refused to do so, but the House of Lords agreed to enter the protest, despite the efforts of some of its members to prevent this.[52] The Lord Lieutenant thereupon prorogued Parliament to March 20, 1770,[53] and by subsequent prorogations did not permit it to meet until February 26, 1771. During the interim a number of the group in opposition to the government lost their places of profit,[54] among them Speaker Ponsonby, the chief of the Undertakers, who was dismissed from his very lucrative post of chief commissioner of the revenue,[55] and the Earl of Shannon, his brother-in-law and fellow Undertaker, who lost his position as master of the ordnance.

---

[51] In order to secure this increase, the government with the consent of the King was led to agree to keep at least 12,000 men in the island at all times and to permit this agreement to be inserted in the bill of supply. See *Charlemont Mss.*, I, 33; see also George Grenville's protest of this concession, made in the British House of Commons on May 3, 1770, and Lord North's reply (*Parliamentary History*, XVI, 948–52). A very good account of the activities of the Irish Parliament in 1769 is given in the *Annual Register*, 1770, pp. 85–90. As the result of the Augmentation Bill Henry Flood no longer pursued his long-time goal to secure the creation of a constitutional militia in line with Molyneux's concepts of parliamentary power for Ireland. See Warden Flood: *op. cit.*, pp. 41–2, and Lecky's *Leaders*, I, 41, 45–6.

[52] *Charlemont Mss.*, I, 28–9. See also *Annual Register, 1770*, pp. 87–8. For Townshend's speech see *Irish Historical Documents*, previously cited, pp. 220–1.

[53] The prorogation of the Irish Parliament caused a great stir. Thomas Allan writing to Sir George Macartney on March 13, 1770, made the following interesting comment: "It is now said the opposition will not take any notice of what has passed in Ireland this winter. I rather believe it, as their Hero Lord Cambden would make but an odd figure if true what is said that it was on his opinion in Council that directions for the prorogation were sent over" (Macartney Letter Books, 3, *loc. cit.*). Camden at the time was Lord High Chancellor; he retained the Great Seal until January 17, 1770, when he disappeared from the Cabinet Council.

[54] *Charlemont Mss.*, I, 29–30.

[55] The revenue board, dominated as it was by Ponsonby, was a haven for sinecures. Thomas Allan—who by the terms of his letter written to Macartney from London on February 23, 1770, was concerned with the financial accounts sent from

There is no doubt that Townshend, acting within the limits of his instructions, had the support of Macartney [56] in his efforts to improve the institutions of Ireland. For example, he sought to place the Irish judges in a position of security and freedom somewhat comparable to the status enjoyed by the judiciary in Great Britian whose members served *quamdiu se bene gesserint* that is, during good behaviour, and were removable only by an address of both Houses of Parliament. In his first address to the Parliament on October 20, 1767, Townsend had stressed how desirable was the independence of the judges in the impartial administration of justice.[57] A bill to this effect, extending the tenure of Irish judges to conform to that of the English judiciary, had been passed and sent to London. When it was returned to Ireland it had been amended by the British Privy Council to provide that the Irish judges might be removed from office only when the Irish Privy Council had so certified, by accepting an appropriate address to the King from both Houses of the Irish Parliament; or when the two Houses of Parliament of Great Britian should address the King asking for such removal. These restrictions on the freedom of tenure of Irish judges by the British Privy Council were resented. As a result, the amended bill was rejected by the House of Commons "not choosing that their Privy Council should interfere with their Address, or that an address of the Parliament of Great Britain should have the same weight as an address of the Irish Parlia-

---

Ireland—stated that a Mr. Jones and a Mr. Millbank (the second, brother-in-law to Lord Rockingham) were both commissioners of the revenue, but that "they never saw Ireland, know nothing of its revenue, their employments perfect sinecures" (Macartney Letter Books, 3, *loc. cit.*)

[56] It is true that Macartney, in the spring of 1770, took exception to the fate of a deserter from the army in Ireland whose execution was permitted by the Lord Lieutenant. The latter, writing to Macartney on April 5, 1770, stated that if "you will cast your eyes over the returns of the army it will be found that lenity hath only been attended with the desertion of at least seven hundred men, & occasioned perhaps more than half that number at Senegal—but allow me to say, Sir George, that you have already heard my determination on this subject some days ago . . . for the good of the service & my duty to my station" (Townshend to Macartney, *ibid.*, 1).

[57] While Townshend had been authorized by the British Cabinet Council to offer this security in general terms, he apparently had gone beyond their intention in his address. Charlemont gives the Lord Lieutenant's explicit words on this point: "I have it in charge from his majesty to recommend this interesting object to parliament, that such provision may be made for securing the judges in the enjoyment of their offices and appointments, during their good behaviour, as shall be thought most expedient" (*Charlemont Mss.*, I, 31). This language was certainly sufficiently general. The British Cabinet Council, however, took serious exception to the public announcement of the proposed change in the status of the Irish judges. The Irish members of Parliament, on the other hand, read into the statement more than Townshend offered in the name of the King.

ment." [58] Also as a result, whether justified or not, Townshend's initial popularity was now undermined.[59] Moreover, Townshend had made a host of powerful enemies by the methods he had used to build up the authority of the Lord Lieutenant and to reduce the control over public affairs previously exercised by the Undertakers. Men who lost their posts sought revenge. Further, as an outcome of his attempts to improve living conditions among the nation's Roman Catholics, he was charged with encouraging "popery as a part of the settled plan of government." In the Dublin *Freeman's Journal* of December 28, 1771, "Hercules," [60] to prove this charge, cited the growth of friaries and nunneries in Dublin where mass was publicly celebrated and festivals of patron saints openly commemorated. In every part of the city, "Hercules" also charged, schools were maintained by "Popish Priests," to which were sent not only the sons of Catholics but even those of "unthinking Protestants on the trifling consideration of convenient vicinity or low prices . . . to the great injury of licenced Protestant Teachers." He especially deplored "the bare-faced insolence, the open parade, and the presumptious magnificence, with which so offensive a number of Mass-houses are constantly and publicly crowded, in the teeth of necessary precautionary Laws . . . made against Popery." He also dealt with the delicate matter of Catholic converts to the Protestant religion. These converts, he asserted:

> "know and pursue their own interest, . . . [which] must be detrimental to Ours; . . . [indeed] it is with no small concern, we behold *Converts* in Parliament; seeing their industry at Elections in favour of Courtiers, and hearing them always vote on the Court-side. Never was a Mortgage-bill or a Lease-bill proposed in favour of Papists till a

---

[58] Thomas Whately to George Grenville, May 21, 1768, *Grenville Papers* . . . (ed. W. J. Smith, 4 vols., London, 1852–3), IV, 296–7.

[59] In referring to the promise embodied in Townshend's address, Charlemont made the following bitter comment: "A recommendation of this sort from the throne is always considered as an absolute and sacred promise from the king, which the viceroy is pledged to perform under the penalty of being accounted either faithless or impotent, of being thought to have wilfully deceived the nation, and to have disgraced the throne by falsehood and imposture, or to have been himself duped and sacrificed by his employers, an alternative which must render him either an object of national resentment and detestation, or of utter contempt" (*Charlemont Mss.*, I, 31).

[60] Hercules Langrishe (later Sir Hercules), an able man attached to Ponsonby, although holding government offices was nevertheless critical of Townshend. Later on he was one of the authors of a volume called *Baratariana*, published in Dublin in 1773, which gave vent to this hostility. It included letters of Flood and Grattan written in the manner of the "Junius" letters. For a comment on the difference between the eloquence of Flood and that of "Junius" see Lecky's *Leaders*, I, 50.

number of *Converts* had seats in our Senate; and if they ever have power enough to carry either of these Bills, we may expect, soon after, the Repeal of all the wise and necessary Laws against Popery; an event which ought to be . . . guarded against, by every true Protestant, every lover of Liberty, every friend of the House of Hanover, every one interested in the Peace and Prosperity of Ireland."

By the time Parliament reconvened on February 26, 1771, the complexion of the House of Commons had been so changed by the work of Townshend and Macartney (in securing adherents in the House of Commons by giving places to some and arousing the hope in others that they would receive similar favours by acting steadily with government) that a motion to address the King to thank him for continuing Townshend in office was carried by a vote of 132 to 107. But rather than present the address, Speaker Ponsonby preferred to resign the office he had held since 1756.[61] His successor was Edmund Sexton Pery, who had proved himself a very able leader of the opposition.[62]

Pery now had the support of the Lord Lieutenant, who also made the new Speaker a member of the Privy Council. Although the government was able to carry its measures through Parliament, the press in Ireland teemed with attacks on Townshend. For example, "Sydney" in the columns of the *Freeman's Journal* of June 30–July 2, 1772, asserted: "Though you well know that your Government is hated, and your Person held in utmost Detestation, you have had the cunning to procure Addresses from a venal Parliament, expressing their entire Approbation of your Conduct, as if the purchased Praises of a few pensioned Slaves contained the sense of the whole Irish Nation." Yet it would scarcely be fair—despite his unpopularity, especially among those who suffered at his hands when opposing his administration—to charge that Townshend was wasteful of the public funds in building up support. The cost of the civil establishment when he took over the government of Ireland on August 19, 1767, was given as £137,753, in comparison to £134,058 shown on September 30, 1772, when he was notified that he was to turn over the office to his successor, Lord Harcourt;[63] the account of

---

[61] Charlemont, very critical of Ponsonby for resigning his post of Speaker, charged him with timidity. See *Charlemont Mss.,* I, 39–40. For Ponsonby's letter of resignation, dated March 4, 1771, see the *Annual Register,* 1771, p. 248.

[62] For a political estimate of Pery as a member of the House of Commons in 1775, see William Hunt: *op. cit.,* pp. 42–3.

[63] The Earl of Harcourt's commission was signed on October 9, 1772; he arrived in Dublin at the end of November.

pensions in August 1767 stood at £86,741 but was only £76,609 in September 1772, not counting an additional charge for pensions "by subsequent King's letters [of] about £5,000"; finally, by not allowing half-pay in the military establishment, as had been usual, this charge in August 1767 stood at £36,481 as against £26,606 in September 1772.[64] Nor is it clear how universal Townshend's unpopularity was.[65] When he left Ireland in December of 1772 there was reportedly "a grand procession to the place of embarkment attended by Lord Harcourt," in the course of which the late Lord Lieutenant "received as great marks of applause from the people as I have ever known given to any man in station however looked up to for popularity."[66]

The administration from November 30, 1772, to early 1777 of Simon, first Earl of Harcourt,[67] an aristocrat of great wealth, was marked by similar evils to those produced by Townshend and his predecessors. Caught in a web of intrigue between the government in England and the rising strength of the Irish leaders, Harcourt

---

[64] "Amount of the Civil Establishments at the Commencement of the Administrations of the following Lord Lieutenants," Townshend Papers, Vol. 6, B.M., Add. Mss. 38497:58.

[65] Townshend wrote not without humour to Macartney on October 1, 1773: "I am like a wreck on yᵉ Coast which is supposed to have some kegs of brandy on board—assailed every moment & trampled on by a most rapacious crew. We have nothing but challengers & low recounters in yᵉ streets lately & mobs following the combatants about every public Place" (Macartney Letter Books, 1, loc. cit.). For an excellent summary of Townshend's "disastrous career" in Ireland, see Lecky's Leaders, I, 43–50.

[66] Robert Waller to Macartney, December 14, 1772, Macartney Letter Books, 5, loc. cit. For the traditional Irish patriot interpretation of the Townshend administration of Ireland see Charlemont Mss., I, 24, 30–1, 35; see also Lecky's History of Ireland, II, 114–16. It may be noted that Townshend, who was created Marquess Townshend in 1786, was honoured with a dinner in Dublin on March 11, 1790, on the occasion of his birthday. Among the fifty people who attended were the Archbishop of Cashell, the Earls of Shannon and Roden, Viscounts Ranelagh and Clonnell, the Bishop of Killaloe and Kilfenora, Chief Justice Carleton, Baron Power, and Lord Montjoy. In his address the Marquess said: "My Lords and Gentlemen. I feel myself much honor'd by your obliging expressions of kindness & esteem and am extreamly sensible of the interest you take in my personal welfare, which I must attribute to my zealous endeavours in executing my Sovereign's most gracious Intentions toward this Kingdom when I had the honor to bear his royal Commission" (Townshend Papers, Vol. 6, B.M., Add. Mss. 38497:80–1). Again on March 11, 1801, once more to honour Townshend on his birthday, a banquet given in Dublin was attended by ninety-four guests with the Lord Mayor leading the list. See ibid., 38497:88–9.

[67] For Harcourt's description of his arrival in Dublin and the departure of his predecessor, see Harcourt Papers (ed. E. W. Harcourt, 13 vols., Oxford, 1876–1903), IX, 43–6; see also Lecky's History of Ireland, II, 116, and William Hunt: op. cit., p. xxi.

may be said to have been a victim of the very system of patronage he served. His instructions directed him to keep a tight watch over all matters having to do with revenue, requests for peerages, and pensions, among other things.[68] But to satisfy those determined to feed at the public trough, as well as his English masters, and to win a majority to his side in the Irish Parliament, he was forced to create new offices and to increase the pension list and the number of peerages. His success in winning over many of the Irish leaders who otherwise would have presented a formidable problem of opposition was primarily due to the highly competent efforts of his Chief Secretary, Colonel John Blaquiere (later Baron de Blaquiere), who was also responsible for carrying through the government measures in the Irish Parliament.[69] Foremost among those brought over to the administration was Henry Flood,[70] one of the first great Irish patriots to seek reforms in the British administration of Ireland. After much intrigue and almost three years of correspondence with Lord North, Harcourt was able to induce Flood to accept a commission as Vice Treasurer and thus a seat in the Privy Council.[71] In addressing the King's minister to thank him for his help in obtaining the place for Flood Harcourt wrote: "I have had the means of doing his Majesty more essential service than I ever expected to have done. I consider the abilities of Mr. Flood as the greatest of acquisitions; and, though they may appear to be purchased at no easy rate, yet, I am inclined to believe, in the course of time, they may prove the means of saving much greater sums." [72]

---

[68] *Harcourt Papers*, IX, 22–37.

[69] Blaquiere had been secretary of legation when Harcourt was ambassador to France from 1768 to the time of his coming to Ireland as Viceroy. For estimates of Blaquiere's ability see Lecky's *History of Ireland*, II, 116, and William Hunt, *op. cit.*, p. xxi; see also, for a patriot bias, *Charlemont Mss.*, I, 35.

[70] For Flood's career see Warden Flood: *op. cit.*; see also Lecky's *Leaders*, I, 35–61.

[71] *Harcourt Papers*, IX, 200, 207, 211, 220–6, 232, 271, 361 and *passim*. For the view that Flood accepted the office of Vice Treasurer not for "personal emolument" but in order to "serve the public" for the good of Ireland in a position of influence, see his letter to the Viceroy dated "1775" and the interpretation of his actions in Warden Flood: *op. cit.*, pp. 93–119, especially pp. 106–8; see also Lecky's *History of Ireland*, II, 140–51, and his *Leaders*, I, 51–4. For the opinion of the Irish patriots that Flood had forfeited his honour in accepting the office of Vice Treasurer, see *Charlemont Mss.*, I, 38–9, 41, 62–3.

[72] Harcourt to North, November 24, 1774, *Harcourt Papers*, IX, 271; see also same to same, October 9, 1775, in which the Viceroy states: "I have, at last, settled everything with Mr. Flood, who accepts of the vice-treasurership. . . . Since I was born I never had to deal with so difficult a man; owing, principally to his high strained ideas of his own great importance and popularity" (*ibid.*, IX, 361–2).

To comprehend fully the political problems that faced the vice-roys in governing Ireland at this period, we must constantly bear in mind the system by which political machinery operated and its emphasis upon places, pensions, and profits.[73] That it was an age when patronage was the commonly accepted privilege of the nobility and of those in power is clearly attested by the record of Lord Harcourt's administration in Ireland.[74] His most serious problem was that expenditures were outrunning revenues.[75] Some means had to be found to bridge the gap. Harcourt planned certain economies to place before Parliament when it should meet on October 12, 1773, but they were insufficient for the needs.[76]

Blaquiere now proposed to the Irish House of Commons that a tax be imposed on the rentals of absentee landlords—a project long held to be of the highest importance by Henry Flood and other Irish patriots.[77] The incomes derived in Ireland on the part of absentees in the 1770's totalled £732,700.[78] But when the news of this pro-

---

[73] An analysis of the political ethics of eighteenth-century Ireland may be found in R. B. McDowell: *op. cit.*, Chap. 2.

[74] See *Harcourt Papers*, IX and X, *passim*. For a succinct analysis of the Irish Parliament and the political system surrounding it in the eighteenth century, see William Hunt: *op. cit.*, Introduction and Appendix to "The Manuscript concerning the Irish Parliament, 1775." The "Manuscript" is an alphabetical list of all the members of Parliament, showing their political disposition together with what places and pensions they had received from the government. Hunt deduces that this "political stock-taking" may be attributed to Blaquiere and that it was drawn up to serve as a guide for dispensing future favours. A similar list, although for an earlier date, is to be found in *Harcourt Papers*, X, 287–371; another, edited by M. Bodkin, "Notes on the Irish Parliament in 1773," (Royal Irish Academy *Proceedings*, XLVII–XLIX, Sec. C.) challenges Hunt's conclusions on Blaquiere's authorship of the 1775 list; while still another, "Contemporary Sketches of the Members of the Irish Parliament in 1782" (ed. G. O. Sayles, *ibid.*, LVI, Sec. C. No. 3), in turn questions Bodkin's arguments while stating conclusively that Blaquiere did not draw up the 1782 list, in which he himself is characterized (p. 236) as "a man of much cabal: and therefore worth managing, which is to be done by a little flattery and attention." All these documents give insight into the structure of Irish politics in the eighteenth century and lead this author to agree with G. O. Sayles's conclusion that the field is ripe for an exhaustive scholarly examination.

[75] By April 24, 1773, Harcourt was writing to Lord North that "the arrears upon the establishment by next Christmas will not fall short of £300,000," and begging him to seek a delay in granting a pension of £3,000 a year to the King's sister, the former Queen of Denmark. See *Harcourt Papers*, IX, 70.

[76] See William Hunt: *op. cit.*, xxii–iii. Although Harcourt was successful in reuniting the revenue boards, which Townshend had divided, this popular action alone resulted in the payment of pensions amounting to £3,600 to the revenue officers eliminated in the process. See Harcourt to North, October 3 and November 9, 1773, *Harcourt Papers*, IX, 71 and 94; see also *Irish House of Commons Journal*, XVI, 344.

[77] See *Charlemont Mss.*, I, 36–7.

[78] The Arthur Young list, which included the names of 195 absentee landlords, was headed by Lord Donegal, who received £31,000; the Duke of Devonshire, the Earl

posal reached England there was great agitation among these absentees, who bitterly opposed the tax.[79] On October 16, 1773, five leading absentees: the Duke of Devonshire, the Marquess of Rockingham, and the Earls of Bessborough, Milton, and Upper Ossory, addressed a letter to Lord North.[80] They stressed the injustice of such a measure. Among other things they declared, referring to residence in England: "We have not hitherto considered such Residence as an Act of Delinquency to be punished, or as a political Evil to be corrected by the penal Operation of a partial Tax." Further, they continued: "We cannot avoid considering this Scheme in the highest Degree injurious to the Welfare of that Kingdom as well as of this. Its manifest tendency is to lessen the value of all landed property there; to put Restrictions upon it unknown in any part of the British Dominions, and, as far as we can find, without parallel in any civilized Country. It leads directly to a Separation of these Kingdoms in Interest and affection, contrary to the standing policy of our ancestors. . . ." In his reply on October 21, 1773, Lord North stated that the Lord Lieutenant had submitted during the summer certain propositions for putting the finances of Ireland on a proper footing, among which was the proposed tax. That in return His Majesty's servants had stated that "if the Irish Parliament should send over to England such a plan, as should appear to be well-calculated to give effectual relief to Ireland in its present distress,

---

of Shelburne, and the Earl of Milton each obtained £18,000; the Dowager Lady Shelburne, £15,000; the Marquess of Rockingham, £14,000; Lord Bessborough, £10,000; the Lord of Upper Ossory, £6,000; continuing down to lesser amounts we come to Colonel Barré with £600, and Edmund Burke with £500. Young states that in compiling the list he was able to correct an earlier list produced by a Mr. Morris with the aid of "a variety of persons living in the neighbourhood of many of the respective estates." See his *Tour in Ireland*, II, 190–3.

[79] There is a great mass of correspondence relating to the absentee tax among the Rockingham Manuscripts; it will be found listed in the Wentworth-Woodhouse Papers, R. 3:5–165. See also Rochford to Harcourt, October 22, 1773, marked "Private and Secret," in which the Secretary of State advised: ". . . all the Lords and gentlemen in opposition here are determined to go to every length to mar, if possible, the absentee tax . . ." (*Harcourt Papers*, IX, 76). North himself on October 29, 1773, wrote to Harcourt: "The cry is universal against it . . . in short it is nearly as unpopular here as it is popular on your side of the water" (*ibid.*, IX, 80).

[80] The letter, it seems, was written by Burke, one of the lesser absentees. See T. H. D. Mahoney: *Edmund Burke and Ireland* (Cambridge, Mass., 1960), pp. 50–8, which vindicates Burke's opposition to the tax. A copy of this letter is among the Wentworth-Woodhouse Papers, listed as R. 3:138. It can be found in print in *Memoirs of the Marquis of Rockingham* . . . (ed. George Thomas, Earl of Albemarle, 2 vols., London, 1852), II, 227, and also—together with replies to the Duke of Devonshire from Lord North—in *Gentleman's Magazine*, XLIII, 602–3, and *Harcourt Papers*, IX, 86–90. See also "A Letter from the Marquis of Rockingham [November 19, 1773] to Sir William Mayne on the Proposed Absentee Tax of 1773," ed. J. E. Tyler, *Irish Historical Studies*, VIII, No. 32, 362–9.

their opinion would be, that it ought to be carried into execution although the tax upon absentees should be a part of it." [81] But the opposition became so great not only in England [82] but also in Ireland —especially among those landowners, it would appear, who were led to feel that the absentee tax would be but a preliminary step to a general Irish land tax—that when the measure was presented to the Irish House of Commons on November 25 it was debated until 2 o'clock the next morning, only to be defeated by a vote of 120 to 106. [83]

With the failure of the absentee tax—again defeated when a second attempt was made to bring it forward during which "Mr. Flood was violent and able in behalf of the bill, in a degree almost surpassing everything he had ever uttered before" [84]—there was an urgent need for some means of raising funds. The national debt by March 25, 1773, stood at £999,686. [85] Accordingly, bills for tontine annuities and stamp duties were introduced. As supply bills they had to be approved in London, but they were materially changed there before their return to Ireland. By December 30, Harcourt wrote to Lord Rochford that "the House was in such a flame last Friday evening, when the tontine and stamp bills received a first reading after their return from England, that it required great management to restrain them from proceeding to acts of intemperance, and rejecting them with precipitation." [86] However, so great was the

[81] See Wentworth-Woodhouse Papers, R. 3:142.

[82] For the lengthy correspondence between Harcourt and North in October and November 1773 over the absentee tax, see *Harcourt Papers*, IX, 80–106, in which the chief minister also makes it plain that regulation of the corn bounty should be a concomitant of the tax bill.

[83] See the circular letter, No. 3, from Rockingham to those opposed to the absentee tax, dated December 1, 1773, Wentworth-Woodhouse Papers, R. 3:156. A very detailed description of the debate in the Irish House of Commons and of the position taken by various members is to be found among the Macartney Letter Books (4, *loc. cit.*) in a letter to Macartney written from Dublin on November 27, 1773, by one of his friends and former supporters in Ireland, George Lill. Harcourt's account of the voting sent to Lord North on November 26, 1773 (apparently within hours after the final vote) speaks of the original question being put in terms of a tax on land of one shilling on the pound—which was defeated by 119 to 107—and of a second question put by Silver Oliver on the basis of two shillings on the pound, vehemently supported by Flood and others but also defeated by a vote of 120 to 106. See *Harcourt Papers*, IX, 110. For diverse accounts of the vote see Warden Flood: *op. cit.*, p. 90; see also the *Gentleman's Magazine*, XLIII, 615–16, which gives the same results of the vote as Harcourt, but adds that it took place as an action of the committee of the whole House of the Irish Commons; see also Lecky's *History of Ireland*, II, 130–2, and William Hunt: *op. cit.*, xxiv–v.

[84] Harcourt to North, November 27 and 30, 1773, *Harcourt Papers*, IX, 115–19.

[85] *Irish House of Commons Journal*, XVI, 249.

[86] *Harcourt Papers*, IX, 142–3 and 144.

influence of the administration—although Harcourt himself appears to have agreed with the Irish leaders that the action in England had been unwarranted—that the Commons, after rejecting the bills as returned, passed virtually the same measures under different titles.[87] Such was the temper of the Irish Parliament by 1774, a year in which the Viceroy worked in close association not only with the members of the Irish House of Commons but also with Lord North and Lord Rochford, keeping in mind his instructions to relieve the hereditary revenue of the King.[88] For the co-operation which he received Harcourt was determined to make reward, and it was at this period that he devoted great energy to finding places for such Irish leaders as Hely Hutchinson and Henry Flood. That his Chief Secretary, Sir John Blaquiere, had a large part in all these efforts is made clear by Harcourt himself in his reports to Lord North on what had been accomplished.[89]

By January 19, 1775, Blaquiere, in London, was sending Lord Harcourt accounts of the action taken in the House of Commons on the American papers.[90] The importance of the American crisis was becoming increasingly apparent as the Continental Association for non-importation and non-exportation took its toll of the Irish economy, already in a sad state, especially in the linen trade, the chief commerce between Ireland and the American colonies.[91] With the

---

[87] Ibid., IX, 146–51, 155, 157, 163–4, 167–8. See also Lecky's: History of Ireland, II, 132–3.

[88] See Lord North's instructions to Harcourt of December 9, 1773: "to improve the public revenue by saving and by better management, to avail the Crown of the expired pensions by avoiding, if possible, the grant of new ones; to defend the hereditary revenue, and to prevent the [revenue] board from recovering that power and patronage which was so grossly abused before the separation of the excise from the customs" (Harcourt Papers, IX, 132–3). This was in reply to Harcourt's communication to North showing the annual deficit as of December 6, 1773, to be some £138,840, which he proposed to make up by duties on stamps, wine, bread, teas, cards, coaches, and muslin to the extent of £88,800; by savings on reuniting the revenue board, parliamentary grants, and stationery in the House of Commons; and by the establishment of writs of assistance in aid of the revenue officers to the extent of £50,000. See ibid., IX, 123–4.

[89] Ibid., IX, passim, and X, 161.

[90] Ibid., IX, 291.

[91] In this connection it is interesting to note that Benjamin Franklin—apparently intrigued by the works of Molyneux and other Irish writers—visited Ireland in 1771, at which time he was impressed by the advantages and disadvantages of that kingdom (Writings of Benjamin Franklin [ed. A. H. Smyth, 10 vols., New York, 1905–7], V, 205 and 255; The Works of Benjamin Franklin [ed. Jared Sparks, 10 vols., Boston, 1836–40], VII, 557–8). As a result he wrote to his son, the Governor of New Jersey, on June 30, 1774, "I should be sorry if Ireland is included in your agreement, because that country is much our friend, and the want of flax-seed may distress them exceedingly" (Writings [Smyth], X, 274). For the subsequent action taken by the Committee of Trade of the Continental Congress in the fall of 1775 to

outbreak of the American War for Independence, Ireland was divided in sentiment. John Ridge, a well-informed Dublin lawyer and one of Burke's most trusted friends, writing to the latter on September 25, 1775, made the following comment: "All the Protestants, as far as I can see, especially the Presbyterians, except a few who have connexions in the army at Boston & a few military Generals are, here with us, friends to the American cause. The Roman Catholics, who receive no favours, no quarter, from their fellow subjects of a different persuasion & are indebted to Government for some lenity in the execution of the laws against them & have no liberty, . . . are ready to give their beggarly assent to Government." [92] Yet when the Irish Parliament opened on the 10th of October of that year, in reply to the speech from the throne delivered by the Lord Lieutenant in the name of the King, according to Harcourt:

> "The House of Commons agreed to a resolution upon a division of something more than two to one, declaring their allegiance to his Majesty, and their abhorrence of the American rebellion. . . . The debate was conducted with great vehemence on the part of Opposition, which was composed of M^r. Ponsonby's and the Duke of Leinster's followings, and a few country members. Our majority consisted of the most respectable people, and the debate mostly, if not entirely, conducted by Sir John Blaquiere and M^r. Scott, whose

---

permit the exportation of flaxseed to Ireland in return for whatever military stores and wool might be obtained from that country, see *Journals of the Continental Congress*, III, 269. It should not be overlooked that there was also some trade in Irish provisions —that is, barrelled beef, pork, and butter—to the British North American colonies (although, of course, the most important Irish provision trade was to the West Indies), as well as some other Irish commodities such as candles, fishing tackle, Kilkenny marble, soap, yarn, ink, among others. In return, the Irish legally and directly imported, in addition to flaxseed, large quantities of barrel staves and some wheat, flour, rum, and lumber, for which the colonies received much needed money. They also imported through Britain substantial amounts of sugar and tobacco, in addition to sizeable stores of tobacco and rum smuggled into the country, some undoubtedly from America. See F. G. James's concise but important study of "Irish Colonial Trade in the Eighteenth Century," *William and Mary Quarterly*, 3rd ser., XX, 574–84.

[92] The letter is among the Fitzwilliam (so-called Milton) Manuscripts now at Lamport Hall, Northamptonshire, England. However, on September 30, 1775, a "Letter from some of the principal Roman Catholics in Ireland addressed to Sir John Blaquiere" offered the fullest assistance, including "two million of loyal, faithful, and affectionate hearts and hands, unarmed indeed, but zealous, ready, and desirous to exert themselves strenuously in defence of his Majesty's most sacred person and government, against all his enemies of what denomination soever, in any part of the world where they may be." This was signed by ten men. See *Harcourt Papers*, IX, 357–8.

zeal and whose abilities are so well known to your Lordship that I shall not add another word." [93]

In the face of this support, the administration on November 23 proposed that to aid in crushing the American revolt, 4,000 of the 12,000 troops stationed in Ireland should be withdrawn and replaced by foreign Protestants without expense to the country. On the 25th this proposal was debated in the House of Commons. Although the withdrawal was approved, the foreign replacements were finally refused.[94]

Such Irishmen as Edmund Burke were horrified at these steps. Writing to Charles O'Hara, a member of the Irish House of Commons, Burke said:

> "Our conduct [of the Parliament of Great Britain] to America, though wicked and foolish, yet is natural wickedness and folly; yours is a species of Turpitude not decent to name. Your Conduct has this aggravation in it, that you had a part assigned you by providence to act, that rarely, if ever happens to a nation, rarely indeed to mankind; you were in the situation, in which you might act as the Guardian Angels of the whole Empire; and without hazard, or danger, or scarcely trouble, have appeared in mediatorial Character of the utmost dignity and Benevolence; and with all certainty, at once have secured your own Liberties and given peace to our general Country." [95]

While it is beyond the scope of this series to examine the events after 1775, it may be stated that the loyalty of Ireland to the King resulted in some dividends, as slow but vastly important changes

---

[93] Harcourt to North, October 11, 1775, *ibid.*, IX, 362–4, in which the Viceroy also refers with pride to his decisive part in managing the decision in spite of "the Presbyterians in the North, who, in their hearts, are Americans . . . gaining strength every day; and letters . . . sent over to encourage Ireland to take an adverse part in the contest." See also *Irish House of Commons Journal*, IX, 172.

[94] The debate on November 25 in the committee of the whole House was one of great intensity with large numbers participating on both sides. In the division over sparing 4,000 of the defence troops the vote was 121 against 76; on the 27th the committee of the whole House voted 106 to 68 against accepting the offer of the same number of foreign troops. The vote of the House accepting the two resolutions as passed in the committee of the whole House was 103 to 58. See Harcourt to North, November 26, 1775, *Harcourt Papers*, X, 32–3. See also Hunt: *op. cit.*, Appendix, pp. 81–2. The debates in the Irish House of Commons on November 25 and 27, 1775, are to be found in Peter Force: *American Archives*, 4th ser., III, 1642–50.

[95] *Correspondence of Edmund Burke* (ed. G. H. Guttridge, Cambridge & Chicago, 1961), III, 243–7; see also Burke to O'Hara, January 7, 1776, in R. J. S. Hoffman: *Edmund Burke, New York Agent . . . and intimate correspondence with Charles O'Hara, 1761–1776* (American Philosophical Society *Memoirs*, Vol. XIL, Philadelphia, 1956), pp. 612–15.

developed in the attitudes of British statesmen toward Irish aspirations as a nation within the Empire. In 1778 the Irish Parliament was permitted to pass an act by which loyal Roman Catholics could lease or purchase lands upon the same basis as Protestants. Also in that year came the formation of the Protestant Volunteers of Ireland, a movement quite independent of the Crown, which neither supported nor opposed it. In the first instance these volunteers were organized to ward off a threatened invasion of Ireland by France, now at war with Great Britian and the Empire. With 80,000 men ultimately under arms and in uniform, led by such an important figure as the Earl of Charlemont in the post of Commander-in-Chief, they became a powerful lever. In 1782, the war against the Thirteen Colonies now lost, a convention of delegates from the corps of these Irish volunteers resolved that the claims of any other than "the King, Lords, and Commons of Ireland was unconstitutional, illegal, and a grievance." In response to this protest the Parliament of Great Britain the following year passed the statute (23 George III, c. 28): "An Act . . . concerning the exclusive Rights of the Parliament and Courts of Ireland, in Matters of Legislation and Judicature; and for preventing any Writ of Error or Appeal from any of his Majesty's Courts in that Kingdom from being received . . . in any of his Majesty's Courts in the Kingdom of Great Britain," thereby granting legislative and judicial independence to Ireland under the Crown in internal matters—a step largely due to the leadership of Henry Grattan and Henry Flood. In 1793 the Catholic Relief Act was a move forward for the Catholics, who could now bear arms, vote as forty-shilling freeholders, accept membership in corporations, and act as grand jurors, although still excluded from Parliament and those offices which required taking the sacrament or were restricted by the anti-Roman Catholic declaration of 1692. But the people of Ireland were so deeply dissatisfied with their unrepresentative and corrupt Parliament that in 1798 under Wolfe Tone a rebellion of the United Irishmen took place; this was followed in 1801 by a political union with Great Britain that was to last until well into the twentieth century.[96]

---

[96] In addition to the great work of Lecky on Ireland during the period under consideration, and other works already cited, see also J. A. Froude: *The English in Ireland in the Eighteenth Century* (3 vols., London, 1872 & 1874, also 1881 edn.), Robert Dunlop: "Ireland in the Eighteenth Century," *Cambridge Modern History,* VI, Chap. 14, Edmund Curtis: *A History of Ireland* (London, 1936), and J. G. S. MacNeill: *Constitutional and Parliamentary History of Ireland till the Union* (Dublin, 1917).

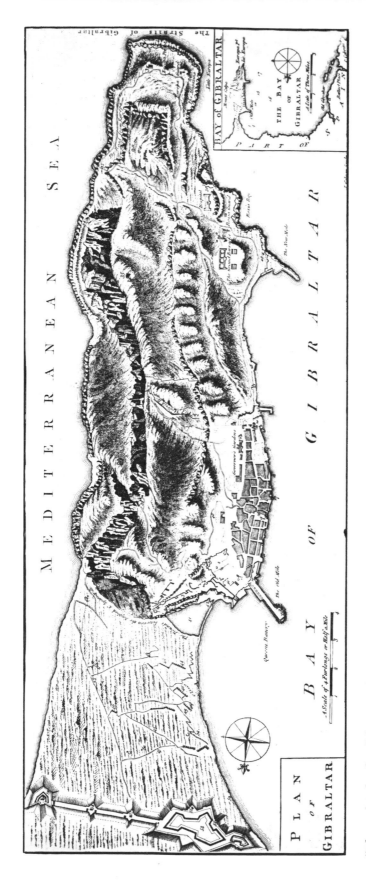

(From *Gentleman's Magazine*, March 1762)

"Plan of Gibraltar" by J. Gibson

CHAPTER II

Mediterranean Outposts

Gibraltar

DESPITE the new military factor of air power, Gibraltar, from its cession by Spain in the Treaty of Utrecht of 1713 to the present, has remained one of Great Britain's prize possessions.[1] Likewise, for over two hundred and fifty years its repossession has been an objective that Spain has sought vainly to achieve, either by peaceful or warlike means.[2] In the words of one scholar, "Gibral-

---

[1] For an excellent study of the circumstances under which Great Britain was able to secure Gibraltar and Minorca see Stetson Conn: *Gibraltar in British Diplomacy in the Eighteenth Century* (New Haven, 1942), Chap. 1, "The English Acquisition of Gibraltar."

[2] For consideration of Gibraltar in earlier volumes of this series see Volume VI, 400–1, 406–7, 425–6; Volume VIII, 11–13, 228, 237, 254. As recently as September 23, 1964, a debate took place in the United Nations Commission on Colonialism when Spain sought the support of this body in reclaiming Gibraltar. At that time Mayor Hidalgo of San Roque in Spain opposed the idea of permitting the people of Gibraltar to vote whether to remain under British rule or to accept Spanish dominion. His position was that the only *true* Gibralterians were the descendants of those who had fled from the Rock (chiefly to nearby San Roque) when Gibraltar was occupied by the English and the Dutch in 1704 in the midst of the War of the Spanish Succession. However, Mayor Hassan of Gibraltar the following day strongly supported the idea of permitting its present residents to decide their allegiance, since earlier in 1964 they had been granted the right of internal self-government. As to Great Britain's attitude, the British government stated in October that it was prepared to discuss with the Spanish government the easing of tensions but not the question of Gibraltar's sovereignty. As a result, the Spanish government in November tightened the customs controls on the only land route between Gibraltar and Spain: see the issues of the *New York Times* (1964) for September 23, p. 15; September 24, p. 3; September 25, p. 11; October 20, p. 17; and November 6, p. 28. Since this time the frontier has been virtually closed. Further, Spain has issued a so-called "Red Book" of 600 pages in which its claims to the Rock are set forth at great length. On December 16, 1965, a United Nations General Assembly resolution "invited" Great Britain and Spain to reach a solution that would be "in the interests of the people of Gibraltar." So far as the 25,000 or so inhabitants are concerned, in their present frame of mind they want neither to come under Spanish control nor to become an independent state—a

tar served as the principal European focus of Anglo-Spanish enmity in the eighteenth century." [3] The terms under which it was acquired provided that there should be religious freedom for those of the Roman Catholic faith, that neither Jews nor Moors should settle in the place, and that no Moorish ships of war enter the harbour (. . . *ut nec Iudaeis, neque Mauris Facultas concedatur in dictâ Urbe Gibraltaricâ sub quocunque praetextu commorandi, . . . neque receptaculum pateat Maurorum Navibus bellicis quibuscunque in Portu distae Urbis . . .).* [4] The question of the bounds of Gibraltar continued to be a problem. Until the signing of the peace the whole isthmus, at the terminus of which the great fortress is located, was under British occupation. In the course of the negotiations the British sought to retain that part of the neck of land extending to a distance of two cannon shots beyond the walls of the fort. The Spaniards, however, held firmly to the position that the jurisdiction of their own Governor had never included "an inch of ground beyond what is contained with his walls, nor any free intercourse otherwise than by sea. . . ." [5] Although the dispute over the adjoining land continued for a century, ultimately a stretch of ground extending about half a mile beyond the cliff was informally conceded by the Spaniards. As a result Gibraltar up to the so-called "British lines" is today somewhat less than three miles in length (beyond which is an area of neutral ground) and approximately half a mile in breadth. [6]

As already noted, most of the native Spaniards fled from the Gibraltar isthmus after its capture in 1704, whereas Jewish and

---

solution the British government may have in mind. According to *The Guardian* of May 26, 1966 (Manchester), the Spanish Foreign Minister presented to the British government a paper that embodies four points: (1) That Gibraltar should now revert to Spain; (2) Spain would permit the British to continue to use Gibraltar as a military and naval base; (3) a "legal regime" for Gibraltar would be created that would permit the present inhabitants to retain both their residence there and their British nationality; and (4) an Anglo-Spanish Convention covering the above points, once signed, would be registered with the United Nations. According to its diplomatic correspondent in the same issue of this paper the British Foreign Secretary has taken the position that the Treaty of Utrecht gave Great Britain solid rights to Gibraltar and that the inhabitants of it also have solid rights which cannot be ignored.

[3] Stetson Conn: *op. cit.*, Preface, p. vii.

[4] For the full Latin text see C. E. Carrington: *Gibraltar, Chatham House Memoranda* (London, 1958), Appendix.

[5] P. R. O. State Papers, Foreign, 94:80, quoted by C. E. Carrington: *ibid.*, p. 11.

[6] The British outer or advanced defence line was maintained at point-blank range of the guns on the Rock. Between this advanced line and that of the Spaniards was neutral ground of 600 toises or approximately a mile. See *ibid.*, pp. 11-13.

other non-Spanish traders settled in the ruins of the town at the base
of the cliff and thereby helped to supply the provisions and other
needs of the garrison. Moreover, the Jews were under the protection
of the Emperor of Morocco and, with the cutting off of trade with
Spain, the English at Gibraltar turned to him for various supplies,
which he agreed to furnish under the condition that both Jews and
Moors have free access to the land at the bottom of the fortress. The
Treaty of Utrecht, however, forbade their presence on the peninsula. Although orders were repeatedly sent by the British government to require the Governor of Gibraltar to adhere to the treaty
terms, they were not obeyed, especially since the garrison was heavily dependent upon the imports from Morocco and the stipulations
its ruler had made respecting the protection of those who owed
allegiance to him.[7] The British had assumed, when they acquired
Gibraltar, that it would become the centre of a vast commerce, as
was already true of Bombay, Madras, and Calcutta in India (and
was destined to be true of Hong Kong and Singapore in the nineteenth century). Therefore it was made a free port soon after its
capture—and has so remained to this day—except for the duties
collected on such items as spirits, beer, and tobacco. However, it
never became a great entrepôt because of its geographical limitations.

In fact, Gibraltar was of so little importance as a trade centre that
in 1718, but four years after the Peace of Utrecht, the British almost
gave it up. For, with the creation in that year of the Quadruple
Alliance—formed by Great Britain, France, Austria, and Holland
for the purpose of stabilizing political affairs in Europe against the
aggression plans of the Spanish Court—Lord Stanhope, Secretary of
State for the Southern Department, journeyed to Madrid to offer the
return of the Rock to Spain should Philip V agree to give up plans
for invading Italy. The offer, however, was rejected, perhaps because Philip's minister, Alberoni, was over-confident about the potential success of what seemed to him at the time a much more
important objective. But, in 1726, the signing of the Treaty of Vi-
enna with the Emperor Charles VI seemed to offer the Spaniards a
favourable opportunity to retrieve Gibraltar forcibly. Late in that
year a force of twenty thousand men under Count de las Torres
began a siege of the Rock. Its fortification had been greatly strength-

---

[7] Stetson Conn: *op. cit.*, pp. 25-6.

ened, however, and its defenders held firm until the Treaty of
Seville in 1729 brought these hostilities to a close.

There is little of importance to record about Gibraltar until, in the
midst of the Great War for the Empire, William Pitt made a surpris-
ing offer in the face of a series of British reverses. For in 1756
Minorca had been lost to the French and, in the following year, the
British forces under the Duke of Cumberland had likewise been
defeated by the French, who then undertook the occupation of the
Electorate of Hanover. With the unfavourable turn of the war in
both Europe and America in that year, Pitt now offered to return
Gibraltar to the Spaniards, provided that they would aid Great
Britain to recover Minorca.[8] But Spain at peace refused the bait,
hoping to reclaim the Rock under more favourable circumstances.
Nevertheless, even in 1762, when Spain in alliance with France
declared war on Great Britain, no direct military effort was made
against Gibraltar. For it was felt in the Court of Spain that by
combining the Spanish navy with that of France, British sea power
would be destroyed; this accomplished, a blockade of the Rock
would force the garrison commanded by Governor Edward Corn-
wallis to surrender. Instead, the Spanish navy was itself largely
destroyed off the coast of Cuba and on the high seas. Not until 1779,
when Great Britain was occupied with the War for American Independence and its naval power in the area of the Mediterranean
greatly reduced, did Spain in alliance with France again give serious attention to Gibraltar. In that year a most determined effort was
made to take it by blockade and siege. The siege was continued
until the preliminaries of peace were signed in 1783. Notable for the
heavy artillery fire exchanged by both sides, it came to be regarded
properly as one of the great sieges of history.[9]

The cluster of odd buildings at the foot of the Rock of Gibraltar in
the middle of the eighteenth century was described by Governor

---

[8] Minorca, it will be noted, was a Spanish possession until the time of its capture
by the English. For an account of Pitt's position as he outlined it to the Duke of
Newcastle see Newcastle to Hardwicke, August 9, 1757, Newcastle Papers, B. M.,
Add. Mss. 32872, folio 493; for the text of Pitt's confidential dispatch to Sir Benjamin
Keene, British envoy at the Spanish Court, August 23, 1757, see William Coxe:
*Memoirs of the Kings of Spain of the House of Bourbon, from . . . 1700 . . .
to . . . 1788* (2nd edn., 5 vols., London, 1815), IV, 187–96; see also Stetson Conn:
op. cit., pp. 164–9.

[9] See [Frederick G. Stephens]: *A History of Gibraltar and its Sieges* (London,
1870), and Wilbur C. Abbott: *An Introduction to the Documents Relating to the
International Status of Gibraltar, 1704–1923* (New York, 1934), pp. 14–15.

Humphrey Bland as forming a kind of Mediterranean shanty town where were congregated "Jews, Genoese, Spaniards, Portuguese, Irish Papists, Scotch pedlars and English bankrupts! . . . the riff-raff of various nations and religions ready to commit any fraud in their power." [10] This description remained true until the end of the eighteenth century; later many important improvements took place.[11] The government of the town was also rudimentary. Civil cases after 1720 were handled in a court merchant and, after 1752, criminal causes were dealt with by three justices of the peace.[12] The garrison, a powerful one at all times, was maintained at a cost of £120,000 in 1760, an expense that continued to rise.[13] In view of the Rock's vast importance in time of war and even in time of peace—lying so close to the piratical Barbary States—this expenditure added to other charges could hardly be considered excessive. It was aptly described in 1782 as "that happy spot, which in the possession of Great Britain, divided France from France, and Spain from Spain, and consequently as a place which ought not on any account to be relinquished." [14]

Minorca

Minorca, won by the British from Spain in 1713, lost to France in 1756,[15] and restored to Great Britain in 1763, remained under British rule until in 1782, while the Royal Navy was largely concentrated in home waters and in the New World, a combined French and Spanish force compelled its surrender. Again captured by the British in

[10] See W. F. Monk: *Britain in the Western Mediterranean* (*British Empire History* series, ed. Sir Reginald Coupland, London, 1953), p. 69.

[11] *Ibid.*, pp. 70–1.

[12] In 1740 Gibraltar was given a civil government. See *The Royal Charter for establishing a Civil Government at Gibraltar* [dated May 10, 1740] . . . (London, 1742); see also *Gibraltar a bulwark of Great Britain . . . with proposals for erecting a civil magistracy there, and for lessening the . . . expence . . . in maintaining that garrison. . . . By a gentleman of the navy* (2nd edn., London, 1725).

[13] For the increasing cost of the Gibraltar garrison from 1718 to 1781, by which year it was £351,000, see John Sinclair: *The Propriety of Retaining Gibraltar Impartially Considered* (London, 1783), pp. 20–1.

[14] John Sinclair to the Earl of Shelburne, July 17, 1782, Shelburne Papers, Vol. 83, Clements Library, Ann Arbor, Mich., quoted by Stetson Conn: *op. cit.*, p. 262.

[15] For the loss of Minorca in 1756 see Volume VI of this series, Chap. 13, which also includes a map of the area facing p. 406; for an important source not cited in that chapter see *Papers Relating to the Loss of Minorca in 1756* (ed. Captain H. W. Richmond, London, 1913), Navy Records Society *Publications,* XLII.

1798 in the midst of the Napoleonic wars, it was finally returned by the Peace of Amiens in 1802 to Spain which still retains it. Apart from the strategic importance of Port Mahon, protected by Fort St. Philip, the island had little value to Great Britain in the eighteenth century.

Unlike Gibraltar, with its polyglot national, religious, and racial elements, Minorca (except for the British garrison) had and has a homogeneous population.[16] The natives had their own mongrel language, were Roman Catholic in faith, and were wedded to political institutions going back hundreds of years. A hardy, impoverished yet carefree people, the Minorcans numbered some 27,000 in 1765.[17] Most of them were engaged in fishing or agricultural pursuits and thus, unlike the inhabitants of the town of Gibraltar, could in good years meet their own simple needs, especially for salt, cotton, wine, fish, honey, vegetables, and fruits.[18]

Under British rule the Minorcans suffered little interference in their religious life or their customs and traditional manner of local government.[19] Much of the land had come into possession of the Church, and was thereby free of taxation; the burden of supporting government therefore rested upon those least able to pay, so that at least a third of the earnings of the average inhabitant went for taxes and dues to the Church.[20] In short, the island was of little economic

---

[16] It is true that there were many strains from earlier colonizations and that at Port Mahon there was even a small Greek colony which had been established in 1745, but its influence on the mores of Minorca was negligible. See F. H. Marshall: "A Greek Community in Minorca," *The Slavonic and East European Review*, XI, 100–7.

[17] D. Fenning, J. Collyer, and others: *A New System of Geography, or a General Description of the World* . . . (2 vols., London, 1765), II, 437.

[18] See Volume VI of this series, p. 404; see also, for the dependence of both Minorca and Gibraltar upon the Barbary States for food supplies, especially to the British garrisons, M. S. Anderson: "Great Britain and the Barbary States in the Eighteenth Century," London University Institute of Historical Research *Bulletin*, XXIX, 87–107.

[19] It is true that under Lieutenant Governor Richard Kane a code of seventeen articles had been issued in 1721 which ended the dependence of the island's Roman Catholics upon Spain and Rome and provided that only native Minorcans could occupy religious posts; also, during the governorship of General William Blakeney in the middle of the eighteenth century, the power of the British Governor over civil affairs was extended somewhat by regulations sent from England in 1753. See W. F. Monk: *op. cit.*, pp. 64–5. For a detailed account of the local government of Minorca in 1741 see John Armstrong: *The History of the Island of Minorca* (2nd edn., London, 1756), pp. 96–108. This volume is in the form of seventeen letters written from June 3, 1740 to February 27, 1756. Armstrong, a military engineer in ordinary to His Majesty, was stationed on the island.

[20] See W. F. Monk: *op. cit.*, pp. 62–3, and especially John Armstrong: *op. cit.*, pp. 109–14.

value to Great Britain. Further, whereas Gibraltar was regarded as impregnable from assault by land, Minorca was wide open to invasion once British sea power had failed in its mission of protecting the waters that surrounded the island, as had been the case in 1756. Yet it was the possession of Port Mahon—which could shelter a fleet as Gibraltar could not—that made it possible for Great Britain to dominate the western Mediterranean during the 1760's and 1770's.

CHAPTER III

India and the United East India Company, 1772-1775

WHILE the Thirteen Colonies struggled from 1763 onward against the supreme authority of the King's High Court of Parliament, India—at least in so far as those parts of it that lay within the control of the United East India Company were concerned—had by 1775 come fully within the orbit of its sovereign powers.[1]

Although in the seventeenth century the King under the royal prerogative had issued letters patent to the old East India Company, by 1698 as the result of disputes that arose over who should be allowed to carry on trade with India and the Far East, the majority in the House of Commons had taken the position that only an act of Parliament, rather than royal patent, could keep Englishmen from trading there. In harmony with this view a statute of that year (9 and 10 William III, c. 44) determined the broad lines upon which a "General Society" for commercial intercourse with India should be established. Likewise, in the reign of Queen Anne, Parliament passed two acts (6 Anne, c. 17, and 10 Anne, c. 28) which had the effect of bringing into existence the United East India Company and providing for its close fiscal relationship to the government. In 1730, by still another act of Parliament (3 George II, c. 16), these financial relations were altered, much to the benefit of the government.[2]

---

[1] P. E. Roberts, in his chapter "The East India Company and the State" (*Cambridge History of India*, V, and Vol. IV of the *Cambridge History of the British Empire*), points out (p. 181) that between 1772 and 1786 all the great statutes were passed that definitely subjected the Company to the control of the Crown and Parliament and converted it into a quasi state department.

[2] For an account of the early English trade with India see Volume V in this series, pp. 231–60; for other accounts of events involving the activities of the United East India Company see in this series Volumes V, Chaps. 8 and 9, VIII, Chap. 6, and IX,

As was emphasized in Volumes XI and XII of this series, in 1767, with the idea of providing an additional revenue for the state, Chancellor of the Exchequer Charles Townshend secured from Parliament two acts particularly related to the Company: one (7 George III, c. 56) to take off the inland duties on tea and also the drawback of duties paid on importation of teas to be re-exported to Ireland and the colonies, and the other (7 George III, c. 57) for payment by the Company to the state over a limited period of £400,000, "in respect to the Territorial Acquisitions and Revenues lately obtained in the East Indies." Two years later, with the expiration of the second statute and after much discussion between the Company and the government, an act (9 George III, c. 24) was passed which preserved for the Company for a period of five years the territorial acquisitions in India, together with the revenue arising from them, on the understanding that during this period the sum of £400,000 would continue to be paid annually into the royal exchequer at the disposition of Parliament. This act also provided that the Company might increase its dividend from ten per cent to twelve and a half per cent, should its revenues justify this, in which case the amount payable into the exchequer would be proportionately increased. However, the statute provided that, should it be necessary to lower the dividend to the one-time six per cent level, there would be no payment into the exchequer.[3]

By 1773 the circumstances of the Company were greatly altered. In that year three acts relating to it were passed. One of them, the Tea Act (13 George III, c. 44, already considered in Volume XII of the series) provided for a drawback of duties on the re-exportation of tea to the colonies and for granting licences to the Company itself to re-export tea duty free. The second, the Regulating Act (13 George III, c. 63), will be discussed more fully later in this chapter. The last, the Loan or Relief Act (13 Geo. III, c. 64), provided for the raising of £1,400,000 for support of the Company's finances. In other words, in 1767 as well as in 1769 the Company was held to be so prosperous that, with certain concessions made in its favour, it could grant to the state the annual sum of £400,000; yet by 1773 it

---

Chaps. 12 and 13; also for maps in this connection see Volume V, facing pp. 234 and 274; Volume VIII, facing pp. 108, 109, 124, 125, 132, 152, 153, 164, 165, and Volume IX, facing pp. 308, 309, 328.

[3] See in this series Volume XI, 89–99, and Volume XII, 12–14. The title of the statute of 1769 is: "An Act for carrying into Execution certain Proposals made by the East India Company . . ."

had become financially involved to such a degree that in order to save it from bankruptcy the government had to bolster it with the sum of almost a million and a half pounds. But to comprehend this development it is necessary to shed some light on what had taken place in India from the time Robert Clive left it early in 1767 to 1773.

To begin with, the idea that the territorial revenues of India, exclusive of trade, were great beyond the present needs of the Company was illusory. "It was the interest of the servants in India, diligently cultivated," wrote James Mill, "perpetually to feast the Company with the most flattering accounts of the state of their affairs." [4] Yet the visions of easily acquired wealth entertained by the owners of East India Company shares had led to speculative activities of two kinds: an attempt to increase the number of votes by splitting the stock, and an effort to gain higher dividends. This speculation was what the previously mentioned legislation passed by Parliament in 1767 had sought to control. For, attendant upon Clive's reports from Bengal, speculation and a boom in Company stock had continued until May 26, 1769, when the news of reverses on all sides in India reached London and panic seized the speculators. By the middle of June of that year the value of shares had dropped from the high of 273 (in 1767) to 239. [5]

Among the items of news which so drastically affected the market in East India Company stock in 1769 was word that Hyder Ali, the powerful ruler of Mysore in southern India, was sweeping victoriously within the Carnatic up to the very gates of Fort St. George at Madras. Happily for the Company, Madras did not fall, but the peace concluding this first war with Mysore was a humiliating one. "The only effect of the struggle" in the words of Henry Beveridge, "had . . . been to entail disgrace on the Company and add enormously to their debt." [6]

---

[4] James Mill: *The History of British India* (3rd edn., 10 vols., London, 1826), III, 383. For a treatment of the financial situation of the Company in the 1760's see again in this series Volume XI, 89–99, especially pp. 89–90 giving figures on the revenue from India in 1766; see also Volume XII, 12–19.

[5] *Ibid.* For a full account of the government intervention in the Company affairs see Lucy S. Sutherland: *The East India Company in Eighteenth-Century Politics* (Oxford, 1952), Chaps. 6 and 7.

[6] See Henry Beveridge: *A Comprehensive History of India* . . . (3 vols., London, 1865–7), II, 281–2. For the campaigns of the first war with Mysore see *ibid.*, II, 217–22, and H. H. Dodwell: "The Carnatic, 1761–84," *Cambridge History of India*, V, 275–9; see also R. C. Majumdar, H. C. Raychaudhuri, and Kalikinkar Datta: *An Advanced History of India* (London, 1948) pp. 682–5.

Turning to the situation in northern India, it may be repeated [7] that before Robert Clive left Bengal for the last time in 1767, he seems to have settled affairs in a manner that left the Company with a sense of security both with respect to its possessions in this area and to the attitude of the native rulers of lands directly west of Bengal and Behar. The Vizier of Oudh, Shuja-ud-daula, after being soundly defeated by Colonel Hector Munro (then Major, later Sir) in the Battle of Buxar and losing his capital, Allahabad, was more than anxious for peace. Again his ally but rival, Shah Zada,[8] while not free to go to Delhi to occupy the imperial throne, had had assigned to him the provinces of Allahabad and Korah, as a result of a treaty that Clive required Shuja-ud-daula to sign on August 16, 1765. This treaty had left Shuja with the title of Vizier as well as that of Nabob of the great principality of Oudh, which was returned to his possession except for the provinces of Allahabad and Korah. But Shuja, an ambitious and restless person, sought to live up to his title of Imperial Vizier by taking direct charge of Shah Alam's affairs. By 1768 he had vastly increased his army and was by every appearance seeking to vitiate Clive's settlement with him.[9]

News of these developments was highly disturbing to the Directors of the Company, as was the news sent by the Select Committee at Calcutta of a declining prosperity in most of northern India as the result of the long period of anarchy, attended by a disappearance of currency, a decay of trade, and a falling off in the cultivation of lands. In this connection the Calcutta Committee stated: "The Majority of the present Princes of Indostan [Hindustan] have no natural right in the Countries they possess. In the general wreck of the monarchy [that is, the Great Mogul Empire] every man seized what Fortune threw into his hands. . . ." [10] Under these disordered conditions, in order to safeguard the possessions of the Company and hold its

---

[7] See Volume IX, Chap. 13, of this series, "The United East India Company Becomes a Political Power."

[8] Shah Zada was proclaimed Shah Alam II, the Great Mogul, by the victorious Afghan, Ahmad Shah, before Ahmad left the Punjab for his native capital of Kabul after crushing the Mahrattas at Panipat. *Ibid.*, IX, pp. 294.

[9] See Sir Robert Barker to Clive, April 21, 1768, Home Ser., Misc., 100: 3–20, India Office, London (now Commonwealth Relations Office). Col. Barker was stationed with a brigade of Company troops at Allahabad at the time of writing; in 1770 he became Commander-in-Chief of all forces in Bengal.

[10] See the letter of the Select Committee in Bengal to the Court of Directors in London, March 28, 1768, Home Ser., Misc., 100: 39–46; see also the Select Committee's letter of September 13, 1768, on the apprehensions that the conduct of Shuja-ud-daula had aroused, *ibid.*, 100: 213–18.

allies in firm dependence, the Select Committee had increased the number of armed troops under its control at Calcutta from one to three brigades—an item of great expense. Thus the hope of a vast surplus in the revenues, anticipated by Clive, could not be realized; nor did it seem possible to lessen the expenditure of the Company's servants, which was exceeding the revenues.

Faced with this situation in India, and in the hope of making great economic reforms, the Directors decided in 1769 to send out a group of three so-called "Supervisors" and to invest them with wide powers over all parts of India where the Company had assumed control. This decision was implemented with the blessings of the government. The men chosen for the important task were considered to be highly qualified by their long residence in India. Henry Vansittart had ably discharged his responsibilities as President and Governor of Fort William between 1759 and 1764; Luke Scrafton was a lawyer who had earlier been Clive's agent at the Court of the Nabob of Bengal and later had become deeply involved in Clive's affairs; while Colonel Francis Forde was distinguished for his military career in India in the late 1750's.[11] Under the terms of their commissions these men were to "Superintend, direct, controul, conduct, manage and Transact" all business and affairs of the Company in and through all parts of India during the goodwill and pleasure of the Company. At the same time they were not to hinder the Governors or Presidents and Councils at Calcutta, Bombay, and Madras in the exercise of the powers and authorities given to them by name or office. The commissions and instructions also charged the Supervisors with the special responsibility to negotiate all treaties, alliances, and other matters relating to peace and war with the native rulers, and they were given authority to make all promotions of Company servants in India, as well as to dismiss or suspend from office any of them of whatever rank.[12]

What could have been accomplished by the presence of the three Supervisors in India can only be surmised. They left on H. M. *Aurora*, which arrived safely at Cape Town but after leaving that

---

[11] See Lucy S. Sutherland: *op. cit.*, pp. 190–200, for a careful analysis of the struggle within the Company and its relationship to the government at the time of the appointment of Supervisors.

[12] For a copy of the commissions dated July 28, 1769, see India Office, Home Ser., Misc., 100:273–9, 347–53; for a copy of the instructions enclosed in a letter from the Company to the Secretary of State, Lord Weymouth, dated August 4, 1769, see *ibid.*, 100:399–430; see also *ibid.*, 204 (1), 1–91, under September 15, 1769.

port disappeared at sea without leaving a trace of those on board. When the Company became convinced that the group had been lost, an offer was made to Edmund Burke in the summer of 1772 to take the headship of a new set of Supervisors. George Dempster, a member of the Board of Directors of the Company and also a member of Parliament, in urging Burke to accept, noted "what a field for Genius probity and industry is open to you in that Country. . . . I have had my scruples hitherto of consenting to very large appointments [in India, but] your acceptance will remove those, for I shall never think we can buy you too dear. . . ."[13] But Burke refused the offer.[14] Had he been willing to accept, one may speculate about the effect of a period of actual service in India upon his attitude toward those entrusted with responsibility in that country, especially so far as the position he was to take years later in the House of Commons at the time of the arraignment of Warren Hastings before the House of Lords was concerned. As for the plan for a new commission of Supervisors, it failed to materialize, chiefly because of differences within the Company over who should be named to it and, finally, of parliamentary opposition to it which resulted, late in 1772, in an act (13 George III, c. 9) forbidding the Company "for a limited Time, from making any Appointment of Commissioners for superintending and regulating Indian Affairs. . . ."

When Warren Hastings had departed early in 1765 from Bengal, where he had been a supporter of the policies of Governor Vansittart, he left having acquired not wealth but a reputation for integrity. He also carried away an intimate knowledge of the people of India, doubtless as a result of his studious habits and his fluency with the native language. It was therefore not surprising that he should have been given a new assignment by the Directors of the Company as second British official at Madras under Governor Josias Dupré. In the spring of 1769 he left England to spend some two years at Fort St. George. While there he carried out certain reforms in the trade investments of the Madras presidency in favour of the native workers.[15] Then in 1771 came his appointment as Governor of Bengal and President of the Council. His administration actually

---

[13] George Dempster to Burke, August 4, 1772: *The Correspondence of Edmund Burke* (ed. Lucy S. Sutherland, Cambridge & Chicago, 1960), II, 321–3.

[14] Burke to the Duke of Richmond, August 4, 1773, *ibid.*, II, 319–21.

[15] See, for example, Hastings to the Council at Madras, December 3, 1771, in M. E. Monckton Jones: *Warren Hastings in Bengal, 1772–1774, Oxford Historical and Literary Studies* (Oxford, 1918), pp. 107–11.

began in the spring of 1772. Here it may be pointed out that at the beginning of 1771 Bengal's bonded debt stood at £612,628; a year later it had mounted to £1,700,000, and by April 1773 it stood at £2,168,691.[16] The new Governor was expected to deal with a financial situation which, serious enough at the time of his appointment, now became almost desperate. Added to the difficulties facing him came the great drought in the basin of the Ganges in 1769 and 1770. As a consequence, the staple food of the inhabitants, rice, failed them. In addition to the famine that ensued, an epidemic of smallpox broke out. One third of the population is said to have perished in these scourges, according to a report made by President Hastings and the Council to the Court of Directors on November 3, 1772.[17] It took time for the country to recover economically from the shock of this terrible visitation.

One of the chief responsibilities that faced Hastings arose from instructions from the Directors of the Company to reorganize the Bengal revenue system.[18] They were persuaded that gross abuses

---

[16] G. R. Gleig: *Memoirs of the Life of the Right Hon. Warren Hastings . . .* (3 vols., London, 1841), I, 208 and 211.

[17] For this report see Sir William W. Hunter: *Annals of Rural Bengal* (London, 1868), Appendix A, pp. 379–98. For the famine itself see *ibid.*, pp. 20–31, and especially Appendix B, "The Great Famine of 1770, Described by Eye-Witnesses," pp. 399–421. As W. H. Moreland and A. C. Chatterjee make clear in their *A Short History of India* (London, New York, Toronto, 1936; 3rd edn., London, 1953), famine had been characteristic of certain parts of India and meant the depopulation of wide areas. In 1943 a serious food shortage occurred in many parts of India, "culminating in an acute famine followed by epidemic diseases in the Province of Bengal" (p. 519) and, even in 1966, near famine conditions exist in many parts of India. Of all the famines that plagued India during the period of English rule, that of 1770 was undoubtedly the most disastrous. Moreover, as Romesh Dutt stresses in his *The Economic History of India* (7th edn., London, 1950), this calamity in no way mitigated the strict collection of the land tax, nor did the Company's servants in Bengal feel that they were called upon to institute any effective measures of relief (pp. 51–3). Under the given conditions doubtless such relief would have been impossible; moreover, the Company shareholders were demanding profits, which further tied the hands of its servants in India. One point that should be made in this connection is that the collection of the land tax was still in the hands of natives whose personal enrichment depended upon the strictest methods of collection.

The letter of the President and Council to the Court of Directors of November 3, 1772, cited above deals with this old and harsh system of tax collection and its injustice toward the people thus exploited.

[18] For the most detailed study of the Bengal revenue system inherited by Hastings see the two books by Professor D. N. Banerjee of the University of Dacca. They are *Early Land and Revenue System in Bengal and Bihar: Volume I, 1765–1772* (London & Calcutta, 1936) and *Early Administrative System in Bengal Volume I, 1765–1774* (London & Calcutta, 1943). These volumes were designed as companion-pieces and are of especial interest since they present with due circumspection the point of view of a patriotic native of India. Their chief importance, however, rests in the careful and illuminating use by the author of quotations from the Company records in his effort (as he states in the Preface of the second work) to be "strictly impartial and scientific."

had developed under the system established by Clive whereby the financial administration of Bengal, Behar, and Orissa was legally vested in the Company by agreement with the Nabob, while the actual collection of the customary taxes remained in the hands of the Nabob's fiscal agents. This was what was termed the dual fiscal system. Hastings was ordered to do away with it and institute machinery that would make it possible for the Bengal Council, acting through its Select Committee, to control all stages of the system from the initial levy upon the ryots (or tenants of land) to the final payment into the treasury at Calcutta. By this the Company hoped to accomplish several things: to readjust the relations of the Company with the ruling native princes of northern India, to prevent the native tax collectors from exploiting the ryots unjustly and diverting revenues illegally into their own pockets, and, finally, to increase the amount of funds at the disposal of the Company in the face of the financial crisis. In carrying out these instructions it seemed necessary to dismiss from his post and place under house arrest at Calcutta Muhammad Reza Khan, the Bengal Nabob's chief minister responsible for the final accounting to the Company for the revenues, and also Shitab Roy, who occupied a similar post in Behar.[19] Thereupon, the collection of the revenue was farmed out to natives who were made responsible to district councils manned by Europeans—a system that after many rather drastic adjustments took deep root in the future government of India. Further, as the Nabob was a minor, his stipulated income was reduced (also on orders of the Company) to sixteen lakhs of rupees, or the equivalent of £ 200,000 sterling, with a saving of eight lakhs or £ 100,000 thereby.[20]

Affairs beyond Bengal, Behar, and Orissa also demanded Hastings's attention and resulted in the undoing likewise of Clive's settlements with the Imperial Vizier of Oudh and Emperor Shah Alam. In

---

[19] To understand the scope of the plans of the Company for the reform of the Bengal revenue system, as well as for other reforms, see the instructions given on September 15, 1769, and March 23, 1770, to the Supervisors sent to India; see also the Directors' letters to the President and Council of Bengal dated March 23, 1770, April 10 and August 28, 1771, March 25, 1772, and April 7, 1773. Most of these are in the form of abstracts made by Hastings and are printed in M. E. Monckton Jones: *op. cit.*, pp. 126–45; see also R. R. Ramsbotham: *Studies in the Land Revenue History of Bengal, 1769–1787* (London, etc., 1926), which is largely taken up with the report of a commission of three presented on March 25, 1778, concerning the revenue of the Province of Bengal. It is called the Amini (Aumeeny) Report. Sir Percival Griffiths in his *The British Impact on India* (London, 1952), Chap. 17, deals with the problem of the collection of the revenue down to the great Indian Mutiny.

[20] In 1772 the lakh, in terms of sicca rupees, was equal to £ 12,500 sterling.

1772, when the Emperor had left Allahabad (the temporary capital granted to him by treaty) to occupy the imperial throne at Delhi under the protection of the Mahrattas, the Governor took the position that by so doing Alam had broken his agreement and was therefore no longer entitled to receive from the Company twenty-six lakhs nor to hold Allahabad and Korah in tribute. These provinces— lying as they did within the confines of Oudh—were therefore turned over to Nabob Shuja-ud-daula. In return the Nabob, by a treaty signed at Benares on September 7, 1773, agreed to pay the Company fifty lakhs, that is, £525,000. In addition, if it should be necessary to defend his claims, he was promised the military assistance of the Company's troops, for which he was to provide the additional sum of two lakhs and ten thousand sicca rupees for each month that a brigade served in Oudh.[21] The Vizier was firmly bound by this treaty, since he realized that it was to his own vital interests to enjoy the protection it afforded. In fact, the following year in pursuing his war against the Rohillas—a conquering people from Afghanistan settled to the north and east of Oudh and ruling over the natives—he asked for and obtained the aid of a brigade of Company troops. By this means Shuja-ud-daula conquered the Rohilla country, an episode that reflected little credit on Hastings and the Calcutta Council, especially as the committing of British troops in a native war of aggression was an interference totally against government policy.[22]

Meanwhile in England the Company was under bitter assault both in Parliament and outside that body. For example, in 1772 *Considerations on India Affairs; Particularly Respecting the Present State of Bengal and its Dependencies by William Bolts, Merchant, and Alderman, or Judge of the Hon. The Mayor's Court of Calcutta* was published. Bolts, while a merchant in Bengal, had acquired great wealth by questionable means, and in the course of his rise had become a Calcutta Alderman. His conduct had led to his arrest and

---

[21] For the Treaty of Benares see "The Benares Diary of Warren Hastings" (ed. C. C. Davies, London, 1948), *Camden Miscellany*, XVIII, 1–40. For Hastings's part in the promotion of the idea of British sovereignty in India see H. H. Dodwell: "The Development of Sovereignty in British India," *Cambridge History of India*, V, Chap. 32.

[22] For a defence of Hastings see Sir John Strachey: *Hastings and the Rohilla War* (London, 1892); for a tempered criticism of Hastings in this connection see P. E. Roberts: "External Relations and the Rohilla War," *Cambridge History of India*, V, Chap. 12; see also R. C. Majumdar, H. C. Raychaudhuri, and K. Datta: *op. cit.*, pp. 691–4, for a carefully buttressed statement regarding Hastings and the war. Burke, as is well known, based some of his most serious charges against Hastings on his participation in this war.

deportation to England in 1768; and his book was a sustained attack on the Company. To support his thesis—that its policy was ruining India—he supplied an Appendix of forty-four documents. The influence of this publication on the public mind was undoubtedly very considerable. In particular, Bolts attacked Governor Harry Verelst, who had succeeded Clive in Bengal and who, as Governor, had brought about Bolts's deportation. As Verelst had given up his post and was in England when Bolts's book appeared, he replied with the publication that same year of his very able and dispassionate *A View of the Rise, Progress, and Present State of the English Government in Bengal.* In it he repudiated the more serious charges directed against the Company.

In the House of Commons the policies of the Company and the situation in India were now being given the most critical scrutiny. Out of the examination came a series of reports: those made by the select committee of the House between May 26, 1772, and June 18, 1773,[23] and those of the committee of secrecy beginning on December 17, 1772, and ending on June 30, 1773. These latter reports covered the entire range of the "Nature, State, and Condition, of the East India Company and of British Affairs in the East Indies," including such items as the appointment of the Supervisors, the financial and business activities of the Company and its servants, and territorial management, especially in Bengal and Behar. Together with the minutes of the meetings of the committee and the appendices, they form a detailed history of the Company and offer itemized accounts of salaries and civil and military lists among other data.[24] Out of this exhaustive investigation came the famous Regulating Act of 1773,[25] which was intended to establish a central power in India that might produce stable government there, but

[23] For the complete report of the House of Commons select committee made on May 26, 1772, and dealing chiefly with the inland private trade and Clive's activities in Bengal, see *Journals of the House of Commons,* XXXIII, 792–944. This report together with its appendices and other select committee minutes and reports for 1772–3 are printed as Nos. 15–19 of the House of Commons *Reports,* II, *Parliamentary Papers . . . 1731–1800.* (These reports are available on Readex Microprint, ed. Professor Edgar L. Erickson.)

[24] For the reports of the committee of secrecy, with appendices, see *ibid.* (Readex), Vols. 32–33, House of Commons *Reports,* II and III, Nos. 20–29. The *Fourth Report* (according to a notation on the copy in the Record Department of the India Library) was written by Edmund Burke. It is largely concerned with the reformation of abuses, the specific objectives of the Regulating Act, and other matters germane to the act.

[25] See especially Lucy S. Sutherland: *op. cit.,* Chap. 9; see also B. B. Misra: *The Central Administration of the East India Company, 1773–1834* (Manchester, 1959), pp. 18–22.

which may also be viewed as an important step in the direction of the assertion of the sovereignty of Parliament over the territories held by the Company.

By the Regulating Act [26] fundamental changes were made in the constitution of the Company. It was now provided that there should be rotation in the election of the twenty-four Directors—six going out each year, after a four-year term of service—and that two years must elapse before any former Director could be eligible for re-election. In the elections there was to be no collusion involving stock-splitting or transfer of stock for additional votes. To vote, a stockholder must own shares valued at £1,000; £3,000 worth of stock entitled the holder to two votes, with £6,000 of stock providing three votes, and £10,000 or more, four votes. As to the government in India, the statute provided for the appointment of a Governor General and four councillors who, acting together as a Council, would have direct control over all matters pertaining to the kingdoms of Bengal, Behar, and Orissa. It was also specified in the statute that Warren Hastings should be the Governor General, with a salary of £25,000 a year, that Lieutenant General John Clavering, George Monson, Richard Barwell, and Philip Francis should be the four councillors, each with a salary of £10,000 a year, and that all should hold office for a period of five years. The five acting together were to make up the Council, the business of which was to be decided by a majority of votes of those present, although in case of a tie the Governor General or, in his absence, the eldest councillor should have a deciding vote—an arrangement that in practice was to prove most unwise, as it led to a struggle for control between Hastings and Francis.[27]

The authority given by the Regulating Act to the India Council over the presidencies of Madras, Bombay, and Bencoolen (the last-named in Sumatra) was limited to the power of forbidding them to

---

[26] For 13 Geo. III, c. 63, "An Act for establishing certain Regulations for the better Management of the Affairs of the East India Company, as well in India as in Europe," see *Statutes at Large* (Eyre and Strahan), VIII, 248–57. The bill received the royal assent by special commission on June 21, 1773.

[27] For voluminous material relating to the opposition to the Governor General by Francis—supported by a majority of the Council—see Indian Office, Home Ser., Misc., 117 (3), 188 (4), (15), all largely concerned with the year 1774. See also Sophia Weitzman: *Warren Hastings and Philip Francis* (Manchester, 1929) and A. T. Embree: *Charles Grant and British Rule in India* (London & New York, 1962), both of which are extremely valuable. Grant, acting as secretary to the Board of Trade in Calcutta, was a warm supporter of Philip Francis and those in opposition to Hastings.

engage in war or to enter into any treaty with the native princes without its consent. A supreme court of judicature likewise was created, to sit at Fort William; it was empowered to settle civil, criminal, admiralty, and ecclesiastical cases involving all British subjects residing in Bengal, Behar, and Orissa, excepting the Governor General and members of the Council. The right of appeal from its judgement was to the Privy Council in England; further, offences and misdemeanours by British subjects were to be tried by a jury. All servants of the Company, including the Governor General, the Council, and members of the supreme court were strictly forbidden to accept any presents from the natives; nor should any other person holding a civil or military office do so, on pain of dismissal. That trade in India might not be the means of exploiting people, it was further provided that no person concerned in the collection of the revenue should be engaged in trade and that no contract involving a loan of money or merchandise should be legal if the rate of interest were above twelve per cent. The act included other commendable features—all designed to promote legitimate trade and hold in check British subjects or others who might attempt to exploit or oppress the natives.[28] Unfortunately, the statute also had some serious defects. The attempt to balance authority between the Governor General and the Council seriously militated against the smooth, efficient management of important Indian affairs. Nor was the position that the supreme court of judicature should occupy vis-a-vis the Council clarified, and this led to needless disputes. Again, the act failed to make explicit the nature of the powers possessed by the Company in its relations with the Nabob of Bengal—something that was purposely left obscure in order to await further developments.

Although it would go beyond the purposes of this series to proceed with the history of the administration of Governor General Warren Hastings, which began in 1774 and continued until his return to England in 1785, it may be said that no one who succeeded him in that high office ever received either such unstinted praise or such unmitigated castigation. Impeached by the House of Commons in 1788 on twenty grave charges of misconduct in office, he was denounced in a series of philippics by such great orators as Edmund Burke, Charles James Fox, and Richard Brinsley Sheridan. The trial held before the House of Lords dragged on until, in 1795, he was

---

[28] See W. H. Moreland and A. C. Chatterjee: *op. cit.*, Chap. 36.

acquitted of all charges but was left an impoverished man.[29] Even the attitude of the House of Commons toward him underwent a decided change in the course of the years. When in 1813 he appeared before that body, meeting as a committee of the whole House concerned with the affairs of India, he was applauded when he entered the chamber—a mark of profound respect—and when he left, all the members rose and remained bareheaded until he had passed beyond the door. Other honours awaited him; Oxford made him a doctor of law and the King made him a member of the Privy Council. Nevertheless, his actions in particular instances were harsh, inflexible, and beyond the limits of plain justice and humanity, especially his treatment of certain natives of high standing, such as the Raja Nandkumar (Nandakuma, Nand Kumar, Nuncumar, Nundcomar),[30] Raja Chait Singh of Benares,[31] and two Begums, mother and grandmother of the Vizier of Oudh; [32] also reprehensible was his decision to honour his treaty with Shuja-ud-daula, and aid him in the Rohilla War. Yet what he did was for the purpose of serving the Company, to extricate it from its financial difficulties, never for personal aggrandizement or enrichment. Moreover, his sustained interest in the welfare of the people of India and his efforts to preserve and make known their great cultural heritage have won recognition, so that no name stands higher among the Governor Generals of India than that of Warren Hastings in the eyes of the descendants of those among whom he laboured.[33]

---

[29] For a recent important study see P. J. Marshall: *The Impeachment of Warren Hastings* (London, 1965).

[30] For a very long letter written by Nandkumar to the Governor General and Council, dated March 8, 1775, and read to the Council on March 11 by Francis, see India Office, Home Ser., Misc., 125:529–52. In this letter the Rajah seeks to vindicate his loyalty to the government of India and complains that Hastings has treated him as an enemy and has cultivated the acquaintance of his enemies; he also lists the various money gifts that came through him to the Governor General. On March 13 Hastings records in a minute his reaction to this attack on him. There follows the discussion of the Council, when it was voted to permit Nandkumar to appear before the Council to prove his charges and his testimony. See *ibid.*, 125:553–621. For the celebrated trial, conviction, and execution of Nandkumar for forgery see especially Sir James Stephen: *The Story of Nucomar and the Impeachment of Sir Elijah Imply* (London, 1885), Henry Beveridge: *The Trial of Maharaha Nanda Kumar; a Narrative of a Judical Murder* (Calcutta, 1886), and Lucy S. Sutherland: "New Evidence on the Nandakuma Trial," *English Historical Review*, LXXII, 438–65.

[31] For Hastings's exactions made upon Raja Chait Singh and the Raja's expulsion from Benares see R. C. Majumdar, H. C. Raychaudhuri, and K. Datta: *op. cit.*, pp. 694–5.

[32] For Hastings's treatment of the Begums of Oudh see *ibid.*, pp. 695–7.

[33] Among works relating to Warren Hastings that have not already been mentioned see Sir A. C. Lyall: *Warren Hastings* (London, 1889) and Keith Feiling:

Before turning from this brief discussion of India in the 1760's and 1770's, it should be stated that some of the defects of the Regulating Act were remedied by the Amending Act of 1781 [34] and by William Pitt's India Act of 1784.[35] These statutes marked the gradual decline in power of the Company.[36] The culmination of the efforts to establish the direct responsibility of Parliament over Company affairs and to create a central authority in India for the stable administration of the British possessions was to come in the next century. With the charter of 1813 the Company lost its monopoly of Indian trade; by the India Act of 1833 it was reduced to the role of political agent for the Crown, which now held its possessions in trust "for the service of the Government of India." The Charter Act of 1853, by its provisions for the establishment of civil service posts, deprived the Company Directors of their patronage privileges. Finally, the Act for the Better Government of India of 1858—in the wake of the great Sepoy Mutiny—took away the Company's last vestiges of power, a step completed in 1861 by the Indian Councils Act.[37]

Thus ended the remarkable United East India Company,[38] while a new India emerged with control over its internal affairs directly administered after November 1, 1858, by the Crown through a Viceroy—who was also Governor General and Commander-in-Chief —operating with an Executive Council.[39]

Warren Hastings (London, 1954); see also B. B. Misra: *op. cit.*, pp. 23–7, for a perceptive treatment of the government of Bengal under Hastings; for other aspects of his administration see N. Majumdar: *Justice and Police in Bengal 1765–1793* (Calcutta, 1960).

[34] See 21 Geo. III, c. 70, which provided reforms of the judicature.

[35] "An Act for the better Regulation and Management of the Affairs of the East India Company, and of the British Possessions in India . . ." (24 Geo. III, c. 25).

[36] See Lucy S. Sutherland: *op. cit.*, Chap. 13.

[37] For developments in the early nineteenth century see B. B. Misra: *op. cit.*; see also *Cambridge History of India*, V.

[38] The Company's formal existence during its period of liquidation actually lasted until 1874.

[39] For an excellent study of the extension of British power in India see Edward Thompson and G. T. Garratt: *Rise and Fulfilment of British Rule in India* (London, 1934). A map on p. 403 shows the extent of British India in 1856 under Governor General Lord Dalhousie. For the acquisitions of the East India Company by the end of the Hastings administration see the frontispiece map in Peter Auber: *History of the Rise and Progress of British Power in India* (2 vols., London, 1846), I.

The best bibliography on India in general remains that in *Cambridge History of India*, V: *British India, 1497–1858* (or *Cambridge History of the British Empire*, IV); for a more recent one on the East India Company for the period 1773–1834 see B. B. Misra: *op. cit.*, pp. 451–9. An effective bibliographic aid is to be found in R. I. Crane: *The History of India: Its Study and Interpretation* (American Historical Association *Publication* No. 17, Washington, D.C., 1958).

CHAPTER IV

The West African Trading Posts and Slavery

UNLIKE the situation in India, the British trading posts and forts in the Gulf of Guinea were under the control of a Company that had been regulated from the time of its incorporation in 1750: the Company of Merchants Trading to Africa, which had taken over the assets of the virtually bankrupt Royal African Company.[1] These trading posts and forts were scattered along a coastal area for some four hundred miles of western equatorial Africa. Interspersed between them were some thirteen posts established by the Dutch. There was no territorial expansion on the Gulf of Guinea to compare with that of the English in North America. In fact, the soil on which the holdings were built was not considered English but the property of the respective native rulers, to whom the Company paid some form of rental. These holdings were within enclosures that contained at most only a few acres, much of it sand. Beyond lay the mysterious interior of Africa, with its steaming, fever-laden jungles and mountains as yet unpenetrated by white men. Life at a trading post was endurable for Europeans only because of the hope of acquiring wealth and then—like those serving in India—returning to England to enjoy it.

The new Company—open to all traders who paid an admission fine of forty shillings—was administered by a committee of nine,

---

[1] For a map of the slaving posts along the Gulf of Guinea in the eighteenth century see Volume II, Revised, of this series, facing p. 268; and for an account of activities of the Royal African Company and the English slave trade down to 1752, see *ibid.*, Chap. 10, "Guinea and the Empire"; see also the important studies by H. A. Wyndham: *The Atlantic and Slavery* (London, 1935), Part I, "The West Coast of Africa," and Part III, Chap. 1, "Negro Slavery"; W. E. F. Ward: *A History of Ghana* (London, 1958), which is a revised edition of his 1948 *A History of the Gold Coast*; and Sir Alan Burns: *History of Nigeria* (5th edn., London, 1955).

resident in England, which made policies for carrying out the Company's main responsibilities, chiefly the maintenance of forts for defence of the posts. Members of the committee were forbidden to engage in African trade and their activities were subject to investigation not only by the Board of Trade but also by Parliament. It was Parliament that appropriated annually the sums of money for keeping the forts in repair—sums varying from £10,000 upward—or, for example, for building a new fort at Anamabo, a project that alone involved the expenditure between 1756 and 1762 of £34,590.[2]

It was charged in the 1770's by dissatisfied merchants, and the charge was apparently true, that the Gulf of Guinea trade under the new Company was not the free and fair commerce intended by the act of Parliament governing the Company, but that the best portion of the trade was under the control—if not directly, at least indirectly —of the committee in England, to the decisive advantage of its members. This control was perpetuated by a group of twelve London, Liverpool, and Bristol men.[3] Despite the requirement that the committee should consist of but nine members, three to be elected annually from each of these cities and none of whom was to act as a committeeman longer than three successive years, the twelve men managed to rotate in such a way as to gain exclusive control of the committee. Further, their appointees in Africa, who occupied such positions as governors of forts, by manipulation of the supplies and by taking advantage of their positions to trade not only with African chiefs and with each other but also with the Dutch—contrary to regulations—were making competition very difficult for the free trader, so it was asserted.[4]

In 1772 the matter came before the House of Commons on a petition of Liverpool merchants "complaining of malversion in the management of the African trade." In the debate that took place on

---

[2] Beyond the cost of building Fort Anamabo, £136,000 was expended on the other posts between 1751 and 1763. See *Considerations on the Present Peace as far as it is relative to the Colonies and the African Trade* (London, 1763), pp. 9–11. This pamphlet is supposed to have been written by John Roberts, who was Governor of Cape Coast Castle in 1753 and again in 1779.

[3] For the importance of Liverpool and Bristol to the slave trade see Averil Mackenzie-Grieve: *The Last Years of the English Slave Trade, Liverpool, 1750–1807* (London, 1941) and *The Trade of Bristol in the Eighteenth Century* (ed. W. E. Minchinton, Bristol Record Society's *Publications*, XX, Bristol, 1957), pp. xiv–xv.

[4] See *Considerations on the Present Peace* . . . , pp. 51–3; see also Richard Brew from Castle Brew, Anamabo, to the Merchants of Liverpool, August 25 and October 1, 1771, in Elizabeth Donnan: *Documents Illustrative of the History of the Slave Trade in America* (4 vols., Washington, 1930–5), II, 536–42.

May 5, many abuses of the committee of the Company were aired and a bill was ordered for "regulating the future elections of committee-men for the African Company." [5] However, on May 20 Edmund Burke presented such cogent arguments against a change that it was agreed to put off the matter.[6]

North of the Gulf of Guinea lay the Gambia River where the English had long been established. Farther north, the areas of the Senegal River and the island of Goree had been in control of the French before 1758, but they fell to the British in that year. By the terms of the Peace of Paris of 1763 Goree was returned to France; the Senegal area, however, was ceded to Great Britain.[7] For a short period Senegal was administered by the African Company by decision of Parliament. But this proved to be unsatisfactory because the French, again in possession of Goree, were seeking to establish a post on the Gambia as well as to reclaim Senegal with its profitable gum trade. Moreover, unlike the activity along the Gulf of Guinea, which was strictly coastal, the gum trade extended up the Senegal River into the interior. Therefore in 1765 the act passed by Parliament in 1763 in favour of the Company was repealed and the Senegal forts and factories were now placed under the direct control of the Crown.[8] Even before the passage of this statute, the King in Council had decided to combine the districts of Senegal and Gambia into a single province to be called Senegambia.[9] This action— implying territorial claims to the regions embraced by the two rivers —was taken by order in Council on November 1, 1765. Charles O'Hara was named Governor of the new province, also in November; [10] further, a legislative council of thirteen was established and a court created to administer English law.[11] Thus, while the British

---

[5] *Parliamentary History*, XVII, 504–7.

[6] *Ibid.*, XVII, 507–12. See E. C. Martin: "The English Establishments on the Gold Coast in the Second Half of the Eighteenth Century," Royal Historical Society *Transactions*, 4th ser., V, 167–89.

[7] For the conquest of Senegal and of Goree see Volume VIII of this series, pp. 173–7; for maps of the area see *ibid.*, facing pp. 176 and 177.

[8] The Divesting Act of 1765, 5 Geo. III, c. 44.

[9] For the steps leading to the creation of Senegambia see Board of Trade *Journal*, *1764–1767*, pp. 110–11, 142, 149, 152.

[10] *Ibid.*, pp. 220 and 223.

[11] See Martin Wight: *The Development of the Legislative Council, 1606–1945* (London, 1947), p. 35; E. C. Martin: *The British West African Settlements, 1750–1822* (London, 1927), pp. 57–66; and by the same author: "The English Slave Trade and the African Settlements" in *Cambridge History of the British Empire*, I, 454–6.

posts along the Gulf of Guinea remained under the African Company, Senegambia was administered directly as a Crown colony under this rather elaborate system until 1783, when Senegal was returned to France and Gambia was once again embraced within the African Company system.

The vast importance of the African trading posts was expressed by one writer in 1763 as follows:

> "The trade carried on between Great Britain, Ireland, North America, the West Indies Islands, and Africa, is of greater advantage to this country [Great Britain], than all other trades whatsoever, arising from the great exportation of British manufactures, East India goods, provisions as well as linens from Ireland, which are paid for with specie, sugar, tobacco, rice, cotton, and other plantation-products; and with the commodities of Africa, such as gold-dust, bees wax, elephants' teeth, gum Senegal, various sorts of dying woods, and particularly Negroes for the plantations. . . ." [12]

The author insisted that above two thirds of all British shipping was dependent on this triangular trade and that a continuous supply of Negroes was "the chief and fundamental support of the British colonies." [13]

While it is true that this trade was triangular in its broad aspects —involving British manufactures carried to Africa, African slaves carried to the British West Indies and the more southern British Continental Colonies, and the produce of these colonies carried to Great Britain—it must not therefore be inferred that the same vessels or the same agents or even the same principal British merchants committed to slaving were necessarily directly concerned in these operations. During the period under review in this series the trade took many relatively complex forms. The slaving vessels necessarily carried from the home base—be it Liverpool, Bristol, London, or some other port—various articles to be used in Africa in trade for Negroes [14] and, after the desired supply of slaves had been purchased, sailed to the New World with this valuable cargo. [15] Once

---

[12] *Considerations on the Present Peace* . . . , p. 7.

[13] *Ibid.*, pp. 7–8.

[14] For example, it is stated that commodities valued at £1,553,994 were sent from England to Africa between the years 1748 and 1754. See Bryan Edwards: *The History, Civil and Commercial, of the British Colonies in the West Indies* (2 vols., London, 1793), II, Appendix, 201.

[15] For the general course of the trade for slaves in Africa and their transportation to the New World, see Volume II in this series, Chap. X, "Guinea and the Empire."

the sale of those thus transported had been accomplished, the ship might return to England well freighted, but more frequently it sailed largely in ballast, carrying bills of exchange on British mercantile firms given by planters, or by those who bought and sold slaves on commission, or by the factors of British merchants who were not themselves directly concerned with this traffic in human beings.[16] The slave ship, in fact, was built for a specific purpose and had decided limitations as a general cargo vessel. Indeed it would appear that most bulky colonial exports—such as casks of sugar and barrels of rice—were carried to their destination in regular broad-bottomed merchant ships.[17]

In the 1750's the chief English slave-trading posts on the Gulf of Guinea had been Cape Coast Castle on the Gold Coast, and Commenda, Succondee, and Dixcove to the west; those to the east were Tantumquerry, Winnebah, Accra, and Whydah.[18] By 1771 the most important posts in this area seem to have been Cape Coast Castle, Anamabo, Winnebah, and Accra.[19] However, it must not be inferred that the shipping of slaves to the English plantations had declined since the middle of the century. From the Gold Coast in 1758, 2,203 were carried away; in 1763 the number was 4,135; in 1770 it was 7,203, and in 1775 it had reached 8,108.[20] The procuring of slaves for America remained the chief objective of the African trade during this period, although there was also a profitable trade in gold, ivory, gum, and some other products. It has been stated that the various Europeans—the English, the Dutch, the French, and the Portuguese —who had established posts on the African continent in the course

---

[16] The late Professor Pares, in dealing with the House of Lascelles, throws light on the changing methods for disposing of slaves in the West Indies; see "A London West-India Merchant House, 1740–1769," *Essays presented to Sir Lewis Namier* (London, 1956), pp. 75–107.

[17] In this connection see R. B. Sheridan: "The Commercial and Financial Organization of the British Slave Trade, 1750–1807," *Economic History Review*, 2nd ser., XI, 249–63. The sale of slaves to planters, or to middle men who in turn sold them to planters or took them to the Spanish possessions, usually involved a chain of fairly long-term credit.

[18] See in this series Volume II, Revised, Chap. 10.

[19] See Richard Brew from Castle Brew, Anamabo, to the Merchants of Liverpool, August 25, 1771, in Elizabeth Donnan: *op. cit.*, II, 536–9.

[20] "The Memorial of the Committee of the Company of Merchants trading to Africa to the Lords Commissioners for Trade and Plantations, [April 15, 1777]," *ibid.*, II, 554. For a good deal of information on the slave trade in the Gulf of Guinea in the 1760's and 1770's, see "Minutes of Enquiry into the Administration of the West African Trade," Board of Trade *Journal, 1776–1782*, pp. 126–46.

of the eighteenth century sometimes carried a combined number of as many as 100,000 Negroes a year to the New World.[21] But this inhuman traffic was not allowed to continue without protest.

Adam Smith, Professor of Moral Philosophy at the University of Glasgow, in his *Theory of Moral Sentiments* (first published in London in 1759) had the following to say of the quality of human fortitude: "There is not a negro from the coast of Africa, who does not, in this respect, possess a degree of magnanimity, which the soul of his sordid master is scarce capable of conceiving. Fortune never exerted more cruelly her empire over mankind, than when she subjected those nations of heroes to the refuse of gaols of Europe, of wretches who possess the virtues neither of the countries which they go to, nor of those which they come from, and whose levity, brutality, and baseness, so justly expose them to the contempt of the vanquished." [22] A few years later, the Virginian, Arthur Lee, while vindicating the conduct of slave owners from the censure of Smith, denounced slavery and the slave trade in a pamphlet published anonymously in which he declared: "Shall a civilized, a Christian nation, encourage slavery, because the barbarous, savage, lawless African hath done it? Monstrous thought!" [23] In America, Anthony Benezet, a French Huguenot who had become a devout member of the Religious Society of Friends in Philadelphia, published in 1766 a powerful tract in which he took to task those who, although great "Advocates of Liberty, remain insensible and inattentive to the treatment of thousands and tens of thousands of our fellow-men, who, from motives of avarice . . . are at this moment kept in the most deplorable state of slavery, in many parts of the British Domin-

---

[21] "One hundred and four thousand one hundred slaves were bought this year [1768] on the coast of Africa. Of these, 53,100 were bought by British merchants" (Thomas Southey: *Chronological History of the West Indies* [3 vols., London, 1827], II, 395). In 1768, by another estimate, the total number of African slaves procured was 97,120; of this total, 59,700 were purchased by British and British colonial slavers, according to Adam Anderson: *An Historical and Chronological Deduction of the Origin of Commerce* (2 vols., London, 1764; revised and continued by William Combe, 6 vols., 1790, Dublin), V, 173. See also E. A. Benians: "Financial Experiments and Colonial Development" *Cambridge Modern History*, VI, 187.

[22] *Theory of Moral Sentiments* (2nd edn., 1761), p. 316. Smith here refers to the overseers of slaves, many of whom especially in the British West Indies were men of very low moral sentiment and conduct.

[23] *An Essay in Vindication of the Continental Colonies of America from the Censure of Mr. Adam Smith, in his Theory of Moral Sentiments. With some Reflections on Slavery. By an American* (London, 1764), p. 44. Lee had just completed his studies at the University of Edinburgh where he received an M.D.

ions." [24] In 1771 appeared the first edition of his equally important *Some Historical Account of Guinea . . . with an Inquiry into the Rise and Progress of the Slave Trade, Its Nature, and Lamentable Effects,* to which he added "a re-publication" of extracts of Granville Sharp's pamphlet on the injustice of slavery (published in London in 1769) [25] together with extracts from the *Virginia Gazette* of March 19, 1767, and from the Bishop of Gloucester's sermon of February 21, 1766, preached before the Society for the Propagation of the Gospel.

In England Granville Sharp was carrying forward the crusade against slavery with equal vigour. He had begun his prolonged struggle on behalf of the slaves in 1765 by befriending Jonathan Strong, a Negro whose freedom from his master he had sought without success to secure. The first of a number of Sharp's tracts against slavery had appeared in 1769, as mentioned, and an enlarged edition of it was published in 1772.[26] In this same year Lord Mansfield, Chief Justice of the Court of King's Bench, laid down his famous decision in the case of Somersett (Somerset), a Negro who had run away from his master in England but had been captured. The specific question before the Court was whether Somersett could be forcibly removed from the kingdom by his master to be sold abroad. In the course of his remarks the Chief Justice took the position that "a Case [before the Court] so odious as the condition of slaves must be taken strictly" and must therefore be supported by some positive law. While paying due attention to an opinion handed down by Attorney General Sir Philip Yorke (later the Earl of Hardwicke) and Solicitor General Charles Talbot (later Baron Talbot) in 1729—that the bringing of a slave into Great Britain or the baptizing

---

[24] Anthony Benezet: *A Caution and Warning to Great Britain and Her Colonies, in A Short Representation of the Calamitous State of the Enslaved Negroes in the British Dominions. Collected from various Authors, and submitted to the Serious Consideration of all, and more especially of Those in Power* . . . (Philadelphia, 1766), p. 3. The authors cited are Burke (*European Settlements*), Thomas Jeffrey, George Whitefield, and George Fox among others.

[25] It was about this time apparently that Sharp entered into a correspondence with Benezet, which continued during the 1770's. See Prince Hoare: *Memoirs of Granville Sharp* (London, 1820); see also Elizabeth Donnan: *op. cit.,* II, liii. The Benezet *Account of Guinea* was published in a "New Edition" (without the Sharp extracts) in London in 1788. For the title of the Sharp tract see footnote 26 following.

[26] The title of the Granville Sharp pamphlet was *A Representation of the Injustice and Dangerous Tendency of Tolerating Slavery, . . . in England* (London, 1769); an Appendix to the 1772 edition relates Sharp's success in the case of Jonathan Strong. See also E. C. Ponsonby Lascelles: *Granville Sharp and the Freedom of Slaves in England* (London, 1928).

of a slave as a Christian did not free him—and a similar opinion of Lord Hardwicke (now Lord High Chancellor) given in 1749, Mansfield argued that the "state of slavery is of such a nature that it is incapable of being introduced by the courts of justice upon mere reasoning, or inferences from principles natural or political. . . ." As he could not find any English law supporting the contention of the plaintiff, he decided that Somersett must be discharged.[27]

The Mansfield decision, however, did not free all slaves who had been brought to England by their planter masters; in fact, "a kind of qualified slavery" continued well into the nineteenth century.[28] Nevertheless the case must be considered a milestone in the movement for the abolition of slavery within the British Empire—a movement which, by the efforts of men such as William Wilberforce, at length brought its goal to reality.[29]

---

[27] For a detailed contemporary analysis of the Mansfield decision see Granville Sharp: *The Just Limitation of Slavery* . . . (London, 1776).

[28] M. A. Thomson: *A Constitutional History of England, 1642–1801* (London, 1938), pp. 419–20. Nevertheless the Mansfield judgement in the case of *Somerset v. Stewart*, 1772, was to result in a social problem—that of free but destitute Negroes, whose numbers were increased later by the arrival of Negro loyalists during the War for American Independence. It was as a result of this problem that Sierra Leone was established by private enterprise in 1787 as a "free settlement" where the black poor might be repatriated. See Martin Wight: *op. cit.*, p. 41.

[29] For the history of the humanitarian movement to abolish slavery, which culminated in the act of 1807, see especially Thomas Clarkson: *History of the . . . Abolition of the African Slave Trade* (2 vols., London, 1808), Reginald Coupland: *Wilberforce* (Oxford, 1923), and F. J. Klingberg: *The Anti-Slavery Movement in England* (New Haven, 1926); see also the section on "Slavery" in *Bibliography of British History: The Eighteenth Century, 1714–1789* (eds. Stanley Pargellis and D. J. Medley, Oxford, 1951), pp. 273–4. For the many tracts and pamphlets on the subject issued during this period see Charles Evans: *American Bibliography*, IV and V, *passim*, and Judith B. Williams: *Guide to . . . English Social and Economic History, 1750–1850* (New York, 1926), II, 412–32.

CHAPTER V

The Empire on the Fringe of the Storm: The British West Indies

I T HAS been calculated that between the years 1680 and 1786 over two million Negroes were transported from Africa to various parts of the British Empire.[1] In the eighteenth century the sugar islands of the West Indies [2] received the largest share of the captive blacks sent to the British colonies. Had most of them survived to old age on the islands and propagated—as they were destined to do after the abolition of slavery within the Empire in the nineteenth century—it is unlikely that by the 1750's there would have been any need or demand for their continued importation. But the simple truth was that, as the late Richard Pares pointed out, "the slave population could not maintain itself; it was always wasting away." [3] Because the average life span of a Negro after arriving on a West Indian plantation was but seven years,[4] it was necessary in order to

[1] Bryan Edwards: *The History, Civil, and Commercial, of the British Colonies in the West Indies* (2 vols., London, 1793), II, 55. In his *L'Histoire philosophique et politique des établissements et du commerce des Européens dans les deux Indes*, which first appeared in Amsterdam in 1770, Abbé Raynal estimated (Book XI, Vol. III, 181) that a total of eight to nine million slaves had been transported to the New World from Africa. See also Adam Anderson's *Origin of Commerce* (6 vols., Dublin, 1790), V, 173 and 276; VI, 922.

[2] For the older British West Indies see in this series Volume II, Chap. 7, "The Caribbean Outpost of the Empire," Chap. 8, "Islands of Cane. Islands of Content-ment. Home of the Old Buccaneers," and Chap. 9, "The Struggle for the Moscovado Markets"; see also Volumes IX, 275–6, and X, 214–20, 223–45, 251–2, 274–5. For developments in the ceded Windward Islands before 1750 see Volume V, Chap. 7, "The 'Neutral' Islands of the Caribbeans"; for the period 1763–75 see Volume IX, Chap. 10, "The Ceded Islands: A Free Port," and Chap. 11, "The Ceded Islands: The Caribs, the Franchise, The Royal Prerogative." For maps of the British West Indies see Volumes II, facing p. 181, and VIII, facing p. 66.

[3] Richard Pares: *Merchants and Planters, Economic History Review, Supplement, No. 4* (Cambridge, 1960), pp. 39–40, 82–3.

[4] [G. M. Butel-Dumont]: *Histoire et Commerce des Antilles Angloises* (Paris, 1758), p. 29.

maintain and expand the sugar economy on those islands to import thousands of slaves each year. As emphasized in an earlier volume of this series,[5] the slavers trading from Liverpool and Bristol to the African coast were the chief suppliers of this demand for slave labour. In the middle of the eighteenth century, according to a computation, 10,050 slaves were carried to these islands, with Jamaica requiring 4,780, Barbados 1,700, Antigua 1,700, St. Christopher 1,200, and Montserrat and Nevis each 335.[6] Between January 1765 and July 1766, Jamaica received 16,760 Negroes, the majority of whom remained on the island with a small proportion sold to the Spaniards.[7]

It is possible to draw an interesting if far from conclusive picture of population fluctuation in the British West Indies from an examination of various official reports and other sources of information provided by Captain Thomas Southey, a commander in the Royal Navy, whose *Chronological History of the West Indies* maintains its high reputation as a painstaking chronicle of developments in the West Indies. The data [8] show the following:

Island	Year	Whites	Black Slaves	Free Blacks
Jamaica	1698	7,365	40,000	
	1734	7,644	86,546	
	1755	12,000	130,000	
	1774	12,737	192,787	4,093
Barbados	1676	21,725	32,473	
	1698	2,330	42,000	
	1748	25,000	68,000	107
	1773	18,532	68,548	

[5] Volume II, Revised, pp. 271–4; see also G. F. Dow: *Slave Ships and Slaving* (Salem, Mass., 1927), Chap. 5, "The Liverpool and Bristol Slavers."

[6] Board of Trade *Journal, 1749–1753*, p. 14.

[7] See Thomas Southey: *Chronological History of the West Indies* (3 vols., London, 1827), II, 388. According to figures presented by Stephen Fuller, London agent for Jamaica, to the Board of Trade early in 1778, from 1765 to 1769 a total of 31,932 Africans were brought to Jamaica and from 1770 to 1774 the total was 44,409. For Fuller's figures see L. J. Ragatz: *The Fall of the Planter Class in the British West Indies* (New York & London, 1928), p. 87.

[8] For the respective figures see Thomas Southey: *op. cit.*, II, 113, 179, 200, 217, 223, 257, 310, 318–19, 343, 367, 374–5, 378, 388, 408, 414–15, 419, 421, and *passim*. These figures should be compared with those given in F. W. Pitman: *Development of the British West Indies, 1700–1763* (New Haven, 1917), Appendix I. For the unreliability of the available figures on the slave population in the British West Indies see Richard Pares: *Merchants and Planters* (previously cited), pp. 83–4.

Island	Year	Whites	Black Slaves	Free Blacks
Leeward Islands	1707	6,957	22,999	
of Antigua, St.	1720	10,458	35,968	
Christopher,	1756	8,613	70,552	
Montserrat, and	1774	6,790	81,270	
Nevis				
Dominica	1763	1,718	5,872	500
	1766	2,020	8,497	
	1773	3,350	18,753	750
Grenada	1763	1,225	12,000	455
	1771	1,661	26,211	415
St. Vincent	1763	695	3,430	1138
	1764	2,104	7,414	
The Bahamas	1722	830	310	
	1734	810	488	77
	1773	2,052	2,241	

This table—manifestly defective as it is—would seem to indicate that there was a constant recruitment of blacks, even when the whites diminished in numbers.

In view of the West India planter's preference for the hardy, warlike Gold Coast Negro, it is not surprising to learn that the period under examination was one of conspiracy and rebellion on the part of the slaves and of legislation to hold them in check.[9] In 1760 Jamaica experienced a series of uprisings among the fiery Koromantyns, starting in St. Mary's Parish in the northeastern part of the island. Spreading westward to Westmoreland and St. James's, the conspiracy was detected before it could take any solid hold in St. Thomas's and St. John's parishes, or in Kingston.[10] "Their generalissimo in the woods," Tacky, apparently a young man of considerable stature around whom the African "priests" had built

---

[9] For an abstract of the laws enacted in Jamaica from 1696 to 1769 for the purpose of controlling the Negroes see [Edward Long]: History of Jamaica . . . (3 vols., London, 1774), II, 485–9.

[10] Bryan Edwards noted that the insurrection of 1760 began among a hundred newly imported Gold Coast Negroes at two plantations, one of which, Trinity Estate, was owned by his relative. Edwards writes: ". . . I do not believe that an individual amongst them had received the least shadow of ill treatment from the time of their arrival there." As testimony to this he stated that the overseer at Trinity, Abraham Fletcher, had shown such "tenderness and humanity [to the slaves in his care] . . . that his life was spared from respect to his virtues" (op. cit., II, 64).

up a legend of invincibility, was ultimately shot. But before these uprisings were finally put down, many planter families were slaughtered under horrifying circumstances. Rather surprisingly, the free Negroes settled in their own "maroon" towns in the more mountainous part of the island gave support to the government in the suppression of the rebellion.[11] About sixty white people were destroyed and not less than a thousand Negroes either were killed in the open, executed after the trial, transported to Spanish America, or committed suicide. Unfortunately, the barbarities perpetrated on the whites were, in turn, practised on the captured leaders of the Koromantyns.[12]

The following year on the island of Nevis a plot was discovered among the Negroes for massacring all the whites at a time when they were sickly as the result of "the want of hurricanes and high winds."[13] Again in 1765 some of the Koromantyns in Jamaica rebelled, but the uprising was firmly put down before much loss of life or property had been sustained.[14] And in 1766 on the same island an uprising in St. Elizabeth Parish was at length quelled by killing nineteen of the rebels, forcing the retreat of the rest, who then dispersed in small bands into the hills; thereafter "a chain of guards" drawn from both the foot and the horse militia protected the settlements.[15] In 1768 on the island of Montserrat, where the Irish were very numerous, "a most horrid and deep-laid plot of the Negroes" was formed to massacre all the white inhabitants during their celebration of St. Patrick's Day.[16] The following year a plot for a general insurrection of slaves in Jamaica was formed; the scheme was first of all to set fire to Kingston at various points and then, when the inhabitants were busy extinguishing the flames, to fall upon them

---

[11] For the settlements in Jamaica of free Negroes called "Maroons" see Volume II of this series, pp. 191–2, and especially R. C. Dallas: *History of the Maroons* . . . (2 vols., London, 1803).

[12] For a detailed account of the rebellion see [Edward Long]; *op. cit.*, II, 447–62; see also Bryan Edwards: *op. cit.*, II, 65–6.

[13] *Annual Register for 1761*, p. 160. In 1756 the population of Nevis by official returns was 1,058 whites and 8,380 blacks. See Thomas Southey: *op. cit.*, II, 319.

[14] Thirteen Negroes were executed, thirty-three transported, and twelve acquitted. See Thomas Southey: *op. cit.*, II, 384.

[15] Lieutenant Emerson Elletson to Brigadier General Lewis, October 18, 1776, Roger Hope Elletson's Letter Book (ms.), Institute of Jamaica, Kingston.

[16] For an account from Montserrat of this conspiracy under date of March 21, 1768, see the *Pennsylvania Gazette*, April 21, 1768. In 1756 the population of Montserrat by official return was 1,430 whites and 8,853 blacks. See Thomas Southey: *op. cit.*, II, 319.

and put them to death. Again, as in the case of the Montserrat plot, the whites were warned by a Negress; three hundred armed slaves were surprised at the place of rendezvous and many of them put to death.[17]

It can be understood that an African born in freedom in the land of his nativity—as many Negroes were who thereafter became slaves by the fortune of war or for some misdeed—would find the condition of slavery intolerable even if treated with consideration by his West India master. But it also appears that on all too many plantations the owner was an absentee living abroad, in which case the care of his plantation might be put in the hands of an overseer, perhaps a man compelled to leave England to escape punishment for his profligacies.[18] In the words of Charles Leslie (in *A New and Exact Account of Jamaica* published in 1739): ". . . it cannot be wondered at . . . when raised to power [such a person], should prove a savage and inhuman Tyrant." The post of overseer—involving as it did the exploitation of slave labour for the profitable management of the sugar plantations—was certainly not one designed to appeal to people of finer sensibilities.

Fear of punishment drove the slave to work, and fear circumscribed his activities during his leisure hours. Fear also dictated the character of the harsh Jamaica black code,[19] in which punishment by mutilation and the most painful methods of execution were sanctioned. In 1764, a temporary act was passed to make this code more

---

[17] *Annual Register for 1769*, p. 110. It is of interest to note that the British settlers in the Belize area of Honduras Bay engaged in cutting logwood and mahogany (a settlement still politically dependent upon Jamaica in the 1760's and 1770's), also had their problems with slave rebellions and runaway slaves; this contributed to their urging during this period that the British settlements in Honduras be recognized as a British colony. See *Archives of British Honduras* (ed. J. A. Burdon, London, 1931), I, 117–25 and 183; see also R. A. Humphreys: *The Diplomatic History of British Honduras, 1638–1901* (London, New York, Toronto, 1961), pp. 3–7, and in this series Volume II, 202–7.

[18] For example, a bill was framed by the Assembly of Jamaica in 1769 to provide a suitable residence for the Governor at Kingston, rather than at Spanish Town, with the stipulation that the landowners of the County of Surrey, within which Kingston lies, should pay for the cost of the mansion. A petition opposing this was signed by the attorneys of twenty absentees, including the attorney for William Beckford, then Lord Mayor of London. The bill was rejected by the Council. See Minutes of the Council, December 19 and 23, 1769, Journal of the Council of Jamaica (ms.) 1769, Jamaica Archives, Spanish Town, cited hereafter as Jamaica Council Journals (ms.). For a study of absenteeism in the West Indies see L. J. Ragatz: "Absentee Landlordism in the British Caribbean, 1750–1833," *Agricultural History*, V, 7–24.

[19] For the laws passed between 1696 and 1750 relating to Negro slaves in Jamaica see [Edward Long]: *op. cit.*, II, 485–9. See also in this series Volume II, pp. 198–200.

effective. The law carried the title, "An Act for raising and fitting out parties for suppressing any Rebellion on this Island during the Continuance of this Act." [20] By it, in order to avoid the inconveniences of martial law in case of a slave uprising, the Governor was authorized to fit out parties which would be rewarded—over and above all plunder—for every rebellious Negro or Mulatto they should kill or take at the rate of £20 per man, £10 per woman, and forty shillings for each child under the age of fourteen. This money was to be paid by the church wardens or "collecting constables" of the parish to which the party belonged. When the Negro had been killed the officer in charge was expected to view the body; in addition, the victim's head was to be brought to the nearest settlement for verification before the reward was paid.

After the suppression of the Jamaica slave rebellion of 1766, Lieutenant Governor Elletson wrote to the *custos* [21] of the several parishes expressing his deep concern over the frequent slave insurrections. He contended that the rebellions were occurring not for lack of "good and wholesome Laws to prevent them," but rather as the result of neglect in strictly enforcing the laws. He therefore called upon each *custos* to require that his parish magistrates prohibit Negroes from leaving their plantations without carrying a ticket and that the slaves be prevented from assembling and beating their drums in violation of regulation. [22]

Although slavery was thus well entrenched in the West Indies, a number of voices were raised against the trade and against the treatment of the Negro as an inferior human being. [23] The Scot Charles Leslie, in the dedication of his book on Jamaica to the Right Honourable the Earl of Eglinton, wrote: "You will see, in the following Sheets, that Slavery is the ruin of Society, and that oppression is still attended with fatal Inconveniences to the Tyrant." [24] This was

---

[20] Temporary Acts of the Assembly, Laws of Jamaica (ms.), 5:127–8, Jamaica Record Office, Spanish Town. Reference has been made (in footnote 18) to the Jamaica Archives. It should be pointed out that at the time the writer of this series was working in Spanish Town the Jamaica Record Office and the Jamaica Archives were housed in separate buildings.

[21] For the unique role of the *custos*, the great landowner placed at the head of each parish in Jamaica, see Volume II of this series, pp. 182–3.

[22] Elletson to the *Custodes* of the several Parishes, November 24, 1766, Elletson Letter Book, *loc. cit.*

[23] [Edward Long]: *op. cit.*, II, 356–8 supports the view of the innate inferiority of the Negro to the Caucasian.

[24] [Charles Leslie]: *A New and Exact Account of Jamaica* (Edinburgh, 1739), which appeared in London in 1740 under the title *A New History of Jamaica* and

also the view of a fellow Scot, the Rev. James Ramsay, who before he took holy orders had been a naval surgeon on board the *Arundel* and who, as a result of his efforts to assist a slave infected with the plague, had become strongly opposed to the institution of slavery. On the island of St. Christopher, while holding the livings of Christchurch and St. Johns', Capisterre, he sought to Christianize the Negroes. This he did, "despite the brutal treatment he . . . received from the sugar growers," and the opposition manifested during the early 1770's by other St. Christopher clergymen.[25] Hostility against his activities in fact became so great that he was forced to withdraw from the island.[26]

If Ramsay was thwarted on St. Christopher in his desire to bring a fuller life to the Negroes, he would have found more favourable conditions on the neighbouring island of Antigua, where Nathaniel Gilbert, landowner, Speaker of the Assembly, and member of one of the leading families of the island campaigned.[27] Gilbert became a fervent Methodist and helped to establish the first Methodist Society in the West Indies. True to his calling, he preached the gospel to the slaves. "Amidst torrents of reproach," we are told, "he persevered till he had formed a society of nearly 200," composed of whites and blacks. Upon his death, the Negro women continued to pray and hold meetings every night until the arrival in 1778 of a Mr. Baxton, the regularly appointed Methodist missionary. By 1783 the number of Methodists in Antigua was 1,000, most of them blacks.[28]

carried its author's name. In this connection the student should consult the section on Jamaica in Elsa V. Goveia's *Study of the Historiography of the British West Indies to the End of the Nineteenth Century* (*Istituto Panamericano de Geografia e Historia, No. 186,* Mexico, 1956), which deals with the historical approach of such writers as Leslie and Long (pp. 49–64).

[25] For Ramsay's indictment of the St. Christopher clergy see the "Leeward Islands," Nos. 22, 26–8, Fulham Palace Manuscripts, Library of Congress transcripts; see also J. A. Schutz: "James Ramsay, Essayist: Aggressive Humanitarian" in *British Humanitarianism: Essays Honoring Frank J. Klingberg* (Philadelphia, 1950), pp. 145–65.

[26] During the War for American Independence Ramsay acted as a naval chaplain, serving under Barrington and Rodney in the West Indies campaign; at its conclusion he settled in England, where he was given the livings of Teston and Nettlestead in Kent. In 1784 came his *An Essay on the Treatment and Conversion of African Slaves in the British Sugar Colonies,* which powerfully helped to promote the anti-slavery movement in England. See F. J. Klingberg: *The Anti-Slavery Movement in England: A Study in English Humanitarianism* (New Haven, 1926), pp. 59–65, and particularly J. A. Schutz: *op. cit.*

[27] See R. B. Sheridan: "The Rise of a Colonial Gentry: A Case Study of Antigua, 1730–1775," *Economic History Review,* 2nd ser., XIII, 356.

[28] See Thomas Coke: *A History of the West Indies* (3 vols., Liverpool & London, 1808–11), I, 213; II, 427–8, 432, 436.

Even more successful in reaching the slaves of Antigua were the missionaries sent by the Moravians or *Unitas Fratrum* (United Brethren), who by 1787, according to Bryan Edwards, had made 5,465 converts. Edwards also indicates that the developing humanitarianism of the latter part of the eighteenth century was first signalled in the British West Indies in Antigua. There the black code was ameliorated to the extent that a Negro slave accused of crime was given a trial by jury, and if convicted of a capital offence was given a respite of four days before his execution, doubtless to allow time for any possible further evidence of his innocence to be brought forward.[29]

No account of the development of humanitarianism in the British West Indies in the eighteenth century would be complete without reference to the Codrington Estates and Codrington College. At his death in 1710, Christopher Codrington—a wealthy Barbadian planter, one-time probation fellow of All Souls, Oxford, and for three years the Governor of the Leeward Islands—willed to the Society for the Propagation of the Gospel in Foreign Parts three plantations (two of them in Barbados and one in Barbuda in the Leeward Islands) and some 300 slaves, in order that an institution of learning and piety might be established and maintained in Barbados. While the benefactor's dream for a seminary for medical missionaries was not to be realized, Codrington College did open its doors in 1745 to offer work at the grammar-school level for both paying and charity students. It continued to function at this level until 1775 and reopened in 1797. (In 1830 studies were undertaken at the college level for a period, but it is as a grammar school, now known as the Lodge School, that it continues to operate.)

Codrington had also been convinced of the need and obligation to Christianize the West Indian Negro slaves. This likewise was the position of the Society, which now faced the difficult problem of seeking to carry out its holy duty by maintaining efficient operation of the Codrington plantations for the support of the College. To realize this secondary aim and to maintain the strength of the labour force it was even thought necessary to make purchases yearly of a certain number of African slaves; in fact, between 1712 and 1761 some 450 Negroes were bought, while others were hired. Although after this period no slaves were imported, in 1766 the Henley planta-

[29] Bryan Edwards: *op. cit.*, I, 448 and 455.

tion, lying not far from the Codrington Estate, was purchased with its 148 Negroes. Also in that year, in the annual sermon delivered before the Society, Bishop William Warburton denounced the African slave trade as contrary to "both divine and human law." To achieve one of the primary aims of the donor as well as its own, the Society moreover continued to send out to the estate clerics who were expected to act as Christian catechists to the Negroes. But the work of conversion proved to be disheartening, as it frequently provoked more opposition than encouragement from the manager or overseer of the estate; nor were most of those sent to bring the Gospel to the benighted well suited for this task. Nevertheless, while the Society before 1775 took the position that slavery and Christianity were reconcilable, it did make great and somewhat successful efforts, especially after 1768, to ameliorate conditions of service of the Codrington Negroes and to encourage other slave-owners on the island to accept the view that only contented and happy people thrive and multiply.[30]

The first Moravian mission in Jamaica was established in 1754, by invitation, among the slaves of the Bogue Estate lying on the Black River in St. Elizabeth Parish. After visiting the Negroes in their huts during two years of prayer and exhortation, the missionaries counted 77 converts "and 400 catechumans, under instruction for holy baptism." In fact, on Sunday mornings a meeting was held for white overseers and bookkeepers, leaving the Negroes to assemble in the afternoons. Although the slaves of this parish rose in revolt in 1760, no Christian convert was found among the rebels. During the first fifty years of the Moravian mission, almost a thousand Negroes were baptized into the faith. In order to operate the plantation of some seven hundred acres called the Old Carmel, which came into the possession of the mission and on which stood the capacious meeting house, the missionaries themselves became slave-owners.

---

[30] See J. H. Bennett, Jr.: *Bondsmen and Bishops. Slavery and Apprenticeship on the Codrington Plantations of Barbados, 1710–1838* (Berkeley & Los Angeles, 1958); *Codrington's Chronicle: An Experiment in Anglican Altruism on a Barbados Plantation, 1710–1834* (ed. F. J. Klingberg, Berkeley & Los Angeles, 1949), especially Chap. 1, "Of the Noble and Generous Benefaction of General Christopher Codrington," by S. C. McCulloch and J. A. Schutz; Chap. 3, "Of the Plantations Intire," by J. A. Schutz and Maud E. O'Neil; and Chap. 5, "Of the Negroes Thereon," by J. H. Bennett, Jr. See also A. G. Spangenberg: *Account of the Manner in Which the . . . United Brethren Preach the Gospel and Carry on Other Missions* (London, 1789), T. J. Hamilton: *History of the Missions of the Moravian Church During the Eighteenth and Nineteenth Centuries* (London, 1900), and J. E. Hutton: *A History of Moravian Missions* (London, 1923).

We are told that they treated their slaves with "the utmost kindness" when they behaved, but did not hesitate to punish them when they acted otherwise.[31]

Whether it was the influence of the Moravians, or that of the anti-slavery literature issuing from the English press by this period, or both, a strong sentiment against the slave trade developed in King-ston, Jamaica. What is most unusual, the movement was promoted by "Mr. Thomas Hibbert, who had been forty or fifty years the most eminent Guinea factor there," but who, in a debating society formed to discuss matters of interest, proposed the question: "Whether the trade to Africa for slaves was consistent with sound policy, the laws of nature, and morality?" After several discussions of the matter the group at length voted against the slave trade by a majority.[32]

In line with these sentiments, the Assembly of Jamaica in 1774 passed two bills placing heavy restrictions on the trade. When this legislation reached the Privy Council in London there was great opposition to it on the part of the Liverpool and Bristol slavers. A meeting called by the Board of Trade on March 6, 1775, to consider the bill was attended by a large body of merchants. Also present was the London agent for the colony, Stephen Fuller, who admitted that the nature of the restrictions placed by the bill upon the slave trade would have the effect of prohibiting it. He gave as his view that the true motive behind the bill was the danger facing the white inhabit-ants of the island from the great disproportion of blacks to whites—over 220,000 Negroes as against a number not exceeding 16,000 of whites of all descriptions.[33] It is of interest to note that three days later Edmund Burke, representing Bristol in the House of Com-mons, appeared before the Board, together with Sir William Mere-dith, a member of the House from Liverpool, to complain of these restrictions on behalf of their constituents.[34] The act was not ap-proved. In the words of the Earl of Dartmouth, Secretary of State for the Colonies and President of the Board: "We cannot allow the colonies to check or discourage, in any degree, a traffic so beneficial to the nation." [35]

---

[31] For the activities of the Moravians in Jamaica in the latter part of the eighteenth century see J. H. Buchner: *The Moravians in Jamaica . . . , 1754–1854* (London, 1854), pp. 24–39.

[32] Thomas Southey: *op. cit.,* II, 420–1.

[33] Minutes of March 6, 1775, Board of Trade *Journal, 1768–1775,* p. 415.

[34] *Ibid.,* p. 416.

[35] Thomas Southey: *op. cit.,* II, 421.

In turning now to consider matters aside from slavery, it may be affirmed that no Assembly was more active in defending its rights in the 1760's than that of Jamaica. During the administration of William Henry Lyttelton (1762–1766), who had been transferred to the island after serving as Governor of South Carolina, several constitutional issues arose. The Assembly most vehemently asserted its exclusive powers over money bills without interference from the Council;[36] it also upheld the privileges of its members to be free from molestation and to have their property exempt from seizure. One of the issues arose in 1764 when the coach-horses of a member, John Oliphant, were seized for debt by the deputy marshall. By order of the Assembly the two men who had assisted the marshall were placed under arrest. They were only released on a writ of *habeas corpus* when an appeal was made to the Governor acting in his capacity as Chancellor. Again they were arrested by order of the House and again released by the same powers. On December 21 the Assembly passed a series of resolves, followed by a motion that it could not proceed to any other business until its prestige had been recognized and suitable reparations made for the indignity suffered by its member.

At this juncture, after a series of prorogations, Lyttelton dissolved the Assembly on the ground that Article 13 of his instructions provided that Assemblymen could not claim a privileged position in order to evade suits brought by creditors. But the new Assembly was equally adamant concerning its privileges and also refused to conduct any business until these should be recognized. As a result it too was dissolved. Nor did the successive members see fit to change their attitude.[37] When they met and organized on August 13, 1765, the Speaker failed to pose the request to the Governor—customary

---

[36] On September 30, 1766, Lieutenant Governor Elletson, who took over the administration that year upon the departure of Governor Lyttelton, transmitted an address of the Council to the King asking for a redress of grievances. This stated that for several years past the Council had been precluded from making any alterations in money bills "contrary to the King's Instructions." Elletson, writing to the Earl of Shelburne, asked if it might be wise "that the Royal Pleasure should interpose before any evil consequence arise." See Shelburne Papers, 52:403–4, Clements Library, Ann Arbor, Mich. It should be pointed out that this claim to the exclusive power of the Assembly over fiscal legislation was modified in 1770 during the administration of Governor Sir William Trelawny, when several bills concerned with the revenue were submitted to the Council. The issue is set forth in some detail in Minutes of the Council, February 15 to April 14, 1770, Jamaica Council Journals (mss.), *loc. cit.*

[37] H. P. Jacobs, in a series of articles on "Roger Hope Elletson's Letter Book," *Jamaican Historical Review,* I and II, deals with the above constitutional issue in the October 1952 number, II, 2:68–9; see also *ibid.,* I, 3:317, 332–4, 336. (The student should note the individual pagination of each number of the *Jamaican*

in all royal colonies—that the House be permitted to enjoy its usual privileges. When the Governor called the members before him in the Council chamber on the 16th for the specific purpose of asking the Speaker whether he would request these privileges, the latter replied he would not. Once more Lyttelton dissolved the Assembly in order "that his Majesty's prerogative suffers no violation." [38] With no money bill passed, but with two regiments of regulars stationed on the island to be paid by the local government, Lyttelton was forced to draw upon the royal exchequer by authority of his instructions. Nor was the home government ever reimbursed, since the Assembly took the position that the Governor's step was designed to subvert their liberties.[39] In the end, after Lyttleton had been recalled, the Privy Council finally framed an instruction that exempted Assemblymen from civil suits for debt while the Assembly was sitting (as well as six days before and after each session) provided that their servants and equipment were absolutely necessary for the performance of Assembly duties.[40] When the Assembly was informed of this instruction, it declared that it already enjoyed

---

Historical Review). For an account of the dispute between Governor Lyttelton and the Jamaica Assembly see *Acts of the Privy Council, Col. Ser., 1745–1766*, pp. 704–13; see also W. J. Gardner: *A History of Jamaica* (London, 1909), pp. 137–41. Mary Patterson Clarke also discusses the constitutional aspects of the issue in *Parliamentary Privileges in the American Colonies* (New Haven, 1943), pp. 88–90 and 252–7.

[38] See *Journals of the Assembly of Jamaica*, V, 529–30.

[39] *Ibid.*, VI, 35–6. The Assembly took the position in 1766 that they were not bound to make any provision for the 36th and 66th Regiments "for any time during which they were precluded from the Constitutional means of making such Provisions"; they nevertheless assured Lieutenant Governor Elletson in an address that they would now proceed to make suitable provision for the troops. For a copy of this address see Shelburne Papers, 52:399–401.

[40] *Acts of the Privy Council, Col. Ser., 1745–1766*, p. 713; see also *Royal Instructions to British Colonial Governors* (ed., L. W. Labaree, 2 vols., New York & London, 1935), I, 115–16. In July 1766 the Assembly addressed Lieutenant Governor Elletson, stating that their ancestors brought with them a right to the laws of England "as their inheritance"; that the House of Assembly had ever held "the same Rank in the System of their Constitution as the House of Commons does in the Mother Country; that . . . all Judges, Magistrates & Public Officers have ever been amenable to the Assembly and their Conduct liable to its Inspection"; that those committed by the House of Commons were never discharged in England by any inferior arrest and they therefore complained of the decree of the late Chancellor as "a most flagrant Violation of their privileges." In reply the Lieutenant Governor agreed that the determination on record in the Office of the Register of the Court of Chancery "appears irregular and unprecedented" and that as Chancellor he had vacated the said proceedings, making them null and void. However, before doing so, Elletson consulted the Council which took the position that the steps taken by Lyttelton as Chancellor could not be supported. For Elletson to the Board of Trade, July 7, 1766, the address of the Assembly, and the Lieutenant Governor's reply, see Shelburne Papers, 52:387–92.

all the privileges possessed by the British House of Commons so that the instruction was unnecessary.[41]

The British West Indies were deeply concerned over the revolutionary movement developing in the Thirteen Continental Colonies in 1774, especially when news arrived of the adoption by the First Continental Congress of the so-called Association. This declared that the North American colonials were not to import any molasses, syrup, coffee, or pimento from the British West Indies after December 1, 1774, and that after September 10, 1775, they were to export no commodities to these British Islands, Great Britain or Ireland. In view of this alarming news, planters of these islands residing in England and merchants trading to them presented a petition to the House of Commons on February 2, 1775.[42] It stated that "the British Property in the West India Islands amounts to upwards of Thirty Millions Sterling, that a further Property of many Millions is employed in the Commerce created by the said Islands . . ." and that any interruption to the commercial intercourse of the islands would be disastrous. They therefore prayed that the Commons adopt appropriate measures to prevent the evils threatened and preserve intercourse between the West Indies and the Northern Colonies as a matter of lasting benefit to the whole British Empire.[43]

On March 17 the House of Commons, meeting as a committee of the whole, reviewed the evidence in support of the petition from the West India planters. As the result of testimony presented by George Walker of Barbados and John Ellis of Jamaica, together with a summary by a Mr. Glover, who "appeared as agent for the petitioners, and manager of the evidence," a clear picture emerged of the economic state of the sugar islands by the end of 1774 and of their commercial interdependence with other parts of the Empire.[44] The

---

[41] *Journals of the Assembly of Jamaica*, VI, 4.

[42] *The Parliamentary Register . . . Debates of the House of Commons [and House of Lords]*, 1774–80, (ed. John Almon, 17 vols., London, 1775–80) I, 131–2, cited hereafter as *Parliamentary Register*; see also Lillian M. Penson: "The London West India Interest in the Eighteenth Century," *English Historical Review*, XXXVI, 373–92, for a broad discussion of the means taken by West India merchants and planters living in London to protect their interests. For the commercial relations of the British West Indies and the North American colonies for the period under review see Richard Pares: *Yankees and Creoles: The Trade between North America and the West Indies before the American Revolution* (London & New York, 1956); see also in this series Volume II, Chap. 9.

[43] *Parliamentary Register*, I, 131, and *Journals of the House of Commons*, XXXV, 91–2.

[44] See *Parliamentary Register*, I, 327–60.

testimony reveals, among other details, the extent to which Great Britain, Ireland, and North America supplied food, especially "corn and provisions," not to mention lumber and other commodities, to the sugar islands, and what they received in return.[45] Also indicated are the kind and value of property in the islands, the extent of absentee ownership, the debts owed to English merchants, and the benefits of the sugar colonies to Great Britain in commercial profits and revenue.[46]

Of especial interest is the petition of the Jamaica Assembly to the King adopted on December 23, 1774. It points out that "weak and feeble as this colony is, from its very small number of white inhabitants, and its peculiar situation, from the encumbrance of more than two hundred thousand slaves, it cannot be supposed that we now intend, or ever have intended, resistance to Great-Britain." Indeed, the people of the colony had never opposed "any law imposed on us by Great-Britain," although sensible of their rights and of "the pernicious consequences" with which some of these laws must be attended, rather relying always "with the most implicit confidence, on the justice and paternal tenderness of your Majesty." Nevertheless the "approaching horrors of an unnatural contest between Great-Britain and her [North American] colonies," bringing with it "the most dreadful calamities to this island," led the people living on it to entreat that they be permitted to act as "humble suitors" for the colonists of America. The petition thereupon sought "to place it in the royal mind, as the first established principle of the constitution," that no laws can affect the people of England but such as receive their assent; it follows therefore "that no one part of your Majesty's English subjects either can, or ever could, legislate for any other part," that those who left England to settle in North America carried with them their rights and privileges, and thus "the people of England had no rights, power, or privilege, to give to the emigrants, as these were at the time of their emigration possessed of all such rights, equally with themselves." It thereupon asserted that the royal prerogative as annexed to the Crown was "totally independent of the people, who cannot invade, add to, or diminish it, nor restrain or invalidate those legal grants, which the prerogative hath . . . very liberally given, for the encouragement of colonization. . . ." As for

---

[45] *Ibid.*, I, 328–36.

[46] *Ibid.*, I, 328–42. For Ellis's evidence on Jamaica's resources and trade, in which he gives the number of Negroes as exceeding 200,000, see *ibid.*, I, 342–6.

the people of Jamaica, they had been promised by royal proclamation that they should have "the same privileges, to all intents and purposes, as the free-born subjects of England." Therefore, although they had received the several acts of Parliament for the regulation of trade "as the salutary precautions of a prudent father, for the prosperity of a wide extended family," they had not conferred on their fellow subjects in England and Great Britain the power to legislate for them and "behold with amazement a plan almost carried into execution, for enslaving the colonies, founded . . . on a claim of parliament to bind the colonists in all cases whatsoever." The petition ended by beseeching His Majesty "to become a mediator between your European and American subjects" and to consider the latter as equally entitled to protection.[47]

This address was doubtless designed among other things to change the policy of non-intercourse with the West Indies agreed upon by the First Continental Congress.[48] Indeed, it carried the implication that the people of Jamaica were very strongly committed to the position taken in North America on colonial rights. The day following the address the Assembly was prorogued and then dissolved, not to meet again until October 31, 1775. During this interval there was a change of attitude on the part of the members of the Assembly.[49] On November 4 a joint committee of the two chambers was appointed to inspect the forts and other fortifications of the island. On the 10th a bill was sent to the Council from the Assembly to raise the necessary money for the proper maintenance of the 50th and 60th British Regiments on the island with the assurance that the

---

[47] See *Journals of the Assembly of Jamaica,* VI, 569–70. When the above petition was presented to the Assembly it was debated; on the division, sixteen favoured and nine opposed it. A committee of five, appointed to wait upon the Governor with the petition, asked him to transmit it to the King "in the most acceptable manner" (*ibid.*). It may be assumed that if all forty-three members of the Assembly were present at the time of the debate, eighteen did not vote.

[48] The address was most favourably received when it appeared in American newspapers. See for example the *Pennsylvania Gazette,* March 1, and the *Connecticut Courant,* March 6, 1775; see also Agnes M. Whitson: "The Outlook of the Continental American Colonies on the British West Indies, 1760–1775," *Political Science Quarterly,* XLV, 56–86, especially 84–6.

[49] It well may be that, in the elections of members, the electors—made up of landholders who had the required yearly income or hereditaments—turned against those who had promoted the petition. Edward Long (*History of Jamaica,* I, 57) stresses the independent spirit of the Jamaica freeholders when it came to elections and points out that in its composition the Assembly was generally inclined to a conservative position; for, to hold a seat in that body, the person elected was obliged to swear that he possessed a yearly income of £300 or gross assets valued at £3,000.

Assembly was giving its full attention to the strengthening of the island's defences. The following day the Assembly sent a bill for laying a duty on tonnage, the proceeds of which were to be applied to the fortifications and for the purchase of gunpowder.[50] On December 22, both the Assembly and the Council framed loyal addresses to the King expressing gratitude for his "most gracious intention to provide for our security by sending Troops to supply the Place of those removed" and assuring him that they would ever be ready "to defend Your Majesty's sacred Person and Government with our Lives and Fortunes. . . ."[51] When adjourning the Assembly that same day, Governor Sir Basil Keith commended both the Assembly and the Council for their "Zeal and Harmony, which must necessarily be productive of every thing I could wish: the Prosperity of this Country, the Advantages of His Majesty's service, and the Ease and Happiness of my administration."[52]

---

[50] See Minutes of the Council, October 31 to November 14, 1775, Jamaica Council Journals (mss.), Spanish Town, Jamaica. See also *Laws of Jamaica*, II, 1760–1792, 181–3.

[51] Minutes, December 22, 1775, Jamaica Council Journals (mss.).

[52] *Ibid.*

CHAPTER VI

The Empire on the Fringe of the Storm: The Bermudas

THE wide-spread slave insurrection which took place in Jamaica in 1760 had ended only after many lives were lost. Far to the northward in the Atlantic Ocean "a dangerous Conspiracy of the Slaves . . . for destroying the white Inhabitants" of the Bermudas occurred in October of the following year.[1] Whether there was any connection between the two events is impossible to say. The population of the Bermudas in 1761 was estimated at about 12,000, almost equally divided between whites and blacks,[2] whereas in Jamaica (as noted earlier) the ratio of Negroes to whites was ten to one. Moreover, Jamaica had been annually importing large numbers of potentially dangerous Gold Coast slaves, while for many years the Bermudas had received almost none, being overstocked with blacks for the island's economy, which produced no great staple export demanding labour. If long hours of toil under intense heat on the sugar plantations of Jamaica had been a factor in producing the rebellion of 1760 there, idleness, rum-drinking, and sheer ennui seem to have been at the bottom of the Bermudian slave conspiracy of 1761.

---

[1] *Ancient Journals of the House of Assembly of Bermuda, 1691–1785* (4 vols., London, 1906), II, 929. Cited hereafter as *Assembly Journals*.

[2] H. C. Wilkinson: *Bermuda in the Old Empire . . . 1684–1784* (Oxford, 1950), p. 244. For the population in 1749, and a general picture of the islands in the middle of the eighteenth century, see in this series Volume II, Revised, pp. 230–8; for a map see *ibid.*, facing p. 238. In 1756 the population was stated to be 6,402 whites and 4,900 blacks, and in 1774, 5,632 whites and 5,023 blacks. See Governor Bruere to the Earl of Dartmouth, March 29, 1774, P. R. O., C.O. 37:36; see also Sir Alan Burns: *History of the British West Indies* (London, 1954), pp. 500 and 515.

How formidable the Bermuda slave conspiracy actually was is not clear.[3] It is apparent, however, that Bermudians were deeply apprehensive lest the horrifying uprisings of Jamaica be repeated on their islands. As a result, many slaves presumed to have been involved in the conspiracy were apprehended, placed in custody, and forced to confess. On October 20 the Assembly moved to bring in a bill without delay that would permit the trial of such offenders "by Commission in a Summary Way and without the Solemnity of a Jury." [4] But, because of the serious drawback to proceeding by formal statute—since such an act could not be effective without royal approval—the two Houses decided on October 21 to address Governor William Popple. From him they sought permission to erect a court with summary powers to try "those guilty of atrocious crimes"; this, they pointed out, could be done without suspending or repealing any law—in view of authority already vested in the Governor and Council "to constitute and appoint a Special Court upon Extraordinary Occasions"—under the terms of an act passed on August 3, 1690.[5] Popple on the 22nd agreed to receive such a bill "provided no Act now in force relating to the tryals of Negroes . . . be thereby repealed." That same day, by disregarding all rules, a bill was accordingly hurried through both the Assembly and the Council and was signed by the Governor.[6]

Nevertheless difficulties arose. Information was still lacking as to the number of slaves involved. On October 28 the Council therefore recommended to the Governor that a reward of £100 be given to any white person furnishing information against a Negro and one amounting to £25 to any free Negro who would do likewise; also to any slave who would inform against his fellow slaves, not only pardon but manumission "under the Public Seal" would be forthcoming.[7] Governor Popple agreed to take these steps. Yet even by the beginning of December, according to the Governor, those discoveries that had been made were imperfect and "tho clear as to bloody intent, not full enough of such proofs as the law requires on

---

[3] See H. C. Wilkinson: *op. cit.*, pp. 242–4, and W. B. Kerr: *Bermuda and the American Revolution* (Princeton, 1936), p. 8, which gives the year of the revolt scare as 1762.

[4] *Assembly Journals*, II, 929.

[5] *Ibid.*, II, 931–2.

[6] *Ibid.*, II, 933–5.

[7] Minutes of the Council, 1746–1765 (mss.), pp. 351–2, Bermuda Archives. Cited hereafter as Council Minutes.

Capital Conviction." [8] On December 7 martial law was declared,[9] and watches or patrols in St. George's Parish and in each of the eight so-called tribes (or parishes) were instituted.[10] Still, sufficient evidence could be produced to bring about the execution of only six slaves.[11] The slaves against whom evidence was inconclusive were ordered to be transported from the island.

While fear of the Negroes persisted in the Bermudas, there was another side to the story of the relations between whites and blacks. For example on May 2, 1762, Mrs. Margaret Spencer, the widowed owner of Peter, a slave in gaol under sentence of transportation, pleaded with the Governor that only through his labour could "she maintain herself and not be a burthen to others." William Cooper in a similar petition stated that he and his wife, both of extreme old age, depended on the support of their slave Tom, now under sentence to be sent abroad. In the same vein Ephraim Gilbert, Gentleman, stressed his great need of his slave, also called Tom. In another case, John Paynter on May 11, in his petition seeking to keep his slave Charles, even offered security for his good behaviour. He argued that the Negro was an experienced pilot who knew every passage around the islands; should he fall into the hands of the enemy—for France and Spain were then at war with Great Britain —the consequences might be very serious.[12] The truth was that most masters were deeply attached to their slaves—economically useless as most of them undoubtedly were except for the tasks they fulfilled in their subordinate position. They were considered an inseparable adjunct to the family group. For the parents of the contemporary generation of slaves had usually been owned by the parents of the present owners; thus both slave-owner and slave had grown from infancy to maturity in intimate association in the same household.[13]

---

[8] Popple to the Assembly and Council, December 2, 1761, *Assembly Journals*, II, 945-7.

[9] Council Minutes, 1746-1765, p. 361. For the fifteen articles and restrictions introduced by the Assembly for the declaration of martial law see *Assembly Journals*, II, 949-50.

[10] *Ibid.*, II, 967-8.

[11] Council Minutes, 1746-1765, pp. 411-12. The owners of these Negroes applied for compensation, which was granted on January 22, 1763. The value placed upon each of those executed ranged from £22 (for the one woman) to £91 in current money. The total compensation granted amounted to £299.—.4.

[12] *Ibid.*, pp. 393-7.

[13] Very naturally some situations were the kind to induce the owner to want to get rid of a slave. For example, even Governor Popple had on his hands two undesirable Negroes, Penelope and her son Julius, both of whom were the property of the King. According to Popple, Julius, with the encouragement of his mother, "had made it a

Yet, as Governor Popple observed to the Assembly on December 2, 1762, there were too many Negroes in the Bermudas; the islands offered so little means for employing most of them effectively. To train them in the techniques of the common trades was "the most pernicious practice," as it discouraged the poorer white inhabitants from following such vocations.[14] Agriculture on the islands consisted almost exclusively of subsistence farming in the eighteenth century, with provisions including some fruits grown in quantity only sufficient to support the population for three months of the year.[15] It is true the islands had at that time one great economic asset, the cedar trees, out of which they constructed a hardy, sea-going sloop for use in the carrying trade. Nevertheless the employment of Negroes in building and manning these vessels caused Governor Popple to request the Assembly to find means of reducing the number of Negroes on the islands so as to provide work for the "industrious but poor white Inhabitants to get bread for themselves and for the support of their Familys."[16] But no such steps were taken, doubtless because of the white people's attitude toward their household slaves.

Indeed many families in the Bermudas were held to be well-to-do, but few if any had sufficient wealth to send their children to England to be educated. This lack of great wealth and of suitable employment for many in the Bermudas persisted, despite the efforts in the spring of 1760 to stimulate trade by repealing an act passed in 1694 excluding Jews from the islands.[17]

During the twenty-five years before the outbreak of the War for American Independence the Bermudas had but two Governors: William Popple, who received his royal commission in 1745, assumed his duties on June 23, 1747, and left the islands on January 2, 1764, and Captain George James Bruere, who was commissioned on

custom for years past of corrupting every wench in the Governor's family . . . contrary to his [the Governor's] express injunctions." As a result both of them had been put out of the house, and Popple had requested the Council to dispose of them and buy others in their place for his household; see Council Minutes, 1746–1765, pp. 408–9.

[14] *Assembly Journals,* II, 946.

[15] D. Fenning, J. Collyer, and others: *A New System of Geography* . . . (2 vols., London, 1765), II, 680; W. B. Kerr: *op. cit.,* pp. 1–2; see also in this series Volume II, Revised, p. 231.

[16] *Assembly Journals,* II, 946.

[17] For the Repeal Act see Acts of Bermuda (mss.), 1775–1793, I, 80, and Council Minutes, 1746–1765, p. 322.

April 18, 1764, and took office on August 9 of that year. Both had great difficulty in securing obedience to the laws of trade and compliance with the requirement that all vessels arriving in the islands from abroad must enter at the custom house located at St. George's, the capital of the Bermudas. For example in 1764, in the interval between Bruere's arrival and Popple's departure, in an attempt to break up the practice of landing goods without payment of duties the collector appealed to the President of the Council, Francis Jones, for military aid in controlling the smuggling at the west end of the islands. But when a detachment of soldiers arrived they were refused quarters in the inns of the district, nor would the justices of the peace support the demand for lodgings. The military experienced the same difficulty to the east at Crow Lane Harbour (now Hamilton, the capital). Bruere brought the matter before the Council in October 1764, at a session which included the examination of witnesses, some of them manifestly defiant, and the presentation of various papers documenting the illegal actions. It was finally voted at this Board that the acts of trade and the Governor's instructions could best be carried into execution "if all vessels arriving at these Islands be obliged to come into the Harbour of Saint George's on their first arrival in order for the greater Ease of Collecting his Majesty's dues." Two members of the Council voted in the negative, and one of them, John Harvey, who in 1766 became Chief Justice, voiced the dissenting view that such a requirement would be a great inconvenience to the inhabitants, whereas duties could just as well be collected at other harbours.[18]

Following the advice of the Council, Bruere issued a proclamation making St. George's the only port of entry. On November 24, 1764, the Governor addressed the Assembly, calling upon it to "disapprove of the . . . Audacious behaviour of Several Captains of Sloops that did presume to Sail and depart from these Islands, without the accustomed Licence of Permit, and some that . . . broke Bulk without making any Entry or Clearance at the Custom House. . . ." In its reply the Assembly asserted that Governor Popple's earlier instructions had been modified and that in 1756 he had laid before its members new instructions providing for a searcher to reside at Ely's Harbour in the west end of the island. It added that the man had remained there for several years until his death, but that no successor had been appointed although the permit to land

---

[18] Council Minutes, 1746–1765, pp. 477–86.

goods had never been revoked. The reply further pointed out that three fourths of all commodities imported, particularly provisions, were sold either at Ely's Harbour or that of Crow Lane.[19] Thus the issue stood, as the result of an appeal made by the Assembly to the King,[20] until in the spring a searcher was again appointed for the west end (with instructions to permit vessels to enter at Ely's Harbour as the only alternative to St. George's).[21] With this accomplished, and in order to satisfy all groups, Bruere wrote to the Secretary of State for the Southern Department, the Earl of Shelburne, pointing out that for many years the inhabitants of the islands had been divided into three parties—one of St. George's, one of "the Center," and one of the "West End"—and therefore recommending that an additional legal port of entry be established at the Crow Lane Harbour under proper regulations. This, he thought, would at least produce unanimity among the Bermudians.[22] But evasion of the trade regulations long continued to be a major problem on the islands.

Another much more notorious practice was that of lying in wait for vessels that might be wrecked or actually using means to lure them onto the reefs and then plundering them. The dangerous Caicos Islands was a favorite resort for the Bermuda marooners and wreckers;[23] but their evil trade was also practised on the coasts of the Bermudas. In 1771 Bruere was compelled to issue a proclamation against what he called a "Notorious Practice" on the part of fishermen and others who, when a ship was in difficulty among the rocks off the islands and before help was requested by the ship's master, would swarm aboard it and would even loot the crew's clothing, shoes, money and other valuables, not to mention additional plunder they took and their demands for "salvage" rights. He therefore forbad this unrequested "assistance" on pain of death.[24] In this

---

[19] *Assembly Journals*, II, 1120–7.

[20] See Board of Trade *Journal, 1764–1767*, p. 294.

[21] Bruere's address to the Assembly, March 19, 1767, Council Minutes, 1765–1781, p. 101.

[22] Bruere to Shelburne, May 18, 1767, Shelburne Papers, 52:553–4.

[23] The practice of sailing to the Caicos Islands for wrecks and also to entice ships onto the shoals was common for many years and persisted late in the century. Governor Bruere wrote to Dartmouth on August 20, 1775: "Our people here frequently pursue a scandalous and villanous Entreprise by going to the Cacoses in search of Wreck Goods; a disgrace to the English flag. . . ." (Bermuda Archives transcript of the Phillipps Mss.); see also H. C. Wilkinson: *op. cit.*, p. 19 *et seq.*

[24] For the Governor's proclamation dated January 5, 1771, see Council Minutes, 1765–1781, pp. 211–12. The occasion of the proclamation was the looting of the ship *Campbell*, Captain James Bruce, bound from Virginia to Glasgow with a cargo of tobacco, pig iron, and lumber. Both whites and blacks, who boarded the vessel

proclamation the Governor also denounced the wicked device of "the putting out of false lights [at night] with the intention of bringing any ship into danger." [25]

The presence of a contingent of regular troops, despite the problem of quartering them beyond the limits of St. George's, undoubtedly had its effect in bringing about some degree of enforcement of the trade laws and respect for government in general. But in 1772 the soldiers were withdrawn and sent to North America. Bruere, writing of the situation to General Gage on December 5 of that year, pleaded that in the interests of law enforcement a replacement detachment be sent to the islands. In reply Gage expressed his regret to hear of "the lawless Proceedings of the People of your Islands," but pointed out that the St. George's garrison had been withdrawn by the King's orders and he could not venture to replace it except by the same authority.[26] The sole defence of the island was therefore left in the hands of the local militia, whose personnel was by no means favourable to securing obedience to British trade and other regulations. Bruere next appealed to Lord Dartmouth for troops, but the Secretary of State for the Colonies answered (on May 3, 1775, in the midst of the American crisis) that the "present state of His Majesties service in North America precludes for the present all hope of our being able to share any part of the King's troops for Service of the Bermuda Islands, or of making them a Station for one of the small Sloops of War. . . ." [27]

Lawlessness was not the only problem the Bermudas had to face. As has been stressed, the inhabitants were able to produce only a limited proportion of their annual food supply and had long depended for the balance on the nearby North American colonies. But in October 1774, the Association of the First Continental Congress resolved to forbid all commercial intercourse with the British West Indies, as well as with Great Britain and Ireland. This was interpreted to include not only the British sugar islands in the Caribbean

---

unasked, "behaved most barbarously, cutting and destroying at a strange Rate, contrary to all the laws of Civil Society," according to Collector of Customs Smith in his long petition to the Governor and Council. Council Minutes, 1765–1781, pp. 206–13.

[25] For the proclamation of January 16, 1771, see Council Minutes, 1765–1781, pp. 211–12.

[26] Gage to Bruere, March, 1773, Haldimand Papers, B. M., Add. Mss. 21, 673:147.

[27] Bermuda Archives transcript of the Phillipps Mss.

Sea but also the Bahamas and the Bermudas (called by the Congress the Summer [Somers] Islands).

Fearful that the population of the islands would face starvation,
some of the popular leaders in the colony—foremost among whom
was Colonel Henry Tucker, head of the powerful Tucker clan—decided in the spring of 1775 to bring unofficial representatives of the
various parishes together at Paget to discuss the problem of obtaining food. Most of the parishes responded. It was then agreed—of
course without the sanction of the Governor—to appeal in the name
of the inhabitants to the Continental Congress to let the islands
continue to be supplied with the customary necessities from North
America.[28] To this end, a delegation headed by Tucker left for
Philadelphia some weeks later. On July 11, 1775, an address by "the
different parishes of the Islands of Bermuda" was read in Congress.[29] It appears that the delegates indicated that a supply of
gunpowder—an article in desperately short supply in the Continental army—was lodged in the unguarded King's powder-house at St.
George's. They may also have intimated that this might be made
available, provided that in return a supply of food was forthcoming.[30]

Other members of the Tucker family seem to have been deeply
involved in the plan to seize the King's powder and carry it to
America. The fourth son of the Colonel, St. George Tucker, had
gone to Virginia to study at William and Mary College; he then read
law and in the spring of 1775 was admitted to the Virginia bar. He
was strongly committed to the American cause. Before returning
home as requested by his father he apparently informed the President of the Congress, in Virginia at the time, that there was "a

---

[28] See the entry for August 1, 1775, *Journals of the Continental Congress,
1774–1789*, II, 239.

[29] The address is among the papers in Tucker House, Williamsburg, Va.; the
substance of it is given by W. B. Kerr, *op. cit.*, pp. 45–6.

[30] On July 17 the Congress again read the address from the Bermudas and then
authorized the President of the Congress, Peyton Randolph of Virginia, to inform
the Burmuda delegates that it was being considered and to request them to send to the
Congress an account of the amount of provisions imported into the islands during the
past years; Randolph was also to furnish them with "a copy of the resolves entered
into on Saturday last respecting the importation of gunpowder." The Saturday resolves read that "for the better furnishing these colonies with the necessary means of
defending their rights," every vessel bringing in gunpowder and other munitions
should in return be permitted to load and export colonial produce to the value of the
imported gunpowder, "the non-exportation agreement notwithstanding." See entries for
July 15 and 17, 1775, *Journals of the Continental Congress, 1774–1789*, II, 184–5 and
187.

considerable Quantity of powder [in the Bermudas] over which there was no Guard," which might easily be secured if wanted. Likewise St. George's elder brother, Dr. Thomas Tudor Tucker, who was practising medicine in Charleston, South Carolina, seems to have "hinted" to the South Carolina Committee of Safety about the availability of the powder.[31] As a result two vessels were dispatched to the islands, the sloop *Lady Catherine*, Captain George Ord, from Philadelphia, and the schooner, *Charleston and Savannah Packet*, Captain John Turner, from Charleston. At this juncture still another Tucker enters the picture—Henry Tucker of Somerset, who lived in the west end of the islands and shared the rather lawless views of the other dwellers there. Acting upon the advice of Colonel Tucker, who had returned meanwhile from Philadelphia, this Tucker organized a raiding party and on August 14 led it at night in sailboats to the unprotected powder magazine which stood at St. George's on a rise close to the Governor's residence and not far from the shore. The party succeeded in breaking into the stronghold and most of the powder-barrels—close to a hundred in all—were rolled down to the boats under cover of darkness and carried to the waiting vessels. In this way part of the powder sorely needed by the American revolutionary forces was shipped to Charleston and the rest to Philadelphia.[32]

Although the Bermuda Assembly meeting on August 16 offered a reward by proclamation of £100 sterling for information that could convict "the Perpetrators of this audacious piece of Villany," and Governor Bruere added a further reward of £30, no evidence was brought to light.[33]

---

[31] See the draft of a letter intended for Richard Rush, Comptroller of the Treasury in Washington, written by St. George Tucker on October 27, 1813, *Virginia Magazine of History and Biography*, XLII, 213–14. Tucker's memory seems to have failed when he referred to the "arrival of Mr. Silas Dean in Bermuda in a Vessel sent by Congress, to bring up the powder in the Magazine there; his reception & intercourse with my father & friends . . . probably confirmed an opinion that I was not wholly ignorant of the affair" (*ibid.*, p. 213). Deane arrived in the Bermudas on his way to France in April 1776, not 1775. See the *Deane Papers*, I, New York Historical Society *Collections*, 1886, pp. 134–5. Deane's own letter from Bermuda to Robert Morris, describing his voyage and the friendly feelings of the people toward the American colonies, is housed in the museum of the United States Naval Academy at Annapolis and is dated April 26, 1776 (according to Professor Vernon D. Tate, Librarian at the Academy) and not 1775, as indicated by H. C. Wilkinson: *op. cit.*, p. 376.

[32] This account is based on the Tucker House Papers, *loc. cit.*, and is treated effectively by W. B. Kerr: *op. cit.*, pp. 46–50.

[33] See Bruere to Dartmouth, August 17, 1775, Bermuda Archives transcript of the Phillipps Mss.

As for the Continental Congress, on November 22, apparently as the result of the seizure of the powder and its delivery, this body agreed: "That the Inhabitants of the Island of Bermuda appear friendly to the cause of America, and ought to be supplied with . . . the produce of these colonies . . . necessary for their subsistence and home consumption," and therefore voted that they should be permitted to import from the colonies annually 72,000 bushels of Indian corn, 2,000 barrels of bread or flour, 1,000 barrels of beef or pork, 21,000 bushels of peas or beans, and 300 tierces of rice. It may be added that this annual supply was allocated among various colonies. For the immediate needs of the Bermudians, the Congress further voted that a cargo of provisions should be sent in the brig *Sea Nymph*, Captain Samuel Stobel.[34] The people of Bermuda were delighted with "the concession" made by the Continental Congress, unwilling as they were to bid open defiance to the power of Great Britain. Under the circumstances Governor Bruere felt himself isolated and was doubtless confirmed in the feeling he had expressed at an earlier date when he wrote to the Earl of Dartmouth that he could not "confide in any person here, at present," as there seemed to be "few friends of government here." [35]

---

[34] *Journals of the Continental Congress, 1774–1789,* III, 362–4.
[35] Bruere to Dartmouth, July 31, 1775, Bermuda Archives transcript of the Phillipps Mss.

CHAPTER VII

The Empire on the Fringe of the Storm: East Florida

LTHOUGH the distance between the Bermudas and the Province of East Florida was great, there was a fairly close connection between the two areas in the 1770's; for the detachment of British regulars which was withdrawn from the islands in 1772, much to the satisfaction of Bermudians—especially the lawless smugglers and wreckers—was sent to East Florida, to the equal satisfaction of the people there. Furthermore, as noted in an earlier volume of this series,[1] a great effort had been made in the 1760's to bring several thousands of the overflow population from the Bermudas to help meet East Florida's crying need for settlers.[2] Although the enterprise was a failure—only some forty Bermuda families eventually settled on lands set apart for them at Mosquito Inlet, about sixty miles south of St. Augustine—it was the forerunner of a much bolder attempt to import settlers for the new province.

The other colonization attempt—the first serious effort to import natives from the Mediterranean area to a North American colony—was promoted by Dr. Andrew Turnbull, a man who had travelled widely and lived in the Levant.[3] He had also acted as British consul

---

[1] For the beginnings of the Province of East Florida see Volume IX of this series, Chap. 8; see also, for much greater detail, the scholarly study by C. L. Mowat: *East Florida as a British Province, 1763–1784* (Berkeley & Los Angeles, 1943), cited hereafter as *East Florida*.

[2] For the settlement efforts of John Savage of Charleston see in this series, Volume IX, pp. 190–1, and for two maps of East Florida see *ibid.*, facing pp. 182 and 183.

[3] The first proposal to bring Mediterranean peoples to settle in the more southern British colonies in North America after the cession of Florida seems to have been made by Archibald Menzies, a Scot who published (on October 23, 1763, from Megerny Castle, Perthshire) a *Proposal for Peopling his Majesty's Southern Colonies on the Continent of America*. In it Menzies recommended that Greeks, Armenians, and Minorcans be brought over to cultivate grapes and olives. A copy of this rare

at the Greek-colonized port of Smyrna in Turkey and had married a native of this Asia Minor city. After returning to England, where he practised medicine, he decided to give up his calling, procure a grant of land in East Florida, and establish a settlement of Greeks upon it. On June 18, 1766, he secured an order in council for 20,000 acres, and in November 1767 he arrived in St. Augustine, eager to carry out his plans.[4] After Turnbull and Sir William Duncan, an associate in the enterprise, had had lands lying just south of Mosquito Inlet surveyed, Turnbull set to work to get them in shape to receive the people he planned to bring.[5] His immediate objective was to recruit within the period of one year some five hundred Greek Christians living in Turkey. Governor James Grant rightly conceived that the project would be attended by vast expense,[6] but this did not daunt the optimistic Turnbull, who had great faith in the Greek spirit of enterprise.[7]

Returning to England in the spring of 1767, Turnbull petitioned

promotion tract is in the John Carter Brown Library, Brown University, Providence, R.I. Dr. Lawrence C. Wroth, then Librarian, points out in his "Source Materials of Florida History in the John Carter Brown Library of Brown University," *Florida Historical Quarterly*, XX, 3–46, that there may be a direct connection between the proposal of Menzies and the Turnbull project, since both men were Scots and both were physicians—that is, if the Dr. Archibald Menzies who accompanied the 1796 Vancouver expedition as a field naturalist was the Menzies who produced the proposal.

[4] At the time that Turnbull received his grant, Sir William Duncan also was granted 20,000 acres. See *Acts of the Privy Council, Col. Ser.*, IV, 815. On May 13, 1767, a grant of 20,000 acres of East Florida land was made to Sir Richard Temple (apparently for George Grenville); at the same time Turnbull secured East Florida grants for four of his children: Nicholas, Mary, Jane, and Margaret. See *ibid.*, V, 590–1. An agreement was signed by Turnbull and Duncan for joint exploitation of their lands for seven years at a cost of £9,000; at the end of this period the agreement was to lapse and a division of the assets to be made under the supervision of an impartial committee. See Dr. Carita Doggett-Corsi: *Dr. Andrew Turnbull and the New Smyrna Colony of Florida* (privately printed in Florida, 1919), pp. 18–21. By marriage Dr. Doggett's name became Corsi and she is often referred to under this name, but the references to her hereafter in this volume will be as Doggett-Corsi.

[5] Governor James Grant to the Earl of Shelburne, January 20, 1767, P.R.O., C.O.5:548, pp. 285–6. According to Carita Doggett-Corsi (*op. cit.*, pp. 24–5), Governor Grant assured Hillsborough that he would assist Dr. Turnbull as the King had commanded. It was the noted surveyor De Brahm who advised Dr. Turnbull to investigate Mosquito Inlet. See also Ralph H. Brown's "The De Brahm Charts of the Atlantic Ocean," *Geographical Review*, XXVIII, 124–32.

[6] Carita Doggett-Corsi: *op. cit.*, pp. 24–5.

[7] Among the Shelburne Papers, 48:393–7, in the Clements Library, Ann Arbor, Mich., is an "estimate of the Expence of settling Twenty Thousand Acres of Land in East Florida with Seventy-five Greek Families . . . also with twenty Negroes to clear the Land the first year." It was calculated that at the seventh year the profits would be £3,114. This seems to have been Turnbull's rosy view of the project he had in mind.

the King for permission to obtain a deactivated sloop of war, which he proposed to fit out as a transport and to man, provision, and navigate at the expense of himself and his partner, Duncan. By this means he would be able to carry "many hundreds of useful subjects to East Florida," who were adept at growing cotton, silk, and other commodities which, he had found, could be produced on the soil of East Florida.[8] He also petitioned that the unused bounty already provided for encouraging the production of cotton, wine, silk, and other desirable articles of commerce in East Florida should be made available for his settlers.[9] Both these petitions were favourably received. Turnbull also finally widened the support of his enterprise by enlisting a third grantee of 20,000 acres, George Grenville.[10]

After making additional arrangements for his settlement, Turnbull in June 1767 sailed in the sloop of war from England for the Mediterranean. At Leghorn in Tuscany he picked up a hundred Italians; at Smyrna in Asia Minor, in the Morea (the present Peloponnesus), and elsewhere, he loaded up large numbers of Greeks despite difficulties in overcoming the opposition of Turkish officials. Finally in Minorca he recruited a considerable number of the Greek-speaking inhabitants, who soon joined the other emigrants concentrated at Port Mahon. In the spring of 1768 some 1,400 prospective settlers left Minorca for Florida in seven crowded vessels. After another vessel had been secured at Gibraltar the flotilla headed across the Atlantic.[11] By June 26 four of the vessels had arrived at St. Augustine; the other three put in an appearance later.

---

[8] For the Turnbull petition to the King see C.O.5:548, pp. 301–3. On March 31 the Earl of Shelburne referred the petition to the Board of Trade which approved the project on April 7, provided that the naval department did not feel it would be attended by "inconveniences." See *ibid.*, p. 305; see also Board of Trade *Journal*, *1764–1767*, p. 379.

[9] For Turnbull's second petition, referred to the Board of Trade on April 9, 1767, see C.O.5:548, p. 309. The Board recommended on the 16th that forty shillings should be given to each of the first five hundred Greeks brought to and settled in East Florida. See *ibid.*, p. 313; see also Shelburne to Grant, May 14, 1767, *ibid.*, p. 317.

[10] To repeat, the grant of 20,000 acres of land in East Florida to Sir Richard Temple in 1767 (*Acts of the Privy Council, Col. Ser., 1745–1766*, p. 815) was designed for George Grenville. See again Carita Doggett-Corsi: *op. cit.*, pp. 18–19. E. P. Panagopoulos in his important study: "The Background of the Greek Settlers in the New Smyrna Colony," *Florida Historical Quarterly*, XXXV, 95–115, refers to "a new and important partner, the Prime Minister of England himself, Lord Grenville." Grenville was of course out of office in 1767 and remained a commoner.

[11] For an excellent description of Turnbull's recruitment of settlers in the Mediterranean see *ibid.*, XXXV, 101–5. The eight vessels carried a total of 1,403 men, women, and children. For the return of these vessels, with the number of settlers in each, see C.O.5:549, p. 257.

This was no mean achievement on the part of the enterprising Dr. Turnbull. Governor Grant was certainly impressed. "This, My Lord," he declared in writing to the Earl of Hillsborough, Secretary of State for the Colonies, "I believe is the largest Importation of White Inhabitants that ever was brought to America at a time. . . ." [12]

By August 1768 the settlers had all been taken to the centre of the Turnbull-Duncan-Grenville land allotment. Called New Smyrna, the grant lay near Mosquito Inlet on a river then named the Hillsborough (now Indian River). Food supplies and huts had been provided in advance, and all seemed to go well at first. [13] Under the supervision of the managers of the estate most of the men set to work willingly. But it would appear that some of them were not accustomed to labour and were at heart mere adventurers. One of them, an Italian named Carlo Forni, launched a mutiny on August 19. Declaring himself "Captain General and Commander in Chief of the Greeks and Italians," he and his followers seized a vessel that had brought provisions, raided the houses for rum and firearms, and threatened with death any who offered resistance. His plan was to sail to Havana, Cuba, with his supporters. Warned by Turnbull of what was taking place, Governor Grant was able to send troops on board the packet sloop *East Florida* and another vessel, the *Juno,* to intercept the escaping vessel, which was carrying some three hundred men, women, and children. Before it could pass the bar of the inlet, a shot was fired across its bows from the *East Florida* and the mutineers surrendered. Although thirty-five of them escaped in a boat to the Florida Keys, they were later captured. [14]

According to Governor Grant, Turnbull's arrangement with the settlers was in fact a fair one. They were to be settled as families and were to receive half of the produce of their labour—"the surest, indeed the only method of making new Adventurers Industrious, for no man in America can be prevailed upon to work for his Master in order to repay the Expence which the Master may have been put to

---

[12] Grant to Hillsborough, July 2, 1768, C.O.5:549, p. 253, and same to same, August 27, 1768, *ibid.,* pp. 281–5.

[13] How many dwellings were built on the Turnbull lands is not clear, but eighty were erected on those claimed by Duncan and forty on the Grenville property. See W. H. Siebert: "Slavery and White Servitude in East Florida, 1726–1776," *Florida Historical Quarterly,* X, 18.

[14] Grant to Hillsborough, August 29, 1768, C.O.5:549, pp. 281–5, and same to same, October 20, 1768, C.O.5:550, p. 2; see also the *Georgia Gazette,* October 19, 1768.

upon his Account." [15] According to Bernard Romans,[16] however, the conditions under which the plantation was worked involved the labourers in hardship and deprivation. He asserted that all were obliged to indent themselves, their wives, and their children for a period of ten years— in what he called a state of vassalage. In return some were given a plot of land to work, but at the end of the period it was to revert to the owner. Others were given no land "and were obliged to work in the manner of Negroes, [at] a task in the field," and received only scanty supplies of maize and pork at a general mess to which they were called by beat of drums. Romans also gives the following account of the mutiny. The men, driven to a state of despair by the manager, a man named Cutler, at last rebelled and cut off one of his ears and two of his fingers.[17] Then, under the leadership of Forni—an Italian of bad principles, accused of the rape of a very young girl—they sought to gain Havana. When brought to trial there was so little evidence against most of the mutineers that bills for crimes deserving capital punishment were presented against only five.[18] Upon their conviction, two of them were reprieved by the Governor; a third was also reprieved but only on condition that he execute the other two, which he was prevailed upon most reluctantly to do after embracing them.[19]

[15] Grant to Hillsborough, July 2, 1768, C.O.5:549, p. 253.

[16] Romans, an engineer and botanist then living in East Florida, served on the grand jury called to consider the fate of the mutineers. See Bernard Romans: *A Concise Natural History of East and West Florida* (New York, 1775); this important work was to have been published in two volumes by subscription but only one appeared. See P. L. Phillips: *Notes on the Life and Works of Bernard Romans,* Florida State Historical Society *Publications,* No. 2 (Deland, Fla., 1924), in which the author discusses fully (pp. 40–4 and 103–11) the anonymous publication of Romans's "Account of the Foundation of New Smyrna" in the *Columbian Magazine* (Philadelphia, August 1788) to which Dr. Turnbull took great exception, and gives in full the Doctor's refutation as it appeared in the December 1788 issue of the same magazine. For biographical and bibliographical notes and documents on Romans see the P. L. Phillips work just cited.

[17] According to the master of the *Juno,* Captain Ryall, who sailed his vessel to the rescue of the colony, Cutler lost his right ear and three fingers of his right hand, and was wounded in the groin. For Ryall's account see the *Georgia Gazette,* October 19, 1768.

[18] The two of the five who were executed were Carlo Forni, the ringleader, and Giuseppi Massodati, who mutilated the manager, Mr. Cutler. Grant to Hillsborough, January 14, 1769, C.O.5:550, p. 56.

[19] Bernard Romans: *op. cit.,* pp. 268–72. Carita Doggett-Corsi, a direct descendant of Turnbull, stressed the point (p. 61) that the mutineers, who at most composed only one fifth of the New Smyrna settlers, never wanted the settlement to succeed and tried to wreck it. After destroying many things they could not take away, they spent three days resting and drinking the rum they had plundered. Her book tends to prove that Romans's criticisms were largely unfounded (p. 33, n2). However, Bruno Roselli (*The Italians in Colonial Florida* . . . [The Drew Press, Florida, 1940], pp. 11–17)

By September all was quiet in New Smyrna,[20] but a new peril threatened. Before the end of the year an outbreak of scurvy carried away some three hundred settlers, mostly elderly people and children.[21] What is more, by the end of 1768 the large sum of £20,000 sterling had been expended in bringing these people to America, and in providing food, clothing, shelter, and other necessities for them. Further sums would have to be paid out to provide them with subsistence and clothing for two more years before any returns could reasonably be expected. In view of these hard facts Governor Grant wrote to the Secretary of the Colonies, the Earl of Hillsborough, warning him that unless he could include the New Smyrna settlement in his budget estimates for 1769 it was likely to perish; for, said Grant, it had already exceeded twice the sum that Turnbull's financial backers had agreed to pay, since over twice as many people had come as had been anticipated. At the same time the Governor spoke in highest terms of Turnbull.[22] As for the Doctor, after the revolt he felt impelled to spend most of his time at New Smyrna instead of leaving affairs in the hands of a manager. When the new year dawned the settlers, now in better health, carried on their activities "chearfully," according to Governor Grant.[23] By March 1769 they had cleared seven miles of land lying along the river and had also put in gardens on their allotments. To relieve their immediate and pressing needs the Governor sent the sloop *East Florida* to Charleston for a supply of maize. Yet the costs of the enterprise continued to mount until by the following summer £28,000 had been spent, and Turnbull's London associates, who had pledged but £6,000, at last became "heartily tired of paying such large & frequent Bills," which had to be honoured if the settlement were not to fail.[24] They finally agreed to honour a total of £24,000, but they would go no farther.

---

makes a strong attack on the Doggett-Corsi history, especially the account of the revolt.

[20] Frederick Mulcaster to [Peter Manigault], September 3, 1768, Manigault Papers, Carolina Library, University of South Carolina, Columbia, S.C.

[21] Grant to Hillsborough, December 1, 1768; C.O.5:550, pp. 5–8.

[22] *Ibid.*

[23] Grant to Hillsborough, January 14, 1769, C.O.5:550, p. 56.

[24] Grant to Hillsborough, March 4, 1769, and same to same, July 21, 1769, C.O.5:550, pp. 86 and 129–30. To help save the colony the British Treasury Board authorized Hillsborough to draw upon the Treasury up to the amount of £2,000. See Thomas Bradshaw of the Treasury to the Board of Trade, March 30, 1769, C.O.5:550, p. 67. Between August 1769 and February 1771, Grant paid out a total of £12,682.12.9 to relieve the New Smyrna settlement. For the "State of Cash paid out

Fortunately the government of the province was able to keep the people of New Smyrna from starving until their crops matured. Although by the fall of 1770 the colony had sufficient food supplies, the settlers were ill-clothed—many going about almost naked—and were obliged to continue to seek shelter from the weather in the small huts hastily constructed in 1768. As Turnbull's credit had run out he could not remedy the situation; but he did try to ease their lot by residing constantly with them and doing as much as any man could "to repair the first fault of exceeding the number of people to be imported." [25] By May 1771 things were looking up at New Smyrna. Turnbull was ready to harvest his crop of indigo, a plant that grew well in the soil of East Florida and matured some two months earlier than the indigo of Georgia and South Carolina.[26] But misfortune still dogged his enterprise.

During the nine years after the establishment of New Smyrna the number of deaths of the settlers totalled 964.[27] Nevertheless the New Smyrna settlement survived and even showed signs of improvement. The people remained in good humour.[28] Unhappily, Turnbull's great supporter, Grant, left East Florida in 1771 and Lieutenant Governor John Moultrie—who then carried on until the arrival of Governor Patrick Tonyn in the spring of 1774—became hostile to the scheme, as did Tonyn himself.[29] Nor did the establishment near New Smyrna of impressive houses on great plantations worked by slaves have a happy effect upon the settlers; for they were looked down on by the wealthy plantation owners and even by the slaves as "poor white trash." [30] Nevertheless Turnbull persisted in his at-

---

of his Majesty's Bounty for the support of the distressed Greek settlement," covering the period August 1769 to February 1771, see C.O.5:552, pp. 41–7. On March 8, 1771, John Robinson, secretary of the Treasury Board, wrote to John Pownall, secretary of the Board of Trade, that with respect to the continued support of "the Greek Colony, their Lordships do not think themselves authorized to allow any farther sum of money for this Service" (C.O.5:552, p. 25).

[25] Grant to Hillsborough, September 1, 1770, C.O.5:550, pp. 145–6.

[26] Lieutenant Governor Moultrie to Hillsborough, May 22, 1770, C.O.5:552, p. 81.

[27] See C. L. Mowat: *East Florida*, p. 72, for the above figure; G. B. Fairbanks in his *The History and Antiquities of . . . St. Augustine . . .* (New York, 1858), p. 170, gives the number as 800.

[28] Lieutenant John Moultrie to Dartmouth, February 19, 1773, C.O.5:545, pp. 289–90; Carita Doggett-Corsi: *op. cit.*, p. 91.

[29] On July 22, 1773, Tonyn's commission received the Privy Seal and he arrived at St. Augustine on March 1, 1774. See Tonyn to Dartmouth, March 7, 1774, C.O.5:554, pp. 15–17.

[30] Carita Doggett-Corsi: *op. cit.*, pp. 91 and 95. For the establishment in East Florida of some eight plantations by people of wealth, see C. L. Mowat: *op. cit.*, pp. 69–70.

tempts to develop his colony. To guard against drought and also to provide for drainage, by 1774 he had installed a system of irrigation at New Smyrna.[31]

Then, in 1776, in the midst of the War for American Independence, Turnbull, under sharp attack by Tonyn, went to England to vindicate himself.[32] To his dismay, upon his return in the fall of 1777 he found that his enterprise had been wrecked. With the encouragement of the Governor the settlers had deserted the colony and gone to St. Augustine.[33] So vanished the New Smyrna settlement, begun in such high hopes of bringing profits to the proprietors and better days to those who had immigrated to East Florida from the Mediterranean.

Another point important to the student interested in the Old British Empire is that out of all the British North American colonies, only East Florida and Quebec possessed no representative Assembly by 1775. All local authority rested in the hands of the Governor, or Lieutenant Governor, and the Council. The ten councillors in East Florida were appointed by the King's mandamus.[34] Some of them however were inactive. Dr. Turnbull, so appointed on May 22, 1767, could seldom be present because of his responsibilities at New Smyrna; Sir Charles Burdett spent most of his time to the north of the province for reasons of health, and John Stuart, Indian Agent for the Southern Department, could not be counted on for active duty as the result of the demands of his work. What is more, Chief Justice William Drayton, who was given a seat in the Council on October 7, 1765, resigned in the fall of 1771 when doubt was expressed as to whether he was entitled to a seat.[35] This left but four active mem-

---

[31] Carita Doggett-Corsi: *op. cit.*, pp. 93–4.

[32] On December 6, 1776, Turnbull presented a memorial to the Board of Trade. In it he stated: "That your Memorialist, having in behalf of Himself and Partners, entered into private Contracts with a great Number of Foreigners who have settled in the Province, the Governor, from his own Authority, insisted on examining all such Contracts, which created such a Diffidence and Apprehension of the validity of the Agreement, as disturbed the Peace, Order, and Industry of the Smyrna Settlement so much, that its Ruin and the Loss of that great Property was with difficulty prevented by your Memorialist" (C.O.5:546, pp. 53–5). Tonyn, it appears, after examining the agreements found that deeds to lands could only go to Protestants whereas the settlers were Catholic; the Governor also drafted a military company from New Smyrna. See W. H. Siebert's study in the *Florida Historical Quarterly*, X, 19.

[33] W. H. Siebert: *Loyalists in East Florida, 1774–1785*, (2 vols., Deland, Fla., 1929), II, 326.

[34] For a list of East Florida members of the Council at the beginning of 1771 with the date of the appointment of each member see C.O.5:552, p. 49.

[35] One issue that led to Drayton's resignation was the question of whether or not the Chief Justice of the province was *ex officio* a member of the Council. Governor Grant apparently thought that this was so. In a letter to the Board of Trade on

bers together with Lieutenant Governor Moultrie. Although the Chief Justice was induced by the Earl of Hillsborough to return to the Council even after the King had accepted his resignation,[36] he displayed consistent hostility to the form of government that existed in the province.[37] In the summer of 1773 he was suspended from the Council for using insulting language to one of its members.[38] However, in his position as Chief Justice he used the Grand Jury presentments to attack Moultrie's administration, both for the things it accomplished and those it neglected.

Beyond Drayton's personal opposition, such as it was, lay a larger constitutional issue: How far could the province be governed by regulations made by the Governor and Council, including even the proclamations issued by the Governor, in the absence of an Assembly empowered to make laws? Drayton took the position that as Chief Justice he must insist upon strict enforcement of the English common law which bound the colony in the absence of a law-making body, and therefore must refuse to recognize as binding any act of the Governor that seemed to run contrary to this law.[39] Never-

December 9, 1765, he wrote: "Mr. Drayton came here in October last to hold the Court of Common Pleas, as Chief Justice of the Province till his Majesty's Pleasure is known. As such he took his seat in Council" (C.O.5:540, pp. 302–3). However the Earl of Hillsborough, writing to Lieutenant Governor Moultrie, indicated that the office did not entitle the Chief Justice to a seat. Another still more important issue was whether the Council had a right to approve or disapprove items of expenditure presented by the Governor. Drayton's position was that this power belonged to the Council. See Moultrie's reply to Hillsborough, August 20, 1772, and Drayton to Dartmouth, August 4, 1773, C.O.5:552, p. 377 and C.O.5:553, pp. 59–60. Soon after Drayton resigned, his close friend Turnbull also resigned from the Council. See Drayton to Lieutenant Governor Moultrie, October 19, 1771, Moultrie to Drayton, October 20, and Moultrie to Hillsborough, October 20 and December 28, 1771, C.O.5:552, pp. 135–6, 139, 141, 227. In 1772 and 1773, to meet the situation of absentee members, five other members were appointed. See Board of Trade *Journal, 1768–1775*, pp. 313 and 374.

[36] Hillsborough to Moultrie, January 11, 1772, Drayton to Moultrie, May 6, 1772, and Hillsborough to Moultrie, August 7, 1772, C.O.5:552, pp. 143, 255, 259.

[37] See C. L. Mowat: *op. cit.*, pp. 45–9.

[38] Moultrie to Dartmouth, August 22, 1773, and Minutes of the Council for August 20, 1773, C.O.5:553, pp. 197–205 and 218.

[39] Drayton, writing to the Earl of Dartmouth on February 15, 1774, pointed out that since no Assembly had been called and "Consequently no Legislative Act passed by which the Laws of England had been Altered or Amended, or new ones made to suit the local Circumstances of the Province . . . I concluded that I was to direct my Conduct . . . according to the Laws or Customs of that Kingdom, so far as they could be adopted to local circumstances. For . . . no Proclamation by the King's Governor has power to change any Part of the Common Law, Statutes or Customs of the Realm, now enforced and made obligatory in this Province by Virtue of the King's Proclamation [of 1763]" (C.O.5:554, pp. 27–32). For an excellent study of Drayton see W. M. Dabney and Marion Dargan: *William Henry Drayton & the American Revolution* (Albuquerque, 1962).

theless it was not until early in 1780 that the government of Great Britain saw fit to take steps to provide East Florida with an Assembly, which met for the first time on March 27, 1781.[40] This delay had apparently been due, in the first instance, to the weakness of the colony in the 1760's and early 1770's [41] and the lack of any serious demand on the part of the people themselves for an Assembly, especially since no taxes were raised and the financial support of the colony was effected solely through annual appropriations by Parliament.[42] When the province began to fill up in the 1770's, the government of Great Britain still hesitated to provide an Assembly, probably because of the strong stand on local rights taken by the North American Assemblies. Nevertheless the promise made in the Proclamation of 1763 that the new acquisitions would be granted legislatures still stood, and the existence of an Assembly in West Florida, as well as one in Grenada, was a constant reminder of an unfulfilled promise to the inhabitants of East Florida.[43]

Despite the grand jury presentment, little general political dissat-

---

[40] Lord Germain to the Board of Trade, January 19, 1780, C.O.5:546, pp. 289–90; Board of Trade *Journal, 1776–1782*, pp. 289–90.

[41] Figures on the population of East Florida are not very satisfactory. De Brahm stated that there were 3,000 people in East Florida "between 1763 and 1771," including 1,400 "Minorcans and over 900 slaves." In addition he indicated that there were 144 married men and 144 single men. For an analysis of his figures see J. R. Dunkle: "Population Changes as an Element in the Historical Geography of St. Augustine," *Florida Historical Quarterly*, XXXVII, 10. See also C. L. Mowat: *op. cit.*, pp. 46–8, and G. H. Fairbanks: *History of St. Augustine*, p. 165. The population of East Florida in March, 1774, when Governor Patrick Tonyn took over the administration, was stated to be 1,000 white inhabitants and 3,000 Negro slaves. See W. H. Siebert in the *Florida Historical Society Quarterly*, X, 23.

[42] In writing to the Earl of Shelburne on July 16, 1767, Governor Grant indicated "that the Legislature is not compleat, an Assembly not yet been called together; of course no internal taxes have been laid; indeed the State of the Province would not admit of them & therefore the civil Establishment is entirely supported by the annual estimate laid before Parliament" (Shelburne Papers, 52:311–12).

[43] On June 21, 1775, the Grand Jury of East Florida—doubtless at the instigation of the Chief Justice—complained of the lack of "a General Assembly of the people by their representatives agreeable to His Majesty's Proclamation of 7th October 1763, on the ground of the Property of the Subject being insecure under the present Deficiency of provincial Laws. . . ." They also requested that their presentment on this subject be published in the *Gazettes* of both Georgia and South Carolina. The court then ordered that copies of the presentment be given to the Governor and Council and be published as desired. On November 1 the Governor and Council, in considering this presentment, took the position that it was unnecessary since the property of the subject was as secure by law in East Florida as in any part of the British dominions. They added that such a presentment constituted an indirect approbation of the opposition to the government of Great Britain voiced in other colonies and tended to discourage loyal subjects from taking shelter in East Florida. See "State of the Charges against Mr. Drayton," C.O.5:546, pp. 27–44.

isfaction was evident in East Florida. The great landowners were deeply loyal to the government at home; there were no town meetings in St. Augustine, nor was a town-meeting spirit prevalent there. Of those settled on the land, few could be called yeoman farmers. In fact a middle class was lacking to bridge the gap between the articulate wealthy and the inarticulate poor. Thus Governor Grant was able to assert in 1769: "None of the people of the province are infected with the spirit of disunion and disaffection which prevails strongly in his Majesty's other American Colonies." [44] This attitude of mind throughout the colonial period helps to account for the fact that in the course of the War for American Independence East Florida offered asylum to many Loyalists who fled from the terror let loose in other colonies, especially after the British evacuation of Savannah and Charleston in 1782. [45]

---

[44] Grant to Hillsborough, February 9, 1769, C.O.5:550, p. 8.

[45] See especially W. H. Siebert's *Loyalists in East Florida* (previously cited) II, 105–31; see also C. L. Mowat: *op. cit.*, pp. 125–6 and 136–7. For other accounts of the War for American Independence and East Florida see Edgar L. Pennington: "East Florida and the American Revolution, 1775–1778," *Florida Historical Society Quarterly*, IX, 24–46, and Burton Barrs: *East Florida in the American Revolution* (Jacksonville, Fla., 1932).

CHAPTER VIII

The Empire on the Fringe of the Storm: West Florida

URNING now to the Province of West Florida (embracing much of the present states of Alabama and Mississippi), the colony did not have "a compleat Legislative Authority" until November 1766, as was explained in a preceding volume of this series.[1] The members of the first Assembly who met at Pensacola in that month apparently felt that the discouragements which had dogged the beginnings of the settlement were behind them and that the province was now on the threshold of a new and brighter day. In harmony with these sentiments they drew up an extended representation to the Board of Trade on November 22, outlining the more pressing needs of the colony—needs which they themselves recognized they had no means of supplying. They therefore looked "to the Generosity of his Majesty, and his Parliament . . ." to meet their urgent requirements.[2]

Pointing to their vulnerability—situated as they were close to Spain's New World possessions and hemmed in on the North by the strong, warlike Creek Indians and the even more powerful Choctaw

---

[1] See Governor George Johnstone's speech of November 3, 1766, "Minutes of the First Session of the Assembly of West Florida . . . ," *Louisiana Historical Quarterly*, XXII, 314–15; for his instructions relating to the calling of an Assembly and its powers see C.O.5:201, pp. 131–81. For maps relating to West Florida see Volume IX of this series, facing pp. 182, 208, 230, 231. For the early history of the Province of West Florida, see *ibid.*, Chap. 9, and Volume X, 329; see also, for a fuller treatment, Cecil Johnson: *British West Florida, 1763–1783* (New Haven, 1943), and C. N. Howard: *The British Development of West Florida, 1763–1769* (Berkeley & Los Angeles, 1947, cited hereafter as *West Florida*), especially for a history of the province's land grants; see further C. E. Carter: "Some Aspects of British Administration in West Florida," *Mississippi Valley Historical Review*, I, 364–75.

[2] See C. N. Howard: *op. cit.*, pp. 111–16; see also Shelburne Papers, 49:547–70 and 52:341–3, Clements Library.

—they asked for the construction of suitable fortifications and, to supplement the regular troops stationed there, for four companies of rangers to "protect the Settlements as they advance." They also sought means to build churches, gaols, and other public buildings in both Pensacola and Mobile, and permission to establish commerce with the Spanish dominions "on a large, generous and extensive Plan." Further, in order to divert the deerskin trade from New Orleans to Mobile, they asked that a premium be granted on such skins equal to the advanced price paid for them by the merchants of New Orleans; then, to encourage the establishment of plantations, they begged for a distribution of slaves as a form of premium to industrious inhabitants wishing to become planters, as well as an extension to West Florida of the encouragement offered to the people of South Carolina and Georgia by way of bounties for the production of indigo, rice, and silk.[3] Among other things required were the development at Pensacola of a naval base for careening and refitting ships of war, the building of a hospital in Mobile, and the provision of other facilities "for the Poor under the affliction of Sickness." In support of the application, they observed: "To see the Fortifications, Churches, Hospitals, and Public Buildings, which are every where erecting in the Spanish Dominions, since the arrival of Don Antonio de Ulloa [Governor of Louisiana] whilst nothing is undertaken on our part is extreamly mortifying to those who consider the changeful State of European Powers." It was estimated that the proposed public works would cost £68,000, at an annual expenditure of £17,150 over a period of four years, and that the annual additional charge to cover the companies of rangers, the distribution of Negroes as premiums, the care of the poor, and the opening up of interior communications would be £11,600.[4]

The memorial from the Pensacola Assembly came before the Board of Trade on May 12, 1767, and after consideration was transmitted to the Secretary of the Southern Department, the Earl of Shelburne, in whose hands it seems to have rested.[5] Apparently in the face of the manifold demands being made for the support of so great an Empire the requests from West Florida seemed quite unrealistic. It would appear, however, that at least the need for main-

---

[3] William Bartram the naturalist, travelling through West Florida in 1775 and 1776, observed that in the high land about Pensacola there were some plantations producing indigo, rice, corn, "Batatas etc." See his *Travels through North and South Carolina, Georgia, East and West Florida* . . . (Dublin, 1793), p. 414.

[4] Shelburne Papers, 52:341–3; and also C. N. Howard's *West Florida*, pp. 114–15.

[5] See Board of Trade *Journal, 1764–1767*, pp. 386 and 388.

taining a military hospital at Pensacola, at an annual cost of about £2,882, was recognized by Secretary at War Lord Barrington, when transmitting General Gage's estimate of the expense involved in those aspects of the colony relating to his department.[6]

In truth the province was still in a formative stage in the 1760's, and so it remained throughout the period of the British régime. Most of the people not in government service seem to have been occupied chiefly in the Indian trade, raising livestock, or subsistence farming. Thus a report sent to the Board of Trade early in 1767 stated that there were no manufactures in the colony other than the production of a small quantity of tar and bricks, and the output from a sawmill making boards and scantlings.[7] In line with the poverty of the people and the dearth of assets for the support of the government, taxation was light. The levy of certain modest import duties and licence fees for the retail liquor trade brought returns which could do little more than provide a payment of ten shillings a day for its members while the Assembly was in session and fifteen shillings for its Speaker.

Lieutenant Governor Montfort Browne, who took over the administration upon the departure of Governor Johnstone for England at the beginning of 1767,[8] wrote to the Earl of Shelburne in June that clearly the chief motive behind the stretching out of the Assembly's business was that the members could "enjoy the enormous salary" they had voted themselves. He added that when he had brought the matter to the attention of the Council, this body had unanimously agreed to his proposal to dissolve the Assembly and order the election of new members in the confidence that there were some people in the province and others expected to come to it who would "be

---

[6] The cost of the colony's defences, not counting the pay and maintaining of the soldiers, amounted to £5,920.8.4½. See Barrington to Shelburne, July 20, 1767, Shelburne Papers, 52:373–4.

[7] Lieutenant Governor Browne to the Board of Trade, January 25, 1767, Shelburne Papers, 52:353.

[8] Governor George Johnstone's administration lasted from October 21, 1764, to January 9, 1767; from January 9, 1767, to April 3, 1769, Lieutenant Governor Montfort Browne was at the head of the province; Governor John Eliot began his administration on April 3, 1769, but died on May 2; thereupon Lieutenant Governor Browne once again took up the reins. Browne was at the head of affairs until his removal from office late in 1769, when he was succeeded by Lieutenant Governor Durnford, who continued in charge from December 26 until August 11, 1770. Peter Chester, the new Governor, continued in office until the capture of Pensacola on May 10, 1781, by the Spaniards. See "List of Commissions . . . to the Royal Governors and others in America," American Historical Association *Report*, 1911, I, 440–1; see also C. N. Howard: "Colonial Pensacola: The British Period. Part III," *Florida Historical Quarterly* XIX, 368–99, and Appendix, "Governors of British West Florida," 399–401.

above appropriating to themselves the small revenue of that infant colony in exorbitant wages." [9]

In justice to the members of the Assembly it should be pointed out that a defence of their conduct appeared in print in 1767 in the form of *A Letter from a Gentleman in Pensacola To His Friend in South Carolina* (dated Pensacola, August 26, 1767). The writer of the pamphlet disclosed that he was acquainted with every occurrence involving the Assembly and Lieutenant Governor Browne. As to the question of the salary voted to members of the Assembly, he stated that at its first meeting this body, "having the example of all the northern Colonies (except one or two) before them, established a salary at ten shillings a day, which in a country where all the necessaries of life are so dear is barely sufficient to pay these unavoidable expenses." Had they received this salary, he contended, they would still not be as well paid as Assemblymen in the northern colonies, taking everything into consideration. But far from applying this salary to their own use, no sooner had the bill which fixed it passed into law, "than they unanimously voted the whole should be applied toward the relief and comfort of the sick and distressed poor people of Pensacola and Mobile, and order'd that the same might be enter'd on the journal of the house, where it now doth, and always will stand as a monument to their benevolence and charity. . . . To shew you in what light the inhabitants consider this matter, which His Honour calls a Grievance . . . I need only tell you, that at the late election, the freeholders made choice of the old members to represent them in the next General Assembly." [10]

During the session of the first Assembly, which lasted from November 1766 until it was dissolved on June 5, 1767, fifteen acts were passed in all. When these measures came before the Privy Council on August 16, 1768, by way of a representation from the Board of Trade, [11] serious objection was found to three of them. One, "An Act

---

[9] Browne to the Earl of Shelburne, June 29, 1767, Shelburne Papers, 52:365.

[10] This publication can be found among the Haldimand Papers, B.M., Add. Mss., 21673:40–3. That the pay of Assemblymen under the law of 1766 was considered high may be indicated by the fact that when a new Assembly met after the election in 1767 their recompense was cut to five shillings per day and that of the Speaker to seven shillings and sixpence. See Assembly Minutes, December 23, 1767, *Louisiana Historical Quarterly*, XXII, 995.

[11] On October 5, 1767, the fifteen acts came before the Board of Trade and were referred to the Board's legal counsel, Sir Matthew Lamb. His report, delivered on May 30, 1768, was taken into consideration on July 21 and on the 29th the Board made its representation. See Board of Trade *Journal, 1764–1767,* p. 419, *Journal,*

appointing the Members of the Assembly and Regulating Elections," was held to be an infringement of the King's prerogative and contrary to the Governor's instructions and was therefore disallowed. The second, "An Act for granting certain Duties to His Majesty" to be applied toward supporting the government of the province, was considered most objectionable since, with few exceptions, it appropriated the entire fund for "an Allowance to the Speaker and Members of the Assembly," something "so flagrantly partial and Oppressive" as to require not only repeal of the statute but precautions to prevent any such improper act being passed in the future. As to the third, "An Act to encourage Foreigners to come into, and Settle in this Province," it too was repealed by Order in Council because it was deemed that its provisions guaranteeing rights and privileges to all people professing the Roman Catholic religion who should come into the province were too general and should be limited to those professing this religion already settled there and thereby qualified for naturalization.[12] The other twelve acts were held to be proper and, when approved, became the nucleus of the code of laws of the short-lived province.[13]

From the year 1767 onward the conviction grew that the future of West Florida lay in the development of the extremely fertile lands east of the Mississippi rather than those of the sandy region along the Gulf of Mexico.[14] In 1768 Lieutenant Governor Browne made a

1768–1775, pp. 41 and 43. For Lamb's report see C. N. Howard: *West Florida*, p. 118.

[12] See *Acts of the Privy Council, Col. Ser., 1766–1783*, pp. 158–9.

[13] For Lamb's report, his legal addresses to the Board of Trade on the fifteen acts, and a list of the acts, see P.R.O., C.O.5:575; see also C. N. Howard: *West Florida*, p. 118. However, it may be pointed out that when Peter Chester became Governor in 1770, he made a study of the laws passed during the administration of Governor Johnstone and Lieutenant Governor Browne and found serious objections to two others of the fifteen acts passed by the first Assembly. One, "An Act for the Granting of Licenses to Retailers of Spiritous Liquors, imposing a Duty on said Licenses: and for regulating of Taverns or Public Houses," passed on January 2, 1767, he felt should be disallowed because the money raised was not to be paid into the account of the treasurer of the province, but turned over directly to the local officials of Pensacola and Mobile for certain local improvements. The other, "An Act for the Order and Government of Slaves," passed on January 2, 1767—providing for the immediate execution of a Negro or slave after conviction—Chester held to be unwarranted as it deprived the Crown of its power to reprieve or pardon the criminal should extenuating circumstances seem to justify the extension of its mercy. See C. N. Howard in the *Florida Historical Quarterly*, XIX, 373–4. The Governor did not perhaps appreciate the difficulty of disallowing a provincial law once approved by His Majesty in Council.

[14] The well-known Indian trader James Adair, a highly educated man who lived among the Indians from 1735 to 1768, wrote his famous *History of the American*

trip into that area and was thrilled by the luxuriance of the natural vegetation.[15] As a result of his enthusiasm, he was instrumental in getting the Assembly in August of that year to draw up a memorial showing the advantages of maintaining troops at the posts on the Mississippi; this was forwarded in a letter to Samuel Hannay, agent for the province.[16] Further, to promote development of the area west of Mobile, one of the acts passed by the Assembly (which met in three sessions from August 1768 to June 29, 1769) was to "Encourage the Settlement of That part of this Province lying to the Westward of Charlotte County." [17] But there was one great drawback to the rapid settlement of the area. Its distance from the seat of government made communications with Pensacola decidedly difficult, and accessibility by way of the Gulf of Mexico was complicated by Spanish control of New Orleans.

In 1764 it had been hoped to make the Iberville River a navigable avenue of approach to the Natchez area, which would permit passage from the Gulf of Mexico into Lake Pontchartrain, and then across Lake Maurepas up the Amite River to the Iberville which receives the flood-waters of the Mississippi. Major Farmer in that year proposed and carried through plans to clear the Iberville of obstructions so as to open up a passage.[18] But by 1766 it was once more impassable. Colonel William Taylor, who was in command of the troops in the Southern District, thought he could solve the problem of opening the Iberville communication by digging a

Indians, particularly those nations adjoining to the Mississippi, East and West Florida, Georgia, South and North Carolina, and Virginia . . . It appeared originally in London in 1775 and was republished in 1930 by the Watauga Press of Johnson City, Tenn., under the editorship of S. C. Williams. Adair was a strong advocate of a western colony to be established on the eastern bank of the Mississippi to which he gave the name Georgiana. This colony was to be located in the country of the Chickasaw Indians where he had lived from 1761 to 1768. An Appendix to his *History* points out the great advantages of establishing such a colony. Also in his *History* is an excellent map of the Indian nations (1775), which is reproduced in Volume XI of this series facing p. 429.

[15] See Browne to the Earl of Hillsborough, July 6, 1768, C.O.5:548, pp. 147–164; see also Cecil Johnson: *op. cit.*, pp. 64–5. William Bartram, who visited Manchac in 1777, mentions (*op. cit.*, pp. 428–9) that Browne had become the proprietor of a large district near a place called "Brown's cliffs" which he held throughout the British period, even when he was Governor of the Bahamas. Browne, his father, his uncle, and his two brothers in 1764 received a grant of 20,000 acres of land in West Florida. See *Acts of the Privy Council, Col. Ser., 1745–1766*, p. 813.

[16] See "Minutes of the West Florida Assembly, 1768–1769," *Louisiana Historical Quarterly*, XXIII, 5–12.

[17] See *ibid.*, XXIII, 12–75, *passim*.

[18] For an account of the early efforts to approach the British lands on the east bank of the Mississippi see Volume IX of this series, pp. 216–18, and also the map facing p. 209.

twelve-by-twelve-foot by-pass canal at a point on the Mississippi where the current was "Thrown with great Impetuosity" and thus avoid the mass of debris that continually choked the Iberville. He predicted the feasibility of the project on his conviction that it would involve no great labour or expense, since the calculated distance of the canal, which need not be more than a thousand yards long, could be dug by twenty men working for two hundred days.[19] Unhappily Taylor was mistaken; the canal route was quite impracticable as planned. General Gage was correctly informed in 1768 that a rise of land some nine miles in length along the Iberville made the elevated bed of that river dry most of the year.[20] Nevertheless the proposal for a canal continued to be entertained by the military engineers as late as 1773.[21]

Despite the difficulties of communication between the coastal areas of West Florida and Manchac[22] and Natchez, these two districts continued to grow in population and wealth as the result of settlers moving in from the North.[23] Although the Assembly made an effort in 1769 to provide the districts with a subordinate but more or less autonomous government, to compensate for their isolation from Pensacola and difficulty of being represented there, this attempt failed to secure the approval of the Privy Council.[24] But the two

[19] For the project see General Gage to the Earl of Shelburne, April 29, 1767, *Correspondence of General Thomas Gage . . . 1763–1775* (ed. C. E. Carter, 2 vols., New Haven, 1931) I, 137–9, cited hereafter as *Gage Correspondence;* see also Shelburne Papers, 51:98–100.

[20] Gage to Hillsborough, January 6, 1769, *Gage Correspondence,* I, 212.

[21] Gage informed Hillsborough on April 24, 1770, that Brigadier (later Major General) Frederick Haldimand, who took over the military command of West Florida from Colonel Taylor in 1767, made "the last Attempt to Send Supplys by that Route," but that intelligent people had assured Haldimand that when the waters of the Mississippi were low, those of Lakes Pontchartrain and Maurepas were much higher. By the end of 1770 Gage had been forced to realize that to dig an adequate, navigable canal would involve vast expense, for it would require a cut of many miles in length and as deep as the bed of the Mississippi at low water, otherwise the waters of the Iberville would "naturaly flow back into the Mississippi, in the Manner they do now, when the freshes [freshets] Subside" (*ibid.,* I, 254). William Bartram had this to say about the Iberville, which he visited in 1777: "The Iberville in the summer season is dry, and its bed twelve or fifteen feet above the surface of the Mississippi; but in the winter and spring has a great depth of water, and a very rapid stream which flows into the Amite, thence down through the lakes into the bay of Pearls to the ocean" (*op. cit.,* pp. 426–7).

[22] William Bartram in 1777 refers to large and commodious buildings at Manchac, "particularly [to] the warehouses of Messrs Swanson & Co. Indian traders and merchants" (*ibid.,* p. 426).

[23] See Cecil Johnson: *op. cit.,* Chap. 6, "Westward Expansion, 1770–1779."

[24] The statute carried the title: "An Act to encourage the settlement of that part of this Province lying to the westward of Charlotte County" (Charlotte County em-

districts were destined, especially after the year 1772, to surpass the coastal area in population. According to Lieutenant Governor Durnford's description of the province in 1774, there were 2,500 white people and 600 slaves living along the Mississippi and 1,200 whites and 600 blacks to the east of Lake Pontchartrain.[25] Likewise Governor Peter Chester[26] affirmed in 1779 that in the Manchac and Natchez districts there was "a greater number of respectable and wealthy planters and settlers than in either of the other Districts of Pensacola and Mobile."[27] As a result, when an Assembly was called to meet on June 6, 1778, these two districts each received a representation equal to that of the district of Pensacola.[28]

The Assembly of West Florida was not a particularly effective body during the period of its existence. In fact it could do little but pass regulations, because of the lack of funds at its disposal. Although the major financial burden for the colony continued to fall upon the people of Great Britain as the result of the annual appropriations voted by Parliament for support of the province's government,[29] this money was not put at the disposal of the Assembly.

As has been indicated, the composition of the West Florida legislature fluctuated. The Assembly that met first in 1766 consisted of

---

braced the town and district of Mobile). This act came before the Board of Trade on December 6, together with five others, and was taken under consideration by the Lords Commissioners on July 19, 1770, along with a report on it by the Board's legal adviser, Richard Jackson. Although praising the general purpose of the act, Jackson objected to it on the grounds that it very improperly created "a Subordinate Province" merely by decision of the West Florida government. The Board therefore sought its disallowance, which was so ordered by the Privy Council on December 9, 1769. See Board of Trade *Journal, 1768–1775*, pp. 139 and 203–4, and *Acts of the Privy Council, Col. Ser., 1766–1783*, p. 286.

[25] For Durnford's description see Cecil Johnson: *op. cit.*, pp. 148–9 and 154–5.

[26] For Chester as Governor see Mrs. Dunbar Rowland: "Peter Chester, Third Governor of the Province of British West Florida under British Dominion 1770–1781," *Mississippi Historical Society Publications*, V (1925).

[27] See "The Answer of Peter Chester, Esquire, Governor of the Province of West Florida to the Petition of Complaint of Adam Chrystie [Speaker of the Assembly] and others" [November 18, 1779], *Louisiana Historical Quarterly*, XXII, 31–46; see also "Papers Relating to West Florida, 1765–1782," in the Manuscript Division of the New York Public Library. This "Answer" by Chester came as a reply to the complaint lodged against him by some of the principal inhabitants of the province that he had acted in violation of his instructions, especially in not calling frequent meetings of the Assembly. This complaint came before the Board of Trade on August 6, 1779; see Board of Trade *Journal, 1776–1782*, pp. 267–8.

[28] "The Answer of Peter Chester . . . " [1779], *loc. cit.*, pp. 31–46. For a survey of the activities of the West Florida Assembly see Cecil Johnson: *op. cit.*, Chap. 4.

[29] For example, in 1764 £5,700 was appropriated by Parliament to maintain the colony; in 1765 it was £5,200; in 1774, £4,850, and in 1775, £5,450. See *Annual Register, 1764*, p. 161; *Annual Register, 1765*, p. 139; *Annual Register, 1774*, p. 252; *Annual Register, 1775*, p. 245.

six members from Pensacola, six from Mobile, and two from Camp-
bell Town; in the Assembly of 1767 the towns and districts of
Pensacola and Mobile each had eight members, while Campbell
Town still had but two. By 1771 representation from the towns and
districts of Pensacola and Mobile had not changed, but Campbell
Town, now "almost deserted," was not included; yet the following
year Charlotte County was represented in addition to Pensacola and
Mobile, and two members appeared for the township of Campbell
Town. Meanwhile an issue had arisen over the holding of yearly
elections, a plan which the town of Mobile favoured but which was
in opposition to the Governor's instructions. As a result, Mobile was
not represented in 1772 and so few members from the other areas
appeared that no quorum for the conduct of business could be
secured. After several prorogations the House was dissolved, not to
be summoned again until 1778. According to Governor Chester, "it
was not the general wish . . . of the Inhabitants of the Province for
several Years that the House of Assembly should be Convened. . . ." [30] In view of the persistent determination of the electors of Mobile to elect members for but one year, no writs of election
were sent to this town, although the "district of Mobile," that is,
Charlotte County, had four members allotted to it, as did the districts of Pensacola, Manchac, and Natchez.[31] Thus the 1778 Assembly, which met on October 1 rather than June 6, concentrated its
efforts not on defensive measures—even though faced with threats

---

[30] "The Answer of Peter Chester . . ." [1779], *loc. cit.*, pp. 31–46, especially
39.

[31] See *ibid.*, 39–43, for Chester's "Answer," which points out that the western part
of the original district of Mobile was "Erected into two Districts: Manchac[k] and
Natchez." As for Mobile and its immediate environs, William Bartram found in 1778
that the "low flat rich islands" of the lower Mobile River were well cultivated with
extensive farms which were "chiefly the property of French gentlemen, who reside in
the city, as being more pleasant and healthy." However, Mobile, which had been
nearly a mile in length, was "now chiefly in ruins, many houses vacant and
mouldering to earth; yet there are a few good buildings inhabited by French
gentlemen, English, Scotch and Irish, and emigrants from the Northern British
colonies. Messers. Swanson and McGillivray, who have the management of the Indian
trade . . . have made here very extraordinary improvements in buildings" (Bartram,
op. cit., pp. 401–2). Pensacola impressed Bartram much more than Mobile. "There
are several hundred habitations in Pensacola," he wrote; "the governor's palace is a
large stone building ornamented with a tower, built by the Spaniards. The town is
defended by a large stockado fortress. . . . Within this fortress is the council
chamber; here the records are kept, houses for the officers and barracks for the
accommodation of the garrison, arsenal, magazine, etc. The secretary resides in a
spacious, neat building: there are several merchants and gentlemen of other professions, who have respectable and convenient buildings in the town" (*ibid.*, p. 414).

of invasion by the American revolutionaries—but on the right of electing members for one year only. As a result on November 5, with nothing accomplished and no prospect that any business would be done, the House was prorogued by Governor Chester and was never again summoned during the existence of the province. In the Treaty of Peace of 1783 both East and West Florida were returned to Spain.

Fortunately for the colony, during the period under consideration the Creek and Choctaw Indians had been fairly quiet.[32] They had become dependent upon the whites, as had other North American tribes, for certain items they regarded as necessary. In view of the location of the Choctaw,[33] the trade with them was of some importance, particularly the exchange of skins and furs for merchandise centring in the port of Mobile (exclusive of pelts that went to New Orleans). For the rest, there were adequate troops to protect the province in the event of an Indian uprising. Thus the extensive financial and military support of the colony by the Crown left no room for the growth of revolutionary sentiment among the inhabitants.

The settlers, far from harbouring a feeling of hostility toward the regular troops in their midst—such as was displayed in Massachusetts Bay—felt infinitely concerned at the mere thought of the disappearance from the colony of this military protection. For example, when Brigadier Haldimand received orders from General Gage in 1768 to withdraw the 21st and 31st Regiments from the province, the settlers were "extremely alarmed" over the prospect that only three companies would remain "for the Protection of an Extensive and most important Frontier"; they therefore represented to Lieutenant Governor Browne "the Danger and fatal Consequences that may attend such a step." [34] Similarly, when the 31st

---

[32] For an excellent treatment of West Florida Indian relations see J. R. Alden: *John Stuart and the Southern Colonial Frontier . . . 1754–1775* (Ann Arbor, Mich., 1944), Chap. 18, "Indian Affairs in the West Florida Area, 1768–75"; see also Helen L. Shaw: *British Administration of the Southern Indians, 1756–1783* (Lancaster, Pa., 1931); and Volume IX of this series, pp. 219–23. For trade relations between West Florida and Spanish New Orleans see the John Fitzpatrick Letter Books (3 vols., mss.) in the New York Public Library for the period from 1768 to 1774. The letters from New Orleans sent during the earlier part of the period covered by this correspondence seem to indicate that Fitzpatrick could more freely conduct his business across the river at Manchac—especially the selling of slaves to the Spaniards.
[33] For John Mitchell's map (1775) of the Southern Indians see Volume IV of this series, facing p. 106; for earlier reference to James Adair's map see footnote 14 above.
[34] Browne to Haldimand, August 14, 1768, Haldimand Papers, B.M., Add. Mss. 21673:86.

Regiment returned to Pensacola in 1770, the event gave the community, according to Lieutenant Governor Elias Durnford, "the greatest satisfaction"; in fact the only complaint voiced was that other military contingents such as the artillery units had not also returned.[35]

Very naturally, with the intensification of the revolutionary movement in the colonies to the north, both West and East Florida received large numbers of Loyalist refugees, including many people of property, most of whom were attracted to the fertile regions of the province lying east of the Mississippi.[36] There they were welcomed with land grants and there they hoped to stay. However in 1778, in the course of the War for American Independence, West Florida was invaded from the north by patriotic colonials under command of Captain James Willing of Philadelphia who in 1774 had opened a store at Natchez but with the outbreak of hostilities had returned to Pennsylvania. Then in 1779 the colony was finally overwhelmed by a Spanish invasion from forces concentrated in Louisiana led by Governor Gálvez. As a result the refugee Tories were again dislodged, to become part of the Loyalist dispersion.[37]

The other parts of North America that received Loyalist exiles were the areas north of New Hampshire and the St. Lawrence River: Newfoundland, Nova Scotia, and the Province of Quebec— none of which participated in the revolt from British rule in 1775. We must now turn to a consideration of developments in these areas before that date.

---

[35] Durnford to Haldimand, March 9, 1770, *ibid.*, 21673:132.

[36] Cecil Johnson: *op. cit.*, pp. 144–8.

[37] See W. H. Siebert: "The Loyalists in West Florida and the Natchez District," *Mississippi Valley Historical Review*, II, 465–83.

CHAPTER IX

The Empire on the Fringe of the Storm: Newfoundland and Labrador

I N the eighteenth century Newfoundland [1] with its great cod fishery served Great Britain in two capacities. Its fish shipped to southern European markets helped to produce a favourable balance of trade; while the annual fishing fleet, which sailed from the coastal towns of western England to catch the cod, helped to train a constant new supply of seamen to produce a favourable balance of naval power. [2]

During the period between the Peace of Paris of 1763 and the outbreak of the War for American Independence (and even long after its end), the interests of the western towns of England and the settled inhabitants of Newfoundland had a great stake in the fisheries; so also did the fishing towns of France and of New Eng-

---

[1] For Newfoundland in the middle of the eighteenth century see Volume III of this series, pp. 248–72; for a map of this area see *ibid.*, facing p. 239.

[2] For the development of this theme see G. S. Graham: "Newfoundland in British Strategy from Cabot to Napoleon" in *Newfoundland Economic, Diplomatic, and Strategic Studies* (ed. R. A. MacKay, Toronto, 1946), pp. 245–64; see also by the same author, "Fisheries and Sea Power," Canadian Historical Association *Report, 1941.* For a broad yet detailed study of the cod fisheries see H. A. Innis: *The Cod Fisheries, The History of an International Economy* (New Haven & London, 1940), and J. D. Rogers: *A Historical Account of the British Colonies, Vol. V Part IV, Newfoundland* (Oxford, 1911); for the fisheries before 1763 see especially R. G. Lounsbury: *The British Fishery at Newfoundland, 1634–1763* (New Haven, 1934). For the political and diplomatic history of Newfoundland during the period under consideration, see John Reeves: *History of the Government of the Island of Newfoundland* (London, 1793) and also D. W. Prowse: *A History of Newfoundland from English, Colonial and Foreign Records* (London, 1896), 1. Even more illuminating for the period 1763–1775 is a brief study by W. B. Kerr: "Newfoundland in the Period before the American Revolution," *Pennsylvania Magazine of History and Biography,* LXV, 56–78, and by the same author: *The Maritime Provinces of British North America and the American Revolution* (Sackville, New Brunswick, [1941]), especially pp. 25–34 and 113–23.

land. It was asserted in 1760 that some 43,000,000 cod were caught by the British during each year of peace and, additionally, that 1,000 tons of cod-liver oil were sent from Newfoundland direct to England.[3] The shipping involved in this fishery had a substantial bearing on the strength of British naval power and on the support of other British interests. With the Great War for the Empire moving toward a climax, strong opposition was voiced in England in the early 1760's to any settlement that would permit the French to return to these fisheries and resume the rights they had held under the terms of the Treaty of Utrecht of 1713. William Pitt was especially insistent upon this point in 1761.[4] In 1762 the question of termination of French fishing rights was still very much an issue in the British Cabinet Council. An official calculation stated that before the formal outbreak of hostilities in 1756 the French employed annually 370 ships, some 60 schooners, 2,240 boats, and 14,800 men in this trade. The value of the fish and oil procured was placed at £467,761. By contrast, the total number of vessels sailing from the west coast of England and the Channel Islands of Guernsey and Jersey was 120;[5] during the season this fleet caught and cured but 60,000 quintals of cod out of a total of 360,000 quintals carried to market by British vessels. The remaining 300,000 quintals were secured "by the inhabitants and by boatmen who sell to the sack-ships and to such of the fishing ships as do not make up their own cargoes." The total value of the cod and the oil procured by these means was placed at £218,000, involving 180 British ships, 3,000 seamen, 3,820 boatmen, and 1,515 boats. Finally, the New England cod fishery in the area about Canso was credited with supplying from 350 to 400 schooners, each with a crew of nine men who caught and cured not less than 300,000 quintals, two thirds of which was carried to European markets and the remainder to the West Indies, with a total value of £180,000.[6] In other words if the above calculations were even approximately correct the value of the French cod fishery surpassed that of the combined fisheries of the

[3] *Pennsylvania Gazette*, January 10, 1760.

[4] For the Duke of Newcastle's memorandum on Pitt's attitude, under April 10, 1761, see Newcastle Papers, B.M., Add. Mss. 32921:381–2.

[5] From Poole went about 35 vessels; from Dartmouth, 20; from Topsham and adjacent places, 15; from Bideford and Barnstable, 20, and from Guernsey and Jersey, some 30. See "Questions and Answers relating to the State of the French & British Fisheries at Newfoundland, 1762," Hardwicke Papers, B.M., Add. Mss. 35913:75–84.

[6] *Ibid.*

English towns, of the inhabitants of the island, and of the New Englanders by almost £70,000.

However, between 1756 and 1763 the French fishing fleet was prevented from resorting to its accustomed haunts by Britain's domination of the seas.[7] As a result the number of British ships going to the island and the Banks greatly increased. In 1760, according to a report sent by Governor Webb,[8] it was 282, and the total amount of cod caught and cured by the crews and the inhabitants was 413,000 quintals,[9] or 53,660 quintals above their combined previous annual average; one may further assume that in the absence of French competition in the markets of southern Europe this cod sold at high prices.

It is therefore not to be wondered at that, for a variety of reasons both economic and strategic, a strong sentiment developed in England for preventing the French from resuming their profitable activities at the conclusion of the war. Nor is it surprising that the French invaded Newfoundland in 1762 to seize its capital, St. John's, doubtless in the hope that such possession would at least put them in a

---

[7] It appears that some French cod-fishing vessels ventured into the more secluded inlets in the extreme northern part of the island, according to Captain Nicholas Darby, a native of Newfoundland, who testified before the Lords Commissioners of Trade on December 6, 1762. See Board of Trade *Journal, 1759–1763*, pp. 310–11.

[8] For the student's convenience in recalling the succession of Newfoundland's Governors from 1760 to 1776, the following list is given:

Governor	Date of beginning administration
James Webb	Summer, 1760
James Webb	Renewal, 1761
Thomas Graves	Summer, 1762
Thomas Graves	Recommissioned in 1763 to govern additionally Labrador, Anticosti, and Magdalen Islands, which had been annexed to Newfoundland by proclamation of October 7, 1763.
Hugh Palliser	June 18, 1764
John Byron	Summer, 1769
Molineux Shuldham	No date given (received the Privy Seal on March 16, 1772) but was on active duty by the summer of 1772.
Robert Duff	July 11, 1775 (without Labrador, Anticosti, and Magdalen Islands, which had been re-annexed to Quebec on September 18, 1774).

See C. M. Andrews: "List of Commissions, Instructions, and Additional Instructions Issued to the Royal Governors and Others in America," American Historical Association *Report* (1911), I, 401–2, which also gives the dates on which the Governors' commissions received the Privy Seal. For the original dates of the commissions see *ibid.*, pp. 481–2.

[9] Governor J. W. Webb to the Board of Trade, February 23, 1761, P.R.O., C.O. 194:15.

stronger bargaining position when peace was finally made.[10] That they expected to remain there, even in the face of the inevitable action they knew would be taken to dislodge them, is indicated by their efforts to strengthen the town's fortifications.[11] Many considerations were involved in making the Treaty of Peace in 1763.[12] In order to retain the right to exploit the cod fisheries, the French agreed to accept many losses either of territory or of important rights in North America, the West Indies, and India. This led Lord Bute and his colleagues in the Cabinet Council—especially the Duke of Bedford who went to Paris to carry on negotiations—to grant some corresponding concessions. To help restore peace and harmony, they agreed by Articles 5 and 6 of the new treaty not only to reaffirm the rights granted in Article 13 of the Treaty of Utrecht, with certain stipulations attached, but also to give the French possession of the small islands of Miquelon and St. Pierre [13] off the southern coast of Newfoundland, likewise with stipulations chiefly to do with fortifications and the number of troops permitted on the islands for purely police duty. In line with the treaty the islands were delivered on July 4, 1763, to the French Governor M. Anjac; thereafter, in consequence of instructions given to Governor Graves of Newfoundland by His Majesty, "all communication has been forbid between his Subjects and those Islands." [14] However, Graves wrote to the Board of Trade on the 20th of October that so many ships were entering St. Pierre that he feared it would become a common mart for French manufactures and East India goods, and one to which the New Englanders would resort unless some method were found of confiscating the ships and cargoes of any British

[10] For the French invasion of Newfoundland and the British recapture of St. John's see Volume VIII of this series, pp. 270–4.

[11] "The Fort of St. Johns has been put in much better state of defence by the Enemy than ever we had it in," wrote Governor Thomas Graves to the Board of Trade, October 4, 1762, C.O. 194:15.

[12] For the Treaty of 1763 see Charles Jenkinson: A Collection of all the Treaties . . . between Great-Britain and other Powers . . . 1648 to . . . 1783 . . . (3 vols., London, 1785), III, 177–191.

[13] That St. Pierre was not an uninhabited island is indicated in a memorial from Samuel Clark and Susannah Young of Poole, England, that came before the Board of Trade in 1762 showing that there were dwelling houses, wharfs, fishing stages and other improvements on it and that about 100 people had made improvements there. See C.O. 5:65, p. 89; see likewise the memorial of Robert Traille of Portsmouth, New Hampshire, who had purchased in 1758 for £750 a part of the island of Miquelon, originally granted in 1722 to Captain Diamond Serjeant by Richard Philips, Governor of Nova Scotia and Placentia, C.O. 194:15.

[14] Governor William Graves to the Board of Trade, October 20, 1763, C.O. 195:15.

subjects who went there to trade. He also stated that the French had settled there in such numbers that they would not find sufficient firewood for the winter nor manage to carry on fishing activities to advantage without sailing as far as the coast of Newfoundland.[15]

While cod could be caught off the coast of Newfoundland, the only area where shore-fishing was permitted to the French was north of Cape Bonavista on the eastern shore and north of Point Riche on the western shore. Yet the fishing privileges within these bounds accorded by treaty to the French were not exclusive, since British subjects could likewise sail to these shores to fish and did so in great numbers, especially after 1756. According to Captain Darby, in 1749 the great schools of cod left the eastern coast and concentrated in the fishing grounds in the area of the Strait of Belle Isle in the extreme northern part of the island. Testifying before the Board of Trade, he affirmed that before the cod migration took place a boat with four men—during the general three-month fishing period—could catch between 500 and 700 quintals of fish on the eastern shore, but that since that time the catch in this area would normally be no more than 200 or 220 quintals; by fishing to the northward, however, a boat with the same complement of men could during the same period procure as much as 1,200 quintals.[16]

Before the war certain difficulties had faced British subjects who had gone into areas where the French were also entitled to fish. The French fishermen, especially those who sailed from St. Malo, came in ships of as much as 500 tons, armed with between sixteen and twenty-four guns and carrying crews of from fifty to seventy men. Upon arriving at the place selected for catching and curing fish, the crews of these ships would form an encampment protected by the guns taken from the ships; further, when British fishermen sought to establish themselves at certain likely places, the French would move in, erect stages and huts, and claim an exclusive right to fish there.[17]

---

[15] *Ibid.*

[16] See the Board of Trade *Journal, 1759–1763,* p. 310. Captain Griffith Williams, who spent some fourteen years in Newfoundland, after reviewing the various areas for the cod fishery wrote in 1765: "But I will take upon me to say, that you need not be jealous of all the Cod Fisheries in the World, had you all to the Northward of Cape Race [Ray] in Newfoundland." Yet he found it necessary to add that "The French have, by far, the best part" of the fishery. See his *An Account of the Island of Newfoundland* . . . (London, 1765), pp. 10–23, also reprinted in *English Historical Documents, 1714–1783* (eds. D. B. Horn and Mary Ransome, Vol. X of *English Historical Documents,* London & New York, 1957), pp. 797–800.

[17] Board of Trade *Journal, 1759–1763,* p. 311.

Some of the practices of the French on the island had clearly violated the stipulations embodied in Article 13 of the Treaty of Utrecht, especially those concerning the erection of fortifications and permanent storehouses. Therefore at the end of the fishing season in 1763, Governor Graves instructed Captain Ruthven of H. M. *Terpsichore* to cruise along the northern shores and destroy all French buildings except the huts and fishing stages, as well as all boats built on the island, and to drive off any French ships lingering there.[18] It may be added that a total of seven vessels of war was assigned to the Newfoundland station in 1763, not only to maintain good order and to enforce the Trade and Navigation Acts [19] but also to keep the fishing activities of the French about the island within treaty bounds.[20]

Nevertheless the British Ministry was determined to carry out in good faith the terms of the Treaty of Paris and on March 14, 1764, agreed to send additional instructions to Governor Hugh Palliser (who succeeded Graves) whereby British and French subjects could carry on their profitable activities in mutual harmony and peace. In this connection the so-called admirals of the harbours [21] were made responsible for seeing that no improper interference with the French fishermen took place, and that "the said subjects of France be permitted . . . in common with our subjects, to chuse their Place or Places of abode there during the Fishing season (which shall be understood to expire on the 20th of October) according as they shall respectively arrive in the said Harbours, and to occupy such space of Beach as shall be proportioned to the numbers of boats they employ. . . ." Moreover, these harbour admirals were given authority to settle all disputes arising between subjects of the two nations, and in so doing to act thereon "with the Strictest Justice

---

[18] Graves to Ruthven, October 15, 1763, C.O. 194:15.

[19] For an additional instruction to Governor Graves in 1763 for the enforcement of the Trade and Navigation Acts see C.O. 5:66, folio 181; this was in harmony with the circular letter sent by the Earl of Egremont on July 9, 1763, to all British Governors in America about the enforcement of the Trade and Navigation Acts. See C.O. 5:66, folio 171.

[20] The Governor's ship, the fifty-gun *Antelope*, with a complement of 280 men was the largest, the *Sky* with 90 men, the smallest. See C.O. 5:66, folio 197.

[21] As in the past, the shipmaster who arrived first in a harbour or cove where he planned to fish and dry his catch was given the post of admiral of the harbour, which carried with it considerable responsibility to see that disputes arising in the harbour were amicably settled. The admiral of the harbour was aided by a vice-admiral and rear-admiral, appointed on the basis of the order in which the next captains arrived at the harbour. See W. B. Kerr: "Newfoundland before the Revolution," *loc. cit.*, LXV, 67.

and impartiality," under the injunction that all the proceedings connected with such disputes and their judgements must be in writing and must be transmitted to the Governor so that they might be either confirmed or annulled as the law required. As to disputes that might arise solely among the French, the admirals were not under any circumstances to interfere but were to consider these matters as beyond their jurisdiction.[22]

As emphasized earlier in this series,[23] the policy of the government in England in the latter part of the seventeenth century was against any colonization of the island; it sought rather to break up such settlements as had appeared. This however was both unrealistic and unsuccessful. In 1761, Governor Webb reported to the Board of Trade that there were 7,910 permanent inhabitants on the island, of which 3,155 were Irish Roman Catholics.[24] It may be assumed that most of these settlers, especially those living in St. John's, had acquired property in land. Nevertheless the convention persisted that no one should claim personal possession of any land along the "French Shore" in face of the acknowledged right of French fisher-

---

[22] For the additional instructions, signed on March 30, 1764, see C.O. 195:9, pp. 266–73. See also Stowe Papers, H. M. 220, Huntington Library, San Marino, Calif., not only for the additional instructions but also for the opinions of the Advocate General, Attorney General, and Solicitor General, which were signed March 19, 1764. It may be noted here that the French ambassador to the Court of St. James drew up "a project of Arrangements" to be agreed upon by Great Britain and France for preventing any dispute between the English and French engaged in the Newfoundland fisheries. For the proposed articles of agreement (fourteen in all, written in French) enclosed in the Earl of Halifax's letter to the Board of Trade of February 25, 1764, see C.O. 194:15. The Advocate General, Attorney General, and Solicitor General were asked for opinions as to the propriety of the French articles. On March 4, 1764, they replied that these were clearly in conflict with 10 and 11 William III, c. 25, "An Act to Encourage the Trade to Newfoundland," and that the Crown could therefore not legally enter into an agreement to adopt them. For this opinion see Stowe Papers, H. M. 220:18, loc. cit., and C.O. 194:15. According to George Grenville, the French ambassador M. de Guerchy, in a memorial concerned with the so-called French Shore, set forth "many new claims" which seemed to lay the foundation for restricting not only the British fisheries but even a part of the territorial rights of Great Britain "to the Southern Part of Newfoundland." See Grenville to the Earl of Halifax, April 28, 1764, Grenville Letter Books, Stowe Papers; see also F. F. Thompson: The French Shore Problem in Newfoundland . . . (Toronto, 1961), pp. 12–13.

[23] See Volume III, 257–8.

[24] Webb to the Board of Trade, February 23, 1761, enclosing answers to the heads of inquiry, C.O. 194:15. For Lord Baltimore's estimate giving the island population in 1753 as between 12,000 and 13,000 permanent inhabitants see "Case of . . . Lord Baltimore . . ." (1754), Calvert Papers, No. 522, Maryland Historical Society, as cited earlier in this series, Volume III, 251. For the Board of Trade estimate of 1765, giving the number of inhabitants including men, women, and children, as not less than 15,000, see ibid.

men to stop there. On May 10, 1765, additional instructions were given to Governor Palliser. These recited that several inhabitants of the island "upon various unwarranted Pretences [had] possessed themselves of, and do claim as their private Property, large Tracts of Land commodious for the Fishery, lying within the several Harbours and Rivers . . . between Bonavista and Point Riche, to the great Prejudice and Discouragement of the Ship Fishery, not only of Our Subjects in general but also of the Subjects of the Crown of France. . . ." The Governor was therefore to give no countenance to these claims and was further instructed that those who came to fish, whether French or British, should have the freedom to choose their stations "as they respectively arrive," but should occupy only the space actually required for their operations.[25] But the French, doubtless fearing that their fishing interest would suffer unless special protection were provided, sent war vessels to the northern Newfoundland coasts in 1764 and, according to Palliser, under this protection the crews of French fishing vessels made unwarranted "encroachments" on the fishing grounds.[26] However, as a result of the Governor's firm policy[27] a fair degree of harmony was maintained between the English and French fishermen, although the latter complained greatly of his rigid interpretation of their rights. For while he permitted the French to remain over the winter with those boats constructed in France and to retain the huts and fishing stages, they were not allowed to use any available timber for building new boats or for repairing their vessels, nor to maintain warehouses for storing the surplus salt that was not used for curing the cod; further, they were forbidden to resort to the coast of Labrador to fish or to have any commercial intercourse with the British colonials.[28]

In fact after 1763 the French cod fishery never recovered the commanding position it had enjoyed before 1756.[29] In order to

---

[25] For the additional instructions to Palliser see C.O. 195:9, pp. 434–6.

[26] On this point, including the petition of the West of England ports against the French encroachments, see Admiral Keppel to William Pitt, April 4, 1765, Chatham manuscript transcripts, Canadian Archives 47:177, and George III to General Conway, August 11, 1765, *Letters of King George III* (ed. Bonamy Dobrée, London, 1935), p. 32.

[27] See *Gazette de Quebec*, September 6, 1764.

[28] For Governor Palliser's "General Account" of the fisheries, December 2, 1766, see C.O. 194:16.

[29] Although 12,455 Frenchmen were employed in the Newfoundland fishery in 1766, utilizing 123 ships and 1,556 boats, they cured but 189,500 quintals of cod

encourage their fishermen to continue to go to the northern shores of the island and compete with the English the French government, it was asserted, provided a special bounty or compensation to every ship that had been obstructed by the English when attempting to secure a place for its fishery.[30] In turn, by "An Act to Encourage the Fisheries" passed by Parliament in 1775, a system of bounties was similarly provided for the seamen from the ports of Great Britain sailing for the Newfoundland fishery.[31]

according to Palliser. See *ibid.* The "First Report from the Committee appointed to Enquire into the State of the Trade to Newfoundland" (*Parliamentary Papers Printed by Order of the House of Commons, 1731–1800*, Vol. 42, *Reports*, XII, "Comprizing No. 107, 1792/3 Newfoundland Trade," to be found in *British Sessional Papers*, ed. E. L. Erickson, Readex Microprint, New York, 1960) gives the following tables for the years 1769–1774 (pp. 57–62):

"A State of the French Fishery," Appendix No. 6.C.

Year	Ships	Boats	Men	Quintals of fish
1769	431	1,455	12,367	215,030
1770	437	1,470	12,855	435,340
1771	419	1,327	12,640	239,864
1772	330	1,468	15,248	388,800
1773	284	1,452	14,476	336,250
1774	273	1,614	15,137	386,215

"A State of the Newfoundland Fishery [British]," Appendix No. 6.H.

Year	Ships	Boats	Men*	Quintals of fish made	Quintals of fish carried to foreign markets
1764	238	1,812	6,156	521,310	470,188
1765	393	1,819	7,031	532,512	493,654
1766	308	2,014	7,215	558,785	523,636
1767	350	2,013	7,012	553,310	533,610
1768	289	2,104	8,064	573,450	542,960
1769	683	2,192	8,420	578,224	544,718
1770	829	2,201	9,395	649,498	610,910
1771	733	2,288	12,122	646,919	560,204
1772	642	2,425	12,698	759,843	481,347
1773	425	2,315	8,490	780,328	489,665
1774	533	2,415	9,998	695,866	516,358

(* on British ships, sackers, and bye boats)

In Joseph Hatton and M. Harvey: *Newfoundland . . .* (Boston, 1883), p. 224, the British export figure for 1763 is given as 348,294 quintals, and the subsequent figures not only vary slightly from those given above in the official report but jump from 1765 to 1785.

[30] Palliser to the Secretary of State for the Colonies, January 4, 1769, C.O. 195:12, pp. 57–62. In 1767 a bounty of 500 livres was given to *all* French ships that went to the French shore; in 1768 this was increased to 1,000 livres for those ships that carried a crew of over sixty men; also in 1767 a bounty was paid to French sack ships that exported cod to the French West Indies. See H. A. Innis: *op. cit.,* p. 183*n*.

[31] For the bounty system see 15 Geo. III, c. 31, par. I. For the effects of the bounty statute upon the Newfoundland fishery see the testimony in the "Report from the Committee appointed to Enquire into the State of the Trade to Newfoundland" (1792/3), *loc. cit.*

The fact that the French were forbidden to resort to Labrador, as being beyond the bounds of the rights they enjoyed by treaty, has already been mentioned. This vast, rather forbidding area had one great asset during the period under consideration: its fisheries. Cod was in great abundance along its southern shores. Labrador had been claimed by France before the war, and in so far as these claims were valid they were surrendered to Great Britain in the Peace Treaty of 1763, with the cession of Canada and all its dependencies. It was therefore decided by the King in Council to annex Labrador to Newfoundland by including it in the commission issued to Thomas Graves, first appointed to act as Governor of Newfoundland in 1762 and recommissioned in 1763.[32] The Labrador shore limits, according to the commission issued to Graves in March of this year, extended southward "from the entrance of Hudson's Straights to the River St. John's, which discharges itself into the sea nearly opposite the west end of the Island of Anticosti. . . ."

Although the New Englanders were not permitted to exploit the cod resources on the Banks or along the coast of Newfoundland, they saw opportunity for enrichment by going to the Labrador coast. Thus when in 1766 the British cruisers on patrol in the waters about Newfoundland arrived on that coast, they found between two to three hundred New England vessels—which had left their ports ostensibly to engage in whaling—fishing for cod and carrying their catch to the French ships moored in the northern harbours of the island.[33] What is more, the crews of these New England vessels were apparently guilty of committing many unlawful acts: destroying the British fishing works, burning the woods, and even killing the natives. They were therefore summarily sent "away a whaling." Reporting his action to the Board of Trade, Governor Palliser stated that the abundance and quality of the fish off Labrador so far exceeded the cod to be procured off Newfoundland that "if ships from the colonies are admitted to carry on that fishery [of Labrador], none can be employed from Britain."[34] Determined to safeguard the interests of the West of England ports, the Governor, under date of August 1, 1766, issued a proclamation that was posted along the Labrador coast. It stated that while vessels from the

---

[32] For Graves's commission dated March 25, 1763, see C.O. 195:9, pp. 150–61.

[33] In 1764 some seventeen vessels were seized for selling their cod catch to the French. See H. A. Innis: *op. cit.*, p. 184*n*.

[34] Palliser to the Board of Trade, October 21, 1766, C.O. 194:16, and Shelburne Papers, 51:253–65.

colonies interested in whaling would still be permitted to land on this coast for the purpose of cutting up their whales, their crews by reason of the outrages they had committed were not to engage in any other activity and if detected in so doing were to be carried to Newfoundland for trial in the general assizes.[35] This proclamation was also published in Boston by order of Governor Bernard, with the advice of the Council.[36]   In explaining his action to the Massachusetts Bay House of Representatives, Bernard stated that it was most important to let whalers know the conditions under which they could carry on activities and that it was the "indispensible duty" of every Governor to republish the proclamations of other governors, but that this action did not necessarily sanction such proclamations.[37] It may be added that by 1767, according to Palliser, the Labrador cod fishery had been taken over largely by the British fishing ships and to them alone was given the privilege of wintering on that coast.[38] He was also able to report that "the mix'd Multitudes of disorderly Crews" from the plantations "have behaved better this year than previously." [39] It should be added that since the government at home was not prepared to exclude colonials from the conti-

---

[35] *Ibid.*, 51:260–4, and C.O. 194:16.

[36] See the *Boston Evening-Post*, August 25, 1766; this proclamation was also reprinted in the *Massachusetts Gazette* on January 8, 1767.

[37] For Bernard's address to the House on February 27, 1767, see *Journals of the House of Representatives for 1766–1767*, p. 340. The members of the House of Representatives had been very much exercised that the Governor should have sanctioned the publication of the Newfoundland proclamation and had stated in a message to Bernard on February 6, 1767: "When we reflected on the heinous charges of Mr. Palliser against the People of this province of robbery, piracy, murder and in effect of treason and rebellion, it was absolutely impossible for us to conceive that any consideration could induce your Excellency and the Council to give them the sanction you have vouchsafed. . . ." The message went on to state that some of the principal traders to Newfoundland and Labrador had been examined and not the least proof obtained of any of the serious charges. See *ibid.*, pp. 257–8. In this connection it should be pointed out that on December 6, 1766, the committee of correspondence of the House prepared a long letter of complaint which stressed among other things "the very extraordinary Conduct: of the Governor of Newfoundland, whereby those engaged in the fishery had suffered very heavy losses." This letter was signed by the Speaker, Thomas Cushing, on December 6, 1766, and directed to Dennys De Berdt, London agent for the colony. Enclosed in the letter were depositions from a number of the people who had gone to Labrador as to the harsh conduct of Captain Hamilton of H. M. sloop *Merlin*. See the Arthur Lee Papers, Vol. 1:27–8, Houghton Library, Harvard University.

[38] Under regulations issued by Palliser on August 10, 1767, no settlement or ownership of property in land was permitted in Labrador and no person was permitted to winter there, with the exception that each of the masters of the first three ships to arrive from England on that coast could leave a crew of twelve men. See C.O. 194:18.

[39] *Ibid.*

nent from participating in the Labrador fisheries (as the Governor had sought to do), the New Englanders continued to resort there until 1775.[40]

But Palliser found himself faced with other difficulties in trying to guarantee the Labrador fishery to the English Bankers. Writing to the Board of Trade on April 6, 1768 he pointed out that "a few Smuggling Traders settled at Quebec" had set forth various claims to over five hundred miles of Labrador shore as well as to numerous islands lying near it. These claims were based on "a pretended old French grant," or on other grants supposed to have been made by General Murray while Governor of Quebec, "which being monopolies I have always considered as illegal and injurious to the common rights of the rest of the King's subjects." [41] Later in the year, again writing to the Board of Trade, Palliser referred to an action brought against him by Daniel Bayne and William Brymer of Quebec in the Court of King's Bench for annulling in 1765 a grant made to them by Governor Murray on April 6, 1763, for carrying on a seal fishery, and for ordering them to quit possession of their holding.[42]

That the government was opposed to monopolies in connection with the fisheries in general, yet desired to give "all possible encouragement to the whale and sea-cow fishery," is indicated by the

---

[40] See W. B. Kerr: *loc. cit.*, LXV, 76.

[41] See C.O. 194:18. There were other claims involving Labrador. For example two Frenchmen—Thomas Cugnet, an agent for the French Compagnie des Indes, and a Monsieur Tachet of Quebec—set forth claims (going back to the French period) to the exclusive possession of land and fishery posts on that part of the coast west of Labrador bordering the Gulf of St. Lawrence. This claim came before the Board of Trade on May 12, 1767. The Lords Commissioners, in a representation to the Privy Council which was supported by the opinion of the Attorney General and Solicitor General, contested both the legality and the desirability of such claims. For an extended account see C.O. 42:28, pp. 221–52. See also, for this period, the petition involving the case of Jean Tachet and the heirs of Messrs. Bissot and Joliet, Canadian subjects of His Majesty, who claimed a deed and grants to certain possessions— among them the island of Anticosti which in 1763 came under the jurisdiction of the government of Newfoundland—whereby they were disturbed in the enjoyment of their privileges. See Shelburne to the Board of Trade, April 28, 1767, Shelburne Papers, 53:61–2, Clements Library; see also Board of Trade *Journal, 1764–1767*, p. 384.

[42] Palliser to the Board of Trade, December 17, 1768, C.O. 194:18; see also Palliser's petition to the Board of Trade, January 6, 1769, and the memorial of Bayne and Brymer to the Board of January 14, 1769, *ibid*. It may be added that the Court of King's Bench declined jurisdiction in the case and proposed instead that it be laid before the Board of Trade; but the Board also declined to consider the case; ultimately a compromise was reached between the parties. See *Acts of the Privy Council, Col. Ser., 1766–1783*, pp. 185–6; see also Board of Trade *Journal, 1768–1775*, p. 8.

instructions given to John Byron, who succeeded Palliser in 1769.[43] With the passage of the Quebec Act in 1774 the territory of Labrador was removed from the jurisdiction of the Governor of Newfoundland and transferred to the government of the Province of Quebec.[44] Nevertheless the Governor of Newfoundland was instructed, as the Commander-in-Chief of His Majesty's ships employed in the protection of the fisheries, to superintend the Labrador fisheries in addition to those of Newfoundland.[45]

Only gradually did Newfoundland become recognized as a colony rather than a fishery island. The exact status of the island was important from the point of view of the applicability of the Trade and Navigation Acts. The instructions given to the Governors before the 1760's were vague on this point. For example, those given to George Bridges Rodney in 1749 simply called on him to report whether or not manufactures from foreign countries or the plantations were being brought to the Island.[46] As a leading authority on the history of Newfoundland before 1763 has pointed out, "the chief difficulty arose from the uncertain position occupied by Newfoundland in the commercial system. No one was at all certain whether the acts of trade applied there, and even the commissioners of the customs classified it as a foreign country in their export and import returns."[47] But this was to change. About 1736 a Court of Vice-Admiralty was established at St. John's—even earlier a "preventive officer" had been posted there—and in 1741 a naval officer was also assigned to this post.[48] This interference in the freedom of action of shipmasters was bitterly resented and apparently the practice of evading inspection of incoming cargoes was wide-spread, doubtless under the persuasion that Newfoundland should be considered (as it long had been) a special case within which the general trade regulations did not operate. However, according to Richard Routh's

---

[43] For Byron's instructions May 10, 1769, see C.O. 5:203, pp. 1–55, particularly instructions Nos. 15–22 relating to Labrador.

[44] By the Quebec Act, which received the royal approval on June 22, 1774, all lands to the south of the territory claimed by the Hudson's Bay Company and stretching to the Gulf of St. Lawrence, as well as the adjacent islands, were included within the limits of the Province of Quebec. See 14 Geo. III, c. 83 par. 1.

[45] For the instructions given to Governor Molineux Shuldham, who succeeded John Byron as Governor in 1772 and retained that post until 1775, see the Earl of Dartmouth to the Lords of the Admiralty of June 16, 1774, and April 28, 1775, C.O. 5:259, folio 159 and folio 197.

[46] For Rodney's instructions see C.O. 5:200, pp. 568–603; for comment on these instructions see in this series Volume III, 260–1.

[47] R. G. Lounsbury: *op. cit.*, p. 202.

[48] *Ibid.*, pp. 326–7.

testimony in 1793 before a committee of the House of Commons, a custom house had been erected at St. John's in 1762, and a Mr. Hamilton sent out as collector, but he "found the People and Climate so disagreeable and the Emoluments so inadequate to his Expectations that he returned to England the same Year and resigned. . . ."[49] According to the witness Thomas Irving, Inspector General of Imports and Exports of Great Britain (also testifying in 1793), officers of the customs were sent out to the island in 1764.[50]

Nevertheless the Commissioners of Customs seem to have been in doubt as to whether the Trade and Navigation Acts actually applied to Newfoundland. In 1765 [51] they presented a memorial to the Lords of the Treasury asking to be informed if these acts were not as applicable to Newfoundland as to the other colonies. This memorial was referred to the Lords Commissioners for Trade and Plantations, who replied on June 5 that they saw "no reason to doubt that Newfoundland is a part of His Majesty's Plantations in America, and consequently that its commerce as well as the ships bound thither are subject to the same regulations and restrictions as are prescribed for the Commerce and Shipping of all other His Majesty's Plantations in America, by the several Acts of Parliament." [52] Acting on the Board of Trade opinion, the Commissioners of Customs in 1766 appointed Alexander Dunn as collector and J. Hays as comptroller of the custom house now re-established at St. John's. Immediately there was complaint on the part of the merchants and shipmasters of the "exhorbitant fees" exacted by these officers, and Governor Palliser was entreated to lay their complaint before the Commissioners of Customs in London.[53] In their letter to the Governor they asserted that "the whole Duties of our Imports in this Island will not pay the Annuity of a Single Officer, if so, of what utility are those Custom House Officers when [His] Majesty's Ships are highly sufficient to prevent any Clandestine Trade?" [54] Faced with this outcry, the collector and comptroller of the custom house

---

[49] See "Second Report for the Committee appointed to enquire into the State of Trade to Newfoundland," 1793, *Reports of the House of Commons, 1731–1800, British Sessional Papers,* XII, 57, and C. R. Fay: *Life and Labour in Newfoundland* . . . (Toronto, 1956), pp. 39–40.

[50] "Second Report for the Committee appointed to enquire into the State of Trade to Newfoundland," 1793, *loc. cit.,* XII, 178.

[51] For a broad view of Newfoundland circa 1765 see Captain Griffith Williams: *An Account of the Island of Newfoundland* . . . (London, 1765).

[52] See P.R.O., Treas. 1:441, folio 206.

[53] Merchants and shipmasters to Palliser, August 28, 1766, C.O. 194:16.

[54] *Ibid.*

also appealed to the Governor, requesting that since no fees for their offices had ever been fixed he would levy them so as "to remove all room for Impositions and Complaints." [55] To reassure the merchants and shipmasters, Palliser informed them that the purpose of the government in erecting a custom house at St. John's was not to subject the fishery to any restraints or changes other than those found absolutely necessary to prevent frauds and abuses in trade. He also agreed with them that an "unregulated" custom house on the island might operate to the prejudice of the fishery and promised to lay their memorial together with his own sentiments before the King's ministers. Nevertheless, he recommended that they pay the same fees as they had paid the previous year.[56] While complaints continued to reach the Governor, it seems clear that after 1772 fees were paid more or less regularly. The matter was definitely settled by an act of Parliament in 1776.[57]

As emphasized in an earlier volume of this series,[58] the government of the island remained rudimentary throughout the eighteenth century. The Governor, who was always a naval officer, was only a part-time official; he arrived at St. John's Harbour late in the spring and left early in the fall, usually making his headquarters on board the ship of war that he commanded. He had no Council and, acting under his commission and instructions, exercised a variety of powers while being answerable only to the government at home. On the local level there were constables and justices of the peace, who were not expected to interfere with the admirals of the harbours, and there was, finally, a court of assize. Not until after the close of the Napoleonic wars, in 1817, was the first full-time resident Governor

---

[55] The Collector and Comptroller of the Customs to the Governor, August 25, 1766, Shelburne Papers, 51:249–51. In their letter the customs officers stated that they were listing the fees usually taken. By 5 Geo. III, c. 45, par. 27, "An Act for more effectively securing and encouraging the Trade of his Majesty's American Dominions; . . . and for regulating the Fees of the Officers of the Customs in the said Dominions," it was recited that at any port where no fees had heretofore been levied the officers of the customs were entitled to equivalent fees received by similar officers at the nearest custom house within the King's dominions. The nearest custom house to St. John's was of course at Halifax; but apparently not having at hand the table of fees levied there, Dunn and Hays relied on a Boston list.

[56] Palliser to the merchants and shipmasters, September 9, 1766, Shelburne Papers, 51:249–50.

[57] See "An Act . . . for regulating the Fees to be taken in the Offices of the Customs on the Island of Newfoundland," 16 Geo. III, c. 47, par. 3. By this law the customs officers were entitled to take fees corresponding to those collected at Halifax, Nova Scotia.

[58] See Volume III, 259–64 and 277–8.

commissioned; it was not until 1825 that he was aided by an appointed Council, nor until 1832 that an Assembly of representatives of the people was called.

In 1763 the Board of Trade, it is of interest to note, requested their secretary, John Pownall, to pose to the English merchants most concerned with Newfoundland the following question: ". . . Whether a more complete and perfect form of civil government in Newfoundland will or will not be for the advantage of that trade and fishery. . . ?" [59] From Poole in southwest England came conflicting replies. John Henning, the mayor, declared that the merchants of their town felt that such a government would be very disadvantageous; [60] George Milner of the same town, on the other hand, took the position that Newfoundland needed such a government more than any other of His Majesty's dominions since the island had witnessed "the most lawless rapine, oppression & injustice." [61] The Glasgow merchants also favoured such a civil government as better for the island than "a military one," [62] while the merchants of Exeter were unanimous in declaring that such a government would be highly prejudicial to the good of the island [63]—an opinion shared by the Bristol merchants, [64] as well as those of Dartmouth. [65] Doubtless the influence of the English merchants resulted in no further steps being taken during the period to improve the type of government long established on the island—a situation that seems to have been perfectly satisfactory to the inhabitants, who were not at all revolutionary-minded.

With the outbreak of the War for American Independence and the closing of the cod fisheries to the rebellious colonials, Americans no longer brought the accustomed food supplies on which the inhabitants of Newfoundland had relied for sustenance. The islanders were therefore much inflamed at what they felt to be an attempt by

[59] See Board of Trade *Journal, 1759–1763*, pp. 416–17 and p. 424.

[60] Henning to the Board of Trade, December 17, 1763, C.O. 194:15.

[61] Reply of December 21, 1763, *ibid.* For efforts on the part of the Society for the Propagation of the Gospel in Foreign Parts to bring religion to the inhabitants of Newfoundland see Ruth M. Christensen: "The Establishment of the S. P. G. Mission in Newfoundland, 1703–1783," *Historical Magazine of the Protestant Episcopal Church*, XX, 207–29.

[62] The Provost of Glasgow to the Board of Trade, December 22, 1763, C.O. 194:15.

[63] The Mayor of Exeter to the Board of Trade, December 24, 1763, *ibid.*

[64] Master of the Society of Merchant Venturers to the Board of Trade, January 10, 1764, *ibid.*

[65] Arthur Holdsworth of Dartmouth to the Board of Trade, March 29, 1764, *ibid.*

their fellow colonials to starve them. The year 1775 was described by one fisherman of the island as "a terrible year of storm and suffering." But the people survived. Moreover, with four or five men-of-war always on the coast, together with a strong garrison and "ten thousand sturdy West Countrymen" arriving from England during the fishing season, the Newfoundlanders could feel secure against any enemy attempt to lay waste their settlements during the war years.[66]

---

[66] D. W. Prowse: *op. cit.*, p. 338.

CHAPTER X

The Empire on the Fringe of the Storm: Nova Scotia

SINCE earlier volumes of this series have dealt with some of the most important aspects of the political and economic history of the Province of Nova Scotia during the period from 1750 to 1775, it seems best at this point to emphasize those factors that were to determine the position taken by the colony in the crisis that developed between Great Britain and the Thirteen North American Colonies.[1]

First of all was the brute fact of British naval dominance of the waters about the peninsula, including the Bay of Fundy, with Halifax as a base of concentration for warships stationed off the northern coast of North America. Then there was Nova Scotia's dependence upon annual appropriations by Parliament for the support of its government.[2] Parenthetically it may be noted that the governments

---

[1] For Nova Scotia see in this series Volume V, Chap. 6, "Land of the Acadians"; Volume VI, Chap. 8, "The Treason of Thomas Pichon," Chap. 9, "Farewell to Acadia," Chap. 10, "The Exiles"; Volume IX, Chap. 6, "The Transformation of Nova Scotia"; and for maps see Volume V, facing pp. 194, 306, 307, and Volume IX, facing pp. 134, 135, 142. For a very thorough study of Nova Scotia during the period under consideration see J. B. Brebner: *The Neutral Yankees of Nova Scotia, A Marginal Colony During the Revolutionary Years* (New York, 1937); see also W. B. Kerr: *The Maritime Provinces of British North America and the American Revolution* (Sackville, New Brunswick, [1941]).

[2] The extent of Nova Scotia's dependence upon annual appropriations by Parliament is understood by the following figures covering the years 1760–1775:

Year	Amounts		
	£	S.	D.
1760	17,636	11	3*
1761	10,595	12	9
1762	5,684	1	10
1763	10,254	15	9¼**
1764	5,703	14	11

of Georgia, East Florida and West Florida were similarly supported by appropriations made by Parliament.[3] Of this group Georgia was the only colony finally to throw in its lot with the revolutionaries, as was indicated in Volume XII of this series.

The Nova Scotia Assembly supplemented the sums furnished by Parliament by certain imposts and an excise on spirituous beverages and other items,[4] which brought in a sum averaging about £2,250 annually between 1758 and 1767.[5] Nevertheless, by that last year the colony had appropriated more than it received from these imposts and was in debt to the amount of £23,252.[6] To ease the financial

Year	Amounts		
1765	11,911	14	11
1766	12,874	16	0*
1767	5,557	11	5
1768	3,895	1	11
1769	4,375	17	11
1770	4,239	0	0
1771	5,796	10	5
1772	5,346	10	5
1773	5,146	10	5
1774	4,346	10	5
1775	4,346	10	5

* includes regular and unanticipated expenses.
** includes earlier expenses not previously paid.
See *Annual Register* for the following years:
1760, p. 187; *1762* (incl. 1761), pp. 155 and 167; *1763*, p. 179; *1764*, p. 160; *1765*, p. 138; *1766*, p. 202; *1767*, p. 218; *1768*, p. 262; *1769*, p. 219; *1770*, p. 236; *1771*, p. 223; *1772*, p. 210; *1773*, p. 227; *1774*, p. 252; *1775*, p. 244.

[3] See the same issues of the *Annual Register* cited in footnote 2 for appropriations made to Georgia and the Floridas. As will be noted, the three southern colonies enjoyed no such liberality as was shown to Nova Scotia.

[4] For the acts granting an excise on wines, tea, coffee, and playing-cards passed in 1765, 1766, and 1767, see *Temporary Acts of the General Assemblies of His Majesty's Province of Nova Scotia, 1758–1766* (Halifax, 1767), pp. 25–30, 43–5, 48–9.

[5] See "Abstract of the State of the Provincial Funds at Nova Scotia from the first . . . General Assembly to the Arrival of . . . [Governor] Lord William Campbell, November 27, 1766," Shelburne Papers, 55:191–2, Clements Library.

[6] *Ibid.* In 1766 according to President Greene of the Council the debt, which amounted to over £20,000, "hangs on the Province" with the Assembly unable to make any provision for it; as a result, "the credit of the Province was at a low ebb." See Greene to the Board of Trade, August 24, 1766, Shelburne Papers, 51:374–5. Out of the funds voted by the Assembly, payments had been made to the assistant judges, the justices of the peace, the provincial treasurer, and the collector of the imposts and excises, along with payments for internal improvements. But the revenue to meet these payments was inadequate. In an attempt to cover the charges against the colony a duty of fivepence a gallon was levied on all imported rum and other distilled spirituous liquors, except those from Great Britain; a duty of two shillings and sixpence per barrel on all but British beer; a duty of a penny a pound on loaf sugar, again excepting that shipped from Great Britain; an excise of tenpence a gallon on all spirituous liquor sold within the province, whether imported or distilled in the colony;

situation, in 1770 the Assembly voted to continue the taxes on tea, coffee, and playing-cards. Although these items had appeared in the tax bill of 1766, they clearly violated British mercantile policy. In a letter to Governor Lord William Campbell [7] of May 23, 1771, the Board of Trade pointed out that the playing-cards taxed were a product of Great Britain and the tea and coffee were particular objects of its commerce, therefore the Board should have recommended disallowance of the law, but did not do so because of "the distrest and almost Bankrupt State of the Public Treasury of the Province." [8] Nor did the financial situation of the province mend thereafter; rather, it declined. In 1774, the largest revenue raised within the colony was but £1,600 as against the demands upon it of £5,400. [9] In December of that year the Assembly raised the duty on imported rum from fivepence to tenpence a gallon, and placed duties of fivepence a gallon on molasses, a shilling a gallon on spirits, sixpence a gallon on wine, and five shillings a hundredweight on unrefined sugar—all in an effort to clear the colony of debt. [10]

But the province remained a British colony chiefly dependent upon the mother country for the maintenance of its government. In the estimates submitted to Parliament for 1775 by the Treasury

---

a duty of sixpence a gallon on all wines, a shilling per pack on all playing-cards, and sixpence a ton on all trading vessels entering Halifax; finally there was a licence fee of £8 per annum for all persons retailing hard liquor or beer within the districts of Halifax, Annapolis, and Fort Cumberland, and £5 per annum for such retailers in certain other parts of the province. See Greene and William Campbell to the Earl of Shelburne, April 4, 1767, Shelburne Papers, 55:182–90. Most of these imposts were to remain in force until 1771.

[7] The following men were commissioned as Governor or Lieutenant Governor of Nova Scotia during the 1760's and 1770's:

Governor	Lieutenant Governor	Date of Commission
Henry Ellis		April 1, 1761
	Jonathan Belcher	April, 1761
	Montagu Wilmot	March 11, 1763
Montagu Wilmot		October 5, 1763
	Michael Francklin	March 28, 1766
Lord Wm. Campbell*		August, 1766
Francis Legge		July 22, 1773

* Campbell was commissioned Governor of South Carolina June 10, 1773. See "List of Commissions . . . Issued to the Royal Governors and Others in America," American Historical Association *Report* (1911), I, 504–6.

[8] "Whitehall Dispatches, 1770–1783," Nova Scotia Archives, Halifax.

[9] For an illuminating discussion of the finances of Nova Scotia in the 1770's see J. B. Brebner: *op. cit.*, pp. 250–4.

[10] *Ibid.* The act is cited as 14–15 Geo. III, c. 11 (Nova Scotia). For the rates established by the act, as well as the rates of import and excise levied on the colony from 1751–1782, see Brebner: *op. cit.*, Appendix A.

Board, not only were the salaries of all provincial officers provided for but also the salary of the London agent, the stipends or allowances to Anglican Church ministers, to schoolmasters serving within the colony, and to the Catholic priest who ministered to the Micmac Indians; also provided for was the cost of maintaining an orphanage and the lighthouse at the entrance of Halifax Harbour.[11] It would be almost inconceivable that the impoverished inhabitants of a virtually bankrupt colony receiving such liberal assistance to protect them from anarchy could have been anything but loyal to the source of their support. Nor was it likely for them to have become greatly exercised over the charges freely voiced by their rich colonial neighbours that the government of Great Britain was seeking to exploit and even enslave Americans.

By 1767 Nova Scotia had an estimated population of 13,374. The majority of these inhabitants—that is, those who had come from New England—numbered 6,913, as against 2,165 from Ireland, 1,946 from Germany and elsewhere in continental Europe, 1,265 Acadians, and 1,085 from Great Britain.[12] The figure of 19,120 settlers reported for 1772[13] shows an increase in population, largely the result of the continued movement of settlers from New England into the newer townships. By that year at least three fourths of the population was made up of those who had come from colonies to the south or who were their offspring.[14] Yet this close connection with New England, which instigated self-supporting Congregational and Baptist churches—in contrast to the Anglican Church establishment whose ministers received financial aid from Parliament—still did

----

[11] For the detailed estimates of 1775 for Nova Scotia see Peter Force: *American Archives*, 4th ser., I, 1709–10.

[12] For the figures found in "Return of the Several Townships in the Province of Nova Scotia . . . January 1767," see Archibald MacMeehan: "Nova Scotia Under English Rule, 1713–1775," *Canada and Its Provinces* (eds. Adam Shortt and A. G. Doughty, 23 vols., Toronto, 1914–17), XIII, 117. President Benjamin Green of the Council, in his dispatch to the Board of Trade of August 24, 1766, estimated that the population of Nova Scotia was 11,272, exclusive of 500 "Neuter French," some 1,500 Indians, and an annual influx of some 50 people who came to fish. See Shelburne Papers, 51:371.

[13] For statistics on the population of Nova Scotia in 1764, 1772, 1781, and 1784, see T. C. Haliburton: *An Historical and Statistical Account of Nova Scotia . . .* (2 vols., Halifax, 1829), II, 274–5. See also J. B. Brebner: *op. cit.*, Chap. 2, "The Incoming Tide."

[14] That there also continued to be a movement of people from Great Britain into the province is indicated by the fact that in 1774 nine vessels arrived in Halifax from such places as London, Scarborough, Newcastle, Sunderland, and Aberdeen, bearing some 700 settlers. See Beamish Murdock: *A History of Nova Scotia or Acadia* (3 vols., Halifax, 1866), II, 518–19.

not bring the inhabitants into the orbit of the American revolutionary movement.[15]

It must be borne in mind that most of the New England communities that sprang up in Nova Scotia in the 1760's and 1770's were isolated ones, located either on lands the Acadians had been required to evacuate or on new lands. Unlike the New England colonies—where a fairly complex system of highways and waterways had long since had the effect of drawing together the towns and hamlets in Massachusetts Bay, Rhode Island, and Connecticut— Nova Scotia, even as late as 1784 according to Colonel Robert Morse, had no roads at all except the highway that ran from Halifax to Annapolis Royal.[16] In this connection one must also remember that the Province of Nova Scotia in 1763 included not only what is now the Province of New Brunswick but also Isle St. Jean—known since 1798 as Prince Edward Island. The latter became a separate province in 1769, but New Brunswick was not created until 1784. The lack of means of transportation and communication—except the passage by water, which might at times prove both difficult and hazardous—kept the rather widely separated communities from frequent contact with each other and focused their concern on local and personal problems, at times even that of mere survival.[17] What the Boston town-meeting might resolve would have little meaning to most of the fishermen-farmers of Nova Scotia, even if they received word of it. Moreover, the majority of the inhabitants of Halifax apparently depended either directly or indirectly for their liveli-

---

[15] See M. W. Armstrong: "Neutrality and Religion in Revolutionary Nova Scotia," *New England Quarterly*, XIX, 50–62.

[16] See the report on Nova Scotia by Col. Robert Morse, *Report on the Canadian Archives 1884* (Ottawa, 1885), p. xxxv. Lieutenant Governor Francklin in a letter to the Board of Trade dated September 30, 1766, pointed out that although many fishery settlements had come into existence along the coastline between Halifax and the Gut of Canso, the only communication between them was by water, except for some paths cut through the woods, and that only the road between Halifax and Windsor (the latter in the area of Minas Basin) was passable for carriages. See the Shelburne Papers, 51:381–3; see also the unpublished study by J. S. Martell entitled "Pre-Loyalist Settlements around Minas Basin . . . 1755–1783" (in the Nova Scotia Archives) for the place of origin of those who established themselves about the Basin. The author states (p. 62) that between 1759 and 1765 "thousands of New England farmers and fishermen formed associated companies and departed for the northern peninsula."

[17] Yet some of the settlers managed to retain business connections with the New England colonies. An excellent example was Simeon Perkins, a native of Norwalk, Connecticut, who settled in Liverpool, Nova Scotia. During the war, while remaining loyal to the King, he also sought to live on peaceable terms with the colonials. See *The Diary of Simeon Perkins, 1766–1780* (ed. H. A. Innis, Toronto, 1948).

hood upon the presence of the British garrison in the town and the ships of war stationed in the harbour.[18]

It is true that certain incidents disclosed a common bond between Nova Scotians and other colonials. In the town of Liverpool on the southeastern coast (originally settled by Connecticut fishermen) when a vessel arrived in the fall of 1765 bearing a newspaper that contained the text of the Stamp Act, the people proceeded to light a bonfire with the document.[19] Likewise after the stamps had arrived in Halifax the stamp-distributor, Archibald Hinshelwood, was hung in effigy on the night of October 12 with suitable "adornments and inscriptions." But the next day the effigy was removed by two prominent citizens without protest or threat.[20] Accordingly the October 19 edition of the *Halifax Gazette* notified its customers that, after November 1, the *Gazette* would supply them with news printed on stamped paper. The printer, however, appears to have had second thoughts after that date. According to the *Boston Evening-Post* of November 25, 1765, he took the convenient way out by placing on board the *Nova Scotia Packet* his supply of stamped paper and addressing it to unnamed Boston printers. When Captain Green discovered this parcel on board he had the papers burnt. To justify his act, he claimed to have had positive orders from the owners of the vessel not to transport any stamped paper. It also appears that after receiving some anonymous threats, the Nova Scotia stamp-distributor kept a guard of regular soldiers to protect his person. But that was the full extent of reaction to the Stamp Act in Nova Scotia.[21] Governor Wilmot was able to write to Secretary of State Conway on February 9, 1766, of his "singular satisfaction" that the people of the

[18] As Lord Campbell noted (in writing from Halifax to the Earl of Hillsborough on September 12, 1768), after the British regiments had left Halifax for Boston the poverty of the people reached great proportions since their "chief dependence was the circulating cash spent by the troops" (P.R.O., Colonial Correspondence, Nova Scotia, A. 3:274, Canadian Archives transcripts).

[19] Governor Montagu Wilmot to the Board of Trade, November 19, 1765, "Whitehall Dispatches, 1770–1783," Nova Scotia Archives, Halifax. This incident was correctly reported in the *Boston Evening-Post* of November 18, 1765; the November 11 edition stated incorrectly that the Liverpool deputy stamp-distributor had received a quantity of stamped papers which the people obliged him to surrender and which they had then made into a bundle and burnt.

[20] See *Boston Evening-Post*, October 28 and November 18, 1765. In reporting the incident this paper refers to the attitude of those who opposed the use of stamps in Nova Scotia and then to their expression of hope that "the Neighboring Colonies will be charitable enough to believe that nothing but their dependent situation prevents them from heartily and sincerely opposing a Tax unconstitutional in its Nature. . . ."

[21] *Ibid.*, December 2, 1765. For Nova Scotia and the Stamp Act see especially the article by W. B. Kerr: "The Stamp Act in Nova Scotia," *New England Quarterly*, VI, 552–66.

colony had submitted "without opposition" to the authority of Parliament.[22]

Even less did the passage of the Townshend Acts produce any protest on the part of the inhabitants of Nova Scotia or any movement to join with the other North American colonies in retaliatory measures against the mother country. For example, when the Massachusetts Bay House of Representatives sent out its famous circular letter of February 11, 1768, addressed to the Speakers of the various Assemblies, Speaker William Nesbitt instead of submitting the letter to the Nova Scotia Assembly placed it in the hands of Lieutenant Governor Francklin, who enclosed it in his letter of March 29 to Lord Hillsborough, Secretary of State for the Colonies. His own letter stated: "I must pray leave to assure your Lordship, that no temptation however great will lead the Inhabitants of this Colony to show the least inclination to oppose Acts of the British Parliament." [23] He also assured Hillsborough on September 9 that he knew of no obstruction to the customs officers in the province.[24] So peaceful was the colony that in July 1768 the British regulars were withdrawn from Annapolis Royal, Fort Cumberland, Amherst, and the St. John River area, and in September two regiments left Halifax for Boston.[25] Yet there was some ineffective opposition to the Tea Act of 1773 when a consignment of tea refused at Portsmouth, New Hampshire, was carried to Halifax for disposal. John Fillis and William Smith, two men both prominent as law officers, raised strong objections on principle to the purchase of the tea.[26] But again this was as

---

[22] Whitehall Dispatches, 1770–1783," Nova Scotia Archives, Halifax.

[23] See Colonial Correspondence, Nova Scotia, A. 3:54–6, Canadian Archives transcripts.

[24] *Ibid.*, A. 3:265. However, there was an incident in 1768 at Liverpool—the scene of some earlier discontent with the Stamp Act on the part of the New Englanders there—that indicated some opposition to the revenue laws. This involved a schooner that had been seized by the revenue officers at the port of New Dublin, north of Liverpool, but had escaped to Liverpool. The attempt of the sheriff and deputy-sheriff of Lunenberg County to seize this vessel met such resistance from a Liverpool mob that the law officers had to give it up. See Emily P. Weaver: "Nova Scotia and New England during the Revolution," *American Historical Review*, X, 55.

[25] See J. B. Brebner: *op. cit.*, p. 163; W. B. Kerr: "The Merchants of Nova Scotia and the American Revolution," *Canadian Historical Review*, XIII, 26–7; T. C. Haliburton: *op. cit.*, I, 247.

[26] For the activities of Fillis and Smith, and the response of the Governor to them, see W. B. Kerr: "Merchants of Nova Scotia . . . ," *loc. cit.*, pp. 29–31. That there was also wide-spread evasion of the trade laws in 1773 in the Halifax area is indicated by a report submitted on October 9 to Lord William Campbell by James Burrow, comptroller of customs at Halifax. See *Manuscripts of the Earl of Dartmouth*, Vol. I, *Historical Manuscripts Commission, Eleventh Report, Appendix*, Part V, 339; see also J. B. Brebner: *op. cit.*, p. 164n.

far as reaction to parliamentary supremacy went in Nova Scotia.

On October 18, 1774, Governor Francis Legge [27] assured the Earl of Dartmouth that—in contrast to the behaviour of the colonials living to the south of Nova Scotia—"the inhabitants have behaved with decorum," and that the East India Company's tea had been "disposed of, purchased and dispersed throughout the country." [28] Moreover, the Governor—after receiving reports that the seaport towns of New England were entering into combinations not to trade with Great Britain or the British West Indies—wrote to the Secretary of State during the summer of 1774 that he would take the opportunity thus afforded to promote trade with the sugar islands, doubtless seeing in the development of such a trade the possibility of at last producing some prosperity for the debt-ridden, improverished colony. [29]

To increase the prospect of a better day for Nova Scotia, the Assembly—dominated by the mercantile interests of Halifax—made a very significant alteration in the impost legislation in November 1774. The new law stated that the importations of British West India products should be free of all provincial duties (except that on rum), provided the imports came directly from these islands and provided that the return cargoes were made up of Nova Scotian products equal to two thirds the value of the goods received. By this law imports from other places would carry a duty of tenpence a gallon on distilled liquors (including rum), [30] fivepence a gallon on molasses, and five shillings a hundredweight on unrefined sugar.

---

[27] For Legge's commission as Governor, dated July 22, 1773, see C.O. 218:7, pp. 319–53; for his instructions, dated August 3, 1773, see C.O. 5:205, pp. 385–422, and C.O. 218:7, pp. 359–436. Legge assumed office on October 15, 1773; for an account of his administration see Viola F. Barnes: "Francis Legge, Governor of Nova Scotia," *New England Quarterly*, IV, 420–47. In *An Essay on the Present State of the Province of Nova Scotia* . . . (Halifax, 1774—a copy of this scarce pamphlet may be found in the John Carter Brown Library, Providence, R.I.), the author, apparently John Day (see Marie Tremaine's *Bibliography of Canadian Imprints, 1751–1880* [Toronto, 1952], item No. 187, p. 84), writes (pp. 10–11) of the high promise the administration of the province showed under Governor Legge, but denounces in most open terms the favouritism and corrupt conduct of some of his predecessors, especially Governor Lawrence. In 1774 Day, a man of political independence, was elected to the Assembly from Halifax; for some years before he had been a member from Newport. See J. B. Brebner: *op. cit.*, p. 229n and p. 267n.

[28] P.R.O., Colonial Correspondence, Nova Scotia, A. 9:125, Canadian Archives transcripts.

[29] See Legge to Dartmouth, July 6, 1774, Colonial Correspondence, Nova Scotia, A. 8:182, Canadian Archives transcripts. In this connection see Viola F. Barnes: *op. cit.*, pp. 426–8.

[30] This duty on rum was designed to protect the Nova Scotia distilleries.

Moreover, to encourage direct West Indies trade in these articles, the statute provided that upon re-exportation there should be a complete drawback of the duties paid on rum, and a drawback of all but a halfpenny a gallon on molasses, while on sugar there should be a drawback of all duties except sixpence a hundredweight.[31] When early in 1775 Parliament cut the New England colonies off from the cod fisheries,[32] an opportunity was thereby opened up for the Nova Scotia fishermen to replace the New Englanders in this highly profitable field of activity.

It should be noted that when the First Continental Congress voted on October 22, 1774, to hold a second gathering in Philadelphia in May of the following year, a resolution recommended that *all* colonies in North America be represented.[33] Accordingly the Speaker of the Nova Scotia Assembly in due time received a letter to this effect, together with a copy of the proceedings of the First Congress. However, all this effort was to no avail. When Governor Legge wrote to Dartmouth in the spring of 1775, he doubtless reflected the viewpoint of most of the Halifax merchants and Nova Scotia fishermen in stating that just as the French had earlier made Louisbourg the centre in North America both of the West India trade and of a flourishing fishery, so Halifax not only might build up its trade as the intermediate port between the West Indies and Canada, but might also become the centre of a great fishery, now that the New Englanders could no longer supply the markets of Spain and Portugal with cod.[34]

Of the other North American colonies, the Province of West Florida corresponded most closely in many respects to the situation found in Nova Scotia in 1775. Both colonies were well removed from those dominated by radical agitators opposed to British policy. Both had representative Assemblies empowered to levy upon the inhabitants but unable to do so except by means of inadequate import duties. Therefore both were dependent upon the generosity of Parliament for support of their governments. Each had a considerable number of former French subjects in their midst; each welcomed

---

[31] For an analysis of the act of November 1774 with a comparison of earlier to later legislation see J. B. Brebner: *op. cit.*, Appendix, pp. 258–61; see also Viola F. Barnes: *op. cit.*, pp. 426–7.

[32] 15 Geo. III, c. 10, par. 7.

[33] *Journals of the Continental Congress, 1774–1789*, I, 102.

[34] Legge to Dartmouth, March 6, 1775, Colonial Correspondence, Nova Scotia, A. 9:226, Canadian Archives transcripts.

the presence of British regular troops and each protested when they departed; finally, each attempted to change certain conditions that stood between them and the potentiality of acquiring wealth. While West Florida sought without success a relaxation of the Trade and Navigation Acts so that its two ports could become centres of a great Gulf of Mexico trade with the nearby Spanish possessions, Nova Scotia in the 1770's similarly sought to develop a West India trade and began to look toward the expansion of its fishery at the expense of recalcitrant New England.

Although by 1775 the population figures for Nova Scotia showed that a predominant number of settlers were of New England origin and background, most of the inhabitants remained loyal to the government of Great Britain. Unwilling to join the rebellious colonies to the south in making war against their King, they were nevertheless equally unwilling to take up arms against their kinsmen and former neighbours in those colonies. For example, the people of Yarmouth stated on December 8, 1775:

> "We do all of us profess to be true Friends & Loyal Subjects to George our King. We were almost all of us born in New England, we have Fathers, Brothers & Sisters in that Country; divided betwixt natural affection for our nearest relations, and good Faith and Friendship to our King and Country, we want to know, if we may be permitted at this time to live in a peaceable State, as we look on that to be the only situation in which we with our Wives and Children, can be in any tolerable degree safe." [35]

The adoption of an attitude of neutrality toward the crisis that faced the Empire seems to have been connected with the hope, on the part of some Nova Scotians at least, that they might thereby provide a bridge, as it were, on which the contending parties within

---

[35] For the Yarmouth petition see J. B. Brebner: *op. cit.*, p. 29. Yet a few active revolutionaries were strongly supporting the rebellious colonials to the south. In the area of the isthmus of Chignecto there was the Scot, John Allan, who had attained the office of sheriff of Cumberland County, and who was also a justice of the peace and a member of the Nova Scotia Assembly. Throughout the war he remained strongly committed to the American cause and made every effort to bring the province within its orbit. There was also Jonathan Eddy, born in Massachusetts Bay and settled in Cumberland County, who in 1775 was deputy provost-marshal and who renounced this office; in 1776 he and a band made up chiefly of transplanted New Englanders sought unsuccessfully to capture Fort Cumberland. Two other members of the Assembly, Sam Rogers of Sackville and William Howe of Chignecto, were deprived of their seats for their revolutionary activities. For an illuminating account of the futile activities of these men see W. B. Kerr: *The Maritime Province of British North America and the American Revolution,* Chaps. 5 and 6.

the Empire could meet and become reconciled. This neutral attitude took shape during a meeting of the General Assembly.[36]

On June 24, 1775, after the beginning of hostilities in Massachusetts Bay, the Assembly tried to restore peace within the Empire. This attempt was in the form of "An Address, Petition, and Memorial" to the King and both Houses of Parliament, emanating from "Representatives of the Freeholders of . . . Nova Scotia." The appeal for reconciliation referred to the "dreadful, and alarming crisis . . . impending over all British America," and declared that Nova Scotians "feel for our Gracious King, We feel for our Mother Country. . . , We feel for the British American Race, once the most Loyall, Virtuous, and happy of mankind. . . ." Acknowledging that the King, the Lords, and Commons in Parliament assembled formed "the Supreme Legislature of this province," they begged to be heard in the hope that their proceedings might possibly "have some influence, with other Assemblies in America. . . ." In harmony with Lord North's conciliatory resolution of February 26, 1775—that if the colonies would tax themselves for the support of the Empire and thereby create a fund that would be at the disposal of Parliament, this body would no longer attempt to tax them—they declared that the tax should be of such a nature that it would "never after be necessary to alter it." The one best suited for this purpose, they felt, would be a duty upon all imported commodities (except salt) that were not the produce of "the British Dominions in Europe and America," the rate of which should be fixed every ten years. As to the application of such a tax in Nova Scotia, they stated: "so Conscious are We of your Justice and Humanity, that we request to know what proportion would be pleasing or Agreeable to you, reminding you to consider that this province having no Manufactories or lucrative Commerce, must ever have a scarcity of Specie." [37]

---

[36] This was the same Assembly elected in 1770 and not dissolved until 1785—apparently as a precaution to keep the colony in check, according to A. L. Burt: A Short History of Canada . . . (Minneapolis, 1942), p. 84.

[37] See Nova Scotia State Papers, Ser. A., Vol. XCIV, 11–30, Canadian Archives transcript. This remarkable paper also concentrated on purely domestic grievances and called for a drastic overhauling of the local government. It is of interest to note that the following recommendations were made: that no native of Nova Scotia be appointed Governor, Lieutenant Governor, or a judge to the province; that members of the Legislative Council be appointed for life and that they should possess property in the colony worth £ 1,000; that elections by ballot for representatives be held every three years, and that the Governor, Council, and judges of the Supreme Court constitute a Court of Vice-Admiralty. The document, carefully edited by the late Professor Brebner, is in the Canadian Historical Review, XV, 171–81.

Thus the Assembly of Nova Scotia proclaimed its loyalty to the King while maintaining a neutral position toward the colonies in revolt. The reasons for the failure of Nova Scotians to join the cause of the New Englanders when the majority of them came from the same stock may well be ascribed to expediency and geography. It would have been most unusual had they not profited from this opportunity to attain some economic stability. But even more important was their inaccessibility—the settlements were too isolated from each other and from the centre of the revolutionary movement for the inhabitants spontaneously to join in mutual thought or action. Also the Bay of Fundy, a body of water separating Nova Scotia from the mainland on which sailed units of the powerful British navy, added to this isolation. Thus such revolutionary action as did take place, in Cumberland County for example, was largely local in nature and ineffective in result. The New Englanders of Nova Scotia were apparently equally reluctant either to fight their fellow New Englanders or to raise the standard of revolt against their King. If there were great principles involved in the American Revolution they were not apparent to most Nova Scotians, even those of New England birth or ancestry.

CHAPTER XI

The Empire on the Fringe
of the Storm: The
Province of Quebec

THE Gulf of St. Lawrence, the St. Lawrence River, and the Great Lakes, together with the streams that fed them and the lands drained by them, have been felicitously called the commercial empire of the St. Lawrence.[1] During the period of French and British control covered by this series the chief exports of the area were fur, fish, and oil.[2] Beyond the valley of the St. Lawrence were few settlements. Detroit, however, because of its strategic situation on the Detroit River had a sizeable permanent white population by the 1760's.[3] Elsewhere in the vast wilderness there were trading posts scattered here and there, such as Michilimackinac, where a small contingent of soldiers was posted and where traders appeared periodically to renew their goods and other supplies, only to disappear again on their way to some near or far-distant Indian village. During the French régime commercial relations had, of course, been limited to France. When the British took over Canada, England undertook to meet the needs of Canadians, old and new, for manufactures and a fur market.

As was noted in Chapter IX of this volume, the Proclamation of 1763[4] transferred from Canada to Newfoundland the jurisdiction

[1] See D. G. Creighton: *The Commercial Empire of the St. Lawrence, 1760–1850* (Toronto, 1937).

[2] See in this series Volume V, Chap. 1, "Les Habitants," and Chap. 2, "The Great Lakes Frontier"; for maps relating to the Province of Quebec as defined in the Proclamation of 1763 see also Volume IX, facing pp. 47 and 162.

[3] For estimates of the population of Detroit from 1760 to 1788, see N. V. Russell: *The British Régime in Michigan and the Old Northwest, 1760–1796* (Northfield, Minn., 1939), pp. 102–3.

[4] See in this series Volume IX, 52–3, for the geographical limits of the Province of Quebec established by the Proclamation of 1763, and Chap. 7, "Canada becomes a British Province."

over the profitable cod and seal fisheries located along the Labrador coast. It was therefore not until after the passage of the Quebec Act of 1774, which restored Labrador to its place within the bounds of the Province of Quebec, that the product of the coastal fisheries again assumed importance among the exports of this colony. Thus from 1764 to 1775 Canada was obliged to look largely to its fur staple as the only export producing the income necessary to pay for the articles required by the inhabitants to supplement what they produced locally. But the Indian trade, and consequently the fur trade, had been placed under severe restrictions in 1764.[5] Instead of the free and easy system under which the French *coureurs de bois* had habitually found their way to the Indian villages and wintered there, the new regulations required natives to bring their fur pelts or skins to designated posts. For example, Indian Superintendent Sir William Johnson reported to the Board of Trade in the fall of 1766 that the Indians living about the Saguenay River were expected to resort to the post at Chicoutimi; "another Post about the Cedars or Carillon on the Ottawa River" was proposed "for the other seven Canada Nations, while at Michilimackinac and La Baye [called also Bay des Puants, La Baye Verte or Green Bay] when established as the Indians have desired, will answer for all those in that country; that then and not till then the trade can be carried on without apprehension of Frauds [or] the hazard of perpetual Quarrels with the Indians. . . ."[6] But, as Johnson also noted in the same communication, the old practice was being continued by "busy Frenchmen who now almost engross the Northern Trade, and who . . . have . . . given sufficient proofs of their invincible dislike of us and their readiness to say anything to the Indians however false as an excuse for the dearness of their Goods. . . ."[7] As for the trade which was to be centred at Michilimackinac, he indicated that Captain Howard, the commanding officer of that post, had admitted to disregarding the regulations by giving permission to "a few Traders [to] go amongst the Indians"—something that the Indian Superintendent insisted had "disobliged the rest [of the traders.]"[8]

[5] See in this series Volume XI, Chap. 12, "Trans–Appalachian Developments: British Policies and Plans for the Management of Western Lands and Indian Affairs," especially pp. 431–40 for the regulation of the Indian trade.

[6] See Sir William Johnson to the Board of Trade, October 8, 1766, C.O. 323:24, T 16, printed in *New York Colonial Documents*, VII, 872.

[7] *Ibid.*, VII, 871.

[8] *Ibid.*, VII, 872.

There was in addition the problem of claims to exclusive trade at
La Baye post under the
dreuil, who paid 25,000
sold his lease to a Wil-
o a monopoly control of
direct opposition to the
ed trade laid down in the
Board of Trade plan of
o Major Robert Rogers,[11]
ilimackinac, resulted in
mmissaries appointed by
carried out. For these
ary of £200 sterling from

ss to and from one of our
be renewed at every Fort,
ny paid five Pounds to Sʳ
uld pass from Schenacady
hird five at Niagara, and a
rader got a single Boat load
Johnson and his commis-
all the Trader's profitts &
rt Mr. Johnson's intentions
erior County under Contri-

his arrival at Michilimac-
nted him with a memorial
their not being allowed to
trade at the Out Posts [13] & [asserted] that if I did not immediately
relieve them, themselves, their Family's & Many of their creditors

---

[9] See Gage to Shelburne, November 11, 1766, *Gage Correspondence*, I, 113–4; for Gage's report on the price paid for various leases by the French see C.O. 5:85, p. 446; see also P. C. Phillips: *The Fur Trade* (2 vols., Norman, Okla., 1961), I, 604.

[10] In this connection see again in this series, Volume XI, Chap. 12.

[11] For the appointment of Major Rogers to command at Michilimackinac see General Gage to Secretary of State Conway, January 16, 1766, *Gage Correspondence*, I, 79–80.

[12] Rogers to Fowler Walker, March 7, 1771, Hardwicke Papers, B. M., Add. Mss. 35915:247–8.

[13] By the term "Out Posts" Rogers meant the places where the traders wintered with the Indians and where, because of the lack of troops, the traders themselves fortified the areas "for the Defence of their own property."

would be totally ruined." Moreover the Indians declared that if traders were not permitted to come to them with goods, "they would take up the Hatchet against their Father, the English." As a result, the new commandant took it upon himself to issue a proclamation stating that "for his Majesty's Interest and the Safety of his subjects . . . the Indian Trade should be free and open . . . and . . . that such as chose to winter at the Out Posts with the Indians should have my passport without fee or reward—they went accordingly and the Trade has been open ever since." [14]

Yet Major Rogers's actions apparently went far beyond assuming responsibility for altering regulations covering the Indian trade. He was subsequently charged with being personally heavily involved in Indian trade, with being away from his post, with selling rum to the Indians, with becoming hopelessly indebted to traders to the amount of 100,000 livres and, finally, with threatening to enter the French service and to encourage the Indians to make war on the English. As a result of these reports Gage relieved him of his command and imprisoned him. When tried by court martial at Montreal, however, Rogers was acquitted.[15] In fact, General Gage himself was among those who strongly approved of his course of action in opening up the trade. Later on, in writing about the trial to the London agent of the Canadian merchants, Fowler Walker (a member of Lincoln's Inn), Rogers said: "I was honoured for what I did instead of being found fault with. I also wrote home to the King's Ministers and set the Commissarys in a proper light and have the pleasure to acquaint you they were all disbanded and the direction of Trade entirely taken from Sr William's hands." [16]

Without placing undue emphasis upon the part played by Rogers in freeing the Indian trade, it seems clear that his action helped to make those responsible for colonial affairs realize that the results of

---

[14] Rogers to Fowler Walker, March 7, 1771, Hardwicke Papers, B.M., Add. Mss. 35915:247–8.

[15] Among the documents relating to Rogers at Michilimackinac see Lieutenant Benjamin Roberts to Governor Guy Carleton, August 20, 1767, Shelburne Papers, 51:256–7, Clements Library, Ann Arbor, Mich.; Governor Guy Carleton to Shelburne, October 9, 1767 (enclosing the deposition against Rogers by his secretary, a Mr. Potter), ibid., 51:351–7; General Gage to the Secretary at War, December 7, 1767, ibid., 51:141; General Gage to Shelburne, January 23, 1768, Gage Correspondence, I, 161–2; and Gage to the Earl of Hillsborough, September 9, 1769, ibid., I, 237. See also Major Rogers's "Journal" for the period September 21, 1766, to July 3, 1767, in the American Antiquarian Society Proceedings, new ser., XXVIII, 231–73, edited and with comments by W. L. Clements, especially 224–31.

[16] Letter of March 7, 1771, B.M., Add. Mss. 35915:247–8.

the Board of Trade regulations in no way justified the expense involved. Therefore it was an easy step to permit the Indian trade in Canada to resume the characteristics it had had during the French period—except that French Canadians and British Canadians now worked together, the former supplying the experience and the latter the capital.

Out of this unity of action came a great trade-expansion movement, especially in the northwest beyond the Great Lakes and toward the region of the Saskatchewan River.[17] But with this expansion the Canadian "pedlars" became competitors of the Hudson's Bay Company factors located at York Factory and other posts on Hudson Bay; for much of the best fur brought by the Indians to the Company posts had come from this river system [18] and from the upper Churchill to the northward. With its prosperity thus threatened, the Company first tried sending white men to winter with the Cree Indians and to take their furs to York Fort in the spring. But when a "pedlar" trading post was set up at Cedar Lake, things took on a most serious aspect. Andrew Graham, at the Severn post located on the Bay, who had previously opposed any inland trading post, now reversed this decision and in 1772 urged the Company to act without delay in setting up such a post. Its committee sitting at Beaver House, London, in 1773 with Graham's warning before it, came to what has been called a "'momentous decision"—the determination to meet the Canadian competition by establishing a post well inland at a place on the Saskatchewan called The Pas.[19] However, it was not here that the Company finally built its inland emporium, but some seventy miles above The Pas on the river at Pine Island Lake, a place called "the key to the entire system of waterways." Westward lay the route to the Rockies; to the north was Lake Athabaska, the Peace River Country, and the vast unknown beyond Great Slave Lake; to the east were the Churchill and the Nelson Rivers, offering easy access to Hudson Bay, Lake Winnipeg, and the Red River Country. Here Cumberland House was built to meet the threat of the Canadian traders—an event that has well

---

[17] D. G. Creighton: *op. cit.*, pp. 28–40; Harold A. Innis: *The Fur Trade in Canada* . . . (New Haven, 1930), pp. 193–8, and especially W. S. Wallace: *The Pedlars from Quebec* (Toronto, 1954), which covers the material of this author's article by the same title in the *Canadian Historical Review*, XIII, 387–402.

[18] See A. S. Morton: *A History of the Canadian West to 1870–1* (London, 1939).

[19] *Ibid.*, pp. 272 and 282, and E. E. Rich: *The History of the Hudson's Bay Company, 1670–1870* (2 vols., London, 1959), II, 11–43.

been called "the turning-point in the history of the Hudson's Bay Company." [20] No longer did the factories cling to the shores of the Bay; rather, once it had pushed that far inland, the Company for its survival and prosperity continued to establish posts at many other places. Nor was this move made any too soon, as a powerful rival was to appear in 1779 in the form of the well-financed North West Company of Montreal; but this phase of the history of the Hudson's Bay Company and its rival are beyond the period covered by this series. It may however be well to point out that Hudson's Bay Company explorer Samuel Hearne—who in 1774 demonstrated great discernment in the choice of the location for Cumberland House—had made inland journeys on behalf of the Company beginning in December 1770 and ending in June 1772. As a result of his explorations he finally reached the mouth of the Coppermine River where it flows into the Arctic Ocean, and thus found the answer to the question whether a northwest passage existed between the Atlantic and the Pacific Oceans, a long-standing concern of the Hudson's Bay Company. [21]

While the economic expansion of the Province of Quebec is linked at this period with the people involved in the Indian or fur trade, the political and constitutional history—from the departure of Governor James Murray [22] in 1767 to the outbreak of the War for American Independence—is closely identified with the activities and leadership of Guy Carleton, who was appointed Lieutenant Governor of the colony on September 24, 1768, and Governor in Chief on January 12, 1768. [23] A native of Ireland, Carleton entered the army at an

---

[20] *Ibid.*, II, 61. See in this connection *Cumberland House Journals and Indian Journal, 1775–82. First Series, 1775–79,* Hudson's Bay Record Society *Publications* (eds. E. E. Rich *et al,* London, 1951), Introduction, and more particularly *The Journals of Samuel Hearne and Philip Turnor,* Champlain Society *Publications* (ed. J. B. Tyrell, Toronto, 1934).

[21] *Ibid.*, II, 55; see especially *A Journey from Prince of Wales's Fort in Hudson's-Bay to the Northern Ocean in the Years 1769, 1770, 1771, and 1772, by Samuel Hearne,* Champlain Society *Publications* (ed. J. B. Tyrrell, Toronto, 1911); see also Glyndwr Williams: *The British Search for the Northwest Passage in the Eighteenth Century* (Imperial Studies, No. 24, London, 1962); the first part of Richard Glover's essay: "The Difficulties of the Hudson's Bay Company's Penetration of the West," *Canadian Historical Review,* XXIX, 240–54; and Gordon Speck: *Samuel Hearne and the Northwest Passage* (Caldwell, Idaho, 1963), pp. 151–247.

[22] For the Province of Quebec under Murray's military and civil leadership, see Volume IX of this series, Chap. 7, "Canada Becomes a British Province."

[23] For Carleton's commission, dated April 12, 1768, see C.O. 43, I, pp. 363–98; for his instructions submitted on March 7, 1768, see C.O. 43, I, pp. 399–516; these instructions are printed in *Documents Relating to the Constitutional History of Canada, 1759–1791* (Canadian Archives, *Sessional Paper* No. 18, 1907; rev. edn., 2

early age and won distinction during the Great War for the Empire for his gallantry in action in the campaigns involving Louisbourg, Belle Isle, Quebec, and Havana; in the Quebec campaign he was Wolfe's chief of staff. As had been true of Murray, in his administration of public affairs Carleton combined the outlook of a military man with a great warmth of feeling for the French, particularly for the Canadian *seigneurs* and clergy. What influence his Irish background may have had in shaping his policies is not clear, but it is at least apparent that he used his influence to prevent Canada from becoming another Ireland.

At the time Carleton became Lieutenant Governor, the population of the Province of Quebec was estimated to be 76,275 people, of whom 54,575 had settled in 110 parishes beyond Quebec and Montreal. Of those living outside these two cities but nineteen were Protestant families; the rest were Roman Catholics. As for the some 450 urban non-Catholics—exclusive of the officers of government and garrison troops—these consisted of merchants, mechanics, and others of the trading class, many of whom seemed to be established in Montreal or Quebec on a temporary basis or only while seeking their fortunes.[24] In other words Carleton was faced, as Murray had been, with the problem of governing a vast body of newly conquered French-speaking Roman Catholics in the midst of whom dwelt a mere handful of lifelong British Protestant subjects, the only inhabitants qualified by law to participate actively in the political life of the province. Upon taking up his duties, and in response to an address by the Council, the Lieutenant Governor emphasized his desire that harmony should prevail between the old and new subjects "so that no Distinction may be noted" except "the great Difference between good Men and bad."[25] As though in response to this call, three days later he received an address from forty-six Quebec merchants and traders (thirty-one of whom were old subjects, and fifteen new) written in parallel columns in both English and French expressing their happiness at his arrival and the hope that with his

---

Parts, eds. Adam Shortt and A. G. Doughty, Ottawa, 1918), I, 301–24, cited hereafter as *Constitutional Documents;* and Francis Masères: *A Collection of Several Commissions, and other Public Instruments* . . . (London, 1772). It should be noted that Carleton was not knighted until 1776 after the siege of Quebec, and only later became Lord Dorchester.

[24] Governor Murray to the Earl of Shelburne, August 30, 1766, Shelburne Papers, 64:317–21.

[25] Carleton to the Quebec Council, September 24, 1766, C.O. 42:26, p. 563.

support the declining fur trade and fisheries would both be re-vived.[26] In fact the first discordant note in Carleton's administration came from members of the Council itself. On October 9, 1766, the Lieutenant Governor, "from prudential Reasons and for private In-formation," singled out five of the thirteen Councilmen to meet together.[27] At his bidding this group consented to suspend an order which the whole Council had issued in August—an order that seemed to undermine the policy of free trade with the Indians guaranteed by the Proclamation of 1763.[28]

This action by Carleton led to a remonstrance, signed and pre-sented to him on October 13, 1766, by five members of the Council. It was chiefly a protest against the idea that the Governor could act with the Council when calling together only part of those entitled to be summoned. It also expressed the fear that members of the Coun-cil who had not been appointed by a royal mandamus were to be treated differently from those who had been so selected.[29] The pro-test resulted in the expulsion from the Council of two of the most able and forceful members: Judge Adam Mabane and Lieutenant Colonel Paul Irving, who as President of the Council had adminis-tered the province after Governor Murray had given up his post and before the arrival of Carleton. By this action Carleton made it plain that the members must not oppose him. On the larger issue involved in the controversy he was undoubtedly right; at least his action received the support of the government at home.

As Carleton became more firmly entrenched in office, he contin-ued to oppose monopolies on the ground that they were a hindrance

---

[26] For the address of the merchants and traders see C.O. 42:26, pp. 571–8.

[27] Carleton to Shelburne, October 25, 1766, C.O. 42:26, pp. 447–51.

[28] This order of August involved a monopoly of trade at five posts within the King's domain granted to Thomas Dunn and John Gray. For the above episode see A. L. Burt: "Sir Guy Carleton and His First Council," *Canadian Historical Review*, IV, 321–32, an article stressing that Carleton did not show the frankness that might have been expected of him, that he could not tolerate opposition to his will, and that "he wanted a subservient Council, and he got it."

[29] For the remonstrance signed by Lieutenant Colonel Paul Irving, who was present at the meeting of the Council on October 9, and by Walter Murray, Judge Adam Mabane, François Mounier, a French-speaking merchant and trader, and Captain James Cuthbert, see C.O. 42:26, pp. 455–8; the remonstrance and Carleton's reply are printed in *Constitutional Documents*, I, 277–9; see also Carleton to Shelburne, October 25, 1766, enclosing the remonstrance, C.O. 42:26, pp. 447–51. For Carleton's letter of October 18, 1766, to the Board of Trade giving his version of the episode, see C.O. 42:26, pp. 667–72, and Shelburne Papers, 64:423–30 and 435–6; see also Adam Mabane to General Murray, October 11, 1766, *ibid.* 64:439. For the composition of the Quebec Council, with the date and status of the appointment (whether or not by royal mandamus) of each member, see C.O. 42:26, pp. 615–16.

to trade and attacked the prevailing system of fees [30] as being both a discouragement to the businessmen and "burdensome on an impoverished people." To Charles Townshend he wrote on November 17, 1766, that he would relinquish all fees and perquisites while in command of the province, as he felt that there was "a certain appearance of Dirt, a Sort of Meanness in Exacting Fees on every Occasion." As for the fees that came to his office for granting licenses, these would no longer be paid to him (as had been customary) but to the provincial Receiver-General for the purpose of providing financial relief to members of the Canadian noblesse who were in distress—in line with the former French government practice of granting many small pensions to them.[31] What concerned him even more was the low state of revenue of the province. Although many public debts had been incurred and there were other demands upon the provincial treasury, there was no public money. Permission had been granted by the Privy Council for a temporary levy of the old duties that had been collected on articles imported from France during the French régime but, according to the opinion of the Attorney and Solicitor General, without an act of Parliament no new duties could be levied.[32] Carleton shared this view, as did most of the inhabitants of the province.[33] It is true that the traditional dues paid by the French *habitants* before the conquest were still collected, but these amounted to a mere trifle in proportion to the contingent expense which was estimated to average annually £5,422.7.8.[34] As a result (as Carleton pointed out to the Earl of

---

[30] For a discussion of fees, along with other aspects of the administration of the Province of Quebec between 1764 and 1774, see W. S. Wallace: "The Beginnings of British Rule in Canada," *Canadian Historical Review*, VI, 208–21.

[31] For the above letter see C.O. 42:26, pp. 695–7; for a list of fees due to the Governor and other officers see C.O. 42:27, pp. 251–69.

[32] *Ibid.*, and Shelburne Papers, 51:297–9. In this connection see Volume IX of this series, pp. 170–2.

[33] When a suit was instituted by the Attorney General of Quebec to require M. Comte Dupré to pay £482 in duties on 28,920 gallons of brandy imported from Great Britain, the jury returned a general verdict that Dupré was not liable to pay these duties. See Carleton to the Board of Trade, November 9, 1766, Shelburne Papers, 51:294.

[34] According to the report of April 15, 1767, from Thomas Mills, Receiver General of Revenue of the province—which itemizes the expenditure and the receipts—the *lots et ventes* and the "fifths" amounted to but £76.13.0, the *cens et rentes* (or quit-rents) on all lands held *en roture* to but 5s 2½d or, with all other sources, a total of £365.16.4½. For the Mills report, enclosed in Carleton's letter to Shelburne dated April 15, 1767, see Shelburne Papers, 51:331–3, and 55:308–51. It should be explained that *lots et ventes* were fines paid to the King upon the alienation of lands; the "fifths" represented the proportion of the purchase money due on the transfer of

Shelburne) the expenses involved in maintaining the colony "fell entirely on his Majesty's Treasury"; [35] yet such a situation need not exist were Canada but given a government with power to act—for example, in 1757 a revenue amounting to £ 13,961.12.10½ sterling had been raised by the French authorities there.[36]

Manifestly the colony needed a stable government to replace the temporary and defective one established by the Proclamation of 1763 and subsequently modified by royal instructions and orders in council, but not strengthened enough to meet the more pressing needs of administration. The ordinances passed during the administration of Governor Murray certainly did not provide adequate power to the government. For instance, there was great dissatisfaction with the ordinance of 1764 relating to the administration of justice, since it governed the appointment of justices of the peace. These men, it was charged, had abused their powers and had oppressed the people. As a result a new ordinance adopted by Governer Carleton and the Council on February 1, 1770, made many important changes in the judicial system.[37] But even more important was the need to resolve the question of which laws were to become permanently established: those of the body of old Canadian law or the law of the conquerors? This decision was clearly beyond the competence of the local government to determine; for it would have to be predicated on the still larger question of what form the government of the province should take.

To Attorney General Francis Masères a government based on a representative Assembly was "at present absolutely impracticable." In view of the qualifications for Assembly seats described in the Governor's commission, very few of the freeholders and planters

lands within the *seigneuries;* and the "twelfths" was the proportion of purchase money due upon *terres en roture,* that is, lands granted by the King on a yearly rental out of his reserved domains. For the management of Canadian finances see H. R. Balls: "Quebec, 1763–1774: The Financial Administration," *Canadian Historical Review,* XLI, 203–14.

[35] Shelburne Papers, 51:331–3.

[36] Revenues collected by edict of the French King in 1757 amounted to £ 8,018.2.3 on imported liquors; on imported dry goods £ 3,363.18.3½, on dry goods exported £ 1,601.15.0½; on *lots et ventes* £ 921.18.11½, and on exported moose skins £ 56.3.4. See "Notes of Proceedings relative to Canada" (apparently largely the work of Maurice Morgann—a man of great ability, who served as a clerk to the Earl of Shelburne and who was sent by him to Canada to report on conditions there), Shelburne Papers, 64:459–66.

[37] For "An Ordinance for the More Effectual Administration of Justice, and for Regulating the Courts of Law in this Province," see *Constitutional Documents,* I, 401–16.

would be eligible. As to the proposal that French-speaking Roman Catholics be admitted to the proposed Assembly, he felt that the experience of the Assembly of the island of Grenada had been such as to give the government at home little encouragement to repeat a similar experiment.[38] There were other complications, according to Masères. While the English settled in the province would "by no means submit to" the idea that the King by his own authority could attempt to govern the colony, at the same time the "better and Substantial part . . . acknowledge that the Parliament of Great Britain has a legal right to make Laws and to lay Taxes in this Colony. . . ." Yet many took the view that once an Assembly had been established, Parliament could no longer exercise supreme power. These people, Masères held, were obviously influenced by the notions prevailing in other colonies of "the independence of the [older North American] Colonies on [i.e., from] the British Parliament." [39] He therefore discouraged the idea of an Assembly. A year and a half later, doubtless influenced by a report that the Earl of Hillsborough favoured the creation of an Assembly to be made up of *seigneurs* and men of property, he suggested, but without enthusi-

---

[38] After the conquest of Grenada, there was such bitter opposition on the part of the British settled there to the admission of French Roman Catholics into the Assembly that this was not accomplished until 1769. However, as early as 1765, Grenada Roman Catholics who had taken the oath of allegiance and had been confirmed in the possession of their lands were given the right to vote for Assemblymen. Further, two French Roman Catholics were admitted to the Council of the island in 1770. See Volume IX of this series, pp. 268–72.

[39] Masères to Shelburne, September 30, 1766, Shelburne Papers, 64:411–20. Masères, in collaboration with Chief Justice William Hey, also published anonymously *Considerations on the Expediency of Procuring an Act of Parliament for the Settlement of the Province of Quebec* (London, 1766); for this pamphlet see *Constitutional Documents*, I, 257–69. In it Masères enlarges on the legal difficulties facing the French Roman Catholics in their attempts to participate in government and to practice their religion; he also expresses his personal unwillingness to accord the *habitants* any political rights until they had embraced Protestantism. While not prepared to grant political power to Catholics, he was ready by act of Parliament to grant them toleration. At the same time he would make their churches partially available for Protestant worship, and where as many as three fourths of the people of a parish were Protestant, a Protestant minister should be appointed for the parish and all relics and symbols of the Catholic religion should be removed from the parish church. Masères, it would appear, was also the author of other writings. Two unpublished works of his relating to Canada, "A View of the Civil Government while it was subject to the Crown of France" and "A Plan for Settling the Laws and the Administration of Justice in the Province of Quebec," were apparently prepared in 1768 and were printed in Montreal in 1857 as appendices to the first volume of *The Lower Canada Jurist*. For a study of their authorship see S. M. Scott: "The Authorship of Certain Papers in *The Lower Canada Jurist*," *Canadian Historical Review*, X, 335–42.

asm, that a single legislative chamber might be created consisting of *seigneurs* and the lesser landholders, each elected by a constituency of its own, "unless it was the intention of government to destroy this constitution of the province and . . . settle everything upon the republican levelling plan of the other colonies, which in my opinion would be both unjust and impolitick." In place of such a proposal, he expressed the wish that Parliament act to impose taxes rather than to create an Assembly.[40]

On the other hand, the Earl of Shelburne as Secretary of State for the Southern Department took a very different position in a letter (addressed either to Hillsborough or to the Board of Trade) dated May 17, 1767:

> "In every Province, which has been lately Settled in America, there has been confusion and uneasiness until that Form of Government has been adopted by which the old Colonies are Governed; I mean by a Governor, Council and Assembly.—A Governor and Council being already appointed, a perfect Tranquility would be Established in Quebec, as in any of the other American Colonies, could an Assembly be called to reduce and assimilate such of the French Laws, as it may be necessary to retain, to the standard of the English Laws, and to make others; nay, more so, in case the Seigneurs of the Country could be chosen members of the Council and Assembly . . . . If the Calling an Assembly be the most eligible Step for the Regulating of Affairs in the Province of Quebec, it ought to be considered of what Members the Assembly should be composed; whether of Protestants alone; of Protestants and Roman Catholics equally; or of Protestants with a limited Number only of Roman Catholics, say one fourth?" [41]

Shelburne then went on to argue that when "Canada fell by Conquest under the Dominion of the King, His Majesty had certainly a Right of establishing such Form of Government therein as He pleased, agreeable always to the Articles of Capitulation [of Montreal of 1760]." Minorca, he pointed out, "is governed by its own Laws; the Roman Catholic religion is even the Established Religion of the Country; and yet Minorca is annexed to Great Britain by Act of Parliament." Further, the "Roman Catholick Inhabitants of Montserrat are allowed several Privileges on account of a noble Defence once made by them when that Island was attacked by the

---

[40] Masères to————, Quebec, May 27, 1768, Hardwicke Papers, B.M., Add. Mss., 35915:280–9.

[41] Shelburne Papers, 64:483–91.

Enemy." [42] He pointed out that in order to enable Roman Catholics to have seats in an Assembly or in the Council, the letters patent and instructions to the Governor would have to be altered—a step that he thought the Privy Council had power to effect, but, if not, must be effected by act of Parliament. An Assembly, a fourth part of which would be French, would make the *habitants* "very happy" and "the Civil Government, the Revenue, and the Affairs of the Church in all other Points might then be regulated by the model of New York, Virginia, or any of the other Provinces." [43] So much for the contrasting views of two eminent men as to how the Province of Quebec should be governed. But what were the steps taken by the British Ministry to grapple with this problem?

In 1766 Charles Yorke, while Attorney General in the Rockingham Administration, drew up a plan of government for the Province of Quebec which gave political recognition to Roman Catholics. The Earl of Northington, the Lord High Chancellor, objected to this upon many grounds. One, that Parliament itself should lay down the plan; for another, that a Roman Catholic could not legally by mere exercise of the royal prerogative hold an office under the Crown, even that of justice of the peace. [44] In spite of this objection and the fall of the Rockingham Ministry before a bill could be presented to Parliament, the Yorke plan was ultimately to serve as a basis for the act passed in 1774. [45]

---

[42] In Montserrat in 1751 the Roman Catholics made up four fifths of the population and among other rights they enjoyed that of franchise. When in 1749 the Assembly of the island enacted legislation to require the oaths of abjuration and supremacy of all voters, the Privy Council disallowed the law. See *Acts of the Privy Council, Col. Ser., 1745–1766*, pp. 101–3.

[43] Shelburne Papers, 64:483–91.

[44] For Northington's views see his letter of August 9, 1767, to the Duke of Grafton, indicating his unwillingness under the circumstances to participate in the framing of a government for Quebec. This letter is published in *Autobiography and Political Correspondence of Augustus Henry, third Duke of Grafton* (ed. Sir William R. Anson, London, 1898), pp. 170–1; see also R. A. Humphreys and S. M. Scott: "Lord Northington and the Laws of Canada," *Canadian Historical Review*, XIV, 42–61; appended to this article is the text of the draft of instructions, approved by the Board of Trade as well as by the Attorney General, which were designed to settle the question of the laws of the colony and the judicial system by means of an ordinance or ordinances that the Governor and Council at Quebec would enact. It was this paper, designed to repeal all the ordinances having to do with the administration of justice in Quebec and to institute a new system, to which Northington raised such objections.

[45] See the Duke of Richmond "Journal," as embodied in the *Memoirs of the Marquis of Rockingham* . . . (ed. George Thomas, Earl of Albemarle, 2 vols., London, 1852), I, 350–5, and Lord Hardwicke to Rockingham, June 30, 1766, *ibid.*, I, 355–6. The plan, dated April 14, 1766, was known as the Yorke-De Grey report

In 1767 the Chatham-Grafton Ministry grasped the nettle when new instructions relative to the judicial system of the province came before the Privy Council for approval on May 29 and were submitted to close scrutiny.[46] Furthermore, on May 20 a vote of the House of Lords sought royal approval to have a body of papers concerning the constitution of the new colony laid before it, which was done.[47] Late in August of that year the Privy Council, turning again to the problem of reorganizing the Canadian government to meet more fully the needs of the inhabitants, came to the conclusion that any move on its part without additional evidence from His Majesty's servants in Canada would be most unwise.[48] Cautious progress therefore seemed to become the watchword of the Ministry in order to avoid serious mistakes. On September 28, 1768, the Council received a report from the Advocate General and the Solicitor General on a plan for establishing the ecclesiastical affairs of the province; this, together with the papers concerning the administration of justice and the revenue, were submitted to the Board of Trade, which was requested to give an additional opinion at the same time on the advisability of the King permitting a "full Legislature" to be convened at Quebec in which Roman Catholics could sit in both houses, as prayed for by the body of merchants "Trading to and deeply interested in the Province of Quebec."[49]

Acting on the determination that no permanent constitution for the colony should be recommended without the most competent and expert advice, the Privy Council instructed the government in Quebec to submit information on conditions in the province for detailed study.[50] In addition, it sent Maurice Morgann, one of

since it reflected also the judgment of Attorney General William De Grey, who succeeded Yorke in that office. See Shortt and Doughty: *Constitutional Documents*, I, 251–7 for the 1765 report; see also *ibid.*, I, 236, for the opinion of the law officers on the status of Roman Catholic subjects in Canada; see further Reginald Coupland: *The Quebec Act* (Oxford, 1925), pp. 56–7, 67n. For a very perceptive treatment of the period, from the fall of the Rockingham Ministry to the eve of the Quebec Act, see A. L. Burt: *The Old Province of Quebec* (Toronto, 1933), Chap. 8, "Toward a New Constitution."

[46] For the instructions and the discussion see *Acts of the Privy Council, Col. Ser., 1766–1783*, pp. 91–9.

[47] *Ibid.*, pp. 90–1.

[48] *Ibid.*, pp. 94–6.

[49] *Ibid.*, pp. 96–7. Governor Carleton himself broached the question of an Assembly in his dispatch to Shelburne of January 20, 1768; see *Constitutional Documents*, I, 294–6.

[50] Among the tasks given to the officers of the colony was an examination of the laws in force there before the conquest and the passing of judgement as to those which should be retained and those to be discarded. Masères, writing on August 14,

Shelburne's advisers, to Quebec to meet with Governor Guy Carleton and to report his findings. The Council marked time until it at last received the detailed and voluminous report submitted by Carleton to the Earl of Hillsborough on September 18, 1769, on the laws and courts of the province.[51] The document came before the Council on October 19, with concomitant dissenting reports from Quebec's Chief Justice and its Attorney General.[52] It may be added that Carleton came to England the following year [53] to present his opinion on the type of permanent constitution that could best meet the needs of the Canadians. He continued to press his views on the government until his efforts culminated in the passage of the Quebec Act; only then did he feel able to return to Canada.[54]

1768, to Richard Sutton, Under Secretary of State to the Earl of Shelburne, indicated that he and Chief Justice Hey had received an impossible assignment. His view was that instead of tampering with the French laws and attempting to codify those that seemed most appropriate for the province while discarding all the rest, the only safe way was to let the law stand as it was. At the same time he admitted the advantages, especially to the English inhabitants, of having the French law codified. For this long letter see Hardwicke Papers, B.M., Add. Mss. 35915:293–301.

[51] For Carleton to Hillsborough, September 18, 1769, and the Carleton report which covers fifty pages of manuscript and was signed by the Governor and Chief Justice Hey, see B.M., King's Manuscripts, 207:23. This report and Masères's dissenting report, together with other important documents relating to the same problem, are to be found in Reports on the Laws of Quebec, 1767–1770 (Public Archives of Canada Publications No. 12, eds. W. P. Kennedy and Gustave Lanctôt, Ottawa, 1931), pp. 51–73.

[52] For Chief Justice Hey's separate and dissenting report dated September 15, 1769, see ibid., pp. 73–8 and for Masères's separate and dissenting report dated September 11, 1769, see ibid., pp. 78–83. See also Acts of the Privy Council, Col. Ser., 1766–1783, p. 97.

[53] Carleton, writing to the Earl of Hillsborough on March 15, 1769, asked to be allowed to return to England for a few months for "many reasons of state as well as to settle private affairs" (C.O. 42:29, pp. 61–8). On July 15 of that year Hillsborough asked the Governor to delay his departure in view of the possibility that the Privy Council might approve a report of the Board of Trade respecting the government of Quebec. But on December 1 Hillsborough gave permission for him to come to England. See C.O. 42:29, pp. 109–11 and pp. 199–200.

[54] Professor G. S. Graham in his British Policy and Canada, 1774–1791: A Study in 18th Century Trade Policy (London, New York, Toronto, 1930) makes the following comment (p. 24): "The Quebec Act has often been considered . . . as the joint product of many minds. But it represented too great a break with continuous, harmonious development to be that. . . . The Quebec act bore indelibly the stamp of one man—Carleton. Only in minor ways did it resemble the view of some of his more understanding contemporaries." Professor Chester Martin, in his Empire of Commonwealth: Studies in Governance and Self-Government in Canada (Oxford, 1929), insists that "William Knox's Extra Official State Papers, published in 1789, disclose . . . hidden principles of American policy which could not be avowed in 1774" (pp. 107–8), with respect to Carleton's influence on the shaping of the Quebec Act; Martin also wrote: ". . . it becomes evident that Carleton's contribution to the gravest political problem that ever confronted the nation was the contribution not of the statesman but of the soldier" (p. 111).

The Privy Council, still moving with the careful deliberation required for so important a matter, on June 14, 1771, called upon the chief law officers of the Crown—Advocate General Sir Charles Marriott, Solicitor General Alexander Wedderburn, and Attorney General Edward Thurlow—to use these Canadian reports, together with other pertinent papers, as a basis "to draw up a general plan of civil and criminal law for the province with the assistance of the Governor, now in England, and of such other persons, as they think fit." They were further requested on July 31, 1772, to be sure to file separate reports and to submit them with "all convenient speed." [55] But Wedderburn was not ready to present his report until December 6, 1772, and Thurlow not until January 22, 1773.[56]

As for Sir Charles Marriott, testifying before the House of Commons on June 3, 1774, he said that it took him more than two years before he was prepared to report to the Privy Council his plan (which covered some three hundred closely written pages), and added: "I saw my difficulties of coming to a decision increased. I

---

[55] C.O. 42:29; see also *Constitutional Documents*, 424n.

[56] *Acts of the Privy Council, Col. Ser., 1766–1783*, pp. 99–100. Abstracts of the above two reports are among the Hardwicke Papers, B.M., Add. Mss. 35915:334–43; see also *Constitutional Documents*, I, 424–45. The Attorney General's report considered the various legal opinions as to the effect of the conquest of Canada upon the laws prevailing there. In his abstract of regulations Thurlow advanced the view that before the legal system for the province could be laid down, the form of government for Canada should be settled, as well as the matter of religion in so far as "it affects the state & becomes an object of establishment or toleration. . . ." Before closing he warned that alterations in the form of government of a conquered country should not be made without "an actual and cogent necessity" and therefore not such a "species of necessity, which I have heard urged for abolishing the laws and government of Canada" (*ibid.*, I, 443–5).

The Solicitor General was much more specific. For example, in his report he gave as his opinion that at that time it would be not only impracticable but dangerous to create a popularly elected Assembly open to Canadians and that an Assembly which excluded them would lead them to feel that they would be "exposed to the oppression of . . . fellow subjects." He then added: "The power to make laws could not with safety be entrusted to the Governor alone; it must therefore, be vested in a Council consisting of a certain number of persons, not totally dependent upon the Governor," who could only be removed by the King's express orders. As to religion, his view was as follows: "There is no instance of any state that has been overturned by toleration. True policy dictates then that the inhabitants of Canada should be permitted freely to profess the worship of their religion; and it follows of course, that the ministers of that worship should be protected . . ."—with the proviso that this protection should not be inconsistent with the sovereignty of the King and civil government of the province, that no ecclesiastical jurisdiction derived from Rome should be permitted, and that the tithes paid by Protestants be used in support of their own religion, *ibid.*, I, 426–9. These and other recommendations made by Wedderburn in the same report were embodied in the Quebec Act, as were the views of the other law officers.

dreaded being hasty or positive, and I thought no trouble too much on such a public subject, which appeared too much for the life of any man, and most certainly for any one man's understanding." [57]

In view of what was felt to be the infinite complexity of the problem of digesting the reports and reconciling differences between the viewpoints of the newer English settlers and the old French inhabitants in the Province of Quebec, the final plan was not ready for presentation to Parliament until May 1774.[58] However, the Earl of Dartmouth wrote to Lieutenant Governor Cramahé on December 1, 1773, promising that the affairs of Canada would shortly be adjusted. "You may be assured that I will not fail . . . to urge the Justice and Expediency of giving all possible Satisfaction to the new subjects [that is, the French Canadians] on the Head of Religion; . . . and that those professing the Religion of the Church of Rome may find within the Colony a resource for every thing essential to the free Exercise of it, in the true Spirit of the Treaty [of 1763, which guaranteed this free exercise]." He was also able to give assurance to Cramahé that the plan would take into account the exclusion of Canadians dwelling beyond the narrow limits of the Province of Quebec (as set up by the Proclamation of 1763) from any form of government other than that of the military post commanders.[59] He undoubtedly had in mind particularly those French-speaking people in the area around Detroit, at Vincennes on the Wabash close to the Ohio River border, and in the Illinois country.

Dartmouth's concern over the situation of French Canadians living west of the Province of Quebec arose as the result of letters

---

[57] *Parliamentary History*, XVII, 1382. Marriott's *Plan of a Code of Laws for the Province of Quebec. By the Advocate-General* (London, 1774) stated (p. 30) that French civil law as applied in Canada may be binding upon such British subjects as adopt it by resorting to this law of their own free will and by acquiring property under its terms, as was true of the particular civil law enforced on the islands of Jersey, Guernsey, and Minorca, as well as in Scotland "or elsewhere in Your Majesty's dominions." This plan is reprinted in *Constitutional Documents*, I, 445–83.

[58] See [Francis Masères]: *An Account of the Proceedings of the British And other Protestant Inhabitants of the Province of Quebec . . . In order to obtain an House of Assembly of the Province* (London, 1775), for a very full account of the proceedings within the province (covering the year 1773 and the early part of 1774) concerned with the creation of an Assembly. In this Masères supports the pretensions of the Protestant old subjects against those of the Catholic new subjects. At the same time he felt that it would be best to have the colony governed for a period of seven years by a council, independent of the Governor and made up only of Protestants. See his letter to Dartmouth dated January 4, 1774, C.O. 42:33, pp. 9–12, printed in *Constitutional Documents* I, 486–98.

[59] P.R.O., C.O. 42:32, pp. 187–91, also printed in *Constitutional Documents*, I, 485–6.

directed to him as Secretary of State for the Colonies which he had
received from America, especially those sent by Colonel Frederick
Haldimand, who was acting head of the military forces in North
America while General Gage was in England, and was thus in
fairly constant communication, as Gage had been, with people in
the great interior.[60] Therefore the letter of December 1 to Cramahé
stressed the necessity of extending the bounds of the Province of
Quebec and, with due caution, added:

> "The Limits of the Colony will also in my Judgment make a neces-
> sary part of this very extensive Consideration [of the future constitu-
> tion of the Province of Quebec]. There is no longer any Hope of
> perfecting that plan of Policy in respect to the interior Country,
> which was in contemplation when the Proclamation of 1763 was
> issued; many Circumstances with regard to . . . parts of that Coun-
> try were then unknown, and there are a variety of other Considera-
> tions that do . . . induce a doubt both of the Justice and Propriety
> of restraining the Colony [Quebec] to the narrow Limits prescribed
> in that Proclamation." [61]

The English-speaking people living within the Province of Quebec, although a very small minority,[62] did not fail to make their
voices heard in the move to persuade the British Ministry to redeem
the pledge of an Assembly given in the Proclamation of 1763.[63] For,

---

[60] See, for example, Haldimand to Dartmouth, August 4, 1773, Dartmouth to
Haldimand, October 14, 1773, and Haldimand to Dartmouth November 3, 1773,
Haldimand Papers, B.M., Add. Mss. 21695:23-4, 40, 42. These letters among other
things considered the problem of how to prevent the settlement at Vincennes—in the
absence of any civil government or laws—from becoming "the Assylum of the lawless
and the Repair of the most Licentious Inhabitants of His Majesty's already most
Extensive Colonies in America," according to Dartmouth's letter of November 3, 1773
(*ibid.*).

[61] *Constitutional Documents,* I, 485.

[62] See Carleton's testimony before the House of Commons on June 2, 1774,
Parliamentary History, XVII, 1368. This figure of 150,000 French Catholics and less
than 400 Protestants was evidently a rough estimate of the population, for Masères,
apparently in 1769, gave the Canadian figure as 90,000 and Thurlow in 1773 put it at
80,000 or 100,000, with both giving the total of British immigrants as 600. See
Constitutional Documents, I, 442; see also *Sir Henry Cavendish's Debates of the
House of Commons in the year 1774 on the Bill for making more effectual provision
for the Government of the Province of Quebec* (ed. J. Wright, London, 1839), pp.
113 and 118-19, cited hereafter as *Cavendish's Debates on the Quebec Bill, 1774;*
and Reginald Coupland: *The Quebec Act: A Study in Statesmanship* (Oxford, 1925),
p. 74.

[63] For the Proclamation of 1763 see *British Royal Proclamations Relating to
America, 1603-1783* (ed. C. S. Brigham), American Antiquarian Society *Transac-
tions,* XII, 212-18, and this author's discussion of it in Volume IX of this series,
Chap. 3.

according to the Proclamation terms for setting up the Provinces of Quebec, East Florida, and West Florida, and assuming control of what had been the French West Indies island of Grenada, the Governors of these dependencies, "so soon as the state and circumstances of these Governments would admit thereof; . . . shall with the Advice and Consent" of the respective Councils, "summon and call General Assemblies within the said Governments," with power to make laws. The clearest evidence of action on the part of the English-speaking settlers of Canada—without reference to earlier demands for an Assembly—may be found in the petition to the Lieutenant Governor and Council, presented in November 1773, asking for a General Assembly "of the Freeholders and Planters of the Province, submitted by his Majesty's antient Subjects." A copy of this petition along with other papers was sent to the chief advocate of the English community in Canada, Francis Masères, who between 1766 and 1769 had been Attorney General of the province but had been given leave by Carleton to return to England.[64]

The petition, according to Lieutenant Governor Cramahé, came from the activity of John McCord, a retailer of spirits, who gathered some of the principal inhabitants at the inn of Miles Prenties in the upper town of Quebec. According to the minutes of the meeting which took place on October 30, 1773, the question was put: "Whether it is not expedient to petition for a house of Assembly. Answer—Yeas 38—to 3 nays." As a result a committee of eleven members was appointed, seven of whom should be regarded as a full committee to draw up a petition. On November 2 eight committeemen assembled. They therewith agreed that a petition for the stated purpose should be presented, first of all to the Lieutenant Governor in Council, rather than to the King; they also resolved that the petition should be translated into French and that some of the principal Canadians be requested to meet with the committee. The letter in French sent accordingly on that day stated that the committee had been nominated *"par une nombreuse assemblée des anciens sujets de sa Majesté."* On November 4 with nine members of the committee and eight Canadians present the petition was read. When the question was put to the Canadians as to whether it should be necessary to convene their fellow Canadians on the question of

---

[64] For the petition, the letter dated January 4, 1774, to Masères, and Masères's letter enclosing the petition to Dartmouth, see C.O. 42:33, pp. 9–12, 21–2, 25–6; these papers are also to be found in *Constitutional Documents,* I, 486–501.

an Assembly, there was unanimous agreement that this should be done. November 8 seven of the committee met but no Canadians appeared. However, one Canadian, a M. Perras, stated in a letter to the committee that he had seen some of his fellow citizens but that they did not appear disposed to attend a meeting called for the purpose in mind. Nevertheless, it was agreed to write to Masères, and to enclose the minutes of the meeting and a copy of the petition presented to the Lieutenant Governor.[65] The Lieutenant Governor, referring to the petitions, affirmed in his letter: "There are not above five among the signers to the two Petitions, who can be properly styled Freeholders, and the Value of Four of these Freeholds is very inconsiderable. The Number of those [signers] possessing Houses in the Towns of Quebec and Montreal, or Farms in the Country, . . . is under thirty." [66]

During the course of the Ministry's development of its plan for reconciling the French Catholic population of Canada to British rule, those responsible were not oblivious to the repercussions that might be felt from the ominous developments in the colonies to the south of the Province of Quebec. This realization could not but foster the feeling that, without further delay, something must be done to persuade both the Canadians dwelling within the province and those French-speaking people living beyond its limits that the government of Great Britain had their interests at heart and was at last prepared to act. [67]

Once the bill was finally completed, after prolonged and sustained effort on the part of those involved in its framing,[68] it seemed

---

[65] For the minutes of the meetings of the English-speaking group, see C.O. 42:33, pp. 13–17; see also Cramahé to Dartmouth, December 13, 1773, with the two petitions asking for an Assembly, one from the citizens of Quebec signed by fifty-two persons and the other of those living in Montreal signed by thirty-four, both dated November 29, and also the minutes of the Council of the province of December 6 and 11. For these see C.O. 42:33, pp. 29–39 and 51–3, and *Constitutional Documents*, I, 487–92.

[66] *Ibid.*, I, 492.

[67] This point is greatly stressed by W. P. M. Kennedy: *The Constitution of Canada, 1534–1937* (London, New York, Toronto), Chap. 7, "The Quebec Act, 1774." It is, however, of no little significance that when the Coercive Acts were under consideration by the Cabinet Council, the possible role of the Province of Quebec in the crisis was not mentioned. "Indeed, during the early months of 1774 the Ministry seems never to have discussed its Canadian policies in Cabinet at the same time as it considered the problem of the American Colonies" (Bernard Donoughue: *British Politics and the American Revolution: The Path to War, 1773–75* [London & New York, 1964], p. 108).

[68] For a list of those who contributed to the final form of the bill see *ibid.*, pp. 120–1.

expedient to have it introduced in the House of Lords—where it was less likely to meet opposition—by the minister best informed on Canadian affairs, the Secretary of State for the Colonies, Lord Dartmouth. This he did on May 2, 1774, when the bill had its first reading under the title "An Act for making more effectual provision for the Government of the Province of Quebec, in North America." After certain papers had been placed before the House, the bill, as was doubtless anticipated, moved through its successive readings apparently without any serious debate. On May 12 it had its second reading. On the 16th certain amendments were accepted, and the following day—after a proviso to the effect that the act would be in force no longer than seven years [69] had been rejected—the bill was passed and sent down to the House of Commons for concurrence.[70]

There was, however, no such smooth sailing of the Quebec Bill through the House of Commons—far from it.[71] On May 18, 1774, it was read and ordered to be printed; on the 20th a request was made for a copy of the Proclamation of 1763, which was presented on the 26th together with a copy of the commission to General James Murray, first Governor of the Province of Quebec, dated November 21, 1763. After a motion in favour of the second reading of the bill, the debate began with a bitter attack by Thomas Townshend, Jr. Lord North, in replying, made clear that no elective Assembly was provided because of the small number of English settlers who, according to parliamentary statutes, alone could be qualified to choose such legislators; therefore, the idea of a Protestant minority electing an Assembly which could pass laws binding on all the French Catholics was thought to be not only unfair but "even cruel." Again, as to the enlargement of the boundaries of the province as

---

[69] The idea of a limit of seven years for rule by Governor and Council was pressed by Attorney General Francis Masères of Quebec. See his letter to Dartmouth, January 4, 1774, previously cited.

[70] For the proceedings on the Quebec Bill covering May 2–17 see *Journals of the House of Lords*, XXXIV, 154, 159, 169, 172, 180–7, 190, 193–4, 201.

[71] See *Journals of the House of Commons*, XXXIV, 778, 785, 792–3, 796, 799, 803, 805, 806, 808, 812. See also *Cavendish's Debates on the Quebec Bill, 1774*. This volume gives in great detail not only the formal proceedings of the House of Commons but also those that took place in the committee of the whole House. Its importance lies in the fact that Henry Cavendish, a member for Lostwithiel (later a baronet), took down in shorthand the debates in the House covering the period from 1768 to 1774. Those having to do with the Quebec Bill were published separately from the general debates of the years 1768 and 1771, which appeared in print in two volumes in 1841 and 1843. The Cavendish shorthand notes are in forty-eight quarto volumes among the Egerton Manuscripts in the British Museum.

contemplated in this act, North declared that this would include "no countries regularly planted by British settlers, but merely distant military posts, at present without any Government but that of the respective commanding officers." To North's arguments, the able lawyer John Dunning in turn replied, stating that an act such as was contained in the bill was "destructive of every principle of freedom, and abounding with mischief," and that, by giving the province "this monstrous southern extent, you run it down upon the back of the planted part of many of our colonies, and take away, by one stroke, the charter properties confirmed by an act of parliament of those colonies. . . ." Other speakers for and against the government likewise put forth their views on the bill. In the course of the debate Charles James Fox pointed out that since the bill made provision for securing tithes for the support of the "Romish clergy," it was a money bill and, as such, had violated the custom and law of Parliament by being introduced in the House of Lords rather than in the House of Commons. However, in a division over this question, it was voted 105 to 29 that the rights of the House of Commons had not been violated.[72]

On May 31 a petition was presented from the Proprietors of Pennsylvania, Thomas Penn and his nephew John, which set forth that the new boundaries of the Province of Quebec would work an injury to them, as a considerable part of their property granted by royal charter was located on the northwest side of the Ohio River and would therefore be comprehended within the limits of the other province. Lord North then rose to state that "it was never the intention of the Bill to affect the just rights of any proprietors, or of any of the Colonies." It was therefore agreed that the petitioners should be heard by counsel when the committee of the whole House should report on the bill. Also read was a petition from the London merchants trading to Canada, which stressed the point that it would be highly injurious to their trade to have the laws of Canada substituted for the laws of England. Further debate ensued; it had to do with the question of whether it was necessary to present certain extensive reports to the House of Commons, the copying of which would consume much time and delay the proceedings. Following this, and after other pertinent papers had been laid before the

---

[72] For the debates on May 26, 1774, including the speeches of Fox, Dunning, and others, as well as Lord North's replies, see *ibid.*, pp. 1–71; see also *Parliamentary History*, XVII, 1357–63.

House—including a petition from the French inhabitants of Canada —key witnesses were called to the bar to testify on conditions in Canada. Among those from the province appearing on June 2 were the Governor, the former Attorney General, and the Chief Justice. The following day consideration was given to a petition from the mayor, aldermen, and common council of London [73] against the bill, especially the clauses governing the substitution of French civil law for English civil law, and the acceptance of Roman Catholicism as "the only legal established religion." After this, other witnesess were heard at the bar. The most important was Advocate General Marriott, who had drawn up the massive report and *Plan for a Code of Laws* mentioned earlier in this chapter (footnote 57). During the 6th, 7th, and 8th of June various provisions of the bill were debated vigorously. On the 8th it was voted to provide a new oath that might be administered to Canadian Catholic office-holders without violating their religious principles—as would have been the case were they required to take the oath provided for by 1 Elizabeth I, c. 1, sec. 19, or by "any other oaths substituted . . . in place thereof," such as that required by 1 William and Mary, Ses. 1, c. 8, sec. 2. The new oath simply stipulated that one should swear to bear true allegiance to the King and to defend his person, crown, and dignity from all traitorous conspiracies and other unlawful acts. However, it specified that any person required to take this oath who refused to do so would incur the penalties embodied in the Act of Elizabeth I.

The question of the extended boundaries, as provided for in the Quebec Bill, was taken up in the House of Commons on the 10th of June in connection with the consideration then of the petition from the Proprietors of Pennsylvania that had previously been tabled. But the Proprietors now declined to be heard by Counsel—doubtless because assurances seem to have been given to them that, in the action just completed by the committee of the whole House, the bill had been amended to protect the territorial rights of the Penn family.[74] The amendment was approved therewith. With this point

[73] For the petition of the Proprietors of Pennsylvania see *Cavendish's Debates on the Quebec Bill, 1774,* pp. 72–3; for the proceedings in the House of Commons of June 2–3, 1774, see *ibid.,* pp. 100–83; for the London petition see *Annual Register, 1774,* XVII, 232–3, and *Gentleman's Magazine, 1774,* XLIV, 247–8.

[74] It should also be pointed out that at the time of laying down the boundary between the Provinces of Quebec and New York, Edmund Burke, acting as the London agent for the Province of New York, had exerted himself on June 6 to secure an amendment to the bill as it came from the House of Lords, so as to give New York a much greater western extension than had been contemplated and thereby to include

clarified, the discussion on that day and on the 13th turned upon such other matters as trial by jury in civil cases—to which the Canadians were opposed, as they were even more strongly to the application of English law to civil cases. A motion that the bill pass its third reading and be returned to the House of Lords with the amendments was agreed to by a vote of 56 to 20.[75]

When the matter of approval of the amended bill came up for debate before the peers on the 18th of the month, the Earl of Chatham spoke against the proposed statute as placing a whole people "under arbitrary power" which was "a most cruel, oppressive, and odious measure." He denounced the suggested substitution for the oath required by the Act of Supremacy of the reign of Elizabeth I as well as the provisions which would permit "unlimited power" to be concentrated in the hands of the Governor, and expressed his fears that such a law "might shake the affections and confidence of his Majesty's Protestant subjects in *England* and *Ireland;* and finally lose the hearts of all his Majesty's *American* subjects."

In his answer to Chatham, Lord Lyttelton said that the bill had been modified in accordance with the ideas of the opposition, especially with respect to the limits of Canada; that Canadians by their good behaviour since the conquest were deserving of a civil code to which they had long been accustomed and which they desired; that the bill was conformable to the genius of the country which would live by it, since it was "consistent with the political notions of the inhabitants, and the form of Government to which they had been accustomed." Before concluding, he denied Chatham's assumption that the form of government planned for Canada would create a sense of separateness from the rest of America, adding that "if

---

within its territorial limits Fort Niagara—which Governor Carleton, according to Burke, wanted as an outpost for the Province of Quebec. See Burke to the New York committee of correspondence, August 2, 1774, in R. J. S. Hoffman: *Edmund Burke, New York Agent* . . . (Philadelphia, 1956), pp. 254–60, *Correspondence of Edmund Burke* (5 vols.+ ed. G. H. Guttridge, Cambridge & Chicago, 1958–65+), III, 13–21; and the *St. James Chronicle,* June 7, 1774; see also Bernard Donoughue: *op. cit.,* p. 124, which makes clear that on June 10 certain amendments were incorporated in the bill that satisfied both New York and the Pennsylvania Proprietors.

[75] For the proceedings in the House of Commons covering the period from June 6 through June 13 see *Cavendish's Debates on the Quebec Bill, 1774,* pp. 183–296, and *Parliamentary History,* XVII, 1363–99; for some additional details see also Peter Force: *American Archives,* 4th ser., I, 185–211. The small number of votes cast on the third reading was occasioned by the drawing to a close of the session. Many members of the House, "fatigued with a long attendance on the *American* bills, were retired into the country" (*ibid.,* I, 214n).

British America was determined to resist the lawful power and pre-eminence of Great Britain, he saw no reason why the loyal inhabitants of Canada should not cooperate with the rest of the Empire in subduing them and bringing them to a right sense of their duty. . . ." Despite the division, the amendments to the bill inserted by the other house were affirmed by a vote of 26 to 7. On June 22 the King, after refusing to receive a petition from the City of London calling upon him to withhold his assent to the legislation, gave his approval to the bill as one "founded on the clearest principles of Justice and humanity; one that would have the best effects in quieting the minds and promoting the happiness of my Canadian subjects." [76]

By the Quebec Act the boundaries of the province were enlarged to comprehend the settlements of French-speaking peoples that lay outside the earlier limits laid down in 1763. However, these territorial additions were clearly tentative since the act itself contained two important provisos: one, "That nothing herein contained, relating to the Boundary of the Province of Quebec, shall in anywise affect the Boundaries of any other Colony"; the other, that nothing in the act should be construed to make void "any right, title or possession, derived under any [previous] grant" of lands within the province "or the Provinces hereto adjoining, but that the same shall remain and be in force . . . as if this Act had never been made." [77]

---

[76] For the proceedings in the House of Lords and the petition from the City of London see *Journals of the House of Lords*, XXXIV, 243–4, 256, 259, and *Parliamentary History*, XVII, 1412–17. The act, cited as 14 Geo. III, c. 83, represents the "first time that Parliament directly constituted a colony. . . ; it was the greatest departure from tradition ever made, and the chief model upon which the Crown colony system was constructed a generation later" (Martin Wight: *The Development of the Legislative Council, 1606–1945* [*Nuffield College Studies in Colonial Legislatures, Vol. I*, ed. Margery Perham, 2nd impr., London, 1947] pp. 37–8).

[77] In studying the Quebec Act the student should refer to *American Archives*, 4th ser., I, 216–20, which presents the alterations made by the House of Commons to the original bill received from the House of Lords. These changes are especially important as they have to do with criminal law, with protection of the rights to lands claimed by the people of other colonies, and with those clauses relating to religion, especially those for the encouragement of the Protestant faith within the province. Of greatest value in dealing with the passage of the act is the Shortt and Doughty *Constitutional Documents*. Reference must again be made to Professor Coupland's extended and important study, *The Quebec Act*. For criticism of Coupland's work by three historians of distinction see the reviews of his book by A. B. Keith in the *English Historical Review*, XL, 337–9, by D. McArthur in the *American Historical Review*, XXXI, 338–40, and by Adam Shortt in the *Canadian Historical Review*, VI, 357–60. A. L. Burt, in Chap. 9 of his *The Old Province of Quebec* cited previously, provides a penetrating discussion of the issues involved in the Quebec Act; see also Victor Coffin: "The Province of Quebec and the Early American Revolution, A Study in English-American Colonial History," University of Wisconsin *Bulletin, Economics, Political Science, and History Series* (Madison, Wis., 1896) I, 275–562, and W. P. M.

With respect to provisions made by the Proclamation of 1763 for the ultimate summoning of a provincial Assembly, the act declared them null and void, as inapplicable to a population that appeared destined to remain for an indefinite period of time predominantly French Canadian in outlook, Roman Catholic in religion, and little interested in political affairs in general. To ease the minds of these inhabitants, it was enacted that they should enjoy the free exercise of their religion, subject to the King's supremacy as established in the reign of Queen Elizabeth I, that the clergy of the Church of Rome should continue to receive their "accustomed Dues and Rights, with respect to such Persons only as shall profess said Religion," and that the King, "for the Encouragement of the Protestant Religion, and for the Maintenance and Support of a Protestant Clergy within the said Province," could make provision to that end "out of the rest of the said accustomed Dues and Rights. . . ." A form of oath that could be taken by a loyal Roman Catholic was, as already indicated, also embodied in the act, as well as a guarantee that all of the King's *Canadian* subjects (except members of religious orders) should enjoy their property in the most beneficial manner and that in all matters of controversy they could resort to the old (French) laws of *Canada* for decisions thereon; [78] provision was also made that these laws should continue in force until altered by the Governor, acting with the advice of a Legislative Council that was to be nominated with the consent of the Governor.

However, in view of the benefits derived during the past nine years by the inhabitants on account of "the Certainty and Lenity of the Criminal Law of England," the British law was to remain in force, also subject to such alterations and amendments as seemed wise to the Governor and Legislative Council. The Legislative Council,[79] to consist of not more than twenty-three or less than

Kennedy: *op. cit.*, Chap. 7, "The Quebec Act, 1774." With respect to the extension of the boundary of the Province of Quebec see Louise P. Kellogg: "A Footnote to the Quebec Act," *Canadian Historical Review*, XIII, 147–56, which stresses both the apprehensions and aspirations of the French-speaking inhabitants who lived in the Illinois country and had been deprived of any settled form of government from 1763 to 1774.

[78] For a most illuminating study of the problems facing English-trained judges in attempting to apply the French civil law that had been in force in Canada see Hilda M. Neatby: *The Administration of Justice Under the Quebec Act* (Minneapolis, 1937).

[79] Martin Wight (*op. cit.*, p. 38) points out that "it is, perhaps, in the debates of the Quebec Bill that the phrase *legislative council* first became current, and in Carleton's instructions that it was first officially employed."

seventeen members, was to be appointed by the King under his signet or sign manual with the advice of the Privy Council. For its legislative functions the Council was to sit at Quebec and operate on a majority basis; a quorum of five only was required when the body functioned as an executive council at the Governor's discretion; it also had the judicial function of a court of civil appeal. In view of the fact that it was "at present inexpedient to call an Assembly," the Council, acting together with the Governor, "for a certain Time and under proper Restrictions," was given a limited power to make ordinances for the peace, welfare, and good government of the province, which, however, could not touch religion, inflict capital punishment, or provide for taxation except for local needs. These ordinances, moreover, were subjected to the approbation or disapproval of the King within a six-month period.[80]

To meet the needs of the province for funds to support its government, Parliament in 1774 supplemented the Quebec Act by the Quebec Revenue Act.[81] This statute substituted other duties for the old ones levied under the French administration on brandy, rum, and other spirits, as well as molasses, which could no longer be legally collected. By this act a distinction was made in rates between these imports, when brought from Great Britain, the British West Indies, or the North American British plantations, and when coming from foreign ports. The act also laid down the cost of a license to operate a house of entertainment within the colony and expressly retained as legally binding all territorial and casual revenues, fines, and rents that had accrued to "His Most Christian Majesty," which were to continue to be collected for supporting the province. By this law it was hoped to make the Province of Quebec self-supporting and its Governor financially independent. The statute, it is important to point out, was passed despite the contention on the part of the American colonials that the Declaratory Act, passed by Parliament in 1766, was *ultra vires*, especially with respect to the assumed right of this body to levy taxes upon those not represented in it.

Reaction to the Quebec Act on the part of the old British subjects within the colony was bitter—deprived as they felt they were of

---

[80] For the functions of the Legislative Council see Carleton's instructions, which were not signed until January 3, 1775, *Constitutional Documents*, II, pp. 594–614; for the limitations of its powers see especially p. 598.

[81] "An Act to establish a Fund toward further defraying the Charges of the Administration of Justice and Support of the Civil Government within the Province of Quebec in America," 14 Geo. III, c. 88.

habeas corpus, juries, English mercantile law, and representative government.[82] But this did not lead them to unite with the rebellious colonies to the southward when the law went into force in 1775, or to deny the power of the King in Parliament to legislate for them. Although a handful did take that position, the rest held that the maintenance of the British connection was a matter of supreme importance. Not even the American invasion shook their conviction that their true destiny lay within the Empire.[83] As for the French-speaking people of the city of Quebec, their clergy in an address hailed Governor Carleton, upon his return on September 18, as the "Conservateur de Nos Lois et Privilèges Religieux," and the laymen in their address called him "notre Protecteur et notre Pére." [84] On the other hand, it would appear that the great body of *habitants* of the province, as distinguished from the *noblesse,* the clergy, and French merchants, was none too happy with the clauses of the act making mandatory the payment of the old feudal dues to the *sei-*

---

[82] William Knox in his anonymous *The Justice and Policy of the late Act of Parliament* . . . (London, 1774)—one of the best, if not the best, contemporary account of the efforts made by the Ministry, the Privy Council, and Board of Trade from 1763 to 1774 to evolve a system of government that could meet the particular needs of the people of Canada, and of the causes for the delay in so doing—stressed the fact that the use of *habeas corpus* and trial by jury were matters that in all the colonies were within the competence of the local legislature. He also emphasized that Parliament—except for the Massachusetts Bay Government Act of 1774—had never determined these matters for the respective colonies. With respect to trial by jury, however, he pointed out (pp. 35–8) that a grand jury in October, 1774, made up of old subjects of the King had considered it a grievance and a violation of their most sacred laws and liberties that Roman Catholics in Canada were liable to all the penalties and disabilities imposed by 3 James I against recusants. Under the terms of the Quebec Act itself and the Governor's instructions, it was the responsibility of the Legislative Council of the province to determine the wisdom or otherwise of introducing *habeas corpus* and the jury system at this juncture. With respect to mercantile law, No. 12 of Carleton's instructions issued on January 3, 1775, "raised the question as to whether the laws of England may not be . . . the rule for the decision in all laws of personal Actions grounded upon Debts, Promises, Contracts, and Agreements, whether of a Mercantile or other Nature. . . ." For Carleton's instructions see *Constitutional Documents,* II, 594–614; for No. 12, see p. 599. In other words, the responsibility for providing a mercantile law under the Quebec Act lay in the hands of the Governor and Legislative Council. It may be noted in passing that excerpts of the Knox pamphlet appeared in the *Quebec Gazette—La Gazette de Quebec* on November 10, 1774, where the authorship was erroneously attributed to Solicitor General Marriott. However, it was reprinted in New York in 1774 as by Knox under its full title: *The Justice and Policy of the Act of Parliament for making more effective Provision for the Government of Quebec, asserted and proved; and the Conduct of Administration respecting that Province, stated and vindicated.*

[83] For the development of this point see D. G. Creighton: *op. cit.,* Chap. 3, "Canada and the American Revolution."

[84] See *The Quebec Gazette—La Gazette de Quebec,* September 22, 1774, for the above addresses.

gneurs and tithes to the Church. It is clear that when the Governor attempted to get the militia under arms and into action, at the outbreak of hostilities between Great Britain and the Thirteen Colonies, these inhabitants did not respond.[85] Instead they considered themselves for the most part as neutrals in the War for American Independence. Nor was this attitude of neutrality to be anything but confirmed in future wars that involved the Empire.

The underlying assumption of the Proclamation of 1763—with its promise of an Assembly—was that the old British subjects would immediately crowd into the Province of Quebec, while many, if not most, of the French-speaking inhabitants would seek out areas where they would be under the protection of the French King. This proved to be false. So also was the underlying assumption of the Quebec Act that Canada would never appeal to the old British subjects as a permanent home and would therefore be destined to remain for an indefinite period of time a rather forbidding region, almost purely French in mores and outlook. Had the men who were responsible for the framing of the Quebec Act been able to peer into the future and see the nature of the transformation that was to take place in Canada, would they have embodied in it those features that tended to make permanent, over and beyond the barriers of language and religion, the separation of the French-speaking and English-speaking peoples? [86] Since they possessed no powers of divination, they surely must, at least in the case of both the Proclamation of 1763 and the Quebec Act, be given credit for employing their best efforts to grapple with a problem so formidable that its proper solution would have demanded a greater understanding and a higher order of statesmanship than existed at that time or yet exists. It is clear, from the background of the Quebec Act, that while the draft-

---

[85] Gov. Carleton to Dartmouth, June 7, 1775, *Constitutional Documents*, II, 663–6; see also Mason Wade: *The French Canadians, 1760–1945* (New York, 1955), pp. 62–7. An examination of *The Quebec Gazette—La Gazette de Quebec* for the years 1774 to 1776 indicates the lack of concern with the American crisis evidenced in the Province of Quebec during the early stages of the war.

[86] In dealing with the Quebec Act, A. R. M. Lower does not visualize any solution of the conflict in Canada between people of different nationalities with fundamentally different outlooks on life. See his *Colony to Nation. A History of Canada* (Toronto, London, New York, 1946), Chap. 6. D. G. Creighton (*op. cit.*, p. 40), on the other hand, takes the position that differences in race, language, and religion at the time of the passage of the Quebec Act had practically nothing to do with the genesis of the political strife that has since afflicted Canada and which, he claims, actually arose out of "the struggle between insurgent commercial capitalism and a decadent and desperately resisting feudal and absolutist state."

ing and passage of the legislation were undoubtedly accelerated by
the crisis looming in the older North American colonies, the act was
not originally designed to bring pressure upon the rebellious Americans but was rather an attempt to grapple with a situation in Canada
that had long cried aloud for attention and for remedial measures.
This does not alter the fact that to the inflamed imaginations of the
New England Congregational clergy and to others both within and
beyond New England, the act was held to be a diabolical scheme
having the primary design of encircling the chief North American
centres of political disaffection with an absolutist political power
allied with an absolutist ecclesiastical power. It therefore could not
fail to give a powerful impetus to the American revolutionary
movement.[87]

[87] In this connection see especially C. H. Metzger: *The Quebec Act: A Primary
Cause of the American Revolution* (U.S. Catholic Historical Society *Monograph
Series*, XVI, New York, 1936) for a discussion of the anti-Catholic prejudice evoked
in the Thirteen Colonies by the Quebec Act at a time when, according to Father
Metzger, the Catholics numbered approximately 35,000 out of a population of well
over 2,000,000. See also his more recent study: *Catholics and the American Revolution: A Study in Religious Climate* (Chicago, 1962).

PART II

A SUMMARY OF THE SERIES

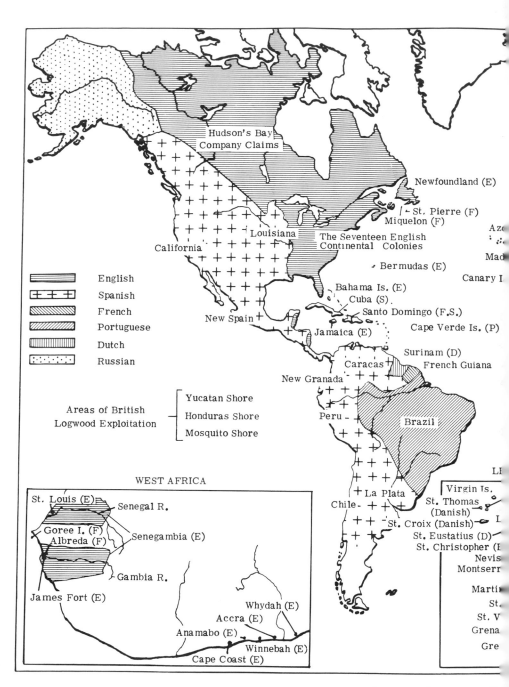

The British Empire B

Legend:
- English
- Spanish
- French
- Portuguese
- Dutch
- Russian

Areas of British Logwood Exploitation
- Yucatan Shore
- Honduras Shore
- Mosquito Shore

Hudson's Bay Company Claims
Newfoundland (E)
St. Pierre (F)
Miquelon (F)
Az
Louisiana
The Seventeen English Continental Colonies
California
Mad
Bermudas (E)
Canary I
New Spain
Bahama Is. (E)
Cuba (S)
Santo Domingo (F.S.)
Jamaica (E)
Cape Verde Is. (P)
Caracas
Surinam (D)
French Guiana
New Granada
Peru
Brazil
La Plata
Chile
LI
Virgin Is.
St. Thomas (Danish)
St. Croix (Danish)
L
St. Eustatius (D)
St. Christopher (E
Nevis
Montserr
Marti
St.
St. V
Grena
Gre

WEST AFRICA
St. Louis (E)
Senegal R.
Goree I. (F)
Albreda (F)
Senegambia (E)
Gambia R.
James Fort (E)
Whydah (E)
Accra (E)
Anamabo (E)
Winnebah (E)
Cape Coast (E)

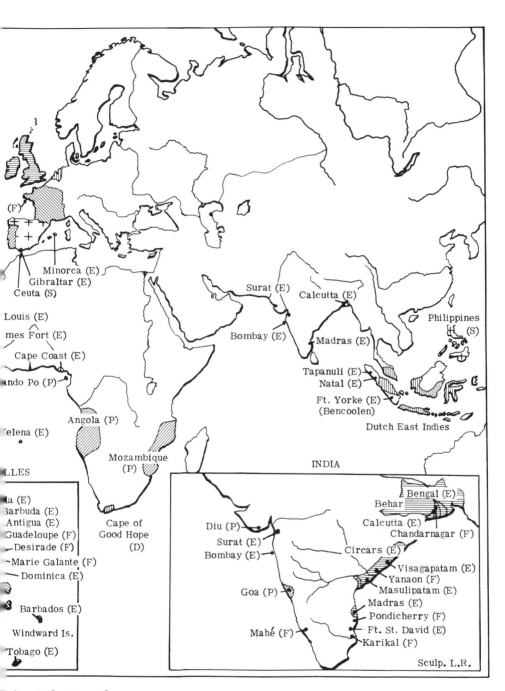

(F)

Minorca (E)
Gibraltar (E)
Ceuta (S)

Louis (E)
mes Fort (E)

Cape Coast (E)

ando Po (P)

Angola (P)

elena (E)

Surat (E)   Calcutta (E)

Bombay (E)   Madras (E)

Tapanuli (E)
Natal (E)

Ft. Yorke (E)
(Bencoolen)

Philippines
(S)

Dutch East Indies

Mozambique
(P)

INDIA

LLES

la (E)
Barbuda (E)
Antigua (E)
Guadeloupe (F)
Desirade (F)
Marie Galante (F)
Dominica (E)

Barbados (E)

Windward Is.

Tobago (E)

Cape of
Good Hope
(D)

Diu (P)
Surat (E)
Bombay (E)

Goa (P)

Mahé (F)

Bengal (E)
Behar
Calcutta (E)
Chandarnagar (F)
Circars (E)
Visagapatam (E)
Yanaon (F)
Masulipatam (E)
Madras (E)
Pondicherry (F)
Ft. St. David (E)
Karikal (F)

Sculp. L.R.

by Lyle Rosenberger

A Summary of the Series

W ITH this volume the objectives of the series—a description and analysis of developments within the Old British Empire from the middle of the eighteenth century to the Declaration of Independence—have been completed. It now remains to characterize and summarize these developments.

By the year 1775, when an open colonial revolt occurred in North America, the Empire embraced many racial as well as national groups. Even within the British Isles—that is, Great Britain, Ireland, and the islands adjacent to and politically dependent on them—there were English, Welsh, Scots, and Irish, as well as the Norman French of the Channel Islands, the Norse of the Orkneys and Shetlands, and the Manxmen of the Isle of Man. This diversity of nationalities within the Isles was reflected in a diversity of institutions, the nature of which had been determined by the need or desirability of substituting either English or Scottish institutions for earlier existing ones. Thus the extension of the power and authority of England over Wales, the Channel Islands, Ireland, and the Isle of Man, and the subsequent political union of England and Scotland—which included the Orkneys and the Shetland islands—brought under one sovereignty peoples of different nationalities, culture, and even institutions and laws. This ability to weave together patterns of cultural diversity was also characteristic of the expanding British Empire as it reached further out into the world.

Before the outbreak of the War for American Independence the British Empire stretched beyond the British Isles to Gibraltar on the Iberian Peninsula, Minorca in the Mediterranean, Senegambia in

Africa (with a government patterned as closely as circumstances would permit after the typical royal colony), the English trading posts on the Gulf of Guinea administered by the Company of Merchants Trading to Africa, and those portions of the subcontinent of India that had come under the political and fiscal administration of the United Company of Merchants Trading to the East Indies. In the New World, starting with the Arctic Ocean and moving southward, there were the possessions of the Governor and Company of Adventurers of England trading to Hudson's Bay, the Crown colony of Newfoundland, the colonies—either royal, corporate, or proprietary—of Quebec, Nova Scotia, Massachusetts Bay (including what is now the state of Maine), New Hampshire, Rhode Island, Connecticut, New York, New Jersey, Pennsylvania, the Three Lower Counties on the Delaware, Maryland, Virginia, North Carolina, South Carolina, Georgia, East Florida, and West Florida. Moreover, the westward extent of some of these colonies, according to royal letters patent or by pretension, was limited only by the Pacific Ocean—as was true of territory claimed by the Hudson's Bay Company, the Provinces of Quebec, Massachusetts Bay, Virginia, North Carolina, South Carolina, and Georgia, as well as the corporate colony of Connecticut—disregarding of course the presence of Spain in that part of Louisiana lying west of the Mississippi. Out in the Atlantic were the Bermudas and the Bahamas, and within the Caribbean Sea were Barbados, the Leeward Islands of Antigua, St. Christopher, Nevis, and Montserrat, and the Windward Islands of Dominica, St. Vincent, Grenada, and Tobago. Far to the west of the Lesser Antilles, among the Greater Antilles stood Jamacia. Again, on the mainland of Central America certain lands bordering the Gulf of Honduras and the Belize River in the logwood region, and on the Mosquito Coast to the south, were also within the sphere of British influence (although British pretensions to these lands were disputed by Spain) and were made dependent on the government of Jamaica. Such was the sweep of the British Empire in 1775.

The Empire had attained these dimensions by voyages of discovery, exploration, colonization, and conquest. It comprehended a variety of Christian groups of European origin, and doubtless a far larger number of both non-Christians and non-Europeans, if one were to include the teeming population of those parts of India dominated by the British by 1775. Some of these non-British peoples, such as the French Canadians, had been incorporated into the

Empire by conquest; others had sought its shelter of their own free will. Like a magnet British North America drew German Protestants of the Rhineland, pietistic sects from Switzerland, Calvinistic Huguenots from southwestern France, and Spanish Jews—all seeking a better way of life. Among other non-Europeans, millions of Mohammedans and Hindus lived within the principalities of India under the firm control of the East India Company. There were, in addition, the Caribs of the island of St. Vincent, various tribes of American Indians, as well as the Eskimos north of the Arctic Circle in the territory granted to the Hudson's Bay Company. These people represented all degrees of civilization and many levels of political, social, and economic status. At the bottom of the scale was the slave. There was white slavery (prescribed for a period of years as a penalty for crime and quite distinguished from voluntary indenture) and black slavery (into which people were sold or were born and died, unless manumitted). This institution of self-perpetuating slavery (so out of accord with present conceptions of Christian principles and virtues) was not everywhere the same in the degree of harshness it imposed upon the Negro torn from his native Africa chiefly to support the colonial plantation economy. Conditions of labour varied according to the geographical area of the Empire and the quality of humanity of the owner or overseer. For the holding of slaves was sanctioned by law, which did not protect the welfare of the Negro as carefully as it provided codes of punishment for him. Happily, by the 1770's a wave of revulsion was felt against this inhuman exploitation and led ultimately to the obliteration of the institution (as is developed and discussed in Chapters IV–VI of this volume).

In view of the admixture of nationalities and races, and the diversity of cultures—with the attending diversity of religious beliefs—the British Empire might well have been the scene of almost indescribable confusion and discord in the period under survey. This was not the case. For what chiefly characterized the government of the Empire—certainly attributable in part to the experience in dealing with the diversities within the British Isles—was its tolerance of differences and, all in all, the even-handed justice that it meted out. Within the vast territorial limits under its authority the government sought (as an ideal, which in practice was fairly well upheld) to establish and maintain what may properly be called a *pax Britannica*—a peace based on the rule of law, wisely administered and judicially enforced, rather than the use of naked force. Thus it supported neither an inquisition nor any other comparable device of suppression. Moreover—apart from Ireland (where the dominant Protestant minority living in the midst of the native Irish demanded the protection of troops and paid for their maintenance), Minorca, and the newly conquered Province of Quebec with its French-speaking inhabitants—no regular soldiers were garrisoned in the midst of the King's subjects to hold them in subjection. In fact, only in time of war had most of the inhabitants of the Thirteen North American Colonies that revolted ever seen a British regular.

Actually the British army was surprisingly weak in the 1760's and early 1770's. For, without taking into account those troops stationed in India and in the pay of the East India Company, the army numbered hardly more than 45,000 soldiers, including the cavalry and artillery regiments—"a paltry handful of troops to guard so vast an Empire," in the words of Sir John Fortescue.[1] The distribution of these land forces in 1763 was as follows: some 17,500 troops were stationed in Great Britain, including about 3,000 invalids; at Gibraltar and in Minorca somewhat over 4,000 men were posted; 12,000 were kept in Ireland, and 10,000 more were allotted to North America and the British islands in the Atlantic Ocean and the Caribbean Sea.[2] Of this total some 7,500 regulars were assigned to North America. In the summer of 1763 these troops were widely scattered, chiefly at various outposts in the Indian country, at Quebec and Montreal, and at such strategic seaports on the Atlantic Ocean and Gulf of Mexico as St. John's and Placentia in Newfoundland, Halifax in Nova Scotia, St. Augustine in East Florida, and Pensacola and Mobile in West Florida. Also a few relief companies destined for the stations in upper New York were maintained at Fort George in New York City and occasionally, before proceeding to the Great Lakes country or to Fort Pitt at the forks of the Ohio, troops might be temporarily cantonned in Connecticut, New Jersey, or Pennsylvania.[3] This pattern of distribution of the forces allotted to North

[1] J. W. Fortescue: *A History of the British Army* (16 vols., New York, 1899–1930), III, 10–11. For a new study of the influence of the presence in North America of British regular troops on the coming of the Revolution see John Shy: *Toward Lexington: The Role of the British Army in the Coming of the American Revolution* (Princeton, 1965).

[2] J. W. Fortescue: *op. cit.*, III, 11.

[3] See Sir Jeffrey Amherst's "Disposition of His Majesty's Forces in North America," August, 1763, C.O. 323:17, p. 45, and in this series Volume X, 200–2, and Volume XI, 128–9 and map on facing p. 45.

America was maintained until at least 1767. Despite the small size of the land forces, the Empire was strong in its ability to defend itself against external threats; for it still could depend upon the Royal Navy, which in the course of the Great War for the Empire had swept both the French and Spanish navies from the high seas.

Just as no empire past or contemporary equalled the extent of the Old British Empire before 1775, so no other approached it in the diversity of the economic pursuits of its polyglot peoples, in their accumulated wealth, and in the spirit of enterprise they displayed. From the looms of England, Scotland, and Ireland poured forth vast surpluses of woollen, cotton, linen, and silk fabrics, as well as numerous other articles, many of them to be sold outside the Empire. From the furnaces and forges of England and the North American colonies came great surpluses of ironware and steel utensils of high quality. Enormous quantities of cured cod, rice, wheat, flour, bread, and other provisions were sent abroad from Newfoundland and North America, while Ireland was a great exporter of barrelled beef, pork, and butter. The British West Indies supplied the needs of Great Britain and the more northern colonies for sugar and at least partially met the needs of the distilleries of Boston, Newport, New York, and Philadelphia for molasses. From the forests, lakes, and rivers of North America were exported to Great Britain abundant ship stores of pitch, resin, turpentine, masts, and ship timber, as well as a wealth of furs and skins. The dependent principalities of India contributed a great variety of cotton fabrics and pepper. Nor must it be overlooked, in enumerating the chief productive activities of the Old British Empire, that probably more ocean-going vessels were built in Great Britain and the colonies in the 1760's than in all of continental Europe combined. Further, no other empire or kingdom had a merchant marine comparable in number or carrying capacity to the combined merchant fleets of the British and the colonials. All this, together with a variety of other fruitful and wealth-producing enterprises, helped greatly to elevate the standards of living, to increase the spread of enlightenment, and to heighten the general well-being within the Empire, at least among those of European lineage.

The Old British Empire was also unique in the extent to which individual freedom existed within it. What other empire permitted a free press to operate not only in the mother country—where in London alone 112 so-called newspapers were published for more than one number during the year 1753 [4]—but in its dependencies? In British North America between 1763 and 1775 over forty newspapers were published for brief or longer periods; pamphlets and books issued by the hundreds from North American presses, some of them extremely critical of the British government—as might be expected amongst a free people.

In line with the spirit of freedom within the Empire—and again setting it off from other imperial systems that had preceded it or that then prevailed elsewhere—was the existence of a complex system of local governments, each of them possessing a surprising degree of freedom of action. This system rested on specific concessions granted by the central government to meet the local needs and aspirations of non-British, as well as British, peoples embodied within the Empire. For example, the people of Minorca were permitted to maintain their own form of local government with a minimum of interference from the British military Governor residing at Port Mahon. Similarly, except for the collection and disbursement of revenue, a comparable administrative relationship existed in those parts of India that had come under the aegis of the East India Company. However, for the administration of British justice among the Company's servants and other British subjects temporarily domiciled within the dependent principalities, courts applying English law had been established. It must be further noted that during the 1770's the Ministry and Parliament became increasingly interested in the Company's methods of administering these principalities and by passing the famous Regulatory Act of 1773 brought the Company's political and fiscal functions under direct government supervision. Thus the native princes continued to rule locally, but with the company administration superimposed or functioning as a parallel system of local government.

The Old British Empire in truth was not a tidy systematic entity in 1775 [5]—a defect that may paradoxically be counted among its merits. While the subject of the constitution of the Empire will be pursued in greater detail later on in this Summary, it may be pointed out now that although an empire, it was nowhere designated as such in the constitutional law that bound it together; nor did it have an emperor at its head. For example, although the supreme authority

---

[4] See in this series Volume I, 71.

[5] For the administrative system as it stood in 1763 see in this series Volume IX, Chap. 1.

over the far reaches of the Empire clearly rested in the King in Parliament, no one was commissioned directly to represent the Crown in those principalities of India dependent on the East India Company or in the vast territory comprehended within the Hudson's Bay Company's domain in North America. Nevertheless the King's Privy Council, aided by the Lords Commissioners for Trade and Plantations, sought to give a quality of uniformity at least to the government of the British colonies and particularly to the royal colonies. This was done by means of letters patent and by commissions and instructions to the Governors of the royal colonies which were framed as nearly alike as the varying local conditions of these colonies permitted. As for the proprietary colonies of Maryland and Pennsylvania,[6] although the Governor in each instance was appointed by the Proprietor or Proprietors subject to royal approval, the extent to which he could be directed by royal instructions in carrying out his duties remained an issue in dispute with the Assembly in both colonies and was never settled during the colonial period. In the case of the purely corporate colonies of Connecticut and Rhode Island, the Governors were seldom instructed by the Crown; when they were, the matter usually related to some quite general concern as, for example, the enforcement of the acts of trade. In fact, the Governors of these corporate colonies had extremely restricted executive authority and as a rule looked to their Assemblies and not to the King for guidance.

Even among the royal colonies in the 1760's and 1770's no Governor was powerful solely by reason of the authority conferred upon him by the Crown. The degree of success he might have in administering his colony depended largely upon his ability to exercise sufficient persuasiveness and tact to win the confidence of the members of his Council and the leaders of the Assembly—and thereby secure approval for a line of action not instigated by people of the colony—or to carry out policies generally approved within the colonies and not specifically prohibited by his instructions. Yet all colonial governments had some restrictions upon their ability to legislate. No law conflicting with a statute of Parliament, or manifestly at variance with principles embodied in the common law, or appearing

---

[6] The question was never clearly settled during the colonial period whether the Three Lower Counties on the Delaware pertained to the Penn family or to the Crown. For an account of the anomalous situation of this colony in the eighteenth century see in this series revised Volume III, 189–93.

to bear unfairly upon any of the King's subjects anywhere, was permitted to stand. And every colony having an Assembly empowered to make laws—with the exception of the corporate colonies of Connecticut and Rhode Island and the proprietary colony of Maryland—was required to submit its acts to the scrutiny of the Privy Council, which possessed the power to validate or disallow them. Further, a law passed in any of the colonies without exception might be carried on appeal from the highest colonial court to the Privy Council which, sitting as a judicial committee, had the final authority to determine the validity of the act. By this means a certain uniformity in colonial legislation was secured.

However, the limitations on the powers of the colonial Assemblies just described did not prevent the growth in prestige of these local legislatures. Just as the House of Commons had become the real centre of authority in Great Britain, especially after the Revolution of 1688-9, so by 1775 in all the older colonies the elected Assembly[7] had assumed an equivalent position. This was the result of the degree of control it had come to exercise over both the appropriation and expenditure of funds, despite royal instructions to the contrary. Even its right to appoint directly and control certain officials had in some of the colonies been won despite the opposition of the Governor acting under his instructions.[8] Whether this drive for power on the part of the colonial Assemblies would stop short of complete independence of the authority of the government of Great Britain was not easy for the British officials to determine, but they noticed an ever-widening assumption by these bodies of legislative authority in local matters. As the late Mary P. Clarke pointed out in discussing the growth of power of the Assembly in the royal colonies: ". . . British officials sometimes urged the governors not to allow to the assembly any rights not exercised by the House of Commons. . . . In the early colonial period the Governor might be concerned to keep the house from assuming an equality with parlia-

---

[7] The word Assembly is, of course, used here to designate the lower chambers of the colonial bicameral legislatures; only Pennsylvania and Delaware were unicameral.

[8] For the dominating position attained by the New York Assembly by the middle of the eighteenth century, as against the powers conferred upon the Governor by his commission and instructions, see Volume III, Revised, of this series, pp. 102–5; for the equally dominant position attained by the Assembly of the proprietary colony of Pennsylvania by 1754 see *ibid.*, VI, 68; see also J. P. Greene: *The Quest for Power. The Lower House of Assembly in the Southern Royal Colonies, 1689–1776* (Chapel Hill, N.C., 1963), Chap. 19, for the progress made by the four colonies of Virginia, North Carolina, South Carolina, and Georgia in wresting power from the Governors from 1763 to 1775.

ment [that is, with the House of Commons]; but as the years wore on, his concern was likely to be that the assembly should not go beyond the precedents set in England."[9] Nor is it surprising that this was the case. Those who assumed leadership in a colonial Assembly were as a rule lawyers well-versed in their calling, great planters, or wealthy merchants, all possessed of considerable prestige and knowledge. As such they were members of a British colonial *élite*.[10] Brought closely in touch with the course of events in Great Britain and of other parts of the Empire by means of the press, if not by personal correspondence, they were generally well-informed as well as determined men, quick to oppose whatever policy might be adopted by the home government or that of another colony if it seemed to affect their local interests.[11] For in their rise to positions of influence these leaders had learned how to use the power they enjoyed, and were frequently most articulate in setting forth their rights and those of their constituents. In other words, they acted very much as did Englishmen in the British Isles in similar positions of influence.

One thing is fundamental to an understanding of the history of political developments within the Old British Empire before 1775—especially in so far as the assertion of colonial rights is concerned—and that is to comprehend the degree to which colonials earlier had felt that their safety and general welfare depended upon the closeness of their connection with the home government. From the very beginning of English colonization of the New World down to the termination in 1760 of the North American phase of the Great War for the Empire, this connection was a matter of first importance in their eyes. Whatever sharp differences existed between any colony and the mother country before this momentous event—and they were many—the outcome had always fallen short of open, declared resistance to English or British policy on the part of the colonials.

Although all the colonies of the Old British Empire had come into

---

[9] See Dr. Mary P. Clarke's *Parliamentary Privilege in the American Colonies* (New Haven, 1943), p. 202.

[10] For a discussion of the British North American *élite* see Volume X, 27–9, of this series, which forms part of Chap. I, "Colonies Ripe for Revolt: The Older British North American Colonies in 1763." This introductory chapter places strong emphasis on the socio-economic forces emerging after the Great War for the Empire.

[11] For emphasis on the close intercolonial connections of mercantile firms in America in the latter part of the eighteenth century see W. S. Sachs: "Interurban Correspondents and the Development of a National Economy before the Revolution: New York as a Case Study," *New York History*, XXXVI, 320–35.

existence by the King's royal prerogative (expressed through letters patent under the Great Seal creating them), before 1760 no colonial Assembly had ever denied the right of Parliament to interfere in its affairs. A series of trade and navigation acts providing various limitations upon the freedom of colonials in their commercial relations within and beyond the Empire had been passed without serious protest from any Assembly. Nor had Parliament limited itself to matters of colonial trade. A number of other restrictions on colonial freedom of action had been embodied in the statutes of the realm. There was a law placing restrictions in the colonies on aliens and others who were not natural-born subjects of the King, a law on the liability of colonial lands for the debts of the owner, one extending to the colonies the British statutes respecting the attestation of wills, another forbidding stock companies and business enterprises that were unlawful in England from operating in the colonies. And there were others for granting naturalization to foreigners dwelling in the colonies, for the holding in England rather than America of trials of colonial Governors charged with misconduct, for protecting the colonial stands of white pine trees considered serviceable to the Royal Navy, for providing legal value to currency issued in the colonies, for prohibiting the exportation of colonial wool, woollen products, and beaver hats (along with a law limiting the number who might be trained as hatters), for restricting the issuing of bills of credit in the New England colonies, and for prohibiting the erection of additional slitting mills and steel furnaces in all the colonies. The active interest of Parliament in the affairs of the colonies from 1660 onwards—whether by prohibiting certain lines of action or encouraging particular enterprises—is attested to by the sixty-eight statutes with direct reference to the colonies that were passed between that year and the beginning of the reign of George III.[12]

While it is true that many of the restrictions placed by Parliament on the colonies were disliked in America, each of them at the time of enactment had a rationale that removed it from the category of mere irresponsible abuse of legislative power. Here was an Empire which was protected at great cost to the people of Great Britain. These same people might well reasonably expect to reap certain benefits from carrying such a burden. They therefore felt justified in requiring that the commerce within the Empire should be so controlled as

---

[12] *Statutes at Large* (Eyre and Strahan), X, see index under Plantations.

to profit them rather than their rivals abroad. As to restrictions other than those having to do with trade, some of them originated in the belief that colonial enterprise should not cause the destruction of a well-established industry in Great Britain, thereby producing unemployment in the British Isles and bringing distress to large numbers of people who would become dependent on the poor rates. Rather, colonials should, it was felt, pursue other fruitful fields of activity. Other restrictions were based upon the view that property—whether in money or land or some other form—should enjoy the same protection in the colonies as in Great Britain.

But in addition to restrictive laws there was beneficial legislation, such as the granting of bounties on masts, ship timber and other naval stores, as well as on indigo shipped to Great Britain, and the concession permitting the direct export of colonial rice to all points south of Cape Finisterre—all of which helped greatly to bring prosperity to several of the colonies. Nor should it be overlooked that in many fields of business activity British colonials were permitted to compete with the people of Great Britain and did so successfully. Colonial cured cod brought premium prices in the markets of southern Europe; the provision trade of the middle colonies to points outside the Empire was great and lucrative; in the building of ocean-going vessels and in the carrying trade of the New World the colonials surpassed their English rivals. In view of the impressive growth of the North American colonies from 1760 to 1775 and the evidence of prosperity and refinement displayed, especially in the metropolitan centres there, one is perhaps justified in concluding that the system of restrictions did not hamper colonial enterprise too seriously. On the contrary it was estimated in the 1740's that the value of colonial exports to the mother country alone amounted to over £5,000,000 sterling and that this commerce to and from Great Britain required the services of some 3,000 vessels, over half of which were owned and profitably operated by colonials.[13]

It may be well to point out that until the middle of the eighteenth century the chief emphasis of British policy toward expansion of the Empire was directed to the development of trade under the mercan-

---

[13] See Volume I, Revised, p. 23, in this series. In referring to the prosperous and expanding condition of the British North American colonies before 1763, O. M. Dickerson very properly asserted: "Such a story of real progress is without parallel in modern history" (*The Navigation Acts and the American Revolution* [Philadelphia, 1951], p. 153).

tilist system. While it is true that no frank repudiation of the trade and navigation system that supported the Empire was made until 1823, after 1748 a gradual change of policy increasingly stressed certain aspects of what can be called "modern imperialism," meaning the effective control of both distant lands and foreign peoples comprehended within the territorial possessions of the expanding state. In connection with this system, strategic and other power considerations of the state rather than direct trade benefits were basic to government policy.

It may be said that the Treaty of Aix-la-Chapelle between Great Britain and France in 1748 was the last time before the days of Gladstone that Great Britain voluntarily sacrificed territory for immediate trade advantages. This date is therefore significant as marking the start of the slow transition of the British Empire from one that was based predominately on mercantilistic principles to one based predominantly on imperialistic principles.[14]

The year 1748 also signals the beginning of the brief period of relative peace that reigned within the Old Empire at the middle of the eighteenth century. For from that date until the beginning of the great international crisis of 1754 a comparative stability marked the

---

[14] For the development of the above distinction see this author's "Acadia and the Beginnings of Modern British Imperialism," *Essays in Modern English History in Honor of Wilbur Cortez Abbott* (Cambridge, Mass., 1941), pp. 177–202, and also his *The British Empire in the Eighteenth Century: Its Strength and Its Weakness* (Oxford, 1952). In his approach to the transition, Professor C. M. Andrews (*The Colonial Period of American History*, I, xiii) stresses the importance of the Peace of Paris of 1763; this was also the thesis embodied in two studies by F. J. Ericson: "British Motives for Expansion in 1763: Territory, Commerce, or Security," Michigan Academy of Science, Arts, and Letters *Papers*, XXVII, 581–94, and *The British Colonial System and the Question of Change of Policy on the Eve of the American Revolution* (Chicago, 1943). S. M. Pargellis (*Lord Loudoun in North America*, New Haven, 1933, p. 1) finds 1757, the year of the coming to power of Pitt, to be of special significance in the transition. In this connection it should be stated that G. N. Clark (*The Wealth of England from 1496 to 1760*, London, 1946) avoids the use of the expression "mercantilism" with its varied connotations in favour of the simple term "protectionism"; while T. S. Ashton (*An Economic History of England: The 18th Century*, London, 1955), expresses his distaste for all such words as "Capitalism, Mercantilism, and Imperialism" (Preface), and therefore avoids the use of them as terms lacking in precision. Nevertheless it seems to serve a useful purpose in dealing with the eighteenth-century British Empire to use the term "mercantilism" as applying to the old British colonial commercial system which, in the words of R. L. Schuyler, "depended for its justification upon the doctrines of mercantilism, that politico-economic complex of principles, policies, regulations, and practices which existed in Europe between the late medieval period and the age of 'laissez-faire'" (*The Fall of the Old Colonial System: A Study in British Free Trade* [London & New York, 1945], p. 3); see also C. M. Andrews: *op. cit.*, IV, Chap. 10, and P. W. Buck: *The Politics of Mercantilism* (New York, 1942), for his emphasis on the structure of the mercantilist states in the seventeenth and eighteenth centuries.

British Empire such as would not occur again in that century. During these years people were proud to be a part of the Empire. Thousands of foreigners sought to establish themselves in North America and thereby breathe the free air of a British dependency. As the Rev. Jonathan Mayhew could declare in the West Meeting-House at Boston in 1750—upon the anniversary of the death of King Charles I—in the Preface to his perfectly proper and loyal sermon of warning, *A Discourse concerning Unlimited Submission and Non-Resistance to the Higher Powers* . . . : "God be thanked one may, in any part of the British dominions, speak freely (if a decent regard be paid to those in authority) both of government and religion; and even give some broad hints that he is engaged on the side of Liberty, the *Bible,* and opposition to Tyranny, Priestcraft, and Nonsense, without being in danger either of the bastille [as in France] or the inquisition [as in Spain]—though there will always be some interested politicians, contracted bigots, and hypocritical zealots for a party, to take offense at such freedoms." Nor is it surprising that the greatest acclaim for Mayhew's truly patriotic *Seven Sermons* . . . (printed in Boston in 1749 and republished in London in 1750) should have come from leading men in England, and that Aberdeen University, not Harvard or Yale, should have honoured him with a doctorate. One may therefore wonder whether Mayhew—that great lover of freedom and supporter of the heritage of the so-called Glorious Revolution of 1688—had he lived, would have welcomed the ties of alliance made with a country the symbol of which to him was the Bastille, or the efforts of patriotic Americans to secure an alliance with a country the symbol of which to him was the Inquisition?

But returning again to 1748, the year that marks the starting point of this series and of the last period in the eighteenth century during which one can view the Empire at peace, this date also marks another phase in British Empire history. For between 1748 and 1754 the gathering of rival British and French forces in North America, the West Indies, and India was to lead to the outbreak of what may well be termed the first modern imperialistic war.[15]

In North America British colonials by 1749 were pressing westward beyond the Appalachian barrier. This movement was bound to

---

[15] See Volumes IV and V of this series for a detailed description of the build-up of rivalry over distant lands within the zones of international friction.

collide with the French movement of expansion into the same area from settlements along the waterways of the St. Lawrence and the Mississippi Rivers. For by 1749 not only were the French firmly planted in Canada to the east of the Great Lakes, but their trading posts were also scattered in the Great Lakes region itself. In the Illinois country they had likewise settled at a number of points along the upper Mississippi and here and there they had established trading posts along the middle course of the river; while near its mouth was located New Orleans, the capital of Louisiana, and to the east was planted the town of Mobile on the Gulf of Mexico. The French logically enough claimed as their own all the lands drained by the St. Lawrence, the Mississippi, and the tributaries of these rivers. The British just as logically pointed to the sea-to-sea grants of land embodied in the seventeenth-century charters of certain colonies—claims which, if upheld, would have deprived the French of all their North American possessions except those in Canada. Here then were rival imperial claims to vast stretches of land and to the right to control the destinies of the native inhabitants on them. It should of course be kept in mind that Anglo-French rivalry was also evident in Africa, India, and the West Indies.

Although the French in North America did not begin to compare with the British settlers in number, they surpassed them in establishing close, friendly relations with many Indian tribes—a great asset in wilderness fighting. As for the British colonials, while they had alliances with the Six Iroquois Confederated Nations in upper New York, and with the Cherokee, the Lower Creek, the Catawba, and the Chickasaw nations to the west of the settled parts of the Carolinas and Georgia, these Indians never offered the type of effective aid that the French could obtain from their native allies in times of hostility.

When in 1749 Céloron de Blainville was ordered by the Governor General of New France to take a force down the Allegheny and into the Ohio River in order to "repossess" the region—a region where for many years traders from Pennsylvania and Virginia had moved about in large numbers without interference and where the British flag flew over their trading posts—this event marked the beginning of a crisis in the history of North America that was to have the most fateful consequences for both the French and the British Empires. For the outbreak of hostilities at the forks of the Ohio—where French and English forces clashed after the French capture of a fort being erected by the Ohio Company of Virginia—ushered in the Great War for the Empire. During the nine years of the war, the hostilities spread to every part of the world where France and Great Britain had interests.[16]

In this decisive war, with the fate of the heart of North America at stake, the French under excellent leadership displayed great capacity for carrying on military operations in the wilderness, even in the face of shortages of various supplies. They had determined as a chief objective to enclose the British colonials securely to the east of the Appalachian Mountain barrier. With the end of the first three years of fighting this objective seemed in sight, for they had inflicted disastrous reverses on both British regulars and colonial troops. But, despite their valiant endeavours to control the vast interior of North America, the French possessed a weakness that was to prove fatal in a prolonged war waged 3,000 miles from the homeland: over-extended lines of communications. For their navy failed to maintain safe, open sea-lanes through which troops and *matériel* to support them could be transported regularly to the New World— and fighting men and munitions, highly expendable in prolonged wars, demand frequent replacement.

The destruction of French naval power in two great sea battles in 1759—one at Lagos off the coast of Portugal and the other at Quiberon Bay off the coast of France—were disasters of the first magnitude. Thereafter, under the dynamic leadership of William Pitt, the British Navy maintained a relentless blockade of the chief seaports of France and the approaches to Canada, while armies in North America under the command of Amherst and Forbes, together with an amphibious expedition up the St. Lawrence led by Wolfe and Saunders, brought about the collapse of French resistance on the continent by 1760. Nor were French possessions in the Caribbean spared the dominating force of the British navy. In 1759 the rich island of Guadeloupe was surrendered; in 1761 the so-called Neutral Island of Dominica fell; the following year French Martinique and Grenada, together with the Neutral Islands of St. Lucia and St.

---

[16] For the unsuccessful diplomatic efforts to reconcile the conflicting claims of Great Britain and France in the Ohio Valley, as well as in the area known by the French as Acadia and by the British as Nova Scotia, and in the West Indies, see Volume V, Chap. 10, of this series; see also the author's "A French Project for Victory Short of A Declaration of War," *Canadian Historical Review*, XXVI, 361–71. A detailed description of the Great War for the Empire during the years of defeat and the victorious years is to be found in Volumes VI–VIII of this series.

Vincent, submitted. The same fate befell the French in India when, after three naval engagements between 1758 and 1759 off the Coromandel coast, the British under Rear Admiral Pocock forced the Comte d'Ache to desert the coast and to sail away to Île de France. With the crushing of the Comte de Lally's army by Eyre Coote in the decisive battle of Wandiwash early in 1760, the last of the French strongholds in India was obliged to capitulate in the spring of 1761. Such was the role played by British naval power.

In an effort to retrieve their losses, the French turned to Spain and, by guaranteeing to indemnify that country for any losses it might sustain from its commitment to the Bourbon Family Compact, brought it into the war early in 1762. But again British sea power was to prove decisive: in the capture of Havana and the conquest of the Philippine archipelago. Nor did the temporary seizure by the French of St. John's, Newfoundland, in 1762 profit them; for after the French fleet had sailed out of the harbour for fear of being bottled up there, the land troops left behind could do little else but surrender to a British expeditionary force.

So far as British hostilities on the continent of Europe were concerned, although the phases of the Great War for the Empire just described remained distinct as a war, to a certain degree this European aspect merged with the German Seven Years' War begun in 1756 when Frederick of Prussia unexpectedly invaded Saxony and began his drive against Austria. While the British granted subsidies to Frederick, they were never at war with either Austria or Russia, Prussia's chief enemies.[17] Their main concern was to preserve the Electorate of Hanover (the personal possession of George III as its Elector) from conquest by the French (allied by subsidy treaties with the Austrians and Russians). Its capture nevertheless occurred when the Duke of Cumberland, with his mixed army of Germans and British, was outmaneouvred by powerful forces under the Maréchal d'Estrées in the fall of 1757 and was compelled to sign the capitulation of Kloster-Seven. This treaty was later repudiated by both George III as the Elector of Hanover and the British Parliament on the ground that the French had violated the terms of peace. From the beginning of the campaign in 1758 to the close of the war

---

[17] For the European "system" of alliance before their reversal in 1755 and the beginnings of the German Seven Years' War in 1756 see in this series Volume VI, Chap. 11, "Britain and her Continental 'System,'" Chap. 12, "The Rivals find new Friends," and Chap. 14, "The American Crisis Ushers in a World War."

on the continent, Parliament subsidized the efforts of Prince Ferdinand of Brunswick to regain Hanover. In the course of hostilities he commanded an army of some 50,000 men, mostly German contingents but also including four British regiments of foot and five of horse under Lord George Sackville (later Lord Germain). Had it not been for the latter's misconduct in the battle of Minden in the summer of 1759, which caused his dismissal from the army, Ferdinand might have destroyed the French opposing him by the skillful disposition of his forces; nevertheless he was able largely to free portions of the Electorate, together with parts of Brunswick and Hesse-Cassel, from the French. This he did by the capture of certain strategic towns and by holding his own in the field until a cessation of hostilities was agreed upon as a preliminary to ending the war.[18]

Upon the signing of the definitive Treaty of Paris with France and Spain on February 10, 1763, Britain's Great War for the Empire was terminated. Five days later, the German Seven Years' War ended when Prussia and Austria concluded a treaty of peace at Hubertusberg (Hubertsberg); for Russia was no longer a belligerent after the death of Czarina Elizabeth early in 1762 and the coming to the throne of Peter III, a great admirer of Frederick of Prussia.

By the Peace of Paris France surrendered Canada to Great Britain, while retaining certain fishing rights off Newfoundland; it also recognized the British claims to all lands in North America east of the Mississippi River, exclusive of the enclave at New Orleans. Spain, to regain Havana, ceded Florida to Great Britain, which in turn later agreed to give up the Philippine archipelago. To carry out the pledge to indemnify Spain for any losses connected with the war, France turned over to that nation New Orleans and what was left of Louisiana west of the Mississippi. In the West Indies, the British returned Guadeloupe and Martinique to France, for which the French were required to cede Grenada and to acknowledge the right of Great Britain to the Neutral Islands of Dominica, St. Vincent, and Tobago. As to India, although the French were permitted to regain all the trading factories they had erected before 1749 in that country, they were severely restricted in their right either to

---

[18] For the progress of the Great War for the Empire and the German Seven Years' War, from 1757 to 1763, and for the termination of the two wars see in this series Volume VII, Chap. 5, "The European Scene. Pitt's Reversal of Policy"; Volume VIII, Chap. 1, "A French Attempt to Conquer the British Isles," Chap. 2, "British Continental Commitments, 1759–60," Chap. 3, "The New King and the German Seven Years' War," and Chap. 12, "The Return of Peace."

maintain armed forces or to build fortifications there. Thus the termination of the Great War for the Empire saw, on the one hand, both France and Spain humbled and, on the other, the British Empire arriving at such a degree of internal strength, accompanied by such an enormous expansion of its limits, that it could well be characterized "*the Great Empire*" in 1763.

During the course of the nine years of war between France and England, some of the British colonies played an important part not only in the military operations in North America but in the Cuban campaign. The New England colonies, particularly Massachusetts Bay and Connecticut, gave impressive aid throughout the period of hostilities; so did New York and New Jersey on a proportionate basis, considering their lesser resources. Pennsylvania's support was sporadic, as was that of Virginia, although both these colonies manned chains of forts to protect their frontier settlements. Maryland refused to be involved in anything but purely defensive measures, while the Carolinas and Georgia held only modest roles in the war isolated as they were from the main theatres of military operations and with the need to keep constant guard over a numerous slave population.

To recompense the individual colonies for the military support they had furnished, Parliament voted reimbursement funds from time to time ultimately totalling £1,072,784 sterling. Of this sum Massachusetts Bay, the largest contributor to the war effort, received close to one third.[19] In fact one is justified in stating that such liberality on the part of a parent state to its colonies had never before been witnessed. It resulted in cutting almost in half the war debts accumulated by Massachusetts Bay and most of the other colonies and in the case of Connecticut reducing them even more. Thus by the end of 1764 all the colonies were pretty largely free of any heavy burden of debt occasioned by the war[20] and could enjoy a corresponding reduction in taxation. On the other hand, Great Britain's public debt in 1763 stood at £146,000,000, of which £137,000,000 was funded, requiring an annual payment of £4,700,000 in interest. With this historically unparalleled national debt to carry and faced also by the need to provide for the adequate defences of the expanded Empire, the people of Great Britain saw little prospect of reducing the heavy load of taxation after the close

---

[19] See Chap. 2, "Parliament Reimburses the Colonies, 1756–1765," in Volume X of this series.

[20] See *ibid.*, Chap. 3.

of the war.[21] On the contrary, an effort was made in 1763 to add to this load by placing a heavy excise tax on the producers of cider and perry. This led to such violent commotions in western England, and was so generally nullified by evasion, that the act was repealed. Nevertheless, in 1766 the strict enforcement of a new act for the taxation of these beverages added some £200,000 to the revenue. In addition, other means were taken by the government to tighten up the domestic revenue measures and thereby reduce the loss of this income through smuggling activities.[22]

One item of expense embodied in the post-war budget which the Ministry felt that the American colonials could and justly should share was the annual cost of maintaining a military force of some 7,500 regulars for the necessary defence of North America—the distribution of which was mentioned earlier in this chapter. A preliminary step was therefore determined upon to prevent the leakage of revenue that resulted from lax enforcement in the colonies of the Trade and Navigation Acts; this step was the adoption of measures in America comparable to those employed in Great Britain. Before this, as a war measure, William Pitt in 1760 had ordered the strict enforcement of these acts to put an end to the lucrative trade between North American colonials and the enemy in the West Indies—an activity which he called "an illegal and most pernicious Trade" having the effect of lengthening the "long and expensive War." [23] As a result, even before the conclusion of hostilities (but after the conquest of Canada), opposition to the rigid upholding of the trade acts was expressed by the Boston merchants in their open hostility to one of the chief weapons for doing away with smuggling—the writs of assistance.

The issue over the writs of assistance was accentuated in 1761 by the stand of James Otis, hired by the merchants to oppose an application by the customs service for such a writ.[24] For the first time the legality of the use of such an instrument in the colonies was challenged in an open court and with it the validity and legality of a law passed by Parliament in 1696 relating to America.[25] This denial of the authority of Parliament was based on the grounds that it was

---

[21] See *ibid.*, pp. 182–3.

[22] See *ibid.*, Chap. 9, "The Search for Revenue at Home," for the purchase of the Isle of Man.

[23] See in this series Volume VIII, 81, dealing with Pitt's circular letter to the Governors of August 23, 1760, printed in *Pitt Correspondence*, II, 320–1.

[24] See in this series Volume X, 124–6.

[25] See 7 and 8 William III, c. 22, par. 6.

contrary to the constitution that protected the rights of the people of the colonies. Far from suffering public disfavour for taking this extreme position, Otis was rewarded by being elected to the House of Representatives; and for a brief period he became a dominant figure on the political horizon of the colony.

The doctrine expounded by Otis raises many questions. Did he mean that Parliament was so limited in its power by the constitution of Great Britain that it could not legally do what it had done for over a century by empowering the fiscal officers of the kingdom to call peace officers to their aid to prevent people in Great Britain from smuggling? [26] Or, if Parliament could so act in Great Britain under the constitution, did he mean that this body could not under the constitution extend such a law to America? In other words, were the people of Massachusetts and the other colonies endowed with privileges and exemptions under the constitution of the Empire that the people of Great Britain did not enjoy? If so, was the statement embodied in Clause 9 of the Statute of 1696, "That all Laws, Bye-Laws, Usages, or Customs . . . in any of the said Plantations, which are in any wise repugnant . . . to this present Act, or to any other Law hereafter to be made in this Kingdom . . . are illegal, null, and void, to all Intents and Purposes whatever," also invalid as a violation of the constitution of Massachusetts Bay? But the constitution of this province was based upon the charter of 1691, which specified that whatever action was taken by the Great and General Court should not be "repugnant or contrary to the Lawes of this our Realme of England," clearly indicating that the inhabitants could not under the limitations of their charter deny or invalidate laws passed by Parliament. [27] Moreover, had not the General Court of the colony as late as 1757 stated that "The authority of all acts of parliament which concern the colonies, and extend to them, is ever acknowledged in all the courts of law, and made the rule of all judicial proceedings. . . . There is not a member of the general court, and we know no inhabitant within the bounds of the government, that ever questioned this authority"? [28] Was not the Otis pronouncement therefore a revolutionary one? And was there not an

---

[26] See 12 Chas. II, c. 19; 13 and 14 Chas. II, c. 11; 9 Anne, c. 6; 3 George 1, c. 7.

[27] For the charter of 1691 of Massachusetts Bay see "Acts and Resolves . . . of the Province of Massachusetts Bay . . . (21 vols., Boston, 1869–1922), I, 1–20.

[28] See Thomas Hutchinson: *History of . . . Massachusetts Bay* (ed. L. S. Mayo, 3 vols., Cambridge, Mass., 1936), II, 47–8.

implication that the people of Massachusetts Bay were now ready to consider themselves exempt from the binding power of any parliamentary legislation that they might dislike? For what other meaning can be attached to the action taken the following year when, on June 14, 1762, the House of Representatives—still agitated over the larger issue involved in the use of writs of assistance—sent instructions to its London agent Jasper Mauduit which openly declared the members' belief that the natural rights of colonials were identical to those of all other British subjects and of all mankind? In these instructions the Representatives based their declaration on the principle that the liberty of men in society consisted in being free of all legislative authority but that established by common consent and the further conviction that to give up such liberty meant to become slaves.[29] Did they not imply by these instructions that both the King and Parliament had long bound colonials without their consent, although to do so was in violation of the laws of nature which alone could bind them?[30]

Again, what import to the ultimate fate of the Old British Empire emerged after the peace settlement from Patrick Henry's action in open court in 1763, when he defended the Virginia Twopenny Act of 1758 as a good law, and accused the King of violating Virginia's rights and acting as a tyrant for having disallowed the act in his Privy Council?[31] Although Henry was charged at the trial with speaking treason, his denunciation of the action of the King in Council only served to carry him to a seat in the House of Burgesses and a position of leadership in the province. Yet before this time no

---

[29] For the influence of Otis on the instructions of the House of Representatives to Mauduit of June 14, 1762, see in this series Volume X, 130–1; see also the author's "Aspects of the Beginning of the American Revolution in Massachusetts Bay, 1760–1762," in American Antiquarian Society *Proceedings*, LXVII, 11–32.

[30] In this connection the student should consult C. F. Mullett: *Fundamental Law and the American Revolution, 1760–1776* (New York, 1933), which gives an account of the writers who had earlier stressed the idea of a fundamental law and indicates the broad scope of its application from the point of view of colonials; see also J. W. Gough: *Fundamental Law in English Constitutional History* (Oxford, 1955), particularly Chap. 11, "The Eighteenth Century" and Chap. 12, "The Last of Fundamental Law"; E. S. Corwin: "The 'Higher Law' Background of American Constitutional Law," *Harvard Law Review*, XLII, 365; and R. B. Morris: *Studies in the History of American Law* . . . (Philadelphia, 1859), Chap. 1. For the history of the law of nature see Sir Frederick Pollock: *Essays in the Law* (London, 1922); see also Margaret MacDonald: "Natural Rights" in *Philosophy, Politics and Society* (ed. Peter Laslett, Oxford, 1950), pp. 35–55.

[31] For a discussion of the Twopenny Acts, the "Parson's Cause," and Patrick Henry's denunciation of the King on November 5, 1763, see in this series Volume X, 145–57.

one in Virginia—so far as the author of this series is aware—had publicly called into question the authority of the King in Council to disallow colonial laws. In fact, of the acts passed in Virginia between 1663 and 1748, seventeen had been disallowed and eight repealed by the Privy Council without its right to do so being challenged or denounced; furthermore, when ten of the Virginia statutes had been disallowed in 1751, following their codification in 1749, there had been no denial of the right or competence of the King in Council so to act.[32]

Thus by the end of the Great War for the Empire, the constitutional connection that had so long been maintained between Great Britain and the colonies was being challenged in its very fundamentals. In Massachusetts Bay, the leading northern colony, the power of Parliament to bind the province by statute had been challenged by James Otis; while in the leading southern colony of Virginia, the authority of the King in Council to nullify a law of the province had been denied by Patrick Henry; in both cases the men who had publicly denied that the government of Great Britain was free to act as it did, had become popular leaders in their communities. It would however take time for such revolutionary doctrines to gain general acceptance. Nevertheless, the education of Americans in constitutional theory proceeded, and progress was especially visible in their postulations of the very limited powers possessed by the government of Great Britain over the colonies. How is this to be explained?

According to Thomas Hutchinson—writing in 1773 as a devoted Loyalist—the rise of American colonial resistance to the authority of the government stemmed directly not from any real oppression by the mother country, but from the destruction of French power on the North American continent.[33] In fact, had the French succeeded in their ambitious plan of firmly enclosing the British in the narrow area east of the Appalachians, is it not apparent that the hostility of the colonials in the 1760's and 1770's would have been directed against the French rather than against the King and Parliament of the mother country? But the war ended otherwise, and a new day dawned for Americans, one with amazing possibilities. In his pamphlet published in 1774 entitled *The True Interest of Great-Britain*

---

[32] See *ibid.*, Volume II, 26–8.
[33] Hutchinson to Dartmouth, December 14, 1773, Massachusetts Archives, 27:286–8; see also L. H. Gipson: *The Coming of the Revolution* (New York & London, 1954), p. 215.

set forth in Regard to the Colonies; and the Only Means of Living in Peace and Harmony with them, Dean Josiah Tucker argued with great force the wisdom of granting independence to the Thirteen Colonies. His reasons for advocating such a step were that it was not the incidents resulting from the Stamp Act or other legislation passed by Parliament that set the colonies on the road to independence, but that "from the Moment in which Canada came into the Possession of the English, an End was put to the Sovereignty of the Mother Country over the Colonies." No longer in fear of a foreign enemy, "it was no wonder they should openly renounce an Authority which they never thoroughly approved of, and which they now found to be no longer necessary for their own Defence."

It seems clear that when politically minded colonials had become convinced that Americans must no longer be subservient to the domination of a Parliament in which they were not and could not be properly represented—and which, they had become persuaded whether rightly or wrongly, did not have their interests at heart— they gave increasing attention to such fundamental matters as the rights of Englishmen under the common law, human rights derived from natural law, and the relation of the individual to government. In so doing they studied the writings of the classical period of Rome; they searched the literature of the seventeenth century, especially that which had its sources in the great English Rebellion and the English Commonwealth period; and they drew abundantly on the writings from the first part of the eighteenth century that reflected the revolutionary traditions of that earlier period.[34] Thus armed, colonial leaders seized their pens. The ideas they expressed were widely disseminated from the pulpit and other public rostrums and especially by the American press in innumerable letters to the

---

[34] In this connection see, among other pertinent studies, Bernard Bailyn: "Political Experience and Enlightenment Ideas in Eighteenth-Century America," *American Historical Review,* LXVII, 339–51; Caroline Robbins: *The Eighteenth Century Commonwealthman: Studies in the Transmission, Development and Circumstance of English Liberal Thought from the Restoration of Charles II Until the War with the Thirteen Colonies* (Cambridge, Mass., 1959); H. T. Colbourn: "Thomas Jefferson's Use of the Past," *William and Mary Quarterly,* 3rd ser., XV, 56–70, and by the same author, "John Dickinson, Historical Revolutionary," *Pennsylvania Magazine of History and Biography,* LXXXIII, 271–92, and especially his recently published book *The Lamp of Experience: Whig History and the Intellectual Origins of the American Revolution* (Chapel Hill, N.C., 1965); Max Savelle: *Seeds of Liberty. The Genesis of the American Mind* (New York, 1948); and Clinton Rossiter: *Seedtime of the Republic. The Origin of the American Tradition of Political Liberty* (New York, 1953).

editors of the forty-three colonial newspapers (published for brief
or extended periods between 1763 and 1775), as well as in broad-
sides, pamphlets, and books. Some of the writings were mere emotional outpourings, but others of a much higher order were addressed to the intellect and sought to rationalize the rights that all
mankind should demand of any government.[35] Taken together these
expressions of intense opposition to the policies of the mother country by their very volume could have had only one effect—the im-
planting in the minds of Americans of a sense of urgency for the
establishment of a new political order. As Professor Bernard Bailyn
has so well expressed it:

> "On such fundamental issues—representation and consent, the na-
> ture of constitutions and of rights, the meaning of sovereignty—and
> in such basic ways, did the colonists probe and alter their inherit-
> ance of thought concerning liberty and its preservation. To conceive
> of legislative assemblies as mirrors of society and their voices as
> mechanically exact expressions of the people; to assume, and act
> upon the assumption, that human rights exist above the law and stand
> as the measure of the law's validity; to understand constitutions to be
> ideal designs of government, and fixed, limiting definitions of its
> permissible sphere of action; and to consider the possibility that
> absolute sovereignty in government need not be the monopoly of
> a single all-engrossing agency but (*imperium in imperio*) the shared
> possession of several agencies each limited by the boundaries of the
> others but all-powerful within its own—to think in these ways, as
> Americans were doing before Independence, was to reconceive the
> fundamentals of government and of society's relation to govern-
> ment." [36]

What proportion of the American people had firmly adopted
revolutionary views before 1775 is difficult if not impossible to determine. Despite the incessant attacks on Parliament and the King in
the British and the colonial press, as well as from the American
pulpit and other public platforms, all colonials were not of one
mind. In fact it is a matter of speculation whether, before the
outbreak of the War for American Independence, there was ever a
majority of one mind. For what has been true of most revolutionary
movements would seem to have been equally true of the dissemina-

---

[35] See in particular Chap. 2 of the notable Introduction to Vol. I of Bernard
Bailyn's *Pamphlets of the American Revolution, 1750–1776* (Cambridge, Mass.,
1965).

[36] *Ibid.*, I, 139.

tion of revolutionary doctrine in America. That is, a comparatively small number of men with dynamic qualities of leadership—and using persuasive pens and voices to appeal to the public in the moments of crisis—enunciated revolutionary political theories and principles, many of which were derived from the past. What is also clear is that a hard core of dedicated men in the various colonies firmly supported the revolutionary views enunciated by these leaders and thus gave to the movement a degree of solidarity and validity never possessed by the Loyalists and one that finally swept along the great body of heretofore uncommitted people.[37]

But to think that relations with Great Britain occupied all the attention of British colonials in North America during the years between 1760 and 1775 would be a gross distortion of the history of the period. The bitter rivalries over lands and boundaries that gradually developed between a number of the colonies were doubtless of much greater importance to tens of thousands of Americans than were the issues between the colonies and the mother country. Nor must the equally bitter sectional conflicts among the inhabitants within such colonies as the Carolinas be overlooked—with the arraying of the underprivileged new settlers of the backcountry against the highly privileged old settlers of the coastal plain. Furthermore, thousands of frontiersmen were pressing into the trans-Appalachian region to occupy lands made available for settlement as a result of a series of Indian land cessions. The chief concern of these pioneers before 1775 was surely not American rights but the acquisition of fertile acres, the building of homes for their families, and security from the Indians. Additionally, there were those who sought western lands in extension of their activities in the Indian trade or chiefly for speculation.[38] In short, it was not on the frontier that the important centres of agitation against the policies of Great Britain were to be found but, logically enough, in the wealthy, leading seaport towns.

When we speak of the revolutionary views of the colonials, this should be clarified in the light of their constitutional connection with the mother country referred to earlier in this Summary. The eighteenth-century British Empire, from the point of view of the government of Great Britain, did possess a constitution—a rather

---

[37] In this connection see M. C. Tyler: *The Literary History of the American Revolution, 1763–1783* (New York & London, 1897), pp. 298–304.

[38] See especially Volume XI of this series, Chaps. 10–15.

complex one, just as was and still is that of Great Britain itself. Nor was it to be found in a single document similar to the constitution adopted by the Thirteen American States in 1787.

Fundamentally, the eighteenth-century imperial constitution was based upon the authority of Parliament as expressed in the Statute of 1696 (7 and 8 William III, c. 7), which laid down the principle of parliamentary supremacy—that is, the right of Parliament to pass laws binding throughout the Empire.[39] In addition, the constitution found expression in the authority exercised by the Privy Council (acting after 1689 as an agency of the King in Parliament) by which it could issue letters patent creating a colony and could subsequently review and validate or veto the laws passed by the colony. Moreover, Parliament itself by formal statute in 1774 provided a government for the Province of Quebec. With respect to the royal colonies, the commissions issued to their Governors under the Great Seal, together with the less formal Governor's instructions and the laws passed by their Assemblies, when once affirmed by the Privy Council, were aspects of the constitution of the Empire. So were charters of the surviving corporate colonies, which in the case of Connecticut and Rhode Island gave them very broad powers of self-government. However, when the Privy Council, acting in its judicial capacity, took a decision on the constitutionality of any colonial issue brought before it, this was held to be decisive and final. This made the Privy Council the final court of appeal as well as the highest interpretive authority of the constitution of the Empire—except for the power of Parliament to clarify or alter any decision that the Council might render.[40]

It should be re-emphasized that the Privy Council, in exercising

---

[39] For a discussion of the elaborate machinery of imperial administration and sovereign control under the constitution, see in this series Volume I, Revised, pp. 13–17, Volume IX, Chap. I, and Volume X, 31 and 410–11. The meaning of the expression "British Empire" and the powers exercised by the "imperial Parliament" (as well as the proper limitations of these powers) in the eighteenth century are dealt with in that excellent book *Empire* (Cambridge, 1961, & New York, 1965), by the late Professor Richard Koebner. The views of Edmund Burke, Benjamin Franklin, Governor Thomas Pownall, Governor Francis Bernard, and Dean Josiah Tucker on the Empire are set forth with skill and understanding.

[40] In this connection see C. M. Andrews: *Connecticut and the British Government* (New Haven, 1915), and by the same author, "The Connecticut Intestacy Law," *Yale Review*, III, 261–92. In the sense that the Privy Council interpreted the imperial constitution whenever an issue arose, its authority can be compared to that exercised by the Supreme Court of the United States under somewhat similar circumstances today.

its weighty authority over the form and functioning of colonial government, customarily reached its major decisions in committee, and on almost all matters relating to the colonies requested the views of the Lords Commissioners for Trade and Plantations (the Board of Trade). This body, in turn, usually sought legal advice from its own counsel and often from the chief law officers of the Crown. It also sought to gather all necessary information, and to this end was free to summon witnesses and to call before it the agent or agents of any of the colonies that might be affected by the Privy Council decision so that the colonial point of view might be fairly and fully presented.[41]

One thing that was especially stressed in connection with the decisions rendered by the Privy Council was whether or not colonials were acting within their constitutional rights. Therefore when a colonial asserted, as Otis did, that an act of Parliament was unconstitutional, this assertion had no more *legal* implication in the eyes of the government than would a similar statement by an Englishman concerning some statute to which he was opposed. So long as a subject recognized his obligation to obey the law in question until it was changed, he was free to protest that it was unconstitutional. Yet to deny the power of Parliament to pass a law and therefore refuse to obey the statute, or to deny the authority of the Privy Council to invalidate a colonial law and thereby refuse to recognize the binding power of an order in council was, in the eyes of the law officers of the Crown, revolutionary. In the words of Blackstone (quoting with approval Coke's *Institutes*): "The power and jurisdiction of parliament . . . is so transcendant and absolute, that it cannot be confined, either for causes or persons, within any bounds." [42] William Pitt, Earl of Chatham, and Charles Pratt, Baron Camden, might in the House of Lords deny the right of Parliament to tax the colonies—claiming it had never before levied internal taxes upon

---

[41] For the important role of the London agents in the middle of the eighteenth century see in this series Volume I, Revised, pp. 10–13; for the most recent studies on this subject—which show how the influence of the colonial agents declined, especially after 1767, with the growth of the revolutionary movement—see Michael G. Kammen: "The Colonial Agents, English Politics, and the American Revolution," *William and Mary Quarterly*, 3rd ser., XXII, 244–63 (this was the subject of his doctoral dissertation at Harvard in 1964), and Jack M. Sosin: *Agents and Merchants: British Colonial Policy and the Origins of the American Revolution, 1763–1775* (Lincoln, Nebr., 1965).

[42] William Blackstone: *Commentaries on the Laws of England* (4th edn., 4 vols., Oxford, 1770), I, 160.

colonials—but in so doing they spoke only in their capacity as individuals.

Significantly, Parliament had finally clarified the issue of its constitutional authority by passing the Declaratory Act of 1766 (6 Geo III, c. 12), reaffirming the principles embodied in the statute of fifty years earlier and re-stating that it had "full Power and Authority to make Laws and Statutes of sufficient Force and Validity to bind the Colonies and People of *America,* Subjects of the Crown of *Great Britain,* in all *Cases* whatsoever." Thus for colonials to deny that they were bound by this statute and to act in line with such a denial was indeed revolutionary. Here was the *real* American Revolution.[43] John Adams, the lawyer, must have held this thought when, referring to the events after 1775, he stated that that war was not "a revolutionary war, for the revolution was complete, in the minds of the people . . . before . . . the skirmishes of Concord and Lexington. . . ." [44] For one must bear in mind that by the autumn of 1774 the colonial leaders—by seeking in the Continental Congress to place restrictions on the use of the sovereign power of the Parliament of Great Britain over the Empire—had repudiated the most fundamental principle of the imperial constitution.

When Parliament laid down the principle of parliamentary supremacy in formulating the comprehensive Statute of 1696,[45] no colonial Assembly—as far as can be determined from available records—denied the binding power of this great constitutional principle, much as individuals might subsequently protest against it or act in violation of some of its provisions or of other statutes. In view of the position taken by colonials in the 1760's and 1770's that Parliament had no right to seek a revenue from America, it is germane to examine the basis for this statute. It carried the title "An Act for preventing Frauds, and regulating Abuses in the Plantation Trade." On the face of it, it was but a measure designed to leave no loop-

---

[43] For this author's use of the term "revolution," and a note on recent literature concerning the American Revolution, see the final pages of this Summary.

[44] Adams to Dr. T. Morse, January 1, 1816, *Works of John Adams* (ed. C. F. Adams, 10 vols., Boston, 1850–6), X, 197. In the above connection see R. G. Adams: *Political Ideas of the American Revolution* (ed. Merrill Jensen, 3rd edn., New York, 1958), Chap. 6, "Some Things Which Parliament Could Not Do." In this chapter Adams stresses the theoretical limitations of the power of Parliament as expressed by Englishmen and Americans in both the seventeenth and eighteenth centuries and the difference in viewpoint of Englishmen and Americans respecting an "unconstitutional" act passed by Parliament.

[45] For the background to the statute of 1696, 7 and 8 Wm. III, c. 22, and analysis of the law, see C. M. Andrews: *The Colonial Period of American History,* IV, Chap. 6.

holes in a system for providing England with additional funds in view of the desperate financial situation facing the government in the midst of a war.[46] In the eyes of those immediately responsible for it, therefore, the statute was designed primarily as a revenue measure to bolster an all but empty Treasury; however it set forth clearly the principle of parliamentary supremacy.

The law seems to have had its inception as the result of the complaint of Bristol and Liverpool merchants that colonial ships were going directly to Scotland and Ireland "to the great prejudice of their Majesties Revenue." [47] The original bill, drawn up by the Commissioners of Customs and also presented to the House of Commons by one of them, was an extremely comprehensive measure. Its supervision, logically enough in view of its purpose, was placed in the hands of the Lord High Treasurer, the Commissioners of the Treasury, and the Commissioners of the Customs, who were empowered to appoint customs officers in the plantations and islands to see that its many provisions were enforced.[48]

To John Adams, writing in 1774, the most comprehensive trade act of all (the Statute of 1696) was not chiefly *regulatory* but was essentially a *taxation* measure. Here are his words:

> "Great Britain has confined all our trade to herself. We are willing she should, so far as it can be for the good of the empire. But we say, that we ought to be allowed as credit, in the account of public burdens and expenses, so much, paid in taxes, as we are obliged to sell our commodities to her cheaper than we can get for them at foreign markets. The difference is really a tax upon us for the good of the empire. We are obliged to take from Great Britain commodities that we could purchase cheaper elsewhere. This difference is a tax upon us for the good of the empire. We submit to this cheerfully; but insist that we ought to have credit for it in the account of the expenses of the empire, because it is really a tax upon us." [49]

Daniel Dulany of Maryland in 1765 pointed out even more fully the degree to which the acts of trade served as devices for taxing the

---

[46] Richard Lodge: *The Political History of England from the Restoration to the Death of William III* (London, 1910), p. 400.

[47] *Journals of the House of Commons*, XI, 188, 195; See also L. A. Harper: *The English Navigation Laws* (New York, 1939), pp. 60–1.

[48] *Ibid.* It may be pointed out that the office of Lord High Treasurer was not abolished until early in the reign of George I.

[49] "Novanglus. . . ," *Works of John Adams . . . , op. cit.,* IV, 46.

colonies. In his *Considerations on the Propriety of Imposing Taxes in the British Colonies* he stated that "A Law which restrains one Part of the Society, from exporting its Products to the most profitable Market, in favour of another; or obliges it to import the Manufactures of one Country that are dear, instead of another that are cheap, is essentially a Tax." In an Appendix to this treatise he also set forth at length the extent to which Virginia and Maryland had contributed to the royal Treasury by this form of taxation.

It would appear that most colonials in 1765 made a distinction, whether rightly or wrongly, between acts regulating trade that would bring a revenue into the British Treasury and those providing for direct taxation. In line with this, the pressure brought to bear upon the Ministry and Parliament resulted in the repeal of the Stamp Act. When the Townshend Revenue Act was passed in 1767 in the hope that Americans would hardly make an issue over import duties of a kind that had long been levied, the cry again went up that Americans were being taxed by a body in which they were not represented and that the attempt to do so was tyranny. To John Dickinson, author of the famous letters by "A Farmer in Pennsylvania," not only was this legislation unconstitutional; it was likewise destructive of the liberties heretofore enjoyed by the colonies. Yet were this position to be generally accepted by Americans, how long would the great body of Trade and Navigation Acts survive—granted the contentions of both Adams and Dulany that they were primarily designed for drawing a revenue from the colonies? Was this not also taxation without representation?

When repealing the import duties on all items in the Townshend Act except the duty on tea, but leaving intact the enactment clause giving the purpose of the act, Parliament in 1770 took a firm stand on the *principle* of its supremacy within the Empire as embodied not only in the Statute of 1696 but also in the Declaratory Act of 1766. Could this half-way measure satisfy colonials after they had forced Parliament to retreat twice within a period of four years? Or would they now begin to share the thinking of Benjamin Franklin, who by 1771 had arrived at the following conclusion: "My opinion has long been that Parliament had originally no Right to bind us by any kind of Law whatever without our Consent." [50] Franklin's position was, in other words, that the whole body of English or British

---

[50] Franklin to Thomas Cushing, June 10, 1771, *Writings of Benjamin Franklin* (ed. A. H. Smyth, 10 vols., New York, 1905–7), V, 324.

legislation relating to the colonies was illegal and a violation of colonial rights; for, by these laws that bound them without their consent, colonials were being treated as unequal to Englishmen at home, a situation that must no longer be tolerated. His revolutionary prescription for remedying this position of inferiority was "never [to] adopt or acknowledge an Act of Parliament [as binding on a colony] but by a formal Law of our own. . . ." [51] By this method a statute would *ipso facto* be null and void in any colony refusing to pass the legislation necessary to implement it, and the colonial Assembly would thus indicate its equality with Parliament. This was indeed a revolutionary proposal.

It is of interest to note that the problem of a more equitable adjustment of relations between Great Britain and the colonies had been the subject of correspondence between Benjamin Franklin and Governor William Shirley as early as 1754. At that time Franklin took the position that the colonies might be well satisfied if representation were given to them in Parliament, provided that all the old trade and navigation and other restraining acts were repealed and that British subjects on both sides of the ocean were put on the same footing. A representation in Parliament, he argued, would be vastly more agreeable to colonials than the system of royal instructions, and more in harmony with the spirit of the English constitution and the principles of English liberty. As a result of placing colonials on a basis of equality with the people of Great Britain, laws subsequently passed by Parliament that might appear to bear heavily upon the colonies would, he felt, be more cheerfully submitted to, since they would then have been enacted by a truly representative Parliament for "the best interest of the whole." [52] Probably no one came closer to the heart of the problem or to a solution that might conceivably have guaranteed the future stability of the British Empire than Benjamin Franklin. But to have urged that the colonies be granted representation in Parliament and that all laws which had bound the colonies since 1660 be repealed—in order to devise a new colonial system more in harmony with the reasonable wishes of the colonists or in a realistic recognition of their maturity and importance as colonials

---

[51] *Ibid.*, V, 324–5.

[52] See Franklin to Shirley, Boston, December 22, 1754, *Franklin Papers* (ed. L. W. Labaree *et al.*, 8 vols.+, New Haven, 1959–65+), V, 449. This letter and others between Franklin and Shirley were the aftermath of the Albany Plan of Union proposed at the Congress held in July of that year. For a discussion of "The Fate of the Plan of Union" see in this series Volume V, Chap. 5.

entitled to the full rights of Englishmen—was a responsibility that no British statesman in the 1760's or 1770's would have accepted. Nor was there any demand for representation in Parliament on the part of colonials. In 1765 the very idea of a representation was openly renounced by the Stamp Act Congress.

Moreover, Franklin's own thinking over the years underwent a drastic change. In 1754 he had regarded the sovereignty of Parliament over the Empire as so firmly rooted that he had proposed that when the Albany Plan of Union should be approved by the colonial commissioners, it should be sent to London to be established by an act of Parliament. He was thus patently ready to disregard the claims of colonials to the right to consultation through their Assemblies in a matter of such vital constitutional importance to them. Moveover in 1755, in the midst of the hostilities, as a measure to bolster the war effort against the French entrenched in what is now western Pennsylvania, he is said to have advocated that "a stamp duty [be] enacted at home for all the colonies." [53] Yet by 1766 his opinion as to the nature of the Empire had become so fundamentally altered that he no longer admitted that the sovereignty of Parliament extended outside Britain; rather, he now saw the colonies as "different States, Subject to the King." [54] Two years later, when writing to his son William, then Governor of New Jersey, he further clarified this new position by stating that the arguments for the view that Parliament had the power to make *no laws* for the colonies far outweighed those that held it had the power to make *all laws* for them.[55] Finally, he came to hold the revolutionary opinion put forth in 1771.

Franklin's changing views on the constitution of the Empire warrant emphasis because of his singularly influential position at this period. For example, as testimony of the degree of trust placed in his statesmanship by his fellow colonials, between the years 1757 and 1775 he was called to act as colonial agent in London not only for the Assembly of Pennsylvania but also for the Assemblies of New Jersey, Georgia, and Massachusetts Bay. If he was a revolutionist at heart—as indeed he was from 1766 onward, which he made abundantly clear in his writings in the press and in private correspond-

---

[53] See *ibid.*, pp. 159–60, and Volume X, 411–12.

[54] See V. W. Crane: "Benjamin Franklin and the Stamp Act," Colonial Society of Massachusetts *Transactions*, XXXII, 71–3.

[55] *Writings of Benjamin Franklin* (Smyth), V, 115.

ence with colonial leaders—so too were those who sought his services and agreed with his views. But one must not be alarmed at the idea that leading colonials became revolutionists. There is not a leading state in the world today that did not secure its present form of government by revolution and revolutionary doctrines. We are all, including the British, the descendants of revolutionists.

The traditional interpretation of the cause of the American Revolution is that it resulted from the assumption by the government of Great Britain that it held the right to raise a revenue in America by some form of taxation, and from its attempt to exercise this right without gaining the prior consent of the governed. But the question must be raised: Was this really the fundamental reason? Or was the Revolution caused by the divergence, already manifest in the 1760's, between the form and spirit of political institutions in England and those in the colonies and the way in which they functioned in both places? But, again, was this the crucial issue in view of the fact that sharp divergencies had existed within the Empire throughout its history? [56] Did not the Revolution more logically flow out of the situation created with the termination of the Great War for the Empire? Was not the victory over the French in North America (as already stressed) too complete and the terms of the treaty of peace too drastic for the British Empire to be maintained without a profound alteration in the relations of the parts to the whole? Had not the North American British colonies as the result of the war years become so powerful and dynamic that they could not much longer be held within the folds of the Empire under such a constitution as had bound them before 1763? Was not Franklin in 1771 reflecting a point of view that but three years later was to be voiced by many leading colonials? What other meaning can be attached to the statement of Thomas Jefferson in his *Summary View of the Rights of British America,* published in 1774, that all attempts to regulate the affairs of the colonies by Parliament were nothing less than acts "of arbitrary power . . . over these States"?

Again, what was really implied when, in its series of resolves indicting the Parliament and Crown of Great Britain for many

---

[56] On this point, among recent studies the following should be consulted: S. H. Beer: "The Representation of Interests in British Government: Historical Background," *American Political Science Review,* LI, 613–50; Louis Hartz: *The Liberal Tradition in America: An Interpretation of American Political Thought since the Revolution* (New York, 1955); and R. B. Ripley: "[John] Adams, [Edmund] Burke, and Eighteenth-Century Conservatism," *Political Science Quarterly,* LXXX, 216–35.

abuses of power, the Continental Congress on October 14, 1774, declared ". . . we cheerfully consent to the operation of such Acts of the British Parliament, as are, *bona fide,* restrained to the regulation of our external commerce, for the purpose of securing the commercial advantages of the whole Empire to the mother country, . . . excluding every idea of taxation, internal or external, for raising a revenue on the subjects in America without their consent"?[57] Was the Congress ever in a position to determine which among the acts of trade did or did not bring a revenue into the British Treasury since they all had this as an ultimate objective? Was the Congress, moreover, at any time in a position to enforce an agreement among colonials to permit Great Britain to regulate the commerce of the Empire? If in the course of the Great War for the Empire many colonial merchants—even in the face of regulations or the fact that the Americans themselves had a most vital stake in the outcome of the war—had traded with the enemy, how could the Congress in time of peace possibly guarantee that trade regulations, even if conceivably devoid of all revenue features, would be any better enforced? In view of the repeated emphasis in the resolutions of the Congress on the *rights* of Englishmen possessed by Americans, can these resolves be considered anything other than a declaration of political equality and self-government? For the concession made by American leaders that Parliament might still regulate colonial trade was meaningless so long as they denied Parliament's right to utilize the proper instrumentalities to enforce such regulations.[58]

At this point a word of caution is needed. The reader should not be misled by some of the pronouncements of colonials in their perfectly legitimate striving for political equality after 1763. For when they branded the conduct of the government of Great Britain as tyrannical, this accusation came, it must be remembered, from the

---

[57] *Journals of the Continental Congress,* I, 63–74.

[58] D. S. Lovejoy (in his important article "Rights Imply Equality: The Case Against Admiralty Jurisdiction in America, 1764–1776," *William and Mary Quarterly,* 3rd ser., XVI, 459–84) when dealing with the basis of American opposition to the policies of Great Britain from 1764 onward writes (p. 483): "A government in London which by Parliamentary statute relegated Americans to an inferior position within the empire was not long to be tolerated." Although this inequality had existed long before the 1760's, when the attention of colonials was drawn to it (according to Professor Lovejoy), it "became a compelling force driving them toward revolution in the years following" (p. 459). He also points out that to John Adams the "mere denial of Parliament's power to tax Americans was a feeble defense of American rights; for it was the [use of the] legislative authority of Parliament over America which was doing the damage, . . ." (p. 483).

lips and pens of people who had become the freest, most enlightened, most prosperous, and most politically experienced of all colonials in the world of the eighteenth century. The very fact that such
statements could be freely printed and circulated was surely not
evidence of British tyranny but rather of British indulgence and the
flowering within the Empire of ideas of English liberty. In all heated
controversy men are apt to overstate their case. This was true of the
colonials between 1760 and 1775. In reality the worst charge that
could be brought against the government of the mother country
from 1760 onward was that—with the best of intentions but very
unwisely, as soon became apparent—it attempted at the beginning
of that year to enforce strictly the old colonial trade regulations and
in 1764 and 1765 sought to secure a revenue by direct means, all for
the partial support of the army scattered along the frontiers for the
defence of North America. In the eyes of the British administration,
the steps seemed only fair and reasonable in view of the burden of
taxation carried by Great Britain. Then in 1767—in the face of the
mounting difficulties that confronted the servants of the Crown in
some of the colonies and with the government now fearful of a
movement that could carry these colonies out of the Empire if
unchecked—came a repetition of the unwise step of attempting to
secure from colonials by import duties a revenue that by paying the
salaries of certain royal officials would place them in a position to
perform their duties while acting independently of the Assemblies.

That the colonials became alarmed and again went into spirited
opposition to the legislation of 1767 is understandable. What else
could be expected from a people so favourably circumstanced and
with such traditions of freedom? Suspicion of the intentions of the
colonies entertained by the government of the mother country and
suspicions of the intentions of the mother country entertained by
leaders in the colonies—spurred on by the press and public orations—gradually mounted to such a point that heated emotion on
both sides swept away any possibility of a cool, objective attempt to
find a peaceful solution to the major problems of political inequality
within the Empire. Under such circumstances both parties resorted
to an appeal to force, with Great Britain contending for the continuing integrity of the Empire and the Thirteen rebellious Colonies
contending for the full measure of the rights of Englishmen. With
the sharpening of the armed conflict and the failure of all attempts
at reconciliation, the American Declaration of Independence logi-

cally followed. Such was the aftermath of the Great War for the Empire!

The American Revolution did not of course dissolve the British Empire.[59] Out of thirty-two colonies—including those on the North American mainland and the island colonies in the North Atlantic and the Caribbean—only thirteen participated in the revolt. How is this fact to be explained? Were they not all bound by the same laws and regulations? Had they not all inherited the same traditions of freedom? Did not all of them have to submit to the same restrictions on their freedom of action?

At least four factors of imperial control and colonial dependency—over and beyond the ties of loyalty to the Crown—must have been weighed heavily in the balance to determine the attitude of, and the decisions made by, the inhabitants of each of the thirty-two colonies. They were: (1) the naval and military strength of government forces in the area of the colony in question, (2) the relative importance of the economic ties that bound it to the mother country, (3) the degree of dependence of its local government upon direct financial support provided by funds appropriated by Parliament, and (4) the extent to which its inhabitants felt they were handicapped by parliamentary legislation. First in importance was certainly the fact that the Royal Navy gave Britain the sea power to hold under firm control every one of the colonies that were beyond the chief centres of the storm. Similarly, adequate royal land forces to control local disturbances were stationed in Newfoundland and the Provinces of Nova Scotia, Quebec, East and West Florida, Jamaica, Antigua, and Grenada. That the presence of British naval and military power in these places was a deterrent to any thought of defying the government of the mother country is evident from the example of Nova Scotia. For even this mainland colony, with its thousands of transplanted New Englanders closely tied by habit of thought and general attitude toward public events to the colonies from which they had come, made no serious effort to revolt in 1775. As to the second factor—the degree to which the prosperity of a colony was dependent on economic ties with the mother country—this, together with British sea power, insured the continued connection of all the British Sugar Islands with the mother country. For the third factor, that of direct financial aid, the governments of New-

---

[59] V. T. Harlow: *The Founding of the Second British Empire, 1763–1793* (London, 1952), Chap. 1, "The Old Empire and the New."

foundland, the Bermudas, the Bahamas, and the mainland colonies of Nova Scotia and the two Floridas were largely, if not totally, supported by funds appropriated by Parliament. Without such support, as the inhabitants of these colonies well knew, they would have faced political and economic chaos. And for the fourth—the extent to which parliamentary regulations seemed adversely to affect the people of the individual colony—the case of West Florida is an excellent example. For, although this colony felt that prosperity was denied it because of parliamentary restrictions against establishing trade relations with the nearby Spanish possessions, there was little it could do about this.

Turning to the Thirteen North American Colonies, where the weight of the Trade and Navigation Acts undoubtedly bore down most heavily, resistance to this regulatory system gradually increased there during the period from 1760 to 1775, powerfully reinforced by the passing of the Sugar Act of 1764, the Stamp Act of 1765, and the Townshend legislation of 1767. The growth in the spirit of alienation from the mother country became especially pronounced at such seaports as Boston, Newport, Providence, New York, Philadelphia, and Charleston, and among the tobacco planters of Virginia. None of the conditions acting as restraints on the loyal colonies was present in the thirteen rebellious ones, with the exception of Georgia, but it too, with a good deal of reluctance and soul-searching, was finally pulled into the revolutionary orbit.

In the case of the Province of Quebec a most serious effort was made by the Continental Congress to induce the French-Canadian Roman Catholics to join the rebellion against Great Britain. But their whole outlook on life was alien to that of the rebellious British Protestant colonials. Moreover, when the King of France had turned his back upon them in 1763, despite their exertions on his behalf, and had given them over to the government of Great Britain, they became disillusioned. As a result most of them adopted a firm neutral attitude toward political events—just as did those Acadians who were permitted to re-establish themselves in Nova Scotia. Furthermore, the subsequent efforts of the American colonials to point out the evils of the Quebec Act to the French Canadians seem to have had the reverse effect of that intended. For it was not difficult for the Catholic population to see a greater threat in the American hatred of "popery" than in the realistic attempts of the British government to provide a workable system of toleration for their religious beliefs.

As for the Kingdom of Ireland, it may be surprising to some readers to realize that with the outbreak of the War for American Independence there was no corresponding uprising among the Irish either of the disfranchised, impoverished, and exploited native Roman Catholics or of the descendants of the tens of thousands of transplanted Presbyterians Scots concentrated in the Ulster section of northern Ireland. This calls for an explanation.

Although the disarmed native Irish seem to have shown little active interest in the American crisis, the Ulster Scots, with large numbers of compatriots dwelling in America (often referred to as the Scotch-Irish), were more open in expressing their sympathy for the colonials. But they could not move. The arm of the Royal Navy stationed in home waters was too powerful a deterrent, as was the well-equipped standing army deployed within the kingdom. Further, the people of Ulster undoubtedly looked upon the troops with mixed feelings; for it must be kept in mind that these transplanted Scots were occupying lands that had once been the property of Irishmen displaced in the preceding century—something the Irish did not forget. The military force thus not only protected the political and religious establishments of the kingdom, but also guaranteed the security of the hold the Ulster Scots had established on the lands of northern Ireland. Despite these factors, the impact of the American Revolution in Ireland caused an agitation in that country which later bore fruit. Due to the leadership of such men as Henry Flood, the Earl of Charlemont, and Henry Grattan, and with the organization in 1778 of the politically oriented and powerful Irish Volunteers—summoned to repel a possible French invasion of Ireland— the severe trade restrictions on Ireland were greatly relaxed by Parliament and Poynings' Law, which had so long bound the Irish Parliament to the British Privy Council, was all but repealed.

Turning to the British situation, just as the colonials before 1775 had been involved in attempts to solve a variety of problems other than those of their relationship with the government of Great Britain, so likewise the British people, especially those in positions of public responsibility, were beset by an even greater number of pressing issues other than the ominous crisis in North American affairs that seemed to threaten the destruction of the Empire. Major concerns were: the near bankruptcy of the great East India Company and the growing anarchy in India; the rise of urban radicalism, which seemed to be striking directly at the traditional form of government of England; and the confusion of aims within the Ministry itself, fostered by the proliferation of political factions. Beyond these matters a bewildering number of other problems, diplomatic, political, economic, and social, cried out for attention. Even a glance at the pages of the sober and restrained *Journals of the House of Commons* for almost any year during the 1760's and 1770's will illustrate the extent to which the attention of the Ministry and Parliament was necessarily distracted from concentrating upon the menacing American situation. In other words, the American Revolution may quite simply be attributed to a failure of British statesmanship after 1763.

Why did the British government hesitate to take certain essential steps in time to stave off a rebellion of the Thirteen Colonies? Many reasons may be assigned for this. To begin with, it is doubtful whether anyone in Great Britain in a position of responsibility felt that it would be possible for American colonials to stage a successful uprising in the face of the Royal Navy's domination of the seas and the valor of the regular army, small as it was. Again, not one of the Ministries during the many changes of administration between 1763 and 1775, however they might differ on the matter of American taxation, could be persuaded that the colonial system was in need of a complete overhaul.[60] To them the proof that the system evolved had been beneficial, not only for Great Britain but for the colonies as well, was shown by the development within the older North American colonies by 1763 of populous and important centres of wealth, culture, and political experience. Furthermore, the system was supported by powerful private commercial interests in Great Britain as well as by public opinion there. It is recorded that even William Pitt, America's great defender, when arguing for the repeal of the Stamp Act in 1766 said that Americans must be informed that if they were not contented with this concession they would have to be taught to submit and that the whole force of Britain should be brought against the colonials if they resisted the Navigation Acts.[61] In other words, the only concession Pitt was prepared to make to the colonies at that time was that Parliament would refrain from levying internal taxes upon them.

The role played by George III in the events leading to the su-

---

[60] In the above connection see C. M. Andrews: "The American Revolution: An Interpretation," *American Historical Review*, XXXI, 219–32.

[61] See Volume X, 393, of this series.

preme crisis that faced the Empire in the 1770's should be assessed at this point. For the King was ultimately made to bear the brunt of American hostility against the British government, as witnessed in the denunciation of his conduct set forth in the Declaration of Independence.

As a constitutional monarch, George III fully accepted the doctrine that sovereignty rested not in his person but in the King in Parliament, and he acted in harmony with this concept. His attitude toward the American crisis was apparently that held by most Englishmen, so far as can be judged from available evidence. Thus early in 1774 he wrote to his chief minister that the fatal compliance in 1766 to the demands of the colonials that the Stamp Act should be repealed had encouraged the increasing pretensions of Americans to independence—which he saw as "quite subversive of the obedience which a Colony owes to its Mother Country." [62] He therefore gave hearty support to the measures formulated by the Cabinet Council and taken by Parliament on the motion of Lord North—in whom he placed his confidence—for restraining the people of Boston and Massachusetts Bay.[63] As Sir Lewis Namier has emphasized,[64] the voluminous correspondence of George III testifies to the accuracy of Horace Walpole's statement that the King "never interfered with his Ministers," but "seemed to resign himself entirely to their conduct for the time." [65] In fact, in face of the American repudiation of the validity of the Coercive Acts in 1774 and the position taken by the Continental Congress toward the limited powers of Parliament, the King's vigorous support of that body in 1775 was to him simply "fighting the battle of the legislature" and was not a contest with the

---

[62] The King to Lord North, February 4, 1774, *Correspondence of King George the Third* (ed. Sir John Fortescue, 6 vols., London, 1928), III, 29. As the late Professor Pares has pointed out, George III "was particularly concerned to resist any threat to established institutions, enforcement of law, or the general principle of 'subordination.' . . . The only great concession he ever made was the repeal of the Stamp Act . . . and he never ceased to repent it, for he believed that it had awakened [in Americans] an insatiable appetite for concessions" (*King George III and the Politicians* [Oxford, 1953], pp. 67–8).

[63] See, for example, the King to Lord North, March 21, 23, 25, April 14, 15, 22, May 4, 6, 1774, *Correspondence of King George the Third with Lord North* (ed. W. B. Donne, 2 vols., London, 1867), I, 176, 177–8, 180–1, 182–4.

[64] See the Romanes Lecture delivered at Oxford in 1952, "Monarchy and the Party System," *Personalities and Powers* (London, 1955), p. 15.

[65] See also Horace Walpole: *Memoirs of the Reign of George III* (ed. G. F. R. Barker, 4 vols., London, 1894), III, 66. For the degree to which George III placed the government in the hands of Lord North and the Cabinet Council see also Herbert Butterfield: *George III. Lord North and the People, 1779–80* (New York, 1950), Introduction, pp. 21–3.

colonies that he himself had brought on.[66] To uphold the Ministry and the majority in Parliament seeking to vindicate this body's sovereignty throughout the Empire, he encouraged the use of the so-called secret service fund to help guarantee the presence of a steady majority of members in the House of Commons that would be similarly committed to this position.[67] In so doing George III was a party to the failure of British statesmanship at this most crucial period in the life of the eighteenth-century British Empire; for under the constitution his influence upon British policy was great. But if he was blind to certain political realities, so was Burke and so was Chatham, as already noted.[68]

In concluding this series certain questions remain in the mind of this writer, the answers to which he has long pondered and continues to ponder. The most germane to the period and subject under consideration is: Was the American Revolution and its sequitur, the War for American Independence, inevitable in the light of all available facts? Or are there no inevitable historical events? Were one to

[66] The King to Lord North, September 10, 1775, *Correspondence of George III* (Fortescue), III, 256; see also Richard Pares: *King George III and the Politicians* and G. H. Guttridge: *English Whiggism and the American Revolution* (University of California *Publications in History*, Vol. XXVIII, Berkeley & Los Angeles, 1942), p. 62.

[67] In this connection the student should consult the *Parliamentary Papers of John Robinson, 1774–1784* (ed. W. T. Laprade, Royal Historical Society [London, 1922], *Camden Third Series*, XXXIII), for an illuminating account of the disbursement of the secret service money in the elections of 1774, 1780, and 1784. Professor Laprade's introduction also serves to correct some of the misconceptions about the extreme corruption characterizing the reign of George III, such as appeared in the works of Edward and Annie Gertrude Porritt: *The Unreformed House of Commons* (2 vols., Cambridge, 1903, 1909), G. O. Trevelyan: *The American Revolution* (6 vols., London, 1905–14, newly reissued in one vol., ed. R. B. Morris, New York, 1964), and of A. M. Davies: *The Influence of George III on the Development of the Constitution* (London, 1921). In support of the Laprade position see Herbert Butterfield: *George III and the Historians* (London, 1957), pp. 238–43.

[68] For an analysis of King George at the time of his accession, together with some additional insights and bibliographical notes, see Volume VIII of this series, Chap. III, "The New King. . . ." For various interpretations of the reign of George III and his relationship to government see especially Herbert Butterfield's *George III and the Historians*. With respect to Chatham, as Sir Charles Grant Robinson has pointed out (*Chatham and the British Empire* [London, 1946, New York, 1962], p. 141): "Chatham accepted the Empire as he found it in 1735; he did not see that by 1760 the structure had decayed, and that the principles on which that structure rested had lost their efficacy, and that an organic reconstruction was essential." Burke, as is well known, was a chief supporter in principle if not in practice of the Declaratory Act pushed through Parliament by the Rockingham administration. No act of Parliament was more bitterly denounced by Americans than this statute. For a valuable bibliographical aid on the reign of George III see J. J. Hecht: "The Reign of George III in recent Historiography: a Bibliographical Essay," *Bulletin of the New York Public Library*, LXX, 279–304.

assume that the second is true, is it inconceivable that, had there been no failure of British statesmanship at this point, alterations might have been made in the constitution of the Empire? Could not this have been accomplished a step at a time from 1763 onward, so that the legitimate aspirations of the colonials for much greater freedom of action might have been realized, while the people of Great Britain could have been reconciled to the hard fact that the seventeenth-century colonial system had by the 1760's become an anachronism requiring drastic reshaping?

Further, the fact that most leading colonials became revolutionaries leads one to speculate upon the environmental factors. For example, if many of those in Great Britain who strongly advised the use of force against the rebellious Americans had been born in America—and thus reared in the midst of all those influences that shaped men's lives in the New World—would they have been Loyalists? Is it not more likely that they would have become revolutionaries? Conversely, if many of the colonials who promoted the American rebellion so ardently had been born in Great Britain, would they have felt other than did the majority of people in the United Kingdom about the revolutionary Americans? To these questions there can of course be no answers. Similarly, one is tempted to speculate upon what might have been the outcome had the leaders of each country had first-hand knowledge of the other land—that is, if communications had been freer and quicker and travel between the two countries had not been so arduous and dangerous. However, in view of the persistence and insolubility of today's crises between nations, as well as within imperial systems, in an age of such ease and speed of communications and travel, this question may perhaps be easily put aside.

Again, when is a government justified in using force to put down an uprising within the limits of its jurisdiction? Was President Lincoln justified in asking Congress in 1861 to permit him to preserve the government of the American union by using force against the seceding states? Was George III justified in calling upon Parliament to sanction efforts of the Ministry to put down an American rebellion in order to preserve the Old British Empire?

The waging of war to people of humane feelings is a terrible thing. Had the government of Great Britain determined to avoid this last resort—and, instead, simply withdrawn its protection from the rebellious Thirteen Colonies, severed all political connection with them, and permitted them peacefully to go their way—how seriously would the vital interests of Great Britain have been affected in the long run? In Dean Josiah Tucker's pamphlet on *The True Interest of Great Britain . . .* , mentioned earlier in this Summary, he argued that the granting of independence was the proper course for Great Britain to pursue with respect to the Thirteen Colonies. This is of course the present-day policy of the British government toward dependencies that desire freedom of action.

In recapitulation: The war begun in 1775 was not waged (as has already been emphasized) to secure the withdrawal of the Thirteen Colonies from the British Empire; rather it had as its original purpose to give these colonies an autonomous position within the Empire—a status to which their leaders felt they had a right both by the common law and the law of nature. But there was really no place under the eighteenth-century British constitution for autonomous local governments. Even the offer made by Lord North in February 1775 fell far short of American demands. By a resolution passed in the House of Commons, after heated debate, agreement was reached that as soon as any colony had contributed its proper proportion to the common defence (which funds should be at the disposal of Parliament) and also made provision for the support of its civil government, no levies would be made on it by the home government. Whatever might have been the reaction in America to such a resolution had it been passed ten years earlier, such a limited constitutional concession in 1775 was both too little and too late to satisfy colonial leaders. For by this time, as Professor Bailyn has so well expressed it in the Introduction of his *Pamphlets of the American Revolution* (I, 20), "the intense political heat" generated in the Thirteen Colonies after 1763 at length fused "long popular, though hitherto inconclusive, controversial, and imperfectly harmonized [political] ideas about the world and America's place in it" into a clear and "comprehensive view unique in its moral and intellectual appeal." Therefore by the beginning of 1776, in the midst of hostilities directed against the King's armies, the rebellious British Americans were well prepared to give an unprecedented welcome to the bitter attack on the British government embodied in Thomas Paine's *Common Sense*, which held up to utter contempt the British monarchy, along with all monarchies, and pointed in magic phrases to the great future that awaited America once it was free of the chains that had bound it to a corrupt and morally decadent Old World.

Thus the receptivity to Paine's demand for independence (which was a culmination of the ceaseless propaganda of the colonial press and the countless exhortations of orators from the pulpit and other public platforms) combined with the critical need for the colonies to become an independent nation in order to gain France as an ally, led the Continental Congress to take a decision destined never to be reversed—that of proclaiming the Thirteen Colonies completely independent of Great Britain and the British Empire.

This brings up for all too brief consideration an aspect of American history of major importance. It is that the success of the revolt in 1775 was not—as was the case in the later revolt within Spanish America—the outcome of a series of separatist uprisings (more or less coordinated for a period) which left at their termination a large number of sovereign, quite independent states. Rather, the success of the American Revolution was due to the unified action taken by the representatives of the Thirteen Colonies in the Continental Congress. This unified action—leading to the adoption of the Articles of Confederation and finally to the drawing up of the Constitution of the United States—came about as the result of the slow growth of an idea: that the security and general welfare of the North American British colonies lay in combining their varied resources. While a number of projects for colonial union had been presented before 1754 by individuals acting on their own initiative,[69] it was only at the Albany Congress held in that year and attended by leading men from seven of the nine northern colonies, that the famous Albany Plan of Union—very properly known as the Franklin Plan of Union—was evolved and approved by the delegates after due deliberation.[70] Despite the fact that the Albany Plan of Union failed to be

---

[69] See Justin Winsor: . . . Narrative and Critical History of America (8 vols., Boston, 1884–9), V, 611–14, and especially F. D. Stone: "Plans for the Union of the British Colonies of North America, 1643–1776," History of the Celebration . . . of the Promulgation of the Constitution of the United States (ed. H. L. Carson, 2 vols., Philadelphia, 1899), II, 439–503.

[70] This writer has felt impelled to arrive at and adhere to the conclusion that while the chief ideas of the historic Albany Plan are to be found embodied in Benjamin Franklin's initial rough sketch called "Short Hints Toward a Scheme for Uniting the Northern Colonies," the structure and language, in so far as was possible, were derived from still another project for union that carried the title "plan of a Proposed Union. . . ." This, it is quite evident, had been drafted with great care before the opening of the Congress, and evidence points to Thomas Hutchinson of Massachusetts Bay as its author. Two historians of distinction, Verner W. Crane and Leonard W. Labaree, have presented at some length their disagreement with this conclusion. For a discussion of the background of the Albany Plan of Union see L. H. Gipson: The British Empire Before the American Revolution, V, Chaps. 4 and 5, and The Albany

approved by any of the colonial Assemblies, it forms a notable land-mark in the constitutional history of what was to become the United States of America.

If contemporary eighteenth-century public statements and private correspondence are safe guides, the evidence is overwhelming that American colonials revolted not to create a new social order but to free themselves from interference by the government of Great Britain. This is the conclusion I have come to as the result of all my years of research for this series and for my volume in the New American Nation series, *The Coming of the Revolution, 1763–1775.* Nevertheless, out of the American Revolution and the War for American Independence emerged inevitable reforms and changes of many types, social and economic as well as political—some of them doubt-less of the kind inherent in any revolutionary movement. For no revolution ever takes place without a ferment of ideas to produce the rationale necessary to justify such an upheaval in the lives of a peo-ple. To Benjamin Rush, addressing the American people at the close of the War for American Independence (in the *American Museum, or Universal Magazine* . . . [1787], I, 8), the real American Revo-lution had only begun. And in this sense the United States in 1966 is still in the midst of the American Revolution. In the present series, however, the term "American Revolution" has been employed, as it is by the political scientist, in its political and constitutional con-notation—that is, to mean the repudiation of the sovereign powers of the King in Parliament.

Such was the revolution that produced the War for American Independence, the first great reversal in the history of the overseas expansion of England. Thus the Declaration of Independence con-stitutes the watershed marking the line of separation between the history of the Thirteen British Colonies and that of the dawning American nation. With this momentous event the present series has reached its logical termination.

Plan of Union, 1754 (Old South Leaflets, No. 9, Boston, 1953); see also his "Thomas Hutchinson and the Framing of the Albany Plan of Union, 1754," *Pennsylvania Magazine of History and Biography,* LXXIV, 5–35; V. W. Crane and L. H. Gipson "Letters to The Editor on the Albany Congress Plan of Union, 1754," *ibid.,* LXXV, 350–62; L. H. Gipson: "The Drafting of the Albany Plan of Union: A Problem in Semantics," *Pennsylvania History,* XXVI, 290–316; V. W. Crane and L. H. Gipson: "Letters to the Editor on the Drafting of the Albany Plan of Union," *ibid.,* XXVII, 126–36; L. H. Gipson: "Massachusetts and American Colonial Union, 1754," American Antiquarian Society *Proceedings,* LXXI, Part I, 63–92; and L. W. Labaree in the *Papers of Benjamin Franklin* (8 vols.+, New Haven, 1965+), V, 378–87.

Note: Recent Literature Relating to the Causes of the American Revolution*

The reasons for the American Revolution have fascinated and challenged historians of every generation since the event itself and seem likely to continue to do so. Charles H. McIlwain in his *The American Revolution: A Constitutional Interpretation* (New York, 1924) finds the explanation (pp. 193–4) in "an infringement of the colonial charters, a violation of the law of nature, which is a part of English law; and a breach of the constitution of the British Empire." However, Max Beloff in the Introduction to his *The Debate on the American Revolution, 1761–1783* (London, 1949) takes the position (p. 8) "that the political thinkers of the period were not concerned with the development of abstract questions about the nature of the state but with the direct issues confronting them, and that the shifting of the grounds of the discussion as it proceeded was primarily a response to the successive situations produced by action on either side." Carl L. Becker in his *The History of Political Parties in the Province of New York, 1760–1776* (Madison, Wis., 1909) arrives at the conclusion that the American Revolution was a two-pronged struggle—for American self rule and to determine who should rule at home: that is, a movement of the common people against the holders of power within the Province of New York.

Turning now to another point of view, in *The American States During and After the Revolution, 1775–1789* (New York, 1924), Chap. 10, Allan Nevins emphasized the importance of the social aspects of the Revolution. Shortly afterwards appeared J. Franklin Jameson's classic *The American Revolution Considered as a Social Movement* (Princeton, 1926). Merrill Jensen in his *Articles of Confederation* (Madison, Wis., 1948) also stressed the struggle between conservative Whigs and the more democratic elements in America as a basic factor of the American Revolution, but in 1957 in his "Democracy and the American Revolution" (*Huntington Library Quarterly*, XX, 321–41) took the position that the Revolution was not a democratic movement at the beginning but later resulted in one. In 1954 F. B. Tolles presented a brief but searching

* Any noteworthy studies that may have appeared after the spring of 1966 are beyond the date of the completion of this volume.

although generally sympathetic critique of the Jameson thesis in his "The American Revolution Considered as a Social Movement: A Re-Evaluation," *American Historical Review*, LX, 1–12. The following year Richard B. Morris in his *The American Revolution: A Short History* (New York, 1955) stated (p. 7) that the American Revolution "was a political revolution rather than an overturn of the social order. . . . It was led by a Whig aristocracy who sought liberation from political and economic restraints imposed by the British government." This was also the position that he took in 1962 in his article "Class Struggle and the American Revolution" in the *William and Mary Quarterly*, 3rd ser., XIX, 3–29.

L. M. Hacker, stressing the economic aspects of the relationship between Great Britain and the colonies, denied that political and constitutional issues brought on the Revolution and saw the causes as stemming rather from "the limitations and penalties imposed upon American economy" by British mercantilism. To him "America is the land pre-eminently where the idea of equality of economic opportunity has flourished" (*The Triumph of American Capitalism* [New York, 1940], pp. 7–8). Going beyond Hacker in an economic interpretation of the crisis that developed, Herbert Aptheker in his *A History of the American People: An Interpretation. The American Revolution, 1763–1783* (New York, 1960) presents (pp. 28–9) the Marxist point of view. The grievances of the exploited colonials that brought on the War for American Independence were: the determination of the government of Great Britain,

> "to monopolize the market for British manufactured goods, hence to restrain local manufacturing; to favor British fur-traders, land-speculators, fishermen, lumbermen; to channelize shipping within the orbit of the British dominion and to monopolize the economic benefits from commerce; to dominate as much as might be the merchandising of colonial commodities; to control the credit and the finances of the colonial economy; to inhibit the westward settlement of the colonial population; to centralize the political machinery of the colonies, throttle democratic developments, and diminish home rule, especially in terms of the purse and the judiciary; to increase the role of the military in colonial life; to raise the revenue needed to run the colonies from within the colonies themselves and, even more important, to protect British capital invested within the colonies."

In contrast to the views of Hacker and Aptheker, O. M. Dickerson praises the system of commercial restrictions before 1763 in his *The*

Navigation Acts and the American Revolution (Philadelphia, 1951).
After surveying the history of this system he writes (p. 147): "Every
colonial power had regulations of some kind designed to confine the
trade of the colonies to the home country. But England's regulations
were different from the others. Under these the British Empire had
prospered while that of every other power had declined." He places
the blame for the Revolution on the fiscal policy of the British
government after 1763. To Randolph G. Adams there was something
much more fundamental. In his *Political Ideas of the American
Revolution: Britannic-American Contributions to the Problem of
Imperial Organization, 1765–1775* (Durham, N. C., 1922, and New
York, 1958) he writes (p. 199): ". . . the social and economic
divergence of Britain and her overseas colonies had by 1765 become
so manifest as to demand a reorganization of the Empire based upon
the facts of the economic world." Max Savelle also stresses the
growing alienation between the mother country and the older North
American colonies in his *Seeds of Liberty: The Genesis of the American Mind* (New York, 1948). After analyzing in detail the pattern
of life in the colonies he arrives at the conclusion (p. 584) that by
the middle of the eighteenth century "American intellectual and
cultural life . . . was not an English culture, except superficially,
but a new national way of life; a variant within the broad culture-
pattern of western civilization as a whole." Thus the American Revolution was promoted to vindicate and maintain this unique culture.
In harmony with this view Eric Robson in his *The American Revolution in its Political and Military Aspects, 1763–1783* (London, 1955)
writes (p. 12): "Conflicting political ideas, not tea nor taxes, caused
the secession of the colonial peoples from the British Empire. Colonial and British political thought and development had come to the
parting of the ways."

In contrast to the above view Clinton Rossiter in his *The First
American Revolution: The American Colonies on the Eve of Independence,* Part I of *Seedtime of the Republic* (New York, 1956),
stresses the pride Americans took in the inherited ideas that motivated them (pp. 224–5):

> "Political thought in the colonies was a proudly conscious extension
> of political thought in England. The more independent and self-
> assertive the colonists became, the more anxious they were to sound
> like trueborn Englishmen. . . . Conservatives, middle-of-the-road-
> ers, and radicals hammered at one another with the slogans of

Whiggery. Rarely if ever in the history of free government has there been so unanimous a "party line" as that to which the colonists pledged their uncritical allegiance. And rarely if ever has the party line been so easily reduced to one comprehensible concept, even to one wonderful word: *Liberty*. Liberty, defined simply and unanimously as that 'which exempts one Man from Subjection to another, so far as the Order and Oeconomy of Government will permit.'"

In other words, men who prided themselves on being Englishmen and on English ideas of liberty promoted the American Revolution.

The unanimity that Rossiter finds in American thought was denied by Philip Davidson. To him a minority set out to control the thinking of the great mass of Americans. In the Introduction to his *Propaganda and the American Revolution, 1763–1783* (Chapel Hill, N.C., 1941) he states: "Had the Revolution been the work of a majority . . . there would have been little necessity for propaganda. . . . The difficulties the leaders faced at every stage of the conflict, the coercion and violence by which thousands were forced into acquiescence or exile, the indifference and malingering of thousands of others, and the constant dissensions which disrupted the leadership itself are sure evidences that the Revolution was at best but the work of an aggressive minority."

J. C. Miller in his two volumes, *Origins of the American Revolution* (Boston, 1943) and the *Triumph of Freedom, 1775–1783* (Boston, 1948), recognizes the importance in the Revolution of the forces demanding a greater degree of democracy in political life, as does E. P. Douglass in his *Rebels and Democrats: The Struggle for Equal Political Rights and Majority Rule During the American Revolution* (Chapel Hill, N.C., 1955). Edmund S. Morgan in his *The Stamp Act Crisis: Prologue to Revolution* (North Carolina, 1953) likewise sees the revolutionary movement in terms of the protection by colonials of their liberty and property and the furtherance of human equality that could only be attained by establishing themselves as a distinct nation.

D. J. Boorstin, on the other hand, in the chapter on "Revolution Without Dogma" in his *The Genius of American Politics* (Chicago, 1953) places stress on the strength of the conservative forces in the American Revolution. R. E. Brown in his *Middle-Class Democracy and the Revolution in Massachusetts, 1691–1780* (Ithaca, 1955) goes beyond Boorstin in picturing American conservatism and the triumph of democracy by 1763. He attacks the Becker thesis. Referring to the American Revolution, Brown writes (p. 401): "It was not, as we have often assumed, a dual revolution in which Americans won their independence from the British on one hand, and in which unenfranchised and underprivileged lower classes wrested democratic rights from a privileged local aristocracy on the other." On the contrary, in his study of Massachusetts Bay he finds "that the Revolution was designed to *preserve* a social order rather than to change it" (p. 405). In other words democracy was a fact in the life of the colony before the American crisis. However, R. N. Lokken in 1959, in "The Concept of Democracy in Colonial Political Thought," *William and Mary Quarterly*, 3rd ser., XVI, 568–80, questions Brown's use of the expression "democracy," especially his application of it to a colony in the eighteenth century under the assumption that the word "democracy" then carried the same connotation that it would have in the nineteenth or twentieth century. Moreover, J. H. Cary in his "Statistical Method and the Brown Thesis on Colonial Democracy," *ibid.* (1963), XX, 251–64, challenges the validity of Professor Brown's manner of using statistics in arriving at his conclusions; to which Brown replies, *ibid.* (1963), XX, 265–76.

Again, John R. Alden in his *The American Revolution, 1775–1783* (New York, 1954), in seeking to throw light on the causes for the War for American Independence, affirms that the Grenville program did not mean "tyranny" in America. The trouble was that this program was not vigorously maintained once it had been adopted. Measures for gradually loosening the imperial bonds could have been much more successful (p. 8):

> "Failure of the British supporters of the post-1763 policy to sustain their program over the objections of those who urged conciliation produced vacillations between harshness and weakness which, in turn, stiffened or invited American resistance. Had the new policy been firmly and steadily pushed in the Stamp Act crisis, it is barely possible that American resistance might have been peacefully overcome. But wiser by far than a consistent course of coercion would have been the abandoning of the effort to turn back the colonial clock. An American policy based upon recognition of the maturity of the colonies . . . might have postponed indefinitely the era of American independence."

Esmond Wright in *Fabric of Freedom, 1763–1800* (New York, 1961) agrees with Alden and writes (pp. 103–4): "The American

Revolution was the product of executive weakness, not tyranny; of parliamentary, not royal, vacillation; and of chronic irresolution before pressure groups, both at home and in the colonies. It was the product also of mounting and mutual anger and bitterness; a situation had been permitted to develop from which there was no escape except by force." To Bernard Donoughue in his *British Politics and the American Revolution: The Path to War, 1773-75* ([London, 1964] p. 1): "The root of the difficulty with the Old Colonies was the extent to which [by 1763] their two and a half million inhabitants had grown apart from the Mother Country." He therefore is led to express doubts as to the ability of any British government to satisfy colonial aspirations short of independence (pp. 282-3): "The question which naturally arises here is whether, had the Government acted upon different premises, and applied different policies there would have been a less tragic outcome to the colonial problem. . . . It is . . . seriously open to doubt whether there was any acceptable constitutional compromise which the Ministry could have offered to the colonial leaders."

The year 1960 saw the publication of Bernhard Knollenberg's *Origin of the American Revolution, 1759-1766* (New York, 1960). This scholarly work develops the thesis that from 1759 to 1766 British officials undertook to carry out a series of new and provocative measures out of which developed wide-spread colonial discontent with the government of Great Britain. From Knollenberg's point of view no one measure alienated the colonials from this alliance but rather an accumulation of justifiable grievances. In 1965 two studies appeared that have bearing upon the theme of the Revolution as a social and intellectual movement. In his "The Revolutionary Character of the American Revolution," published in the July number of the *American Historical Review* (1965), LXX, 998-1014, William H. Nelson of the University of Toronto, among other things, has this to say:

"The Revolution was genuinely two-sided: it meant alienation, but it also meant liberation. The American colonies had, perhaps since their founding, dissented in varying degree from the established social, ecclesiastical, and governmental arrangements in England. Now, suddenly, they were able, through the Revolution, to transform mere dissent into a new system, positive and ultimately lawful. Americans articulated a remarkable ideology. . . . The heart and center of this ideology is political individualism: individual man—

his life, liberty, and pursuit of happiness—became the central concern of the whole political order."

The next work, *Pamphlets of the American Revolution, 1750–1776,*
Volume I, 1750–1765, edited by Bernard Bailyn with the assistance
of Jane N. Garrett (Cambridge, 1965), is one of major importance to
this theme. When completed in four volumes it will be by far the
most comprehensive exposition and analysis of contemporary writings on American revolutionary thinking. The roots of this trend of
colonial thinking, according to Professor Bailyn, lay not only in the
thought of the classical writers of antiquity but also and especially in
the views embodied in the works of "seventeenth-century heroes of
liberty" and subsequently transmitted to the revolutionary generation by such early eighteenth-century radicals as John Trenchard,
Thomas Gordon, and Bishop Hoadly. The ideas thus communicated
became powerful weapons against the established order of things.
Giving force and glowing meaning to all this inherited volume of
polemical writing against constituted authority, was the conviction
of many Americans that they were being made the victims of a
conspiracy. After reading American pamphlet literature covering
the years 1750–1776, Professor Bailyn says (Vol. I, p. x): "In the end
I was convinced that the fear of a comprehensive conspiracy against
liberty throughout the English-speaking world—a conspiracy believed to have been nourished in corruption, and of which, it was
felt, oppression in America was only the most immediately visible
part—lay at the heart of the Revolutionary movement." Yet, Bailyn
feels, there was within the Empire fear of another and equally
ominous conspiracy (p. 88): "Paradoxically, however, and significantly, the opponents of the Revolution—the administration itself—were equally convinced that they were victims of conspirato-
rial designs. Officials in the colonies, and their superiors in England,
were persuaded as the crisis deepened that they were confronted by
an active conspiracy of intriguing men whose professions masked
their true intentions." Thus, he suggests, two groups of conspirators
were thought to be arrayed against each other.

As a postcript to this Summary, Gordon S. Wood's "Rhetoric and
Reality in the American Revolution" has just appeared in the *William and Mary Quarterly* (1966), 3rd ser., XXIII, 3–32, seeking to
survey the recent literature bearing upon the Revolution. To Wood
such writers as Carl Becker in his *Declaration of Independence: A*

Study in the History of Political Ideas (New York, 1922), Philip Davidson in his *Propaganda and the American Revolution, 1763–1783* (Chapel Hill, N.C., 1941), and Arthur M. Schlesinger in his *Prelude to Independence: The Newspaper War on Britain, 1764–1776* (New York, 1958)—whom he groups together as the "progressive historians"—saw the revolutionary leaders as using ideas to cover up the real purposes of their opposition to the government of Great Britain. Opposed to them in their outlook, according to Wood, is another "group" of historians whom he calls the "neo-Whigs." The leaders of this group are Edmund S. Morgan, Jack P. Greene, and Bernard Bailyn. Citing Edmund S. Morgan's "The American Revolution Considered as an Intellectual Movement" which appeared in *Paths of American Thought* (eds. A. M. Schlesinger, Jr., and Morton White, Boston, 1963) and his "Colonial Ideas of Parliamentary Power, 1764–1766" published in the *William and Mary Quarterly* for 1948 (3rd ser., V, 311–41), Jack P. Greene's "The Flight from Determinism: A Review of Recent Literature on the Coming of the American Revolution" from the 1962 spring number of the *South Atlantic Quarterly* (LXI, 235–59), and Bernard Bailyn's introductory essay to his *Pamphlets of the American Revolution, 1750–1776*, Wood points out that all three stress the vital importance of the political *principles* enunciated by the colonial leaders to an understanding of the basis for the revolutionary movement of the 1760's and 1770's, and the secondary importance of whatever other motives may have helped to generate the American Revolution—although he feels that Bailyn has built on far the most comprehensive foundation of the three. In ending his essay Wood says (p. 32): "Precisely because they sought to understand both the Revolutionary ideas and American society, the behaviorist historians of the Progressive generation, for all of their crude conceptualizations, their obsessions with 'class' and hidden economic interest, and their treatment of ideas as propaganda, have still offered us an explanation of the Revolutionary era so powerful and so comprehensive that no purely intellectual interpretation will ever replace it."

Finally, in completing this note on the recent literature concerned with the American Revolution, it may not be unfair to point again to my own conclusions embodied in my volume in the New American Nation Series, *The Coming of the Revolution, 1763–1775*, as well as in this summing up of the present series. As a final word I might say that I myself believe in the usefulness of the various approaches and interpretations of the specialists; I also realize that since each new study provokes consideration of additional aspects of the question under review, one cannot hope ever to see a complete synthesis of all viewpoints, nor yet a single definitive approach. Such indeed is the nature of history.

PART III

HISTORIOGRAPHY

Historiographical Sketches Relating to the History of the British Empire, 1748-1776[1]

THE written history of a period, such as the one with which this series is concerned, is drawn from a wide variety of sources. These, however, vary greatly in value. As a result the historian who desires to maintain or to set a certain standard of excellence in his writing is charged with the responsibility of locating and bringing under examination at least the most important and authoritative of these sources. In so doing he must exercise the highest powers of discrimination in order to select from them the data that will be embodied in his work. Naturally the degree of success that he attains in his endeavours to chronicle faithfully what has happened and why it so happened will go far toward determining the reliability and degree of permanence of his work. Thus the historian's art is one of selectivity as well as of presentation.

But the writing of history—involving as it does so many processes, from the original concept of what it is that should be studied to the completion of the published .work—is subjective to a degree not always clearly appreciated by the reading public. Historians like all other writers are creations of the age in which they live and thus

---

[1] Two useful studies relating to historiography have been issued in America by the Social Science Research Council. The first was published in 1946 as *Bulletin 54* under the title *Theory and Practice in Historical Study: A Report of the Committee on Historiography,* and was prepared by a group of distinguished historians; it included a fairly comprehensive reading list on historiography and the philosophy of history. This was followed in 1954 by *Bulletin 64* under the title *The Social Sciences in Historical Study. A Report of the Committees on Historiography.* Taken together the two reports indicate the ever-widening scope and complexity of historiography and stress the importance of careful preparation and general qualification in those who would hope to succeed in this field of scholarly activity.

A select list of studies on historiography germane to the period under review will appear in Volume XIV of this series.

heirs to certain preconceptions. They are creatures of a specific environment binding each of them to the past in a variety of ways that influences their individual intellectual development and consequently their evaluation of the sources on which they base their interpretations of historical events. Because of this, it is but commonplace to state that no two scholars working independently— although equally intent upon arriving at the ascertainable truth about certain events in the past and using the same sources—will arrive at identical interpretations of a common subject. Hence the enquiring reader, eager to master a particular period of history, should welcome a variety of works concerned with it, and the individual attitudes of the various authors; for he must be aware that no one historian or school of historians can possibly be definitive and must recognize that each really serious effort to evoke the past usually contains valuable insights as well as blind spots.

Again, in dealing with such a field as American colonial history American scholars must always decide whether to adopt the imperial approach to the study of English colonial expansion in the New World or the contrasting, more characteristic national approach of most American writers concerned with the same period. This second approach assumes the existence of the United States of America and then probes into the past in order to uncover the beginnings and development of a group of Thirteen English Colonies destined to become the nucleus of a new nation. The imperial approach, by comparison, views English colonization of the New World simply as a part of the history of the rise and decline of the British Empire. In this approach London, the capital of the Empire, is always the nerve centre, and the history of the American colonies is placed in the wider context. Such, obviously, has been the approach of this series and of a number of histories and specialized studies written particularly by American historians—the British historian customarily writes from an imperial point of view, whether he approves or denounces the conduct of the government.

But this historiography will not attempt to examine the respective merits of the national and the imperial approaches to the subject. It will consist simply (in contrast to the fairly comprehensive bibliography that will appear in another volume) of a series of brief essays dealing only with certain of those writers whose works have in some measure affected the public view of the period of history of the British Empire under survey. To have included all historians of merit who have contributed to an understanding of this period would have demanded much more space than is available. Neither, proceeding on these terms, can it take into consideration the indispensable works of the compilers, archivists, and editors who have brought together governmental documents—such as parliamentary papers and colonial records—so basic to the historian's research, nor examine the authors or editors of the more general histories and studies of institutions that encompass the period. These must be left to the general bibliography.

In undertaking this task, it seems natural and proper to begin with some of those British writers who were contemporary or nearly contemporary to the events they sought to describe and proceed, so far as possible, upon a chronological plan based on the date of publication of the major contribution or contributions of each individual. We shall then consider the works of two Canadian historians and, finally, a selected list of American historians, also in the chronological order of their writings.

British Historians

George Bubb Dodington, Baron Melcombe
(1691–1762)

ORN in 1691 the son of Jeremias Bubb, George Bubb took the name Dodington in 1720 from his mother's brother George, who had left him a large estate upon his death that year.[1] Before this he had already entered Parliament and had also been employed as envoy extraordinary to the Court of Spain. In 1724 he became a lord of the Treasury, and later, Treasurer of the Navy, an employment he resigned in 1740 in order to join the group in opposition to the government centred round the Prince of Wales at Leicester House. However, upon the death of the Prince of Wales he made peace with the Pelhams and in 1755 again held the post of Treasurer of the Navy, only to lose it the following year when William Pitt came briefly to power. The year before his death, with Lord Bute in the ascendancy, he was finally created Baron Melcombe of Melcombe Regis in Dorset. His power, such as it was, rested in his control (by virtue of his wealth) of a number of seats in the House of Commons.

The *Diary* left by Lord Melcombe covers the years 1749 to 1761 and throws considerable light on the political manoeuvring of the various factions during that period. Melcombe's estate went chiefly to Thomas Wyndham of Hammersmith, upon whose death the Melcombe diary came ultimately into the possession of Henry Penruddocke Wyndham in 1777. After much hesitation and delay, Wyndham, a scholarly man and a leading authority on the topography of

---

[1] See L. C. Sanders: *Patron and Place-hunter: A Study of George Bubb Dodington, Lord Melcombe* (London, 1919).

England, decided to publish it. The *Diary* was issued in 1784.[2] The task of bringing it out was manifestly a distasteful one to Wyndham; he could not forbear placing on the title page a quotation from Rabelais: *"Et tout pour la trippe,"* and one from the *Diary* itself: "And all for quarter day" (the day when payment is made in England on rentals, etc.). In the Preface, the editor gave as his own opinion that Dodington's political conduct had been "wholly directed by the base motives of avarice, vanity, and selfishness" (p. viii). He was nevertheless persuaded that Dodington had prepared his diary for ultimate publication, and that it was his obligation to fulfill that intention. Yet, Wyndham acknowledged, by publishing it and by treating the character of the "Author thus freely, I shall appear as a very extraordinary Editor. . . ." (p. x). Wyndham also added an Appendix, containing another group of revealing documents found among the Dodington manuscripts.

The *Diary* is almost unique in exhibiting with utmost frankness the day-by-day details of the fortunes and misfortunes of a prominent political figure whose chief passion was grasping for political power and royal favour. Yet Dodington's very honesty in recording accurately his conversations with leading men and in tracing the course of events makes his work important to any historiography that covers the last decade of the reign of George II.

Tobias George Smollett (1721–1771)

In 1790, nineteen years after the death of novelist Tobias George Smollett, his five-volume edition of *The History of England from the Revolution to the death of George II* was published in London. A non-controversial piece of work, it had appeared originally in 1757 in four volumes designed to capitalize on the public's interest in Hume's two-volume history of the Stuart period and bring the story forward to 1748.[1] To accomplish his task, Smollett wrote at the rate

---

[2] *The Diary of the Late George Bubb Dodington* . . . *1749 to* . . . *1761* (ed. H. P. Wyndham, Salisbury, 1784; London, 1785, 1809, 1823, 1828).

[1] See David Hume's *The History of Great Britain* . . . (2 vols., Edinburgh, 1754, 1757) and Smollett's *A Complete History of England Deduced from the Descent of Julius Caesar, to the Treaty of Aix-La-Chapelle, 1748*, etc. (4 vols., London, 1757–8).

of close to a century a month. His work stirred up the wrath of Hume and others; it was also received somewhat coolly by William Pitt, to whom it was dedicated without permission.

The great popularity of Smollett's work may be judged by the fact that it was re-issued in numerous editions, without reference to the earlier version of the work. The hero of the history is William Pitt. The final chapter presents a most favourable picture of Great Britain—the piety of the clergy, the progress of the arts and sciences, and the triumph of British armies. Although in 1762 Smollett undertook the editorship of the short-lived, partisan *Briton,* which sought to defend Lord Bute from the attacks of John Wilkes's *North Briton,*[2] there is little trace in his *History* of the bitter partisanship that characterized the work of Hume.

Far removed from the *History of England* was Smollett's *The History and Adventures of an Atom,* which had issued from the press in London in 1769. In this curious and fanciful work, with its many elements of coarseness, the author (using the name Nathaniel Peacock) attacked with heavy-handed and bitter satire almost everyone prominent in political life from 1754 to 1768, not excluding George II, George III, and Pitt. Placing these figures against the background of real events, Smollett distorted the events somewhat by imagination and open partisanship.[3] In contrast to this, his *History* was important as the first series to chronicle systematically the political and military events from 1688 to 1760. It is well to add that in writing this detailed account the author had at his disposal a staff of assistants. Other writers interested in the same period often leaned on Smollett's *History,* without always acknowledging their debt. The work therefore cannot be ignored in the historiography of the later years of the reign of George II.

[2] The first issue of the *Briton* appeared on May 30, 1762, for the express purpose of defending Lord Bute; subsequent issues appeared until the last one on February 12, 1763, by which time Wilkes's *North Briton* had come to prominence, aided in effect by the attention given it in the *Briton.*

[3] In *The History and Adventures of an Atom,* the setting is supposedly Japan and to those who came under his scrutiny Smollett accorded fictitious Japanese names. Although the leading people mentioned in this narrative are easily identifiable to the student acquainted with the history of the period, others should consult the volume by William Davis: *A Second Journey Round the Library of a Bibliomaniac* (London, 1825), pp. 115–18.

William Belsham (1752–1827)

Dodington and Smollett dealt with the reign of George II. Among the first of the writers to deal comprehensively with that of George III was William Belsham, essayist and historian, and brother of the distinguished Unitarian divine, Thomas Belsham. In 1796 he published four volumes of *Memoirs of the Reign of George III to the Session of Parliament Ending A.D. 1793*.[1] The popularity of this work is indicated by the fact that it went through five editions (the last appearing in six volumes in 1801) before it reached the final form embodied in his *History of Great Britain from the Revolution, 1688, to the Conclusion of the Treaty of Amiens, 1802* which came from the press in 1805 and 1806 in twelve volumes.[2]

Of the Whig historians none was more outspoken than Belsham and none offered more severe condemnation of the policies of the British government toward America. For example, in dealing with the maintaining of the armed forces that the Grenville Ministry considered necessary for the protection of the extended Empire after the Peace of Paris in 1763, Belsham made an unfavourable contrast between the modest reduction of these forces and the drastic reduction that had been made after the Peace of Aix-la-Chapelle in 1749. To him the peacetime military establishment of 1764 was "enormously extravagant." Even though a large part of this force was needed among the newly conquered French in Canada, in the areas of danger from powerful, hostile Indian tribes in other parts of North America, and at other critical points in the New World, Belsham recorded that "for the support of this unnecessary and unaccountable force, America was to be plundered, harassed, and oppressed."[3] As for the Stamp Act passed by Parliament to help support this force in America, he stated that it "afforded a most striking and hideous specimen of the despotism which would be

---

[1] It may be noted in passing that in 1793 Belsham published his two-volume *Memoirs of the Kings of Great Britain of the House of Brunswick-Luneburg*, the second volume of which is concerned in part with the period between the Peace of Aix-la-Chapelle and the death of George II. Although this work went into a second edition in 1796, it seems to have had little influence on historiography.

[2] It is to the twelve-volume edition that reference will be made in this essay.

[3] *History of Great Britain*, V, 112n.

eventually exercised when the new system [of American taxation] should be fully established."[4] Indeed, he concluded that in "his attempts to force his wretched innovations upon America, Mr. Grenville must surely have been actuated by the very demon of folly!"[5]

Belsham also seems to have kept alive the idea that after the retirement of Bute from the Ministry, this Scottish Earl continued to exert an evil power over the affairs of state. In dealing with the Townshend legislation of 1767 relating to America, he stated that "through some unaccountable fatality, or more probably, from the secret operation of that invisible and malignant influence which seemed perpetually to shed its poisonous and deadly dews over the political atmosphere, the project was revived, incredible as it may seem, of drawing a revenue from America."[6] As for George III, while characterizing him in 1781 as "grave, temperate, devout," Belsham commented: "But the virtues of the man, . . . afforded a very inadequate compensation for the errors and imperfections of the monarch; under whose reign it may be justly affirmed, that from the almost perpetual predominance of evil councils, the people suffered all that could be inflicted under the restraints of a constitution radically excellent."[7] Here, then, is the work of a patriotic Englishman of liberal but strong views surveying in retrospect the events which (as the result of misguided statesmanship) had deprived Great Britain of its fairest possessions, the Thirteen Colonies. Yet he gave no consideration to the extraordinary problems of maintaining the great Empire administered by Great Britain before 1775 in such a way as to ensure an equitable division of the financial burdens. It is therefore not surprising that there were some who reacted violently to Belsham's interpretations. In reviewing the last two volumes of the fifth edition of the *Memoirs*, a writer in the April 1803 number of the *Edinburgh Review* declared: ". . . by the illiberality, party spirit, and intemperate ardour for the propagation of his political opinions, which Mr. Belsham displays, he has forfeited the title of historian, for the more appropriate, though less respectable, name of zealot, or pamphleteer. The bitter and licentious spirit in which he had indulged his pen throughout his former volumes [Vols. I–IV] has now risen to a height more intolerable to the reader,

---

[4] *Ibid.*, V, 155.
[5] *Ibid.*, V, 171.
[6] *Ibid.*, V, 233–4.
[7] *Ibid.*, VII, 263.

and disgraceful to the writer." [8] Strongly partisan as it is, Belsham's work has nevertheless played a part in shaping interpretations of the history of this period.

John Adolphus (1769–1845)

In 1802 *The History of England from the Accession of King George the Third, to the Conclusion of Peace in the Year 1783* issued from the press in three volumes. They were written by John Adolphus, who assisted Archdeacon William Coxe in his preparation of the *Memoirs of Sir Robert Walpole* published in 1798. Adolphus had previously written studies of the chaotic conditions of revolutionary France. It is clear that he now turned with a sense of relief and pride to a description of Great Britain, whose stable constitution under the reigning monarch was—he declared in the Preface to his work— "entitled to veneration from every observer, and to support from all those whom birth or accident has made partakers of its blessings." Adolphus therefore wrote as a conservative who had faith not only in the institutions of his country but also in the men who had guided and were guiding its destinies. He was fully aware that in the work of some of his predecessors

> "bitter calumny or fulsome adulation had disfigured most of their characters; and that the real image of persons, as well as the true colour of events, could with difficulty be discerned through the noxious mist or splendid vapour. . . . That men should be steadfastly patriotic, and, in their pursuit of the public good, always temperate, just, and self-denying, is very desirable; but the historian feels, with regret the necessity of recording the aberrations of the most elevated minds; and that work must be a romance, not a history, which fails to shew that individuals, whose general views have been directed to the benefit of their country, have been, in occasional acts, rash, vain, factious, arbitrary, or absurd." [1]

It was in such a spirit—in sharp contrast to that in which Belsham recorded his *Memoirs of the Reign of George III*—that Adolphus's

---

[8] *Edinburgh Review*, II, 177–84.
[1] *The History of England*, Preface.

The History of England emerged. It had gone through three revised editions when the author decided late in life to present the complete history of the reign of George III. Volume I of this new version appeared in 1840 and Volume II the following year. They cover the history of George III to 1778, and therefore go somewhat beyond the period with which this historiographical essay is concerned.[2] These later volumes, as one might conjecture, are superior to those of the earlier editions since during the intervening thirty-eight years many additional sources of information had become available. Yet the interpretations of events and the characterizations of individuals do not reflect much change. Adolphus's views on such figures as George III, Lord Bute, the Duke of Newcastle, William Pitt, George Grenville, and Lord Mansfield are in fact not far removed from views held in the twentieth century by many distinguished scholars. A contemporary, reviewing *The History of England* when it first appeared, wrote in the *Edinburgh Review:* "The characters appear fairly drawn, though they chiefly consist of the most brilliant and favourable features of each character"; the same writer also praised the "perfect impartiality" displayed by the author "in narrating events."[3]

Adolphus's innate conservatism prevented him from viewing the crisis that developed between Great Britain and the North American colonies with more than a moderate sense of detachment. For example, he called the procuring by Benjamin Franklin of confidential, private letters—written by Governor Francis Bernard and Lieutenant Governor Hutchinson to a friend in England, who was not in office—and the sending of those letters to Massachusetts Bay, "a treacherous and unwarrantable act."[4] Nevertheless, he did not spare Solicitor General Wedderburn for his "vituperative" denunciation of Franklin in the proceedings before the Privy Council on January 4, 1774.[5] While his praise of the character of George Washington was unstinting, his estimation of the Declaration of Independence as a document may be judged by his statement that "at

---

[2] Adolphus never lived to conclude his task. He had published Volume VII in 1845 and was working on Volume VIII when he passed away, leaving the series incomplete and without the useful supplement of an index.

[3] See the *Edinburgh Review*, I, 317–30. The reviewer points out certain errors of fact in *The History* as well as Adolphus's failure to illuminate some important aspects of the period.

[4] John Adolphus: *History of England* (1841), II, 28–9.

[5] *Ibid.*, II, 40–7.

no preceding period of history was so important a transaction vindicated by so shallow and feeble a composition." [6] At the same time, the student will find little fault with Adolphus's detached presentation of the debates in Parliament on American affairs, in which he places equal emphasis on the positions of those who opposed the government policy toward the colonies and of those who supported it.

Adolphus's style is formal and displays little in the way of colour or drama, for his *History* is pre-eminently a work of scholarship. The reader, in utilizing the fairly copious footnotes, is never left in doubt as to the sources from which the author drew his information or the quality of these sources. Professor Herbert Butterfield has summarized the importance of the *History* in the following terms: "The first serious attempt to produce what we would call a 'historical' reconstruction of the early years of George III's reign, was that of John Adolphus. . . . It would not be incorrect to say that he produced the classical Tory defence of George III." That the influence of Adolphus has lasted is also suggested by Butterfield in the section of his *George III and the Historians* entitled "The Return to Adolphus." [7]

Robert Bisset (1759–1805)

Another work of merit, which corresponds closely in spirit to Adolphus's *History*, is Robert Bisset's *History of the Reign of George III. to the Termination of the Late War*, which first came from the press in six volumes in 1803 and was issued in greatly revised form in 1810 in four volumes. Bisset had already published, in 1796, *A Sketch of Democracy*, concerned with those states that had possessed a democratic form of government in ancient times; and he arrived at the conclusion that this type of government was in its nature vicious. Two years later (1798) his *The Life of Edmund Burke, Comprehending an Impartial Account of his Literary and Poetical Efforts and a Sketch of the Conduct and Character of His*

---

[6] *Ibid.*, II, 227–9, 353–6.
[7] *George III and the Historians* (London, 1957), pp. 61 and 181–90.

most eminent Associates, Coadjutors and Opponents appeared; this
was revised and reissued in two volumes in 1800. Although an
admirer of Burke's genius, Bisset did not hesitate to criticize the
great orator when he felt he was wrong.

In the Preface to his *History of . . . George III* Bisset acknowledged the difficulty of writing of "present times" without "prejudice
and partiality"; but such problems disappeared, he felt, in the case
of the writer not connected with any political party and therefore
without motive for distorting the truth. He was led to his theme as
he regarded "with proud pleasure . . . the efforts of my country,
displaying in arduous struggles the exhaustless abundance of British
resources, and the invincible force of British character. . . ." What
further impelled him to undertake the task was his conviction that
Belsham and Robert Macfarlane (who like Belsham had published a
four-volume history of the reign of George III) [1] were both "re-
peaters of party notions and reports, rather than original composers
of authentic and impartial history. . . ." Therefore, where Belsham
found "mean and unworthy motives" for the actions of the King and
others, Bisset generally discovered higher motives. Only in his treatment of the New Englanders did he depart greatly from this rule.
On this subject he wrote: "The puritanism which they inherited
from their forefathers, with its concomitant hypocrisy, incorporated
itself with their commercial conduct; and avarice is never keener
than after a coalition with fanatical austerity, and never with more
ardour uses the ministry of fraud, than when arrayed in the garb of
sanctity." In contrast, when dealing with the Stamp Act crisis Bisset
gave a fair presentation of the position of the colonials and of others
who opposed the act; for example, he wrote: "The constitution of
the American colonies was similar to the polity of Britain, in establishing provisions for the security of property, liberty, and life;
they therefore possessed the right of taxing themselves by their
representatives. This was a privilege which the Americans thought
inherent in them as British subjects, and . . . its practical enjoyment constituted a great part of their comfort and happiness;
and . . . inspirited those exertions which rendered them so beneficial to the British empire." He then raised the question "whether an
adherence to a system of experienced benefit daily increasing, or the

---

[1] Robert Macfarlane: *The History of the Reign of George III* (4 vols., London,
1770–96). The second and third volumes were by an unacknowledged hand.

adoption of new schemes of doubtful operation and certain opposition was most likely to continue and extend that benefit for which colonies were established." [2] This is writing in the modern spirit.

That the influence of Adolphus in shaping the historiography of the period was ultimately greater than that of Bisset may be attributed to the fact that his research into the sources was deeper, his sense of discrimination in the use of authorities more exacting, and his work therefore carried greater weight among scholars.

James, 2nd Earl Waldegrave (1715–1763)

The year 1821 brought the publication of the *Memoirs from 1754 to 1758 by James Earl Waldegrave one of His Majesty's Privy Council in the Reign of George II and Governor to the Prince of Wales afterward George III*. This volume was edited by Henry Richard Vassall Fox, 3rd Lord Holland, although he refrained from signing his name to the Foreword addressed "To the Reader." The importance of the *Memoirs* lies in the fact that Waldegrave enjoyed the trust of George II and was employed by him on more than one occasion in confidential matters of state. Furthermore, as Governor to the Prince of Wales, he was for a period of years thrown into close association with both him and his mother, the Princess Dowager. He also came into intimate contact with such men as Newcastle, Pitt, and Fox at a most critical period in the history of Great Britain and the Empire, and was therefore able to present a number of notable pen portraits of them.

At the beginning of the *Memoirs* Waldegrave wrote: "I will advance no facts which are not strictly true, and do not mean to misrepresent any man; but will make no professions of impartiality, because I take it for granted that it is not in my power to be quite unprejudiced." Although critical of many of his contemporaries, he made no judgements. A writer in the *Edinburgh Review* for 1822 gives the following high praise to the author of the *Memoirs:* "Through the whole of his narrative, there is an appearance of truth and impartiality, seldom found in those who have taken part in the

---

[2] Robert Bisset: *The History of the Reign of George III. to the Termination of the Late War* (Philadelphia, 1810), I, 279 and 289–90.

political struggle they describe." [1] This has also been the opinion of most historians concerned with the period of history that Waldegrave covered. However, the most significant review of his work appeared in the July 1821 number of the London *Quarterly Review*. It was from the pen of the notable John Wilson Croker (1780–1857), a founder of the paper and a constant contributor to it over the years. [2] Croker, quite dubious of the historical value of all memoirs, said of their authors: "it is only their *admissions against* themselves which can be safely relied on. . . ." In this vein he points out, for example, that Waldegrave was unable to appreciate or sympathize with the attitude manifested toward him by the Princess Dowager during the later period of his governorship of Prince George. In fact, the student of history of this period would do well to read the Croker article, together with the *Memoirs*, to get a balanced view of what took place in the household of Prince George. Croker—despite certain reservations, including those against memoirs in general— paid tribute to Waldegrave and affirmed that "his lordship is not merely a candid but an enlightened historian—his facts are accurate—his feelings good—and his principles honourable. . . ." [3] Before closing his essay he made the following interesting statement: "We understand that the sum so liberally given for Lord Waldegrave's Memoirs has awakened out of the dust of the family scrutoirs 'Memoirs of his own Time by Horace Walpole,' that Mr. Murray [4] has purchased them at a magnificent price [£2,000], and that they are in the press, and will shortly be given to the world." [5]

Horace Walpole (1717–1797)

The Memoires of the Last Ten Years of the Reign of King George the Second, although completed some months prior to the death of

---

[1] *Edinburgh Review*, XXXVII, 1–9.

[2] For Croker's relations with the *Quarterly Review* see the October 1884 issue, CLVIII, 527. For additional light on Croker see *The Croker Papers.—The Correspondence and Diaries of the late Right Honourable John Wilson Croker, LL.D., F. R. S., Secretary to the Admiralty from 1809 to 1830* (ed. Louis J. Jennings, 3 vols., London, 1884).

[3] *Quarterly Review*, (1821) XXV, 392–414.

[4] John Murray, publisher of the *Quarterly Review*.

[5] *Quarterly Review*, XXV, 392–414, especially p. 414.

Horace Walpole, the fourth Earl of Orford, in the summer of 1796, remained unpublished by the terms of his will. The manuscript was kept under seal until the sixth Earl of Waldegrave, the last custodian, turned it over for editing to Lord Holland, who also edited the *Memoirs* of the second Earl of Waldegrave. The Walpole manuscript appeared in print in 1822, more than sixty years after the death of George II and long after the protagonists in Walpole's reminiscences (covering the period beginning with 1751 and ending with the death of the King) had passed from the scene.

It should be mentioned that, before 1822, various editions of Walpole's multitudinous, delightful, and illuminating letters had reached the public. The year after his death *The Works of Horace Walpole* had appeared in five volumes, containing between three and four hundred of his letters; in 1818 came his letters to George Montagu and his letters to the Rev. William Cole and others, and in 1820, four volumes of *Private Correspondence of Horace Walpole, Earl of Orford*.

These collections of letters form an important background for the *Memoires,* which they supplement in certain instances and contradict at times. As a reviewer of the *Memoires* remarked of Walpole: ". . . his *Letters* are deserving of unqualified commendation. They are full of wit, pleasantry, and information. . . . As an historian, his principal merit is the minute information he gives of the characters and motives of the persons with whom he acted; and his chief defect, an unjust propensity to satire, and disposition to refer to mean or interested motives the conduct of every man opposed to him, or connected with persons he disliked." [1] In his estimate of Walpole as a writer, this same reviewer affirmed that "his historical works are inferior to his Letters." [2] This estimate of the Walpole *Memoires* was combined with a review of the Waldegrave *Memoirs*. The critic, despite some reservations on both publications, said of them: "So far from finding them barren or unsatisfactory, we are inclined to regard them as the most valuable addition made to English memoirs, since the publication of Burnet's History of his Own Time; [3] and with the exception of Lord Clarendon's account of

---

[1] *Edinburgh Review,* XXXVII, 19–46.
[2] *Ibid.*
[3] Bishop Gilbert Burnet (1643–1715): *History of his own Time* (2 vols., London, 1723, 1734).

his own life,[4] we know of no works in our language that contain such minute and circumstantial details from an eyewitness, or so many persons remarkable in our history." [5]

An important review of Walpole's *Memoires* was printed in the April 1822 *Quarterly Review*. Internal evidence suggests that it came from the pen of John Wilson Croker, whose connection with this periodical has already been mentioned in the sketch on Walde-grave (footnote 2). At the outset Croker stated: "Horace Walpole is an old hero of ours"; he then lauded Walpole's reports of speeches in the House of Commons as superior to any other published reports adding, ". . . nothing that we have met equals [their] brilliancy, vivacity and truth. . . ." [6] But with this, his approval of the *Memoires* ended—despite the presence of "many striking passages, some interesting anecdotes, and a few curious facts . . . thinly scattered through a thousand quarto pages [and] generally purchased at the expense of truth and justice. . . ." As to Walpole's statements of fact, the reviewer found them to be correct in the main, but felt that the "malignity" of his colouring of these facts into a veritable "*code of libel*" vitiated the work as history. For Walpole pictured all public men, apart from his cousin General Conway, "as the most infamous tribe of villains that ever existed," according to Croker, and demon-strated toward them "the feelings of a tiger-cat, sometimes sportive, sometimes ferocious, always cruel." [7] If a base motive, rather than a lofty one, could possibly be attributed to anyone, it was always chosen. Croker concluded that it was impossible, within the limits of his review, to mention the hundreds of instances "of detraction and misrepresentation" embodied in the *Memoires;* this, to him, con-victed the writer "of all the arts of calumny, misrepresentation and falsehood." [8]

Yet Walpole's writings, despite the blemishes that characterize them, were much too significant to be ignored. In 1825, some three years after the publication of the *Memoires* of the reign of George

---

[4] Edward Hyde, first Earl of Clarendon (1609–1674): *True Historical Narrative of the Rebellion and Civil Wars in England* (3 vols., Oxford, 1702–4), in which were incorporated the most important details of Hyde's life; and in 1727 was published A *Collection of several Pieces of Edward, Earl of Clarendon, to which is prefixed an Account of His Lordship's Life, Conduct, and Character by a learned and impartial pen* (8 vols., [Oxford]).

[5] *Edinburgh Review*, XXXVII, 19–46.

[6] *Quarterly Review*, XXXVII, 184.

[7] *Ibid.*, XXVII, 179, 182, 187.

[8] *Ibid.*, XXVIII, 215.

II, there came from the press *Letters from the Honble. Horace Walpole, to the Earl of Hertford, during his Lordship's Embassy in Paris,* which included some letters to the Rev. Henry Zouch. In 1833 three volumes of the highly important *Letters of Horace Walpole, Earl of Orford, to Sir Horace Mann, British Envoy at the Court of Tuscany* were printed; in 1837 the public was presented with a new edition of the *Private Correspondence* (first published in 1820), which omitted certain passages "unsuited to the taste . . . of Female Readers of any refinement"; in 1840 six volumes of the *Letters of Horace Walpole, Earl of Orford* were issued, containing several hundred letters that either had never before been printed or had never been included in any of the collected works; and in 1843 and 1844 appeared in four volumes *Letters of Horace Walpole . . . to Sir Horace Mann at the Court of Florence, from 1760 to 1785,* thus completing a work of real importance to historians.[9]

This prolific publication of Walpole's correspondence finally led to the project for bringing out his memoirs covering the first years of the reign of George III. When the sixth Earl of Waldegrave had turned over to Lord Holland the Walpole memoirs concerned with the last ten years of the reign of George II, he had also placed in Holland's hands the manuscript relating to George III. But nothing was done with it. On Waldegrave's death these memoirs came into the possession of Lord Euston (later Duke of Grafton) as executor. He thereupon chose as editor Sir Denis Le Marchant, who had distinguished himself both in public life and in his writings on public affairs. As a result in 1845 the four volumes of *The Memoirs of the Reign of King George III* followed under Le Marchant's editorship. In reviewing the books for the December 1845 number of the *Quarterly Review* a writer (again by internal evidence the magazine's editor, Croker) stated that, as "to naked facts and the mere succession of events," the *Memoirs* now before him were "in general accurate." He also pointed out that Walpole, during the period when his cousin General Conway was a member of the

---

[9] The student using the original edition of Walpole's letters to Sir Horace Mann should consult especially the lengthy and carefully prepared reviews of the volumes that appeared in the *Edinburgh Review* for July 1833, LVIII, 227–58, and in the London *Quarterly Review* for September 1843 and October 1844, LXXII, 516–52, and LXXIV, 295–416. Needless to say, those turning to the correspondence today should consult the truly notable series *The Yale Edition of Horace Walpole's Correspondence,* ed. W. S. Lewis and staff. At the time of writing the six volumes of the Walpole-Mann correspondence published in the Yale edition bring it to March 1768.

highly confidential Cabinet Council, was even "better informed *than he ought to have been* on many cabinet questions"—something that certainly added importance to his record of the events of the years 1765 to 1768. Nevertheless, the reviewer felt impelled to denounce what he considered to be a "disregard of truth, a perversity of judgment, and a rancour of feeling" in these *Memoirs*. The review, covering some forty-five pages, quotes Walpole against Walpole and calls in other contemporary writers to refute the assertions of the author on certain events, thus "recording a solemn . . . protest against the . . . historical value of the Memoirs of Horace Walpole." [10]

In his important work on historiography, *George III and the Historians*, which appeared in 1957, Professor Herbert Butterfield devotes a chapter to "Horace Walpole's Memoirs." In it he stresses the fact that Walpole gave a retrospective view of the significance of events embodied in his memoirs as though he were recording his own views on the events at the time they took place. Butterfield therefore warns the reader of the *Memoirs* that it is necessary to reconcile Walpole's recollections of events with the frequently widely divergent outlook expressed in his letters written at the time they happened. Butterfield very properly concludes his Walpole essay with the following caution: "Horace Walpole, therefore, has left for the historian two great bodies of material and two imposing sets of opinions and reactions, both of which require a careful critical apparatus." [11]

William Coxe (1747–1828)

The Rev. William Coxe, Fellow of King's College Cambridge, Archdeacon of Wiltshire, was the author of numerous works, including *Memoirs of Sir Robert Walpole*. After finding that Horace Wal-

---

[10] *Quarterly Review*, LXXVII, 253–98. It should be pointed out that in 1894 these *Memoirs*, after being re-edited by G. F. Russell, were republished in four volumes. Walpole also left a journal covering the events of the reign of George III not included in the *Memoirs*. In 1859 it was published under title *Journal of the Reign of King George the Third, from 1771 to 1783. By Horace Walpole*.

[11] *George III and the Historians* (London, 1957), pp. 108–18.

pole's *Memoires of the Last Ten Years of the Reign of King George the Second* were "deeply imbued with the prejudices and antipathies of the writer," and that the "misrepresentations, and errors with which it abounded" were "calculated to create an impression, highly unfavourable to the character of Mr. Pelham," he decided to provide the public with a fair account of the activities of this statesman as George II's chief minister. This Coxe did although he was "under increasing infirmities of age, and a total defect of sight." [1] The memoirs appeared in two folio volumes in 1829, the year after Coxe's death, entitled *Memoirs of the Administration of the Right Honourable Henry Pelham* . . . Having had access to the vast body of Newcastle Papers, and the papers of other leading figures for the period that he described, the Rev. Coxe was able to produce an exceedingly valuable record of public events during the years from 1743 to the death of Pelham in 1754. The work was enhanced by the inclusion of a number of important letters as an Appendix. Unfortunately, Coxe's literary style in this work did not measure up to his scholarly standards, and both style and scholarship undoubtedly bear the marks of his physical handicaps. Nor are the *Memoirs* easy reading, in spite of the minor corrections made since their appearance.

The unsigned account of Coxe's life in the *Dictionary of National Biography* has stated: ". . . his chief article of faith seems to have been the impeccability of the whigs." The reader therefore will look in vain for any account of the methods used by Pelham and the Duke of Newcastle, his brother, to ensure a complacent House of Commons; moreover, the internal history of Great Britain for the period is too much neglected in favour of foreign affairs. [2] Nevertheless the *Memoirs* take a high place in the historiography of the period for their reliability.

---

[1] *Memoirs of the Administration of the Right Honourable Henry Pelham* . . . (2 vols., London, 1829), Preface, pp. vii and viii.

[2] For an appreciative sketch of the life of Coxe see his obituary in *Gentleman's Magazine*, 1828, Part II, 86–9. It may be noted that some of the omissions in Coxe's work have more recently been filled in by John B. Owen in *The Rise of the Pelhams* (London, 1957), in which Owen speaks of the *Memoirs* in terms of respect.

Philip Henry Stanhope, Viscount Mahon
(1805–1875)

To counteract the work of William Coxe with its strong Whig bias (not to mention the writing of Horace Walpole, with its almost constant spirit of condemnation of the people involved), we now come to a work which, like that of John Adolphus, presents the conservative point of view: Lord Mahon's *The History of England from the Peace of Utrecht to the Peace of Versailles, 1713–1783.* This was issued in seven volumes between the years 1836 and 1854.

The success of Mahon's *History* was immediate. By 1858 it had passed through four editions and appeared in a fifth and revised one, which incorporated corrections of errors in the earlier editions.

Mahon, who became the fifth Earl Stanhope in 1855 on the death of his father, was a man of excellent education. Soon after securing a degree at Oxford he entered the House of Commons and was active in political affairs from 1830 to 1852. He then gave his chief attention to cultural matters, serving as a trustee of the British Museum, as honorary Antiquary of the Royal Academy of Arts, and as an examiner in the new school of jurisprudence and modern history at Oxford. Like Adolphus, Mahon was intensely proud of England. In the Introduction to his *History,* he states:

> "The era of the Georges in England may be compared to the era of the Antonines at Rome. It was a period combining happiness and glory—a period of kind rulers and a prosperous people. While improvement was advancing at home with gigantic strides, while great wars were waged abroad, the domestic repose and enjoyment of the nation was scarce for a moment ever broken through. . . . Unlike the era of the Antonines, this prosperity did not depend [in the words of Gibbon] 'on the character of a single man.' Its foundations were laid on ancient and free institutions, which, good from the first, were still gradually improving, and which alone, amongst all others since the origin of civil society, have completely solved the great problem how to combine the greatest security to property with the greatest freedom of action."

While acknowledging the existence of corruption and faction, which offered a basis for "most loud and angry complaints," Mahon writes: "How much has prosperity been felt, but how little acknowledged! How sure a road to popularity has it always been to tell us, that we are the most wretched and ill-used people on the face of the earth!" In attempting to unfold a small period of history with its "mingled mass of national wisdom and national folly," the writer assures the readers of one thing: his "honesty of purpose." Then, manifestly with Walpole's writing in mind, he states: "I feel that unjustly to lower the fame of a political adversary, or unjustly to raise the fame of an ancestor—to state any fact without sufficient authority, or to draw any character without thorough conviction, implies not merely literary failure but moral guilt." [1]

Mahon's work has many excellent qualities. The style is simple and straightforward without any straining for literary effect. The descriptions of leading people, whether Whig or Tory, are fair. Mahon stressed George III's lack of education and of taste in *belles-lettres* and pointed out certain peculiarities of the King's speech that gave the impression of "shallowness." At the same time he pronounced the King to be "truly and emphatically an honest man," who gave to his "exalted duties . . . conscientious and constant attention," and affirmed that, after the period of "the sway of the northern Favourite . . . the taint of the factions which Junius adorned and envenomed,—and the odium of the North American contest," no one among the world's rulers, "not even our own Elizabeth were ever more deeply rooted in the hearts of the people that they ruled." [2] Of both the Earl of Bute and the Duke of Newcastle Mahon was critical. Among other reproofs of their actions, he suggested that "the cabals of Bute were to the full as numerous and crooked as Newcastle's." [3] As for George Grenville, he characterized him as "an excellent Speaker [of the House of Commons] spoiled," and spoke of his two chief measures—the expulsion of John Wilkes from Parliament and the taxation of America—as having "long since been acknowledged not only as disastrous, but as in the highest degree unwise." [4] William Pitt, later Earl of Chatham, he described

---

[1] Lord Mahon: *History of England from the Peace of Utrecht to the Peace of Versailles. 1713–1783* (5th edn., 7 vols., London, 1858), I, Introduction. This revised edition is the one recommended for general use.

[2] *History* (1858), IV, 207–8.

[3] *Ibid.*, IV, 215.

[4] *Ibid.*, V, 34.

as one "who made himself the first man in England, and England the first country in the world."[5] Of Charles Townshend, he said: "His application was great—his ambition unbounded. No man had more quickness of wit, or less reserve in displaying it . . . but it was not free from that drawback . . . a fickleness and unsteadiness of purpose." Yet, before his untimely death in 1767, Townshend seemed well on the way to attaining "the main power of the State . . . [for] of late he had found no rival in the House of Commons, and would bear no superior in the Cabinet."[6] If Mahon doubted the capacity for leadership of Charles Townshend, he had praise for Lord North, the King's chief minister, whose figure was "overgrown and ungraceful" and who was extremely near-sighted, but who met the eloquence of Charles James Fox, Edmund Burke, Colonel Barré, and others, with "a flow of good sense and sterling information, enlivened by never failing pleasantry and wit . . . conjoined with high character and with steady courage. . . ."[7]

Mahon was accused by the learned reviewer of Walpole's *Memoires* (in the December 1845 number of the *Quarterly Review*)[8] of falling into the Walpole "snares—habitually quoting, and sometimes copying without quoting—his malicious romances," despite his (Mahon's) assertions that "on no occasion would he readily trust Horace Walpole as to *motives*."[9] Although Mahon was well-versed in the history of England, and had access to the most valuable manuscript material relating to it,[10] he had, rather surprisingly, only a superficial knowledge of the American colonies and consequently of the story of British expansion in North America down to 1775. Following publication of Volumes V and VI of the original edition, which in 1851 covered the period 1763 to 1780, a very able review appeared in the July 1852 number of the *North American Review*.[11]

---

[5] *Ibid.*, III, 12.

[6] *Ibid.*, IV, 27; V, 184.

[7] *Ibid.*, V, 254–5.

[8] *Quarterly Review*, LXXVII, 274. The writer, by internal evidence, was clearly the magazine's owner, John Wilson Croker. For Croker see the essay on Waldegrave, *supra*, footnote 2.

[9] *History* (1st edn.), IV, 14.

[10] *Ibid.*, I, 2–3.

[11] *North American Review*, LXXV, 125–208. The review of these same volumes in the *Quarterly Review* (XC, 507) for March 1852 states: "His diligence and impartiality are universally recognized. . . . His pen is always under guidance of conscience. A fine sense of justice and scrupulous regard for truth is perceptible throughout. . . ."

At the outset the reviewer acknowledged:

> "Lord Mahon is a better historical writer than either of the eminent
> persons who have treated any portion of English history between the
> Revolution of 1688 and the accession of George the Third. He is a
> more reasonable, at all events a more moderate, Tory than Mr.
> Adolphus, who began at the latter era [that is, with the reign of
> George III]. Indeed, one chief merit of his book is the fair and
> generous spirit which for the most part pervades it. It is quite plain
> that he means to maintain good faith with subjects and readers, to
> tell the story frankly and truly, and impartially to award praise and
> blame."

After this initial compliment, the remainder of the long article is
given over to showing the *History's* shortcomings in relating events
that took place in America. This is done, however, in a spirit of
moderation, as is the reviewer's effort to bring to the attention of
readers certain errors of fact and of interpretation in Mahon's volumes. This well-tempered and important review—together with
Volume V of George Bancroft's *History of the United States* covering the period 1763 to 1766, which appeared the same year incorporating other information then available—suggested many ways for
Mahon to improve his work. Thus the revision of it that came out
six years later met some of the criticism previously levelled against
it. In fact the late Professor A. F. Pollard, who wrote the biography
of the Earl of Stanhope for the 1898 edition of the *Dictionary of
National Biography,* made the claim for Mahon's *History* that it "still
remains the best narration of English history during the eighteenth
century." Although this claim can no longer be sustained, Mahon's
work was an important contribution to the historiography of the
period.

James Grahame (1790–1842)

No other British writer ever developed the passionate love for the
United States that James Grahame embodied in his work; yet Grahame was writing about a country he had never visited. His grandfather, Judge Thomas Grahame of the Admiralty Court of Glasgow,

is said to have been the first British judge to decree the liberation of a Negro slave brought into Great Britain, which he did "on the ground, that a guiltless human being, in that country, *must* be free"—a judgement that preceded by some years the more celebrated decision of Chief Justice Mansfield.[1] Further, Judge Grahame was opposed to British policy on the issues that led to the War for American Independence. James's father, Robert—also a lawyer and a writer to the signet, who became a man of wealth and attained the office of Lord Provost of Glasgow by election—likewise strongly favoured the American side of the struggle.[2] With this family background it is perhaps not surprising that James Grahame became an ardent supporter of the idea that colonies, and particularly the British North American colonies, were destined for independence.

After attending the University of Glasgow, and also Cambridge for a brief period, he followed his grandfather and father into the practice of law and became a barrister. He was successful in this field, but his heart was not in it. Deeply influenced by religious ideas, his "views coincided with those professed by the early Puritans and the Scotch Covenanters." But after 1824 it was to history rather than to the Gospel that he dedicated the remaining years of his life. "For a considerable time," he wrote to his friend John Frederick W. Herschel, the astronomer, "I have been meditating a great literary work. . . . It is a history of North America,—the most interesting historical subject, I think, a human pen ever undertook."[3] In 1827 he published in London the first two volumes of his history. Before the end of 1829 the remainder of the work—carrying the account to 1776—was completed. During the next seven years, Grahame laboured to eliminate every possible blemish from the text, although his health was undermined by his great exertions. At last in 1836 his complete revised history appeared from the London press of Smith, Elder & Co. in four volumes. It was published under the title *The History of the United States of North America, from the Plantation of the British Colonies, till their Revolt and Declaration of Independence.*

It is a matter of considerable interest to note that *The History* was

---

[1] "Memoir of James Grahame, LL.D.," *The History of the United States of North America, from the Plantation of the British Colonies till their Assumption of National Independence* (2nd edn. enlarged and amended, 2 vols., Philadelphia, 1850, 1852), I, v.

[2] *Ibid.*, v–vi.

[3] *Ibid.*, I, x.

ignored in Great Britain. This was true not only when the first two volumes appeared but also when the complete work was published. In fact, in order to bring out the 1836 edition Grahame was obliged to assume the entire cost of publication, a venture "which resulted in a loss of one thousand pounds sterling. . . ." [4] Surprisingly enough, despite the excellence of the work, only one major review of it ever appeared. This was Charles Francis Adams's critique of the first two volumes in the January 1831 number of the *North American Review,* in which he stated: "Mr. Grahame has published what we conceive to be the best book that has any where appeared, upon the early history of the United States. He has corrected, with a proper boldness, the mistakes, whether of ignorance or malignity, which his predecessors in the same labors had committed." [5] It is true that in the review of Volume III of George Bancroft's *History of the United States* (which appeared in the January 1841 issue of this same periodical), William H. Prescott paid the following tribute to the work of Grahame: "The most thorough work, and incomparably the best on the subject, previous to the appearance of Mr. Bancroft's, is the well-known history by Mr. Grahame, a truly valuable book. . . . Mr. Grahame's work, however, with all its merit, is the work of a *foreigner.*" [6] This review prompted Grahame to write to Prescott in reply: "When I look into the works of some of your greatest American writers, and see how daintily they handle certain topics, . . . I must respectfully doubt, if, as yet at least, an American is likely to be the best writer of American history." He added, nevertheless: "That the greatest and most useful historian that has ever instructed mankind will yet arise in America, I fondly hope, desire, and believe." [7]

Undaunted by the general silence in the British periodicals respecting his achievement, Grahame set to work on a second revised edition of *The History.* This, however, was not destined to appear until after his death. In 1845, as the result of activity on the part of the Massachusetts Historical Society, a four-volume second edition was printed in Boston by Little & Brown; the following year Blanchard & Lea of Philadelphia brought it out in two quarto volumes; in 1850 and again in 1856 the same firm reissued the revised edition.

---

[4] *Ibid.,* I, xvii.
[5] *North American Review,* XXXII, 174–95.
[6] *Ibid.,* LII, 83–4.
[7] Grahame's "Memoir," *op. cit.,* I, xxiii.

Thus, although scorned in Great Britain, Grahame's work was welcomed in the United States.

Only the last portion of Grahame's history deals with the period that concerns us. Throughout it carries the well-developed thesis that the logical and proper end of colonies that prosper and expand is the establishment of independence from the parent state. An equally developed second thesis, dealing with the British trade and navigation system, laid down the proposition

> "that a political connection between two countries of which the weaker is not entirely enslaved, founded upon or interwoven with such a commercial system, manifestly carried within itself the principles of its own dissolution. . . . Assuredly, even although no other subject of quarrel had presented itself, the commercial restrictions alone must in process of time have occasioned the disruption of the American provinces from the British Empire. Every step in the progressive advancement of those distant communities was a step towards potential independence."

Before ending his *History*, Grahame also declared with great insight:

> "Had Britain, after the treaty of Paris [of 1763], discerned the change which her relation with America had actually undergone, and liberally recognized it; had she, instead of aggravating the pressure of her commercial restrictions, and introducing new regulations still more arbitrary and severe, begun with prevenient grace to relax those bonds; and finally, acknowledging the national maturity of her colonies, declared them independent; and, trusting to their grateful friendship, sought to negotiate with them a commercial treaty beneficial to her own people,—would the consequences of this policy, more magnanimous than any nation had ever yet shown itself equal to, have proved more conducive than the scenes which actually ensued to the happiness of Britain, America, and mankind in general?" [8]

Indeed, perhaps the chief criticism that can be made of Grahame's *History* is that it was a century ahead of its time when it was issued in Great Britain, and this possibly explains the icy silence of the writing public there towards it.[9]

---

[8] Grahame: *History*, II, 365–6 and 555.

[9] For an excellent survey of Grahame's work see Michael Kraus: *A History of American History* (New York, 1937), pp. 194–8.

Henry Peter Brougham, Baron Brougham
and Vaux (1778–1868)

Among the vast number of works produced by Lord Brougham—a Scot who entered the House of Commons in 1810, became extremely active in public affairs, and in 1830 attained the high position of Lord Chancellor—the only writing that need be mentioned in the present historiographical survey is his interesting and provocative *Historical Sketches of Statesmen who Flourished in the Time of George III.*[1] In preparing these *Sketches,* he stated, his purpose was to record "for the warning or for the encouragement of the great [men of public affairs], the errors of [or] the wisdom, the vices or the virtues, of their predecessors."

The first and second of the three series of sketches appeared in 1839. Here in separate essays are portrayed (among others) George III, the Earl of Chatham, Lord North, Edmund Burke, and Lord Mansfield. Of George III he wrote: "The American war, the long exclusion of the liberal party, the French Revolution, the Catholic question, are all sad monuments of his real power." A fundamental point that concerned Brougham was whether the King's interference in public affairs was "unconstitutional." "Does the king of this country hold a real or only a nominal office? Is he merely a form, or is he a substantive power in our mixed and balanced constitution?" Some people regarded the only true power vested in the Crown to be the choice of ministers and thought that even the exercise of this power was actually controlled by Parliament. Brougham, however, could not comprehend this theory of a monarchy. "It assigns to the Crown either far too much revenue, or far too little power. . . . To affect living under a kingly government, and yet suffer no kind of kingly power, seems extravagantly absurd." Thus Brougham leads the reader to the conclusion that George III acted constitutionally in exercising his power, but that "he took the wrong direction."[2]

Lord Chatham he characterized as "the person to whom every one

---

[1] Brougham's *Historical Sketches* . . . (3 vols., London, 1839–43; new edns.: **6** vols. 1845, 2 vols., Philadelphia, 1840 and 1842).

[2] *Historical Sketches of Statesmen* (Phila. edn.), I, 2, 10, 17–19.

would at once point, if desired to name the most successful statesman and most brilliant orator that this country ever produced, [yet]
impracticable, difficult beyond all men to act with, overbearing,
impetuously insisting on his own views being adopted by all as
infallible, utterly regardless of other men's opinions when he had
formed his own, [and] as little disposed to profit by the lights of
their wisdom as to avail himself of their co-operative efforts in
action. . . ."³ While praising Lord North for many noble qualities
of character, Brougham wrote that the "American war is the great
blot upon his fame; . . . the policy toward our colonies, of which
he had been the leading advocate in Parliament, and for which he
was primarily responsible as minister, can admit of no defence;
nor . . . is it possible to urge, even in extenuation of his offending,
that he was all along aware of the King's egregious folly, which
obstinately persisted in a hopeless and ruinous struggle against the
liberties of his people." ⁴

Burke, according to Brougham, was "among the most extraordinary persons that have ever appeared," but despite his almost in-
comparable gifts he "was deficient in judgment" and inconsistent.
"It would, indeed be difficult to select one leading principle or
prevailing sentiment in Mr. Burke's latest writings, to which something extremely adverse may not be found in his former . . .
works." ⁵

Without quite according the foremost place as a lawyer to a
fellow Scot, Lord Mansfield, Brougham praised his wisdom at bar
and bench as well as when presiding in the House of Lords. In fact,
Lord Camden, Mansfield's opponent, was in the writer's eyes "a man
inferior to him in everything but courage . . ." for a certain timidity held this great man (Mansfield) from accepting the highest posts
of responsibility in the government.⁶

---

³ *Ibid.*, I, 23, 44.
⁴ *Ibid.*, I, 54–5.
⁵ *Ibid.*, I, 125, 132, 136.
⁶ *Ibid.*, I, 93, 104.

Thomas Erskine May, Baron Farnborough
(1815–1886)

Leaning heavily upon the memoirs and correspondence of certain eighteenth-century protagonists by then published—such as those of Horace Walpole, for example—Thomas Erskine May in 1861 and 1863 published his two-volume *Constitutional History of England since the Accession of George the Third, 1760–1860*. May had already brought out *A Practical Treatise on the Law, Privileges, Proceedings, and Usage of Parliament* (1844), and *Rules, Orders, and Forms of Procedure of the House of Commons* (1854), both of which were held in the highest esteem, as his *Constitutional History* was also destined to be. Indeed, one may say that the last constituted something of a landmark in British historiography. A revised edition of the *Constitutional History* appeared in 1863 and 1865, and a third edition in 1871. Not only did it have many reprintings, but as late as 1912 a new edition, edited by Francis Holland, carried the *Constitutional History* down to 1911.

Departing from the views of writers like Adolphus, May set the background for his work in the first chapter, "Influence of the Crown during the Reign of George III." In it he stressed the fact that George's mother, "ambitious and fond of power . . . derived her views of the rights and authority of a sovereign from German courts; and encouraged the prince's natural propensities by [giving him] the significant advice of 'George, be king.'" [1] He also pointed to the influence exerted by Lord Bute, who taught the king-to-be "that his own honor and the interests of the country required the extension of his personal influence, and a more active exercise of his prerogatives." May then added that the "chief obstacle to this new policy of the court was found in the established authority of responsible ministers, upheld by party connections and parliamentary interest." [2] Nevertheless, the King and Bute, his minister,

---

[1] *Constitutional History of England* (2 vols., New York, 1886), I, 22.
[2] *Ibid.*, I, 23.

"were resolved to carry matters with a high hand, and their arbitrary attempts to coerce and intimidate opponents disclosed their imperious views of the prerogative. . . . [But] these stretches of prerogative served to unite the Whigs into an organized opposition. . . . It now became their office to assert the liberties of the people, and to resist the encroachments of prerogative. Thus the king's attempt to restore the personal influence of the Sovereign, which the Revolution had impaired, so far from strengthening the throne, advanced the popular cause. . . ." [3]

Again, of the withdrawal of Bute from public life May writes: "The fall of the King's favored minister was even more sudden than his rise." Bute, however, did not "propose to relinquish his own power together with his office; he retreated to the interior cabinet, whence he could direct more securely the measures of the court. . . ." [4] Here then we have the Princess Dowager and Lord Bute urging George III to reassert the royal prerogatives that the Crown had lost as the result of the Revolution and to undermine "the established authority of responsible ministers." Here we also have Bute driven from public office as the result of public resentment and then retreating to the "interior cabinet" in order to direct the measure of the Court in greater security.

Such views of George III—although they were generally accepted throughout the nineteenth century—are no longer held by leading historians, whether authorities in the field of political or constitutional history. George III is today regarded as a monarch who was dedicated to maintaining the constitution of England as altered by the Revolution; nor were there in his time "responsible ministers" in the sense that they exist today or even at the time May wrote—that is, responsible to the majority in the House of Commons. Nor is the view any longer accepted that Lord Bute remained the secret and malign influence behind the throne after he surrendered the seal of office. Moreover, important policies were determined primarily by his ministers and not by George III acting alone. As the late Professor Maitland has so well stated: "George III, though he had a will of his own and strong views of policy, did not interfere with this arrangement. At the deliberative meetings of the Cabinet Council the king was not present; the formal meetings of the Privy Council at which he was present were not meetings for debate or discussion,

---

[3] *Ibid.*, I, 32.
[4] *Ibid.*, I, 33–4.

but merely meetings at which the king would give his formal assent and authority to matters which had been already before the Cabinet and about which the king's pleasure had been already taken." [5]

James Anthony Froude (1818–1894)

Among the historians whose work demands a place in this historiography, none wrote more brilliantly than James Anthony Froude. And yet, no history should be used with greater caution than that which came from his pen. While a student at Oriel College, Oxford, he was brought in touch with the Tractarian Movement, the leaders of which were John Henry Newman, a fellow of his college, Richard Hurrell Froude, Froude's elder brother, also a fellow at Oriel, and John Keble. Froude ultimately reacted strongly against the views of the sponsors of this movement and their efforts to recover the values of mediaeval Catholicism, which finally carried Newman into the Roman Catholic Church.

After Froude had written his *History of England from the Fall of Wolsey to the Defeat of the Spanish Armada* (1870–1875), in which his hostility to the Roman Catholic Church was clearly displayed, he turned to the preparation of *The English in Ireland in the Eighteenth Century*. It is in Volume II of this work that he came to grips with the problems facing Ireland during the period of concern to the present series. In this connection he wrote:

---

[5] F. W. Maitland: *The Constitutional History of England* . . . (Cambridge, 1909), p. 395. M. A. Thomson, in his *A Constitutional History of England, 1642–1801* (London, 1938), considers the reigns of George I, George II, and George III, and the relation of these monarchs to their ministers. Of the authority that they exercised in dismissing a minister and in consulting those outside the Ministry, he writes: "Nor did any of these actions violate any established constitutional convention. The King in matters constitutional was almost always conservative." He further concludes, with particular reference to George III, that there "is no proper foundation for the belief, once prevalent, that he attempted to subvert the constitution" (p. 367). The viewpoints of other historians on George III's conception of his constitutional position are presented elsewhere in this historiography. Sir Lewis Namier, as will be noted later, was particularly active in modifying the opinion of George III held by such writers as May.

"A free government depends for its successful working on the loyal cooperation of the people. Where the people do not cooperate, the forms of liberty are either a mockery, or an instrument of disunion and anarchy. Had the Irish been regarded from the outset as a conquered people whom a stronger neighbor had forced, for its own convenience, into reluctant submission, Ireland would have escaped the worst of her calamities. Her clans would have been held in awe by an army; public order would have been preserved by a police: but her lands would have been left to their native owners; her customs and laws might have been untouched, and her religion need not have been interfered with. . . . [However,] the nature of the English constitution forbade an experiment which might have been dangerous to our own liberties. . . . We imposed upon her our own modes of self-government; we gave her a parliament, we gave her our trial by jury and our common law; we assimilated the Irish Church to our own; and these magnificent institutions refused to root themselves in an uncongenial soil." [1]

The work embodied a theory of government that, though at one time widely held, has since proved erroneous. Thus, in thinking of the relations between England and Ireland and in justifying the domination of the one over the other, he stated in Volume I: "In a world in which we are made to depend so largely for our well-being on the conduct of our neighbors, and yet are created infinitely unequal in ability and worthiness of character, the superior part has a natural right to govern; the inferior part has a natural right to be governed. . . . Yet Ireland would neither resist courageously, nor would she honorably submit." For the Irish, "though they would make no stand for liberty, as little could endure order or settled government." [2] This reflects the conclusions of his contemporaries, Darwin and Spencer.

Those who attempted to assess the value of the work varied in opinion. A writer who reviewed *The English in Ireland* in the January 1873 and April 1874 numbers of the *Quarterly Review* declared: "At last we have a picture and a judgment of Ireland by a hand at once competent, candid, and unsparing. Mr. Froude is too practised an historian, and has too disciplined a mind, not to make sure of the completeness, as well as the essential correctness, of his facts; though some of them no doubt may be open to question, and many

---

[1] *The English in Ireland in the Eighteenth Century* (3 vols., London, 1872–4; New York, 1873–4), II, 1–2. A new edition appeared in 1881.
[2] *Ibid.*, I, 2 and 12.

more are sure to be fiercely controverted." At the same time the reviewer admitted that there was a certain weakness in the book. "Impartial the work certainly is not, and scarcely pretends to be . . . its tone is often extravagantly, almost savagely severe, . . . Irish faults and crimes are hunted down with a ferocity which has something of the bloodhound in the relentless pertinacity of its pursuit." [3]

To combat Froude's strictures on Ireland there came from the New York press in 1873 *English Misrule in Ireland. A Course of Lectures by the Very Rev. Thomas N. Burke . . . in reply to James Anthony Froude,* and in 1874 W. H. Flood published his *Notes and Historical Criticism on Mr. A. Froude's English in Ireland in the 18th Century* (Torquay). The April 1874 number of the *Fortnightly Review* carried a review by Professor J. E. Cairnes, which presented the work most unfavourably. G. P. Gooch, in his study of nineteenth-century historiography, while agreeing that Froude has included in his work a good deal of valuable material, called it "morally indefensible and politically mischievous." [4] But the most notable refutation of many of Froude's charges against Ireland and the Irish was included in W. E. H. Lecky's great work on the eighteenth century.

William Edward Hartpole Lecky (1838–1903)

Of all the historians who wrote on England in the eighteenth century none penetrated more deeply into the heart of his subject than William Edward Hartpole Lecky. Born and educated in Ire-

---

[3] *Quarterly Review,* CXXXIV, 169–85. In reviewing Volumes II and III, the same critic again stressed Froude's defects as a historian, with his "savage scorn" and "lively rage," but held that while the work relied too greatly upon the secret papers of the government, yet "in the main the picture is undoubtedly true and its value lies in its resolute and unflinching outspokenness" (*ibid.,* CXXXVI, 498–526).

[4] *History and Historians of the Nineteenth Century* (London, 1920), p. 338. In *Some Modern Historians of Britain, Essays in Honor of R. L. Schuyler* (eds. Herman Ausubel *et al.,* New York, 1951, pp. 49–65) Beatrice Reynolds writes the essay on Froude. It is largely taken up with a consideration of Froude's earlier work on England under the Tudors, although his view of England's lost opportunity for remaking Ireland after the battle of the Boyne—by the absorption of the natives through British emigration there and by more enlightened legislation favouring that kingdom—is also mentioned (p. 59).

land, Lecky held a degree from Trinity College, Dublin.[1] He became
the author, (among other works) of *A History of the Rise and
Influence of Rationalism in Europe*, which appeared in two volumes
in 1865, and *A History of European Morals from Augustus to
Charlemagne*, also in two volumes, which came out in 1869. Lecky
thereupon turned to the writing of his eight-volume *History of
England during the Eighteenth Century*, the first two volumes of
which appeared in 1878 and the final two (VII and VIII) in 1890.

In his Preface to Volume I Lecky pointed out that it was not his
purpose to write a chronological history of the period or to present
in detail either military events or those "personal and party incidents
which form so large a part of political annals." His desire was rather
to illuminate "the permanent forces of the nation . . . the more
enduring features of national life." He therefore fastened upon a
topical development in his series, and dealt in great detail with such
subjects as the monarchy, the aristocracy, and the "democracy"; the
religious establishment and the dissenters; the growth of the power
of Parliament and of the press; the history of political ideas; and the
broad culture of the English nation. Moreover, he went beyond
England to place considerable emphasis in his volumes upon Scotland, even more on the American colonies, especially in treating the
American Revolution, and most upon his native land. In fact, in 1892
those portions of the *History of England* relating to Ireland were
issued separately in five volumes and reprinted many times under
the title *A History of Ireland in the Eighteenth Century*. It may be
added that the sections relating to America and the revolt of the
colonies were in turn brought together by Professor James A. Woodburn of Indiana University, supplemented with notes and published
in book form in the United States in 1898 under the title *The
American Revolution, 1763–1783*. . . . All these publication efforts
give testimony to the high regard in which this important work was
held.

In the Preface to his *History of England* Lecky did not fail to pay
tribute to Lord Mahon's "very valuable history," but he made clear
that he himself had in mind a quite different purpose from Mahon's
and expressed the hope that the reader would not think of his work

---

[1] James Johnston Auchmuty of Trinity College, Dublin, in his *Lecky: A Biographical and Critical Essay* (Dublin, 1945), has given the public by far the most
discriminating account of Lecky's career and of the influences that motivated his
thinking and laid the basis for his career in history.

as written "in any spirit of rivalry, or with any wish to depreciate the merits of its predecessor." [2] In fact, it is clear that the only historian whom Lecky felt called upon to challenge strenuously was Froude; this he did in his reviews in *Macmillan's Magazine* after the publication of the three Froude volumes.[3] These articles, while recognizing the great literary merits of *The English in Ireland* and the extent of Froude's research, took strong exception to his defence of the Irish penal laws, to his spirit of intolerance, and to the use he made of the authorities on which he relied. "It is written with very great power," wrote Lecky to a friend, referring to Froude's work, "and its single object is to blast the character of the [Irish] people, representing them as hopelessly, irredeemably bad, justifying every past act of oppression, and trying to arouse to the utmost, sectarian passions both against and among them." [4]

In view of Lecky's deep desire to correct what he felt were Froude's distortions of Irish history, it is perhaps not surprising that *The History of England* is badly out of balance. For example, out of a total of 642 pages in Volume II some 345 pages are allotted to Ireland; in Volume IV, of a total of 560 pages, 248 pages; in Volume VI, out of 611 pages, 310; of the 465 pages in Volume VII the majority relate to Ireland, and, finally, Volume VIII is given over entirely to Ireland. The book in reality could better have been called "Great Britain and Ireland in the Eighteenth Century." In contrast to Froude's work there is a spirit of detachment in the text of Lecky's *History*, although this is not always evident in the footnotes.[5] For Lecky, although a devoted Irishman, was at the same time dedicated to the British connection, and even opposed Gladstone's plan of Irish home rule.

From the standpoint of present-day scholarship, the chapters on Ireland stand on a higher plane than do those relating to England,

---

[2] *History of England in the Eighteenth Century,* I, Preface, pp. v and vi.

[3] See *Macmillan's Magazine,* XXVII, 246–64, and XXX, 166–84.

[4] Lecky to Arthur Booth, February 1, 1878, *A Memoir of the Right Hon. William Edward Hartpole Lecky . . . By his Wife* (New York, London, Bombay, Calcutta, 1909), p. 140.

[5] For example, at one point in dealing with the fatal consequences of the suppression of the Roman Catholic religion, Lecky quotes Froude against Froude by arraying the earlier *History of England* against the *English in Ireland* and charging that in the latter Froude "intended to blacken to the utmost the character of all Irish people, and especially of the Irish Catholics" (*England in the Eighteenth Century,* II, 101*n*). For Lecky's further criticism of Froude's distortions of Irish history by his misuse of sources see also *ibid.,* II, 127*n,* 154*n,* 169*n,* 180*n,* 201*n,* 280*n,* 308*n,* 341*n,* 360–1, 377*n,* 408*n.*

since Lecky leaned too heavily at times on such authorities as Walpole's *Memoires* and *Letters*, rather than on more reliable sources, in writing of developments in England. Further, in dealing with English constitutional history he followed all too readily the error of his fellow historian Macaulay, by associating the nineteenth-century cabinet form of government with the outcome of the Revolution of 1688 in the statement: "The formation of a ministry, or homogeneous body of ruling statesmen of the same politics, deliberating in common, and in which each member is responsible to the others, has been justly described by Lord Macaulay as one of the most momentous and least noticed consequences of the Revolution." [6] Again, his characterization of George III as being guilty of inflicting "more profound and enduring injuries upon his country than any other modern English king," would not be accepted today without fundamental qualification by most serious students of British history.[7]

However, in turning to the American colonies and the crisis that developed in their relations with the mother country, it is manifest that Lecky strove to present fairly and with sympathetic understanding both sides of the issues that brought on the War for American Independence. This is evident in his treatment of the passage and the repeal of the Stamp Act, of the Townshend revenue and law-enforcing measures, of the Tea Act, and of the Coercive Acts and the Quebec Act of 1774. His grasp of eighteenth-century British colonial history was far better than that of Lord Mahon. In fact, taking *England in the Eighteenth Century* as a whole, one does not hesitate to agree with G. P. Gooch's verdict that it has assumed "rank as a classic." [8]

---

[6] *Ibid.*, I, 223; see also the article reviewing Volumes I and II of Lecky's *History* in the *Quarterly Review* (1878), CXLV, 504–5, in which the writer points out that it took rather more than a century after the Revolution for the Cabinet form of government to reach maturity.

[7] *History of England*, III, 14.

[8] *History and Historians of the Nineteenth Century*, p. 366. Students interested in an appraisal of Lecky's various writings should read the brilliant essay on this subject by Charles F. Mullett in *Some Modern Historians of Britain: Essays in Honor of R. L. Schuyler* (New York, 1951), pp. 128–49.

William Hunt (1842–1931)

The year 1890 which signalled the completion of Lecky's great work on *England in the Eighteenth Century* also saw the publication of Volume XXI of the *Dictionary of National Biography* containing a life of George III by the Rev. Dr. William Hunt. This biographical article therefore enjoyed the prestige of a place in that notable series while it was still under the editorship of Leslie Stephen.

Hunt had distinguished himself as an undergraduate at Oxford by winning a first class honours degree in law and history. For a period of years thereafter he was an examiner in history at the university, and at the same time vicar of the parish of Congresbury in Somerset. But in 1882 he gave up his pastoral activities and went to London in order to devote himself to literary activities of a historical nature. It may be noted in passing that he contributed to each of the sixty-three volumes of the *Dictionary of National Biography (D.N.B.)*, close to six hundred biographies in all. Further, he was not only editor of the series called *The English Church,* but contributed a volume to it. He was also a joint editor with Reginald L. Poole of *The Political History of England,* Volume X of which he wrote under the subtitle *The History of England from the Accession of George III to the Close of Pitt's First Administration* (1760–1801). It was published in London in 1905, the year of his election as President of the Royal Historical Society. His last work, published in 1907 and entitled *The Irish Parliament, 1775,* was the editing of a most revealing eighteenth-century manuscript mistakenly attributed to Colonel John Blacquiere, serving at the time as Chief Secretary for Ireland under Lord Lieutenant Harcourt.

Hunt's approach to the beginning of the reign of George III is clearly set forth in the article on that monarch in the *D.N.B.* "George," he writes, "began his reign with a determination to break the yoke of the whig oligarchy, and to recover for the crown its power which it had lost since 1688—" as the result of the English Revolution. He then continues: "In his struggle with the whigs and his work of building up the prerogatives he used the services of a number of politicians who attached themselves to him personally, rather than to any minister or faction, and were called by those who opposed his policy the 'king's friends.' He thus renounced the proper sphere of a constitutional monarch in favour of that of a party leader." This statement assumed that in the 1760's the proper constitutional role of the King was to stand aloof from party and public issues, a position that was true of the monarchy when Hunt wrote in the 1880's. Nevertheless, in his volume on the *Political History of England* Hunt states of George III: "In religion, tastes, and prejudices he was in sympathy with the great mass of his people; and in matters in which his policy and conduct seem most open to censure, he had the majority of the nation with him." [1] At the same time Hunt affirmed that it was George III who insisted on formulating national policy and that the Ministry was left simply to carry it out. "Ministers might or might not be agreed on matters of the first importance" he wrote; "all the agreement between them which was necessary was that each in his own sphere should act as an agent of the king's policy." [2] This was in harmony with his statement in the *D.N.B.* that with Lord North at the head of the Ministry in 1770 the King for a period of twelve years, "carried out his own system of government, and the affairs of the country were directed by an irresponsible king acting through responsible ministers." Thus Hunt apparently accepted the view that by 1770 ministers were "responsible" to Parliament and to the electorate (as they were at the time he wrote) and yet he finds that these "responsible ministers" simply carried out the irresponsible King's policy, whatever it was. In the words of Professor Herbert Butterfield: "the work of William Hunt illustrates the point that no amount of learning can redeem historical work if the student is defective in imagination. Hunt declares that George III's relations with his ministers and with 'the King's friends' are unconstitutional in the 1760's because the fact is self-evident to him—such relations would obviously have been unconstitutional in the closing decades of Victoria's reign." [3] In other words, Professor Butterfield does not criticize the way Dr. Hunt marshals his facts but rather his interpretation of them. This criticism must be borne in mind in reading Hunt's work and assessing him as a historian.

---

[1] *Political History of England*, X, 3.
[2] *Ibid.*, X, 7.
[3] *George III and the Historians* (London, 1957), p. 179. Butterfield's section on William Hunt in this work is presented on pp. 176–80.

Sir George Otto Trevelyan (1838–1928)

Of the British historians whose writings have dealt with the period embraced in this series, Sir George Otto Trevelyan went farthest in indicting the government and people of Great Britain and in giving unstinting praise to the American colonials. In this respect his work is almost unique. Trevelyan was the nephew of the historian Thomas Babington Macaulay, whose life and letters he prepared for the press and with whom as a youth he had established a close relationship. After a period of study at Cambridge, where Trevelyan ranked high as a student, he became a writer whose literary style compared favourably with that of his uncle; also, like him, he entered politics as a Liberal member of Parliament. By 1880 he had written the delightful *Early History of Charles James Fox*, which dealt with Fox's career down to the year 1774.

In 1897 Trevelyan retired from public life in order to devote his time to writing.[1] To exercise his talents he chose a great theme: *The American Revolution*. Part I of this work appeared in 1899 and carried the story of the American revolt from 1766 to 1776; in 1903 Part II was published in two volumes that traced the course of events to 1787; finally the task was terminated with two additional volumes published between 1912 and 1914 under the title *George the Third and Charles Fox, the Concluding Part of the American Revolution*. What Trevelyan insisted upon in every page of *Part I* (the portion of *The American Revolution* that is of immediate concern to this historiographical essay) and felt a responsibility for telling the world, was that the government of Great Britain was completely in the wrong on the issues that led to the disruption of the Old British Empire. Professor Richard B. Morris, in his one-volume condensation for American readers, comments in the Introduction: "To say that the publication of Trevelyan's *The American Revolution* marked an international event in history and belles lettres, would scarcely be doing full justice to the work's impact. . . . It

---

[1] For the events in the life of Trevelyan see *Sir George Otto Trevelyan, a Memoir by his son, George Macaulay Trevelyan* (London & New York, 1932).

constituted a bridge to renewed understanding between the British and American peoples. . . ."[2]

This remarkable book, instead of beginning with the inception of the revolutionary movement in America at the conclusion of the Great War for the Empire, starts with the year 1766 in the midst of the crisis.

After a digression in Chapter I about Charles James Fox's changes of heart and habits, Trevelyan paints a picture of the unrestrained joy that greeted the repeal of the Stamp Act in the following words: "In the spring of 1766 a new chapter of peace and good-will . . . had opened before the delighted eyes of all true fellow-countrymen on either side of the Atlantic. . . . The mother-country had erred, had suffered, had repented, and now retrieved her fault." Nevertheless, the King was not reconciled, and "when, in spite of his efforts, the work of pacification was accomplished, George the Third never forgave his wise and faithful servants for having saved him from himself."

In view of the fact that the repeal was carried out by the Marquess of Rockingham, the King dismissed him and turned again to William Pitt, but in so doing courted disaster. For, "under cover of a name which has elevated and adorned the annals of our Parliament, was formed a bad and foolish administration which woefully misdirected our national policy." Following the lead of the Ministry —which Chatham was no longer able to guide—the House of Commons on June 2, 1767, passed a series of resolutions imposing duties upon a number of commodities admitted into the British colonies and plantations. Thus, says Trevelyan:

> "the step was taken, and taken in the name of Chatham, which in one day reversed the policy that he had nearest at heart, and undid the work of which he was most justly proud. The Boston massacre; the horrors of the Indian warfare; the mutual cruelties of partisans in the Carolinas; Saratoga and Yorktown; the French War; the Spanish War; the wholesale ruin of the American loyalists; the animosity towards Great Britain which for so long afterwards coloured the foreign policy of the United States;—all flowed in direct and inevitable sequence from that fatal escapade."[3]

---

[2] George Otto Trevelyan: *The American Revolution* (one-volume condensation, ed. R. B. Morris, New York, 1964), Introduction, p. xi.

[3] *The American Revolution, Part I, 1766–1776* (London, 1899), pp. 28–32.

But prior to this statement Trevelyan makes the point that:

> "The undisguised tyranny of the seventeenth century had worked its own cure by the sturdy opposition which it evoked from all classes, and almost every creed. By the time George the Third had been on the throne ten years . . . a despotism of a subtle and insidious texture was being swiftly and deftly interwoven into the entire fabric of the Constitution. The strong will, the imperious character, and the patient, unresting industry of the King, working through subservient Ministers upon a corrupt Parliament, had made him master of the State as effectively, and far more securely, than if his authority had rested on the support of an army of foreign mercenaries. The purpose to which he was capable of putting his all but unlimited authority was soon to be written in blood and fire over the face of the globe." [4]

In the face of this menace to English liberty, Trevelyan continues, the American colonials rallied to defend the English constitution from the King who was seeking to destroy it, and to their eternal credit and glory, Charles James Fox and other British Whigs gave their moral support to those who finally took up arms to protect these traditional and precious constitutional rights. In defending this thesis Trevelyan most scrupulously excludes all facts that might have thrown any doubts upon its validity. Those that he does use are marshalled with such skill and presented with such animation and artistry as to produce the effect that he had in mind. These defects notwithstanding, we still have in *The American Revolution, Part I,* a notable contribution to our historical literature.

In a brief review in the October 1899 issue of the *American Historical Review,* Frederick Jackson Turner stated that *The American Revolution, Part I,* represented "an important reaction from the recent American tendency to state the English side of the case, in this momentous struggle between mother country and colonial dependencies." Turner found the book "delightful reading," but he deplored Trevelyan's failure to discriminate between the cultures of the various sections of the British colonies along with his neglect "of the eighteenth-century legal, administrative, and political contentions between the authorities of the mother country and the colonies," something that "constitutes a grave limitation on the value of the book as a study of the origin of the war for independence." [5] To

---

[4] *Ibid.,* p. 20.
[5] *American Historical Review,* V, 141–4.

Herbert L. Osgood, Trevelyan's work was "not a balanced or well rounded history of the Revolution in either its political or social phases. . . . [In fact,] to the scientific historian, to the sober student of social and political forces, it will not be wholly convincing or satisfactory." [6]

In view of the underlying assumption of Trevelyan's *History*, it is perhaps understandable that the book came as a distinct shock to British scholars. In the London *Quarterly Review* for July 1899, there is a long unsigned article dealing not only with the Trevelyan history but also with the works of a number of American writers, all having to do with the American Revolution. It will be of interest to the reader to note that the books included are *The Literary History of the American Revolution, 1763–1783* by Professor Moses Coit Tyler; *The Story of the Revolution* by Henry Cabot Lodge; *The Life of Thomas Hutchinson, Royal Governor of the Province of Massachusetts Bay* by James Kendall Hosmer; *With the Fathers: Studies in the History of the United States* by John B. McMaster; *The Formation of the Union, 1750–1829* by Albert Bushnell Hart; *The United States of America, 1765–1865* by Edward Channing; and *The Provincial Governor in the English Colonies of North America* by Evarts Boutell Greene. Except for Lodge, the reviewer has warm praise for each of these American authors, for their spirit of historical detachment and their honest presentation of facts. Of Lodge the writer points out that "he has carried into literature and politics a respectable degree of scholarship, marred by much apparent acerbity of temper, an incurable passion for ultra-republican theories, and a confirmed dislike of Great Britain. . . . In the picture which he gives us of the Revolution there are no shadows. All the figures are those of heroes." Turning to Trevelyan, the reviewer then writes:

> "His latest work has come to us as a rather disagreeable surprise.
> Animated by a spirit not that of history, and we should hope not that
> of politics, he has gathered up all the Whig traditions, animosities,
> and jealousies of the eighteenth century, and has flung them by way
> of defiance on the threshold of the twentieth, at a time when the
> dying nineteenth century had come to look upon them with some-
> what of disdain. . . . He has exhibited a singular and, to us, quite
> unjustifiable hatred of King George III, of the Parliament, of English
> laws, English policy, and English society during the memorable
> period covered by his volume." [7]

[6] *Political Science Quarterly*, XIX, 502–5.
[7] *Quarterly Review*, CXC, 221–54.

With that, the reviewer proceeds to challenge in detail the real relevance of much that Trevelyan wrote on the state of affairs in the American colonies and Great Britain in the eighteenth century.

In much the same spirit, J. A. Doyle (author of *English Colonies in America*, 5 vols., London, 1882–1907), in reviewing the Trevelyan volume in the July 1899 number of the *English Historical Review*, wrote:

> ". . . if a historian must needs take sides Sir George Trevelyan has taken the right one. . . . Neither Sir George nor any other writer can exaggerate the blundering incapacity of the British policy, civil and military alike. But it is a very different thing to say as Sir George Trevelyan does, often in words and always by implication, that all the moral and civil virtue was on the side of the colonists. He represents, indeed, a phase of thought which American writers themselves have by this time wholly outgrown. . . . Indiscriminate praise and indiscriminate invective invariably bring their own Nemesis by missing the real points where praise and blame are appropriate."

Trevelyan, says Doyle, leaves the impression that "All Americans are enlightened patriots; all the adherents of George III are ignorant and wrong-headed oppressors. Thus praise and blame alike miss the mark." In closing his review, and referring to Trevelyan's active political career, Doyle posed the question: "Can a strong party politician write a history of a period in which party issues must meet him at every turn?" to which he replied: "The practical exigencies of politics leave no place for those nicely balanced judgments, or for that thoughtful and discriminating analysis of actions and motives, which are the first duty of the historian." [8] Such was Doyle's opinion of the limitations placed on the ardent politician who would play the role of historian.

We must now turn to the work of a group of academic historians who, although they held certain different points of view concerning the history of the period covered by this series, were more restrained than Trevelyan in the positions they took on the great issues and therefore far more interested in penetrating beyond the inherited traditions of the past to get to the facts.

---

[8] *English Historical Review*, XIV, 596–604.

Denys A. Winstanley (1877–1947)

Denys A. Winstanley's career was closely identified with Trinity College, Cambridge, where he did his undergraduate work and where he became a fellow and also a vice-master. His first contribution to the history of the period embraced by this series was his "George III and his First Cabinet," which appeared in the October 1902 *English Historical Review*.[1] In 1910 the University of Cambridge Press published his *Personal and Party Government: A Chapter in the Political History of the Early Years of the Reign of George III, 1760–1766*; in 1912 came his *Lord Chatham and the Whig Opposition*, also from Cambridge University Press; finally, in 1922 the same press brought out his *The University of Cambridge in the Eighteenth Century*, which is largely concerned with the activities of Thomas Pelham-Holles, first Duke of Newcastle, as High Steward and later as Chancellor of the University, and only indirectly related to the building up of his political power.[2]

In *Personal and Party Government* Winstanley laid down the proposition that the "great 'Revolution families' . . . established themselves in power by using the influence of the crown against the crown itself"; and it was left for George II to discover that, in order to protect himself from the "Jacobites, he had sold himself into slavery to the whigs. . . . Parliament which in former days had resisted the crown in the name of the people, now prevailed against the king in the interests of the whig aristocracy." [3] When George III came to the throne, Winstanley continues, he determined "to inaugurate a new epoch in the relations between the crown and the cabinet, to wrest from his ministers the power which they had stolen from the monarchy, and, without transcending the limits of his prerogative, to exercise a decisive influence over the national destinies." [4] The study also has as a major thesis the opinion that during the period under consideration the Duke of Newcastle in his stand

[1] *English Historical Review*, XVII, 678–91.
[2] For an interesting review of *The University of Cambridge* by L. G. Wickham Legg, Fellow of New College, Oxford, see *ibid.*, XXXVIII, 601–4.
[3] *Personal and Party Government*, p. 9.
[4] *Ibid.*, p. 23.

for government by party was right, as against William Pitt, who stood in opposition to this view.[5]

These interpretations by Winstanley were destined to be challenged by some later historians, as will be subsequently noted. This was also true of certain statements made in his *Lord Chatham and the Whig Opposition*. For example, he asserted that it was never George III's "intention to bring about a revolution in the government or to trample under foot the privileges acquired by the nation in its contest with the Stuarts; but he firmly believed, and with some justice, that the politicians, who had driven James II from the throne and excluded his son from the succession, had never intended to reduce the kingship to a condition of subservience." Another much more debatable interpretation lay in the following statement: "The constitution had developed on other lines than those laid down by the statesmen responsible for the Revolution settlement; and the royal authority had been usurped by a narrow oligarchy which had taken advantage of a disputed succession and a foreign dynasty to acquire supremacy in the state. The whigs had triumphed over the family which they had placed upon the throne; and when George III succeeded his grandfather, the royal power appeared to have reached the nadir of its fortunes."[6] Then, according to Winstanley, came a revolution: "Parliament, which remained as corrupt as before, was now tied by gold chains about the throne. . . . No longer could parliament be considered an effective check upon the despotic tendencies of the crown, since the astute policy of George III rendered the Bill of Rights and Act of Settlement . . . almost constitutionally valueless. Parliament, which had previously been the puppet of the whig nobility, now became the slave of the court."[7] *Lord Chatham and the Whig Opposition* is, nevertheless, a work of first-class scholarship, based upon a careful examination of various sources including at least a hundred volumes of the vast collection of Newcastle Manuscripts in the British Museum. Its main thesis speaks of the great need in the 1760's for a government with strong party connections—something quite opposite to the conceptions of both George III and the Earl of Chatham at the time Pitt formed his administration in 1766. To Winstanley, the hope of the

---

[5] For William Hunt's review of *Personal and Party Government*, in which he takes issue with Winstanley, see the *English Historical Review*, XXV, 785–7.

[6] *Lord Chatham and the Whig Opposition*, pp. 1–2.

[7] *Ibid.*, pp. 15–16.

nation at this period was the Rockingham Whigs, "the foremost champions of the party system so fiercely attacked by the court, and it was on this point that Pitt was in complete disagreement with them . . . 'Men not measures' became his watchword, and the destruction of the party system his goal. . . ." Thus Chatham repudiated the enlightened principles held by, and rejected the support of, the only group of men who could have aided him in carrying on a creditable administration of the government.[8]

Professor Basil Williams, reviewing *Lord Chatham and the Whig Opposition*, suggests that Winstanley's lack of appreciation of Pitt's ideal of government caused him to be somewhat unfair to the minister and that the Winstanley charge that Pitt's watchword was "men not measures" is inaccurate. On the contrary Williams claims, Pitt's watchword was "measures not men." Far from accepting the view that Pitt had failed the nation in his unwillingness to support the Rockinghamites, or Rockingham Whigs, Williams maintains that no one in the Rockingham party had any commanding influence in the House of Commons, and that the members of the party owed more to Pitt than he did to them, but that they finally failed him.[9]

Basil Williams (1867–1950)

Unlike Winstanley, with his long and uninterrupted academic career at Cambridge, Basil Williams, after receiving his degree at Oxford, turned to a variety of activities: clerk in the House of Commons; secretary to the Transvaal Education Department; special South African correspondent for *The Times;* Ford Lecturer at Oxford; Professor of History at McGill University and later at the University of Edinburgh. Although he published certain studies relating to England in the early part of the eighteenth century, his chief contributions to the period covered by this series are to be found in *The Life of William Pitt, Earl of Chatham,* which appeared in 1913 in two volumes, and in *The Whig Supremacy, 1714–1760*

---

[8] *Ibid.,* pp. 31–3.
[9] *English Historical Review,* XXVIII, 168–70.

(a volume in *The Oxford History of England* series), which was published in 1939.

Before dealing with Williams's biography of *Pitt*, however, mention must be made of the publication in 1905 at Stuttgart, Germany, of Dr. Albert von Ruville's three-volume *William Pitt, Graf von Chatham*, which came out in London and New York two years later, translated by H. J. Chaytor and Mary Morison. This was the first detailed scholarly biography of Pitt and it was based not only upon printed materials but also upon such manuscript sources as the Newcastle Papers in the British Museum and the papers in the Record Offices of London and Berlin. Far from being a biography with pro-German leanings, it took, if anything, a pro-British position over the charge that Great Britain had betrayed King Frederick of Prussia at the Peace of Paris in 1763. On the other hand, there was no hero worship of the great man whose life was portrayed. Von Ruville dealt with his subject with the cold detachment that he might have shown had he been writing the life of a leading figure from the days of the old Roman Empire. What doubtless added to the importance of his work in the eyes of the public was the fact that the English version carried a general Introduction by the distinguished British historian, Professor Hugh E. Egerton of Oxford (1855–1927). While acknowledging the great importance of this work, Egerton was led to express the feeling that von Ruville "carries his impartiality to such lengths as sometimes to appear lacking in sympathy." Egerton was also critical of certain inferences that von Ruville drew from his facts. Indeed, no one should turn to the body of this work without a careful reading of Egerton's Introduction. The importance attached by the scholarly public to this life of Pitt is further indicated by the amount of space accorded in the January 1908 *English Historical Review* to a review by L. S. Leadam, a leading authority on eighteenth-century Great Britain. Leadam dealt with equal acumen not only with the work in translation but with the original German text. Again, what has been said of the Egerton Introduction applies even more strongly to the Leadam review, if the reader of von Ruville is to get a balanced view of Pitt's public career.[1]

Eight years after von Ruville had given his work to the public, Basil Williams presented his study of the life of Pitt. It may be noted

---

[1] *English Historical Review*, XXIII, 159–65.

that, although Williams was critical of Winstanley's treatment of Pitt in *Chatham and the Whig Opposition,* he cited it fairly frequently and also availed himself of Winstanley's "accurate and extensive knowledge of Chatham and the period" by seeking his advice and having him read the proofs of his own biography of Pitt. As for von Ruville, Williams only mentions his *William Pitt, Graf von Chatham* once and refers but twice to his *William Pitt (Chatham) und Graf Bute* which had appeared in 1895; and in the comprehensive bibliography of his own Pitt biography Williams's entire reference to von Ruville's large and important work reads as follows: "Especially useful for information from the Prussian archives and based on much general research. The author's suggestions to Pitt's discredit are generally more ingenious than convincing."

Yet Williams himself was critical of Pitt's arrogance, of his passion for ostentatious display, and his reckless extravagance. At the same time, his life of that great historic figure is a study that only a patriotic Englishman, who was both a distinguished scholar and an ardent admirer of his subject, could write. Although other biographies of Pitt have followed since,[2] the Williams work remains highly regarded, and this is so despite its apparent lack of appreciation of the strength of the positions on political issues taken from time to time by Pitt's opponents. The historian W. L. Grant (one of the co-editors of *Acts of the Privy Council, Colonial Series*), in reviewing Williams's *Life of William Pitt* in April 1914,[3] was justly critical of it in certain respects, especially the treatment of the peace negotiations with France in 1761 and 1762. Yet he doubtless voices the opinion of most serious students of the period when he calls it "much the best life of Lord Chatham which has yet appeared," and also when he states, "compared to the *Life* by Dr. von Ruville, Mr. Williams shows not only a sounder judgement, but also greater breadth of reading in both published and unpublished materials."

The Basil Williams contribution of 1939 to the *Oxford History of England* series: *The Whig Supremacy, 1714–1760* also seems

---

[2] See Brian Tunstall's *William Pitt . . .* (London, 1938), which treats Pitt's rivals with great fairness; J. C. Long's *Mr. Pitt and America's Birthright* (New York, 1940); and the three-volume work by O. A. Sherrard, which appeared under the following titles: *Lord Chatham: A War Minister in the Making* (1952), *Lord Chatham: Pitt and the Seven Years War* (1955), and *Lord Chatham and America* (1958). For reviews of the last two volumes of Sherrard's trilogy by the author of this series, see the *American Historical Review,* LXI, 628–30, LXIV, 366–7.

[3] *English Historical Review,* XXIX, 379–81.

destined to hold its own as a work of great importance in the field of eighteenth-century history. Shortly after its appearance it was reviewed in the January 1940 *English Historical Review* [4] with great expertness and equal fairness by Richard Pares, at the time a lecturer in history at New College, Oxford. Pares gave as his opinion that the book would probably "long remain the best work of its kind on the general history of England in this period"; at the same time he deplored the fact that the author seemed to have benefited so little from "the formidable attack on accepted traditions" that the recent studies published by Professor Namier had inspired; he also pointed out certain errors of the kind likely to occur in any book concerned with so many aspects of world affairs. Although the book was presumably "reprinted with corrections" in 1942, 1945, 1949, and 1952, it was not until a second edition was published in 1962—some time after Williams's death—that the necessary revisions were introduced by Charles H. Stuart of Oxford University.[5] Brought up to date *The Whig Supremacy* stands today as one of the most authoritative works on eighteenth-century England.[6]

Sir Lewis Namier (1888–1960)

The fundamental premises underlying the work of George Otto Trevelyan and other writers who followed the Whig interpretation of the history of the early years of the reign of George III were drawn sharply into question by the writings of Sir Lewis Namier. Born in Warsaw of a Jewish landowning family that had become Roman Catholic, reared in Galicia, he received his advanced educa-

---

[4] *Ibid.*, LV, 136–9.

[5] The original text is altered as little as possible in the 1962 edition, and the reviser's changes and corrections—based chiefly on the researches done by the Namier school of historians—are not marked out. However, there are forty-seven emendations inserted in the footnotes, enclosed in brackets and initialled by Mr. Stuart; some of these are merely explanatory, but others distinguish the opinions of the reviser from those of the original author.

[6] It would be unfair not to point out that the outstanding study by John B. Owen, Fellow of Lincoln College: *The Rise of the Pelhams* (London, 1957) exhibits a more authoritative mastery of source materials relating to political life in England in the 1740's than does the Williams study.

tional training at Balliol College, Oxford, graduating with a first class honours in history. He became a naturalized British subject before the World War of 1914, in which he served as a private during the first year, and worked in the Foreign Office before beginning his distinguished career as teacher and scholar.

Few people have surpassed Namier in his expressions of admiration for the twentieth-century British form of government and no other historian has defended from attack with such singleness of purpose the mixed monarchical-parliamentary form of government that existed under George III. His first important work on the eighteenth century, *The Structure of Politics at the Accession of George III*, appeared in 1929 in two volumes; in the Preface to the one-volume second edition of it, published in 1957, Namier wrote: "I have corrected mistakes, clarified points in the light of new information, and have made minor additions: the sum total of these alterations has wrought much greater change than appears on the surface."

In *The Structure of Politics*, the author—after the most extensive and intensive research, the results of which were presented in great detail—attempted to answer such questions as: Why did men seek to enter Parliament? What was the electoral structure of England in 1760? What inferences can be drawn from the general election of 1761? To what use was the secret service money put while the Duke of Newcastle was in charge of the British Treasury? By finding answers to such questions, he felt, he was able to test the validity of the Whig assumptions that the reign of George III revealed an unprecedented scene of corruption of both the electorate and the elected, whereby the King was able to secure a sufficiently numerous body of obedient followers in Parliament (known as the "King's Friends") to enable him to force through his own policies in any legislation passed by that body.

The Structure of Politics, certainly a remarkable book, was followed by another, almost equally notable: *England in the Age of the American Revolution*, published in 1930. This was manifestly intended as the first volume of a promised study of the four Parliaments of George III and of the factors that led to the American Revolution. Like *The Structure of Politics*, however, it is limited to a study of a brief period before the Peace of Paris of 1763. After a challenging introductory chapter entitled "The Social Foundations" follows "Book I. Government and Parliament under the Duke of

Newcastle" in five chapters, the last of which ends with the sentence "My next book, if ever written, will be on 'The Rise of Party.'" Thus what Namier left the world in these five chapters was in reality an elaborate but exceedingly important introduction to his projected series on England and the American Revolution.[1] In addition, he left a series of essays which further illuminated his views. Among these, and perhaps the most important, was his "Monarchy and the Party System," delivered at Oxford in 1952 as the Romanes Lecture.[2] This was reprinted in the volume of essays published in 1955 under the title *Personalities and Powers* and again in a second volume of essays called *Crossroads of Power* issued posthumously in 1962. In it and in other essays, as well as in the volumes that have been cited, Namier sought to make clear the fundamental differences between the "mixed royal-parliamentary" government of the period of George III—as part of the intervening transition period from royal to parliamentary government—and the parliamentary government of the twentieth century.

What were the chief differences as Namier saw them? First of all was the absence of political parties in the modern sense; for most men sought seats in the House of Commons not so much in support of or in opposition to specific political issues but primarily to serve personal interests. In order to maintain themselves in their posts the so-called "King's Friends"—usually men with a professional interest in holding office on a civil service basis—could be counted on to support any policy backed by the King. Yet, the combined strength of these office-holders and other placemen beholden to the Crown could not command a majority in Parliament; for the powerful, conservatively inclined independent country gentlemen—especially those who were not seeking office but who sat in the House of Commons—frequently voted against the Court. In between these groups were the professional politicians—those seeking or holding the great offices and therefore intent on enlarging their following—and their placemen, and the balance of the political

[1] In the Foreword to John Brooke's *England in the Age of the American Revolution: The Chatham Administration, 1766–1768* (London, 1956), Namier stated that when he came to revise his *England in the Age of the American Revolution* he would call it "Newcastle and Bute," reserving the earlier title to appear as a series banner as Brooke had done.

[2] The lecture as delivered did not contain all the detail included in the printed version, according to the best recollection of the writer of this series who was present on that occasion.

factions seeking power. The ministers of state, as was true of the Ministries of George I and George II, were appointed by George III and the freedom of these appointments was limited only by the test that the Ministry must be able to carry on the business of state both in and out of Parliament. Once the King had given his confidence to an administration, the Cabinet Council formulated policies and, after securing the King's approval, implemented them. Contemporaries living under this mixed form of government, Namier has pointed out, were bound to be unaware of the "insoluble contradictions of a political system which, incongruously, associated a royal executive with parliamentary struggles for office. Yet the two had to coexist in an organic transition from royal to parliamentary government." [3] Finally, Namier maintained that the traditional charge of resort to wholesale corruption by George III's ministers in order to secure a majority in Parliament favourable to their policies was only partly true, as he demonstrated by a study of the expenditure of the secret service funds while the Duke of Newcastle was First Lord of the Treasury.

Reviewing *The Structure of Politics* soon after its publication, D. A. Winstanley (whose work is discussed in a previous sketch) stated that Namier had done "a very notable service to history by his masterly analysis of the Duke of Newcastle's secret service accounts. He has shown not only that there is no indication of the secret service money being used by Newcastle to purchase votes for particular divisions [in the House of Commons], but that the fund itself was far less tainted than its name implied." [4] Professor Theodore C. Pease, an American historian deeply interested in the period of British imperial history under survey, in his review of the Namier book spoke of having the feeling that for the first time the student was presented with "really adequate data regarding the English political system of the eighteenth century"; he added that "by a careful analysis, item by item, of Newcastle's secret service accounts, Mr. Namier disposes of the theory that bribery and buying of seats from secret service funds was the means by which the government got its majorities." [5] This same scholar later reviewed *England in the Age of the American Revolution* and found, as perhaps the most

---

[3] *Crossroads of Power: Essays on Eighteenth Century England* (London, 1962), pp. 214–27; see also *The Structure of Politics at the Accession of George III* (2nd edn., London, 1957), Chaps. 1 and 4 and Appendix.
[4] *English Historical Review*, XLIV, 657–60.
[5] *American Historical Review*, XXXIV, 824–6.

revealing statement in it, Namier's idea of "virtual representation" pointing to the fact that Parliament really represented not only the inhabitants of Great Britian but also its land, that is, the material resources of the island. In Namier's view, as Pease indicated, the "first British Empire suffered disruption because Englishmen failed as yet to distinguish . . . between the distant, sublimated authority of the Crown, symbolically 'paternal' [in the American Continental Colonies], and the direct governmental power which in a free country is wielded by the sons of the soil." [6] Professor H. Hale Bellot of the University of London wrote of Namier's *Structure of Politics,* "no student but must follow with delight the workings of so powerful and original a mind, and observe with humble admiration so signal an exhibition of learning and technical skill." With reference to *England in the Age of the American Revolution,* Bellot stated: "Mr. Namier has rewritten the history of the origin of the 'king's system,' . . . and his interpretation is quite new." [7]

In an equal spirit of acclaim for his major contribution to historiography, Namier was knighted in 1952, and in 1956 a group of sixteen historians— including Professor Richard Pares,[8] Lucy Sutherland,[9]

---

[6] *Ibid.,* XXXVI, 583–5.

[7] *English Historical Review,* XLVII, 677–9.

[8] Richard Pares will be treated under a separate heading.

[9] Dr. Lucy Stuart Sutherland, Principal of Lady Margaret Hall, Oxford, although a contributor during the early days of her career as a historian to studies of early English history, has become one of the leading authorities on certain aspects of the history of England in the eighteenth century, especially those relating to politics in London and to the activities of the United East India Company. Among her more important studies are: "Edmund Burke and the First Rockingham Ministry," *English Historical Review,* XLVII, 46–72; *A London Merchant 1695–1774* (London, 1933), describing the activities of William Braund, who was interested among other things in chartering ships to the East India Company; *The East India Company in Eighteenth-Century Politics* (Oxford, 1952); "Henry Fox as Paymaster General of the Forces," *English Historical Review,* LXX (1955), 229–57, in collaboration with J. Binney; *The City of London and the Opposition to Government, 1768–1774* . . . (London, 1959); *The City of London* . . . *1756–7* (Oxford, 1960), reprinted from the British Academy *Proceedings,* XLVI; "The City of London in Eighteenth-Century Politics," in *Essays Presented to Sir Lewis Namier* (eds. Richard Pares and A. J. P. Taylor, London, 1956), pp. 49–74, and the editing of *The Correspondence of Edmund Burke, Volume II, July 1768–June 1774* (Cambridge & Chicago, 1960). *The East India Company in Eighteenth-Century Politics* reflects most strongly the influence of Namier in her probing of that smaller part of her evidence which reveals the mainsprings of action and generally in her mastery of detail; it is a book especially designed to meet the needs of the specialist in the field of eighteenth-century history. Dr. Sutherland, despite the use of the Namier techniques, cannot be classified as one of this school. As an independent worker she has arrived at her own conclusions. One need only contrast her view of Burke with that of Sir Lewis to illustrate the point. For Dr. Sutherland's testimonial to Namier see "Sir Lewis Namier, 1888–1960," British Academy *Proceedings,* XLVIII, 371–85.

Romney Sedgwick,[10] and Betty Kemp [11]—dedicated a volume of *Essays* to Namier. In the Preface it was stated: *"The Structure of Politics at the Accession of George III . . .* marked an epoch. . . . The political history of England has been permanently reshaped; and its study will continue to bear the stamp of Sir Lewis Namier's inspiration." [12] Already the excellent study by John Brooke: *The Chatham Administration, 1766–1768* (London, 1956), and the equally excellent one by John B. Owen: *The Rise of the Pelhams* (London, 1957), may be singled out among other works that are products of the inspiration of, and the techniques employed by, Namier.

In 1958 Namier delivered the Leslie Stephen Lecture at the University of Cambridge on "Charles Townshend." This paper, which appeared as one of the essays in *Crossroads of Power,* was the basis for the book of the same title completed by Sir Lewis's closest associate, John Brooke.[13] This book is likely to stand indefinitely as the chief authority on the life of Townshend—that brilliant but irresponsible statesman who, as Chancellor of the Exchequer in the Chatham Ministry, helped lead the government to make certain fatal decisions regarding the American colonies. Nor should one fail to point out that Sir Lewis was a leading force in reviving the plan for *The History of Parliament,* and was influential in effecting agreement that it should follow his method of historical approach. He also accepted responsibility for the section of the *History* relating to the eighteenth century and approached his task in a way which would place the period "in historical perspective" by "analyzing the infor-

---

[10] Romney Sedgwick, formerly a fellow of Trinity College, Cambridge, edited *Letters from George III to Lord Bute, 1756–1766* (London, 1939). The Introduction (pp. vii–lxvii) is a notable contribution to an understanding of George both as heir to the throne and as the young King. The dating and classification of the three hundred and thirty-nine letters presented in this volume illustrate the high standard of scholarship that Sedgwick, under the aegis of Namier, brought to bear on this undertaking.

[11] In *King and Commons, 1660–1832* (London & New York, 1957), an important contribution to English constitutional history, Betty Kemp develops the concept that between 1716 and 1783 there was a constitutional balance of power between the King and the House of Commons and that from 1784 to 1832 this balance was overturned to the disadvantage of the King. For criticism of certain aspects of her thesis see Herbert Butterfield in *History,* XLV, 266, and Basil Henning in the *American Historical Review,* LXIII, 661–2.

[12] *Essays Presented to Sir Lewis Namier,* Preface, p. v.

[13] Namier and Brooke: *Charles Townshend* (London, 1964). Brooke contributed the final chapter, as well as certain supplements and revisions to earlier chapters; he also collaborated with Namier on *The History of Parliament,* as will be referred to later, in which the article on Townshend was written by Namier.

mation given, and revealing the underlying realities of political life."
As a result the first volumes of *The History of Parliament* to issue
from the press have been those on *The House of Commons,
1754–1790*, a collaboration of the late Sir Lewis and John Brooke.[14]

But all has not been praise in the evaluation of Sir Lewis Namier's
major works and his other writings on eighteenth-century history. In
fact, the eminence of his position as a historian has been seriously
challenged, and the subject is a very live one today. Passing over the
writings of Professor Herbert Butterfield, which must be left for
treatment under a separate heading, let us turn to those of W. R.
Fryer of the University of Nottingham. In 1957 his article "The
Study of British Politics between the Revolution and the Reform
Act" was printed in *Renaissance and Modern Studies*; this was
followed by his "King George III: His Political Character and Conduct, 1760–1784, a New Whig Interpretation," published in the 1962
volume of the same journal;[15] then in 1963 Fryer summarized his
conclusions in *The Burke Newsletter* in an article: "Namier and the
King's Position in English Politics, 1744–84."[16] "The fault that I find
with Namier," Fryer wrote, "is not defect of knowledge, but erroneous perspective." Fryer took serious exception to such Namier
statements as: "The Executive was the King's as truly as it is now
[that] of the President in the United States; he, too, had to choose
his Ministers: but from among Parliamentary leaders."[17] To Fryer,
by 1760 constitutional *convention* if not constitutional *propriety*,
rather than constitutional *law*, had limited the ability of the King to
choose his ministers freely; for convention dictated that the minister
be selected either from recognized leaders in the House of Commons or from the ranks of peers of eminence or repute in the House
of Lords. The selection of Lord Bute was thus a violation of constitutional convention and of constitutional propriety.[18] In this Fryer
parted company with Namier over the degree of independence of
action enjoyed by George III. He also asserted that "in this period of
British history there was in fact no real 'balance' between Crown
and Parliament, that the King had no secure 'independence' in the

---

[14] Namier and Brooke: *The History of Parliament: The House of Commons,
1754–1790* (3 vols., London & New York, 1964).

[15] *Renaissance and Modern Studies*, I, 91–114; VI, 68–101.

[16] *The Burke Newsletter*, V, 246–58.

[17] "King George III: A Study In Personality," *Crossroads of Power*, p. 127, and
Personality and Power, p. 42.

[18] *Renaissance and Modern Studies*, VI, 82–4.

conduct of his executive functions, and that the House of Commons was in a position of ultimate supremacy over the executive. . . . " [19] By taking this position he was inevitably led to question the legitimacy of Namier's concept of mixed monarchical-parliamentary government and consequently the entire basis upon which the Namier studies had been erected. In Fryer we therefore have a return to the Whig conception of the eighteenth-century limited monarchy.

Another attack on the Namier approach to history has come from Professor Harvey C. Mansfield, Jr., of Harvard, in his paper "Sir Lewis Namier Considered," printed in the November 1962 *Journal of British Studies*.[20] Mansfield, writing as a political scientist, has called into question Namier's credibility as an authority on English politics in the 1760's and especially the argument that there was no danger of tyranny in Britain in the early 1760's. In this connection he has taken issue with Namier's claim that there was no evidence of the influence of Bolingbroke's writings upon George III, and has contended that in the early period of the King's reign—in harmony with Bolingbroke's injunctions—he sought to carry out a political reformation which was "to be accomplished by the King alone, acting with his advisers rather than with his ministers"; [21] that is, by an inner Cabinet acting behind the Cabinet Council (a charge which was also levied by Edmund Burke and others). The King's failure to accomplish this reformation was due to the fact that he could not find the proper support at hand. One of Mansfield's additional major criticisms of Namier's work is its anachronic approach to eighteenth-century politics, with its insistent emphasis on the need for a twentieth-century British party system as the solution to the major problems of the eighteenth century, rather than the treatment of the problems from the point of view of those living at the time. Thus Mansfield writes: "But this obvious superiority of modern party government is the basis for Namier's apology for George III as a constitutional monarch; and this apology is the essence of his entire work on the eighteenth century, which aims at destroying the legend that George III's accession brought danger of tyranny." [22]

If historicism is based upon the assumption that human thought is never free from historical conditions, the question must be raised

---

[19] *Ibid.*, VI, 99, "Additional Note."
[20] *Journal of British Studies*, II, 28–55.
[21] *Ibid.*, II, 35–6.
[22] *Ibid.*, II, 41.

whether Namier was a historicist. "If he were," in Mansfield's view, "then the whole of his work would not rest on the clear superiority of party government; for this clear superiority, according to the most advanced variety of historicism, would itself be historically conditioned." [23] The gauntlet thus thrown down against Namier and his work was picked up by Professor Robert Walcott of the College of Wooster, Ohio, author of *English Politics in the Early Eighteenth Century* (*Harvard Historical Monographs*, No. 28, Cambridge, Mass., 1956), a historian whose writing has been greatly influenced by that of Sir Lewis. In his article " 'Sir Lewis Namier Considered' Considered," which appeared in the May 1964 *Journal of British Studies*, he took up seriatim the various charges levelled against Namier by Mansfield and answered them in considerable detail. Using his own historical outlook upon the events during the end of the reign of George II and the early years of that of George III,[24] Walcott's chief complaint was that Mansfield repeatedly made misleading citations from Namier's writing, thus distorting the true meaning. The same issue of this periodical carried Dr. Mansfield's reply, "Sir Lewis Namier Again Considered." Namier's "near-contempt for ante-Namier historians," he charged, "has its source in his clear contempt for eighteenth-century statesmen. . . . He exalted eighteenth-century 'materials' and 'information' at the expense of eighteenth-century issues, as seen in the opinions of eighteenth-century statesmen." [25]

This critical dialogue is but a small part of the swelling literature still being written by those holding diversified opinions of the work of Sir Lewis Namier,[26] a man of brilliant mind and a historian who

---

[23] *Ibid.*, II, 51.
[24] *Ibid.*, II, 85–108.
[25] *Ibid.*, III, 109–19.
[26] See, among other writings that have not already been mentioned, "The Political System of the Eighteenth Century," anonymous, *The Times Literary Supplement*, January 31, 1928; "L. B. Namier," by Catherine S. Sims in *Some Modern Historians of Britain* (eds. Herman Ausubel, J. B. Brebner, and Erling Hunt, New York, 1951), pp. 341–57; "Prophet and Pedant," anonymous, in the *New Statesman and Nation*, June 25, 1955; "Namier Inc." by John Raymond in the *New Statesman*, October 19, 1957; "The Structure of History," anonymous, in *The Times Literary Supplement*, November 22, 1957; "Ascetic History," anonymous, in *The Times Literary Supplement*, January 1, 1960; "Party, Purpose, and Pattern: Sir Lewis Namier and His Critics," by Dr. Jacob M. Price of the Department of History, University of Michigan in the *Journal of British Studies*, I, (1961), 71–93; "The Namier Way," by J. B. Owen in the *New Statesman*, January 26, 1962; "On and Upward with the Arts. The Flight of Crook-Taloned Birds," in two Parts by Ved Mehta in *The New Yorker*, Part I, December 8, 1962, pp. 59–147, and especially Part II, December 15, 1962, pp.

has perhaps made a major contribution by the very fact of the controversial discussion provoked by his work and his approach to history. But we must now turn to the writings of the most formidable opponent of Namier and his school, the Master of Peterhouse, Cambridge, Professor Herbert Butterfield.

Herbert Butterfield (1900–   )

Professor Harold T. Parker of Duke University, in his essay on Herbert Butterfield, wrote: "Among contemporary British authors Professor Herbert Butterfield of Cambridge University has probably been most successful in communicating a historian's wisdom, not only in his volumes of essays but also in his narrative histories which at their best exemplify with remarkable fidelity the theory of historiography to which he is devoted." [1] Thus we are presented with a historian interested primarily in ideas. If Namier's distinction as a scholar rests largely on the depth and exactness of his research, Butterfield's lies chiefly in his ability to illuminate with penetrating vision the larger significance of events.

Butterfield's career since he entered Cambridge as a young scholar has been continuously identified with this great institution of learning. In 1923 he became a fellow of Peterhouse, in 1930 a lecturer in history at the university; in 1944 Professor of Modern History, and in 1963 Regius Professor of History; in 1955 he also became Master of Peterhouse. As was true of Namier's writings,

47–129; "Namier on Eighteenth-Century England," by Dr. D. I. Gaines of the City College of the University of the City of New York in *The Historian,* February, 1963, pp. 213–25; "Sir Lewis Namier," by Professor H. R. Winkler of Rutgers, The State University, in the *Journal of Modern History,* March, 1963, pp. 1–19; "Names and Namierism," a most revealing article by John Brooke, Namier's closest associate during the last nine years of his life, in *History and Theory:* III, (1964), 331–47; and finally (at the present date of writing) the devastating essay by J. H. Plumb, Fellow of Christ's College, Cambridge, in the *New York Review of Books,* December 3, 1964. At the moment of publication an additional essay has come to hand by Sir Isaiah Berlin: "L. B. Namier," in the November 1966 *Encounter,* XXVII, 32–42, probably the most penetrating study of the lot.

[1] H. T. Parker: "Herbert Butterfield," *Some 20th-century Historians: Essays on Eminent Europeans* (ed. S. W. Halperin, Chicago, 1961), pp. 75–101. It may be noted that these *Essays* were dedicated "to Bernadotte E. Schmitt, Scholar, Teacher, and Friend, from his Former Students" at the University of Chicago.

Butterfield's publications relate to a number of fields, but only those that have a bearing on the historiography of the period of this series need be considered. In 1931 he brought out his *The Whig Interpretation of History*, in which (p. 11) he states his thesis as follows: "It is part and parcel of the whig interpretation of history that it studies the past with reference to the present; and though there may be a sense in which this is unobjectionable if its implications are carefully considered, and there may be a sense in which it is inescapable, it has often been an obstruction to historical understanding because it has been taken to mean the study of the past with direct and perpetual reference to the present." In 1944 came his *The Englishman and his History;* in 1949 his *George III, Lord North and the People, 1779–1780;* in 1957 his *George III and the Historians;* and in 1958 a concise summing up of his views on the reign of George III in "George III and the Constitution," published in *History,* February 1958.

George III and the Historians is of particular interest to students of the history of the period under review. It consists of three so-called "Books," the first of which carries the title "The Historian and his Evidence" and stresses the need to train the critical faculties if one is to avoid many of the pitfalls facing anyone seeking to write history. The second book, "George III and His Interpreters," is a survey of the writings of those leading historians who were concerned with the reign of George III before the appearance of the works of Sir Lewis Namier and his "school"; it constitutes an important contribution to the historiography of the period. The third book, called "George III and the Namier School," is a penetrating analysis in seventeen sections of the importance of the contributions made by Namier and his followers. While according high praise to Namier himself, Butterfield takes John Brooke, one of the Namier school, severely to task. In writing *The Chatham Administration,*[2] says Butterfield, Brooke failed to realize that here in the formation of the Chatham Ministry was an administration uniquely designed to realize George III's desire of carrying on his government by individuals without any relation to party groups. Finally, in his article "George III and the Constitution" published in the February 1958 *History,* Butterfield summarizes his views of the strength and weakness of

[2] John Brooke: *The Chatham Administration, 1766–1768* (London & New York, 1956).

the Namier school of historians. He insists that their weakness is due mainly to the fact that, in their over-emphasis on structural analysis, they neglected the importance of ideas and convictions of people; they also failed to give credit to the work of historians who preceded them and who had arrived at conclusions corresponding to their own—thus presenting their own conclusions as more novel than they actually were; further, so absorbed were they in analyzing factional struggles within Parliament itself that they failed to give proper emphasis to the importance of events beyond its doors.

But as the result of his criticism of the Namier school, Professor Butterfield has himself come under strong attack. This is especially evident in the article "Party, Purpose, and Pattern: Sir Lewis Namier and his Critics" by Dr. J. M. Price of the University of Michigan, which appeared in the October 1961 *Journal of British Studies.*[3] Before turning his attention to Butterfield, Price stresses that the great contribution of the Namier school of historians to understanding the history of the period lies in the precise way in which they have analyzed and described "the locus and transmission of power, through the observable phenomenon, political behavior. . . . What people in power and in politics say is interesting and sometimes significant; what they do is usually more important." To determine how men in Parliament were informed, Sir Lewis and his followers studied "the tangled fabric of kinship and interest which bound men together in the politics of the midcentury." Price maintains that "the perfection of these biographical and quantitative research techniques" has meant little to Butterfield, for in his writing one looks "in vain for those fine distinctions between actual institutions and the words used to describe them so basic in understanding their work." Price also challenged what he felt was Butterfield's assumption: namely that "to investigate the ties of interest, dependency, consanguinity, proximity, friendship, etc. that encouraged men to act together in politics is to deny any role at all to ideology as a determinant of men's political actions." He concludes that "when Butterfield says the historian should spend less time analyzing the structure of the house [the House of Commons] and more time analyzing the contents of debates he may be . . . taking a methodologically retrograde step."

Thus we see that Namier's great work cannot easily be brushed

---

[3] *Journal of British Studies,* I, 71–93.

aside. But neither can the perceptive writings of Butterfield—which include his wealth of ideas on so many facets of the historian's craft contained in books that are not the main subject of this essay—for, again in the words of Professor Parker, "he has set a new standard of philosophical narrative by his technique of walking alongside each historical character, by his imaginative sympathy, and by his insight and wisdom. To read his books is, for the professional historian, to raise one's conception of achievement and to renew the springs of one's aspiration." [4]

Richard Pares (1902–1958)

Son of Sir Bernard Pares, the distinguished student of Russian life and Russian affairs, Richard Pares himself achieved distinction at Oxford as a classical scholar but thereafter turned to modern history. In 1924 he became a prize fellow at All Souls, Oxford; in 1927 he was appointed to an assistant lectureship in history at University College, London, and the following year he went to the West Indies and to New England to engage in research. Upon his return in 1929 Pares again settled at Oxford, this time as a lecturer in history at New College and as a fellow of All Souls. In 1939 he accepted the appointment of joint editor of the *English Historical Review*, a post he held for almost twenty years. In that same year he entered the Administrative Civil Service to make his contribution to the British war effort during the Second World War. At its conclusion (having been awarded the C. B. E.), he was elected to the chair of history at the University of Edinburgh, where he remained from 1945 until physical disability compelled him to resign in 1954. When he re-received an appointment as a special research fellow at All Souls College, he returned to Oxford, which became the centre of his scholarly activities until his untimely death in 1958.[1]

Pares was distinctly a historian's historian. His numerous writings

---

[4] H. T. Parker: *op. cit.*, p. 101.

[1] See the sketch of the career of Pares by Dr. Lucy S. Sutherland presented as an Introduction to *The Historian's Business and other Essays* by Richard Pares (eds. R. A. and Elisabeth Humphreys, Oxford, 1961).

assume far more information, a far greater background knowledge of the period to which he directed his talents, than most general readers would be expected to possess; yet sophisticated as his work was, it was never obscure. While such contemporaries as Namier and Butterfield concentrated upon England in the eighteenth century, Pares set out to deal with the vastly larger subject of the British Empire.

In his first major work, *War and Trade in the West Indies, 1739–1763*, Pares displayed his maturity as a scholar by evaluating the relative importance of the source materials he consulted in order to fathom the motives of statesmen; in his narrative of the critical events, he also set a standard of historical detachment that can only receive praise; moreover his treatment of the many aspects of the history of the West Indies, and especially the overseas relations of England and France during the period covered in the book are of the greatest value to the student of European expansion. Yet the work is difficult reading and, because of the topical method employed, repetitious in spots; nor was Pares at home with the Spanish side of the story he relates—as he himself disclosed in his Preface forewarning the reader of the book's shortcomings. Nevertheless, *War and Trade in the West Indies* represents a major contribution to the history of the British West Indies; as such it can stand on its own merits, even though it is but a by-product "of a fuller history" he had planned to undertake.[2] Two years later a companion piece to this volume came out under the title *Colonial Blockade and Neutral Rights, 1739–1763* (Oxford, 1938). This study helped to fill in the lacunae, particularly on such topics as privateering and the famous Rule of War of 1756, the rule of international law dealing with the doctrine of "Continuous Voyage," and the role of prize courts in time of war.[3] These two works, together with the article "American versus Continental Warfare, 1739–63" which appeared in 1936,[4] placed Pares in the foreground of those scholars interested in the mercantile history of the eighteenth-century British West Indies.

[2] *War and Trade in the West Indies, 1739–1763* (Oxford, 1936), p. ix. For reviews of this work see A. P. Newton in the *English Historical Review*, LIII, 143–4; F. W. Pitman in the *American Historical Review*, XLIII, 148–50, and L. H. Gipson in the *Journal of Modern History*, IX, 375–7.

[3] For an excellent review of this important study see D. J. L. Davies in the *English Historical Review*, LIV, 333–5; see also L. H. Gipson in the *Journal of Modern History*, XI, 79–80.

[4] *English Historical Review*, LI, 429–65.

Pares's *A West-India Fortune,* published in London in 1950, which relates the history of the Pinney family both on the island of Nevis, as sugar planters, and in Bristol, as sugar brokers, is also a valuable contribution to the economic and social history of the West Indies. An even more important study dealing with commerce in this area is his *Yankees and Creoles: The Trade between North America and the West Indies before the American Revolution,* which appeared in London and New York in 1956. This revealing volume presents in detail the multifarious problems facing the North American owners and captains of vessels who resorted to the West Indies in search of profitable markets for their commodities in exchange for the coveted produce of the sugar islands.[5] In 1956 Pares also published "A London West-India Merchant House, 1740–1769," as his additional contribution to the *festschrift* to Sir Lewis Namier which he co-edited.[6] This study is concerned with the Lascelles family of London, a family deeply involved in public service as well as planting and trade in Barbados.

In addition to the projected history of the British West Indies that failed to materialize, Pares had also agreed to write the history of the reign of George III to 1815 (designed to follow Basil Williams's *The Whig Supremacy, 1714–1760*) for the *Oxford History of England* series—a task which his growing physical disabilities unfortunately compelled him to forego. He had done the foundation work on the history of the King with such meticulous care, however, that some of the results of his labours were able to be presented in a paper, "George III and the Politicians," read before the Royal Historical Society in 1950 and published the next year.[7] This was followed by the six Ford Lectures, delivered on the same subject at Oxford in 1951 and 1952, which appeared in book form in 1953.[8] This is another study of the structure of politics, but with no particular thesis to expound; some of its points of view are stated with the diffidence of one always looking for more light, but others are expressed with far more finality.

---

[5] For an excellent brief review of *Yankees and Creoles* by W. T. Baxter see the *English Historical Review,* LXXII, 178–9.

[6] *Essays Presented to Sir Lewis Namier* (eds. Richard Pares and A. J. P. Taylor, London & New York, 1956).

[7] *Transactions* of the Royal Historical Society, 5th ser., I, 127–51.

[8] *King George III and the Politicians* (Oxford, 1953). The lectures (which the author of this series had the pleasure of hearing) were delivered by Professor Pares from his wheelchair to an audience that on each occasion packed the auditorium in the Examination Schools—a tribute to his prestige as a historian.

To Professor Pares, George III, despite his many faults of character, was not a bad King. Nor was he one who sought to alter the
results of the Revolution of 1688 in order to regain the prerogatives
claimed and exercised by the Stuarts. In the King's view the eighteenth-century English constitution provided for a balance of power
between the monarch and Parliament. If he opposed the Old Whigs
it was because he felt that they were attempting to deprive his office
of that which still rightly belonged to it—admittedly after it had
been shorn of most of the great prerogatives. In other words, in *King
George III and the Politicians* Pares presented the monarch as one
who defended, rather than endeavoured to destroy, the constitution
of the nation as he found it when he ascended the throne. As to the
influence of Namier's *Structure of Politics* on Pares, M. A. Thomson—author of the *Constitutional History of England, 1642–1801*
(1938)—in reviewing *King George III and the Politicians* in the July
1953 *English Historical Review* very properly stated: "Professor
Pares has been stimulated by Sir Lewis Namier, as also by Mr.
Romney Sedgwick,[9] but his response to these stimuli has been to
exercise an independent judgement on the questions they have tack-
led or suggested and to raise further questions of his own." Thomson
goes even further in his praise of this work; he concludes his review
by saying that he "is unable to think of any other single work written
during this generation on eighteenth century England from which
he has learnt more." [10] This may well be the view of many other
scholars. Undoubtedly as evidence of the high esteem in which
Pares was held as historian, scholar, and teacher, the Clarendon
Press at Oxford reprinted in 1961 some of his briefer studies in the
volume entitled *The Historian's Business and other Essays* (mentioned in the footnote at the beginning of this sketch). A careful
re-reading of each of these essays will repay the scholar handsomely.
Prior to the appearance of *The Historian's Business*, the monograph
"Merchants and Planters" was brought out by the Economic History

---

[9] Reference is made to the *Letters from George III to Lord Bute, 1756–1766*
(London, 1939) edited by Sedgwick. See Pares's very discriminating review of this
book in the *English Historical Review*, LV, 475–9.

[10] *English Historical Review*, LXVIII, 447–9. While Namier confined his attention
chiefly to the early years of the reign of George III, Pares's analysis covers the entire
reign under the respective chapter headings: "Amateurs and Professionals in Politics,"
"King, Lords, and Commons," "George III and the Parties," "The Appointment and
Dismissal of Ministries," "The King and the Cabinet," and "The Decline of Personal
Monarchy."

Society in 1960 as another posthumous publication.[11] In conclusion, it should be said that it is difficult to discuss the wealth of productivity of Professor Pares without a tribute to the courage of the man, whose intellectual brilliance and dedication to the task at hand for years so greatly overcame his physical infirmities.

J. Steven Watson (1916–   )

J. Steven Watson, a student and a tutor at Christ Church, Oxford, was joint editor of that useful and scholarly work *The Law and Working of the Constitution, Documents 1660–1914* (2 vols., London, 1952). It was also he who succeeded in bringing out *The Reign of George III, 1760–1815* (Oxford & New York, 1960) as Volume XII in *The Oxford History of England* series—after the assignment had passed successively from Professor G. S. Veitch to Professor Richard Pares, whose growing disabilities obliged him to relinquish it.

Watson's treatment of the reign of George III represents the repudiation of the Whig interpretation of the period, and shows evidence of the influence of the Namier school. For example, Watson states that the King was not a subverter but an upholder of the constitution. In fact, throughout this comprehensive volume he demonstrates his independence of thought. He presents Bute in a much more favourable and convincing light than Pares had, and shows Newcastle more clearly than did Namier. While he gives Pitt a heroic cast, his picture of him—especially as the Earl of Chatham—is far less heroic than that drawn by Basil Williams. If his presentation of the situation in Scotland and Ireland and of the colonial crisis in North America that led to open hostilities in 1775 can be regarded as somewhat defective to the specialist in these fields, yet his account of political, social, and economic develop-

---

[11] See the *Economic History Review Supplement*, No. 4 (London, 1960). See also the review by Bernard Bailyn in the *William and Mary Quarterly*, 3rd ser., XVII, 536–8. This work, which consists of four essays, represents the final word of Pares on the trade of the West Indies, but does so in conjunction with an examination of the tobacco colonies, and with some illuminating findings on the subject of planter debts.

ments in England is illuminating and of great value. Doubtless most discriminating readers will agree with the opinion given by Professor D. B. Horn of the University of Edinburgh when, in reviewing *The Reign of George III* in the *English Historical Review,* he writes that it is "a book which will be referred to with gratitude by students on specific points and which yet also presents to the general reader a lively and well-informed narrative of British history in the reign of George III," but contains, unhappily, "far too many slips and misprints," blemishes that a second edition could easily remove.[1]

Mr. Watson, as one of the more recent group of historians, should not stand alone; yet, because of the nature of my approach to these historiographical essays—that is, concentration chiefly on those historians who have contributed more than one major work dealing with the period and subject of my series and whose works have affected historical judgements—I am forced to neglect some of the more contemporary British historians now producing valuable monographs and books, not to mention teachers, editors, and compilers. In the interests of time and space, these must be reserved for the general bibliographical guide to follow in this series.

Similarly, limitations of space preclude a survey in these brief sketches of the work of specialists relating to the history of certain areas in the Empire, including Africa, India, the West Indies, and Canada. Thus the work of such meritorious historians of the West Indies as Edward Long and Bryan Edwards has been passed over, as has that of many fine scholars writing about India, Canada, and elsewhere.[2]

---

[1] See the *English Historical Review,* LXXVII, 115–18. For other reviews see those by I. R. Christie of University College, London, in the *American Historical Review,* LXVI, 721–3; Professor G. H. Guttridge of the University of California in the *Journal of Modern History,* XXXIII, 201–2; A. L. Rowse of All Souls College, Oxford, in the *New York Times Book Review,* November 27, 1960, which is most laudatory; and the anonymous review in the *Times Literary Supplement,* October 7, 1960, which is unnecessarily severe.

[2] For the works of the specialists dealing with various parts of the wider British Empire—including topical guides, reference works and bibliographies—see the general bibliography to follow in this series. Special mention must be made here, however, of Elsa V. Goveia's *A Study on the Historiography of the British West Indies* (Mexico, 1956), which is an invaluable historiographical aid for the period, as is the fine book by H. P. Beers: *The French in North America: A Bibliographical Guide* . . . (Baton Rouge, La., 1957), especially in its historiographical chapters.

Canadian Historians

As HAS just been mentioned, these historiographical sketches are far from being all-inclusive and do not begin to cover all the British Empire historians who write about the period 1748 to 1776. Thus this brief section on Canadian writers does not take into account François Xavier Garneau, Henri Raymond Casgrain, nor yet my old friend A. L. Burt. The omission of A. G. Doughty and others who gathered and edited so much valuable Canadian source material is also regrettable, but the limitations of time and space have allowed for only two exceptions: the two Canadian historians who are the subject of the sketches to follow, each of whom has shed great light on what has been called the Atlantic Community.

Harold Adams Innis (1894–1952)

Professor Donald G. Creighton of the University of Toronto, in his book *Harold Adams Innis: Portrait of a Scholar* (Toronto, 1957) affirmed (p. 103) that Innis before his death had become "the greatest Canadian national historian." This assertion would hardly be questioned by any historian who has used his work.

Born on a rather unproductive Canadian farm near Otterville in the Province of Ontario, Innis began his education in a one-room rural school; in 1905 he entered the Otterville High School and from there, in due course, the Woodstock Collegiate Institute. Next he enrolled at McMaster University (then located at Toronto), where he became increasingly interested in economic history and where he secured his baccalaureate. Soon after taking his degree, he enlisted in the Canadian army during the First World War and went overseas, only to be wounded at Vimy Ridge and invalided back to Canada. Upon his recovery, he entered the University of Chicago where he received his doctorate in political economy in 1920. In that year he also began his career at the University of Toronto, starting as an instructor in political economy and slowly advancing in rank until in 1937 he became head of the department and in 1947, Dean of the School of Graduate Studies as well. In addition to his academic responsibilities, he performed some valuable public duties, including service on two important Canadian investigation commissions.

The most significant of Innis's contributions to the historical literature of the period 1750 to 1775 lies in two of his books, each characterized by its mastery of the subject in hand. One of them, *The Fur Trade in Canada: An Introduction to Canadian Economic History,* was first published by the Yale University Press in 1930.[1] It was very properly called by the reviewer in the *English Historical Review* (XLVII, 169–70), "a most important contribution to our interpretation of Canadian history." It should be added that the two large volumes by Professor E. E. Rich of Cambridge University entitled *The History of the Hudson's Bay Company* (London, 1958–9) supplement rather than displace the Innis work. This may also be said of the great series of documents relating to the activities of the Company published since 1930 by the Hudson's Bay Record Society, which also sponsored Rich's *History.* Closely related to Innis's *Fur Trade in Canada,* but emphasizing only one aspect of this trade, is a brief but enlightening study by Murray G. Lawson with a Foreword by Professor Innis that appeared in 1943 from the University of Toronto Press; it is entitled *Furs: A Study in English Mercantilism, 1700–1775.*

The other important contribution made by Innis to an understanding of the period is the volume in the series issued under the

---

[1] *The Fur Trade in Canada* was republished in Toronto in 1956; it is now available in paperback from Yale University Press (New Haven, 1965). The General Preface of the original volume stated: "The history of the fur trade here presented by Doctor Innis may be regarded as an introduction to the analytic study of that industry which appears in another volume, *The Fur Trade of Canada* (Toronto, 1927)."

direction of the Carnegie Endowment for International Peace, *The Cod Fisheries: The History of an International Economy*, published in 1940 by the Yale University Press and reissued in Toronto in 1954. Mention should be made of two other brief Innis studies relating to the subject of the fisheries: one, "An Introduction to the Economic History of the Maritimes, including Newfoundland and New England," appeared in 1931 in the annual *Report* of the Canadian Historical Association; the other, "Cape Breton and the French Régime," was published in 1935 in the Royal Society of Canada *Transactions*, Section 2. *The Cod Fisheries*, as W. P. Morrell points out in his review of it in the *English Historical Review* (LVII, 271–4), represents "the first attempt to tell the whole complex story [of the cod fisheries] in a single volume." As the book is heavy in detail, it would be well for the student to use with it such works as Griffith Williams's *An Account of the Island of Newfoundland . . .* (1765), Ralph G. Lounsbury's *The British Fishery at Newfoundland, 1634–1763* (published by Yale University Press in 1934), and Edward Ackerman's *New England's Fishing Industry* (published in 1941 by University of Chicago Press), the last despite its emphasis on the modern side of the industry.

Innis's final contribution to the historiography of the period under review was his editorial work on *The Diary of Simeon Perkins, 1766–1780*, published in 1948 as Volume XXIX of the *Publications* of the Champlain Society.

John Bartlet Brebner (1895–1957)

Among Canadians who contributed significantly to the history of the period with which this historiography is concerned is the late John Bartlet Brebner. Born at Toronto, Brebner after two years at the university enlisted in the Canadian armed forces in 1915 and served throughout the First World War. When he had been mustered out of the service he entered Oxford University, where he secured an honours degree in 1920. He then returned to the University of Toronto to lecture in modern history for five years before he joined the staff of the Department of History at Columbia University as an instructor. In 1927 he was awarded his doctorate by this institution and by successive promotions at length became in 1954 the holder of the Gouverneur Morris chair in history, a post which he held from 1954 until his death three years later.

Brebner's first book, *New England's Outpost: Acadia before the Conquest of Canada,* which was based on his doctoral dissertation, appeared in 1927 as one of the Columbia University *Studies in History, Economics and Public Law.* It deals with the history of Acadia (or Nova Scotia) from 1640 to 1760. But it is the last six chapters (covering 1754 to 1773) that are of special interest to this historiography, setting forth the background for the expulsion of the Acadians from their lands as the result of a plan entered into by Governor Charles Lawrence of Nova Scotia and Governor William Shirley of Massachusetts Bay. Thoroughness of research and clarity of style, together with a spirit of detachment in dealing with issues that continue to arouse emotions, characterize the writing.[1]

Brebner's first book was followed in 1933 by his *Explorers of North America, 1492–1806* as part of *The Pioneer Histories* series. This volume is concerned with the objectives of the explorers and sheds light upon the process of the opening up of the North American continent. In 1937 came his *The Neutral Yankees of Nova Scotia: A Marginal Colony during the Revolutionary Years,* an important work which carries forward the story of Nova Scotia from 1760—the point where Brebner stopped in his *New England's Outpost*—to the year 1782.[2] Nova Scotia, originally planted by the French as Acadie (or Acadia) was between 1760 and 1775 colonized largely by New Englanders, who were given the lands that had been cultivated by the exiled Acadians. But after the termination of the war between Great Britain and France, hundreds of the exiles— at last ready to take an oath of loyalty to George III—were permitted to return to Nova Scotia and were given new allotments of

---

[1] For comments of reviewers see H. P. Biggar in the *English Historical Review,* XLIII, 267–8; Archibald MacMechan in the *Canadian Historical Review,* IX, 63; L. S. Mayo in the *American Historical Review,* XXXIII, 667–8; and A. R. M. Lower in the *New England Quarterly,* I, 264–6. It should be pointed out that the author of this series (Volume VI, Chaps. 8–10) gives a different interpretation of a number of incidents in the history of Nova Scotia covering the period 1750 to 1760 to that of Professor Brebner.

[2] One unusual feature of the *Neutral Yankees of Nova Scotia* is an Appendix (pp. 362–5) in which Brebner lists revisions that should be made to his *New England's Outpost,* something that only adds to the confidence one has in the integrity of his quest for the truth.

land to the east of the Bay of Fundy. During the period of the crisis that developed between England and the American colonies they remained neutral. So too, surprisingly enough, did all but a few of the thousands of transplanted New Englanders. In his study Brebner makes clear why this was the case. The two books taken together represent the most scholarly account of a colony that, had circumstances been different, might have become a fourteenth colony to revolt from Great Britain.[3] Nor must we overlook what may be considered in some respects a still more important contribution to an understanding of the history of the period. This is the first four chapters of Brebner's *North Atlantic Triangle: The Interplay of Canada, the United States and Great Britain* (published in 1945 as the concluding volume of a series of twenty-five issued by the Carnegie Endowment for International Peace).[4] This volume presents a broad survey of the early relations between what are now the three great Atlantic English-speaking nations. Also serving somewhat the same purpose—except that it is presented in the single dimension of the Canadian point of view—is Book 1 of his *Canada: A Modern History* (published posthumously in 1960 in *The University of Michigan History of the Modern World* series, as a general history without annotation, edited by Allan Nevins and H. M. Ehrmann). Unfortunately, this final volume from the pen of Professor Brebner bears the marks of a tired, ailing man.[5]

---

[3] For reviews of *The Neutral Yankees of Nova Scotia* see particularly Chester Martin in the *Canadian Historical Review*, XVIII, 437–40; Viola F. Barnes in the *American Historical Review*, XLIII, 411–12; A. R. M. Lower in the *New England Quarterly*, X, 798–9; W. B. Kerr in the *Mississippi Valley Historical Review*, XXIV, 235–6; and L. W. Labaree in the *Journal of Modern History*, X, 108–9.

[4] For the review by the writer of this series of *North Atlantic Triangle* see *New York History*, XXVII, 96–8. In this connection it may be noted that Brebner did a special wartime history in collaboration with Allan Nevins (*The Making of Modern Britain: A Short History*, New York, 1943), in which Chap. 6, "World Wars for Empire," gives a broad view of the eighteenth-century British Empire in an imperial light.

[5] For examples of critical opinion on *Canada: A Modern History* see C. P. Stacey's review in *Canadian Historical Review*, XLII, 55–6, and A. R. M. Lower's in *American Historical Review*, XLVI, 489–90. For an appreciation of Brebner see D. G. Creighton: *Canadian Historical Review*, XXXIX, 182–3.

American Historians

I n turning to the American writers who helped to illuminate the history of the period covered by this series, among the contemporaries we come first to the work of William Douglass: *A Summary, Historical and Political, of . . . British Settlements in North-America* (2 vols., Boston, 1747, 1751), a useful summary, as the title suggests, but for the first half of the eighteenth century only. Then there is President Thomas Clap of Yale, who brought into print *The Annals of Yale-College . . . to 1766* (New Haven, 1766), and Amos Adams, author of *A Concise Historical View of . . . New-England* (Boston, 1769), later superseded by Palfrey's history of that area. In addition one could point to numerous contemporary works by travellers, botanists, cartographers and other specialists. However, the first man who set a critical standard for the writing of history concerned with the period 1748 to 1776 is Thomas Hutchinson.

Thomas Hutchinson (1711–1780)

Thomas Hutchinson not only was a historian of the first rank among American colonials, but also attained distinction in other lines of activity: in the field of colonial finance, whereby Massachusetts Bay became a sound-money colony; in ably defending the rights of Massachusetts Bay in the boundary dispute with New York; in serving the province in turn as Speaker of the House of Representatives, as a member of the Governor's Council, as Lieutenant Governor, as Chief Justice of the Superior Court of Judicature, and finally, as Governor. Yet in 1774 he left the colony, never to return, and by the time he died, a Loyalist refugee in England, he had sunk into relative obscurity.

On October 22, 1778, while in exile, Hutchinson wrote in his diary: "I finished the revisal of my History, to the end of my Administration and laid it by." [1] However, it did not appear in print until fifty years later. The first edition was published in London in 1828 under the editorship of his grandson, the Rev. John Hutchinson.[2] The edition designed for the American market carried the title *The History of the Province of Massachusetts Bay, from the Year 1750, until June, 1774;* that for the British market was entitled *The History of the Province of Massachusetts Bay from 1749 to 1774, comprising a detailed narrative of the origin and early stages of the American Revolution* and included a Preface and a dedication to the Lord Chancellor, Boston-born Baron Lyndhurst, son of the distinguished Bostonian portrait painter, John Singleton Copley. The appearance of this volume thus completed Hutchinson's great historical trilogy on Massachusetts Bay, for two volumes had been published in Boston: *The History of the Colony of Massachusetts-Bay, from the first settlement . . . until . . . 1691* in 1764 and in 1767 *The History of the Province of Massachusetts-Bay, from . . . 1691, until the year 1750.*[3]

Charles Deane, of the publishing committee of the Massachusetts Historical Society, read a paper before that body in 1857 on "Hutchinson's Historical Publications." In it he paid this tribute to Hutchinson: "Governor Hutchinson's historical labors are of the highest value, and Massachusetts owes him a debt of gratitude for what he

[1] *The Diary and Letters of His Excellency Thomas Hutchinson . . .* (ed. P. O. Hutchinson, 2 vols., London, 1883–6), II, 218.

[2] The interesting circumstances under which Vol. III was published are described by Mr. Charles Deane in the Massachusetts Historical Society *Proceedings*, III, 144–6.

[3] While Hutchinson was still engaged in the writing of this volume at his Boston mansion, where he kept his papers and books, rioters broke into the house on the night of August 26, 1765, and destroyed or scattered its contents. As Hutchinson noted in the Preface to Vol. II, the manuscript and other papers that survived the onslaught were picked up and taken to the home of the Rev. Mr. Eliot, minister of the New North Church. Fortunately only a few pages of the manuscript itself were lost. However, many original records were destroyed, so that Hutchinson was obliged to make clear in the Preface that he had been deprived of some papers for the period 1730 to 1750 "which would have enabled me to render it more particular and circumstantial."

has done to illustrate her annals, . . . as his work will ever be regarded as of the first authority by the student of our history, it can never be wholly superseded. . . . Hutchinson's mind was eminently a judicial one; and candor, moderation, and a desire for truth, appear to have guided his pen." Commenting on the volume of his *History* describing the events between 1750 and 1775 that led to the Revolution, Deane concluded with the statement: "His subject was a delicate one; but it is treated with his usual good judgment, and with an excellent spirit." [4] In view of the circumstances under which the last volume was written, this is an eminently fair statement. [5]

As already stressed in this historiography, it is extremely difficult for any one engaged actively and prominently in public life to write with detachment about those events and the personalities connected with them, especially when this record is a part of the author's own personal history. This was true in the case of Hutchinson's writing of the history of Massachusetts Bay from 1750 to 1774. For example, he rather deserts the calm measured terms used throughout the balance of the work when describing the activities of James Otis, and particularly his own appointment as Chief Justice of the Superior Court of Judicature instead of Otis's father, who had apparently been promised a seat on the bench. Doubtless as a result of reports made to him at the time, Hutchinson's version of the incident declared that the younger Otis "vowed revenge" if his father failed to win the appointment and from "so small a spark a great fire seems to have been kindled." [6] In this connection it must also be pointed out that

[4] Massachusetts Historical Society *Proceedings*, III, 134–50. See also L. S. Mayo's valuable paper on Hutchinson's historical work in the American Antiquarian Society *Proceedings*, New Series, XLI, 321–39.

[5] In *The Life of Thomas Hutchinson, Royal Governor of the Province of Massachusetts Bay* (Boston & New York, 1896, pp. 87–8) J. K. Hosmer writes: "In the main, he is fair-minded, and in the circumstances surprisingly calm," and adds, although his history is without purple patches and brilliant descriptions, it "is the work of a thoughtful brain, whose comments on politics, finance, religion, . . . are full of intelligence and also full of humanity." The high standing that Hutchinson's history still enjoys is indicated by the publication of a critical edition, ed. Lawrence Shaw Mayo, under the general title *The History of the Colony and Province of Massachusetts-Bay* (3 vols., Cambridge, Mass., 1936). In 1949 Catherine Barton Mayo supplemented her late husband's edition with *Additions to Thomas Hutchinson's "History of Massachusetts Bay,"* published in the American Antiquarian Society *Proceedings* for 1949 and in a separate reprint (Worcester, Mass., 1949). This study contains many important additions which Hutchinson himself made to his completed manuscript; the two works should therefore be used together.

[6] *The History of the Province of Massachusetts Bay, from the Year 1750, until June, 1774* (London, 1828), pp. 87–8. Yet, in justice to Hutchinson (with respect to the truth of these statements), Governor Bernard wrote to the Earl of Shelburne on

Hutchinson's *History* fails to indicate that one of the basic causes of Otis's (and others') opposition to him was the fact that he, together with a small group of wealthy men closely associated with him by marriage and other ties, tended to monopolize the chief offices of the province. At the same time, in dealing with the trying circumstances of the Stamp Act rioting in Boston that resulted in the wrecking of his home, Hutchinson maintains his judicial calm,[7] as he also does over such other incidents as the so-called "Boston Massacre,"[8] and the "Boston Tea Party."[9] Bearing in mind that he wrote as an acknowledged Loyalist, it must be noted too that he was aware of the fact that most of the people of the province were committed to the defence of what they considered to be their rights—rights which, all in all, are fairly presented. In describing colonial leaders who opposed him, he was most generous in his characterization of the redoubtable patriot Joseph Hawley as a man of "singular scrupulosity." But he displayed no such detachment in writing of Samual Adams, who was accused not only of preventing (by intimidation of the sheriff) the sale of his late bankrupt father's estate but of "defalcation" in connection with the office of town collector of taxes. Adams was also pictured as acquiring "a talent of artfully and fallaciously insinuating . . . a prejudice against the characters of all whom he attacked" and by this means "robbing men of their characters, and injuring them more than if he had robbed them of their estates."[10] But these are exceptions to the general tone of the volume which is distinguished, as were the two preceding volumes of his *History* and the supporting documents in the Appendix, by its candour and a manifest desire to present without prejudice the stirring events in which he himself played so leading a role.[11]

December 22, 1766 (Shelburne Papers, 51:507–11, Clements Library, and also P.R.O., C.O. 5:892) that "Otis Junior did not confine himself to hints but declared openly with oaths, that if 'his father was not appointed judge, he would set the whole province in a flame, though he perished in the attempt.'" Bernard's letter stated that two gentlemen of credit had made depositions respecting Otis's threat. For a discussion of this event see Volume X, 121–2, of this series.

[7] *History of Massachusetts Bay, 1750–1774*, pp. 120–7.

[8] *Ibid.*, pp. 270–80.

[9] *Ibid.*, pp. 422–41.

[10] *Ibid.*, pp. 294–6.

[11] See, for example, Hutchinson's treatment of his ancestor, the famous Anne Hutchinson, in Vol. I (Mayo edn.), 50 and 62–3.

Peter Oliver (1713–1791)

If, in the writing of the history of the beginnings of the American Revolution, Thomas Hutchinson had pretty well subdued his emotions so as to present fairly both sides of the great public issues that arose, the same cannot be said of his close friend Peter Oliver. Both Hutchinson and Oliver came of well-to-do Massachusetts Bay families; both received their education at Harvard; both entered business and prospered, Hutchinson by trade and Oliver by his iron works at Middleboro in Plymouth County. Further, both men became members of the Governor's Council; both were appointed to a place on the bench of the Superior Court of Judicature; both attained the office of Chief Justice; as Loyalists both suffered the confiscation of their property, and both, while in exile in England, sought to write a true account of the revolt of Massachusetts Bay against British rule. By 1778 Hutchinson had completed his task and by 1781 Oliver his. Hutchinson's history was first published in 1829,[1] but it was not until 1961 that the Oliver history—until then available only in manuscript—appeared in print. Competently edited by Douglass Adair and J. A. Schutz, who have provided an illuminating Introduction, and issued by the Huntington Library, it carries the title: *Peter Oliver's Origin & Progress of the American Rebellion. A Tory View.*[2]

While Hutchinson wrote two substantial volumes covering the history of Massachusetts Bay before 1750, Oliver, with a very differ-

---

[1] Peter Oliver had apparently read the manuscript of Hutchinson's history. Referring to the two volumes which had been published, Oliver stated: "a Continuation of which, to the breaking out of the present Rebellion he left prepared for the Press; as Publication of which would be a valuable Present to the Publick, as it would be a Register of Facts, which neither the Talent of historick Writing, or Truth itself would blush to Patronize" (*Peter Oliver's Origin & Progress of the American Rebellion. A Tory View* [eds. Douglass Adair and J. A. Schutz, San Marino, Calif., 1961], p. 30).

[2] The original manuscript of Oliver's history has never been located, if it still exists. A fair copy of it is among the Egerton Manuscripts in the British Museum; a second copy, of later date, is in the Huntington Library at San Marino, Calif. In publishing the collated version of the two manuscripts the editors divided the book into chapters with appropriate headings. They also supplied the last part of the title: *A Tory View.*

ent purpose in mind, merely summarized the early history in an introductory statement (which in print occupies less than twenty-five pages) primarily designed to give the reader a background to the events that took place. The *Origin and Progress* is in the form of a letter to a friend and is dated from London, March 11, 1781. Before concluding his introductory statement, Oliver warns his hypothetical correspondent:

> "You will be presented with such a Detail of Villainy in all its Forms, that it will require some Fortitude to meet the Shock. You will see Religion dressed up into a Stalking horse, to be skulked behind, that Vice might perpetrate its most atrocious Crimes, whilst it bore so fair a Front to mislead & deceive the World around. In short, you will see every Thing, sacred & profane, twisted into all Shapes to serve the Purposes of Rebellion; & Earth & Hell ransacked for Tools to work the Fabrick with." [3]

In dealing with the immediate causes for the rebellion, Oliver felt impelled to refer to the plurality of offices held by Thomas Hutchinson, which included the posts of Lieutenant Governor, Chief Justice of the province, and judge of the probate court for Suffolk County, "the most important County of the Province." He then remarked: " . . . the Envy of Ambition in some, & the Envy of Avarice in others, were roused at the Possession of so many by one Man. But let it be remembred, that the pecuniary Stipends of this Province, to their Servants, were similar, in profit, to the Wages of Sin, for no Man could get a Living by them; & those three united in Mr. *Hutchinson* . . . did not afford him a decent Support for his Family." As to Hutchinson's relinquishment of the office of judge of probate, Oliver quotes Hutchinson as having stated: "it gives me so much Pleasure to relieve the Widow & fatherless, & direct them what Steps to take in managing their Estates; & also in reconciling contending Parties; that I would rather resign my other Offices, & discharge this alone without Fee or Reward." [4] In fact to Oliver, who had known him from an early age, Hutchinson was a symbol of the finest type of manhood: "the Scholar, without Pedantry—the polite Gentleman, without Affectation—the social Companion, without Reservedness—affable, without the least Tincture of Pride . . . liberal in his Charity, without Ostentation or Partiality. . . ." [5]

---

[3] *Peter Oliver's Origin & Progress* . . . , p. 26.
[4] *Ibid.*, p. 33.
[5] *Ibid.*, p. 34.

In contrast, James Otis, according to Oliver, took to heart the maxim of one of Milton's devils: "Better to reign in Hell than serve in Heaven," and "carried his Malevolence to so great a Length, that being often thwarted in his Opposition to Government, he took to the Course of Dram drinking, & ruined his Family . . . & the last I heard of him was, that he seemed to be a living Monument of the Justice of Heaven, by his being a miserable Vagabond, rolling in the Streets & Gutters, the laughing-Stock of Boys & the Song of the Drunkard." Nor was Oliver any more complimentary to Samuel Adams. In his effort to delineate his features, he drew upon the observation of "a celebrated Painter in *America,* vizt. 'That if he wished to draw the Picture of the Devil, . . . he would get Sam Adams to sit for him.'" To Oliver, Adams's outstanding characteristic was "the Malignity of his heart," and the "employing his Abilities to the vilest Purposes. . . . He was so thorough a *Machiavelian,* that he divested himself of every worthy Principle, & would stick at no Crime to accomplish his Ends." As for John Hancock, he "was as closely attached to the hindermost Part of Mr. *Adams* as the Rattles are affixed to the Tail of the Rattle Snake. . . . His understanding was of the Dwarf Size; but his Ambition . . . was upon the Gigantick." Although Hancock, according to Oliver, might have been "a most useful member of Society . . . Mr. *Adams,* who was restless in endeavors to disturb ye Peace of Society, & who was ever going about seeking whom he might devour, seized upon him as his Prey, & . . . Adams, like the Cuddle fish, would discharge his muddy Liquid, & darken the Water to such an Hue, that the other was lost to his Way, & . . . in the Cloudy Vortex would again be seized, & at last secured." [6]

Nor was the clergy of the province in general described other than as "a set of very weak men. . . . Among those who were most distinguished of the Boston Clergy were Dr. *Charles Chauncey,* Dr. *Jonathan Mayhew* & Dr. *Samuel Cooper*; & they distinguished themselves in encouraging Seditions & Riots, untill those lesser Offences were absorbed in Rebellion." Of the three, Dr. Cooper was the most dangerous to the public peace. He was "a young man—very polite in his Manners—of a general Knowledge—not deep in his Profession, but very deep in the black Art. . . . No Man could, with a better Grace, utter the Word of *God* from his Mouth, & at the same

---

[6] *Ibid.,* pp. 36–40.

Time keep a two edged Dagger concealed in his Hand. His tongue was Butter & Oil, but under it was the Poison of Asps." Recording the conduct of the merchants was likewise to Oliver a "disagreeable Task"; for "the Inhabitants of the *Massachusetts Bay* were notorious in the smuggling Business, from the Capital Merchant down to the meanest Mechanick." Indeed, "some of those Smugglers have acquired so strong an Habit of Smuggling, that they have openly declared, that if they could gain more by a legal Trade they would prefer the former." [7]

All this helps Oliver to answer to his own satisfaction the rhetorical question raised at the beginning of his treatise: why Massachusetts Bay— "a Colony, wch. had been nursed, in its Infancy, with the most tender Care & Attention; which had been indulged with every Gratification that the most froward Child could wish for; which had even bestowed upon it such Liberality, which its Infancy & Youth could not *think* to ask for; which had been repeatedly saved from impending Destruction, sometimes by an Aid unsought—at other times by Assistance granted to them from their own repeated humble Supplications"—should "plunge into an unnatural Rebellion, . . . this surely . . . must strike [one] with some Degree of Astonishment; & . . . [make one] anxiously wish for a Veil to throw over the Nakedness of human Nature." [8]

In view of the spirit in which the *Origin & Progress of the American Rebellion* was written, one may understand why it did not appear earlier in print. On the other hand its publication serves a useful purpose in presenting the emotional reactions of a stalwart and able Loyalist to events in which he himself was deeply involved.

Alexander Hewat (1745–1829)

The Rev. Alexander Hewat was born in Scotland and received his education in theology at the University of Edinburgh. In 1763 he

[7] *Ibid.*, pp. 42–6.

[8] *Ibid.*, p. 3. For reviews of Peter Oliver's *Origin & Progress of the American Rebellion* see J. R. Alden in the *American Historical Review*, LXVII, 796; R. L. Calhoun in the *William and Mary Quarterly*, 3rd ser., XIX, 303–4; and Malcolm Freiberg in the *Mississippi Valley Historical Review*, XLVIII, 693–4.

emigrated to South Carolina and there became pastor of the First Presbyterian Church, known as the Scots Church, at Charleston. After serving in this capacity for some twelve years, he went to England about the year 1775 and seems to have spent most of his remaining years in London.

Hewat's favourable reception in Charleston is indicated by the fact that he not only enjoyed the friendship of Lieutenant Governor William Bull but was also admitted to membership in the St. Andrew's Society. That he cherished the friendships formed in Charleston may be judged from his continued correspondence with friends in that town and from his will, in which he left £50 to his former church there. In 1779 his *An Historical Account of the Rise and Progress of the Colonies of South Carolina and Georgia* was published in two volumes in London.

Hewat, a Loyalist, was a man of moderate views and of scholarly instincts. In sketching the history of South Carolina and Georgia from their beginnings down to the repeal of the Stamp Act his achievement was such that patriot David Ramsay remarked in the Preface to the first volume of his own historical account that, in comparison to other histories of South Carolina,

> "Dr. Hewat's historical account of the rise and progress of the colonies of South Carolina and Georgia, was read with much more advantage—on it greater reliance was placed—and of it more use has been made, than of all the histories which had preceded. To him every carolinian ought to be obliged for preserving many useful facts which otherwise would before this day have been forgotten. His valuable work was written shortly before the american revolution when tradition went further back and was more recent than at present. Much of the information contained therein is said to have been derived from lieutenant governor William Bull who had been a public officer since 1740, and who was the son of lieutenant-governor Bull, and the grandson of Stephen Bull, who had held public offices in succession from the very first settlement of the colony." [1]

It is therefore small wonder that Ramsay and later writers especially concerned with the history of South Carolina as a colony have leaned upon Hewat from time to time.

In his account of the South Carolinians Hewat stresses the fact that "a noble spirit of benevolence pervaded the society." Charleston

---

[1] David Ramsay: *The History of South-Carolina from its first Settlement in 1670, to the Year 1808* (2 vols., Charleston, 1809), I, x–xi.

was not a place of sloth and indulgence but "was like a bee-hive, and there were none that reaped not advantages more or less from the flourishing state of trade and commerce." Yet agriculture, though highly profitable, was carried on by overseers of plantations in a manner that he regarded as slovenly.[2] Turning to the background events of the American Revolution after the Peace of Paris of 1763, Hewat writes:

> "Every member of the vast empire might perceive, that some com-
> mon tax, regularly and impartially imposed, in proportion to the
> strength of each division, was necessary to the future defence and
> protection of the whole. In particular, the people of Great Britain,
> when they looked forward to the possible contingency of a new war,
> and considered the burdens under which they groaned, had a melan-
> choly and dreadful prospect before them; and the parliament consid-
> ered it as their indispensible duty to relieve them as much as
> possible, and provide for the safety of the state by a proportionable
> charge on all its subjects. For as the exemption of one part from this
> equal charge was unreasonable and unjust, so it might tend to
> alienate the hearts of these subjects residing in one corner of the
> empire from those in another, and destroy that union and harmony
> in which the strength of the whole consisted."[3]

However, Hewat pointed out that this plan did not take into account the fact that Americans were "jealous of their liberties, proud of their strength, and sensible of their importance to Britain." More-over, "their great distance, their vast extent of territory, their numer-ous ports and conveniences for trade, their increasing numbers, their various productions, and consequently their growing power, had now prepared and enabled them for resisting such laws as they deemed inconsistent with their interest, or dangerous to their lib-erty." As for the colonists of New England, when Parliament now moved to secure a colonial revenue they

> "were alarmed with the most terrible apprehensions and suspicions,
> openly affirming, that the King, Lords and Commons had formed a
> design for enslaving them, and had now begun deliberately to put it
> in execution. Immediately they entered into associations for distress-
> ing the mother country. . . . They pretended that they were driven
> to such measures by necessity; but in reality they had nothing less in

---

[2] Alexander Hewat: *An Historical Account of the Rise and Progress of the Colonies of South Carolina and Georgia* (2 vols., London, 1779), II, 294–302.
[3] *Ibid.*, II, 308.

view than their favourite plan of independence, for the accomplishment of which it required time to secure the union and help of the
other colonies. . . . Hence the seeds of disaffection which had
sprung up in New England spread through the other colonies, inso-
much that multitudes became infected with republican principles,
and aspired after independence." [4]

Such was Hewat's explanation for the revolt of the North American
British Colonies.[5]

The point should again be stressed that Hewat's *History* is of
greatest importance as a source for the colonial background of South
Carolina.

Thomas Jones (1731–1792)

Thomas Jones, a former Justice of the Supreme Court of the
Province of New York and a great landowner there, wrote between
the years 1783 and 1788, while in exile in England as an American
Loyalist, his *History of New York during the Revolutionary War.*
Under the editorship of Edward Floyd de Lancey it was published
in two large volumes in 1879 by the New York Historical Society. It
is by far the most detailed account of the progress of the War for
American Independence, especially as it relates to New York, prepared by any Loyalist writer.

After securing a degree at Yale, Jones probably studied law in the
office of his father, David Jones, who was Speaker of the New York
Assembly for fifteen of the twenty-one years he was a member, and
who afterwards was elevated to the post of Justice of the Supreme
Court of New York. Upon the senior Jones's resignation from the
bench in 1773 for reasons of health, Thomas took his father's
place—having meanwhile developed a successful law practice and
served as Recorder for New York City. He continued to serve in that
capacity until in 1776 in the midst of the War for American Independence the Court ceased to function under the authority of the

---

[4] *Ibid.,* II, 308–9, 313–14, 329.
[5] For a treatment of Hewat as a historian see Michael Kraus: *A History of
American History* (New York, 1937), pp. 122–4.

Crown. After suffering imprisonment three times at the hands of the revolutionaries, Judge Jones left with his family for England in 1781. As the act of attainder passed in 1779 by the Assembly against him and others who were loyal to the government of Great Britain threatened not only confiscation of property but also the death penalty, should they still be within the state when peace was made, he never returned to America.

Thus it was as an exile and stirred by deep emotions that Thomas Jones wrote his *History*.[1] That it contains numerous errors is clear—and perhaps not too surprising in view of the fact that it was largely written in the little village of Hoddesdon in Hertfordshire where he settled and remained until his death. That it was also slanted throughout to vindicate the Loyalist point of view is equally clear. But it was written by a man of high intelligence, who had been in close touch with New York provincial affairs, had occupied posts of great importance in the colony, and had therefore had access to much official information. In other words, the *History*— written in the white heat of resentment and for this reason to be used with caution—is not a mere fabrication and presents many valuable insights. Moreover, the very extensive notes supplied by the editor at the end of each volume serve both to illuminate and, at times, to correct the text.[2]

To Judge Jones three men were largely responsible for the revolt of New York against the mother country: William Livingston, John Morin Scott, and William Smith, Jr.[3] All were Presbyterian in religion and republican in politics. This "triumvirate," the author asserts, "determined, if possible, to pull down Church and State, to raise their own Government and religion upon its ruins, or to throw the whole province into anarchy and confusion." To this end they gathered around them in their Whig Club a number of people who "took active parts, in the late unnatural, unprovoked, American

---

[1] Professor Richard B. Morris called the Jones *History* nothing less than "venomous"; see his sketch of the life of William Smith in the *Dictionary of American Biography;* see also H. P. Johnston: *Observations on Judge Jones' Loyalist History of the American Revolution. How Far is it an Authority?* (New York, 1880), especially pp. 7–11.

[2] Again the student is advised when reading the Jones *History* to have at hand the Johnston *Observations,* which refutes specific points in it. These refutations are embodied in nineteen sections, each of them under a proper heading.

[3] See Dorothy R. Dillon: *The New York Triumvirate. A Study of the Legal and Political Careers of William Livingston, John Morin Scott, William Smith, Jr.* (New York, 1949).

rebellion," and who at the meetings of the Club customarily drank toasts to "the immortal memory . . . of Oliver Cromwell," or of John Hampden or Hugh Peters or General Ludlow—all identified with the great English rebellion of the seventeenth century against Charles I. Thus "the Colony, in a short time, from a state of happiness, became a scene of confusion, of uproar, and disorder, thanks to the triumvirate of Livingston, Scott, and Smith, and to them only." [4] Their influence in New York politics, according to Jones, was such that even the royal Governor of New York, Sir Henry Moore, was won over to "the republican interest, which he espoused with great warmth. . . ." [5] The newspapers were used to serve the ends of this group. For example, "The American Whig" essays that appeared in the local press between March 1768 and July 1769 were largely from the pen of William Livingston, who was doubtless aided by Scott and Smith. That Livingston as early as 1769 had in mind the separation of the colonies from Great Britain, Jones sought to prove by quoting the following statement by "The American Whig": "This country will shortly become a great and flourishing empire, independent of Great Britain; enjoying the civil and religious liberty, uncontaminated, and deserted of all control from Bishops, the curse of curses, and from the subjection of all earthly Kings; the corner stones of this great structure are already laid, the materials are preparing, and before six years roll about, the great, the noble, the stupendous fabric will be erected." Jones, who in 1784 was busy writing his *History,* comments: "How well this prediction has been verified the times at present show." [6]

Jones also included among the chief enemies of established order the Whig Captain Alexander McDougall, a privateersman in

---

[4] Thomas Jones: *History of New York during the Revolutionary War and of the leading Events in the Other Colonies at that Period* (ed. E. F. de Lancey, 2 vols., New York, 1879), I, 2–7. As to the reputed connection of the three men with the activities of that revolutionary group, the New York Sons of Liberty, this is not confirmed by the available evidence. See Dorothy R. Dillon: *op. cit.,* pp. 95–6.

[5] Thomas Jones: *op. cit.,* I, 18–19. Cadwallader Colden seems to agree with Jones about Sir Henry's conduct. Writing to Sir Jeffrey Amherst on June 24, 1766, he stated that the Governor "openly caressed the Demagogues—Put on a Homespun Coat, the Badge of the Faction, & suffered the Mob to insult the officers of Government without interposing. He went in Person to the Coffee House to publish every Piece of News which he thought would please them, & it plainly appears from his Speech that he is more carefull not to displease the Assembly, than to enforce the Resolution of the House of Commons" (*Colden Letter Books* [2 vols., New York Historical Society *Collections,* 1876 and 1877], I, 112).

[6] Thomas Jones: *op. cit.,* I, 24.

the late war and subsequently keeper of a "Slop-Shop" resorted to by sailors. McDougall, "a strong republican, a rigid Presbyterian" was likewise "a principal promoter and encourager of the unhappy disputes which raged with such violence in the colony for many years, terminated in a rebellion, in a dismemberment of the empire, in almost a total destruction of thirteen valuable provinces, and in the loss of not less than 100,000 brave men."[7] It should be noted that Judge Jones, writing this statement apparently in 1784, was under the impression that conditions were much more chaotic than they actually were in what had been the American colonies.[8]   In dealing with the Stamp Act, Jones makes a point of stressing the united opposition of all groups in America to this measure of the British government. He also argues that in the critical year 1774 the same unity was true of *all parties, denominations and religions, apprehending at the time, that the Colonies laboured under grievances which wanted redressing. . . . To redress which, and to form a happy, perpetual, and lasting, alliance, between Great Britain and America,"* are the reasons he gives for the New York Loyalists joining in the selection of delegates to the Continental Congress and in other measures. But the sanguine hopes of these Loyalists, he claims, were blasted when the "republicans," having by illegal means come into control of affairs in the province, "fined, imprisoned, robbed, and banished his Majesty's loyal subjects with a vengeance."[9] However, the major part of the *History* lies beyond the chronological limits of this historiography, since it relates the progress of the War for American Independence and the subsequent betrayal, as the author saw it, of the Loyalists by the government of Great Britain in the Peace Treaty of 1783.

One person above all others abhorrent to Jones was his fellow Loyalist, William Smith. Smith, earlier a member of the New York "triumvirate," according to Jones, was "a rigid Presbyterian—a factious republican—a hater of monarchy—an enemy to Episcopacy, a leveller in principle, and a sly, arch, hypocritical ringleader of sedi-

---

[7] *Ibid.*, I, 24–6.

[8] *Ibid.*, I, 24n.

[9] *Ibid.*, I, 34–5. At this point in the Jones narrative there is some confusion which the editor sought to clarify in the notes, *ibid.*, I, 438–67. In the course of his *History* Jones does not spare the British military commanders; he is especially severe in his treatment of the activities of General James Robertson, appointed military Governor of New York in 1779 who, he affirms, plundered the Loyalists equally with the revolutionaries by setting up the so-called "courts of police." See *ibid.*, II, 17–25.

tion." Jones charges that over the course of the thirty years after he entered public life, Smith "greatly improved in all that art, cunning, chicanery, dissimulation, hypocrisy, and adulation, which he possessed in so eminent a degree while a youth; and which ever was, and ever will be, the true characteristic of a person professing the religion of a New England dissenter, and the politics of an English republican." [10] These quotations from Jones's *History* give the texture of his interpretation of the events that led New York to seek with other colonies to break the ties that had bound it to Great Britain.

We must now turn to consider the historical work of Jones's mortal enemy, William Smith.

William Smith (1728–1793)

William Smith and Thomas Jones had certain things in common. Both were of well-to-do New York families; both went to Yale for their education; each had a father who attained high rank in the law and who was awarded a place on the Supreme Court and on the Governor's Council of the province; each followed his father's profession with great success and each was able to take his father's place on the bench; each suffered exile as a Loyalist; finally, each left in manuscript an account of the revolutionary movement in New York highly subjective in character. Yet Smith's standing as a historian is much higher than Jones's in that his work was much broader in scope and his analyses of situations much deeper.

Like Thomas Hutchinson, William Smith (in the midst of a busy professional career and before passions had been aroused by the crisis in Great Britain's relation with the Continental Colonies) gave his efforts to recording the early history of his own colony. His *History of New-York from the First Discovery to the Year M.DCC.XXXII* was published in London in 1757. In the same year the partisan *A Review of the Military Operations in North America . . .* (covering the period 1753 to 1756) also appeared, written in collaboration with William Livingston and John Morin

---

[10] *Ibid.*, I, 41n., 167–8.

Scott. All three men were by now closely associated in public affairs and would later organize the Whig Club. Smith also continued to write what he called his "Historical Memoirs of the Province of New-York," which finally extended to the year 1783.[1] The first part of these memoirs, for the period 1733 to 1762, appeared in 1830 together with the reprinting of the *History of New York to 1732*.[2] Still remaining in manuscript was Smith's record of the events covering the years 1763 to 1783. It was not until 1956 that the portion of the memoirs concerned with the crisis years (supplemented by certain of Smith's letters) was printed privately in typescript by W. H. W. Sabine—who also acted as editor—under the title *Historical Memoirs from 16 March 1763 to 9 July 1776 of William Smith, Historian of the Province of New York, Member of the Governor's Council, and the last Chief Justice of that Province under the Crown, Chief Justice of Quebec*.[3]

Taken as a whole the Smith history of New York compares quite favourably with the Hutchinson history of Massachusetts Bay. While it is weak in dealing with the early period, when the Dutch were in control of the province, it embodies an interesting and valuable account of the state of the province in the middle of the eighteenth century with respect to its boundaries, its internal subdivisions, its trade, its inhabitants (especially the complexity of their religious life), and its political institutions, including the laws and courts. The portion of the history germane to this essay also throws much more light on activities within the New York Governor's Council than does Hutchinson's history of Massachusetts Bay;[4] but the latter is far more illuminating in such other respects as its

---

[1] The manuscript of these memoirs is in the Manuscript Division of the New York Public Library, together with many of William Smith's letters and other papers. See E. B. Greene and R. B. Morris: *A Guide to the Principal Sources for Early American History (1600–1800) in the City of New York* (New York, 1953), pp. 102–3, 117, 175, 354.

[2] *The History of the Late Province of New-York from its Discovery to the Appointment of Governor Colden, in 1762* (2 vols., New-York Historical Society *Collections* for 1829 and 1830).

[3] It should be mentioned that Smith kept a diary for the period 1784–93, which is in the possession of the Smith family in Canada. The first portion of the diary, ed. L. F. S. Upton, was published in 1963 by the Champlain Society as *The Diary and Selected Papers of Chief Justice William Smith, 1784–1793. I. The Diary, January 24, 1784 to October 5, 1785.*

[4] See *The History of the Colony and Province of Massachusetts-Bay* (ed. L. S. Mayo, 3 vols., Cambridge, Mass., 1936) and *Additions to Thomas Hutchinson's "History of Massachusetts Bay"* (ed. Catharine Barton Mayo, Worcester, Mass., 1949).

well-integrated account of local developments from 1750 to 1774. Further, the Smith history, beyond the first volume, is in the form of an extended diary and has the value of presenting a day-by-day view of the shifting political scene, while the third volume of the Hutchinson history was written sometime after the events described and can therefore claim the advantage of perspective. There is also much less personal and censorious writing in Hutchinson's history than in Smith's.[5] The political outlook of the two men, at least up to the outbreak of hostilities in 1775, is sharply at variance— Hutchinson remains the consistent conservative, Smith the ardent Whig.

There was, finally, a quality of indirection in the conduct of Smith that was absent in Hutchinson. This may be illustrated by the McDougall incident. In 1769 Alexander McDougall wrote a letter addressed "To the Betrayed Inhabitants of the City and Colony of New-York," which he signed "A Son of Liberty." This appeared in the *New York Gazette: or, the Weekly Post-Boy*. Smith agreed with the rest of the Council that the article was "a false, seditious, and infamous libel" against the Governor, Council, and Assembly, and pressed for the prosecution of McDougall. Notwithstanding this action, he wrote a letter, published in the March 19, 1770, edition of the same newspaper under the caption "Copy of a late letter from an eminent Counsellor & a Friend of Liberty to his Correspondent in this City," in which he denounced Lieutenant Governor Colden as a foe to liberty for seeking to prosecute McDougall.[6]

---

[5] For example, Smith, who hated Cadwallader Colden, writes of him that the "Folly of his Hopes can be surpassed only by his own Wickedness & Avarice" (*Historical Memoirs from 11 March 1763 to 9 July 1776* . . . p. 217). The animosity directed toward Colden seems to have developed after the appearance in 1757 of Smith's *History of New-York . . . to the Year M.DCC.XXXII.* In it, in referring to Captain Laughlin Campbel's plan to form a settlement in Upper New York and of his failure to secure a land grant, Smith writes that the project was "unfortunately dropped, through the sordid news of some persons in power, who aimed to share in the intended grant." See the 1757 edition of the *History*, pp. 179–80, and New-York Historical Society *Collections*, IV, 247–8. Colden, who at the time of the episode was surveyor-general of the province and a member of the Governor's Council, took violent exception to this statement and wrote to Smith on January 15, 1759, that his account was "in every circumstance a misrepresentation of Facts. It is in the principal part absolutely false & an egregious calumny of the persons who at that time had the administration of Government in their hands." *The Letters and Papers of Cadwallader Colden*, New-York Historical Society *Collections* (9 vols., New York, 1918–37), V, 283–6.

[6] See, in *Historical Memoirs. . . ,* pp. 75–6, Sabine's editorial comment showing the changes Smith made in the draft of the letter and his (Smith's) attempt to intimate that the letter was written by John Dickinson.

The foregoing comparisons must not, however, leave the impression that Smith's contribution to the history of New York should be neglected. It is definitely an important original source.[7]

Jeremy Belknap (1744–1798)

Among the eighteenth-century writers who confined themselves to the history of a single colony the name of Jeremy Belknap justly ranks high. Between the years 1784 and 1792 three volumes of his *The History of New-Hampshire. Comprehending The Events of one complete century and seventy-five years from the discovery of the River Pascataqua to the year one thousand seven hundred and ninety. . . .* appeared in Boston. From the date of publication to the present this work has maintained its standing as an authoritative treatment of the history of colonial New Hampshire.[1]

Born in Boston and educated at Harvard, Belknap became pastor of the Congregational Church at Dover, New Hampshire, in 1766. After remaining there for twenty years, he settled in Boston in 1787 as pastor of the Federal Street Church, a post that he continued to hold to the end of his life. His love of history and his determination to rely on only the more authentic sources in the writing of it may well be attributed to the fact that as a youth he attended Old South Church in Boston. Here he came under the ministry, and therefore the happy influence, of the "accurate and indefatigable" Thomas Prince, a clergyman who spent years collecting the materials for *A Chronological History of New England in the Form of Annals,* which appeared in 1736 and was republished in 1756. According to the announcement, Prince's work was to have carried the story down

[7] For Smith see R. A. Wines: "William Smith, the Historian of New York," *New York History,* XL, 3–17; see also Smith's "Observations on America" (an attempt to explain the loss of the colonies), as edited by Oscar Zeichner in *New York History,* XXIII, 328–40, and M. L. Maturin: "William Smith, the Historian," *Magazine of American History,* VI, 418–39.

[1] In 1813 a 2nd revised edition of this work appeared, "with large additions and improvements published from the author's last manuscript." It is this edition that is used in the present historiographical survey. For Belknap see J. S. Bassett: *The Middle Group of American Historians* (New York, 1917, pp. 24–43), and C. W. Cole: "Jeremy Belknap: Pioneer Nationalist," *New England Quarterly,* X, 743–51.

to 1730, but it never got beyond 1633.[2] Belknap was also influenced by Hutchinson's *History of Massachusetts Bay* and paid tribute to that author's "extensive and accurate" knowledge "of the antiquities of the country." [3] A third and powerful influence on Belknap's writing was that of Ebenezer Hazard (who did much to illuminate early American history).[4] The close association of the two men in their historical activities is indicated in their voluminous correspondence, begun in 1779 and continued to the year of Belknap's death.[5] It may be noted that four years before Belknap died, he was instrumental in bringing about the founding of the Massachusetts Historical Society, the first of its kind in the United States.

The spirit in which *The History of New-Hampshire* was written is indicated clearly in the Preface to Volume I. In it Belknap wrote: "The authorities from which information is derived are carefully noted in the margin. Where no written testimonies could be obtained, recourse has been had to the most authentic tradition, selected and compared with a scrupulous attention, and with proper allowance for the imperfection of human memory. After all, the critical reader will doubtless find some chasms which in such a work it would be improper to fill by the help of imagination and conjecture." [6] Working in this careful manner, Belknap explained, it took "off and on nine or ten years" to complete the first volume. Referring to a statement by Dr. Samuel Johnson in the *Rambler* that no writer "has a more *easy* task than the historian," Belknap pointed out to his friend Hazard that if Johnson

> "had to write the History of a country, and to search for his materials wheresoever they were likely or *not likely* to be found; if he was to

[2] According to Belknap, for a period of over fifty years Prince was engaged in gathering source materials relating to New England, all of which were deposited at Old South Church. Those that survived the war were used by Belknap. See *The History of New-Hampshire*, I, Preface, p. iv.

[3] *Ibid.*, I, 2.

[4] Between 1775 and 1789 Hazard was involved in the American postal service; at the same time he devoted what time he could to collecting the source materials on early American history which resulted in the publication of his *Historical Collections . . . Intended as materials for a history of the United States of America.* The two folio volumes, which appeared in 1792 and 1794 respectively, embodied many important state papers and other documents from the latter part of the fifteenth century down to and including the year 1664. But there Hazard's ambitious enterprise ended.

[5] For this correspondence see the Massachusetts Historical Society *Collections*, 5th ser., II and III.

[6] *History of New-Hampshire*, I, v.

find that the 'treasures' contained in 'records' are to be explained by private papers, and that these are to be sought in garrets and rat-holes of old houses, when not one in a hundred that he was obliged to handle and decipher would repay him for the trouble; that 'tradition,' whatever it might 'pour down,' is always to be suspected and examined; and that the means of examination are not always to be obtained,—in short, if he had to go through the drudgery which you and I are pretty tolerably acquainted with, and to humour the passions of those we are obliged to, all the while, he would be fully sensible that to write an History as it should be is not so easy a work." [7]

Volume II of Belknap, which is of particular concern to this historiography, is fully in harmony, as might be expected of one in his position, with the interpretation placed on events by American tradition. For example, in describing the plan of the British Ministry after the Peace of Paris of 1763—a plan that was to bring on the American revolt—Belknap wrote:

"In no age, perhaps, excepting that in which Rome lost her liberty, was the spirit of venality and corruption so prevalent as at this time, in Britain. Exhausted by a long war, and disgraced by a peace which deprived her of her most valuable conquests, the national supplies were inadequate to the continual drain of the exchequer. A New ministry, raised on the ruin of that by which America was conquered and secured, looked to this country as a source of revenue . . . and . . . extended their system of corruption into America . . . the pretence was, 'to defray the expenses of protecting, defending and securing it'. . . . Notwithstanding this pretext, it was our opinion, that the grand object was to provide for dependents, and to extend the corrupt and venal principle of crown influence, through every part of the British dominions." [8]

On the other hand, in dealing with the royal government in New Hampshire under John Wentworth, Belknap wrote with fairness and appreciation of this Governor's efforts in behalf of the colony. Nor is his account of the growth of the revolutionary movement in New Hampshire tinged with denunciation or bitterness. The same may be said of his account of the controversy between New Hampshire and New York over the contested lands. With respect to Volume III, all

---

[7] Belknap to Hazard, January 13, 1784, Massachusetts Historical Society *Collections,* 5th ser., II, 294–5.
[8] *History of New-Hampshire,* II, 247–8.

that need be said is that it constitutes an invaluable survey of the resources, both natural and human, of the province, and later state, of New Hampshire. In short, the Belknap *History* is an admirable work and one which evoked from George Bancroft the following generous comment: "His *History of New Hampshire* would do credit to the literature of any nation. . . . It would not be easy to name any local history in any European language, superior to the History of Belknap." [9]

David Ramsay (1749–1815)

Among the early American patriotic writers concerned with the period covered by this series none is closer in spirit to Alexander Hewat than David Ramsay, although he viewed the coming of the Revolution in a very different light.

A native of Pennsylvania and a student of medicine who came under the tuition of Dr. Benjamin Rush at the College of Pennsylvania, Ramsay after a short sojourn in Maryland settled permanently in Charleston, South Carolina. There he was not only successful in his profession but from 1776—like so many American physicians, such as Rush in Philadelphia and Joseph Warren in Boston, for example—was active in political affairs. He served in the South Carolina House of Representatives almost continuously from 1776 to the conclusion of hostilities, later represented his state in the Continental Congress, and still later was a member of the state senate. He therefore had special qualifications for writing *The History of the Revolution of South-Carolina, from a British Province to an Independent State,* which was published at Trenton in two volumes in 1785 while he was serving as a member of the Continental Congress in Philadelphia. In limiting his account to the state of his adoption he noted candidly in the Preface, using the third person, that: "He would have been pleased could he have extended his plan; and his work, perhaps, would have been more acceptable: but his knowl-

---

[9] *North American Review* (April 1838), XLVI, 480, and Sidney Kaplan: "The History of New-Hampshire: Jeremy Belknap as Literary Craftsman," *William and Mary Quarterly,* 3rd ser., XXI, 18–39.

edge of the affairs of the middle and northern states was not sufficiently particular to warrant his attempting the history of the whole." He also stated that despite his care "to guard against partiality, he expects to be charged with it by both of the late contending parties. The suffering Americans . . . will accuse him of too great moderation, and of being too sparing of censure. Europeans who have heard much of American cowardice, perfidy and ingratitude, and more of British honour, clemency and moderation, will probably condemn his work as the offspring of party-zeal." It was in such a spirit that Ramsay wrote his *History*. In place of a picture of colonial oppression after the conclusion of the late war with France, he presented the following view: "Few countries have at any time exhibited so striking an instance of publick and private prosperity as appeared in South-Carolina between the years 1763 and 1775. . . . Wealth poured in upon them from a thousand channels. . . . They were also completely satisfied with their government, and wished not for the smallest change in their political constitution." Nevertheless, "the parliamentary claims of taxation and unlimited supremacy . . . created suspicions in the minds of the jealous colonists, that the mother-country harboured designs unfriendly to their liberties." For now was to come the plan for an American revenue laid by Parliament. The minister was prompted to embark on his innovation "by the immense load of national debt incurred during the war. . . . They conceived that every part of their dominions should pay a proportion of the publick debt; and that the parliament of Great-Britain, as the supreme power, was constitutionally invested with a right to lay taxes on every part of the empire. This doctrine . . . so conformable to the letter of the British constitution . . . was reprobated in the colonies as subversive of their rights, and contrary to the spirit of the same government, when the empire became so far extended as to have many distant representation assemblies." As the result of the colonial resistance to the Stamp Act, the Townshend Revenue measures to the Tea Act of 1773, and the measures taken against Massachusetts Bay in 1774, a "general confederacy . . . opposing the execution of these constitutional acts" was created.[1]

In a similarly temperate spirit, Ramsay turned to consider the role

---

[1] *The History of the Revolution of South-Carolina* . . . (2 vols., Trenton, 1785), I, 7–17.

played by the people of South Carolina in the War for American Independence, which lies beyond the scope of this series. His *The History of the American Revolution* (2 volumes, London & Philadelphia, 1789) was the first general history of that war and the first history to stress the social forces that promoted it. In 1793 it was reprinted in Dublin. *The History* was introduced by an "Advertisement by an English Friend" in which it was stated that this work "is at once short and full, as well as judicious, authentic, and impartial, and is clearly the best extant on the subject." It very naturally deals in much greater detail with the events leading up to the outbreak of hostilities in 1775 than does the earlier work. In his Preface Ramsay states: "At present I thought it prudent to publish little more than a simple narration of events, without introducing my authorities. Several of these are already in my *History of the Revolution of South-Carolina*, and such as are printed may be found in the periodical publications of the day." While the book therefore has some of the characteristics of a compilation of other printed accounts of the American Revolution, its chief value is that it expresses the sentiments of an active participant in the movement for independence—one who had been held prisoner by the British for a period—far removed from the arm-chair category of compilers of history. Ramsay's view of the origin of the idea of American political independence was that at the beginning of the war there was no desire for such a step but simply a demand for the redress of grievances. Nevertheless, the commencement of hostilities "exhibited the Parent State in an odious point of view, and abated the original dread of separating from it." At the same time he admits that the "eagerness for independence resulted more from feeling than from reasoning." Yet the step once taken resulted in certain advantages to those who had been colonials. "The Americans no longer appeared in the character of subjects in arms against their sovereign, but as an independent people, repelling the attacks of an invading foe." [2]

Ramsay is a historian in the best sense of the word. He gives his

---

[2] *The History of the American Revolution* (2 vols. in one, Dublin, 1793), I, 297, 301, 307. Ramsay was also the author of other works: in 1809 he published in Charleston his two-volume *History of South Carolina from . . . 1670 to the year 1808* which is still less original than the two histories dealt with in the text; in the Preface he acknowledges his dependence upon Alexander Hewat's *An Historical Account of the Rise and Progress of the Colonies of South Carolina and Georgia* which appeared in two volumes in London in 1779, George Chalmers's *Political Annals of the Present United Colonies . . . to . . . 1763, Book I*, published in London in 1780, and Governor John Drayton's *A View of South-Carolina, as Respects*

own interpretations even when leaning on other writers for details if they reflected his view of passing events. In fact, there are few writers who sought to deal with the revolutionary movement upon whom one can rely with greater confidence, although he is mistaken here and there in some points of fact. Professor Page Smith in his important article, "David Ramsay and the Course of the American Revolution," which appeared in the January 1960 *William and Mary Quarterly,* very properly calls *The History of the American Revolution* "a remarkable achievement." [3] A more recent reassessment of Ramsay and his work is to be found in the new book by Robert L. Brunhouse: *David Ramsay, 1749–1815: Selections from his Writings,* published by the American Philosophical Society in 1965. [4]

William Gordon (1728–1807)

A cloud hangs over the work of the Rev. William Gordon, who in 1788 published in London his four volumes on *The History of the Rise, Progress, and Establishment of the Independence of the United States of America.* As a dissenting minister, Gordon was the pastor of a meeting house at Ipswich, Suffolk, for twelve years. Then, after spending six years at the Gravel Lane Meeting House at Southwark, he decided to go to America in 1770. From 1772 to 1786 he was pastor of the Roxbury Third Congregational Church, close to Boston. After resigning this charge, he returned to England in order to publish his history and there spent the rest of his days.

While in America, Gordon, whose sympathies were strongly

---

her Natural and Civic Concerns, issued from the Charleston press in 1802. Ramsay was also the author of the *History of the United States from their first Settlement as English Colonies . . . to the Year 1808* (3 vols., Philadelphia, 1816–17), as well as a *Universal History Americanised* (9 vols., Philadelphia, 1819) and a *Life of George Washington* (New York, 1807).

[3] *William and Mary Quarterly,* 3rd ser., XVIII, 51–77; see also by the same author *The Historian and History* (New York, 1964), pp. 165–76. For other views of Ramsay as a historian see O. G. Libby: "Ramsay as a Plagiarist," *American Historical Review,* VII, 697–703; E. D. Johnson: "David Ramsay: Historian or Plagiarist?" *South Carolina Historical Magazine,* LVII, 189–98; R. L. Meriwether: "David Ramsay," *Dictionary of American Biography,* XV, 338–9; and Michael Kraus: *A History of American History* (New York, 193f), pp. 127–9.

[4] American Philosophical Society *Transactions,* LV (Philadelphia, 1965). This work on David Ramsay contains his collected letters, together with four of his shorter works, and a bibliography of his writings.

American, enjoyed the acquaintance of many leading people, including George Washington and Horatio Gates.[1] A man with a very active mind, Gordon participated freely in public events, revolutionary and other, and was in no wise hesitant about offering advice to those in authority on the weightiest of problems.[2] That he was highly regarded by many is shown by the fact that he received honourary degrees from Harvard, Yale, and the College of New Jersey, was an Overseer of Harvard, and served as chaplain of the two houses of the General Court of Massachusetts Bay. Yet his frankness of expression offended many people and led to dismissal from his post as chaplain upon the charge that he "grossly reflected" on the General Court. There is evidence that he was equally frank in the first draft of his history. According to John Adams (writing to Vice-President Elbridge Gerry a quarter of a century after its appearance in print), when Gordon sought to publish his manuscript he was told that "the style was so bold that it would damn the work, and that many things were so favourable to America and others so disgraceful to Britons that neither would be borne. Accordingly the style and spirit was altered and accommodated more to the British taste and feelings. In this labour of love he had the assistance of some of the dissenting clergymen; and among them I can name the Drs. Towers, father and son. Had the original manuscript been printed, the work would have appeared very differently."[3]

According to a contemporary who went to England in 1790, when

[1] In the Massachusetts Historical Society *Proceedings* LXIII, 303–613, are to be found a large number of letters written by Gordon, fifty-four of them to Washington and forty-five to Gates; they begin in the spring of 1770, with a letter to James Bowdoin, and end in the fall of 1799. For years Gordon was rather intimately associated with Jeremy Belknap and Ebenezer Hazard in collecting materials relating to the history of the American colonies. Belknap thought his *History* "jejune, stiff, and unanimated." Hazard, although not approving the style, felt that the book was "valuable, as containing a great deal of useful matter." See the *Belknap Papers*, Part II, Massachusetts Historical Society *Collections*, 5th ser., III, 105, 107. For numerous references to Gordon's relations with the two men see the index to the *Belknap Papers, ibid.*, III, 451.

[2] As a strong advocate of freedom of the individual, Gordon did not hesitate in 1776 to express publicly the fact that there was something irreconcilable between both the Declaration of Independence and the Virginia Bill of Rights and maintainance of the institution of slavery. These convictions were set forth in an article in the short-lived *New England Chronicle* of October 3, 1776.

[3] J. T. Austin: *The Life of Elbridge Gerry, with Contemporary Letters* (2 vols., Boston, 1828–9), I, Appendix, 520. Adams was in London as American envoy to the Court of Great Britain at the time Gordon's *History* was published. His reference to the Towers was to Joseph and his son, Joseph Lomas, both of them dissenting preachers. Joseph Towers wrote a great deal of biography. For brief lives of the two see the *Dictionary of National Biography*.

he was introduced to one of Gordon's relatives and asked him about the success of the *History,* the man smilingly replied: "It was not Doctor Gordon's history." In extenuation of this remark the relative said that upon Gordon's arrival in England he had placed the manuscript in the hands of an intelligent friend, who after reading it gave his opinion that it could never sell and moreover "was full of *libels* against some of the most respectable characters in the British army and navy—and that if he possessed a fortune equal to the duke of Bedford's he would not be able to pay the damages that might be recovered against him, as the *truth* would not be allowed to be produced in evidence." The friend thereupon advised Gordon "to place the manuscript in the hands of a *professional gentleman,* that it might be new *modelled.*" This Gordon agreed to do.[4] Another contemporary affirmed that once this professional rewriting was done Gordon, "indignant at the purgation, went to work and rewrote his history: the latter is thought to have been much less perfect than the original copy."[5]

The *History* took the novel form of a series of letters from and to America, starting with a letter supposedly written from Roxbury on December 26, 1771, and ending with a letter likewise from Roxbury dated June 30, 1783. Volume I, which carries the narration down to the summer of 1775—and is therefore of special concern to this series—includes thirteen letters, four from England, the balance from America. Whether or not the original manuscript took the form of hypothetical letters is, of course, impossible to state definitively. In the Preface to this volume Gordon writes that "by keeping to such form, and making the narration agree with the moment to which it related, and by introducing the various insertions necessary for the authenticating of facts; a present ideal existence of past events might be produced in the mind, similar to what is felt when a well-executed historical painting is examined. The better to secure this point, several parts are written in the present tense." In further justification of this form of presentation, Gordon states that the use of letters rather than chapters was "not altogether imaginary," as from the moment of his arrival in America in 1770 he had continued "a correspondence with gentlemen in London, Rotterdam and Paris,

---

[4] "Recollections of a Bostonian" first appeared in the *Boston Centinel* (1821–2) and selections were reprinted by Hezekiah Niles in his *Principles and Acts of the Revolution in America* . . . (Baltimore, 1822), pp. 479–86, especially p. 483.
[5] *Ibid.*

answering in general to the prefixed dates." He also points out in the Preface that at the beginning of 1776 he conceived the idea of preparing a history of the Revolution and that in gathering materials for it he was permitted to examine certain records of the Continental Congress and papers belonging to Washington, Gates, Greene, Lincoln, and Otho Williams, as well as thirty folio manuscript volumes of the records of Massachusetts Bay down to the year 1763. He also consulted the Thomas Hutchinson papers that survived the sacking of the Boston mansion.

It must be borne in mind that, like David Ramsay, Gordon was exceedingly active in the cause of colonial freedom. He wrote numerous letters to the press and associated intimately with many of the revolutionary leaders; his history should therefore carry weight. However, it remains under the heavy indictment of the late Professor O. G. Libby of the University of North Dakota in his "A Critical Examination of William Gordon's *History of the American Revolution*" which appeared in the 1899 *Report* of the American Historical Association. In this devastating study Libby, employing the word "theft," concludes "that Gordon was neither a man of unimpeachable veracity nor a great historian, and that his history must be rejected wholly as a source for the American Revolution." [6] To prove his point Libby displays in parallel columns the version of events as presented in the *Annual Register* and in the *History* and demonstrates the extent to which Gordon leaned upon the periodical without acknowledging his debt to it. He also shows by a similar procedure Gordon's reliance upon Ramsay and, in a later study, the reverse process of Ramsay's reliance on Gordon. [7]

A constant problem faces the scholar dealing with writings in this early period of British and American historiography; it involves the question of who borrows from whom and the ethics of borrowing. Take, for example, the *Annual Register*. When Edmund Burke or someone else prepared the material for this monthly publication, the sources of his information were seldom disclosed and results of his compilation were therefore doubtless considered common property and were used as such. [8] Gordon maintains in the Preface to his

---

[6] *Annual Report of the American Historical Association for the Year 1899* (2 vols., Washington, 1900), I, 367–88.

[7] "Ramsay as a Plagiarist," *American Historical Review*, VII, 698.

[8] This point is well illustrated in Professor Libby's article in the *Proceedings* of the Wisconsin Academy of Sciences and Arts, XIII, 419–25, in which he shows that seven books concerned with the Revolutionary War (not counting Ramsay or Gordon) and

History that what concerned him above all else was the truth. It is significant that he uses the expression "compiler" in describing his work: "The compiler of the present history." He then goes on to affirm "that he has paid sacred regard to truth . . . and has laboured to divest himself of all undue attachment to every person, country, religious name or profession. . . ." Writing on February 16, 1789, to President Washington, who had paid for forty-two sets of the *History*, Gordon expressed the wish "that if your Excellency discovers any capital mistakes, you would be so obliging as to point them out in order to future correction." He also mentioned in this letter that the costs of printing the work had been very great—"not far short of £700 sterling for the twelve hundred and fifty sets." [9]

Accepting the fact that Gordon was, as he described himself, the "compiler" of his history, that part of it which covers the period up to the beginning of hostilities is not open to serious criticism so far as stating the ascertainable facts (no matter where they were procured) is concerned, nor does it rely excessively upon the *Annual Register*. Professor Libby's first citation of such reliance does not occur until page 379 of the London edition of 1788, which consists of a general observation about the division (in the year 1774) of the American people into three classes in their attitude toward political issues. Libby detected four other citations from the *Annual Register* in this volume, each of which involved but a few lines out of a total of 504 pages. In justice to Gordon it should be said that his account of the course of events in the 1770's down to the outbreak of hostilities, especially those relating to Massachusetts Bay, is especially important and presents fresh light on many incidents. Such was the reaction of the historian, George Bancroft, who although critical of certain aspects of Gordon's *History* wrote of it: "His work, notwithstanding all its faults, is invaluable." [10] That it was highly esteemed in the United States is indicated by the fact that in addition to the London edition three American editions were printed.

One final observation must be made about the *History*. By 1788

published between 1778 and 1798 were "all copied, more or less closely from the British *Annual Register*"; see also *American Historical Review*, VII, 697n.

[9] Massachusetts Historical Society *Proceedings*, LXIII, 553–4.

[10] *A History of the United States* . . . (10 vols., Boston, 1834–74), IX, 123n. Bancroft in this connection stated that "Gordon was capable of prejudice, and was no critic; [yet] when he cites a document, I hold it certain that he cites it truly, for I have found it so in every case where I have had occasion to verify his citations; when he tells a story, I hold it certain that some one had told it before. . . ." (*ibid.*).

Gordon came to have a much less unrestrained admiration for America than he had shown, for example, in 1775 and consequently a less hostile attitude toward the British government. Writing to John Temple from his home at Jamaica Plain on March 15, 1786, he declared: "The spirit of the Americans in continuing to abuse Britain, etc., tho' peace has been established, has reconciled me greatly to the thought of leaving the continent where I should have had no quiet in case of a future rupture, unless I would have gone with them in all their extravagances." [11] This doubtless accounts for the fact that when in his *History* he described the actions at Lexington and Concord he was much more moderate in his criticism of the British than he had been in his long letter to the press of May 17, 1775, entitled "An account of the commencement of Hostilities between Great Britain and America, in the Province of the Massachusetts-Bay. By the Reverend Mr. William Gordon of Roxbury, in a Letter to a Gentleman in England." [12] In fact, one may venture the opinion that the revised manuscript of the *History* was a more balanced, more impartial, account of the War for American Independence than was the first account. Histories of wars prepared under conditions of emotional strain are less likely to stand the test of calm historical judgement than those composed at a later period when emotions have calmed. Even so, the Gordon *History* is ardently pro-American in spirit.

Jonathan Boucher (1737–1804)

If the Rev. William Gordon was wholly committed to the American patriot course when he wrote his *History*, the Rev. Jonathan Boucher was equally committed in his loyalty to the government of Great Britain in writing *A View of the Causes and Consequences of the American Revolution, in Thirteen Discourses Preached in North America between the Years 1763 and 1775: with an Historical Preface*. This work was published in London in 1797.

---

[11] Massachusetts Historical Society *Proceedings*, LXIII, 610. In this same letter Gordon also complains that he was being "abused in the public papers."
[12] Peter Force: *American Archives*, 4th ser., II, 625–31.

Born in England in Cumberland County and reared in poverty, Boucher nevertheless succeeded in acquiring a fair educational foundation in the free schools of his county and, after acting as an usher of the school at St. Bees, was recommended by its master for the position of tutor to the two sons of a planter living at Port Royal in Virginia. In 1759 he went to that colony, but returned to England in 1762 to take holy orders. From that time until 1770, when he removed to Maryland, most of his effort went into the ministry of St. Mary's in Carolina County, Virginia. To supplement his income, he tutored a number of boarding-school boys, among them young Custis, the stepson of Colonel George Washington. He remained on terms of intimacy with Washington for a number of years,[1] as well as with the Rev. James Maury of Fredericksville Parish in Louisa County.[2]

His first charge in Maryland was at the parish church of Annapolis and while in that colony he grew particularly close to Governor Robert Eden. In his *Reminiscences* he wrote:

> "The times grew dreadfully uneasy, and I was neither an unconcerned nor an idle spectator of the mischiefs that were gathering. I was in fact the most efficient person in the administration of Government, though I neither had a post nor any prospect of ever having one. The management of the Assembly was left [by the Governor] very much to me; and hardly a Bill was brought in which I did not either draw or at least revise, and either got it passed or rejected. . . . All the Governor's speeches, messages, etc., and also some pretty important and lengthy papers from the Council were of my drawing up."

All this activity was at least suspected by the "noisy patriots" and made Boucher a very "obnoxious person."[3] From Annapolis he went as rector to Queen Anne's Parish in Prince George's County. There he carried on his work until the fall of 1775, when the revolutionary spirit reached such a point that he and six other ministers of the Church of England in Maryland felt it necessary to desert their parishes and flee to England.

---

[1] See *Letters of Jonathan Boucher to George Washington* (ed. W. C. Ford, Brooklyn, N.Y., 1899).

[2] For Boucher's relations with Maury see *Reminiscences of an American Loyalist, 1738–1789* (edited by his grandson, Jonathan Boucher, Boston & New York, 1925), pp. 60–1.

[3] *Ibid.*, pp. 92–3.

Twenty-two years afterwards, while Boucher was the vicar of Epsom in Surrey, his *A View of the Causes and Consequences of the American Revolution* was published. Boucher's book on the Revolutionary War, like Gordon's, is unusual in form; but instead of being written as letters, it is presented as a series of thirteen discourses. Selected from sermons he delivered in Virginia and Maryland between 1763 and 1775 dealing with the political issues of the day, these discourses are preceded by a "historical preface" ninety pages in length, and the whole is dedicated to "George Washington, Esquire." [4]

The Preface to the volume embodies the thesis that the controversy between the mother country and the colonies "in its origin, progress, and termination, was entirely an affair of party . . . a struggle for pre-eminence between Whigs and Tories," and adds: "To assist . . . future enquirers in this arduous investigation, [into the causes of the revolt] this Volume of Sermons is now, with all due deference, submitted to the Public." Furthermore (it continues), when "the future historian of the American revolt shall recollect . . . how much the Continental Colonies were favoured by the terms of the Peace of 1763, he will also recollect with how much unmerited obloquy those wise men were aspersed, who then foresaw and foretold that it would not be long before the Colonists would be led to think of independence." But the centre of disaffection was always in the more northern colonies, for "that spirit of Republicanism which . . . overturned the Constitution of Great Britain in 1648 . . . was carried over to . . . America by the first Puritan emigrants" and its principles transplanted "into a more genial soil. . . . How they have thriven by transplantation, the revolution of America shews." [5] As Boucher expressed it even more forcibly in one of his discourses: "I believe the people of the four New England governments may challenge the whole world to produce another people who, without actually rebelling, have, throughout their whole history, been so disaffected to government, so uniformly

---

[4] The dedication, covering four pages, was designed to heal the breach that occurred between the clergyman and the influential General of the Continental Army before Boucher left America. For on August 6, 1775, he had written a letter expressing his deep indignation because Washington had failed to intervene in his behalf while he was being "run down, vilified, and injured in the manner which you know has fallen to my lot . . ." (*Reminiscences*, pp. 136–41).

[5] *A View of the Causes and Consequences of the American Revolution* (London, 1797), Preface, pp. xxi–xxiv and xxix.

intolerant towards all who differ from them, so dissatisfied and disorderly, and, in short, so impatient under every proper legal restraint not imposed by themselves." [6]

In support of this thesis the Preface quotes with approval the statement made by Israel Mauduit in *A Short View of the History of the New-England Colonies, with Respect to their Charters and Constitution* . . . (London, 1769 and 1776, p. 5): "In all the late American disturbances, and in every attempt against the authority of the British Parliament, the people of Massachuset's Bay have taken the Lead. Every new move towards independence has been theirs; and in every fresh mode of resistance against the law, they have first set the example, and then issued out admonitory letters to the other Colonies to follow it." [7]

Yet, as one who had resided in both Virginia and Maryland, Boucher found an explanation for the favourable response of certain southern colonies to the revolutionary steps taken by Massachusetts Bay. "Among other circumstances favourable to the revolt of America, that of the immense debt owing by the Colonists, to the Merchants of Great Britain, deserves to be reckoned as not the least. . . . The being overwhelmed with debt seems always to have been an essential ingredient in the character of a conspirator: in all ages, and in all countries, insurrections have been extended chiefly by 'men that are in trouble, and men that are in debt.' " [8]

At the heart of Boucher's position was his full acceptance of the doctrine of non-resistance to legal government as "a tenet of our Church" and his approval of such a statement as: "A rebel is worse than the worst prince, and a rebellion worse than the worst government of the worst prince, that hath hitherto been." [9] The deep

---

[6] *Ibid.*, p. 474.

[7] *Ibid.*, Preface, pp. xxix–xxx. Earlier editions of Mauduit's pamphlet carry the title *A Short View of the History of the Colony of Massachusetts Bay* . . . (London, 1769, 1774, 1776).

[8] *A View of the Causes and Consequences of the American Revolution*, pp. xl–xlii.

[9] *Ibid.*, pp. 485–6. The basis for the discourse on the doctrine of non-resistance was a famous sermon delivered by the Provost of the College of Philadelphia (later the University of Pennsylvania), the Rev. Dr. William Smith of the Anglican Church on June 23, 1775, in Christ Church, Philadelphia, at the request of the officers of the Third Battalion of the City of Philadelphia. It appeared in print not only in Philadelphia but also in London, Bristol, Belfast, Dublin, and elsewhere. Smith voiced his opposition to British measures toward America, and accepted the doctrine of Locke on the right of a people to resist, in the following words: "A continued submission to violence is no tenet of the Church of England." And again: "The doctrine of absolute Non-resistance has been fully exploded among every virtuous

sincerity of Boucher's beliefs and his courage in upholding them before the world are shown by his refusal to make any concessions to those in his own parish engaged in the revolutionary movement; and his defiance of the enemies of the government to which he was loyal is demonstrated by his preaching with a brace of pistols on the lectern beside the Bible. If the doctrine of non-resistance is no longer accepted by enlightened people in quite the terms that he expounded it, other of his views are. As one writer has expressed them: "His closely inter-related concepts of freedom of conscience, liberty under law, and voluntary obedience to government, all essentials of a free society, are proof of his faith in man as a rational animal." [10]

It may be well to close with the tribute paid to Boucher's book by Moses Coit Tyler: "Nowhere else, probably, can be found so comprehensive, so able, and so authentic a presentation of the deeper principles and motives of the American Loyalists, particularly from the standpoint of a high-church clergyman of great purity and steadiness of character, of great moral courage, of great learning, finally, of great love for the country thus torn and distracted by fratricidal disagreements." [11]

Mercy Otis Warren (1728–1814)

If among writers Jonathan Boucher was perhaps the most extreme of American Tories, Mercy Otis Warren was perhaps the most extreme of American patriots. Daughter of Colonel James Otis and sister of the more famous James Otis, she was a lady of talent. In 1754 she had married James Warren of Plymouth. Warren, a man of independent views that ultimately brought him into disfavour, was for a time President of the Massachusetts Provincial Congress,

---

people." For this sermon, published with a Preface, see *The Works of William Smith, D.D. late Provost of the College and Academy of Philadelphia* (2 vols., Philadelphia, 1803), II, 251–86.

[10] R. G. Walker: "Jonathan Boucher: Champion of the Minority," *William and Mary Quarterly*, 3rd ser., II, 3–14.

[11] *The Literary History of the American Revolution, 1763–1783* (2 vols. in one, New York & London, 1897), I, 320–1.

Speaker of the House of Representatives of Massachusetts, and, from 1776 to 1781, a member of the Navy Board. Among his close acquaintances and those of the Otis family were many of the most important patriotic leaders of that province. A number of them, respecting Mrs. Warren's intelligence and her abilities as a writer, gladly entered into correspondence with her.[1] Thus, at the time she began to work on a history of the American Revolution (apparently in 1778) she had at her disposal the undiluted written sentiments of many of the leading men in the patriotic party. When in 1805, at the age of seventy-seven, she brought out in Boston her *History of the Rise, Progress, and Termination of the American Revolution, Interspersed with Biographical, Political and Moral Observations,* her three-volume work embodied these sentiments fully.

No account left by anyone who lived through the stirring events of the Revolution more accurately sets forth the patriotic fervour of the times than the work of Mrs. Warren. In the Preface to her *History* she writes: "The historian has never laid aside the tenderness of the sex or the friend; at the same time, she has endeavoured, on all occasions, that the strictest veracity should govern her heart, and the most exact impartiality be the guide of her pen." Yet she uses little shading in drawing the characters of those most intimately identified with the great drama that was unfolding—they are either black or white. Mercy Warren's chief accusation and explanation for all that happened in the developing crisis between Great Britain and the colonies is that the measures directed against Americans were "instigated by a few prostitutes of power, nurtured in the lap of America, and bound by every tie of honor and gratitude, to be faithful to the interests of their country." These disloyal people, she claims, "did not hesitate at a junction with the accumulated swarms of hirelings, sent from Great Britain to ravish from the colonies the rights they claimed both by nature and by compact." She pays her compliments especially to the "hard-hearted judges of admiralty, and the crowd of revenue officers that hovered about the custom houses," saying of them: "Peculation was generally the prime object of this class; and the oaths they administered, and the habits they encouraged, were favorable to every species of bribery and corruption."[2]

---

[1] Before the appearance of her *History,* Mrs. Warren had already written some political satires, poems, and plays.

[2] *Op. cit.,* I, 37–8.

In describing the character of Thomas Hutchinson, Mercy Warren showed no restraint: [3]

> "It is ever painful to a candid mind to exhibit the deformed features of its own species; yet truth requires a just portrait of the public delinquent. . . . Soon after the recall of Mr. Bernard, Thomas Hutchinson, Esq. a native of Boston, was appointed to the government of Massachusetts. All who yet remember his pernicious administration and the fatal consequences that ensued, agree, that few ages have produced a more fit instrument for the purposes of a corrupt court. He was dark, intriguing, insinuating, haughty and ambitious, while the extreme of avarice marked each feature of his character."

For it was Hutchinson, she contends, who "had seized the opportunity to undermine the happiness of the people, while he held their fullest confidence, and to barter the liberties of his country by the most shameless duplicity, . . . [as] laid open by the discovery of a number of letters under his signature, written to some individuals in the British cabinet." [4] By this means Hutchinson was "convicted as the grand incendiary who had sown the seeds of discord, and cherished the dispute between Great Britain and the colonies. . . . So deeply riveted was this opinion among his enraged countrymen," continues Mrs. Warren, "that many apprehended the summary vengeance of an incensed populace would not suffer so notorious a parricide to repair quietly to England." [5]

The merit, therefore, of the *History of the Rise, Progress, and Termination of the American Revolution* lies not in the accuracy or comprehensiveness of the work, both of which are wanting, but in its reflection of the spirit of the patriotic people of Massachusetts Bay in the 1770's. [6]

---

[3] It would doubtless be impossible to determine to what degree Mrs. Warren's attitude to Hutchinson was influenced by the fact that he was given the post of Chief Justice of the Superior Court of Judicature by Governor Bernard in 1760 although her father, Colonel Otis, had been promised this honour by the two previous administrations. That her brother James was deeply enraged seems quite clear. See Israel Williams Papers, 2:155, Massachusetts Historical Society.

[4] These were the Hutchinson-Oliver letters addressed to Thomas Whately, then a private citizen. Sent to Boston by Benjamin Franklin, the letters led to an issue that is dealt with in Volume XII of this series, pp. 57–64.

[5] *History of the Rise, Progress, and Termination of the American Revolution*, I, 78–9, 81, 97–8, 123. It is of interest that in 1781 the Warrens purchased the Hutchinson home at Milton where they resided for a decade. See G. P. Bauer: "Mercy Otis Warren" *Dictionary of American Biography*, XIX, 484.

[6] It may be mentioned in passing that in her *History* (III, 391–5) Mrs. Warren, who was an ardent Jeffersonian Republican, made some comments on John Adams, the Federalist, which offended him so deeply that they led to a heated exchange of

Abiel Holmes (1763–1837)

An examination of early American historical writing discloses the initial difficulty facing anyone who sought to compress into a unified narrative the manifold developments in each of the Thirteen Colonies. The sources for such a history were scattered and in many cases not easily accessible, even assuming that the potential historian had the time and the means to engage in extensive travel and research. In fact it was not until the year 1805 that the Rev. Abiel Holmes—father of the still more famous Oliver Wendell Holmes and pastor of the First Church at Cambridge, Massachusetts—after many years of labour, which also involved travel, brought out in two volumes his *American Annals; or a Chronological History of America from its Discovery in MCCCCXCII to MDCCCVI.* More than twenty years later a second revised and enlarged edition appeared in 1829 under the title *The Annals of America, from the Discovery by Columbus in the Year 1492, to the year 1826.*[1]

In the Preface to the second edition Holmes states:

> ". . . while local histories of particular portions of America have been written, no attempt has been made to give even the outline of its entire history. To obtain a general knowledge of that history, the scattered materials, which compose it, must be collected, and arranged in the natural and lucid order of time. . . . If history, however, without chronology, is dark and confused; chronology, without history, is dry and insipid. In the projection, therefore, of this work, preference was given to that species of historical composition, which unites the essential advantages of both."

letters between the two. As these comments relate to a supposed change in attitude toward Great Britain on the part of Adams after the close of the War for American Independence, it is only necessary to refer the curious reader to the letters themselves, which are printed in the Massachusetts Historical Society *Collections,* 5th ser., IV, 321–503.

[1] In the *North American Review* for October 1829 (XX, 428–41) there is a long, favourable review of the *American Annals* that ends with the statement: "It is the best repository of historical, chronological, and biographical knowledge respecting America, that can be found embodied in one work." For the life of Holmes see "Memoir of the Rev. Abiel Holmes, D.D. LL.D., etc. by Rev. W. Jenks, D.D." published in 1839 in the Massachusetts Historical Society *Collections,* 3rd ser., VII, 270–82.

Under the given conditions, Holmes performed this task admirably.

His work elicited the following praise from George Bancroft: "Take it all in all, the *Annals* of Holmes constitute a work, which in its kind has never been equalled among us, and has few parallels anywhere. . . ." [2] Professor M. A. De Wolfe Howe of Harvard pointed out in the *Dictionary of American Biography* that Holmes's work "marked an important step in American historiography," and also set a certain scholarly standard that made it much more than mere annals. [3] In the second edition, for example, at the beginning of Volume I there is a "Catalogue of the Authors" used in the work, which contains a list of 272 titles printed in English, French, Spanish, Dutch, Swedish, or Latin; ten manuscript collections are also listed. Reference to these sources is made in the footnotes, some of them very brief, scattered throughout both volumes, and in the "Notes and Illustrations" found at the end of each volume along with the "Tables" which precede the index in the second volume.

Volume II, which begins with the planting of the colony of Georgia, is particularly germane to the present historiography. As might be anticipated, the narration of events is uniformly interpreted in a manner favourable to Americans; yet there is an absence of the bitterness against the government of Great Britain that one might have expected from a writer who believed so firmly in the justice of the colonial position. For example, in dealing with the background of the Declaration of Independence Holmes states: ". . . independence was not the object of the controversy, on the part of the colonies, but constitutional liberty. Oppression, by demanding more than is due, loses the benefit of legal claims. . . . To declare themselves independent, was no more than to announce to the world the real political state in which Great Britain had placed them." [4] It is not without significance that the only reference to King George III, in connection with the causes leading to the Declaration of Independence, is that the "British King had entered into treaties with . . . princes of Germany, for . . . men to be employed in America." [5] This may be contrasted with the Declaration of Independence itself, in which the King is excoriated as the chief source of all the

---

[2] The tribute by Bancroft comes in the midst of a long review of the *Documentary History of the American Revolution* by M. S. C. Clarke and Peter Force in the *North American Review*, April, 1838, XLVI, p. 481.

[3] *Dictionary of American Biography*, IX, 160–1.

[4] *The Annals of America* . . . (Cambridge, Mass., 1829), II, 237–8.

[5] *Ibid.*

grievances that were rending the Old Empire. In the rather full index to the *Annals* the King's name does not appear. Holmes was far too well informed a scholar to have left out inadvertently what has been assumed by so many other historians as the King's responsibility for bringing on the crisis that led to the War for American Independence. On the contrary, the implication in his work is that the Ministry and Parliament must bear the burden for the various measures of colonial administration directed toward America after 1763, and that the King only approved these when recommended to his attention.[6] Thus Professor Lewis B. Namier, in his revisionist writings of a century later, is really reverting to the Holmes position with respect to George III and British policy toward America.

Benjamin Trumbull (1735–1820)

It is remarkable that Benjamin Trumbull, who served in 1776 as a chaplain in the revolutionary armed forces and afterwards as the captain of a company of volunteers, became the leading colonial authority on the history of colonial Connecticut but never wrote anything about the American Revolution. Benjamin belonged to the Hebron, Connecticut, branch of the Trumbull family and was related to the Lebanon, Connecticut, branch which produced not only the Revolutionary War Governor Jonathan Trumbull but also his son, the Revolutionary War painter John Trumbull. It may be noted that in 1766 the Lebanon branch of the family changed the spelling of the family name from Trumble to Trumbull and in 1768 the Hebron branch adopted the same spelling. While the Lebanon Trumbulls were identified with Harvard at this period, the Hebron family looked to Yale. There, in 1759, Benjamin took his degree. The following year, after receiving a licence to preach, he was installed as the pastor of the North Haven Congregational Church, where he remained until his death some sixty years later.

Among Trumbull's literary efforts was a brochure published in 1766 in the form of a letter addressed to the Governor's Council

---

[6] See *ibid.*, II, 119, 124, 131–2, 144, 147, 148, 153, 159, 171, 181, 185–6.

stressing the importance of Yale College to the cause of religion and
to the country. In 1774 he came to the defence of Connecticut's
claims to land now lying in northern Pennsylvania in his pamphlet,
*A Plea, in Vindication of the Connecticut Title to the Contested
Lands, Lying West of the Province of New–York, Addressed to the
Public.* But his lasting fame resulted from the publication in New
Haven of *A Complete History of Connecticut, Civil and Ecclesiasti-
cal, from the Emigration of Its First Planters, from England, in the
Year 1630, to the Year 1764; and to the Close of the Indian Wars,*
which appeared in two volumes in 1818.

It would seem that by the early 1770's, if not before, Trumbull had
decided that the time was ripe for a history of the colony and that
he would undertake the project. In the Preface to Volume I he gives
an account of his efforts toward this end: his collecting of books and
manuscripts, his perusal of the official records, his journeys to all the
principal towns of the colony to study local papers and burial monuments, and his examination of the great collection that the Rev.
Thomas Prince of Boston had made for his *Chronological History of
New England in the Form of Annals.* By 1774, just when he felt that
he was at last in a position to begin writing the projected history, he
was forced to delay the enterprise; for "the war commenced between Great-Britain and her colonies, and the universal attention
was turned to a very different object." Moreover, within a few years
after the peace, he was invited "by a vote of the General Association
of the state, to compile a different history"—a history of the United
States of America down to 1792, including three complete centuries. As a result of this urging he spent some ten years collecting
materials for his new project. However, before he was able to complete the first volume some of his colleagues in the Ministry persuaded him to attempt to get out the first volume of the Connecticut
history on the ground that it might assist him in introducing "a
larger work." This he was able to do in 1797.

Trumbull then turned back to the history of the United States.
The first and only volume to be published appeared in 1810 under
the title *A General History of the United States of America; from
the Discovery in 1492, to 1792: or, Sketches of the Divine Agency, in
their Settlement, Growth, and Protection; and especially in the late
Memorable Revolution. In Three volumes. Volume I exhibiting A
General View of the Principal Events, from the Discovery of North
America to the Year 1765.* An unusual aspect was that it was
published in that year not only in Boston but also in Philadelphia,

New York, Baltimore, New Haven, Hartford, and Portland. This *History* was largely a skillful compilation of the writings of earlier historians. Yet here and there Trumbull introduced his own interpretation of events. For example, in dealing with the letters patent for the Province of Pennsylvania granted on March 4, 1681, to William Penn he writes:

> "This conveyance greatly encroached on the patent both of Maryland and Connecticut. Both these patents were older, by half a century, than Mr. Penn's, and on each of the territories which they conveyed there had been made very considerable settlements. As the patents were construed, that of Mr. Penn encroached on the territory granted to lord Baltimore one whole degree, or sixty nine English miles and a half. It granted a tract of country on the northern part about 290 miles across the whole territory conveyed in the ancient patent, fifty years before to Connecticut." [1]

The *History of the United States* did not live up to its promise. Instead of dealing with the events up to the year 1765, it ended abruptly with those of 1761.

With this contribution to the history of the United States behind him, Trumbull now returned to his account of Connecticut and, as has been indicated, succeeded by 1818 in reissuing Volume I, with corrections and additions, and in producing Volume II, which carried the general story down to the year 1764. However, in dealing with the controversy with Pennsylvania over western lands, he extended his account beyond the period of the War for American Independence and up to the final settlement of the Connecticut claims, when the Continental Congress granted to the state the so-called Western Reserve beyond the Pennsylvania boundary—a grant which he called "New-Connecticut." He also inserted an Appendix which gave an account of the educational system in Connecticut in 1818.

What characterizes the Connecticut history as a whole is the quality of calm temper and fairness, even when dealing with matters upon which the author held deep convictions. In fact it is so soundly conceived and is carried out with such careful use of the available sources that it may still be read with profit, at least on the subject of the internal aspects of the colony. [2] As might be expected

---

[1] *A General History of the United States* . . . I, 195.

[2] George Bancroft makes the following comment on Trumbull and his major work: "It excells Hutchinson in spirit, and equals it, nay, surpasses it in research. . . . He read all sorts of records; he picked up and tested traditions; he was wise in the

of an author with a lifelong concern for spreading the Christian Gospel, he devotes about one third of the work to the ecclesiastical affairs of the colony. Yet even this portion is not without interest, and it illuminates much of the history of Connecticut. As stressed, Trumbull seemed to be disinclined to extend his writing to include any account of the revolutionary movement against the government of Great Britain. Thus he leaves his readers with the following picture of America at the conclusion of the peace made with France in 1763:

> "The extent of territory ceded to the colonies, the safety of their commerce and fishery, the prodigious scope which presented itself for both, the increase of wealth, the extent of settlement, the advancement of population, and the general diffusion of happiness, all united their influence to bring in a full tide of gladness. . . . The colonies gloried in their prince, and in their relation to Great Britain. . . . They were impressed with a grateful sense of the royal beneficence, and parliamentary goodness, in the grants which had been made for their assistance, in defraying the expenses of the war. They were entirely satisfied with the British government, and conceived themselves to be peculiarly happy in the protection and privileges which they enjoyed, as British subjects. This was the general feeling and happy state of the country, at the return of peace." [3]

But he stops short of analyzing why, if this were the case, the colonies were so ripe for revolt a little more than a decade later.

William Henry Drayton (1742–1779) and John Drayton (1766–1822)

Memoirs of the American Revolution, from its Commencement to the Year 1776, inclusive; as relating to the State of South-Carolina: and occasionally referring to the States of North-Carolina and Geor-

---

theology of Hooker and Stone; he knew the hills and valleys, the towns and the villages of his commonwealth, and in fact he got Connecticut by heart before he began writing its history. Europe he knew but little of; and in reference to it he makes mistakes or betrays ignorance; but Connecticut he knew thoroughly" (April 1838 *North American Review*, XLVI, 477–8).

[3] *A Complete History of Connecticut*, II, 455–6.

gia appeared in two volumes published at Charleston in 1821. It is in a sense a composite work by William Henry Drayton and his son, John.[1] At his death the elder Drayton left a two-volume manuscript of his memoirs, covering the period from the fall of 1773 to the close of 1776, together with other writings and important papers bearing upon the American Revolution. Since these writings contained much information that had not previously been published in any history, John Drayton in the summer of 1819 decided to put the material in shape for publication and to supplement it with a view of events in the twenty-year period preceding the point where his father's memoirs began. To do this, he made use of additional official records, which he lists in the Preface of Volume I. At the time he undertook this task he was Judge of the United States Court for the District of South Carolina. It may also be mentioned that early in the century he had prepared and published his own valuable *A View of South-Carolina, as Respects her Natural and Civil Concerns,* written largely while he held the office of Governor of the state.

Among other interesting aspects of the *Memoirs* is the fact that William Henry Drayton spent over ten years of his youth in England, attending Westminister School and Balliol College, Oxford. Upon his return to America he was for some years a strong friend of the British administration, but by 1774 he had become its implacable foe. In his pamphlet *A Letter from Freeman of South-Carolina to the Deputies of North-America, Assembled in the High Court of Congress at Philadelphia* he even denied the right of Parliament to legislate for America in his assertion that "the British Parliament ought not to have, and cannot of right possess any Power to Tax, or in any shape to bind American Freeholders of the British Crown, . . . because their consent is not signified in Parliament, by a *Representation of their own election*" (p. 12). Yet, while denying the supremacy of Parliament over the colonies, he held that they were nevertheless under the Crown of Great Britain.[2] But in the spring of 1776—some weeks before the Declaration of Independ-

---

[1] In connection with this essay the student should consult W. M. Dabney and Marion Dargan: *William Henry Drayton & the American Revolution* (Albuquerque, N.M., 1962) and C. L. Mowat: "The Enigma of William Drayton," *Florida Historical Quarterly,* XXII, 3–33.

[2] By reason of his authorship of the "Freeman" pamphlet, Drayton was dismissed from his post as an assistant judge of the province. See *Memoirs of the American Revolution* . . . I, 157–60.

ence—while acting in the capacity of Chief Justice of the province under the revolutionary government of South Carolina, he charged the grand jury in Charleston that as "George the Third . . . has endeavoured to subvert the Constitution of this country, by breaking the original contract between King and People; . . . the law of the land authorizes me to declare, and it is my duty boldly to declare the law, that George the Third . . . has abdicated the government, and that the throne is thereby vacant; that is, he has no authority over us, and we owe no obedience to him." [3]

The *Memoirs* themselves, conceived as they were by one holding such views, do not display the extreme bitterness that might be expected. Emphasis is placed upon the two factors which (from the authors' viewpoint) formed the basis of colonial opposition to the government of Great Britain: first, that the attempt by George III and Bute to raise a revenue in America at the conclusion of the Peace of 1763 went against the traditional and confirmed policy of the British government; second, that by the time peace was established in 1763, Americans had begun to think of themselves as forming a distinct nation and as facing a fundamentally different situation. Thus the *Memoirs,* logically enough, stress the point that no "nation could be free or happy, when their property might be taken from them by a power, over which they had no control," and that, with the coming of the peace "the American mind began to expand. And the situation of the Colonies at the peace of 1763, was contrasted with what it had been in former years: when Spain inclosed them in one side, while France stood ready to attack them on the other." [4] For, according to the Draytons, to the colonials the "ideas of liberty and independence, were equally great: and the removal of hostile neighbours, not a little increased an impatience among them, of being controlled by a parliament, in which they were unrepresented; and which was separated from them, by the vast Atlantic." [5]

The chief concern of the *Memoirs,* as the full title implies, was the political developments in South Carolina and the growing breach between those Carolinians in authority who attempted to enforce British regulations and those who sought to be free from them. The

---

[3] For Chief Justice Drayton's charge to the grand jury on April 23, 1776, see Peter Force: *American Archives,* 4th ser., V, 1030.

[4] *Memoirs of the American Revolution* . . . I, 9.

[5] *Ibid.,* I, 13.

value of this aspect of the work is considerable, particularly as the text is reinforced by official documents at the end of each chapter except the last.

George Bancroft (1800–1891)

George Bancroft may well be called a giant of American historiography. Those scholars who have drawn upon the large collection of his manuscripts reposing in the Manuscript Division of the New York Public Library cannot but pay grateful tribute to his zeal, industry, and foresight in securing copies of those documents, in both the Old World and the New, that could illuminate and give weight to his writing.[1]

A native of Massachusetts and the son of a Congregational minister whose church was at Worcester, Bancroft early displayed qualities of mind that indicated a future as a writer. He was also fortunate in his education. At the age of eleven he went to Phillips Exeter Academy. Two years later he prepared to enter Harvard, where he had four profitable years as an undergraduate. Then, as a result of the encouragement and financial support extended by the president and members of the governing body of the college, he was privileged to study abroad, mostly at the University of Göttingen, in order to round out his formal education under such distinguished men as, for example, Professor Arnold H. Ludwig Heeren. Upon his return to America he held a tutorship in Greek at Harvard for a year, during which time he also preached from various pulpits in the area. In 1823 he participated actively in the founding of a boys' school at Northampton, Massachusetts, and became one of the headmasters. But by 1831 he had severed his connection with the school, because he felt he was not fitted for a teaching career.[2] Meanwhile, however, he had been establishing himself as a writer by his contribution of a series of articles to the *North American Review*, that most influential journal founded in Boston in 1815.

---

[1] For the two fullest accounts of the life of Bancroft see R. B. Nye: *George Bancroft, Brahmin Rebel* (New York, 1944), and M. A. De Wolfe Howe: *The Life and Letters of George Bancroft* (2 vols., New York, 1908).

[2] *Ibid.*, I, 201.

Parenthetically, he had also delivered a Fourth of July oration at Northampton in 1826 that gave expression to the strong democratic views he held even at this period. In it he declared: "The government is a democracy, a determined, uncompromising democracy. . . . The popular voice is all powerful, with us; this is our oracle; this, we acknowledge, is the voice of God." [3]

It is not clear from his own records when Bancroft first conceived the idea of writing the history of his country. What is clear, however, is that his marriage and his subsequent separation from teaching activities brought him the independence to pursue such a project. The result was a powerful work that was to bring him fame and, within his lifetime, the gratitude of the people of the United States. [4]

Volume I of Bancroft's *History of the United States from the Discovery of the American Continent* appeared in Boston in 1834. In the Preface he wrote:

> "I have formed the design of writing a History of the United States from the Discovery of the American Continent to the present time. . . . I can find for myself no excuse but in the sincerity with which I have sought to collect truth from trust-worthy documents and testimony. . . . I have applied, as I have proceeded, the principles of historical skepticism, and, not allowing myself to grow weary in comparing witnesses, or consulting codes of laws, I have endeavored to impart originality to my narrative, by deriving it from writings and sources which were the contemporaries of the events that are described."

The book was a great success, as were the subsequent volumes of the series. Volume II appeared in 1837 and Volume III in 1840; the three completed that part of his *History* which Bancroft called "the Period of Colonization."

---

[3] *Ibid.,* I, 186.

[4] During the period that Bancroft devoted himself to writing, he also became active in public affairs as a leading member of the Democratic Party in Massachusetts. In 1837 President Van Buren appointed him collector of the port of Boston, a post he held with credit until 1841; in 1845 he became President Polk's Secretary of the Navy and the following year was named Minister to Great Britain. It was during the period of his three years at the Court of St. James that he gathered voluminous transcripts of documents and other papers housed in both public and private depositories not only in Great Britain but also in the archives of France, Holland, and Spain. In this worthy enterprise he was accorded every possible facility and encouragement. Moreover, upon his return to the United States—when he established himself in New York—he continued to work industriously at gathering material for the completion of his great project. For an extended account of his activities in gathering such data for subsequent volumes of his *History* see the Preface to Volume VI.

In 1852 he was able to publish Volumes IV and V of his series; these carried the subtitles "The American Revolution. Epoch First. The Overthrow of the European Colonial System, 1748–1763" and "The American Revolution. Epoch Second. How Great Britain Estranged America, 1763–1766." Two years later came Volume VI, under the subtitle "The Crisis," covering the years 1766 to 1774. Volume VII published in 1858, and Volume VIII published in 1860, both have the subtitle "The American Revolution. Epoch Third. America Declares Itself Independent"; the two cover the years 1774 to 1776. Volumes IX and X, which appeared respectively in 1866 and 1875,[5] are subtitled "The American Revolution. Epoch Fourth. The Independence of America is Acknowledged"; they embrace the years 1776 to 1782.

The extraordinary popularity of Bancroft's series may be shown by the fact that the reissue in 1874–5 had reached the twenty-fifth edition of Volumes I and II, the twenty-third of Volume III and IV, the twentieth of Volume V, the eighteenth of Volume VI, the twelfth of Volume VII, the ninth of Volume VIII, the fifth of Volume IX, and the first of Volume X.[6] As J. Franklin Jameson rightly said: "The book at once took rank as the standard history of the United States."[7]

Omitting other contributions made by Bancroft to historical literature, both within and beyond the series, it is Volumes IV to VII on the American Revolution, covering the period from 1748 to 1776, with which this historiography is particularly concerned. Volumes IV, V, and VI were well documented by footnote references to authorities. Unhappily, Volume VII, concerned with the most critical period of May 1774 to June 1775, was published without citing sources. The Preface contains the following statement: "In preparing the volume, there has been no parsimony of labor; but marginal references to the documents out of which it has mainly been constructed are omitted. This is done not from an unwillingness to subject every statement of fact, even in its minutest details, to the severest scrutiny; but from the variety and multitude of the papers which have been used, and which could not be intelligibly cited,

---

[5] In 1866 Bancroft became United States Minister to Prussia and remained there until 1874.

[6] See M. A. De Wolfe Howe: *op. cit.*, II, 333.

[7] J. F. Jameson: *The History of Historical Writing in America* (Boston & New York, 1891), p. 103.

without burdening the pages with a disproportionate commentary." [8] Nevertheless these four volumes represent a remarkable achievement and, along with the other six, a valuable contribution to historical literature. Yet, by the time of the author's death in 1891, Bancroft's great *History* had begun to fall into disfavour. It is therefore important to determine why this happened.

First of all, Bancroft reflected strikingly the rather uncritical temper of the period in which he wrote. Furthermore, he was inclined to broad generalizations that could not be sustained under critical analysis. For example, in the 1830's he wrote in the Introduction to Volume I: "The United States of America constitute an essential portion of a great political system, embracing all the civilized nations of the earth. At a period when the force of moral opinion is rapidly increasing, they have the precedence in the practice and the defence of the equal rights of man." Yet at that very time, the moral opinion of some other countries respecting the rights of man was far in advance of that in many parts of the United States, where the institution of human slavery was not only protected but defended on moral grounds. This looseness in expression is strongly manifested in Volume IV, which deals with the years 1748 to 1763. While the subtitle "The Overthrow of the European Colonial System" is one that might be calculated to attract the attention of the reader, it is incorrect and quite misleading; the same comment can be made of the title of Chapter I, "America Claims Legislative Independence of England," which is concerned with the year 1748. In this chapter Bancroft, in describing the significance of the American Revolution, goes back to the Middle Ages and in highly embellished prose writes:

> "But a new principle, far mightier than the church and state of the Middle Ages, was forcing itself into power. Successions of increasing culture and heroes in the world of thought had conquered for mankind the idea of the freedom of the individual; the creative but long latent energy that resides in the collective reason was next to be revealed. From this the state was to emerge, like the fabled spirit of beauty and love out of the foam of the ever-troubled ocean. It was the office of America to substitute for hereditary privilege the natural equality of man; for the irresponsible authority of a sovereign, a dependent government emanating from the concord of opinion; and as she moved forward in her high career, the multitudes of every

---

[8] As is well known, the so-called "Centenary Edition" of the *History*, published in 1876 in six volumes, is also without footnotes.

clime gazed towards her example with hopes of untold happiness, and all the nations of the earth sighed to be renewed." [9]

There is not a single line in this quotation that a scholar could not challenge on the ground of accuracy. The same may be said of such a statement as: "A nation without union, without magazines and arsenals, without a treasury, without credit, without government, fought successfully against the whole strength and wealth of Great Britain. An army of veteran soldiers capitulated to insurgent husbandmen," [10] or that relating to the beginnings of the war for American Independence: "As the fleets and armies of England went forth to consolidate arbitrary power, the sound of war everywhere else on the earth died away. Kings sat still in awe, and nations turned to watch the issue." [11]

It should be emphasized that in writing his *History* Bancroft had a thesis to prove. Abundant original sources were available to him and he resorted to them, but it is clear that he used only those authorities that supported the point of view that dominated his thinking. Even these he used with startling freedom—altering and transposing passages at will—in order to produce the desired effect.[12] For example, while in England he was given the opportunity to examine the vast collection of the Duke of Newcastle Papers [13] relating to domestic and foreign affairs. These documents disclose a high order of intelligence on the part of the Duke. Nevertheless, Bancroft attempts to explain Newcastle's advancement to the head of the government in 1754 by asserting that it was a result of his "imbecility." Moreover, without a shred of evidence he writes that it was the practice of Newcastle to entrust "the royal prerogative [in America] to men of broken fortunes, dissolute and ignorant, too vile to be employed near home. . . ." [14] In my own experience of working for many years with the Newcastle Papers, especially those having to do with the Governors of the royal colonies, I can point to no man sent to America by the Duke who fitted this category. On the contrary the evidence shows that Newcastle, in making appointments to this high colonial office, sought to secure the services of the best men he could find. In 1752 he wrote to Andrew Stone:

---

[9] *History of the United States* (1st edn.), IV, 12.
[10] *Ibid.*, IV, 14.
[11] *Ibid.*, VI, 528.
[12] In the above connection see R. B. Nye: *op. cit.*, p. 193.
[13] See *History of the United States* . . . VI, Preface, iii–iv.
[14] *Ibid.*, IV, 18 and 20.

". . . my point is always to serve honest deserving men"; and to Horatio Walpole in 1754 he declared: "I wish I knew who were the two best men in England for [the governorship of] New York and Jamaica and I would recommend them immediately against all competitors; for we will have the best men we can find." [15] Nor do Bancroft's characterizations of Thomas Hutchinson (a royal Governor, but not a Newcastle appointee)—as one whose "sordid nature led him to worship power," as one guilty of "hypocrisy" and "duplicity," who "could stoop to solicit justice as a boon," or as a man whom "a small temptation not only left . . . without hardihood to resist oppression but would easily bend . . . to become its instrument" [16]—do justice to the man who, for devotion to a principle, sacrificed both wealth and high position to choose exile from the native land he loved so dearly.

It is abundantly clear that at the points where Bancroft gave rein to his deeply ingrained patriotic feelings and preconceptions he cannot be trusted. Yet, in fairness to him, it must be said that portions of his *History* were written with a certain detachment and great learning. Granting his limitation of being able to see only one side of every question that touched America, it may be stated that he was, all in all, fair in his treatment of George Grenville and Lord North. For instance, his account of the passing of the Stamp Act, based upon wide research, is well documented. In it he pointed out that it was not Grenville but Jenkinson who pressed for a stamp tax in America, a measure for which Grenville, however, assumed responsibility as the King's chief minister. Again, according to Bancroft, "Grenville did not propose a requisition on the colonies, or invite them to tax themselves; the delay [of one year] granted was only for form's sake, and with the hope of winning from them some expression of assent. . . ." [17] With respect to American independence from

---

[15] Newcastle to Andrew Stone, May 2–13, 1752, and Newcastle to Horatio Walpole, May 14, 1754, Newcastle Papers, B.M., Add. Mss. 32727, folios 63–5, and 32735, folios 268–72.

[16] Bancroft's *History* IV, 28; VI, 41 and 304. "The fate of Hutchinson was a strange one," wrote Bancroft in 1838. "He was philosophic, if to know somewhat of the selfish principles in man be philosophy; otherwise he was blind, except to facts. He felt himself that he had not solved the problem of the causes, which gave being and progress to Massachusetts; and it is said that tears used to gush from his eyes as he reflected on his career, and yearned for the land from which his blindness to popular life had estranged him" (*North American Review*, XLVI, 477).

[17] *History of the United States* . . . V, 190. In a footnote Bancroft quotes Burke's speech on American taxation in which he denied that the colonies were ever given an option of taxing themselves, calling any such statement a "falsehood." (*The Works of*

Great Britain, he was surely right when he marshalled evidence to prove that the surrender of Canada by France in 1763 meant the inevitable downfall of the Old British Empire in North America,[18] or when he demonstrated that Samuel Adams was the first American leader, at least as early as 1768, to dedicate himself to breaking the political ties that bound the colonies to Great Britain, a dedication he held to the end.[19]

The character of Bancroft's *History*, its strength and weakness, is well described by Francis Bowen, editor of *North American Review*, in his review of Volume IV in the April 1852 issue:

> "His manner had one signal excellence, which would have atoned for many faults; it was never feeble, prosy, or dull. One other quality it had, which contributed largely to the success of the work, though we are not sure that it will add to its merits in the estimation of posterity. It was animated throughout by a fervid spirit of patriotism; a love of country too exalted to be discriminating, and an admiration of the American polity, which would brook no limitations and admit of no defects, colored his pages so highly, that the historian seemed to give place to the eulogist, and the leading [American] personages of the story to be uniformly represented as saints or heroes. Foreigners are apt to ridicule such manifestations of national feeling, and even Americans would require its expression to be more temperate. The historian who would write for posterity must remember, that distance of time has the same effect as distance of place in sobering the judgment, and reducing all colors to a uniform neutral tint." [20]

Such was a contemporary's discerning judgement on Bancroft's great work and such has been the judgement of most later critics. John Spencer Bassett, writing during the early years of the twentieth century, expressed a similar feeling when he noted that "Bancroft's *History* is now out of date, and a changing age treats it with disdain. . . . His quick and nervous summation of facts is not suited to the careful weighing of evidence." [21] However, Edmund S.

---

the *Right Honourable Edmund Burke* [2 vols., London, 1803], II, 394–7). Bancroft adds the comment: "it was a falsehood"; he then states that the Massachusetts Bay Assembly was misled into the belief that Grenville had made such an offer by a letter from Jasper Mauduit—a letter based in turn on misinformation regarding Grenville's statement to the London colonial agents. See Bancroft's *History*, V, 190n.

[18] *Ibid.*, IV, 460–2.
[19] *Ibid.*, VI, 192, 253, 469.
[20] *North American Review*, LXXIV, 507–15.
[21] J. S. Bassett: *The Middle Group of American Historians* (New York, 1917), p. 183.

Morgan—while admitting that Bancroft "was not always scrupulous in his use of quotations, though he wrote the extravagant prose of the nineteenth century, though he saw the hand of God operating in places where we would not detect it,"—affirms that the "first, and in many ways the greatest, historian of the Revolutionary period was the Jacksonian Democrat, George Bancroft." [22] This agrees with the view expressed by N. H. Dawes and F. T. Nichols in their article "Revaluing George Bancroft," which appeared in the June 1933 *New England Quarterly:* "George Bancroft's *History* lacked the pagan splendor of Prescott, the blood and iron, and fire of Motley, and the exquisite beauty of expression which was peculiar to Parkman; but Bancroft was the historian of America as no man ever was, or probably will be." [23]

[22] E. S. Morgan: *The Birth of the Republic, 1763–89* (Chicago, 1956), p. 158.

[23] *New England Quarterly*, VI, 292. For a measured judgement of Bancroft as "the first American historian to bring to a study of the Revolution the research techniques of modern scholarship" but who was also "unconsciously a mythmaker," see Page Smith: *The Historian and History* (New York, 1964), pp. 177–80. This myth-making was also emphasized earlier in Sydney George Fisher's paper, "The Legendary and Myth-Making Process in Histories of the American Revolution," presented before the American Philosophical Society in 1912. Referring to Bancroft's *History,* Fisher states that it was "the most violently partisan and timorously defensive history of the Revolution that had appeared. It was most cautiously written, with the greatest dread of the slightest admission, and with intense straining to make out a perfect [American] case. Entirely devoid of candor . . . his omission of everything that did not support the English whig theory . . . made his work more violently and narrowly one-sided than the partisan pamphlets of the period of which he was writing" (American Philosophical Society *Proceedings,* LI, 68–9). On the other hand, the excellent article by Michael Kraus in the December 1934 *New England Quarterly,* "George Bancroft, 1834–1934," points out with justice that some parts of the *History* are so excellent "that the disrepute into which Bancroft's work has fallen as a whole should not blind even the present-day student to the value of these useful parts." Kraus also states that what "invalidates most of Bancroft's material on the colonial period is the point of view which he adopted as a clue to America's early history"—that there was an urge in the colonies, from an early period, for political independence. This point of view, consistently maintained by Bancroft, went hand in hand with his thesis that in "their struggles with king and parliament the colonists were right, and their opponents were wrong. Bancroft belonged to that school of historians which the late Professor Osgood called 'prosecuting attorneys' " (*New England Quarterly*, VII, 662–86). See also the essays on George Bancroft in Michael Kraus's *A History of American History* (New York, 1937), pp. 215–38, and in his *The Writing of American History* (Norman, Okla., 1953), pp. 115–27; Harvey Wish: *The American Historian. A Social-Intellectual History of the American Past* (New York, 1960), Chap. 5, "George Bancroft and German Idealism," an especially provocative essay; and "George Bancroft," by Watt Stewart in *The Marcus W. Jernegan Essays in American Historiography* (ed. W. T. Hutchinson, Chicago, 1937), Chap. 7.

Richard Hildreth (1807–1865)

In describing the movement within the American colonies that led to the Declaration of Independence and the establishment of the American Union, the account left by the historian Richard Hildreth offers a sharp contrast to that written by George Bancroft. In many respects it is remarkably modern in approach; it is also markedly different from most of his other writing. Quite absent in this phase of his historical work are any emotional overtones.

Like Bancroft, Hildreth at an early age entered Phillips Exeter Academy where his father, Hosea Hildreth, was a professor of mathematics; also like Bancroft, he went from there to Harvard. After graduation in 1826, a period of eighteen years followed during which he combined an active law practice with even more active efforts in writing for newspapers and ardently promoting such reforms as the abolition of slavery, the cause of temperance, and the revision of the banking system. During the latter part of this period, he spent some three years in British Guiana for his health. His sojourn there, however, did not seriously interrupt his literary labours.

Hildreth's writings up to 1849 were by and large polemical in tone. Among them were *The Slave: or Memoirs of Archy Moore,* which appeared in Boston in 1836 and enjoyed a very wide circulation; *Despotism in America; or, An Inquiry into the Nature and Results of the Slave-Holding System in the United States,* published in 1840; and his *Theory of Morals . . .* which came out in 1844 and struck at accepted social and religious beliefs and practices.[1] The Puritans of New England, with their belief in a state establishment of religion, came under his condemnation, but so too did the members of the Society of Friends, who opposed any such establishment.[2] He also excoriated the institution of slavery entrenched in

---

[1] See D. E. Emerson: *Richard Hildreth* (Johns Hopkins University *Studies in Historical and Political Science,* LXIV, No. 2, Baltimore, 1946), Appendix II, "Bibliography of Published Writings of Richard Hildreth."

[2] See, for example, in his *The History of the United States of America from the Discovery of the Continent to the Organization of Government under the Federal Constitution* (3 vols., New York, 1849), I, 399–405.

the South. In view of his confirmed attitudes as to what had been wrong with American life during the colonial period, it is not surprising that when Hildreth turned to writing the history of the American people he should produce a very different work than had Bancroft, who saw little but the fulfilment of the highest goal in American progress from British colonial dependence to independence as a distinct nation. For Hildreth simply set as his standard: "relating plain facts in plain English; with no interest but justice, and no aim but truth. . . ." [3]

In the Preface to Volume I of his *History of the United States of America . . . 1497–1789* Hildreth wrote:

> "Of centennial sermons and Fourth-of-July orations, whether professedly such or in the guise of history, there are more than enough. It is due to our fathers and ourselves, it is due to truth and philosophy, to present for once, on the historic stage, the founders of our American nation unbedaubed with patriotic rouge, wrapped up in no fine-spun cloaks of excuses and apology, without stilts, buskins, tinsel, or bedizzenment, in their own proper persons, often rude, hard, narrow, superstitious, and mistaken, but always earnest, downright, manly, and sincere. The result of their labors is eulogy enough; their best apology is to tell their story exactly as it was." [4]

Such was the spirit in which Hildreth wrote. His style, consistent with his purpose, was sober, unadorned, and without the highly coloured descriptions of events or sweeping generalizations in which Bancroft delighted and which delighted the reader of his works in his own generation. It is possible, as Russel B. Nye asserts, that "Hildreth wrote American history admittedly as Bancroft's ri-

---

[3] *Ibid.* (revised edn., 6 vols., New York, 1880), I, xi.

[4] *Ibid.* (1849 edn.), I, iii. In a long unsigned review of the six volumes that appeared in the *North American Review* for October 1851 the writer, while acknowledging the impressiveness of Hildreth's performance, is very critical of it: "As a historian of the Puritan fathers of New England, indeed, he lacks the first requisite for the successful performance of his task,—the power to appreciate their motives and understand their purposes. He has exaggerated all their faults, and hardly given us a glimpse of their virtues." Indeed, according to this review, his *History* "is written with a pen steeped in gall; it is bitter and denunciatory from beginning to end"; and, finally, "Mr. Hildreth's performance . . . begins with a sweeping censure of its predecessors, and aspires to present the history of America for the first time in its true character. It is not a feeble or careless production; the author of it is an independent thinker, a correct writer, and has other eminent qualifications for his task. . . . His work is most faulty in the very respect in which he seems most ambitious to excel; and he has thus shown, though in a manner which he did not intend, that freedom from prejudice is the first requisite of a historian" (*North American Review*, LXXIII, 411–47).

val, as an antidote to the elder man's effulgent, flowing narrative and his dramatic presentation of events." [5] At least it is quite evident that, in the first edition of his *History,* Hildreth chose to ignore the fact that Bancroft had already published his first three volumes of history covering the period of colonization down to 1748. In the Preface to Volume I, Hildreth could therefore write: "No other work on American history, except mere compends and abridgments, embraces the same extent of time; none comprehends the same circuit of inquiry, or has any thing like the same plan and objects. Nowhere else can be found in the same distinct completeness the curious and instructive story of New England theocracy, the financial, economical, and political history of the colonies and the Revolution, the origin and shaping of our existing laws and institutions, state and national, the progressive, social and intellectual development of our people." [6]

The reader turning from Bancroft to Hildreth will certainly find the second rather dry reading, especially the portions concerned with the eighteenth century down to the passage of the Stamp Act in 1765. The succinct presentation is suggestive of a textbook, as is the lack of footnotes. Nevertheless, the *History* indicates an excellent mastery of the impressive body of printed authorities listed chronologically at the end of Volume III. To illustrate the point, in his determination to avoid the use of emotional appeal Hildreth gives an extremely matter-of-fact account of the issue over the writs of assistance; [7] the same thing may be said of his treatment of the Virginia Twopenny Acts. [8] He reveals the acquiescence of the colonies to a variety of acts of Parliament relating not only to trade but to quite other fields. [9] He points out that before 1764 Parliament had never used its "super eminent powers" to levy taxes for a revenue,

---

[5] R. B. Nye: *George Bancroft, Brahmin Rebel* (New York, 1944), p. 186. A. M. Schlesinger Jr.'s excellent article "The Problem of Richard Hildreth" in the June 1940 *New England Quarterly* expressed the opinion that the charge that Hildreth, the Federalist, wrote in answer to Bancroft, the Democrat, was not proven. See *New England Quarterly,* XIII, 223–45. For an extended note on the subject see D. E. Emerson's *Richard Hildreth,* Appendix I, "Hildreth on Bancroft's History," pp. 163–8. The writer takes the reasonable position that "Hildreth's inspiration came from his own interest in history, from his definite opinions concerning American history, and especially from very deep convictions about the way that history should be written" (p. 164).

[6] *History of the United States . . .* I, v.
[7] *Ibid.,* II, 498–500.
[8] *Ibid.,* II, 508–9.
[9] *Ibid.,* II, 516–17.

and that Grenville in introducing such a plan was bringing forward something new; [10] but at the same time he quotes with candour the view expressed by James Otis (in his *The Rights of the British Colonies Asserted and Proved*, published in Boston in 1764, pp. 39–40) that, while any kind of tax levied by Parliament on its colonies was "absolutely irreconcilable with the rights of the colonists as British subjects and as men," it would nevertheless "be an end to all governments if one, or a number of subjects or subordinate provinces, should take upon them so far to judge of the justice of an act of Parliament or to refuse obedience to it"; therefore, since forcibly resisting Parliament and the King's laws is high treason, "let the Parliament lay what burdens they please on us, we must, it is our duty to submit, and patiently bear them till they will be pleased to relieve us." Hildreth's laconic comment on this was: "But this doctrine of patient submission to injustice was not of a sort to go down in America." [11] In giving an account of the Stamp Act riots, he asserts that the rioters who wrecked the Hutchinson Boston mansion were "the dregs of the population . . . maddened with liquor and excitement," apparently stirred to violence by a sermon delivered by the Rev. Jonathan Mayhew the day before the riot, based on the text: "I would they were even cut off which trouble you." [12]

Yet in his quiet way Hildreth shows a firm commitment to the American cause. In doing so, it is interesting to note, he makes no accusation of George III as a tyrant. In fact, when the King's name is mentioned at all it is incidentally and, like Holmes, it does not even appear in the general index. In other words, to Hildreth the measures that alienated the colonials from the mother country were fundamentally ministerial and parliamentary in origin. It is therefore not surprising that in dealing with the Declaration of Independence, he is silent on its indictment of George III as the chief source of the miseries inflicted on the American people. Indeed, he seemed loath to embark upon its contents and instead limited his discussion to the parts of the original draft that Congress had deleted in order not "to offend friends of America in Great Britain" or to antagonize such a colony as Georgia that favoured "that execrable traffic" the slave trade. [13] As A. J. Kelly points out,

---

[10] *Ibid.*, II, 518. Hildreth as a rule is very careful; he does, however, refer to the Chancellor of the Exchequer as "Lord" Grenville.

[11] *Ibid.*, II, 522–3.

[12] *Ibid.*, II, 527–8.

[13] *Ibid.*, III, 136–7.

Hildreth "succeeds in discussing the Revolution with the detachment of a scholar dissecting ancient history. There is hardly a spark
of hatred toward England in the entire theme. He is sympathetic
with the ideal of American liberty, but that is as far as his sense of
fairness will allow him to proceed." [14]

If the first three volumes of Hildreth's *History of the United
States* are remarkable for the author's spirit of historical detachment
and his attempt to present without embellishment the truth about
the growth of the colonies and their ultimate separation from Great
Britain, the next three volumes (issued in 1851 and 1852) which
carry the title: *The History of the United States of America, From
the Adoption of the Federal Constitution to the End of the Six-
teenth Congress* and bring the story down to 1821, show a return to
the more partisan approach that characterized many of his earlier
journalistic efforts.[15] But these volumes, in which he takes a stand as a
champion of the Federalists and Whigs, lie well beyond the limits of
this historiographical essay.[16] As to the first three volumes which do
concern us, Charles Kendall Adams had high praise for them.
"These volumes" he wrote, "completed as early as 1850 still probably form the most valuable single work on American History." [17] If
such is not the judgement of the present-day scholars, they will at
least be likely to agree with G. P. Gooch, who wrote of Hildreth that
"his business-like narration taught Americans that their history must
be studied in the same critical spirit as that of other countries." [18] It
may also be added that it is Hildreth's spirit rather than Bancroft's
that animates twentieth-century historical writers in their search for
an understanding of the past.

---

[14] A. H. Kelly: "Richard Hildreth" in *The Marcus W. Jernegan Essays in American Historiography* (ed. W. T. Hutchinson, Chicago, 1937), p. 34. Kelly seeks to
explain Hildreth's detachment in writing his first three volumes (which include the
revolt of the colonies from Great Britain) as the result of his strong support of
Federalism, which was pro-British, as against the Jeffersonian anti-British attitude.

[15] See J. F. Jameson: *The History of Historical Writing in America* (Boston & New
York, 1891), pp. 112–13.

[16] The six volumes were published as a set between 1856 and 1860; then came the
revised set of 1863, and in 1880 a second revision of it.

[17] *A Manual of Historical Literature* (New York, 1889), p. 569.

[18] *History and Historians of the Nineteenth Century* (London, 1920), pp. 407–8.

Francis Parkman (1823–1893)

No other historian who has written on the British colonies has received more discriminating acclaim from his contemporaries, and none has better retained his high standing among the scholarly public to this day, than Francis Parkman.[1]

Parkman inherited wealth from his grandfather, an opulent Boston merchant, and therefore never lacked financial resources to meet his daily or scholarly needs. His father, the Rev. Francis Parkman, was for thirty-six years the respected pastor of the Unitarian New North Church in Boston. By education also Francis was well prepared for the career he was to follow, especially his training in English literature and composition at the Boston private school he attended before entering Harvard at the age of seventeen. His early wandering among the woods, streams, and mountains of New England was another facet of the educational background that led toward his future calling as a historian. While he did not distinguish himself as an undergraduate, he did well in the subjects that appealed to him and, beyond that, read widely for his own improvement. The year before he took his baccalaureate degree he went to Europe for the sake of his health and spent some months in Sicily and Italy. Then in 1846—having completed the work for a degree in law—he made his memorable trek into Indian country. This took him to the Rockies, where he spent some weeks living among the Sioux and other Indian tribes. Out of this experience came the

---

[1] Among other biographies and studies of Parkman see C. H. Farnham: *A Life of Francis Parkman* (Boston, 1923), valuable as from the pen of one closely associated with the historian over a period of years; H. D. Sedgwick: *Francis Parkman* (Boston & New York, 1904), a volume in the *American Men of Letters* series; and especially Mason Wade: *Francis Parkman: Heroic Historian* (New York, 1942), a most penetrating biography by one who was both a New Englander and a Roman Catholic and who therefore saw sympathetically both sides of the issues between Catholic New France and the Protestant British colonies which Parkman sought to describe. Two other works of great value in discovering the nature of the man are: *The Journals of Francis Parkman* (ed. Mason Wade, 2 vols., New York & London, 1947), and the *Letters of Francis Parkman* (ed. W. R. Jacobs, 2 vols., Norman, Okla., 1960); while the section on him in H. P. Beers's *The French in North America: A Bibliographical Guide . . .* (Baton Rouge, La., 1957), pp. 90–6 and *passim,* throws useful light on the process whereby Parkman gathered the material for his volumes.

delightful book *The California and Oregon Trail,* which was published in 1849 and quickly became a classic.

In making the western trip, Parkman had two objectives: he wanted to know the Indians at first hand, for, since his youth, he had been fascinated by the untamed wilderness country of North America and its native inhabitants; and he also wanted to restore his health, a goal which the European trip had failed to accomplish. Although he achieved the first objective, he returned in worse physical condition than before. His eyesight had all but failed him, he was affected by a nervous condition, especially in his hands, and also afflicted by gout. Moreover, in the years to come a rheumatic condition in his knees, as well as insomnia, became increasingly serious handicaps. One might therefore have anticipated that Parkman in the face of such disabilities and with no need to earn a living, would have settled down to the quiet life of a valetudinarian. Far from it! His zest for achievement seems only to have been sharpened. The life story of his battle and triumph against these formidable odds is as inspiring as the books he wrote. For years a wire frame guided his hand (when he could write) but some days he might be able to compose only six lines; on others even this was beyond him, since he was often incapacitated for periods of days or even weeks and at such times was unable to approach any mental or physical labour.[2]

This was not all. The ambitious plan that he had formulated for his life's work in history called for the use of vast numbers of original documents. Much of the material needed was in the Old World, both in England and on the Continent. Copies of these sources had to be made for him and then read and re-read to him. Thereafter he cited them with accuracy in the footnotes. The amazing thing is that there is no trace of either incapacity or self-pity in his writing. Its buoyancy and sparkle carries the reader along with never a hint—except in a Preface—of the suffering of the man who poured forth such luminous descriptions of the New World or recounted so lucidly the events that held his attention.

---

[2] In 1864 Parkman sent an autobiographical letter to his friend, the Rev. Dr. G. E. Ellis; the first part of it is missing, but the remainder is published by W. R. Jacobs in *Letters of Francis Parkman* I, 175–84. A second autobiographical letter written on October 28, 1886, was sent to Martin Brimmer with instructions that, after the author's death, it should be turned over to the Massachusetts Historical Society. This letter is to be found in the Appendix of N. D. Sedgwick's *Francis Parkman,* pp. 327–38. These two letters set forth in full the difficulties faced by the historian.

Parkman's first purely historical undertaking—one fully in harmony with his almost passionate interest in the American Indian—was to describe the downfall of Indian prowess in North America as an outcome of the bloody war that took place in the Great Lakes region and the Valley of the Ohio during the years 1763 and 1764. In so doing he unfortunately neglected to deal with the war waged against the Cherokee between 1759 and 1761 that resulted in breaking the power of this great warrior "nation"—surely a vital part of the story of how the frontiers advanced despite Indian resistance, which was Parkman's theme. Nevertheless his *Conspiracy of Pontiac and the Indian War after the Conquest of Canada,* which appeared in two volumes in 1851, was a triumph of artistic execution and deservedly passed through many editions[3] although subsequent research has indicated that in choosing his title Parkman was misled by the sources he used. For Pontiac, though a chief leader of the revolt itself, was not himself responsible for the great Indian conspiracy. In the presence of Sir William Johnson and the chiefs of five of the Indian tribes most deeply involved in the recent war, Pontiac on July 28, 1766, stated that all but one of the war belts that touched off the uprising were sent by the Seneca Indians. He claimed that they were the real conspirators, and challenged the assembled Indian leaders to deny this fact.[4] No evidence to the contrary seems to exist. In certain other respects, too, Parkman's work should be used with caution.[5]

In addition to his passionate commitment to telling the story of the American wilderness in terms of the impact of the white man upon it and upon those who had long dwelt within it, Parkman also became thrilled with the idea of chronicling the history of French colonization in North America and the long struggle between the French and the English for mastery of that continent. But for years

[3] For analyses of Parkman as a literary historian see Howard Doughty: *Francis Parkman* (New York, 1962); O. A. Pease: *Parkman's History. The Historian as Literary Artist* (New Haven, 1953); W. R. Jacobs: "Some of Parkman's Literary Devices," *New England Quarterly,* XXXI, 244–52; and David Levin: *History as Romantic Art: Bancroft, Motley, Prescott, and Parkman* (Stanford, 1959).

[4] See "Sir Willm Johnson's Transactions held with Pontiac and other Western Chiefs at Ontario in July 1766," in Johnson to the Board of Trade, August 20, 1766, P.R.O., C.O. 323:24.

[5] See, by the author of this series, *The British Empire Before the American Revolution,* Volume IX, Chap. 6, "The Great Indian Uprising, 1763," and H. H. Peckham: *Pontiac and the Indian Uprising* (Princeton, 1947). For a defence of Parkman see W. R. Jacobs: "Was the Pontiac Uprising a Conspiracy?" Ohio Archeological and Historical Society *Quarterly,* LIX (1950), 26–37.

after the publication of the Pontiac book he was too incapacitated to carry on his historical work. However, in 1865 came his *Pioneers of France in the New World,* recounting early French exploration and settlement. Two years later *The Jesuits in North America* appeared, followed in 1869 by *The Discovery of the Great West* (in a later edition renamed *LaSalle and the Discovery of the Great West*). After a break of five years came *The Old Régime in Canada* and, in 1877, *Count Frontenac and New France under Louis XIV.* These volumes, concerned with the seventeenth century and the first half of the eighteenth, lie outside the scope of consideration of this essay; nevertheless, it should be noted that they established the reputation of Parkman as a historian of the first order. In 1884 *Montcalm and Wolfe* issued from the press in two volumes; it concentrated on the rivalry between France and Great Britain in North America from 1745 up to the disappearance of French power as a result of the Treaty of Peace of 1763. This work does fall within the scope of our present interest.

Montcalm and Wolfe is a powerful book, such as only a great literary artist and dedicated scholar, committed to a high standard of historical accuracy, could produce. Yet the title given to it, while achieving a dramatic effect, greatly over-emphasized the importance of the personal contribution of James Wolfe to the destruction of the French New World Empire. After all, the major credit for the British triumph in North America—an event with vastly important implications for the future of this continent—should properly go to William Pitt rather than to Wolfe. Again, in seeking to account for the defeat of the British force sent against Fort Duquesne in 1755, Parkman, lacking the adequate source material, did not take into consideration the peculiar circumstances that brought about the disaster.[6] But the historian of today cannot ignore Dinwiddie's failure to provide the promised powerful Indian support which Braddock had been led to expect and greatly deserved. Parkman also ignored the failure of Lieutenant Colonel Gage, commander of the British vanguard, to take the precaution exercised earlier on the march of seizing the dominating hills. For it was from the cover of these high positions that the Indians later poured the most deadly fire upon Braddock's troops. Nor does Parkman deal with Gage's further failure to risk the necessary losses entailed in pressing the

---

[6] *Montcalm and Wolfe* (2 vols., Boston, 1884), I, Chap. 7, "Braddock."

troops forward out of the trees and into the open country just beyond what became the scene of total British defeat—a movement which, had he advanced, might have led to the capture of the French fort and a great victory. Nevertheless, the description of the Braddock expedition constitutes a high order of historical literature, if not of military history. At the same time one of the most important contributions made by *Montcalm and Wolfe* to our understanding of the history of this period lies in Parkman's scholarly treatment of the problem of the so-called "neutral" Acadians dwelling within the bounds of the peninsula of Nova Scotia. The evidence he marshals in this work indicates that as a wartime expedient—the dispersion of these people among the British colonials to the southward seemed to present the one practicable solution to a problem otherwise bristling with danger, from the point of view both of Governor Charles Lawrence of Nova Scotia and Governor William Shirley of Massachusetts Bay, the two men largely responsible for the decision.[7]

It should be added that Parkman's treatment of the wartime history of Nova Scotia led to a rather bitter exchange of letters between Parkman and his old Canadian friend, the Abbé Henri Raymond Casgrain, who wrote his *Un Pèlerinage au Pays d'Évangéline* (Quebec, 1887) as a public reply to *Montcalm and Wolfe*.[8] Philip H. Smith, a popular writer, also attempted to demolish the reputation of Parkman's book by publishing in 1884 *Acadia, A Lost Chapter in American History;* but, unhappily for its reputation, Smith's work was based upon false information, as Parkman pointed out in the January 22, 1885, number of *The Nation*.[9]

---

[7] *Ibid.*, I, Chap. 4, "Conflict for Acadia" and Chap. 8, "Removal of the Acadians." Parkman supplemented the evidence respecting the Acadians in his *A Half-Century of Conflict* (2 vols., Boston, 1892), II, Chap. 22, "Acadian Conflicts," and also Appendix C, pp. 321–60, "Shirley and the Acadians."

[8] Parkman replied by letter on October 23, 1887, to Casgrain's book, a copy of which the Abbé had sent to him. Pointing out his suppression in it of vitally important facts, Parkman ended with the statement: "Evidence has been given to prove that, if the Acadians were victims, the French were more to blame than the English. It is not enough to evade and ignore such testimony, as you have done. You must meet it squarely and answer it if you can, or else you will lose your case by default" (*Letters of Farncis Parkman*, II, 211–14). See again Parkman to the Abbé, November 4, 1887, in reply to the letters of October 27, 1887, and also on August 30, 1888, in *ibid.*, II, 215–16 and 225–6. The Casgrain letters to Parkman are among the Parkman Papers in the Massachusetts Historical Society.

[9] In the November 6, 1884, issue of *The Nation*, Parkman, in a brief answer to Smith and to other writers opposed to his account of the Acadians, referred to Longfellow's "Evangeline" as a "graceful and touching poem and a charming ideal

In considering the historical work of Parkman, one must keep in mind that in some respects it falls far short of what is expected of the present-day historian. It neglected diplomacy, as well as many highly important strategic, tactical, and logistical problems; without a treatment of these aspects, the steps taken by Great Britain and France during the war years cannot be clearly grasped. The war that Parkman describes is not the highly complicated world-wide war of 1754 to 1763, but merely a phase of it—the North American wilderness phase. Yet he accomplished this limited task so brilliantly that one may justly honour him with the title Master Historian.

John Gorham Palfrey (1796–1881)

Among the New England writers who made important contributions to the early history of the United States during the so-called Middle Period was John Gorham Palfrey.[1] It is interesting to note that he—as well as fellow historians George Bancroft, William Hildreth, and Jared Sparks—received his early training at both Phillips Exeter and Harvard. Upon securing his baccalaureate in 1815 he prepared for the ministry and in 1818 he was installed as the minister of the Unitarian Brattle Square Church in Boston. There he remained until his appointment in 1831 as Dexter Professor of Sacred Literature at Harvard. Already a contributor to the *North American Review,* he purchased that highly influential journal in 1835 and continued to write for it even after he had sold his interest in it in 1843. Although he had resigned from the faculty at

---

picture" and then added: "But the history of humanity, to be good for anything, must rest not on imagination but on truth." See also Parkman's reply to Smith in the February 25, 1885, *Boston Evening Transcript* (reprinted in Jacobs's *Letters of Francis Parkman,* II, 170–4). For a rather extended treatment of the Acadians see, in the author's present series, Volume V, Chap. 6, "Land of the Acadians," and Volume VI, Chap. 8, "The Treason of Thomas Pichon," Chap. 9, "Farewell to Acadia," and Chap. 10, "The Exiles." According to W. R. Jacobs (in *Letters of Francis Parkman,* II, 174n.), Parkman summarized his position as follows: "That the Acadia story is a most deplorable one nobody will deny. That this unhappy people were deeply sinned against is equally true; but the chief offense has been laid at the wrong door."

[1] For an excellent recent study of Palfrey's career, see F. O. Gatell's *John Gorham Palfrey and the New England Conscience* (Cambridge, Mass., 1963).

Harvard in 1839 on account of the multiplicity of his activities, he continued to accept new offices. In 1844 he became Secretary for the Commonwealth and in 1847 began his one term as a member of Congress. Later, in 1861, he received the appointment of postmaster at Boston, a position he held for the next six years.

In view of the variety of public services undertaken by Palfrey—which undoubtedly absorbed much of his energy and attention—it is doubly surprising that in the early 1850's he should have committed himself to a major scholarly task and one that would demand the closest application for its completion: the writing of a history of New England down to the outbreak of hostilities between Great Britain and the colonies in 1775. Having drawn upon the materials that were readily available in America, he went to England in 1856 to work in the British Museum and to consult the manuscript collections in the Colonial Office and in other depositories. As a result, Volume I of his *History of New England* appeared in 1858. In 1860 Volume II came from the press and Volume III followed in 1864. These three volumes form a unit and each carries the subtitle "During the Stuart Dynasty." They are concerned with the period of New England history ending with the downfall of the Andros régime that coincided with the Revolution of 1688 in England. Volume IV, which brought the New England story down to 1741, was not published until 1875. Before his death in 1881, Palfrey had largely completed his work on the manuscript of the final volume that would carry the series to the beginning of the War for American Independence, but Volume V was not destined to be published until 1890, when it appeared under the editorship of his son, F. W. Palfrey. The two last volumes carry the title *The History of New England from the Revolution of the Seventeenth Century to the Revolution of the Eighteenth.*

Palfrey's *History* is a remarkable achievement. It is much more than the local history of the New England colonies, for it stresses throughout the interrelation of this area with England and does so with real erudition. Unlike Hildreth's *History of the United States,* Palfrey's text is illuminated throughout with footnotes that add immeasurably to its value for the student; it is moreover thorough if not exhaustive in its careful marshalling of the facts.

A critique of Volume I in the April 1859 *North American Review* (doubtless written by Francis Bowen, owner and editor of the *Review* at this period) referred to the author's "rare gifts as an historian," his "unimpassioned impartiality of narrative," and his "conscientious and painstaking industry . . . needed, not so much for the narrative of actual events on this side of the ocean, as for the often obscure and difficult investigation of their Transatlantic causes and relations." It also mentioned his "candor . . . signally conspicuous in dealing with . . . fixed historical prejudice."[2] In reviewing Volume II in the same magazine, the writer (again apparently Bowen) pointed out that the threads of the story "are so blended as to give perfect unity to the narrative, making it the veritable history of New England, and not what we should have had from a less skilful hand, the histories of the separate Colonies, held together only by the binder's thread and the covers." This reviewer further affirmed that in view of the emphasis placed on "institutions and customs, the domestic, social, political, and religious life," the *History* would "bear favorable comparison" with Macaulay's description of England.[3] J. Franklin Jameson, writing near the close of the last century, also gave the work high praise when he designated it "probably the best single large piece of work that has been done in America on any part of our colonial period."[4]

Volume V of Palfrey's series is of particular concern to this historiographical essay. In its Preface (prepared toward the end of 1876 and therefore some four years before his death) Palfrey spoke of his enfeebled state of health and stressed the effects this produced on the writing of history. But the same deep love for, and pride in the people of New England burned as brightly as ever, as he wrote: "The work which in five generations was done in New England for the continent and the world, was done by Englishmen of Puritan training. As far as human judgment may trust itself, no other class of men contemporary with them was equal to the achievement." In helping to explain this, he pointed out the homogeneous character of the population of New England, and added that despite the differences that arose among them "all had the same generous aims, and the same guiding and fortifying principles of truth, honor, uprightness, and religion."[5]

Palfrey's efforts to be objective in his approach are clearly de-

---

[2] *North American Review,* LXXXVIII, 462–3.

[3] *Ibid.,* XCI, 421–2.

[4] *The History of Historical Writing in America* (Boston & New York, 1891), p. 123.

[5] Palfrey's *History of New England* . . . V, vii–viii.

monstrable. For example, he seeks to be fair to New Englander Thomas Hutchinson, of whom he writes: "His eloquence, activity, courteous manners, superior abilities and extensive knowledge easily gave him the lead in the House [of Representatives], of which he was made Speaker after a short service." Again, when Hutchinson, as Lieutenant Governor, was temporarily placed at the head of the government in Massachusetts Bay, he is shown as displaying "his shining qualities to advantage [which] contributed to strengthen his hold on the public respect." [6] Yet in the Preface to Volume III, in referring to the "cycle of New England," which he thought of as eighty-six years, he cannot forbear to write:

> "In the spring of 1603, the family of Stuart ascended the throne of England. At the end of eighty-six years, Massachusetts having been betrayed to her enemies by her most eminent and trusted citizen, Joseph Dudley, the people, on the 19th day of April, 1689, committed their prisoner, the deputy of the Stuart King, to the fort in Boston which he had built to overawe them. Another eighty-six years passed, and Massachusetts had been betrayed to her enemies by her most eminent and trusted citizen, Thomas Hutchinson, when, at Lexington and Concord on the 19th of April, 1775, her farmers struck the first blow in the War of American Independence." [7]

Hutchinson's crime, according to Palfrey, was that he was loyal to the King and the government in Britain rather than to New England, which should have been the paramount duty of every native. Nevertheless, in his desire to be fair even to the British government, he did take issue with the statement made by that eminent New Englander, John Adams, that when "the British ministry received from General Amherst his despatches, announcing the conquest of Montreal, and the consequent annihilation of the French government in America, in 1759 [1760], they immediately conceived the design, and took the resolution, of conquering the English colonies, and subjecting them to the unlimited authority of Parliament." [8] In commenting on this, Palfrey made clear that in the process of examining the official papers in London he had "searched in vain for proof" of such a design at that period.[9] Also, far from upholding the position taken by John Dickinson in his "Letters from a Farmer in

---

[6] *Ibid.*, V, 230–1.
[7] *Ibid.*, III, viii.
[8] John Adams to William Tudor, March 29, 1817, *Works of John Adams* (ed. C. F. Adams, 10 vols., Boston, 1850–6), X, 246.
[9] *History of New England . . .* V, 236n.

Pennsylvania" that the acquisition of Canada by Great Britain was "greatly injurious to these colonies," [10] Palfrey emphasized the fact that this acquisition put an end to the sufferings of British colonials at the hands of the French and Indians. "With intervals, and with different degrees of horror," he wrote, "this barbarity of Indian war under French influence had been going on for more than eighty years. It could not stop too soon; and for putting an end to it . . . the name of Chatham should be dear to humanity." [11]

Palfrey's account of the developing crisis between Great Britain and the colonies is presented solely from the colonial point of view, yet it is even tempered and sticks closely to the facts.[12] In evaluating Palfrey's contribution to historical literature the British writer G. P. Gooch stated:

> "Bancroft's idealisation of Puritan America was repeated by Palfrey, who wrote a 'History of New England' to the outbreak of the War of Independence. His admiration for the colonists is too great and his gratitude for their services to political liberty too deep to allow him to be critical. Without applauding religious intolerance, he finds excuses for it; but his book is learned, clear, and accurate. He had delved deep in the English archives, and no previous historian had so closely studied the interaction of Old and New England during the critical decades of the Puritan era. Though inferior in popularity to Bancroft, he reached a higher level." [13]

This must surely be the judgement of most scholars who have studied the role of New England during the colonial period.

Sydney George Fisher (1856–1927)

Sydney George Fisher was descended on his father's side from John Fisher, who accompanied William Penn on his first voyage to

---

[10] *Writings of John Dickinson* (ed. P. L. Ford, Historical Society of Pennsylvania Memoirs, XIV, Philadelphia, 1895), 360.

[11] *History of New England* . . . V, 172.

[12] James Truslow Adams has this to say of Palfrey's *History:* "In the relations between England and the colonies, Palfrey could see little but tyranny on the one side and God-fearing patriotism on the other. Nowhere does he show any real understanding of motives and problems. The work is strongly biased, also, by his inability to admit any flaws in the Puritans" (*Dictionary of American Biography,* XIV, 170).

[13] *History and Historians of the Nineteenth Century* (London, 1920), p. 407.

Pennsylvania, and on the side of his mother, Elizabeth Ingersoll, from Loyalist Jared Ingersoll, graduate of Yale, leading Connecticut lawyer, and Judge of the Middle District Court of Vice-Admiralty at Philadelphia. It is therefore not surprising that, at the age of forty, he turned his attention to the writing of colonial history. Although a native of Pennsylvania, where he spent his early years, he received his formal education in New England: first at St. Paul's School, New Hampshire, then at Trinity College, Connecticut, and lastly at the Harvard Law School. Thereafter, like his father, he entered the practice of law in Philadelphia. But, also like his father, his chief claim to fame is not in the preparation of legal briefs but in other writings, especially in the field of history.

His first historical work, published in Philadelphia in 1896 under title *The Making of Pennsylvania,* was concerned with the nature of the various groups, religious and national, in the province and its struggles over boundaries during the colonial period. This was followed a year later by two more volumes: *Pennsylvania, Colony and Commonwealth* and *The Evolution of the Constitution of the United States, showing that it is a Development of Progressive History and not an Isolated Document Struck Off at a Given Time or an Imitation of English or Dutch Forms of Government.*

The Evolution of the Constitution is a much more scholarly piece of work than the other two, which were popular in style and addressed to the general reading public. In it Fisher made available to students for the first time a carefully collated analysis of certain specific provisions of colonial charters and early state constitutions that dealt with governmental powers, to show how, by the slow process of evolution, many of these same concepts came to be embodied in the constitution of the United States. This was followed by another popular work, *Men, Women and Manners in Colonial Times,* published in 1898 in two volumes. In 1899 came *The True Benjamin Franklin,* an entertaining book that went into seven editions. As in Paul Leicester Ford's *The True George Washington,* published in 1896, the title employed the word "True" only in the sense that the work sought to discard the mythical aspects of the subject— generally presented to the American public stripped of all blemishes—and to humanize the man while not detracting from his great achievements. It may be noted in passing that in 1927, the year of Fisher's death, an edition of *Benjamin Franklin* came out omitting the word "True."

Fisher's next work (after *The True William Penn* in 1900) was *The True History of the American Revolution,* published in 1903. It is of secondary interest that in the same year he published *The American Revolution and the Boer War: An Open Letter to Mr. Charles Francis Adams on his pamphlet, "The Confederacy and the Transvaal"*—a brief pamphlet, which held up to scorn Adams's opposition to a continuation of the struggle on the part of the Boers.

In the Preface to *The True History of the American Revolution,* Fisher especially indicts those who preceded him in writing about the American Revolution for their failure to make use of the original authorities "rather more frankly than has been the practice with our historians." He seems to have levelled this charge particularly against Bancroft, Hildreth, and Fiske, whose works had been the general guides from which school books and other compilations had been prepared.[1] Fisher expressed special dissatisfaction with any description of the Revolution "which treats the desire for independency as a sudden thought, and not a long growth and development, or which assumes that every detail of the conduct of the British government was absurdly stupid, even from its own point of view, and that the loyalists were few in numbers and their arguments not worth considering." [2] Yet, as Professor Claude H. Van Tyne noted in his review of this book, Fisher was apparently unaware that others had already reached the same conclusion, so that he was but highlighting "certain facts about the Revolution upon which the best historians and teachers of history have been agreed for twenty years." [3] Further, the author was not always correct in his facts, as the result of placing so much reliance on printed materials. For example, in referring to the reimbursement of the colonies for their expenses incurred in the prosecution of the Great War for the Empire, he mentions the granting to them of only £133,333 (the sum appropriated by Parliament in both 1761 and 1762 for these services),[4] whereas the total amount of parliamentary reimbursement was actually £1,072,784 sterling.[5] Nevertheless, at the time of

---

[1] S. G. Fisher: "The Legendary and Myth-making Process in Histories of the American Revolution," American Philosophical Society *Proceedings,* LI, 53.

[2] *The True History* . . . (Philadelphia & London, 1903), p. 5.

[3] See Van Tyne's review in the July 1903 *American Historical Review,* VIII, 773–6.

[4] This figure was given in the *Statutes at Large,* a source not mentioned in Fisher's work. See, in this connection, *The British Empire before the American Revolution,* Volume X, 48–9.

[5] See *ibid.,* X, 50, which gives the figures drawn from the minutes of the British Treasury Board.

publication the merits of the book were considerable. It was well written; it held the attention of the reader; and it was the work of one who probed critically the arguments put forth on both sides of the controversy.

Once one accepts Fisher's underlying thesis in *The True History of the American Revolution*—that the real promoters of the American Revolution aimed at nothing less than American independence—one can accept its narration of events as generally convincing. At least it helped to give the readers of any one of its many editions a viewpoint far removed from that of Fourth-of-July orations. Not the least interesting part of *The True History* is its conclusion. This denied that the American Revolution taught Great Britain a lesson on how properly to govern colonies, while pointing out that Parliament still claimed and exercised "the same supreme and omnipotent power in every British colony that it has in London." It should be remembered that the book appeared in 1903.

In 1908, *The True History*, now reshaped, rewritten, expanded, and greatly improved, appeared in two large volumes under the title *The Struggle for American Independence*. In the Preface Fisher still maintained, as he had in his earlier book, that the American people "have little or no conception of what the Revolution really was, no conception of the nature of the original evidence; and the unwillingness of our writers of general histories to cite that evidence keeps it a sealed book to the public." He also insisted that no complete history of the Revolution had yet been written "dealing frankly with all the contemporary evidence and withholding nothing of importance that is found in the original records." [6] This he sought to accomplish. While he drew fully upon printed sources, including some contemporary newspapers, to enrich his abundant footnotes, the vast contents of documentary evidence still in manuscript (and some of the greatest importance) quite escaped him—for he doubtless laboured under the impression that all the really important papers on both sides of the dispute had found their way into print. Within these limitations Fisher gave the world an important book and one that made good use of the sources at his command to develop the thesis implicit in its title—that the aim of the American radicals after the conquest of New France was independence. In it, he presents the viewpoint of the Loyalists of one shade or another,

---

[6] *The Struggle for American Independence* (Philadelphia & London, 1908), I, Preface, v–vi.

as well as that of the patriots.[7] In his treatment of the British policy toward the colonies (like that of Holmes and Hildreth) the name of George III scarcely appears; he emphasizes rather that it was the "Tory" policy of the Ministry that prevailed in the face of the ineffectiveness of Whig opposition both in and out of Parliament.

Professor James A. Woodburn of Indiana University—who brought together in one volume those portions of Lecky's *History of England in the Eighteenth Century* that directly related to the Thirteen older North American Colonies, and who disagreed vehemently with Fisher's main points of departure from the more traditional interpretations of the rise of the Revolutionary movement in America—in reviewing *The Struggle for American Independence* wrote:

> "The volumes bear the stamp of originality—they lead a departure from beaten paths. There is much of interesting detail and the author shows a wealth of knowledge as well as an acquaintance with scholarly and scientific methods. Grounds for the author's conclusions are given, but the reader will hardly escape the feeling that in his treatment of the controverted political questions of the period the author has been a one-sided rather than an all-around impartial historian. Yet one wishing to know the whole story of the Revolution must feel grateful to Mr. Fisher for his volumes." [8]

Edward Channing (1856–1931)

During the early years of the present century four men stood out as students of American colonial history: Charles M. Andrews, Herbert L. Osgood, George Lewis Beer, and Edward Channing. Although Channing turned his back on colonial history after 1912, his work in that field warrants consideration in this historiographical essay.

Edward Channing was the product of New England and exhibited some of the finest traits that have been characteristic of many New Englanders of the past: an enquiring mind, a high sense

---

[7] For his attempt to determine the strength of the Loyalists see *ibid.*, I, Chap. 21.
[8] *American Historical Review*, XIV, 143–5.

of professional responsibility, and a spirit of dedication to the specific task in hand. It was his good fortune as a junior at Harvard to have come under the instruction of Henry Adams, who was offering a course in mediaeval institutions—an experience which so impressed Channing that he decided to become a historian. To fulfill this ambition he took two additional years of postgraduate work at Harvard, receiving his doctorate in 1880. It would appear that while still an undergraduate, he had conceived the idea of writing a history of the United States based upon the sources.[1] But he deferred this project in order to make himself better qualified for so formidable an undertaking. In 1883 he became an instructor in history at his *alma mater;* by 1897, he had advanced to the rank of professor.

Channing's first important contribution to American colonial history was *Town and County Government in the English Colonies of North America;* it appeared in 1884 as Number X in the second series of Johns Hopkins University *Studies in Historical and Political Science.* In this study he steered clear of the theories of the so-called Teutonic school of writers. This was followed by the first brief but illuminating study of the English trade acts, which was published under the title "The Navigation Laws" in the American Antiquarian Society *Proceedings* of 1890. The paper analyzed the legislation passed by Parliament before 1760, a date that roughly marked a dividing line between what Channing considered to be the earlier liberal and later "illiberal colonial policy which finally resulted in the American Revolution. . . . The change really consisted in making the Navigation Laws a reality and in forcing the colonies to bear their share of the burdens necessarily incurred in carrying out an imperial policy." [2] Before 1760, he affirmed, the trade laws were a positive advantage to the colonies, for "colonial shipbuilders, colonial shipowners, colonial shipmasters and colonial seamen were given a share in the monopoly of the carrying trade of the English Empire." [3]

Passing over Channing's other historical activities, such as the writing of textbooks which proved to be quite profitable to him, we

---

[1] See S. E. Morison: "Edward Channing. A Memoir," Massachusetts Historical Society *Proceedings,* LXIV, 250–84, also printed in Morison's *By Land and By Sea: Essays and Addresses* (New York, 1953), Chap. 14.

[2] American Antiquarian Society *Proceedings,* new series, VI, 160–79, especially p. 160.

[3] *Ibid.,* VI, 167.

come to the year 1905 when, in his fiftieth year, he was able to bring out the first volume of his *History of the United States*—a series that was to fulfill his chief ambition in life. The series was addressed not to the general reader but rather to his fellow historians and especially to the younger writers and teachers of American history looking for scholarly guidance. It placed a good deal of emphasis upon England, and later Great Britain, as the centre from which colonization of the Thirteen Colonies had flowed. Yet the title of the series, along with the subtitle of Volume I, "The Planting of a Nation in the New World, 1000–1660," tends to show that the author viewed the history of early English New World colonization as a necessary and inevitable preparation for the final establishment of an independent United States of America. This outlook was reinforced in the Preface, in which he stated that a chief purpose of the *History* was to describe "the development of the American people," adding that the "growth of the nation will, therefore, be treated as one continuous development from the political, military, institutional, industrial, and social points of view." [4]

Volume II of the *History* issued from the press in 1908, carrying the subtitle, "A Century of Colonial History 1660–1760"; [5] it was followed in 1912 by Volume III, subtitled "The American Revolution, 1761–1789." [6] Also published in 1912 was that valuable source book, *The Barrington-Bernard Correspondence and Illustrative Matter, 1760–1770, drawn from the "Papers of Sir Francis Bernard"* (*sometime Governor of Massachusetts-Bay*), which Channing edited with the aid of Archibald Cary Coolidge. Again in that same year, a Boston press published the famous *Guide to the Study and Reading of American History* prepared by Channing in collaboration with Albert B. Hart and Frederick J. Turner. This took the place of the earlier *Guide* produced by Channing and Hart in 1896, and was not fully displaced as an indispensable aid to students until the appearance in 1954 of the *Harvard Guide to American History*.

Three more volumes of the *History*, published between 1917 and

---

[4] *A History of the United States* (6 vols., New York, 1905–1925), I, Preface, p. v.

[5] See in this connection the unsigned review of Vol. II that appeared in the *American Historical Review* (XIV, 364–6), apparently written by C. M. Andrews, which stresses the magnitude of Channing's achievement while pointing out some of the defects of the book.

[6] Vol. III was very competently reviewed by C. H. Van Tyne in the *American Historical Review*, XVIII, 603–5. This review, like the one of Vol. II, emphasizes the great merits of the volume while criticizing Channing's rather narrow outlook.

1925, brought the story of the growth of the American nation down to the close of the Civil War, called by Channing "The War for Southern Independence." He had planned to continue the *History* to the year 1900, but never wrote the concluding volumes because of failing health. Nevertheless the work represents a great achievement, and it is unlikely that any future historian will ever duplicate the same scholarly standards maintained throughout the series. And yet the question of its permanence as a contribution to history may be raised, in view of the vast assortment of materials that has to be surveyed and evaluated for each epoch of the history of the United States for a work of this nature.[7] Did Channing himself finally become disillusioned as to the ability of one man, no matter how well endowed and trained, to accomplish the task adequately within the span of years allotted to him?[8] Was he not primarily a specialist in American colonial history and one who richly deserved the praise accorded in 1912 to his three volumes on the colonial period by Professor Andrews: "All things considered, the best account of the colonies prior to 1765 will be found in Edward Channing's *History of the United States* (Vols. I–III, 1905–1912) . . ."?[9]

The merits embodied in the volumes that fall within the proper scope of this historiography, II and III, are many. They impart a unified view of the gradual development of each of the Thirteen Colonies destined to form the early United States of America, with the emphasis on the political problems that faced each of them. Critical notes at the end of each chapter, together with footnotes, help to illuminate the text. There are also valuable chapters dealing with such subjects as labour, non-British immigration, religion, education, industry, and commerce as they affect the American colonies. But there is something of fundamental importance missing in the setting. Only infrequently is the reader made aware that the

---

[7] In the general bibliographical note on p. 25 of Vol. III Channing wrote: "The material, in print and manuscript, relating to the Revolutionary period is vast in extent and still unsatisfying. In the Record Office, in the British Museum, in the Royal Institution, and in countless muniment rooms and boxes in private houses and corporations in England are masses of manuscripts, while the storehouses in American libraries and public depositories are even greater in extent. . . . It is impossible for any man within the scope of a single lifetime to master even a tithe of this material. . . ."

[8] In 1926, the year after the publication of the sixth volume of his *History*, Channing wrote a rather revealing letter on December 23 to this author in reaction to a prospectus of the plan for this present series. It was a letter of encouragement in which he stated: "I have been over your programme and wish I were doing the job, myself."

[9] C. M. Andrews: *The Colonial Period* (New York, 1912), p. 253.

Thirteen Colonies were units within the framework of an expanding British Empire, or that the government put forward sustained efforts to make this Empire as economically self-contained as possible, or of the extent to which colonials benefited from the opportunities for enrichment embodied in such a mercantilist policy. Nor would a student who had studied the correspondence of George III be likely to agree with Channing that the King was "shrewd and unpitying" as a politician or that his "whole ambition was to place the kingship back where it had been in the days of the early Stuarts." [10]

It is clear that Channing sought to be fair when, in dealing with the issues that led to the revolt of the American colonials, he presents the arguments of both sides as to whether the Parliament of Great Britain had the legal right to levy taxes on the colonials.[11] At the same time few scholars today, fresh from a study of British colonial policy covering the two decades preceding the outbreak of colonial hostilities in 1775, would be apt to subscribe to Channing's assertions that the American colonials "were patient and long-suffering" and "only prolonged misgovernment on the part of the rulers of Britain compelled them to declare themselves independent of that empire from which they had sprung." [12] Was he not, despite his efforts to maintain an attitude of historical detachment, too good a New Englander to be thoroughly objective in dealing with the eighteenth-century British Empire? [13]

Herbert Levi Osgood (1855–1918)

If Francis Parkman chronicled the struggles that took place between red men and white men for control of the North American

---

[10] Channing: *History of the United States*, III, 30.

[11] *Ibid.*, III, 67–71.

[12] *Ibid.*, II, 599.

[13] The student interested in Channing's career should consult not only S. E. Morison's delightful memoir of Edward Channing, already cited, but also J. A. DeNovo: "Edward Channing's 'Great Work' Twenty Years After," *Mississippi Valley Historical Review*, XXXIX, 257–74; R. A. Fahrney: "Edward Channing" in *The Marcus W. Jernegan Essays in American Historiography* (ed. W. T. Hutchinson, Chicago, 1937), pp. 294–312; Michael Kraus: *The Writing of American History* (Norman, Okla., 1953), pp. 232–41; and C. R. Fish: "Edward Channing: America's Historian," *Current History*, XXXIII, 862–7.

372 HISTORIOGRAPHY

wilderness, Herbert Levi Osgood was the historian who dwelt learnedly and in detail on the growth and evolution of the institutions brought by the English-speaking people who established colonies along the North Atlantic seaboard.[1]

It is an interesting fact that so many great American historians of the nineteenth century and early years of the twentieth were New Englanders by birth and ancestry. Osgood was a native of Maine. He was fortunate enough to attend Amherst College at a time when its faculty included such scholars and teachers as Julius Hawley Seelye, Professor of Philosophy, Anson Daniel, Morse Lecturer on Political Economy and later Professor of History and Political Science, and John William Burgess, Professor of History, Political Science, and Political Economy. The last exerted the greatest influence on Osgood. Following the example of Burgess, who had spent some two years studying in Germany, Osgood, not long after getting his Amherst degree, went to the University of Berlin for the academic year 1882–3 and worked under the leading historians there. He also came in contact with doubtless the greatest of German historians, Leopold von Ranke, then in his eighty-eighth year but busy working on his *Weltgeschichte*. Osgood adopted von Ranke's approach to historical writing as his own.[2]

Between 1883 and 1889 Osgood taught in the Brooklyn High School and was also a part-time graduate student at Columbia, working under the guidance of Professor Burgess who was now lecturing there on constitutional law and political science. Upon receiving his doctorate he went to England in 1889 to delve into the vast manuscript collections at the Public Record Office in London. He remained for fifteen months, gathering materials for what was to be his life-work, a political history of the English colonies on the North American continent. On his return to New York he joined the faculty at Columbia and by 1896 had become a full professor.

At a meeting of the American Historical Association held at New Haven in December 1895, Osgood presented a paper on "The Study

---

[1] See especially D. R. Fox: *Herbert Levi Osgood, an American Scholar* (New York, 1924); see also H. J. Coppock: "Herbert Levi Osgood," *Mississippi Valley Historical Review*, XIX, 394–403; E. C. O. Beatty: "Herbert Levi Osgood" in *The Marcus W. Jernegan Essays on American Historiography* (ed. W. T. Hutchinson, Chicago, 1937), pp. 271–93; and Michael Kraus: "Herbert Levi Osgood" in *The Writing of American History* (Norman, Okla., 1953), pp. 251–7.

[2] See Osgood's tribute to von Ranke in the review of the latter's *Zur eigenen Lebensgeschichte* in the September 1891 *Political Science Quarterly*, VI, 560–2.

of American Colonial History," in which he questioned the validity
of any account of the American Revolution that did not take into
consideration the forces that had brought the British Empire into
existence. He also expressed the view that in any study of English
expansion the "political and constitutional side . . . should be
given the first place, because it is only through law and political
institutions that social forces become in the large sense operative."
To illustrate, he referred to the "acts of trade," as "a natural and
necessary phase in the development of colonization not, as Bancroft
persists in calling them, 'a badge of servitude.'"[3] His course in
American colonial institutions was directed to that end. Students
flocked to his graduate seminar and, under his guidance, completed
some fifty doctoral dissertations in the broad field of early American
political institutions. Meanwhile, Osgood was busy with the task of
carefully outlining and writing the first part of his monumental
work, a history of the American colonies in the seventeenth and
eighteenth centuries.

The American Colonies in the Seventeenth Century appeared in
three large volumes in 1904 and 1907. It is only necessary to note
that Professor Charles M. Andrews, in reviewing Volume III in the
April 1908 American Historical Review, was impelled to state that
Professor Osgood had completed "a study of the colonies in the
seventeenth century which may justly be deemed the most important interpretation of our colonial history that has thus far been
made."[4]

The writing of The American Colonies in the Eighteenth Century
proceeded much more slowly. Osgood had earlier made clear that
the "seventy years lying between 1690 and 1760 is to a large extent
an unknown period." For, outside "the external history of the
French and Indian wars" [manifestly referring to Parkman's
achievement] "absolutely no satisfactory work of a general character
has been done."[5] While much of the source material in England for
the seventeenth century had come into print by the twentieth, at
least in calendar form, most of that for the eighteenth century still
lay in manuscript and was widely scattered. It is therefore not
surprising that Osgood—so busily engaged both in teaching and
writing (except for one period of sixteen months spent in research in

---

[3] American Historical Association Annual Report, 1898, pp. 63–6.
[4] American Historical Review, XIII, 605–9.
[5] American Historical Association Annual Report, 1898, p. 63.

London in 1909 and 1910 and a second brief sojourn there five years later)—did not live to see the publication of the last of his great labours. Yet before he passed away on September 11, 1918, he had all but completed his final work. It appeared in 1924 in four volumes under the supervision of Dixon Ryan Fox, his son-in-law. The new series, covering the history of the British North American colonies from the Revolution of 1688 to the Peace of Paris of 1763, is still by far the most complete account left by any writer of the history of the individual Thirteen Colonies for this period.[6] For purposes of organization Osgood divided this series into three parts, each with a subtitle. Part I is called "The Colonies During the First Two Intercolonial Wars, 1690–1714"; Part II, "The Colonies During the Interval of Peace Between the Second and Third Intercolonial Wars, 1714–1740," and Part III, "The Growth of the Spirit of Independence during the Period of the Third and Fourth Intercolonial Wars, 1740–1763." It is with Part III that this historiographical essay is especially concerned, although certain sections of Part II (such as, for example, the founding of the colony of Georgia) also fall within its scope.

While Osgood was primarily concerned in his series with treating the development of each of the Thirteen North American Colonies and paid very little attention to the growth of the British Empire elsewhere, he does place a good deal of emphasis on the role of the British executive authority in imperial affairs. Nevertheless, quite missing is the sort of stress on the strained relations between the mother country and the colonies between the years 1740 and 1763 that one might have expected in view of the announced central theme of Part III, "The Growth of the Spirit of Independence. . . ." In considering this criticism of *The American Colonies in the Eighteenth Century*, it must be borne in mind that Osgood did not live to complete the work and that had he done so it would have included, we are informed, a chapter on American slavery together with other chapters comparing the institutions of the British continental colo-

---

    [6] Charles M. Andrews, in reviewing *The American Colonies in the Eighteenth Century* at some length, criticized certain aspects of it. Nevertheless, he very properly called it "a really great work, which within its limits is a veritable encyclopedia of accurate knowledge and commentary concerning eighteenth century [American] colonial history . . ." (*American Historical Review*, XXXI, 533–8). The British historian H. E. Egerton stated in his review that, within the limitations the author set for it, "*The American Colonies in the Eighteenth Century* shows a high-water mark of learning and of luminous judgement which will secure for it a place among the classics of American history" (*English Historical Review*, XLI, 132–3).

nies with those of the British West Indies and with Ireland, as well as a final summary chapter of comparable breadth to the excellent chapter that concluded his *The American Colonies in the Seventeenth Century.*[7]

Further, there is reason to believe that Osgood's final goal was to write a series of volumes upon a subject that seems to have interested him more than any other, but which he felt could not be wisely undertaken until the colonial background up to 1763 had been completed. This was the American Revolution.[8] Here he would, of necessity, have concentrated on the more purely imperial relations between Great Britain and the colonies. However, we are not left in the dark about his views on the great event and as these views are so fundamentally different from most writers who preceded him and many others who came after him, it is important that they be mentioned here.

In the September 1887 *Political Science Quarterly* Osgood contributed an article on "England and her Colonies." Its object in dealing "with the constitutional relations existing between England and her colonies" was "to show that the supremacy of king and Parliament over them was complete," and that this control "was exercised in every department of government activity, judicial, legislative, ecclesiastical, military; that the right of the mother country to this control was uniformly asserted until the fortune of war compelled her to acknowledge America as an independent nation." The English colonies "were colonies of the English crown; their inhabitants were its subjects. The true doctrine of sovereignty and allegiance necessitates this conclusion." But by the Revolution of 1688 these Crown powers were transferred by statute from the King acting alone to "the King in Parliament" in so definite a manner "as never afterwards to be seriously called in question." Before this transfer of Crown power, while there "were ample precedents for the exercise of the rights of British sovereignty in America . . . those rights had not yet been called into the fullest operation. Their legitimacy however was in general fully acknowledged by the colonists." Colonial society, by reason of the great liberty permitted in establishing governments, developed freely and in a manner "far different from anything which existed in the mother country.

---

[7] D. R. Fox: *op. cit.,* pp. 102–3.

[8] This was the view of Professor Fox, the fellow historian who knew Osgood most intimately; see *ibid.,* pp. 59–60.

. . . In this divergence of social organization and interests, as between the colonies and the mother country, lay the germ which might develop into resistance on the part of the plantations, if at any time England should attempt to enforce her rightful supremacy over them." In Puritan New England especially, the theory of the social contract gradually developed. Such a theory was consistent with the facts and aims of a democratic form of government. The theoretical basis of the "American revolution, as truly as the French, was the outgrowth of the doctrine of natural rights and social contract." The "unconstitutionality of parliamentary taxation without representation was that in a state of nature no one could be deprived of his property without his consent. Were it otherwise, men would be slaves. Such a proceeding therefore is a breach of the law of nature, and no law of society can make it just." In the words of the Massachusetts General Court in 1765: " 'there are certain essential rights of the British constitution of government, which are founded in the law of God and nature, and are the common rights of mankind.' The path between this and the 'unalienable rights' of the Declaration of Independence is direct." This theory of government held by colonials was revolutionary—"one under which no government can be successfully carried on. When they came to erect a government of their own, they had to abandon it." Osgood concludes his article in the following words: "The theory as well as the action of the colonists was revolutionary." [9]

Charles McLean Andrews (1863–1943)

Charles McLean Andrews is undoubtedly the greatest master of the materials basic to an understanding of early British colonial

---

[9] *Political Science Quarterly*, II, 440–69.

That Osgood continued to maintain this position is indicated by his article "The American Revolution," which appeared in the March, 1898, number of the *Quarterly*. In it he argued that "the American leaders, as soon as they awoke to a realizing sense of the power which lay at the centre of the old constitution of the British Empire, demanded a new constitution, one in which Parliament by solemn agreement and enactment should set a definite limit to the exercise of its powers. But in their argument and in their acts they ignored the fact that Parliament had never set any such limit, and they conducted themselves as if they were already living under the new constitution which they desired. Hence arose the revolutionary character of their argument . . . " (*Political Science Quarterly*, XIII, 41–59).

history produced by America so far. His chief interest lay in political institutions. No other person in Great Britain, the United States, or elsewhere ever remotely challenged him in his mastery of his chosen field.

Born in Wethersfield, Connecticut, of Puritan ancestry, Andrews studied at Trinity College in his native state, and did his graduate work at Johns Hopkins, where he received his doctorate in 1889. His commitment to institutional studies was evident early in his career, doubtless as a result of the emphasis placed upon such studies by Herbert Baxter Adams and others under whom he worked. Adams had been trained in Germany and had introduced the seminar method of instruction at Johns Hopkins. Out of this seminar came Andrews's first publication, a study of local institutions called *The River Towns of Connecticut: A Study of Wethersfield, Hartford and Windsor*, which appeared in 1899 in the *Johns Hopkins Studies in History and Political Science*. Then began a connection with Bryn Mawr College which continued until in 1907, when he returned to Johns Hopkins to take the place of his former teacher, Adams, who had passed away. But his stay in Baltimore was only temporary, for in 1910 he accepted the chair of Farnam Professor of American History at Yale. There he continued his multifarious historical activities until his retirement in 1933.

During his graduate studies Andrews came closely in touch with the work of the so-called Teutonic school of historians. These men saw a very direct connection between early Germanic institutions and those of England and later of America, a connection which Andrews however rejected, as is indicated in his study, *The Old English Manor*, published in 1892 in the *Johns Hopkins Studies*. Passing over other works that do not bear directly upon the period of this historiography,[1] we come to the *Guide to the Manuscript Materials for the History of the United States to 1783, in the British Museum, in Minor London Archives, and in the Libraries of Oxford and Cambridge*, prepared by Andrews in cooperation with Frances G. Davenport and published in 1908 by the Carnegie Institution of Washington. This invaluable contribution to historical scholarship was followed in 1912 by *The Colonial Period*, a little book rich in content but popular in form, which broke with previous writings in

---

[1] For a list of the principal writings of Andrews see "Charles McLean Andrews: A Bibliography," compiled by George Wilson Pierson and Leonard W. Labaree with the aid of Andrews, *William and Mary Quarterly*, 3rd ser., I, 15–26.

this field by giving equal attention to the island colonies of Great Britain before 1775 and to the American continental colonies. In that same year the Carnegie Institute brought out Volume I of Andrews's *Guide to the Materials in American History, to 1783, in the Public Record Office of Great Britain;* Volume II followed in 1914. This work was of outstanding importance, not only as a calendar of the vast contents of this repository covering the specified years, but also for the illuminating essay that prefaced each separate division of the manuscript collections. Every subsequent serious student of American colonial history is indebted to Andrews as a result.

But Andrews did not limit his interest simply to the study of political institutions. In a paper on "Colonial Commerce" presented before the American Historical Association in 1913 he called attention to the importance of commerce, which "yields to no other phase of our history in the influence it has exercised upon the life of the period to which it belongs." [2] That same year in a paper entitled "Anglo-French Commercial Rivalry, 1700–1750, The Western Phase," presented before the International Congress of Historical Studies and later expanded for publication in the *American Historical Review,* he drove home the point that the "rivalry between England and France is perhaps the most conspicuous feature of eighteenth-century history from 1700 to 1763." That this rivalry was based largely upon commercial considerations and involved commercial supremacy as an objective on the part of each country, he illustrated amply and in detail. [3] In 1918 the Colonial Society of Massachusetts (*Transactions,* XIX) published his "The Boston Merchants and the Non-Importation Movement," in which he traced the activities of "the Society for encouraging Trade and Commerce within the Province of Massachusetts Bay" from its founding in 1763 to 1768, and disclosed how the more radical Boston element gained the upper hand during the mounting American crisis. In this connection he showed the impact on other colonies—especially at the American ports south of Boston—of the weapon of non-importation of goods from the mother country, as the Massachusetts Bay merchants exercised their leadership. [4] It should be mentioned that

---

[2] *American Historical Review,* XX, 43–63.
[3] *Ibid.,* XX, 539–56, 761–80.
[4] The Colonial Society of Massachusetts *Transactions,* XIX, 159–259; also reprinted by the Harvard University Press, Cambridge, Mass., 1917.

1918 was the very year that Arthur M. Schlesinger published his notable *The Colonial Merchants and the American Revolution,* which in much greater detail confirmed Andrews's findings.

Andrews also expressed an interest in social history. In 1919 his *Colonial Folkways: A Chronicle of American Life in the Reign of the Georges* appeared as a volume in *The Chronicles of America* series. In this compact, small volume we find the first general account of the way of life of American colonials—high, low, and middle class in social order—their dress, dwellings, and diversions, their intellectual and religious proclivities, their means of livelihood and of intercommunication.

Further, turning aside from his more institutional studies, he produced in 1924 (revised in 1931) *The Colonial Background of the American Revolution: Four Essays in American Colonial History,* his most important contribution to an understanding of the growth of those forces—including the divergent attitudes of the British on the one hand and the American colonials on the other—which from Andrews's point of view made the American Revolution inevitable. Although lacking footnotes, bibliography, and index, this statement of his views, confirmed by long and deep study of source material drawn from both sides of the Atlantic, can still be read with great profit. It was supplemented by his address delivered as President of the American Historical Association in 1925: "The American Revolution: An Interpretation," [5] which strongly justified the movement that led to the revolt of the American colonies. It ended with the statement: "The American revolutionists had an ideal of living; it can hardly be said that in 1776 the Englishmen of the ruling classes were governed in their colonial relations by any ideals that were destined to be of service to the future of the human race." Indeed in this address Andrews almost excelled Bancroft in his castigation of the government of Great Britain. But it seems to have been true that after the American Revolution British policy towards the remaining colonies, as well as toward those that subsequently came into existence, was not radically altered for a considerable period of time. Yet there was no additional movement for revolt within the Empire and no marked evidence of discontent. As Robert Livingston Schuyler pointed out: "The American Revolution did not, however, cause the British Government to abandon the commercial principles of the old

---

[5] *American Historical Review,* XXXI, 219–32.

colonial system or to adopt a more liberal policy of colonial government; much less did it cause it to favor the independence of
Britain's remaining colonies." [6] Again one may ask: Was it basically
colonial discontent with British policy rather than the loosening of
the bonds of loyalty—as the result of the outcome of the Great War
for the Empire—that brought about the shattering of the Old British
Empire?

In referring to the period 1754 to 1765 George Louis Beer wrote:
"In the annals of the British Empire during this decade, the most
vital fact was the conquest and subsequent retention of Canada. It
made the American Revolution inevitable." [7] Here is a factor that for
some unexplained reason Andrews ignored. Was it not true that
British colonial policy in its broad outlines did consider the welfare
of the colonies? Is it not fairer to say that the flexibility with which
British administration of the colonies functioned had enabled the
North American colonies in particular to experience an amazing
growth in population, in wealth, and in political experience, as the
result of the large measure of self-government accorded to them?

In Volume I of *The Cambridge History of the British Empire*
(published in 1929) two very pertinent chapters were written by
Andrews, the only American contributor. Entitled "The Acts of
Trade" and "The Government of the Empire, 1660–1763," these
chapters displayed his great mastery of the intricacies of the British
colonial institutional history of the seventeenth and eighteenth centuries. They are still of major importance to students of this period.[8]

It should also be pointed out that from the time of his acceptance
of the teaching post at Yale until his retirement, Andrews devoted
much energy to guiding his large group of graduate students in their
studies. In addition he was involved in a variety of other activities.
After his retirement he at last felt sufficiently free to concentrate his
attention on his dream of writing a detailed history of the colonial
period. According to his master plan, it was to be a work in seven
volumes covering the entire period of English colonization in the
New World down to 1776.[9] In 1934 he brought out Volume I of *The*

---

[6] *The Fall of the Old Colonial System: A Study in British Free Trade, 1770–1870*
(London & New York, 1945), p. 67.
[7] *British Colonial Policy, 1754–1765* (New York, 1907, 1922 edn.), p. 313.
[8] *The Cambridge History of the British Empire* (Cambridge & New York,
1929), I, 268–99, 405–36.
[9] See C. M. Andrews: "On the Writing of Colonial History," *William and Mary
Quarterly*, 3rd ser., I, 27–48, which outlined in detail the projected history. This

Colonial Period of American History, carrying the subtitle "The Settlements," a subtitle also employed for Volumes II and III published respectively in 1936 and 1937. Of these three volumes, Andrews said that he had limited his "field of observations to the period from the founding of Jamestown to the overthrow of the proprietary governments" [10]—a period falling largely within the seventeenth century and therefore not germane to this historiographical essay. Mention may be made, however, of the award to his work of the Pulitzer Prize in 1935 and, in 1937, of the gold medal given by the National Institute of Arts and Letters for writings of distinction in the fields of biography and history. In 1938 came Volume IV of the series, subtitled "England's Commercial and Colonial Policy." Once again Andrews went back to the beginnings of English colonization in the New World; while his chief emphasis was on the origins of this policy in the seventeenth century, he gave a great deal of attention to the maturing of it in the eighteenth. This is therefore a work that should not be neglected by those interested in how the British Empire was governed during the second half of this century or by those concerned with various aspects of mercantilism as a system. At the same time it is not an easy book to read, since it is addressed—along with the first three volumes—primarily to the specialist in colonial history. In all these volumes Andrews wrote from the standpoint of one viewing colonial history from London.

Unhappily, Andrews made no progress beyond Volume IV of the series because of physical incapacitation. In Volume V he had planned to "show colonial life in the eighteenth century in its manifold varieties" and thereby to uncover "trends and divergencies indicating a progressive movement . . . of what may be called an Americanizing process." Volume VI would have dealt with "certain very important political aspects" of the period from 1700 to 1763, including among other things the growth in power of the colonial assemblies; and Volume VII with the course of events from 1763 to 1776, when open conflict developed as the result of the conflicting

---

article was published after Andrews had passed away; in fact, it was his desire that it should not be published until after his death. See *ibid.,* I, 27n. Andrews's students were aware of his projected history many years before he could embark upon it. The author of this historiographical essay had the privilege of completing his graduate studies under the guidance of Andrews, who was an inspiring, generous, but exacting teacher. In conversation with him in 1918 about his contemplated series, he spoke of being "not as yet ready" to undertake it.

[10] *The Colonial Period of American History: The Settlements* (New Haven, 1937), III, 326.

issues of local "self-government on one side, and centralization on the other."

In summarizing the work of Charles M. Andrews, it may be said that he brought to it the application of a highly refined and exacting historical methodology, as well as an unrivalled knowledge of the sources of colonial history. He recognized fully that no exposition, no interpretation, of past events could be definitive. In the Preface to his *The Colonial Background of the American Revolution* he had stated: ". . . I bring this brief survey of the subject to the attention of my fellow workers in the field of American history, fully aware of the tentative character of many of its conclusions." The constant revision he made of his other contributions to colonial history shows that this attitude was basic to his approach. The impressive extent of his achievement lies in his attempt to uncover a past that is at best difficult to establish even in part. His care in distinguishing between ascertainable, attested facts as against the legendary and the uninformed statements of contemporaries; his insistence also that the history of the colonies founded by England in the New World must not be approached as mere background for the history of the American nation but rather as a projection of English civilization—these are among Andrews's chief claims to greatness as an institutional historian.[11]

George Louis Beer (1872–1920)

Professor Curtis Nettels, in an important study published in the September 1933 *New England Quarterly,* affirmed with reluctance that "the writings of G. L. Beer have probably exerted a greater influence in shaping modern views of British colonial policy than the works of any other historian." [1] This estimate has been heartily endorsed by other scholars.

---

[11] Among other accounts of the career of Andrews the scholar see A. S. Eisenstadt: *Charles McLean Andrews: A Study in American Historical Writing* (New York, 1956), and also "Charles McLean Andrews" in *Some Modern Historians of Britain: Essays in Honor of R. L. Schuyler* . . . (New York, 1951) pp. 215–34; Leonard W. Labaree: "Charles McLean Andrews: Historian, 1863–1943," *William and Mary Quarterly,* 3rd ser., I, 3–14; and Lawrence H. Gipson: "Charles McLean Andrews and the Re-orientation of American Colonial Historiography," *Pennsylvania Magazine of History and Biography,* LIX, 209–22.

[1] *New England Quarterly,* VI, 491–512. The title of Professor Nettel's article is "The Place of Markets in the Old Colonial System."

Beer, the son of a well-to-do New York tobacco importer, was born on Staten Island. At the age of sixteen he was ready to enter Columbia College, where he secured his baccalaureate in 1892. He returned to take graduate work with the faculty of political science, where John W. Burgess, Herbert L. Osgood, and E. R. A. Seligman were the dominating scholars. His master's thesis was published in 1893 as a volume in the Columbia University *Studies in History, Economics and Public Laws* under the title *The Commercial Policy of England toward the American Colonies.*[2] It was an outstanding piece of scholarship, especially for a man but twenty-one years of age.

The Commercial Policy of England . . . was written with so much discriminating judgement and such a spirit of detachment toward one of the most important and difficult themes in English colonial history that it is still recognized as an authoritative statement. This is so despite the fact that it leaned wholly upon printed material, as attested by the footnotes and the bibliography, and that it has certain shortcomings. For example, in stating that the English mercantile system "was a policy of unconscious ignorance, not of conscious malice,"[3] Beer committed himself to a position—that mercantilism was born out of ignorance—which is sustained neither by his later writings nor by the writings of such historians as Charles M. Andrews or Lawrence A. Harper. The same may be said of his statement in the concluding chapter: "Up to 1763 England acted consistently on a false, but historically justifiable, economic principle."[4] Granted that mercantilism as it evolved into an accepted principle of statecraft during the seventeenth and eighteenth centuries is not regarded as acceptable state policy in the twentieth century, neither is the institution of feudalism nor that of monarchy as it existed at an earlier time in English history; but this does not prove that the institutions did not play a vitally important role in the development of England. Beer places the dividing line between the period when the chief reliance of the British government was on mercantilistic principles and when its reliance on political principles began at the year 1763. This date can be strongly defended, as it has

---

[2] The Beer study was reprinted in 1948 as a separate volume by the New York firm of Peter Smith.

[3] *The Commercial Policy of England toward the American Colonies* (New York, 1948 edn.), p. 9.

[4] *Ibid.*, p. 144.

been by Professor Charles M. Andrews,[5] but to the writer of this series the date 1749 is more acceptable as marking the fundamental reorientation of British colonial policy.[6]

For the next ten years after the publication of *The Commercial Policy of England* . . . Beer devoted most of his talents to his tobacco import business (although part of the time he also lectured in history at Columbia). He was so successful at this enterprise that he was able to retire at the age of thirty-one. He then turned again to the study of British policy toward the colonies. To gain some deeper insight on the subject, he spent over a year in London at the Public Record Office, delving into the vast manuscript collections there. Upon his return to New York he determined to deal first of all with those aspects of this policy that represented a fundamental shift from the earlier purely mercantilistic approach. From this, in 1907, came his *British Colonial Policy, 1754–1765*, a study of the period from the beginning of the Great War for the Empire to the repeal of the Stamp Act. Although Beer wrote in the Preface of this book that his plan was to treat "the entire subject" of British policy, "apart from the controversies of the American Revolution," he felt impelled to deal with the preliminaries of the revolutionary movement.[7] His reason for stopping short of the year 1775 is given in the summary of the contents of the volume: "The question of defence was predominant throughout the transitional years from 1754 to 1765, and gives a certain unity to the period. . . . The controversies that led ultimately to the American Revolution, grew out of this military question, and . . . the inherent difficulty of creating an efficient and equitable system of defence in a decentralized empire." [8] This development was inevitable in view of the virtual breakdown of the requisition system (treated in full in Chapter 4). In this connection, especially in the light of charges that he was biased in favour of the British, it should be made clear that Beer held no brief either for British policy or against the colonial position. To him, "the fundamental question at issue [in 1765] was the political independ-

---

[5] *The Colonial Period of American History* (4 vols., New Haven, 1934–8), IV, 426.

[6] See L. H. Gipson: "Acadia and the Beginnings of Modern British Imperialism," *Essays in Modern English History in Honor of Wilbur Cortez Abbott* (Cambridge, Mass., 1941), pp. 177–202.

[7] *British Colonial Policy, 1754–1765* (New York, 1907, reissued in 1922), Preface v–vi.

[8] *Ibid.*, p. 314.

ence of the American colonies. . . . This movement [for independ-
ence] came into violent conflict with British imperialism, whose aim
was to increase the administrative efficiency of the Empire. Both the
British and the colonial ideals were justifiable from their respective
viewpoints, each one being in harmony with one of the two underlying tendencies in modern historical evolution." [9] He also stressed the
point that the movement for American political independence was
inevitably bound up with another historical event of great importance—the conquest and subsequent retention of Canada, bringing
with it the insoluble problem of providing equitably for North
American security.[10] Further, Beer found that during the period
surveyed in *British Colonial Policy* an important change took place
in British commercial policy. For, after analyzing the "purely commercial regulations of the years 1764 and 1765," he wrote: ". . . it is
apparent that their aim was to encourage and not to restrict colonial
industry." [11] Yet this change in policy in no wise checked the revolutionary movement, which in his opinion came about not primarily
from economic considerations but rather as the result of disputed
rights. As to the *right* of Parliament to tax the colonies, he stated:
"From the legal standpoint, this view was unassailable. It was somewhat vulnerable from the historical standpoint, as Parliament had
hitherto not exercised all its legal power, notably that of taxation. It
[Parliament], however, totally failed to take into account that the
colonies were growing to political maturity, and that they resented
the idea of subordination implied in the doctrine of parliamentary
supremacy." [12]

In his review of *British Colonial Policy, 1754–1765*, in the July
1909 *American Historical Review*, Charles H. Hull of Cornell University [13] pointed out that the book differed radically both in method
and in viewpoint from all other works concerned with the same
period, and added that these "differences, with scarcely an exception, are to Mr. Beer's credit and to his reader's profit." Here, based
on a systematic examination of the records, was the attitude of those

---

[9] *Ibid.*, pp. 314–15.
[10] *Ibid.*, p. 313.
[11] *Ibid.*, p. 226.
[12] *Ibid.*, pp. 311–12.
[13] The review was signed simply with the initials C. H. H. However, Professor Hull
was himself deeply concerned with British colonial policy and was the logical person
to review the book; see the American Historical Association *Annual Report for 1908*,
I, 121.

responsible for the welfare of the British Empire during this critical period of British history, presented with great fullness and fairness. The study of how they discharged their responsibility was "a work which needed to be done . . . it needed to be done as Mr. Beer has done it, in a spirit of sympathetic appreciation for their difficulties, but not of blind acquiescence in their conclusions." So highly did Hull rate the work as a contribution to historical knowledge that he concluded his review with the statement that "upon its own direct subject, it is not only unrivalled but unapproached by any one." [14]

In 1908 Beer published his *The Origin of the British Colonial System, 1578–1660,* which again showed his mastery of sources and ability to interpret them.[15] This work was followed in 1912 by *The Old Colonial System, 1660–1754. Part I, The Establishment of the System, 1660–1688,* which appeared in two volumes in 1912. It was also well received, although the reviewers made it clear that Beer, in concentrating on the purely economic aspects of the British system, had neglected political and other considerations.[16] Nevertheless, the volumes were so highly regarded by scholars that they received the Loubat Prize in 1913 (for the best original work published in the English language on the history, geography, archaeology, ethnology, philology, or numismatics of North America during the preceding five years). With this work completed, Beer faced the task of filling in the gap between the years 1688 and 1754, which he planned to do in some four or more volumes. Although he gathered much material and prepared the first drafts of a considerable number of chapters, his interest was deflected by the outbreak of the First World War and a call to activities of a public service nature, which seemed at the time much more important to him. As a result,

---

[14] *American Historical Review,* XIV, 817–19. W. L. Grant, Professor of Colonial History at Queen's University, Ontario, Canada, praised the work highly but at the same time expressed the feeling that Beer "in his reaction against the school of Bancroft, . . . does rather more than justice to the mother country and rather less to the colonies" (*English Historical Review,* XXIII, 371–3).

[15] See C. M. Andrews's review in *American Historical Review,* XIV, 808–10.

[16] See C. M. Andrews's review in the *American Political Science Review,* VII, 509–11, that of W. T. Root in the *American Historical Review,* XVIII, 798–800, and that of O. M. Dickerson in the *Political Science Quarterly,* XXVIII, 515–17. H. E. Egerton, Beit Professor of Colonial History at Oxford, has the following comment to make on Beer's writings: "Few writers have deserved better of those interested in colonial history than Mr. Beer. Concentrating from the first upon a single aspect of the subject, he has brought to bear upon it so much learning and research that it is not too much to say, in spite of brilliant treatment of particular portions of the subject by Professor Ashley and others, that the establishment, development, and operation of the English economic colonial system has first found in him its serious historian" (*English Historical Review,* XXVIII, 573–6).

the great study that was to have comprehended a review of the English colonial system from 1578 to 1765 was never completed. Beer died on March 15, 1920, at the age of forty-eight.[17]

Claude Halstead Van Tyne (1869–1930)

Claude Halstead Van Tyne, like Sydney George Fisher, dedicated himself to presenting the American Revolution in a new light based not upon traditional interpretations but upon an impartial evaluation of all obtainable evidence.

Although Van Tyne began his career in the business world, he gave up his post as a bank cashier at about twenty-three to enter the University of Michigan, from which he received his baccalaureate in 1896. During the academic years 1897 to 1898 he studied abroad at Heidelberg, Leipzig, and Paris. On his return he entered the graduate school of the University of Pennsylvania, where he won his doctorate in 1900. His dissertation appeared in print two years later under the title *The Loyalists in the American Revolution*. Although criticized by Victor Coffin (not unjustly) as a "loosely arranged group of essays, in texture often rather chatty, without adequate framework, not showing full grasp of the material nor effective synthetic power," [1] the work cannot be dismissed lightly since it is really the first important attempt to give a unified account of the struggles and fate of a large segment of the population of the North American colonies.

In 1903 Van Tyne returned to the University of Michigan as

---

[17] It may be noted in passing that members of the Department of History at Columbia University, as well as Professor E. R. A. Seligman and others anxious to salvage for the scholarly world as much as possible of Beer's unfinished study, sought in vain to secure funds that would facilitate the editing and publication of those portions of the manuscript that might have been placed in final form. It may also be added that the author of this series was requested to serve as editor for this project and had tentatively agreed to do so. For studies on Beer the scholar and public servant see *George Louis Beer: A Tribute to His Life and Work in the Making of History and the Moulding of Public Opinion* (New York, 1924), contributed by a number of leading American and English admirers of his work; see also Grace A. Cockroft: "George Louis Beer," *Some Modern Historians of Britain: Essays in Honor of R. L. Schuyler* . . . (New York, 1951), pp. 269–85; Arthur P. Scott: "George Louis Beer" in *The Marcus W. Jernegan Essays in American Historiography by His Former Students* (Chicago, 1937), pp. 313–22; and Michael Kraus: "George Louis Beer," *The Writing of American History* (Norman, Okla., 1953), pp. 257–60.

[1] *American Historical Review*, VIII, 776.

assistant professor and within two years had contributed *The American Revolution, 1776–1783* as Volume IX of *The American Nation* series. In the first chapter of this book he sought to summarize the causes of the War for American Independence. Reflecting on the disputes that arose between Great Britain and the older North American colonies between 1761 and 1775 as the result of the growing divergencies in their points of view respecting colonial rights, he stated: "It is plain to-day that the only way to keep up the nominal union between Great Britain and her colonies was to let them alone. The colonies felt strongly the ties of blood, interest, and affection which bound them to England. . . . They [also] felt only the normal adult instinct to act independently. Could the British government have given up the imperial idea to which it so tenaciously clung, a federal union might have been preserved." [2] As the result of his writings and other qualifications, Van Tyne was made a full professor and head of the Department of American History in 1906 and was later appointed head of a united Department of History.

To the October 1913 *American Historical Review* Van Tyne contributed an important article entitled "Influence of the Clergy, and Religious and Sectarian Forces, on the American Revolution." In this paper he sought to present "all those causes, remote and immediate, of the American Revolution" which were traceable to this influence. Although he had set himself a task far too ambitious for a single paper, he managed to emphasize forcefully the role played by the American Congregational and Presbyterian clergy in creating among their congregations and colonials in general a climate favourable to rebellion against the King and Parliament. In discussing the causes for the American Revolution, he voices his opinion "that the historical muse has been too much of a worldling, and has worshipped too partially the golden calf of economic causes." To support this position, in his conclusion he says: "Conflicting political ideas, and not tea or taxes, caused the American secession from the British empire, and the Puritan clergy had a large part in planting the predominant American political ideas which were antagonistic to those dominant in England." [3]

Owing to his occupation with various professional responsibilities, it was not until 1922 that Van Tyne was able to put into print the first volume of what was designed to be his life-work, under the

---

[2] *The American Revolution, 1776–1783* (New York & London, 1905), p. 17.
[3] *American Historical Review*, XIX, 44–64.

serial title: *A History of the Founding of the American Republic.*
This first volume, called *The Causes of the War of Independence,*
was not so much the work of independent research that might have
been expected as a highly useful summary of others' labours. As
Arthur M. Schlesinger noted in the January 1923 *American Historical Review:* "Had the present volume appeared twenty years ago, it
would have created a sensation and have marked an epoch in American historiography. Appearing, however, in the year 1922, its chief
service is to correlate and synthesize the results of special researches
into Revolutionary history made by a host of students in the intervening period, and, by showing the essential harmony of their conclusions, to give to their findings a new validity." [4] *The Causes of the
War of Independence* leans heavily upon Clarence W. Alvord's
Mississippi Valley in British Politics, Arthur M. Schlesinger's *Colonial Merchants and the American Revolution,* and the constitutional
writings of Andrew C. McLaughlin, among others.[5]

The people of the colonies, Van Tyne states, had been permitted
for over a century to develop ideas incompatible with imperial
restraints. Quoting with approval Horace Walpole's statement that
at the close of the War with France in 1763 the English ruling class,
"born with Roman insolence," was behaving with "more haughtiness
than an Asiatic monarch," [6] Van Tyne asserts that it was "in this
spirit that the English rulers undertook to set bounds to the independence already won, [and] to establish a system of real British
control in America." [7] Of the British conception of the constitutionality of the sovereignty of Parliament throughout the Empire, Van Tyne writes: "Such a position left the colonists to
accept subordination to an absolute government or to deny the
authority of Parliament altogether." [8] Yet, while granting the British
position on the omnipotence of Parliament as the legal embodiment
of political power, he arrives at the conclusion that George III was

[4] *Ibid.,* XXVIII, 327–9.

[5] See the excellent article by P. G. Davidson, Jr., on Van Tyne in *The Marcus W.
Jernegan Essays in American Historiography* . . . (Chicago, 1937), pp. 339–53.

[6] *The Letters of Horace Walpole* (ed. Mrs. Paget Toynbee, 19 vols., Oxford,
1903–1925), VII (1904), 365.

[7] *The Causes of the War of Independence* (Boston & New York, 1922), p. 85.

[8] *Ibid.,* p. 222. In an important article entitled "The Background of American
Federalism," Professor Andrew C. McLaughlin of the University of Chicago wrote, in
1918, that Englishmen "asserted the indivisible character of legislative power, and
almost at once took a position which, if insisted on in practice, left nothing to the
colonists but a choice between acceptance of an absolute government at the head of a
centralized empire on the one hand, and the total denial of all parliamentary
authority on the other" (*American Political Science Review,* XII, 228).

the master mind who determined the fate of the British Empire. With the disappearance of the Duke of Grafton as the chief minister, he maintains, the King instead of seeking the aid of Chatham or Rockingham turned to Lord North, who "did his master's bidding, not only then, but for a dozen years thereafter, at the cost of dismembering the British Empire, and the eternal blackening of his own reputation." [9] In terminating the volume Van Tyne further clarifies his thesis on King George's responsibility in these terms: "It was the failure of a Parliament, corrupted by George III, to heed the warning of England's greatest living statesmen, Burke and Pitt and Fox and Camden and Barré, that brought about the rending of the empire." Yet, admitting that the King's position reflected the current opinion of the politically active majority in England who opposed the great minority statesmen, he adds: "The nation was, therefore, on the eve of disaster, as any nation is like to be when its greatest minds and characters are forced to defy and to try to defeat the convictions of a majority of their countrymen." Nevertheless, in his concluding sentence, while stating that the "British Empire was doomed to be broken asunder," he now finds it "brought to that disaster by the insistent demand of Englishmen in America for the full enjoyment of those liberties which England had fostered beyond any other country of the world." [10]

In 1929 the second volume of the projected trilogy was published: *The War of Independence; American Phase* . . .[11] This carried the history of the war from Lexington to the creation of the French Alliance by the Continental Congress. Although this study is beyond the scope of this historiography, it should be noted here that it is unquestionably the best book produced by Van Tyne, for it displays a far greater mastery of the source material—he drew, for example, upon the great manuscript resources of the William L. Clements Library on the University of Michigan campus—and a far greater degree of independent historical judgement. In recognition of its merits he was awarded the 1930 Pulitzer Prize in History. Unhappily, it came to him posthumously; for on March 21, before the announcement of the award, he had passed away.

---

[9] *The Causes of the War of Independence*, p. 273.
[10] *Ibid.*, p. 478.
[11] *The War of Independence; American Phase, Being the Second Volume of a History of the Founding of the American Republic* (Boston & New York, 1929).

Carl Lotus Becker (1873–1945)

At the time he was working, no historian exemplified more fully the application of scientific techniques to the writing of history than Carl Becker (the name he preferred to use). But Becker himself would have repudiated the idea that he was a "scientific" historian.

Carl Becker was born on an Iowa farm in Black Hawk County. His parents were solid, hard-working, prosperous people whose outlook was conventionally orthodox. After a year at Cornell College at Mount Vernon, Iowa, he transferred to the University of Wisconsin and in 1896 received his bachelor's degree. He was fortunate to have spent his undergraduate days in the environment of such members of the faculty as the historians Frederick Jackson Turner, Charles Homer Haskins, and Victor Coffin, a Canadian, under all of whom he studied. But Turner's influence on his intellectual orientation was especially profound. As Becker himself later expressed it, "I, like I know not how many other lads of nineteen, was straightway a devoted disciple and questionless admirer of 'old Freddie Turner.' I didn't care *what* he offered. For him I would even study history." [1]

Yet, except in one essay on Kansas, Becker never followed his master into the field of American westward expansion or into analysis of the influences of the advancing frontier upon American life and institutions. After two years of graduate work in history at Wisconsin, he held a fellowship at Columbia, where he worked under Herbert L. Osgood, John W. Burgess, and James Harvey Robinson; but he returned to Wisconsin for his doctorate, received in 1907. So much for his formal education. He taught at Pennsylvania State College (now Pennsylvania State University), Dartmouth, the University of Kansas, and the University of Minnesota, before becoming John Stambaugh Professor of European History at Cornell University in 1917, a post he occupied for the remainder of his working career.

---

[1] Carl Becker: "Frederick Jackson Turner" in *American Masters of Social Science* . . . (ed. H. W. Odum, New York, 1927), p. 276; see also Carl Becker: *Everyman His Own Historian: Essays on History and Politics* (New York, 1935), p. 194.

Becker's first important contributions to history came in 1901 with his articles in the *American Historical Review* for that year: "Nominations in Colonial New York" and "Growth of Revolutionary Parties and Methods in New York Province, 1765–1774." [2] These were followed in 1903 by his "The Nomination and Election of Delegates from New York to the First Continental Congress, 1774" in the *Political Science Quarterly*.[3] What he sought to describe in these articles was the transition of the government of the Province of New York from "a virtual aristocracy to a democracy in the middle and last half of the eighteenth century." [4] These brief studies, which showed great maturity for a young man still in his twenties, were later revised and embodied in his doctoral dissertation: *The History of Political Parties in the Province of New York, 1760–1776*, published by the University of Wisconsin Press in 1909 as a volume in its history series. Professor Arthur M. Schlesinger of Harvard, in a Foreword prepared for the edition re-issued in 1906, wrote: "It is seldom that a doctoral dissertation becomes a minor classic of historical literature, but *The History of Political Parties in the Province of New York, 1760–1776* by Carl Becker, written over fifty years ago, is still a seminal work for students of the American Revolution . . . in research method as well as in content, objectivity and interpretation it is a model of what a work of historical scholarship should always strive to be."

But even this remarkably fine book has been challenged at fundamental points. For example, Becker took the position that during the colonial period in New York provincial politics were controlled by a few powerful families closely linked by marriage and that the political parties were based not so much on differences of political or economic principles and practices as on personal loyalty—citing in this connection the rivalry of the de Lancey and Livingston groups. Again, according to Becker, the principal instrument of political control in New York was based on the economic relations of tenant to proprietor, as the result of which the tenants voted in accordance with the wishes of the great landed proprietors. Professor Milton M. Klein of Long Island University has questioned the validity of each of these propositions in a carefully documented paper, "Democracy and Politics in Colonial New York," [5] which should be read side by

---

[2] *American Historical Review*, VI, 260–75, and *ibid.*, VII, 56–76.
[3] *Political Science Quarterly*, XVIII, 17–46.
[4] *American Historical Review*, VI, 260.
[5] *New York History*, XL (July, 1959), 221–46.

side with Becker's *History of Political Parties in the Province of New York, 1760–1776*. Klein also challenged another fundamental thesis put forward by Becker: that the Revolution was fought not only for home rule but to determine who should rule at home. An indirect comment on this Becker thesis was also made by Professor Richard B. Morris of Columbia University in a brilliant paper first presented at a gathering of the Conference on Early American History and later printed in the January 1962 *William and Mary Quarterly* under the title "Class Struggle and the American Revolution." In this study Morris did not limit himself to an examination of the course of events in only one colony but dealt with all the colonies and arrived at the following conclusions: "We did not declare our independence of George III in order to reform the land laws, change the criminal codes, spread popular education, or separate church and state. We broke with England to achieve political independence, freedom from external controls, emancipation, if you will, of the bourgeoisie from mercantilist restraints. . . . If in its origins and common purpose the American Revolution was an anti-colonial war fought for independence and national identity, it was also marked by liberative currents, class conflicts, and egalitarian urges." [6]

In 1915 Becker contributed to *The Riverside History of the United States* his delightful volume *Beginnings of the American People,* only the second part of which covers the period embraced in this historiography. Although based on available printed materials and devoid of footnotes, the book represents the efforts of a first-class philosophical mind to present an interpretation of the War for American Independence. The same comment may be applied to his *The Eve of the Revolution: A Chronicle of the Breach with England,* also devoid of footnotes, which appeared in 1918 as a volume in *The Chronicles of America* series. As Becker explains in the Preface, this is not so much a history of the period between 1763 and 1776, as a book in which he "chiefly endeavored to convey to the reader, not a record of what men did, but a sense of how they thought and felt about what they did."

Doubtless Becker's most important contribution to colonial history was *The Declaration of Independence: A Study in the History of Political Ideas.* Published in 1922, it had reached its sixth printing by 1956. In various illuminating chapters the Declaration is

---

[6] *William and Mary Quarterly,* 3rd ser., XIX, 3–29.

considered from the angle of the philosophy of natural rights, from that of the theory of the British constitution, and from that of the political philosophy of the nineteenth century. Becker notes that of the premises for the position taken by the colonial leaders in 1774, the two major ones were: "(1) that all men have imprescriptible natural rights; (2) that the British empire is a voluntary federation of independent states." The basis for the first premise, he points out, was the wide-spread belief in natural rights held in the eighteenth century. As to the second premise, he has this comment to make: "In order to find a logical defense of their activities, American patriots were forced, in successive stages of the controversy, to restrict the authority of Parliament over the colonies more and more, until the act of separation made it necessary for them to deny that it had any authority over them at all." While giving the Declaration high praise as one of the great historic documents of the eighteenth century, Becker felt that it contained flaws. In suggesting that its "style is always a bit fragile," he asks "is it not because the thought is a bit fragile also, too easily satisfied with what is open and visible, and therefore lacking in depth and subtlety, ignoring all that must be ignored if the life of man is to be understood and described, even with the felicity of genius, at the level of common sense?" [7]

Passing over other writings, such as his brilliant *The Heavenly City of the Eighteenth-Century Philosophers* (published in 1932), we must mention his presidential address before the American Historical Association in 1931, "Everyman His Own Historian," which became the title-piece of a volume of essays in 1935 (cited in the first footnote of the present sketch). In this address Becker made his case against the so-called "scientific" historians, whose ideal in approaching their work was that of absolute detachment; he also strongly defended and aligned himself with the so-called "relativists" among students of history—that is, those stressing the pragmatic approach to the truth of the past and emphasizing the fact, implicit in this approach, that what they wrote was based upon the climate of opinion prevailing in their time. [8]

---

[7] *The Declaration of Independence. A Study in Political Ideas* (New York, 1956), pp. ix–x and xiv–xv.

[8] Maurice Mandelbaum in his *The Problems of Historical Knowledge* (New York, 1938) attacked the historical relativism of Becker and of other writers, especially Croce; Becker's review of this book in the *Philosophical Review*, XLIX, 361–4, defended his own position on relativism but indicated that he had modified it in some respects. For further searching criticism of the relativist attitude toward history see

It is clear that Becker showed little interest in the field of institutional history. His importance as a historian, in fact, lies in the emphasis that he placed upon people as individuals, and their ideas on contemporary events and the past, whether or not these ideas were correct. If the measure of his influence on historical writing may be gauged by the number of studies that have attempted to analyze the significance of his approach to history, then his influence has been considerable. Yet, like his great teacher and life-long inspiration, Frederick Jackson Turner, his own output was relatively modest. Nevertheless, among American historians perhaps only Turner's writings have received more serious attention than those of Carl Becker.[9]

Clarence Walworth Alvord (1868–1928)

The entire period of Clarence Walworth Alvord's creative life as a scholar was devoted to analyzing and portraying the development of the great Mississippi basin in the eighteenth century. No one else has treated the subject on so large a scale.

B. J. Loewenberg's "Some Problems Raised by Historical Relativism," *Journal of Modern History*, XXI, 17–23, and W. H. Coates's "Relativism and the Use of Hypothesis in History," *ibid.*, XXI, 23–7. These two papers were read at the 1947 meeting of the American Historical Association. In 1956 came a much more direct attack upon Becker's approach to history: Perez Zagorin's "Carl Becker on History. Professor Becker's Two Histories: A Skeptical Fallacy," *American Historical Review*, LXII, 1–11, in which Zagorin questioned the following statements by Becker: "Let us then admit that there are two histories: the actual series of events that once occurred; and the ideal series that we affirm and hold in memory. The first is absolute and unchanged—it was what it was whatever we do or say about it; the second is relative, always changing in response to the increase or refinement of knowledge" (*Everyman His Own Historian*, p. 234). Zagorin concluded his study by stating that "the motive of two histories will not survive criticism, and that if we wish to speak intelligibly, we can speak only of one history, that for which there is evidence." But Leo Gershoy in the same issue of *American Historical Review* (pp. 12–17) came strongly to the defence of Becker.

[9] For Becker see especially George H. Sabine: "Carl Lotus Becker," an essay introducing Becker's *Freedom and Responsibility in the American Way of Life* (New York, 1945); Charlotte Watkins Smith: *Carl Becker: On History and the Climate of Opinion* (Ithaca, N.Y., 1956); Cushing Strout: *The Pragmatic Revolt in American History: Carl Becker and Charles Beard* (New Haven, 1958); and Burleigh Taylor Wilkins: *Carl Becker: A Biographical Study in American Intellectual History* (Cambridge, Mass., 1961), which also contains a full bibliography of Becker's writings and related works.

Born in Greenfield, Massachusetts, educated at Phillips Academy, Andover, and at Williams College, with two years at Friedrich Wilhelm University in Berlin and part of a year at the University of Chicago, Alvord became identified with the University of Illinois in 1897 at the age of twenty-nine. There he spent his most fruitful years. Beginning as an instructor in the preparatory division, he slowly advanced in rank and responsibility. In 1901 he became an instructor in history in the university proper and in 1913 finally attained the rank of full professor, a position he retained until he resigned in 1920 to accept a chair in history at the University of Minnesota. However, he forsook his post at Minnesota after three brief years to go abroad. This was not only for reasons of health but also in order to have access to the vast manuscript collections in London that would enable him to proceed with his plan for continuing his work on the history of the Mississippi Valley. Unfortunately, he made all too little progress on this project before his death in 1928 at Diano Marina on the Italian Riviera.[1]

Alvord's deep involvement in the history of the Old West—that is, the West of the colonial period—can be dated from 1905. In that year he was sent by the State Historical Library of Illinois into the area of the eighteenth-century French settlements bordering the Mississippi River in what was earlier known as the Illinois country. There, in the courthouse of Belleville, he discovered two large collections of records in French relating to the villages of Cahokia and Kaskaskia. His appointment as general editor of the Library's historical collections followed and during his editorship some fourteen volumes of the *Collections* of the Illinois State Historical Library were published. In 1907 the *Cahokia Records* appeared as a volume in this series, buttressed by an extensive and illuminating Introduction prepared by Alvord. Of especial interest and value for the period under consideration in this historiography are Volumes X, XI, and XVI of the *Collections* (issued respectively in 1915, 1916, and 1921 as Volumes I, II, and III in the so-called "British Series"). They consist of documents concerned with the Illinois country, and carry the titles: *The Critical Period, 1763–1765; The New Regime, 1765–1767;* and *Trade and Politics, 1767–1769.* All three volumes

---

[1] See Marion Dargan, Jr.: "Clarence Walworth Alvord" in *The Marcus W. Jernegan Essays in American Historiography*, pp. 323–38, and especially Solon J. Buck: "Clarence Walworth Alvord, Historian," *Mississippi Valley Historical Review*, XV, 309–20.

were carefully edited by Alvord with the assistance of Clarence E. Carter, who had taken his doctorate at Illinois and was at the time a professor of history at Miami University in Ohio. Each volume was provided with an Introduction, critical footnotes, an excellent index, and, if the document was in French, a parallel translation in English. In support of this scholarly activity, the University of Illinois Historical Survey had already been created, of which Alvord was made the director. Further, in 1913, in order to celebrate fittingly the first century of Illinois as a state in the American Union (1818), the Illinois Centennial Commission appointed him editor-in-chief of the *Centennial History of Illinois,* published in five volumes. Volume I, written by Alvord himself, was subtitled, "The Illinois Country, 1673–1818." When it appeared in 1920 it was widely and fittingly acclaimed. Meanwhile in 1912, in collaboration with Lee Bidgood, Alvord had brought out *The First Explorations of the Trans-Allegheny Region by the Virginians, 1650–1674,* and the following year, when the Mississippi Valley Historical Association launched the *Mississippi Valley Historical Review,* Alvord became its managing editor, a post he held until 1923.

One might have thought that Alvord would have been content with these responsibilities. But in 1917 he brought out two volumes of what he hoped would be his most important contribution to historical literature: *The Mississippi Valley in British Politics: A Study of the Trade, Land Speculation, and Experiments in Imperialism Culminating in the American Revolution.*[2] This impressive pioneering effort sought to illuminate the role of the trans-Appalachian West in British politics between the years 1763 and 1774. Very properly, in view of the complexity of the many problems that faced him and the vast quantity of original material that demanded evaluation, Alvord wrote with due modesty in the Preface: "It is not to be expected that I have always followed the best trace, or that I have never pointed out a closed trail for the true road, but it is my hope that the journal of my explorations may assist later discoverers and that in the end the true connection between British politics and the Mississippi Valley may be made known." While many historians since 1917—particularly such writers as V. W. Crane, R. A. Humphreys, Sir Lewis Namier, John Brooke, R. A.

---

[2] See Professor O. G. Libby's review of *The Mississippi Valley . . .* in the *Mississippi Valley Historical Review,* IV, 131–3.

Billington, J. R. Alden, and J. M. Sosin—have modified and corrected a number of Alvord's statements and have challenged certain of his points of view, the work was an important pathmaker for other scholars and as such, in the eyes of a committee of historians, amply merited the Loubat Prize. Yet the title of the book is misleading in its implication that British politics, as related to the Mississippi Valley, culminated in the American Revolution. The late Carl Becker, although he praised the book, wrote: "Professor Alvord often implies that the connection [between British politics concerning the West and the Revolution] was important; but I confess not to have understood very well what he thinks the precise nature of that connection was" [3]—a statement that others who have read the book could echo. It is clear, again quoting Becker, that Alvord did not have "what some people would call the synthetic mind." Further, in view of the emphasis placed upon parts of the Old British Empire lying outside the Mississippi Valley, such as the Province of Quebec, the title is not sufficiently comprehensive.

It may be said in conclusion that Alvord's place in the historiography of the period is certainly an honourable one, especially in view of his excellent work as an editor and the stimulus his various scholarly activities gave to a generation of young historians. As evidence of this high respect the Mississippi Valley Historical Association created the Clarence Walworth Alvord Memorial Commission, dedicated to the furtherance of studies relating to the West, from which in 1942 appeared a volume concerned with missionary activities in the old Northwest: *Documents Relating to Northwest Missions, 1815–1827*, edited by Grace Lee Nute and published for the Commission by the Minnesota Historical Society.

Thomas Jefferson Wertenbaker (1879–1966)

A native of Virginia, born at Charlottesville, Thomas Jefferson Wertenbaker has embodied in his writings the finest traditions of the enlightened Southerner. His undergraduate and graduate in-

---

[3] *American Historical Review*, XXII, 671–4.

struction was received at the University of Virginia, where he was awarded his doctorate in 1910. Before gaining his Ph.D, however, he had spent a year as editor of the *Baltimore News,* had then served for two years as associate professor of history and economics at the Agricultural and Mechanical College of Texas, and another year as instructor in American history at his *alma mater.* After 1910 his professional career was chiefly identified with Princeton University, where he passed successively through the various ranks and in 1925 attained the chair of Edwards Professor of American History, a chair he held until he became a professor emeritus in 1947. It may also be noted that he was editor of the New York *Evening Sun* from 1918 to 1923, was visiting professor at the University of Göttingen in 1931, and in 1939–40 and again in 1944–5 was Harold Vyvyan Harmsworth Professor of American History at the University of Oxford.

Wertenbaker's contribution as a historian falls largely in the field of seventeenth-century American history, especially such works as *Patrician and Plebeian* (1910), *Virginia Under the Stuarts, 1607–1688* (1914), *The First Americans* (which is Volume II of *A History of American Life,* 1927), *Torchbearer of the Revolution: The Story of Bacon's Rebellion and Its Leader* (1940), *The Puritan Oligarchy: The Founding of American Civilization* (1947), *Bacon's Rebellion, 1676* (1957), and *The Government of Virginia in the Seventeenth Century* (1957). However, many of his other books— such as *The Planters of Colonial Virginia* (1922), *The American People. A History* (1926), *Norfolk—Historic Southern Port* (1931), *The Founding of American Civilization: The Middle Colonies* (1938), *The Old South: The Founding of American Civilization* (1942, reissued in 1963), *Princeton, 1746–1896* (1946), *Father Knickerbocker Rebels: New York City during the Revolution* (1948), *The Golden Age of Colonial Culture* (1949, last reprinted in 1963), and *Give Me Liberty: The Struggle for Self-Government in Virginia* (1958)—throw much light on the period under survey in this series and especially on social and economic developments.

In *The Planters of Colonial Virginia,* Chapter 8, "Beneath the Black Tide," Professor Wertenbaker analyses both the social and economic consequences of the institution of Negro slavery on eighteenth-century Virginia. His thesis is that one looks in vain for the very important yeoman class of farmers which in the seventeenth century had cultivated the soil and prospered in the colony. For, in the face of slavery, this yeoman group either migrated from Virginia to other colonies or to the frontiers, or sank in poverty to become "poor white trash," or rose to the level of the gentry by acquiring slaves. The dominant role of the yeoman farmer in the seventeenth century is characterized as follows (p. 59): "Prior to the slave invasion which marked the close of the Seventeenth century and the opening of the Eighteenth, the most important factor in the life of the Old Dominion was the white yeomanry." But this thesis on the earlier importance of the yeoman was challenged by a fellow Virginian, Philip Alexander Bruce, who contended (in the April 1923 *American Historical Review*) that even in the seventeenth century the "social importance of the yeoman, like his economic, was altogether numerical. He had none in the ordinary sense of the word." [1] Yet the picture drawn in *The Planters of Colonial Virginia* of the unhappy effects of the spread of slavery, with the increase in luxury and the disdain of manual labour among the white population, is a memorable one.

Honoured with the name of one of the great founders of the American nation, Professor Wertenbaker views the history of the period with which this historiography is concerned much as his great namesake saw it. The following examples of this viewpoint are embodied in his *The American People*. In describing George III he writes (p. 51): "Of simple habits, industrious, chaste, religious, he might have served his kingdom well but for his determination to restore the despotic power of the Crown." Again, in describing how the King turned to George Grenville in carrying out this objective in the colonies, he adds (p. 52): "Reactionary, precise, of great industry and little vision, Greenville was just the man to lash the Americans into obedience." Moreover, he says, George III found his main support in the Tories when pursuing his colonial policies and (p. 56): "The passage and repeal of the Stamp Act was but an incident in the clash between two systems—the despotic system of the English Tories and the liberal system of America." Therefore with the passage of the Townshend Acts the "colonists now realized that England was determined to crush their liberties" (*ibid.*).

One of Wertenbaker's most notable achievements was his study of the transit of European civilization to North America. The first volume to appear in this series was *The Founding of American*

---

[1] *American Historical Review*, XXVIII, 552-3.

Civilization: The Middle Colonies. Professor Leonard W. Labaree wrote appropriately of this interesting book: "It is a striking evidence of the originality of the author's thought and of the vitality of American historiography in general that a period already covered by several excellent multiple volume histories can receive a further extensive treatment so fresh and so illuminating." [2] In demonstrating that the New World environment and culture affected the Old World civilization brought to the Middle Colonies by the settlers, this study illustrates the results most fully by showing the modifications produced in architecture.

An even more important contribution to our knowledge of colonial culture in the period before the American Revolution is to be found in Wertenbaker's *The Old South: The Founding of American Civilization.* While this study ranges from the seventeenth century to well into the nineteenth, it is especially valuable for correcting many popular misconceptions of the civilization in the South. For example, he stresses the existence of five distinct cultural areas (p. 9): "the tobacco country, the rice and indigo country, the mercantile belt, the naval stores and timber belt, and the back country"—each sharing close economic ties but with interests and ways of life that were in many respects in marked contrast. In this work he also emphasizes the importance of the fact that the yeomen of Virginia outnumbered the great aristocratic planters in the 1760's and 1770's by as much as twenty-five or more to one in such Piedmont Counties as Prince William and Culpeper. Nevertheless, little is said about the life of the yeoman, while that of the planters of the Chesapeake area is portrayed with great charm and depth. It was the group of great planters, he argues, who were the chief landwasters and most responsible for the perpetuation of the curse of slavery; this group also not only dominated the social life of Virginia but was entrenched in the central government at Williamsburg as well as in the local government at county and parish level.

In harmony with the spirit of this volume is Wertenbaker's informative *The Golden Age of Colonial Culture,* a small book embodying lectures delivered at New York University on the Phelps Foundation. In it he analyses the level of culture at Boston, New York, Philadelphia, Annapolis, Williamsburg, and Charleston, covering the period from the middle of the eighteenth century to the out-

[2] *Ibid.,* XLIV, 344–6.

break of the War for American Independence. He is especially enthusiastic about the culture of Annapolis, Williamsburg, and Charleston, has praise for that of Philadelphia, less for that of New York, and least for that of Boston.

In *Father Knickerbocker Rebels* Professor Wertenbaker concentrates upon the history of New York City between the years 1765 and 1783. He tells a fascinating story which (in the words of E. Marie Becker of the New York Historical Society) "reconstructs the scene in all of its fullness and interprets the life of the people as if he were a contemporary." [3] Yet it is a one-sided story. The heading of Chapter 1, "Liberty Assailed," gives the theme of the book. The description of the constitutional relationship of the colonies to Great Britain would be accepted by few students today versed in the history of the British Empire in the eighteenth century. For example, writing of the year 1765 (p. 3) he states that American colonials "had established what in time became thirteen semi-independent little republics, each ruled by an elective Assembly. For Parliament, in which they were not represented, to attempt to govern the colonies at this late date, was to render these Assemblies nullities and reduce the people to slavery." Again, referring to the people of New York, he asserts (*ibid.*) that the "right of being taxed only by themselves was 'fundamentally interwoven' in their constitution." Still further, in dealing with the Sugar Act of 1764 (p. 5), he contends that "when Prime Minister George Grenville decided to collect the duties and sent a bevy of revenue vessels to America to prevent smuggling, the colonial merchants faced ruin." Nor does he explain why the Ministry and Parliament felt, upon the conclusion in 1763 of the war with France, that it would be proper to require the colonials to make an additional contribution to the support of the Empire beyond that made as the result of the navigation and trade restrictions.

This failure to set forth more than the American patriotic side of the conflict between those in authority in Great Britain and the colonials is also evident in another delightful book, *Give Me Liberty: The Struggle for Self-Government in Virginia,* most of which is devoted to the history of Virginia before the middle of the eighteenth century. In writing of the outcome of the Great War for the Empire Professor Wertenbaker presents an interesting point of

---

[3] *Pennsylvania Magazine of History and Biography,* LXXIII, 399–401.

view (p. 207): "It has often been said that had the French power in
America not been broken, the colonists would not have dared to
rebel against Great Britain. It would be more to the point [to say]
that if the French threat had not been removed the British government would not have dared to drive the Americans into rebellion."
But can this contention be easily defended? Assuming that the
French had won the war—and thereby had consolidated their position west of the Appalachians and had continued to hold in alliance
the powerful, warlike Indian tribes that could be let loose at any
moment against the British colonial settlements—would there have
been an American rebellion, even if the British government had
then insisted that the Americans make some specific contribution to
the British Treasury for their own defence? Is it likely, further, that
they would have sought an alliance with the French against a
government seeking to protect what remained of their once great
land claims? Again, in what sense did Professor Wertenbaker use
the word "supreme" in the following statement with reference to the
year 1763 (p. 216): "The [Virginia] Assembly, after a century and a
half of battling with Kings and Governors, had made itself to all
intents and purposes supreme" when its acts were disallowed by the
Privy Council (as were ten of those passed in 1748)? Did the
Assembly deny the right of the King's government to nullify a
Virginia law until some years later?

But such challenges as may be made to Professor Wertenbaker's
interpretation of political events must not obscure the rich legacy of
cultural history which he left to the world.

Oliver Morton Dickerson (1875–   )

Oliver Morton Dickerson was fortunate enough to have pursued
both his undergraduate and graduate studies at the University of
Illinois at a time when its prestige for historical studies was very
high. Not only was Clarence Walworth Alvord there, busily engaged in his investigation of the history of the Old West, but Evarts
Boutell Greene (author of *The Provincial Governor in the English
Colonies of North America* [1898] and *Provincial America, 1690–*

1740 [1905]) was still Dean of the College of Literature and Arts and only later went to Columbia University as DeWitt Clinton Professor of History. The quality of training that Dickerson received may well be judged by his doctoral dissertation which, when rounded out, was printed in 1912 under the title *American Colonial Government, 1696–1765: A Study of the British Board of Trade in its relation to the American Colonies, Political, Industrial, Administrative.* The significance of this work was immediately recognized. In a review of it Professor Charles M. Andrews wrote: "Dr. Dickerson has written a book of first importance for the study of American colonial history"; and added that the multifarious phases of the work of the Board of Trade were handled "with skill and scholarly acumen." [1] In fact *American Colonial Government, 1696–1765* represents perhaps the most comprehensive and judicious assessment of the work of the Board of Trade in relation to the American colonies for the specified years that exists; it still stands as an authoritative guide, despite the excellent work in the same field of such other scholars as the late Professor A. H. Bayse and Professor Mary P. Clarke. [2] The heart of Dickerson's study has to do with how the tradition of American political liberty grew and "how, athwart all the schemes for the enlargement of imperial control, rose the colonial assemblies with their resistless, creeping encroachments upon the prerogative" (Preface, p. 13). Dickerson found that the trade policy of the Board was not "excessively narrow, but was intended to make the colonies and the home country mutually helpful to each other industrially. . . . To this end it favored bounties, drawbacks, discriminating tariff duties, and the expenditure of money for popular instruction in new and promising enterprises." Again, in describing the Board's responsibility for making recommendations to the Privy Council to be used as a basis for its decisions in reviewing colonial legislation, he states, the Board "was not arbitrary or tyrannical, but acted with the judicial fairness of a court of first instance" (Resumé, pp. 364–5). Thus Dickerson's early work embodied an understanding of, and a not unsympathetic attitude toward, the problems of administration of the expanding British Empire.

---

[1] *American Economic Review*, II, 613–15.

[2] A. H. Bayse: *The Lords Commissioners of Trade and Plantations. . .*, *1748–1782* (New Haven, 1925); see also Mary Patterson Clarke: "The Board of Trade at Work," *American Historical Review*, XVII, 17–43, and the Introductions to the Board of Trade *Journals*.

It was not until 1936, a quarter of a century after his first book, that Dickerson made his next contribution to the historiography of the period under review. This was his *Boston under Military Rule, 1768–1769: As Revealed in "A Journal of the Times,"* a compilation of articles dealing with day-to-day incidents in Boston. Secretly prepared by a small group of extreme radicals, these accounts were first sent to New York for publication in Holt's *New-York Journal, or, the General Advertiser,* and then, after also appearing in Philadelphia in the *Pennsylvania Chronicle,* were printed in the *Boston Evening-Post.* Although reviewers pointed out the danger of accepting such propaganda at face value,[3] Dickerson contended that the accounts were in the main truthful. He did however admit that there were exaggerations and that they were prepared with "almost diabolical cleverness" for the purpose of stirring the American public against British rule. In 1939 Dickerson's interesting and valuable chapter on "Writs of Assistance as a Cause of the Revolution" appeared in *The Era of the American Revolution. Studies Inscribed to Evarts Boutell Greene* (ed. Richard B. Morris). In this essay he treats the 1761 controversy in Massachusetts Bay over writs of assistance as but an "interesting episode" in the history of that colony, rather than as the beginning of the American crisis; for his emphasis is on the opposition of the American courts to attempts to use these writs in the colonies south of Massachusetts after the passing of the Townshend Acts in 1767. In 1947 Dickerson supplemented this study by commenting in the *William and Mary Quarterly* on a document indicating the role played by the Attorney General of Massachusetts Bay, Jonathan Sewall, in protecting John Hancock's boat the *Lydia* from seizure for allegedly bringing to Boston harbour goods not covered in the manifest.[4]

By 1949 Dickerson had turned in another direction with his publication in the September *New England Quarterly* of "England's Most Fateful Decision."[5] This had to do with the determination of the government of Great Britain to set up a board of American Customs Commissioners. Dickerson advanced the thesis that this board "in

---

[3] For critical reviews of the book see "W. L. B." in the *English Historical Review,* LIII, 364–5; A. M. Schlesinger in the *New England Quarterly,* X, 386–7; M. W. Jernegan in the *Mississippi Valley Historical Review,* XXIV, 381–3; and T. S. Anderson's brief comment in the *American Historical Review,* XLIII, 218.

[4] "Opinions of Attorney General Jonathan Sewall of Massachusetts in the Case of the *Lydia,*" *William and Mary Quarterly,* 3rd ser., IV, 499–504.

[5] *New England Quarterly,* XXII, 388–94.

seven short years dragged with it the inevitable political separation of most of the colonies under its control from the rest of the Empire" (p. 391). This short piece was followed in 1951 by *The Navigation Acts and the American Revolution*. The book is divided into two parts: "Part One. The Cement of Empire" and "Part Two. Dissolving the Cement of Empire." The viewpoints of Part One had been essentially embodied in his *American Colonial Government*, but were now re-enforced by an abundance of data indicating that, in its actual functioning, the eighteenth-century British trade and navigation system was a source of strength and prosperity to the continental colonies and was accepted by the inhabitants in this light. The thesis of Part Two is that this beneficent system was altered in 1764 by "a new plan of regulating colonial trade for revenue purposes, which resulted in a change in the constitutional relations of the colonies to the home country" (p. 190). But the chief damage done to the old cement of Empire as the result of the new revenue legislation, according to Dickerson, was caused between "the years 1768 and 1772 by the tactless, arbitrary, and mercenary operation of these laws by a new race of customs officers and particularly by the conduct of the American Customs Commissioners at Boston" (p. 208). This period Dickerson describes as "The Era of Customs Racketeering"—the title he gives to Chapter 9. The impression left by the author is that the older legally-minded, self-restrained customs officers had given place to those seeking "plunder" by securing "personal profit from customs extortions" (p. 210). But the question remains, who were the racketeers, those who made their fortunes bribing customs officers or the venal customs officers? Although rich in statistical data and penetrating in analysis, the book should be used with caution, especially in view of its emotional, *ex parte* marshalling of evidence.[6] The same caution, unhappily, must be applied to the three articles that he wrote after the publication of *The Navigation Acts and the American Revolution*. They are entitled: "British Control of American Newspapers on the Eve of the

---

[6] For reviews of *The Navigation Acts and the American Revolution*, see L. H. Gipson in the *American Historical Review*, LVII, 687–90; G. H. Guttridge in the *English Historical Review*, LXVII, 585–6; E. S. Morgan in the *William and Mary Quarterly*, 3rd ser., IX, 262–4; S. E. Morison in the *New England Quarterly*, XXV, 266–8; and Aubrey Land in the *Mississippi Valley Historical Review*, XXXIX, 104–5. The student should also read the thoughtful letter to the editor by Irvin Mark in the *William and Mary Quarterly*, 3rd ser., IX, 588–91, which calls into question the validity of the thesis embodied by Professor Dickerson in this study.

Revolution," "The Commissioners of Customs and the 'Boston Massacre,'" and "Use Made of the Revenue from the Tax on Tea," and appeared respectively in the *New England Quarterly* for December 1951, September 1954, and June 1958.

Arthur Meier Schlesinger (1888–1965)

Arthur M. Schlesinger, a first-generation American born in Xenia, Ohio, to a family with a deep love of books, received his baccalaureate from Ohio State University in 1910. While a student there working under Dean George Wells Knight, he developed a deep interest in history. To pursue this interest he enrolled in the graduate school of Columbia University, where he enjoyed a fellowship for two years. Returning to Ohio State as an instructor in history, he advanced to the rank of full professor before leaving in 1919 to become head of the Department of History at Iowa State University. He remained in this position until 1924, when he was named Francis Lee Higginson Professor of History at Harvard, a post he held until in 1954 he became a professor emeritus. In the course of his career as a historian (primarily of the national period) he made many contributions to the advancement of historical studies in the United States, especially in the field of social history.[1]

While a student at Columbia, Schlesinger had the opportunity to work in the seminar on colonial history conducted by Professor Herbert L. Osgood, who had already published his *The American Colonies in the Seventeenth Century* and was engaged in research on and the writing of *The American Colonies in the Eighteenth Century*. Out of this relationship with Osgood and his particular field of interest appeared in 1913 Schlesinger's "Colonial Appeals to the Privy Council," published in two issues of the *Political Science Quarterly*. The article showed an excellent grasp of institutional

---

[1] Professor Schlesinger is the author of a most interesting and instructive autobiography, *In Retrospect: The History of a Historian* (New York, 1963). For a review of it by one of his former students, Cushing Strout, see the *American Historical Review*, LXIX, 868–9.

history.[2] It was followed five years later by the publication of Schlesinger's doctoral dissertation, *The Colonial Merchants and the American Revolution, 1763–1776.* Issued in 1918 as one of the Columbia University's *Studies in History, Economics and Public Law,* this work has proved his most important contribution to colonial history. Of it Professor Charles M. Andrews commented in the October 1918 number of the *American Historical Review:* "In his elaborate study of the colonial merchants and the American Revolution, Professor Schlesinger has made the most important original contribution to colonial history that we have had in a long time. His work is noteworthy not only for the light which it everywhere throws on the events of the pre-Revolutionary period, but also for its value as a model of creative research." Andrews also stressed that Schlesinger "approached a very large and important task with energy, and courage, and enthusiasm, and has handled the data which he has collected not only with insight and understanding but also with remarkable firmness, fairness, and dispassionate judgment." [3] Not the least of the merits of the book is its thorough examination, evaluation, and wise integration of a wide variety of sources. Moreover, the account in it of the so-called "Association" promulgated by the Continental Congress in 1774 is by far the most complete and, all in all, the most satisfactory that we possess.

As the title of the book indicates, emphasis is placed upon the situation in which the colonial merchants found themselves as the result of the legislation affecting the colonies passed by the Parliament of Great Britain from 1763 to 1776. These laws were enacted not only for the purpose of more strictly regulating American trade but also with the idea of providing a fund through the taxation of the colonials whereby the latter would make some contribution, in the first instance, to the costs of providing for colonial defence and, later, in order to strengthen the independence of the executive and the judiciary in those colonies where they were held in subservience to the colonial Assembly. Professor Schlesinger wisely refrained from sweeping generalizations about the position taken by the merchants in the growing crisis. As a body they were, he noted, opposed to the Sugar Act and the Stamp Act; but in face of the violence of

---

[2] *Political Science Quarterly,* XXVIII, 279–93, 433–50. This study may still be read with profit although it has been largely superseded by Joseph Henry Smith's book published in 1950 on *Appeals to the Privy Council from the American Plantations,* with an Introductory Essay by Julius Goebel, Jr.

[3] *American Historical Review,* XXIV, 104–5.

the radicals, especially during the crisis of 1765 to 1766, many drew back; when finally compelled to make a choice between revolution and loyalty to the Crown, hundreds chose exile rather than be a party to rebellion.

On the situation facing the merchants during the critical years 1764 and 1765, Schlesinger had this statement to make, the first portion of which may be questioned: "Threatened with bankruptcy by the parliamentary legislation of 1764–1765, the merchants of the commercial provinces were the instigators of the first discontents in the colonies."[4] He repeated this in a paper presented before the American Historical Association in 1918, "The American Revolution Reconsidered," but modified it to state that as the result of the Grenville legislation bankruptcy was threatening "the great mercantile houses of Boston, New York and Philadelphia."[5] Moving ahead to the year 1773, Schlesinger emphasized in both the book and the address that the merchants were motivated to take the lead in opposing the Tea Act by the fear that the East India Company would establish a monopoly in the sale of tea.[6] But a recent detailed study of the trade of one of these cities, *The Maritime Commerce of Colonial Philadelphia* by Arthur L. Jensen, casts doubts on this thesis, at least so far as the Philadelphia merchants are concerned.[7]

Again, in referring to the situation after the Peace of Paris of 1763, Schlesinger says: "George III, who had ascended the throne in 1760, was already devoting every political and financial resource in his power to the task of converting the British government from an aristocracy of great Whig families into a personal autocracy. His parliament and ministers did not seek to reflect the aspirations of

---

[4] *The Colonial Merchants and the American Revolution, 1763–1776* (New York, 1918), p. 591. More recent research has challenged the view that the enforcement of the Sugar Act and the Stamp Act would have led to the bankruptcy of the merchants, as asserted by the commercial interests. See in this series Volume X, Chaps. 11 and 12.

[5] *Political Science Quarterly*, XXXIV, 61–78, especially 69.

[6] *Ibid.*, 72, and *Colonial Merchants*, pp. 262–304.

[7] After stressing the position taken by colonials that the Tea Act was designed to support a new and dangerous assumption of power by Parliament and that the action against it in Philadelphia was not by the merchants as a group but rather by the mechanics and small tradesmen, Jensen writes: "Finally, if it was the merchants who were worried by the threat of an East India Company monopoly in the colonies, it seems strange that they did not express this fear in their private correspondence. Not one merchant whose papers were used for this study even so much as mentioned a personal fear of monopoly as a reason for opposing the Tea Act" (p. 205). For a comment on the Jensen book as a reply to Schlesinger's *The Colonial Merchants and the American Revolution*, see Professor Bernard Bailyn's review in the *Journal of Economic History*, XXV, 156–8.

the British public and therefore lacked a potent incentive for the
formulation of a conciliatory program of colonial subordination." [8]
No view could be more out of line with the findings of such scholars
as the late Professor Richard Pares, the late Sir Lewis Namier, and
Namier's chief critic, Professor Herbert Butterfield, all three of
whom were persuaded by the evidence that George III was thoroughly committed to the constitutional principles of the limited
monarch—based upon the idea of the sovereignty of the King's
High Court of Parliament.[9] Nor is it evident that the British people
were not in sympathy with the program of the Grenville Ministry to
lift from their shoulders some of the financial burden of providing
for the defence of North America.

Again, speaking of William Pitt, few students of the life of this
great statesman would now agree with Schlesinger's statement: "If
his counsels had been followed by the government, it is entirely
possible that the colonial revolt might have been forestalled by
some plan of imperial federation." [10] The most that can be said of
Pitt's position was that he opposed the taxation of the colonies by
Parliament along with all measures taken by the Ministry and Parliament to enforce the collection of a revenue in the American
colonies. On the other hand, he was totally committed both to the
trade and navigation system and to the laws passed for the enforcement of this system and took the responsibility in 1760 of calling on
the navy to cooperate with the customs officers to that end. In fact,
the Pitt enforcement measures helped to bring on the American
crisis. Further, in favouring the repeal of the Stamp Act in 1766, Pitt
declared: "At the same time, I assert the authority of this kingdom
over the colonies, to be sovereign and supreme, in every circumstance of government and legislation whatsoever. . . . Taxation is
no part of the governing or legislative power." [11]

---

[8] *Political Science Quarterly*, XXXIV, 65. See also the repetition of this statement
in Schlesinger's *New Viewpoints in American History* (New York, 1922), p. 164.

[9] For Pares see his *George III and the Politicians* (Oxford, 1953); for Namier see
his *Structure of Politics at the Accession of George III* (2 vols., London, 1929), and
especially his Romanes Lecture delivered at Oxford in 1952 on "Monarchy and the
Party System" in *Personalities and Powers* (London, 1955), reprinted in *Crossroads
of Power: Essays on Eighteenth Century England,* (London, 1962); for Butterfield
see his *George III, Lord North and the People 1779–80* (London, 1949), *George III
and the Historians* (London, 1957), and especially "George III and the Constitution,"
History, XLIII, 14–33.

[10] *Political Science Quarterly*, XXXIV, 65.

[11] *Parliamentary History*, XVI, 99.

Passing over Schlesinger's other contributions to historical literature that are not relevant to this historiography,[12] we come to four excellent but brief studies that have as their theme the American colonial press and political propaganda and mob action. In 1935 appeared "Colonial Newspapers and the Stamp Act";[13] this was followed in 1936 by "Politics, Propaganda, and the Philadelphia Press";[14] in 1937 by "Propaganda and the Boston Newspaper Press, 1767–1770";[15] and in 1955 by "Political Mobs and the American Revolution, 1765–1776."[16] Then, two years later, came his masterly *Prelude to Independence: The Newspaper War on Britain 1764– 1776* (New York, 1957). As Professor Richard B. Morris stated in the *New York Times Book Review* (January 19, 1958), the book "relates with impressive documentation and keen discernment" the battle waged by the American press on the eve of the Revolution to win over to the cause of liberty the great body of uncommitted colonials. In the process of this struggle, as Schlesinger's study makes clear, any colonial press inclined to favour the government of Great Britain was given short shrift unless protected by British military forces—as Boston printer John Mein found out in 1769. *Prelude to Independence* thus forms an admirable companion piece to the *Colonial Merchants and the American Revolution, 1763–1776.*

Leonard Woods Labaree (1897–   )

Leonard Woods Labaree was born in Persia of American missionary parents. He was provided with excellent schooling for his future role as colonial historian. From the Hotchkiss School in Connecticut

---

[12] Schlesinger is the author of the well-known textbook *Political and Social History of the United States, 1829–1925* (New York, 1925, revised edns. 1933, 1941), as well as *The Rise of the City, 1878–1898* (New York, 1933), *Learning How to Behave, a Historical Study of American Etiquette Books* (New York, 1946), *Paths to the Present* (New York, 1949, revised edn., 1963), *The American as Reformer* (Cambridge, Mass., 1950), and *The Rise of Modern America, 1865–1951* (New York, 1951).

[13] *New England Quarterly*, VIII, 63–83.

[14] *Pennsylvania Magazine of History and Biography*, LX, 309–22.

[15] Colonial Society of Massachusetts *Transactions*, XXXII, 396–416.

[16] American Philosophical Society *Proceedings*, XCIX, 244–50.

he went to Williams College where he took a baccalaureate in 1920; then followed work in the Yale graduate school and a doctorate in 1926 under the guidance of Professor Charles M. Andrews. Out of Labaree's studies at Yale and research in America and England came his important work on *Royal Government in America: A Study of the British Colonial System before 1783,* published in 1930.[1] For the first time the student of institutional British colonial history was given a well-rounded view of the actual functioning of the royal provinces as units of government from 1675 (the year of the establishment of the Lords of Trade) to the close of the War for American Independence. The study deals with the island colonies as well as those in North America; further, it stresses the underlying policies held by the government on the royal provinces and the serious problems that arose in attempting to implement these policies. As a result Labaree's book not only took the place of the earlier and much more limited pioneer study by Professor Evarts Boutell Greene, *The Provincial Governors in the English Colonies of North America* (published in 1898), but was also awarded the Justin Winsor Prize by the American Historical Association; it remains the standard work in its field, despite the appearance, also in 1930, of Arthur Berriedale Keith's *Constitutional History of the First British Empire.*[2]

To honour Professor Andrews upon his retirement in 1931 from the chair of Farnam Professor of American History the *Essays in Colonial History Presented to Charles McLean Andrews by his Students* was published. Labaree, at the time an assistant professor of history at Yale, not only assumed the editorship of this volume but also furnished an illuminating essay, "The Early Careers of the Royal Governors," in which he tests out the accuracy of the charge made by General John Huske in the late 1750's that most offices in America in the gift of the Crown were filled "with broken Members of Par . . . . . t, of bad, if any, principles, pimps, valet de chambres, electioneering scoundrels, and even livery servants." By studying the careers of two hundred and fourteen men who held commissions as royal Governors, Labaree arrived at the conclusion that

---

[1] For an especially discriminating review of *Royal Government in America* see that by the British scholar R. A. Humphreys in the *American Economic Review,* XXI, 511–13.

[2] For Labaree's review of Keith's *Constitutional History* see the *American Historical Review,* XXXVI, 581–2.

most of them were "honest men, . . . no more given to riotous
living than others of their class and period, with education and
experience quite up to the standard for office holders of their day."

In 1933 the Connecticut Tercentenary Commission issued Labaree's unconventional local history of *Milford, Connecticut, The
Early Development of a Town as Shown in Its Land Records.*
Although this brief study of a typical Connecticut town is largely
concerned with the seventeenth century, it covers the eighteenth
century and even includes a reference to the twentieth. It represents
the type of institutional study designed to show the coordination of
the church and government with the land system in Puritan New
England.

In 1935 Labaree's *Royal Instructions to British Colonial Governors, 1670–1776* appeared in two volumes (as a publication of the
American Historical Association, supported by the Beveridge Memorial Fund). This is an indispensable aid to all serious students of
British colonial history. It represents a great and exacting labour,
collating over twenty thousand articles of instructions issued to the
various Governors of the royal colonies during the period under
review (except those for Newfoundland, which "followed a pattern
of their own" and therefore could not be collated with the instructions of the more typical royal colonies). Among other things the
instructions throw interesting light on the attitude of the mother
country toward the colonies. They also enable one to determine
what may be called the durable lines of British colonial policy and
those that were changed by circumstance; and to differentiate
those instructions applicable only to certain geographical areas from
others applicable to all colonies. A word of caution to the student
may be appropriate in connection with the use of the *Royal Instructions* however, for they are presented without explanation or interpretation (except for the fairly brief but excellent Introduction).
Thus there is nothing, for example, to indicate to what extent the
instructions were or could be enforced, and the student must search
elsewhere for the answers to such questions. In reviewing this work,
Charles F. Strong pointed out some of the conclusions that may be
drawn from examining the instructions: "All in all, one is impressed
with the tolerance and good will which the home government displayed in the face of colonial tendencies to evade the instructions;
and in this policy of moderation were some of the causes of the
triumph of the colonial assembly [over the prerogative of the

Crown] and of the severance of the ties between thirteen of the colonies and the mother country." [3]

Among other by-products of Labaree's study of royal government is his short but interesting article, "The Royal Governors of New England," which appeared in 1937 in the *Publications* of the Colonial Society of Massachusetts. This survey of the careers of the royal Governors from 1676 to 1775, carried out in an objective spirit, shows the Governors in a far more favourable light than that shed by such historians as Bancroft.[4] Then, in 1945, the American Antiquarian Society *Proceedings* published Labaree's "The Nature of American Loyalism," which analyzed the different types of loyalism expressed by those who refused to be party to the disruption of the Old British Empire.[5] This led in 1948 to the publication of *Conservatism in Early American History,* a study of such topics as the nature of the ruling families in colonial America; the relationship of land holding to aristocratic tendencies; the position of the great merchants of the leading seaports in relation to the artisans and small shopkeepers; the opposition of conservative clergymen to those of the clergy who sought to break down the established churches; and the part played by education and social theory in moulding the outlook of colonial America. In it Labaree considers the forces of conservatism in the American colonies during the century before the Declaration of Independence. It should be added that the volume was the product of a series of lectures supported by the Stokes Foundation and delivered at New York University in 1947.

As the result of his thorough and exacting formal training as a historian, and also by reason of his specialization in the history of the eighteenth-century British Empire, Professor Labaree is exceptionally well qualified for the task in which he is now engaged. According to arrangements entered into by Yale University and the American Philosophical Society, and with the encouragement of a generous gift from *Life* magazine, he took over the editorship of *The Papers of Benjamin Franklin* . . . in 1953; his associate editor until after the appearance of Volume V was Dr. Whitfield J. Bell, Jr., who was succeeded by Dr. Ralph L. Ketcham. In 1959 the first volume issued from the press. At the compilation of this historiography (1966) seven other volumes had appeared, bringing *The Papers* to

[3] *Journal of Modern History,* VIII, 360–1.
[4] Colonial Society of Massachusetts *Transactions,* XXXII, 120–131.
[5] American Antiquarian Society *Proceedings,* LIV (1944), Part 1, 15–58.

the end of December, 1759. Using a chronological arrangement the
editors are incorporating all the important correspondence and writings by Franklin that have come to light, as well as such letters and
other communications to him as justify inclusion. The high standards set and carried out in the editing of *The Papers* merit the
warmest praise as an achievement that will be hard to surpass. Even
in the account of the framing of the Albany Plan of Union of 1754
(Volume V, pp. 378–87), at which point Professor Labaree's interpretation differs markedly from the explanation presented by the
author of this series,[6] he shows a desire to do justice to an opposing
view. Professor Max Savelle, who has had the responsibility of reviewing the successive volumes in the *American Historical Review*,
wrote of Volume I: "This major project in historical publication is
off to a superb start."[7] It continues to maintain this high quality.

Max Savelle (1896–   )

Max Savelle, born in Mobile, Alabama, was given his training as a
historian at Columbia University, where he was both an undergraduate and a graduate student. In 1932 he received his doctorate and,
in that same year, published his *George Morgan, Colony Builder*.
This scholarly work is largely concerned with the activities of
George Morgan from 1765 to 1789—his efforts along with others to
exploit the resources of the West, particularly in the Illinois country
—and with his attempt, in what was Spanish territory at the time, to
build a colony called New Madrid on the west bank of the Mississippi. Of special value to the student of late American colonial
history is the account given of the ambitious yet financially disastrous operations in the Illinois country of the Philadelphia firm of
Baynton, Wharton, & Morgan covering the years 1765 to 1771. In
the writing of this book Savelle drew not only upon manuscript
sources available in the United States and in Great Britain but also
upon those in the Spanish Archives.

Between 1926 and 1932 Savelle served as an instructor at Colum-

---

[6] For a discussion of the Albany Plan of Union see the final pages in the Summary
of the series, Part II, of this volume.

[7] *American Historical Review*, LXVI, 170–1.

bia. He was then called to be a professor of history at Stanford University, where he remained until, in 1947, he accepted a chair in history at the University of Washington which he still holds. In 1939 he contributed "The American Balance of Power and European Diplomacy, 1713–78" to *The Era of the American Revolution: Studies Inscribed to Evarts Boutell Greene* (ed. R. B. Morris). This study deals with the balance of power among the European nations having claims to New World territory, as the colonial balance of power took its place in international law beside the older European concepts of balance of power. When this balance was lost by France as the result of the outcome of the war waged between 1754 and 1763, the only French hope of restoring it, as Savelle makes clear, was to give moral and other support to the British North American colonies in their efforts to break the ties that bound them to Great Britain. When the Comte de Vergennes became committed to this policy, the French-American military convention of 1779 and the ultimate winning of independence by the Thirteen Colonies resulted. The essay, a brief, valuable study in the field of European diplomacy, was followed in 1940 by a full-length work in the same field, *The Diplomatic History of the Canadian Boundary, 1749–1763*. This volume constitutes an important contribution to *The Relations of Canada and the United States*—a series subsidized by the Carnegie Endowment for International Peace and published by Yale University Press. The work is much broader than the title would suggest, as it brings into the picture not only the claims and counter claims of Great Britain and France to the Hudson Bay area, Nova Scotia, and the trans-Appalachian area, but also the pretensions of those two powers in the West Indies. Based upon an abundance of source materials used with great skill, it sets forth the futile attempts of the Anglo-French Joint Commission to solve the question of boundaries between the years 1750 and 1755, and the war that followed this diplomatic failure and resulted in the loss of all France's claims in North America.[1]

---

[1] For reviews see L. H. Gipson in the *American Historical Review*, LXVII, 394–5, and in the *Political Science Quarterly*, LVI, 470–1; A. B. Corey in the *Canadian Historical Review*, XXII, 323–6; and W. D. Oberman in the *Mississippi Valley Historical Review*, XXVII, 626–7. Another scholar to employ the diplomatic or what he calls the "international" approach is Professor Richard W. Van Alstyne: *The Rising American Empire* (Oxford & New York, 1960) and *Empire and Independence: The International History of the American Revolution* (*America in Crisis* series on American Diplomatic History, New York, London, Sidney, 1965); see also his shorter

Two years after the publication of *The Diplomatic History of the Canadian Boundary*, Savelle's textbook, *The Foundations of American Civilization*, came from the press. In contrast to other such works in American colonial history, it devotes much more attention to the British West Indies and to the diplomatic aspects of early American history. Economic and social phenomena are likewise stressed. One scholar, however, complained that Savelle's statement that the colonists "discarded their cultural heritage or remodeled it into a new form," could lead one to "conclude that European civilization and institutions were almost obliterated." As an example of the author's emphasis upon American uniqueness, the reviewer noted his "failure to mention English constitutional history among the sources from which the United States Constitution was drawn." [2]

Professor Savelle's most ambitious work up to the present was published in 1948 under the title *Seeds of Liberty: The Genesis of the American Mind*. With a wealth of illustrative material he surveys colonial religion, science, economic and social thought, politics, literature and the other arts, with special emphasis on the period between 1740 and 1760. During these twenty years he sees the fashioning of what he calls the American mind (as contrasted to the English or British mind) with its distinctive outlook on life. The book is enriched by illustrations and maps. It is a veritable storehouse of information and should not be neglected by any student interested in the approach of the eighteenth-century colonial to the manifold problems of living.

The thesis advanced in *Seeds of Liberty: The Genesis of the American Mind* is stated clearly in the Preface (pp. x–xi):

". . . it was the fathers of the Revolutionary generation who really formulated the American way of life for which that generation fought. The Revolution was, in fact, essentially a civil war fought for a recognition and acceptance, by the mother country and the world, of the new pattern of culture that had been established by those who

studies in the *Huntington Library Quarterly*, XXV, 1–28; XXVI, 201–33; XXVII, 311–46. Using Britain as the centre of focus, Professor Van Alstyne makes his greatest contribution in the area of the international aspects of the War for American Independence; he is less firm in his grasp of some of the details of the domestic colonial background that he touches on.

[2] C. P. Gould in the *Mississippi Valley Historical Review*, XXIX, 458–9. In 1964 a new edition of *The Foundations of American Civilization*, revised and expanded with the help of Robert Middlekauff of the University of California, came out under the title *A History of Colonial America*.

preceded the young men who made independence a practical reality: the older generation, which, while the Revolutionary generation
was still in its teens, formulated and brought to maturity the ideal of
life and liberty that those younger men were to find worth fighting
for."

In other words, the Revolutionary War was fought by colonials not
merely for freedom from taxation by the government of Great Britain, or even more broadly for freedom from interference by that
government in the ways colonials sought to make a living, but for a
much larger objective, namely, "recognition and acceptance, by the
mother country and the world, of the new pattern of culture" that
had been established in America by 1760. This is indeed a startling
explanation of the American Revolution. For the patterns of colonial
culture that had evolved by 1760 embraced not only concepts of
individual liberty but, inconsistently, concepts of perpetual slavery
embodied in local law for those colonials who were black (p. 243).
By contrast, the mother country's concepts of liberty forbad the
institution of slavery. One is therefore left to ponder the question:
Were American colonials more deeply committed to the idea of
individual liberty than the people of Great Britain? Again, granted
that the Revolutionary War in America was a civil war between
those who, as conservatives, held to the British political connection
and those who, as radicals, sought to loosen and break that connection, does it follow that colonials should readily be classified in
other respects as conservative or radical? Is it true to say that "the
reactionaries in religion and philosophy stemmed from the conservative middle class among townsmen and farmers; [while] the
radicals in philosophy and religion were apparently the poor, the
frontiersmen, and self-made men like [Ethan] Allan and [Benjamin]
Franklin" (p. 179)? These and other questions emerge as one reads
this challenging book.[3]

Professor Savelle has made other valuable contributions to the
period. In 1952 he wrote the section on "Road to Revolution" for
Problems in American History, edited by R. W. Leopold and A. S.
Lind; in 1957 he published *A Short History of American Civilization*

---

[3] For reviews of *Seeds of Liberty: The Genesis of the American Mind* see
especially L. W. Labaree in the *American Historical Review*, LIV, 609–11; E. S.
Morgan in the *Mississippi Valley Historical Review*, XXXV, 495–6; Adrienne Koch in
the *New York Times Book Review*, May 23, 1948; and L. B. Wright in the *Political
Science Quarterly*, LXIV, 315–16.

in collaboration with Tremaine McDowell; and in 1964 he produced *The Colonial Origins of American Thought,* a selection of readings from original sources to which he has added illuminating comments.

Julian Parks Boyd (1903–   )

Julian Parks Boyd was born in Converse, western South Carolina, and attended Duke University, where he received a baccalaureate *summa cum laude* in 1925 and, the following year, a master's degree. He thereupon entered the graduate school of the University of Pennsylvania as a fellow and, in addition to his course work, also acted as an assistant in the Department of History during the academic year 1927–8. Next he accepted the post of editor for the Wyoming Historical and Geological Society at Wilkes-Barre, Pennsylvania; he remained there until 1932, when he received an appointment as Director of the New York State Historical Association. He resigned this post in 1934 to accept the assistant librarianship of the Historical Society of Pennsylvania at Philadelphia and in 1935 became its Librarian as well as Editor of its publications, including the *Pennsylvania Magazine of History and Biography.* After five years (during which he made the periodical one of the most reputable American scholarly journals), he was called to Princeton University to act as Librarian and, in 1952, was appointed Professor of History there.

Boyd's first contribution to the history of the period under review here was an illuminating article, "The Sheriff in Colonial North Carolina," which appeared in the April 1928 *North Carolina Historical Review.* As editor of the Wyoming Historical and Geological Society publications, he faced a much more difficult task; for his chief responsibility was the collection and editing of the widely scattered papers relating to the so-called Susquehannah Company. This company had come into existence in Connecticut in 1753 for the purpose of settling lands within the bounds of the royal patent given to William Penn in 1681, the central third of which was considered to lie within the sea-to-sea bounds of Connecticut, as laid down in 1662 by a royal charter to this colony. The history of the controversy—which resulted in bitter contests between the Connecticut settlers in the Wyoming Valley and the Proprietors of Pennsylvania and their supporters—was presented by Boyd in four volumes, published between the years 1930 and 1933, bringing the story from the spring of 1750 down to the summer of 1772. Each volume presents a most complete documentation of the sources and contains a lengthy, carefully written Introduction, which seeks to interpret with detachment the progress and significance of one of the most notable boundary disputes in American colonial history.[1] While in the midst of this large editorial enterprise, Boyd also found time in 1931 to contribute an article on "Connecticut's Experiment in Expansion: The Susquehannah Company, 1753–1803" to the *Journal of Economic and Business History,* which carries the account of the dispute to its termination.[2]

Boyd's next contribution to the historiography of the period came in 1938 in the form of a seventy-page essay on "Indian Affairs in Pennsylvania, 1736–1762" embodied in *Indian Treaties Printed by Benjamin Franklin, 1736–1762,* a collection in facsimile of thirteen Indian treaties with a brief Introduction by Carl Van Doren. This was followed in 1941 by *Anglo-American Union: Joseph Galloway's Plans to Preserve the British Empire, 1774–1788.* As the title implies, the study is concerned neither with Galloway's life nor his political activities, but simply with a series of plans to save the Old British Empire from disruption. Boyd repeatedly refers to his subject as a conservative, but in some important respects Galloway did not play such a role—his effort, for example, to overthrow the Pennsylvania Proprietors was not the work of one who may properly be called a conservative. Nor can the plan—presented to the Continental Congress in 1774 and advocated in a major address—whereby a colonial union should be created among the Thirteen North American Colonies whose government should possess the power to annul any law

---

[1] *The Susquehannah Company Papers, Volume I, 1750–1755, Volume II, 1756–1767, Volume III, 1768–1769, and Volume IV, 1770–1772* (Wilkes-Barre, 1930, 1931, 1933). For a review of Vols. I–III see L. H. Gipson in the *American Historical Review,* XXXVIII, 338–40.

[2] *Journal of Economic and Business History,* IV, Part 1 (1931–2), 38–69. A similar article, *The Susquehannah Company: Connecticut's Experiment in Expansion,* appeared in 1935 without annotation as Tercentenary Commission of the State of Connecticut *Publications,* XXXIV. An additional study on this subject by Boyd, "New State Movements in New York and Pennsylvania," *Quarterly Journal of the New York State Historical Association,* XII, No. 3, deals with the post-revolutionary aspects of the dispute.

passed by the British Parliament relating to their affairs be called anything short of a revolutionary measure. Granted that Galloway was opposed to any steps directed toward the independence of the colonies, his virtual repudiation of the terms of the famous Declaratory Act of 1766 and his preference for giving the colonies a wide range of autonomy, free at least from interference by Parliament, would have been regarded in 1766 by such men as Rockingham, Burke, and even Pitt as an extremely radical proposal. It was still a decidedly radical proposal in 1774.

If Galloway fares rather badly at the hands of Dr. Boyd, the same cannot be said of Thomas Jefferson. In 1943 Boyd's *The Declaration of Independence; the Evolution of the Text as shown in Facsimiles of Various Drafts by its Authors, . . .* appeared, as a publication of the Library of Congress (a revised edition was published two years later by Princeton University Press). It is a work of meticulous scholarship. While Boyd gives due credit to the earlier work of Carl Becker (*The Declaration of Independence: A Study of the History of Political Ideas* [2nd edn., New York, 1942]) and the still earlier work of J. H. Hazelton (*The Declaration of Independence, Its History* [New York, 1906]), his own work marks a decided advance in the critical handling of data, which he supports with facsimiles of original documents as he shows the transformation of the Declaration of Independence from its earliest ascertainable form to the copy engrossed on parchment and signed by the delegates. Yet even this impressive record of how this great document took its final shape was further clarified by Boyd upon the later discovery among the Jefferson Papers in the Library of Congress of a fragment of manuscript in Jefferson's hand which preceded the so-called "Rough Draft" and which indicates, therefore, that the latter should properly be called the "committee draft," since it was prepared by the committee of five appointed by Congress to bring in a formal Declaration of Independence.[3]

In 1943 an act of Congress authorized the Thomas Jefferson Bicentennial Commission "to prepare as a congressional memorial to Thomas Jefferson" a new edition of his writings "at a cost not to exceed $15,000 for the preparation of the manuscript" and to employ a historian for this purpose. On March 12 of that year the

---

[3] J. P. Boyd: "New Light on Jefferson and His Great Task," *New York Times Magazine*, April 13, 1947, pp. 17 and 64–70.

Commission appointed Dr. Boyd as editor of this scholarly undertaking. Asked to report on the scope, probable cost, and length of
time this enterprise would involve, Dr. Boyd submitted his findings
the following September. Shortly after this, Princeton University
undertook to sponsor the new edition with the aid of a subvention of
$200,000 from the New York Times Company. These offers were
accepted by the Commission, and in the spring of 1944 an office was
established in the Princeton University Library for the editor and
his small staff, composed at the time of Dr. Lyman H. Butterfield
and Miss Mina R. Bryan. Boyd then proceeded with the demanding
work of gathering reproductions of the original documents of all
Jefferson's papers and of arranging them for publication with elaborate and illuminating footnotes and editorial comments. The plan
for this challenging task calls for some fifty volumes in all. In 1950
the first two volumes of *The Papers of Thomas Jefferson* were issued. Volume I covers the years 1760–76; Volume II brings the series
to June 1779; other volumes, moving forward chronologically, have
followed at more or less regular intervals. Dr. St. George L. Sioussat,
who reviewed the first six volumes, doubtless voiced the views of
American scholars in general when he wrote in measured under-
statement: "This great series is henceforth to be regarded not only as
an accomplishment in itself but also as a standard of which any who
undertake similar editorial enterprises will have to take account." [4]
Many historians would even agree with Dr. Douglass Adair, who in
reviewing Volume I wrote: "Indeed, it can be predicted (with a
sober and strict concern for the exact meaning of greatest) that the
Jefferson Papers when completed will probably stand as the greatest
technical triumph of historical scholarship produced in the twentieth century." [5]

   Agreed that this high appraisal of *The Papers of Thomas Jefferson*
is warranted, one must however point out that even so impressive an
edition of the papers does not diminish the weakness of the purely
biographical approach to a study of the history of the revolt of the
Thirteen North American Colonies in 1775. Although the side of the
American patriots is presented with extraordinary fullness, as one
would obviously expect from the writings of Jefferson or any of his
American contemporaries, almost no light is shed on the anxious

   [4] *American Historical Review*, LIX, 938–40; see also *ibid.*, LVI, 118–22 and
585–7, for other reviews of *The Papers of Thomas Jefferson* by Sioussat.
   [5] *Pennsylvania Magazine of History and Biography*, LXXIV, 406–9.

efforts of the government of Great Britain to adjust the financial burdens of state during the 1760's and earlier years of the 1770's so that these might be justly apportioned among the units of the Empire; there is also an absence of light on how deeply the Ministry, the majority of the members of Parliament, and apparently most of the people of Great Britain, felt about the principle of the sovereignty of Parliament as the proper unifying agent within the British Empire. While today's student of American history can well understand why men rallied to save the American union in the 1860's, anyone reading *The Jefferson Papers* would scarcely be made aware why self-respecting, even liberal-minded Englishmen or British Americans ever rallied to save the British Empire in the 1770's. Nevertheless *The Jefferson Papers* will surely stand as a monument to American historical scholarship.

Among other shorter studies that have come from the pen of Professor Boyd, his "The Disputed Authorship of The Declaration on the Causes and Necessity of Taking up Arms, 1775," printed in 1950 in the *Pennsylvania Magazine of History and Biography*, may be singled out as additional evidence of his meticulous scholarship.[6]

Carl Bridenbaugh (1903–   )

Among historians concerned with the second half of the eighteenth century, none has dealt so fully with the social and intellectual aspects—with special emphasis on urban life—as Carl Bridenbaugh. Born in Philadelphia, he received his formal education at Dartmouth and the University of Pennsylvania, and, under the guidance of Professor Arthur M. Schlesinger, took his doctorate at Harvard in 1936. He taught at the Massachusetts Institute of Technology and Brown University before becoming the director of the Institute of Early American History and Culture at Williamsburg in 1945. In 1950 he accepted the Margaret Byrne chair in American History at the University of California at Berkeley, but in 1962 returned to Brown as University Professor of History.

---

[6] *Ibid.*, LXXIV, 51–73.

As early evidence of his sustained interest in American culture, Professor Bridenbaugh's "Colonial Newport as a Summer Resort," covering the period 1729 to 1775, appeared in 1933.[1] This study emphasized the important point that mingling of people from different colonies on a social basis at a resort of this kind helped to break down the isolation of colonial groups, as families from the South consorted with residents of other colonies. Again, in 1935 the April number of the *Pennsylvania Magazine of History and Biography* (LIX, 34–80) reprinted "Patrick M'Robert's *Tour Through Part of the Northern Provinces of America, 1774–1775,*" first published in Edinburgh in 1776, to which Bridenbaugh contributed the Preface. This was followed in 1938 by his important and scholarly *Cities in the Wilderness: The First Century of Urban Life in America 1625–1742.*

In the Preface to *Cities in the Wilderness* Bridenbaugh makes the following observation:

> "Emerging from forty years' preoccupation with the significance of the frontier in early American history, historians are now beginning to realize that much that was characteristic of life in the colonies did not necessarily bear the stamp of frontier democracy and individualism. Commercial as well as agrarian interests dictated political if not also social revolution; most of the intellectual activity and much of the social and political advance of the eighteenth century depended upon an urban rather than a rural environment; certainly a large part of our radical thought came neither from farm nor forest but from the seaboard towns." [2]

To illustrate and document this point of view Bridenbaugh concentrated his attention upon "five representative towns": Boston, Newport, New York, Philadelphia, and Charles Town (Charleston). This volume contains (and marshals with skill) an immense amount of data drawn from town and provincial records, newspapers, letters, diaries, and other sources, such as contemporary maps and illustrations. Political history is only treated incidentally; however, a great deal of emphasis is placed upon social and economic aspects of urban life—the various ways people earned their livelihood, as well as their (non-economic) relations with one another. The book is a major contribution to American colonial history, especially valuable

---

[1] Rhode Island Historical Society *Collections*, XXVI (1933), 1–23.
[2] *Cities in the Wilderness* (New York, 1955 [first published in 1938], Preface, p. vi).

for its description of the evolution of five villages into towns and of these towns into cities, in the American connotation of the word.[3]

Against the background furnished by *Cities in the Wilderness* Carl Bridenbaugh, in collaboration with his wife Jessica, brought out in 1942 their *Rebels and Gentlemen: Philadelphia in the Age of Franklin*. It is the story of the rise of Philadelphia covering the years 1720 to 1775, when it became not only "the leading commercial entrepôt of the colonies" but also a chief centre, if not the chief American centre, of the so-called age of enlightenment. This city, they declared, "was probably the leading, certainly the most unfettered, middle-class community of the Western world, . . . where admission to the middle class was freest, its opportunities and privileges greatest, and the literate base of society most broad."[4] Although the book is based upon printed material and has no footnotes, both the comprehensive bibliographical note at the end and the text itself indicate the breadth of material covered. The emphasis throughout is on social and cultural developments. "No brief review," declared Professor Richard H. Shryock of the University of Pennsylvania, "can do justice to this remarkable synthesis and interpretation of the history of colonial Philadelphia."[5]

In 1948 came Bridenbaugh's critical edition of Dr. Alexander Hamilton's delightful *Itinerarium* describing his journey in 1744 from Annapolis to York, Maine, and back.[6] This was followed in 1949 by *Peter Harrison: First American Architect*, concerned with the American career of the designer of many fine colonial structures (such as King's Chapel in Boston) who also became the British customs collector of the port of New Haven and remained a firm but quiet Loyalist. In 1950 two more Bridenbaugh works appeared: a little volume (the first in the *Williamsburg in America* series) entitled *Seat of Empire: The Political Role of Eighteenth-Century Wil-*

---

[3] Wayne E. Stevens of Dartmouth College in reviewing *Cities in the Wilderness* declared that it was a volume "destined to exert a profound influence upon the study of early American history in years to come" (*Mississippi Valley Historical Review*, XXVI, 248–9).

[4] *Rebels and Gentlemen: Philadelphia in the Age of Franklin* (New York, 1942), pp. 363–4 and 367.

[5] *Pennsylvania History*, X, 219–20; see also F. B. Tolles in the *New England Quarterly*, XV, 751–2, and N. G. Goodman in the *New York Times*, October 11, 1942.

[6] *Gentleman's Progress: The Itinerarium of Dr. Alexander Hamilton, 1744* (Chapel Hill, N.C., 1948). *The Itinerarium* was first published in 1907 in a private limited edition, ed. A. B. Hart.

liamsburg [1750–1779], and *The Colonial Craftsman,* a most illuminating volume originally prepared as the Phelps Lectures for New York University.

In 1951 Bridenbaugh presented three challenging lectures at Louisiana State University; these were published the following year by the press of that university as *Myths and Realities: Societies of the Colonial South.* In it are described "The Chesapeake Society," "The Carolina Society," and "The Back Settlements." Among the historical myths that the author questioned was the idea of a "South" in the later use of the term, the idea of a "leisured" planter class, the idea that Negro slaves were "contented," the idea of the existence of political "sectionalism" in either Maryland or Virginia, and the idea that the "backcountry" was a melting pot for nationalities—an area that lacked roads, knew little town life, and was backward in education. The conclusions arrived at in this very readable and stimulating book have not been permitted to stand without challenge, however. Louis B. Wright, another distinguished authority in the field of colonial culture, wrote that "the professional historian will find something to question and to arouse him to further investigation, or to a fresh assessment of the evidence upon which Mr. Bridenbaugh has based his generalizations. *Myths and Realities* will be certain to provoke discussion and Mr. Bridenbaugh deserves our thanks for so fearlessly providing a useful stimulant." [7]

To carry the theme of *Cities in the Wilderness* forward to the separation of the Thirteen Colonies from the mother country, Bridenbaugh brought out in 1955 his *Cities in Revolt: Urban Life in America, 1743–1776.* This book—divided into two parts: "Part One. War, Expansion, and Prosperity, 1743–1760" and "Part Two. Depression, Tension, and Revolt, 1760–1776"—continues his study of the significant developments in Boston, Newport, New York, Philadelphia, and Charles Town (Charleston). The author contends that in these populous centres "signs of the divergence between loyal colonialism and a new American nationality are discernible after 1743," although their citizens had no clear under-

---

[7] *American Historical Review,* LVIII, 638–40. Richard B. Morris, in challenging Bridenbaugh's statement that "no sustained effort to analyze and depict the life of the Southern provinces has yet been made," writes that "it would seem ungracious to end this review without reminding the reader of the major contributions to innumerable problems treated in this book which have been made by Philip A. Bruce, Thomas J. Wertenbaker, Thomas P. Abernethy, Louis B. Wright, and Wesley Frank Craven" (*Mississippi Valley Historical Review,* XL, 115–16). See also Howard Mumford Jones in the *William and Mary Quarterly,* 3rd ser., X, 263–7, and J. Carlyle Sitterson in the *New York Times Book Review,* November 9, 1952.

standing of what was actually taking place in this gradual shifting
of loyalties. Bridenbaugh makes no attempt to give a history of
the Revolution in this provocative book; instead, he provides the
reader with a study "of the locale and the conditions in which
the uprising took place and of the people who participated in
it." [8] In this task he has eminently succeeded—marshalling an enormous amount of data (political, economic, and social) covering a
variety of aspects of urban development that point to the growing
maturity and complexity of city life in British North America before
the outbreak of the War for American Independence. The book,
taken with his earlier publications, distinguishes Professor Bridenbaugh as the master historian of the American colonial city. An
occasional statement in *Cities in Revolt* may however take one by
surprise, such as the assertion that "the mercantile dynasties of the
five cities and their growing satellites coalesced into the only recognized colonial social class" (pp. 71–2)—thus denying this status to
the aristocratic planter group. In view of the fact that the book is
heavily laden with quotations, it is most unfortunate that conditions
of publication did not permit the inclusion of footnote references;
these references, available to the scholar in mimeograph form, show
the wide variety of sources used by the author.[9]

In 1962 Bridenbaugh's *Mitre and Sceptre: Transatlantic Faiths,
Ideas, Personalities, and Politics, 1689–1775* was published. It deals
with a very important subject and supplements, if not supplants,
Arthur Lyon Cross's scholarly *Anglican Episcopate and the American Colonies,* published in 1902; for it includes much source material not contained in the earlier book. It is also far more doctrinaire.
Embodied in this study is the thesis that "in England's American
colonies the most enduring and absorbing public question from 1689
to 1776 was religion"; also the companion thesis that the "Anglicans
aimed at nothing less than the complete reordering of American
Society." [10] A third thesis is to be found in the statement that the
"American Revolution of 1760–1775 resulted quite as much from a
religious as from a political change in the minds and hearts of the

---

[8] Preface, p. vii.

[9] For access to the footnotes see *Cities in Revolt,* p. 434; a copy is also available in
this author's collection at Lehigh University Library. Bernard Bailyn of Harvard
University evaluates the book in his review in the *William and Mary Quarterly,* 3rd
ser., XIII, 258–61, as do J. B. Hedges of Brown University in the *American Historical
Review,* LXI, 654–5, and L. B. Wright of the Folger Library in the *Mississippi Valley
Historical Review,* XLIII, 113–15.

[10] *Mitre and Sceptre: Transatlantic Faiths, Ideas, Personalities, and Politics, 1689–
1775* (New York, 1962), Preface, pp. xi and xiii.

people." [11] Further theses are implied in the headings of the two subdivisions of the book. The first is called "Ecclesiastical Imperialism, 1689–1760," and the second, "No Bishop, No King, 1760–1775." How far these theses are established by the author and are acceptable will be disputed among historians. In fact students who have read *Cities in Revolt* are hardly prepared for these new and rather startling interpretations, especially in view of the statement (p. 355): "Any hope of success for an American episcopate died with the repeal of the Stamp Act." Nevertheless, *Mitre and Sceptre* is a book of great learning and should be read by all serious students of American colonial history for the light it throws on religious developments.[12] It especially highlights the fact that what men assume to be true is almost as important to the historian as what is true, since men tend to act on the basis of what they are persuaded are the facts in any situation. Bridenbaugh does not claim that any of the King's first ministers, during the critical years between 1760 and 1775, ever seriously contemplated sending an Anglican bishop to America, nor can such a claim be supported by the evidence— irrespective of the desires of such men as Archbishop Secker in England or those in America supported by the Society for the Propagation of the Gospel in Foreign Parts.

John C. Miller (1907–   )

Of all those who have described the background and the progress of the American Revolution, no one has presented his findings in a more entertaining manner than John C. Miller. Born at Santa Bar-

---

[11] *Ibid.*, p. 20.

[12] For important reviews of *Mitre and Sceptre* see J. P. Greene in the *William and Mary Quarterly*, 3rd ser., XX, 597–602, J. A. Schutz in the *New England Quarterly*, XXXVI, 117–19, Michael Kraus in the *American Historical Review*, LXVIII, 412–13, and Conrad Wright in the *Mississippi Valley Historical Review*, L, 107–8. Thomas P. Govan, in a review article entitled "The Historian as Partisan, Prosecutor, and Judge," is very critical of the spirit in which *Mitre and Sceptre* has been written: "Mr. Bridenbaugh is not merely a judge, he is also a prejudiced and partisan prosecutor, and suggests that historians who attempt to be neutral, or even fair, in their presentation of evidence, are trying to strike 'some kind of Olympian balance among the issues or between the parties' " (*Historical Magazine of the Protestant Episcopal Church*, XXXII, 49–56).

bara, California, he attended school in Tacoma, Washington, and did both his undergraduate and graduate work at Harvard, receiving his baccalaureate *summa cum laude* in 1930, his master of arts degree in 1932, and his doctorate in 1939. Between 1939 and 1950 he taught history at Bryn Mawr College, advancing from the rank of assistant professor to that of associate professor; he then went as a professor of history to Stanford University, where he now holds the Edgar E. Robinson Chair.

Professor Miller's first contribution to historical literature, "Religion, Finance, and Democracy in Massachusetts," appeared in the March 1933 *New England Quarterly* [1] while he was still a Harvard graduate student. This article deals with a rebellion threatened during the early 1740's by debtors and religious enthusiasts against the economically conservative and religiously orthodox holders of power in Massachusetts Bay. The attempt to establish a land bank, with its threat to all creditors, and the excitement of the Great Awakening, with its blow at ecclesiastical conformity, are well portrayed. In dealing with the land-bank crisis, Miller affirms that with "the aid of Parliament the rise of democracy in Massachusetts was staved off for a generation"—and thus parts company with Professor Robert E. Brown whose thesis on democracy will be dealt with in a later section of this historiography. This essay by Miller was followed by another, "The Massachusetts Convention, 1768," published in the *New England Quarterly* (September 1934), which challenged the view that radical frontier communities pressed their democratic ideas on the more conservatively inclined Atlantic seaboard towns. The second article made clear that, in the issue involving the sending of British troops to Boston, it was the radicals of this town who sought without success to persuade the other towns to join them in resistance and that it was reaction against this rebellious position which caused the Convention to fall under the control of the moderates.

Miller's doctoral dissertation, *Sam Adams, Pioneer in Propaganda*, written under the direction of Professor S. E. Morison, appeared in 1936. The theme is much the same as that in the "Religion, Finance, and Democracy" article: the struggle between the aristocrats and the yeomen and mechanics, but now with Thomas Hutchinson dominating one group and Samuel Adams the other. In the book, Adams

---

[1] *New England Quarterly*, VI, 29–58.

is pictured as the period's most dangerous enemy to the British government. "Boston was controlled by a 'trained mob' and . . . Sam Adams was its keeper," Miller writes (p. 53), and by 1768 it was clear that Adams had determined to break the political bonds that tied the Empire together. To accomplish this "he made it his policy to provoke the British government to attempt the punishment of the colonies—a step certain to put provincial radicals in power" (p. 301). Hoping to achieve this end in 1770, "the instruments he used to bring about the [Boston] Massacre were his 'Mohawks' from North Boston" (p. 186). Although he failed in that venture, the passing of the Tea Act in 1773 gave him his golden opportunity. He "determined not to permit the tea to be landed" (p. 289). After planning against the likely contingency that the tea ships would not be permitted to return to England without landing their cargo, Adams, late in the afternoon of December 16, arose in Old South Meeting House and declared that " 'this meeting can do nothing further to save the country.' His words were the signal for a wild war whoop from the galleries and the street outside. . . . Most of those 'Naragansett Indians' were Adams's followers from the North End," who dumped the tea into the harbour (pp. 293–4). He was at last in control of Massachusetts Bay. Thus, at the gathering of the Continental Congress in 1774 Adams, with the aid of "a few staunch friends with whom he could speak plainly and prearrange the proceedings" (p. 318), transplanted the caucus from Faneuil Hall to Philadelphia and "overthrew the conservatives in Congress just as he had driven the Tories out of the Boston town meeting" (p. 342). In other words, we have here a Samuel Adams who was the real father of the War for American Independence, and a study in which the great agitator's triumph is related with artistry in an account based upon the use of a wide range of printed and manuscript sources. In the main its basic conclusions do not differ greatly from the more pedestrian and somewhat more cautious account of Adams by Ralph V. Harlow: *Samuel Adams, Promoter of the American Revolution: A Study in Psychology and Politics,* which appeared in 1923.[2]

Another major work by Professor Miller, *The Origins of the American Revolution,* was published in 1943. Reissued in 1959, the book contained both an Introduction and a Bibliography, missing in the

---

[2] For two reviews of *Sam Adams, Pioneer in Propaganda* see R. V. Harlow in the *New England Quarterly,* IX, 731–4, and Philip Davidson in the *American Historical Review,* XLII, 788–90.

original edition.[3] Professor Carl Bridenbaugh's review of the 1943 edition stated that Miller had "produced a fine volume as notable for its urbanity and judiciousness as for its ripe scholarship and crystal clarity."[4] That this was the consensus of the general reading public is indicated by the book's choice by the Book-of-the-Month Club. The chief complaint voiced by most historians was that the author had failed to recognize adequately the contributions of other writers in his field. As Professor John A. Krout pointed out: "But if his data are often refreshingly novel, his conclusions seldom challenge the findings of his predecessors over the years, from Bancroft to Andrews; in his general viewpoint he is probably nearer the former than the latter. In fact, despite his rewarding quest for new material, he is deeply indebted to the pioneer research of others. It is difficult, therefore, to understand his apparent reluctance to give any indication in his numerous footnotes that he is acquainted with the writings of some of the most important historians of the Revolutionary Era."[5] Professor Nettels made the same criticism; he was also critical of other characteristics of Miller's writing: "Most of the quotations are of a derogatory nature, and from this fact arises the distinctive character of the book. . . . His book takes precedence over others by virtue of his superior skill in stripping human frailty of its garments of respectability, in order that deformities may be exposed."[6] A master of the apt phrase and broad generalization, Miller holds the attention of the reader as few writers covering the background of the American Revolution have done. But this gift has its dangers, especially when the highest degree of accuracy is demanded.[7] In the review of *The Origins of the American Revolution* by the present writer it was emphasized that Professor Miller's chief objective was not the production of a scholar's handbook on the background of the Revolution, but rather "the presentation of the ideas and actions of the men of the eighteenth century, irrespective

---

[3] The first edition was published by Little, Brown & Co. of Boston; the new edition came from the Stanford University Press.

[4] *New York Times Book Review*, August 8, 1943.

[5] *Political Science Quarterly*, LVIII, 611–14. Professor Verner W. Crane writes in the same vein in his statement: "The author has conspicuously neglected to place his own researches in relation to the formidable body of scholarship in his field" (*American Historical Review*, XLIX, 494–5); see also the review by Carl Bridenbaugh already mentioned.

[6] See Curtis Nettels in the *Journal of Southern History*, IX, 562–3.

[7] The author of this series found that upon his initial reading of the volume he was impelled to place numerous question marks in the margin, especially in the first three chapters.

of what later generations may have thought of them and how they may have weighed them. . . . The more restricted purpose has been brilliantly achieved; the very limitations of the book make possible some of its excellence." [8]

As a sequel to *The Origins of the American Revolution,* Miller produced *Triumph of Freedom, 1775–1783* in 1948. It possesses all the conspicuous virtues of the earlier book and presents the same difficulties to the scholar intent on measuring the reliability with which the author used his source materials. To Dr. Bernhard Knollenberg: *Triumph of Freedom, 1775–1783* is an interesting work; but, because of lack of documentation, its authenticity is problematical and its value limited." [9] On the other hand, Professor Charles F. Mullett commented: ". . . in one very tangible respect the book's most conspicuous feature is the dearth of footnotes—and this on pages sprinkled with quotations and statements sufficiently original to warrant citations! If this be academic treason, let us applaud it. Is not a scholar to be trusted?" [10] Accepting the book's limitations, one may affirm that it is certainly one of the most comprehensive and most readable accounts of the War for American Independence that has been written. [11]

In conclusion it may be said that Professor Miller's writing would have had a far greater impact on his fellow historians had he been prepared to sacrifice some of its characteristic popular features in favour of the more conventional canons of historical scholarship.

Bernhard Knollenberg (1892–   )

Born in Richmond, Indiana, Bernhard Knollenberg attended Earlham College, where he received his baccalaureate in 1912. He thereupon enrolled in the Harvard Graduate School, was awarded

---

[8] See *Pennsylvania History,* XI, 230–1.

[9] See the *American Historical Review,* LIV, 147–9.

[10] *Journal of Southern History,* XV, 103–5.

[11] For an extended and highly competent review of the *Triumph of Freedom, 1775–1783,* indicating both its strong and weak features, see Professor Merrill Jensen in the *William and Mary Quarterly,* 3rd ser., V, 580–5. Professor Miller's more recent writings have been on subjects beyond the scope of this historiographical essay: *Crisis in Freedom: The Alien and Sedition Acts* (1951), *Alexander Hamilton: Portrait in Paradox* (1959), and *The Federalist Era* (1960).

his master's degree in 1914, and entered the Harvard Law School; in 1916, having received a law degree, he was admitted to the bar and began to practise law. From 1929 to 1938 he was with the New York firm of Lord, Day, & Lord, which he left to become Librarian of the Yale University Library, a post he held until 1944. Meanwhile he had become involved in government service. For years he held important posts in connection with the administration of Lend-Lease, the Office of Strategic Services, and the United States Commission on the North Atlantic Fisheries. But his greatest interest remained in the field of history.

In 1940, while still acting as Librarian at Yale, Knollenberg brought out his challenging *Washington and the Revolution, A Reappraisal: Gates, Conway, and the Continental Congress.* This study (for it is not a history of Washington and the American Revolution) seeks to do justice to some of those who, as a result of the mystique that had enveloped the life of Washington, have fared rather badly in earlier writings on the annals of the War for American Independence. In his effort to correct the distortion of the history of this war, Knollenberg succeeded admirably. The value of his legal training, especially in the careful weighing of evidence, is clearly demonstrated throughout. Nor does he, at least in the eyes of this writer, seriously minimize the real greatness of Washington by the presentation of detailed proof of his very human qualities.[1]

Reference may also be made to Knollenberg's *Pioneer Sketches of the Upper Whitewater Valley, Quaker Stronghold of the West,* published by the Indiana Historical Society in 1945, although it lies beyond the period under consideration here, as does his "John Adams, Knox, and Washington" (published in the October 1946 American Antiquarian Society *Proceedings*), an article that throws new light on the relations between John Adams, Henry Knox, and George Washington during the early years of the American nation. More pertinent to this historiography is Knollenberg's editing of the illuminating letter written by Jonathan Williams, when visiting his great-uncle, Benjamin Franklin, in London. Williams upon gaining entrance to the House of Lords on January 20, 1775, heard Lord Chatham deliver his great speech and gave the substance of it in this unsent letter, along with a *résumé* of other speeches supporting or opposing Chatham's motion to withdraw the troops from Boston.

---

[1] For two rather sharply contrasting reviews of *Washington and the Revolution* see L. M. Sears in the *Mississippi Valley Historical Review*, XXVIII, 261–2, and T. S. Anderson in the *American Historical Review*, XLVII, 350–1.

The document, preceded by an Introduction, was published in 1949 as one of the Indiana University Library *Publications* under the title *Franklin, Jonathan Williams and William Pitt. A Letter of January 21, 1775.* In 1952 the *Correspondence of Governor Samuel Ward, based chiefly on the Ward Papers covering the Period, 1725–1776* was competently edited by Knollenberg for the Rhode Island Historical Society. This volume presents the letters written or received by Ward during most of the critical years preceding the Declaration of Independence, and when he was acting as chairman of the committee of the whole in the course of the deliberations of the Second Continental Congress.

The editing of the Ward *Correspondence* was but one phase of Knollenberg's historical activities. For in 1960 his *Origin of the American Revolution, 1759–1766* appeared. This is a work of great learning, addressed primarily to fellow historians. Out of a total of 486 pages, only 237 are devoted to text dealing with the period shown in the title; the remainder of the book contains an epilogue covering the period 1766 to 1775, appendices, footnotes, bibliography, and index. In the book, the Duke of Newcastle receives his due as one opposed to "novel or harsh measures of colonial government" (p. 13); indeed, Knollenberg ventures the opinion that from "the standpoint of British relations with the colonies, the retirement of Newcastle was calamitous. Had he remained in office, the provocative colonial measures from 1763 to 1765. . . , it is reasonable to believe, would not have been taken" (p. 23–4). Knollenberg also shows a sympathetic attitude toward Grenville, when (beset by distracting problems of administration as the King's chief minister) he was led to make his "disastrous" proposal to tax the colonies (pp. 30–1).

Knollenberg's book embodies a thesis, supported with skill and heavy documentation. It is that the cause of the alienation of British colonials from Great Britain lay in the projection from 1759 onward by the British government of certain definite policies that were incompatible with the spirit of the constitution of the Empire before that date. The chief causes for this alienation he finds as follows: the disallowance by the Privy Council in 1759 of the Virginia Twopenny Acts; the issuance in 1761 of general writs of assistance, especially those involving the customs service in Massachusetts Bay; the order, also in 1761, by the Privy Council forbidding the Governors of New York and New Jersey to issue judges' commissions that were not revocable at the pleasure of the Crown; the effort from 1759 onward by the Archbishop of Canterbury and the Society for the Propagation of the Gospel in Foreign Parts to establish an Anglican episcopacy in America; the determination of Parliament, in 1763, to bring about the rigid enforcement of the Navigation and Trade Acts and, in 1764 and 1765, to raise a revenue in the colonies (pp. 1–4). To Knollenberg the "stereotyped system of British Government . . . was, on the whole, satisfactory to the colonial 'yokefellows'. . . . Had the relationship not been disturbed by the many new and vexing British measures introduced from 1759 to 1765 . . . it might, I think, have endured (subject to occasional political readjustments notably such as were made half a century later in the British Empire and in Great Britain itself) for many generations, perhaps even to this day" (p. 5). In developing this thesis, Knollenberg argues that the way in which the Anglo-French war was fought and ended (with the Peace of Paris in 1763 and the collapse of French authority in North America) did not have any serious effect upon the attitude of colonials toward the mother country (pp. 8–9). But the question may well be raised—even if it cannot finally be answered—is it at all likely, had the war ended in a French victory with the British colonials securely enclosed to the east of the Appalachian mountain chain, that any or all of the governmental measures enumerated above would have led to a revolt on the part of Americans or to their subsequent appeal to France for aid in freeing them from the parent state? Granted that this point has not been sufficiently weighed, the book is nevertheless a very important contribution to the literature of the background of the War for American Independence. In fact, no more powerful brief in behalf of the colonials exists.[2]

Knollenberg's latest work, published in 1964, carries the title *George Washington: The Virginia Period, 1732–1775*. It may be regarded as a companion study to *Washington and the Revolution, A Reappraisal*. Like the earlier work it is addressed primarily to his

---

[2] While Philip Davidson provides a sympathetic review of the book in the *American Historical Review*, LXVI, 1057–8, S. E. Morison is more critical of the soundness of the Knollenberg thesis in his review in the *New England Quarterly*, XXIV, 265–6. C. R. Ritcheson, reviewing the book in the *Mississippi Valley Historical Review*, XLVII, 682–3, takes the position that Knollenberg has "an unfortunate tendency to accept evidence as meaningful only as it is useful to the thesis [inherent in the book]. Britain has again been hauled to the bar. The case for the prosecution has been made as tellingly as it is ever likely to be, . . . The judge would do well, however, to hear from other quarters before rendering his verdict." Doubtless the most perceptive review to appear was that by M. M. Klein in the *William and Mary Quarterly*, 3rd ser., XVIII, 277–80, in which he states both the strength and the weakness of the book at some length.

fellow historians. The purpose of the book is clearly stated in the Preface: "Previous biographers, faced with the dearth of contemporary evidence concerning Washington's early life, have filled the gap with so many dubious reminiscences and conjectures that readers of a scholarly bent who wish for an account based solely on contemporary evidence do not know where to turn. My first object is to supply this need." Knollenberg maintains that there was a need for a biography "based on the same critical approach to Washington's own statements as to other evidence," a need also for an account of Washington that will refrain from "undue glorification . . . because his glorification has often been at the expense of injustice to the reputation of others." He has given us just such a book. Out of 238 pages less than 120 are devoted to the text; the rest is made up of appendices, notes, bibliography, and index. As in his earlier work, he portrays a Washington with human failings, but there emerges at the same time the rare man who, as the Commander-in-Chief of the American armies, refused any monetary reward other than his actual expenses. "Many sought and some found the opportunity to profit financially from the war. . . ; but, from the time of his election to the chief command, Washington dedicated himself unreservedly to service of the public; first to the winning of the war and from then on to establishment of a nation designed to perpetuate the ideals for which he and his soldiers had fought" (pp. 116–17). Had the book been available before Volume XI in this present series went to press, the chapters (13 and 14) on Washington as "Planter and Businessman" and "Washington's Bounty Land" would have been cited for the light they shed on the land-speculation activities of Virginians.

Not undeservedly Knollenberg—despite the fact that some of his conclusions have been, and will continue to be, questioned—may be termed a historian's historian.

John Richard Alden (1908–   )

John Richard Alden, a native of Michigan, took his formal training in history, both undergraduate and graduate, at the University of Michigan. It was there that he came under the tuition of Profes-

sor Verner W. Crane, who directed his attention to the opportunities
for creative scholarship in an investigation of the receding western
frontiers during the latter part of the eighteenth century. Upon
receiving his doctorate in 1939, Alden taught for brief periods at
Michigan State Normal College and at Bowling Green (Ohio) State
University. Then, in 1945, he went to the University of Nebraska as
associate professor of history and there attained the rank of full
professor; in 1955 he accepted an appointment at Duke University,
where he now holds the James B. Duke chair in history.

Alden's first contribution to historical literature was in the form of
an enlightening article, "The Albany Congress and the Creation of
the Indian Superintendencies," published in 1940 in the *Mississippi
Valley Historical Review*.[1] Four years later he produced his *John
Stuart and the Southern Colonial Frontier: A Study of Indian Relations, War, Trade, and Land Problems in the Southern Wilderness,
1754–1775* (Ann Arbor, Mich., & London, 1944). The importance of
this book lies in the fact that for the first time the student of late
colonial history was given a comprehensive and scholarly account of
the problems presented by the impact of advancing white settlement in the lands to the east of the lower Mississippi River and by
intercolonial rivalry over trade with the Indians settled in that area.
Alden's study takes sharp issue with some of the views of certain
writers—for example, Clarence W. Alvord, Thomas P. Abernethy,
Clarence E. Carter, and Archibald Henderson—over such matters
as the relation of the office of Superintendent of Indian Affairs to
that of Commander-in-Chief of the British forces in North America
(pp. 140–6), the Indian Treaty of Hard Labor (p. 270), the running
of the famous Donelson line to mark the Virginia-Cherokee frontier
(pp. 344–50), and the legality of the Transylvania project promoted
by Judge Richard Henderson (p. 293).

In 1948 Alden's study of *General Gage in America: Being Principally a History of His Role in the American Revolution* was
published. As most of this book relates to the activities of Gage
before the outbreak of hostilities, the term "American Revolution"
seems to have been used by Alden in the sense given to it by John
Adams, that is, the progress of the revolutionary movement from
1763 to 1775 in contrast to the War for American Independence
waged from 1775 to 1783. There had long been a need for a book on
Gage, since he held the highly important post of Commander-

---

[1] XXVII, 193–210.

in-Chief of all British forces in America during the critical years between November 16, 1763, and September 26, 1775, when his recall to England reached him at Boston (his later dismissal from his command, while inactive and at home, occurred on April 18 1776). The study is a good one, based soundly upon such abundant sources as the Gage Manuscripts in the Clements Library at Ann Arbor, Michigan. Alden takes an understanding attitude toward Gage and an objective view of the very great responsibilities which faced him and necessitated so many critical decisions. The picture one gets is of a man lacking military genius, yet sensible and modest—a man who was loyal to the King and the service to which he had been called, but at the same time on friendly terms with many Americans, one of whom he married. Indeed Gage before 1774 was perhaps the most popular among colonials of any of the British generals who served in America in the eighteenth century.[2]

With the Gage task well accomplished, Alden turned to a more difficult one: a study of the life of British-American General Charles Lee. This, entitled *General Charles Lee: Traitor or Patriot?*, was published in 1951. The facts of Lee's unusual career are stated fully and sympathetically in this scholarly work which nevertheless does not overlook Lee's faults of character. To Alden, after weighing the evidence, Lee was neither a traitor nor guilty of any major blunders at Monmouth. Moreover, Alden affirmed that in "generalship" Lee "seems to have been superior to Washington and Nathanael Greene; and he brought to the American army experience, confidence, zeal, and an almost amazing energy."[3] While one may question these conclusions,[4] it is even more difficult to agree with the following

---

[2] Bernhard Knollenberg called *General Gage in America* "an exceptionally valuable and interesting volume in the field of British colonial history. . . . Professor John Richard Alden . . . has the intelligence to ask significant questions, the perserverance to find answers to most of them, and the integrity to let the reader know when he has not." (*Saturday Review of Literature,* June 5, 1948). See also C. E. Carter in the *American Historical Review,* LIV, 370–1, and W. B. Willcox in the *Mississippi Valley Historical Review,* XXXV, 294.

[3] *General Charles Lee: Traitor or Patriot?* (Baton Rouge, La., 1951), p. 306.

[4] In turning to the Lee volume, the student would do well to read the review of it by Professor William B. Willcox, of the University of Michigan, that appeared in the *American Historical Review,* LVII, 462–3. Willcox, a specialist in the War for American Independence, questions the superiority of Lee over either Washington or Greene as a military commander. Professor John C. Miller of Stanford University, who has also written on the war, goes even further to question Lee's standing as a general in a review that appeared in the *William and Mary Quarterly,* 3rd ser., VIII, 598–600. See also the review by Professor Carl Bridenbaugh in the *New York Times Book Review,* June 10, 1951.

estimate of Lee, the patriot, given by Alden: "As a fervent supporter
of the 'liberties of mankind' and a propagandist he was one of those
responsible in major degree for the Revolutionary War. . . ." [5]

Professor Alden's next contribution to historical literature came
with the publication in 1952 of *The War of the Revolution* in two
volumes—a work that had been left in manuscript at the death of
the Delaware lawyer, Christopher Ward—which Alden competently edited and also supplemented with a chapter on the aspects
of the war that took place west of the Appalachians. Two years later
came his own excellent *The American Revolution, 1775–1783*, a
volume in *The New American Nation* series. Only the first two
chapters of this book lie within the scope of this historiography.
The first, "The Coming of the Revolution," is of especial interest. In it Alden surveyed the period from 1763 to 1775 and stated
among other things that: "George III purchased support in order to
restore the royal power; [in addition] his long campaign to re-
establish monarchical authority produced other and greater evils. A
core of politicians seduced by cash and position came in increasing
numbers to occupy Cabinet seats and other posts of authority, especially after 1767. . . . As his purpose to rule as well as reign became evident, bitter opposition sprang up. Many enemies of the
King would have been content to reduce the authority of George III
to the proportions of that exercised by George II; others . . .
desired also to take further moderate steps toward political democracy." According to Alden, among the "series of ill-advised measures" of the Grenville Ministry that "goaded the colonists into open
revolt" were that:

> "It undertook to restrict settlement on and speculation in the lands
> beyond the Alleghenies recently won from France; to maintain a
> standing army of redcoats . . . in America; to compel the colonists
> under certain circumstances to provide quarters, supplies and trans-
> portation for segments of this army; to make permanent the offices of
> two royally chosen superintendents of Indian affairs. . . ; to reno-
> vate the customs service in America and to enforce the long laxly
> executed Acts of Trade; to expand restrictions upon colonial paper
> currencies. . . ; to lessen the trade between the colonies and the
> foreign islands of the West Indies by imposing a tax of threepence
> per gallon upon molasses imported from those islands; and to secure

---

[5] *General Charles Lee: Traitor or Patriot?*, p. 306.

a revenue from America through the tax on molasses and, especially, through the famous Stamp Act."

These measures, Alden asserts, were regarded by the colonials "to be violations of colonial charters, well-established customs, and the rights of Englishmen. In brief, they were 'unconstitutional.' " [6] These statements require a brief comment.

With respect to the charge that George III sought powers not exercised by his grandfather, it is the view of such authorities on his reign as the late Professor Richard Pares, the late Sir Lewis Namier, and Professor Herbert Butterfield, that this was not true. They also take the position that if George permitted the use of bribery to strengthen the hands of his Ministry, this had been done on an even wider scale by George II. Again, the measures concerned with America were not advanced by the King but by the Ministry, and when George III had once approved a measure, he gave both it and the Ministry his firm support. Nor is it clear that the members of the Ministry had been "seduced" to advocate the polices toward America which they themselves had conceived as the Privy Councillors responsible for the appropriate lines of action. Furthermore, Alden does not make clear upon what basis he can state that in the eyes of colonials the various measures enumerated above were "unconstitutional." The only legislation before 1774 so regarded, it would appear, were those statutes designed to secure a revenue in America by taxation. It is true that other measures may have been disliked by Americans, but that does not mean that they were considered "unconstitutional" before 1774.

In 1957 at Baton Rouge—as Volume III of *A History of the South*—Professor Alden's *The South in the Revolution, 1763–1789* was published; a work written in a judicious tone and a spirit of detachment. What adds to its value is its broad approach to the history of the South during the specified years. Indeed, the reader is made to realize that for the period from 1763 to 1775 one cannot speak of the "South" in the conventional sense that was to be employed later; for it was then an area in which many decidedly different outlooks were held on political, economic, and social matters.

---

[6] *The American Revolution, 1775–1783* (New York, 1954), pp. 3–5. For this volume see especially the review by Theodore Thayer, *William and Mary Quarterly*, 3rd ser., XI, 476–8; see also reviews by Carl Bridenbaugh, *New York Times*, February 21, 1954; Merrill Jensen, *Saturday Review of Literature*, February 27, 1954; F. B. Tolles, *American Historical Review*, LX, 118–20; Aubrey Land, *Mississippi Valley Historical Review*, XLI, 319–20; and C. F. Mullett, *Journal of Southern History*, XX, 410–11.

As might be expected, Alden is at his best in dealing with the frontier problems facing the southern colonies before 1775; he is not however quite so sure in some other matters. Professor Merrill Jensen of the University of Wisconsin in the *William and Mary Quarterly* for 1958 not unjustly points out that Alden underestimated the financial plight of the government of Great Britain after 1763; Jensen also questions Alden's handling of the British land tax and his implication that under Grenville an innovation was made by the Sugar Act in 1764 in giving the American Vice-Admiralty Courts power to try customs cases. The reviewer takes the author further to task for his failure to point out that the *revenue* feature of this act was held to be an innovation and a grievance in the eyes of colonial merchants, especially that part of the act whereby anyone accused of attempting to evade it was held to be "guilty until he proved his innocence."[7] The book is nevertheless one of great merit.

Edmund Sears Morgan (1916–   )

Although born in Minneapolis, where his father, Edmund Morris Morgan, Jr., was a professor of law at the University of Minnesota, Edmund Sears Morgan moved with his parents to New England at an early age. In due course he entered his father's college, Harvard, where he came under the tutelage of S. E. Morison and Perry Miller. After receiving his baccalaureate in 1937 he enrolled in the London School of Economics, where he studied economic history and political thought under R. H. Tawney and Harold Laski. Returning to Harvard, he completed his doctorate under Professor Miller. His dissertation dealt with domestic relations in seventeenth-century New England, and part of it appeared in print in 1944 under the title *The Puritan Family: Essays on Religious and Domestic Relations in Seventeenth-Century New England.*[1] In 1945 he became an instructor in history at the University of Chicago, but left the follow-

---

[7] *William and Mary Quarterly,* 3rd ser., XV, 394–6. For other reviews see D. J. Mays in the *Mississippi Valley Historical Review,* XLV, 129–30; W. M. Wallace in the *Maryland Historical Magazine,* LIII, 79–81; and Philip Davidson in the *American Historical Review,* LXIII, 1003–4.

[1] For the profound influence of Perry Miller's writings see Morgan's "Perry Miller and the Historians" in the American Antiquarian Society *Proceedings,* LXXIV, 11–18.

ing year to go to Brown University, where he remained until 1955. During this period he advanced to the rank of professor, a title he continued to hold when called to Yale where he is now.

In 1948 the *New England Quarterly* published Professor Morgan's enlightening article, "Thomas Hutchinson and the Stamp Act." This paper made clear that—contrary to the view held by most of Hutchinson's contemporaries about his attitude to taxation—Hutchinson in fact opposed internal taxation of the colonists by Parliament and, in an effort to ward off such taxation in 1764, sent to Richard Jackson in England an essay on colonial rights.[2]

Also in 1948, an article on "Colonial Ideas of Parliamentary Power, 1764–1766," appeared in the *William and Mary Quarterly*.[3] In it Morgan challenged the views of Randolph G. Adams, Carl Becker, and other historians (who held that colonials before 1765 had virtually conceded the right of Parliament to tax them), by asserting that "it was not the Americans who drew the line between internal and external taxation," and adding that when colonials "objected to the Townsend duties in 1767, they had in no way changed the conception of Parliamentary power which they had avowed at the time of the Stamp Act; they still admitted the authority of Parliament to regulate trade and to legislate in other ways for the whole Empire; they still denied that Parliament had a right to tax them."[4] This essay—concerned with a point of fundamental importance to the history of the relations of the colonies with Great Britain between the years 1763 and 1775—should have taken more fully into account the fact that the Connecticut Assembly in 1764 in its *Reasons Why the British Colonies, should not be charged with Internal Taxes, By Authority of Parliament* had recommended that Parliament, instead of imposing stamp taxes, could secure an American revenue "in such Manner as to leave . . . the People in the full Possession and Enjoyment of their just Rights and Immunities. . . . by a Duty . . . on the Importation of Negroes, and [export duties] on the Fur Trade, etc. . . ."[5] Moreover, Benjamin Franklin, when examined at the bar of the House of Commons in 1766, indicated that "the Colonies have always submitted to external taxes, and

---

[2] *New England Quarterly*, XXI, 459–92; for a clarification of certain lines in the now mutilated Hutchinson manuscript see *ibid.*, XXI, 492.

[3] *William and Mary Quarterly*, 3rd ser., V, 311–41.

[4] *Ibid.*, V, 340–1.

[5] See *Connecticut Colonial Records*, XII, 651–71. For the appointment of a committee to draw up the *Reasons* see *ibid.*, p. 256.

object to the right of parliament only in laying internal taxes";
Franklin also strongly defended the distinction made by colonials
between the two types of taxes.[6] Even in 1767, it should be pointed
out, when some 240 New York merchants petitioned against regulations that they asserted were clogging trade, they called for permission to import foreign-produced rum into the continental colonies
and argued that Parliament by charging "a moderate Duty, would
add considerably to the Revenue, prevent Smuggling, [and] promote the Petitioners Navigation."[7] Thus it was regulation, not external taxation, that the New Yorkers objected to in 1767.

Professor Morgan's next contribution to a reinterpretation of the
background of the American Revolution was his article, "The Post-
ponement of the Stamp Act," which came out in 1950 in the *William
and Mary Quarterly*.[8] In it he wrote: "Both the events themselves
and the subsequent misrepresentation of them reveal something of
the confusion, misunderstanding, and duplicity which plagued
Anglo-American relations in the period leading up to the Revolution."[9] To Morgan, Grenville was guilty of duplicity in that he had at
first "expressed his willingness to let the colonies raise the money
[they were expected to contribute to defence of North America] in
any way they saw fit,"[10] and had then changed his mind and determined to act by parliamentary statute. This calls for further clarification.

On March 9, 1764, Grenville (as Chancellor of the Exchequer, as
well as First Lord of the Treasury and the King's chief minister)
among other resolutions presented one to the House of Commons in
the following terms: "That . . . it may be proper to charge certain
Stamp Duties in the said Colonies and Plantations." However, he
did not ask for a stamp bill to be brought in at the time but only
sought the sentiment of the House as to the propriety and legality of
such a bill so that, should it seem desirable, it could be introduced
the following year. The question that arises is simply this: Did
Grenville in his speech imply that he was "willing to give to the
Provinces their option to raise that or some equivalent tax, Desirous
as he express'd himself to consult the Ease, the Quiet, and Good will

[6] "The Examination of Doctor Benjamin Franklin," *Writings of Benjamin Franklin*
(ed. A. H. Smyth, 10 vols., New York, 1905–7), IV, 424.
[7] *Journals of the House of Commons*, XXXI, 159.
[8] *William and Mary Quarterly*, 3rd ser., VII, 353–92.
[9] *Ibid.*, VII, 355.
[10]*Ibid.*, VII, 359.

of the Colonies?" This was the impression that Jasper Mauduit, London agent for Massachusetts Bay, got from his brother Israel's report of what Grenville said and this was the view he conveyed to the House of Representatives in a letter written soon after, on March 13.[11]

There is hopeless confusion as to just what Grenville said. For example, Edmund Burke in his great speech on American taxation labelled the report that Grenville had granted such an option to the colonies a "falsehood"—spread, according to Burke, "with a malignant intention." [12] Whatever Grenville may have said about the colonies in his speech, it is clear that, in the words of Burke, "he never could have proposed that they should tax themselves on requisition," and that no formal offer was ever made by his Ministry to permit the colonies to raise the required sum as they saw fit.[13] In fact, the first and only official communication of the Ministry's intentions concerning a proposed stamp tax was embodied in the circular letter sent to all the Governors by the Secretary of State for the Southern Department of August 11, 1764, requesting them to forward information that would be useful to Parliament in framing an American stamp bill.

The above-mentioned studies served as a foundation for the preparation of the well-written and well-received book, *The Stamp Act Crisis: Prologue to Revolution*,[14] which Professor Morgan brought out in 1943 in collaboration with Helen M. Morgan. This book embodied, as well as re-emphasized, the reinterpretation of late American colonial history already presented in the earlier studies,

---

[11] *Ibid.*, VII, 355 and 357.

[12] See *Works of the Right Honourable Edmund Burke* (12 vols., London, 1899), II, 42 and 44. George Bancroft, after reviewing the evidence, re-echoed Burke's statement with the terse comment: "it was a falsehood" (*History of the United States* [Boston, 1852], V, 190 and note). Edward Montague, London agent, apparently supported the version given by Mauduit in a letter supposedly written on April 11, 1764, to the House of Burgesses, to the effect that Grenville said "it would be as satisfactory to him if the several provinces would among themselves, and in modes best suited to their circumstances, raise a sum adequate to the expense of their defence." (For a version of the Montague letter see the *Virginia Gazette* [Purdie and Dixon], October 3, 1766.) The most authoritative account of Grenville's actual remarks of March 9 is contained in the shorthand notes of Nathaniel Ryder, a member of the House of Commons. Ryder, after giving Grenville's opinion that stamp duties were "the best plan," wrote that the minister expressed his "wish to follow to a certain degree the inclination of the people in N. America, if they will agree to the end." (For the Ryder note on Grenville's remarks on stamp duties see in this series Volume X, 259; the Ryder Parliamentary Notes are among the manuscripts in the Harrowby Manuscript Trust, Sandon Hall, Staffs., Eng.)

[13] Burke's *Works*, II, 42.

[14] *The Stamp Act Crisis: Prologue to Revolution* (Chapel Hill, N.C., 1953).

but with a wealth of additional illustrative detail including interesting studies of such leading figures as Governor Francis Bernard, Thomas Hutchinson, Jared Ingersoll, John Hughes, and John Robinson.[15]

Before the appearance of *The Stamp Act Crisis*, Morgan's brief but entertaining *Virginians at Home: Family Life in the Eighteenth Century* had appeared (1952) as Volume II of the *Williamsburg in America* series. Then, in 1956, came his slender but provocative volume *The Birth of the Republic, 1763–89* in the *Chicago History of American Civilization* series. In it he sought, in summary fashion and along traditional lines, to highlight the forces that brought about the American Revolution, the independence of the Thirteen Colonies, and the establishment of a federal government under the Constitution of 1787. The protection of property and liberty, the furtherance of human equality, and the growing realization by Americans that they could only find their true identity if constituted as a distinct nation, were to him the chief principles underlying the actions taken during the years 1763 to 1789 in opposition to the policies of the government of Great Britain.[16]

---

[15] For leading reviews of *The Stamp Act Crisis* see O. M. Dickerson in the *American Historical Review*, LIX, 132–3; C. R. Ritcheson in the *William and Mary Quarterly*, 3rd ser., X, 633–5; S. E. Morison in the *New England Quarterly*, XXVI, 260–2; and J. R. Alden in the *Mississippi Valley Historical Review*, XL, 525–6. In referring to the causes of the American Revolution, Page Smith states in his *The Historian and History* (New York, 1964), pp. 190–1, that an interpretation had been slowly taking form from the time of Sydney George Fisher which "seemed, generally speaking, clear and stable and satisfyingly impersonal. The Revolution was the outcome of forces rather than 'the result of the actions of wicked men' . . . On to this settled and orderly scene burst Edmund and Helen Morgan's *The Stamp Act Crisis: Prologue to Revolution* . . . Their argument, like that of David Ramsay a hundred and sixty-five years earlier, hinged on the decisive character of the Stamp Act and threatened at once to undermine the whole painstaking, if jerry-built, structure of interpretation that had been erected by a dozen twentieth-century historians." For the Morgans argued, Page went on to state, that the "opposition [to the Stamp Act] was . . . almost entirely on the grounds of abstract principle—the constitutional principle of no taxation without representation."

[16] Most of the reviewers found little fault with *The Birth of the Republic*; see for example J. R. Alden in the *American Historical Review*, LXII, 637–8; R. E. Moody in the *New England Quarterly*, XXX, 532–4; and A. C. Land in the *Mississippi Valley Historical Review*, XLIII, 669–70. However, to Professor Max Savelle its defects were so serious as to demand a full-length review of the book. This appeared in the *William and Mary Quarterly*, 3rd ser., XIV, 608–18. To Savelle, nowhere in it was there "evidence of any comprehension of what the English leaders really thought about the Empire or why they thought as they did, or, indeed, any recognition that their philosophy of the Empire had any genuine validity for them" (p. 609). Moreover the book, Savelle felt, "leaves an unavoidable impression of patriotic bias, of a sort of Bancroft-in-modern-dress oversimplification. And patriotism, noble sentiment though it be, is no substitute for historical objectivity" (p. 610). In a "Letter to the Editor" Irving Brant framed an answer in which he stated that he agreed "with

At the meeting of the Mississippi Valley Historical Association in 1956 Professor Morgan presented his next challenge to current interpretations of the American Revolution in his paper "The American Revolution: Revisions in Need of Revising," printed in the January 1957 *William and Mary Quarterly*. In it he pointed out the difficulties of reconciling the disparate recent views on the causes of the American Revolution held by the so-called imperial school of historians, with the views of those historians who have been especially interested in a study of the social and economic history of eighteenth-century America, and those of the Namier school of historians, who have emphasized in their studies of the reign of George III that men in positions of power and responsibility in England were interested primarily in local and personal interests and gave little thought to imperial policy. Further, he stressed that these conflicting interpretations of the American Revolution have discredited the more traditional Whig interpretations: the imperialist school has affirmed British "beneficence and farsightedness" in the administration of the Empire; the social and economic school has presented the revolutionary patriots as "hypocrites pursuing selfish interests," and the Namierites have shown eagerness "to exonerate George III and discredit the English Whigs." All these modern schools, Morgan suggests, leave unexplained the position taken by such leading patriots as George Washington, John Adams, Thomas Jefferson, and Benjamin Franklin. "What I would suggest," he writes, "is that the Whig interpretation of the American Revolution may not be as dead as some historians would have us believe, [and] that George Bancroft may not have been so far from the mark as we have often assumed." The answer to the question ("Why the American Revolution?") that moved Bancroft, he feels, lies in a study of local American institutions which may illumine "how a great nation with great principles of freedom was forged from thirteen quarrelsome colonies."

In 1958 Professor Morgan's useful historiographical pamphlet, *The American Revolution: A Review of Changing Interpretations*, appeared as one of the series of publications issued by the American Historical Association's Service Center for Teachers of History.[17] In

Professor Morgan on nearly all of the challenged facts and conclusions . . ." (*ibid.*, XV, 137–9).

[17] The Morgan article, with the addition of bibliographical footnotes, is also embodied in *Interpreting and Teaching American History*, pp. 38–55. This volume, eds. W. H. Cartwright and R. L. Watson, Jr., was published in 1961 by the National Council for Social Studies, a Department of the National Education Association.

it George Bancroft occupies the centre of the stage. Admitting that Bancroft "abused quotations shamelessly [and] chopped truths in half and sometimes offered up the smaller part," Morgan adds that his importance lies in the fact that "though he has been proved wrong at many points, no one else has yet been able to bend his bow. No one has yet rewritten the history of the Revolution on the grand scale." The work of various scholars who have sought, since Bancroft's time, a clearer understanding of the American Revolution is thereupon brought under survey and the degree of success of their efforts is assessed. One thing that troubles Morgan is that in seeking to overthrow the Bancroft interpretation there are certain inconsistencies in the historians' new views: "If the Navigation Acts were fair, if Americans were not initially attached to any particular view of Parliament's authority, if George III was no tyrant, why should the colonists have sought independence? What, again, *was* the Revolution? If Bancroft's answer was wrong, what should we put in its place?" In concluding his essay Morgan warns, however, that it "would be wrong to leave the impression that the imperial, the social-economic, or the Namierist interpretation is now finished. Each has made a lasting contribution to our knowledge of the Revolutionary period. Each is still inspiring new studies. [Yet,] we must not expand particular insights into a complete explanation. We must continue to ask, for we still do not fully know, what the Revolution was."

It is necessary only to mention that Morgan's next book, *The Puritan Dilemma: The Story of John Winthrop,* also issued in 1958, is a contribution of real importance to the history of seventeenth-century New England Puritanism; this is likewise true of *Visible Saints: The History of a Puritan Idea,* his Anson G. Phelps Lectures delivered at New York University and published in 1963 by the New York University Press.[18]

In 1959, in order to supplement and reinforce his *The Stamp Act Crisis* and to provide a valuable aid to the enquiring student, Morgan brought together a representative body of source material published under the title *Prologue to Revolution: Sources and Documents on The Stamp Act Crisis, 1764–1766.* Three years later he produced his finest and most mature contribution to the historical

---

[18] Also not germane to the period under consideration is the address by Morgan: "The American Indian: Incorrigible Individualist" in *The Mirror of the Indian* published by the Associates of the John Carter Brown Library (Providence, 1958), pp. 3–19.

literature of the period with which this historiographical essay is concerned: his *The Gentle Puritan: A Life of Ezra Stiles, 1727–1795* (New Haven, 1962). This is intellectual as well as social history at its best, covering the career of a leading New England Puritan, with emphasis upon Stiles's eager acceptance of the Enlightenment as a student at Yale; his inward struggles over religious belief as a Yale tutor; his outward happy relations with the cosmopolitan inhabitants of Newport as pastor there of the Second Congregational Church; and, finally, his singularly successful period of achievement as President of Yale between the years 1778 and 1795.[19]

Robert Eldon Brown (1907–   )

Professor Brown is the author of three challenging books, and co-author of a fourth, all of which relate to the period with which this series is concerned. Born at Hamilton, Kansas, in 1907, he was graduated from the University of Washington in 1938 and enrolled in the graduate school of the University of Wisconsin. In 1943 he returned to the University of Washington as an instructor and remained there until 1946, when he received his doctorate at Wisconsin. His thesis was entitled "The Road to Revolution in Massachusetts." After a year in the United States Army as a historian, he went to Michigan State College (now University) as assistant professor of history; in 1954 he was advanced to the rank of associate professor, and in 1956 to that of professor of history. In 1954 he received the Beveridge Award from the American Historical Association, for his *Middle-Class Democracy and the Revolution in Massachusetts, 1691–1780* which appeared in print the following year.

What Professor Brown did in this work was to make clear in most

---

[19] For reviews of *The Gentle Puritan* see S. H. Brockunier in the *American Historical Review*, LXVIII, 146–8; C. W. Akers in the *New England Quarterly*, XXXV, 531–3; W. J. Bell in the *William and Mary Quarterly*, 3rd ser., XXI, 121–3; and C. K. Shipton in the *Mississippi Valley Historical Review*, LXIX, 316–17, in connection with which Shipton also reviewed Louis L. Tucker's *Puritan Protagonist: President Thomas Clap of Yale College* (Chapel Hill, N.C., 1962).

Since this sketch was written Professor Morgan has edited *The American Revolution: Two Centuries of Interpretation* (Englewood Cliffs, N.J., 1965). This useful book presents the interpretations of a number of historians past and present who have sought to answer the question: "Why the American Revolution?"

painstaking detail the extent not only of economic democracy in Massachusetts Bay (based largely upon the ability of the poor man to secure land and become a freeholder), but also of political democracy. This he did by an examination of tax returns, wills, inventories, and other evidence of the possession of the kind of property that would entitle the owner to the right of franchise.[1] Two chief theses underlie the book: first, that before the American Revolution the economic, social, and political life of Massachusetts Bay was dominated by a very widely based middle-class democracy, and not by a seaboard aristocracy of those with wealth, those professionally identified with this wealth, or those having inherited influence as members of old established families;[2] second, that the War for American Independence was fought not for the reasons usually assigned by most historians but simply to preserve this middle-class democracy in the face of the British government's determination to destroy it and to substitute for it a compliant aristocracy.[3]

The word "democracy" is extremely difficult to clarify in terms of the American scene.[4] In an article on "Liberal Democracy and Social Control" (1957) Professor Andrew Hacker of Cornell University

---

[1] For a criticism of the validity of Professor Brown's statistical method of arriving at his conclusions see Professor John Cary's "Statistical Method and the Brown Thesis on Colonial Democracy" and Brown's reply, *William and Mary Quarterly*, 3rd ser., XX, 251–76.

[2] That Professor Brown felt that his findings on economic, and concomitantly political, democracy in Massachusetts Bay were applicable to other colonies as well is indicated by his interesting article, "Economic Democracy Before the Constitution," which appeared in the fall (1955) number of *American Quarterly*, VII 257–74.

[3] For reviews of *Middle-Class Democracy and the Revolution in Massachusetts* see R. B. Morris in the *American Historical Review*, LXII, 636–7; C. K. Shipton in the *Political Science Quarterly*, LXXI, 306–8; R. P. Stearns in the *William and Mary Quarterly*, 3rd ser., XIV, 100–3; R. J. Taylor in the *Mississippi Valley Historical Review*, XLIII, 111–13; and Richard Pares in the *English Historical Review*, LXXII, 122–6, a review especially notable at once for its fairness and for its examination of the validity of certain of Professor Brown's assertions. The most lengthy challenge to the Brown thesis is contained in a paper presented by Professor Merrill Jensen at the Conference on Early American History in 1957; see *Huntington Library Quarterly*, XX, 321–41. Far from agreeing that the men who were leaders in the colonies brought on the American Revolution to preserve democracy, Jensen holds that they did not believe "in democracy," nor was it "a democratic movement except by inadvertence. The pamphleteers . . . were concerned with the formulations of constitutional arguments to defend the colonies and their legislatures from interference by parliament. . . . The ardent leaders of the fight against British policies showed no interest in, or sympathy for, the discontent of back-country farmers or religious groups such as the Baptists. Instead, they temporarily joined with their political enemies to suppress or ignore it." Jensen therefore concludes, after presenting examples of the changes brought about, that the American Revolution was a democratic movement not in origin but in result.

[4] As Roy N. Lokken has pointed out in "The Concept of Democracy in Colonial Political Thought" (*William and Mary Quarterly*, 3rd ser., XVI, 568–80), the word

stated that "the basis of power of liberal democracy has traditionally been deference to a ruling class. . . . For almost a century and a half, America had just such an unquestioned class.'. . . And the social control which permitted this class to hold informal sway was the very traditional one of deference. . . . It means more simply that the bulk of the community defers to a small section and does not think to question that this class will hold the important positions and make the vital decisions." [5] If Hacker's statement on liberal democracy is true of the national period, it is equally true of the colonial period, which was dominated to an even greater extent by a comparatively small ruling group.

In Massachusetts Bay the chief concentration of this ruling group was in the town of Boston and its environs, where the only centre of higher education, Harvard College, was situated. Here, likewise, were the press, the merchant group that helped to support the newspapers by advertising, the chief legal lights, and the most influential Congregational ministers—all shapers of public opinion. There seems to be little doubt that, once the revolutionary movement got under way in the 1760's, a struggle took place within this numerically small but dominant group as to whether or not it was in the best interests of colonials to cut loose from outside political interference. Those who favoured resistance to continuation of the control long exercised by the government of England or Great Britain embodied in their ranks the most influential lawyers, preachers, publishers of newspapers, and politicians. These men, by their exhortations from the press, pulpit, or other public forum, stirred up the people throughout the colony.

So far as this statement of the location of effective power in public affairs can be substantiated, the ruling group that moulded the thinking and actions of the middle-class democracy of Massachu-

---

"democracy" was seldom applied by colonials to their own institutions and when used in their writings usually referred to classical examples of a type of government to be avoided, unless combined with monarchy and aristocracy. In referring to Professor Brown's book, Lokken complained that it neglected to present "a study of the political ideas of eighteenth-century Massachusetts or, for that matter, of the English-speaking world as a whole," and did not "attempt to define what the colonists meant by the term 'democracy'" (p. 59).

[5] See *American Political Science Review*, LI, 1009–26. Samuel Dubois Cook in his critique of Hacker's theory of the basis of American social control writes: "Hacker's construction contains insights into the historic pattern of power. No amount of sentimentality about egalitarianism can deny or obscure the gulf between the promise and fulfilment of liberal democracy" (*ibid.*, LI, 1027–39).

setts Bay was a seaboard *élite*. Therefore, granted that most adult males could qualify for the franchise—as Professor Brown has sought to demonstrate—the source of their ultimate commitment to the cause of political freedom would seem to have been the influence upon their thinking exercised by this seaboard *élite*. As Professor William Nelson of the University of Toronto has stated: "The Revolution was genuinely two-sided: it meant alienation, but it also meant liberation"[6]—on the one hand instilling a hatred of the government of Great Britain in place of the old sentiments of loyalty, and on the other promoting visions of the great future that awaited a liberated America.

Such an interpretation helps to harmonize the concept of a middle-class democracy in Massachusetts Bay with the view of Professor Arthur M. Schlesinger that colonials "unhesitatingly took for granted the concept of a graded society," at the top of which was an "aristocracy" of talent and wealth. Those who composed this ruling group by and large "considered themselves trustees for the common good. . . . In all the colonies men of quality occupied responsible posts in every sphere of official activity." This was possible because of "the conviction that only the rich and wellborn possessed the required wisdom and capacity. . . . Nor did their role . . . excite resentment among the mass of the population. Men in every walk of life not only accepted the concept of a layered society, but believed in its rightness."[7]

Assuming that both Schlesinger's and Brown's views are correct, the two concepts may be reconciled on the basis that the ruling *élite* had become convinced that its own power was threatened by the new British measures. In order to preserve its control, therefore, the *élite* was pushing the general mass of the people to revolt against the threatening authority of the mother country by persuading the colonials that they must preserve an existing middle-class democracy, without avowing that such a democracy was, in effect, itself controlled by this same aristocratic ruling group.

In 1956 Professor Brown produced *Charles Beard and the Constitution: A Critical Analysis of "An Economic Interpretation of the Constitution"* in eleven chapters, each paralleling Beard's chapters,

---

[6] "The Revolutionary Character of the American Revolution," *American Historical Review*, LXX, 988–1014.

[7] "The Aristocracy in Colonial America," *Massachusetts Historical Society Proceedings*, LXXIV, 3–21.

which are placed under relentless scrutiny. The book is germane to this historiography only in the extent to which it is based upon a consideration of American pre-revolutionary political institutions. In it Brown re-emphasized his findings associating the prevalence of middle-class democracy in colonial times with the wide-spread possession of property and the franchise. He sought to show how untenable was Beard's thesis that people whose wealth was largely in personalty rather than in land dominated the Constitutional Convention of 1787 in order to secure their class ends; he also judged Beard's second thesis, that "the Constitution was put over undemocratically in an undemocratic society" (p. 194) to be equally untenable.[8] As an addendum to this study, Boston University Press published in 1963 a volume entitled *Reinterpretation of the Formation of the American Constitution,* which embodied three lectures delivered by Professor Brown at Boston University[9]—lectures that served to summarize his two earlier books.

Virginia, 1705–1786: Democracy or Aristocracy?, published in 1964 and written by Professor Brown and B. Katherine Brown, his wife, is his fourth study to challenge early scholarship on the eighteenth century. This book places all students of American colonial history in debt to the Browns for their account of the voting franchise, the electorate, election practices, and the electoral record in eighteenth-century Virginia, with separate chapters devoted to each of these topics. But the authors' efforts to prove that other writers have been mistaken in dealing with the lack of democracy in eighteenth-century Virginia have led them to undervalue such works as the late Charles S. Sydnor's *Political Leadership in Eighteenth-Century Virginia* (1951) and his *Gentlemen Freeholders: Political Practice in Walington's Virginia* (1952), Bridenbaugh's *Seat of Empire: The Political Role of Eighteenth-Century Williamsburg* (1950), and his *Myths and Realities: Societies of the Colonial South* (1952); and especially Jack P. Greene's "Foundations of Political Power in the Virginia House of Burgesses, 1720–1776," *William and Mary Quar-*

---

[8] For reviews of *Charles Beard and the Constitution* see H. C. Syrett in the *Political Science Quarterly,* LXXI, 608–9; E. C. Kirkland in the *American Historical Review,* LXII, 152–3; C. B. Swisher in the *Mississippi Valley Historical Review* (now *A Journal of American History*), XLIII, 338–9; Maurice Klain in the *American Political Science Review,* L, 1154–6; W. A. Williams's long review in the *William and Mary Quarterly,* XIV, 3rd ser., 442–8; and H. H. Bellot in the *English Historical Review,* LXXII, 568–9.

[9] For reviews of Brown's *Reinterpretation . . .* see E. L. McKitrick in the *American Historical Review,* LXIX, 236–7, and Staughton Lynd in the *Political Science Quarterly,* LXXIX, 116–18.

terly, 3rd ser., XVI, 485–506. They do not refer at all to Greene's *The Quest for Power: The Lower Houses of Assembly in the Southern Royal Colonies, 1689–1776*, doubtless published too late in 1963 to be available. While a careful study of aristocracy in Virginia is needed, it may be stated here that in the view of eighteenth-century Virginians a new *élite* was constantly being recruited from families that previously could not qualify. "Based largely upon wealth," according to Professor Greene, "this native aristocracy was never a closed social group; social lines remained fluid throughout the eighteenth century. Newcomers or older settlers who gained wealth were readily accepted by established families. . . . This constant replenishing of the gentry was an important factor in maintaining its vigor. . . ."[10] This group directed the political destinies of eighteenth-century Virginia after achieving the role of leadership by reason of the education and immersion in public affairs that its wealth permitted. Even the Virginia study by the Browns presents evidence of the aristocratic aspirations of the people: for example, they make the point that the man who did not own a slave sought to procure one; those who owned only one or two sought to add to them so that in time they might acquire the means to enter the ranks of the great families.[11]

What mars Professor Brown's important contributions to our understanding of the late colonial period is a certain belligerence toward fellow workers in this field; added to this is his tendency to avoid all evidence that might call into question the viewpoints he has put forward with such great skill. In fact one cannot avoid contrasting the spirit in which Brown has written with that of Jackson Turner Main, whose excellently researched book on *The Social Structure of Revolutionary America* (Princeton, N.J., 1965) suggests that in viewing the trend toward an egalitarian middle-class society of rather conspicuous social mobility during the period from 1763 to 1788, conclusions must remain quite tentative until all the local records have been examined.[12]

❉   ❉   ❉   ❉

[10] Jack P. Greene: *The Quest for Power* . . . (North Carolina, 1963), pp. 23–4.

[11] For reviews of *Virginia, 1705–1788: Democracy or Aristocracy?* see Carl Bridenbaugh in the *American Historical Review*, LXX, 472–3, and Emory G. Evans in the *Virginia Magazine of History and Biography*, LXXIII, 356–8.

[12] In further contrast to the careful documentation of Professors Brown and Main is the intriguing work by W. S. Sachs and Ari Hoogenboom: *The Enterprising Colonials: Society on the Eve of the Revolution* (Chicago, 1965), which suggests new approaches, but fails to document them adequately.

In concluding these sketches the author is fully aware of his sins of omission (whatever may be those of commission). But he can assure the reader that in the *Bibliographical Guide* to follow in the series, the important work of those not here included will be given all due recognition possible.

General Index

Historiographical Index

Adair, Douglass: editor of Oliver's *American Rebellion*, 302; on the work of Boyd, 422

Adams, Amos, early history of New England by, 298

Adams, Charles Francis: on Grahame's *History*, 251; pamphlet by, attacked by Fisher, 365

Adams, Charles Kendall, on Hildreth, 353

Adams, James Truslow, on Palfrey, 363n

Adams, John, on the work of Gordon, 322; and Mercy Otis Warren, 332n–3n

Adams, Randolph G.: work of, on the American Revolution, 218; views of, challenged by Morgan, 442

Adolphus, John, historiographical essay on, 235–7

Alden, John Richard: on the causes of the American Revolution, 220; historiographical essay on, 436–41

Alvord, Clarence Walworth: Van Tyne's dependence on the work of, 389; historiographical essay on, 395–6

Andrews, Charles McLean: on Channing's work, 370; on Osgood's work, 373, 374n; historiographical essay on, 376–82; on Dickerson's work, 404; on Schlesinger's work, 408

Aptheker, Herbert, work of, on the causes of the American Revolution, 217

Auchmuty, James Johnston, on Lecky, 260n

Bailyn, Bernard, work of, on American revolutionary thought, 222

Bancroft, George: on Belknap, 318; on Gordon, 325 and n; on the work of Holmes, 334; on Trumbull, 337n–8n; historiographical essay on, 341–8; on Hutchinson, 346n; Hildreth as a rival of, 350–1

Bassett, John Spencer, on George Bancroft's work, 347

Becker, Carl Lotus: work of, on the nature of the American Revolution, 216; historiographical essay on, 391–5; on Alvord, 398; work of, praised by Boyd, 421; views of, challenged, 442

Beer, George Louis: on the conquest of Canada and the American Revolution, 380; historiographical essay on, 382–7

Belknap, Rev. Jeremy: historiographical essay on, 315–18; association of, with Gordon, 322n

Bell, Whitfield J., Jr., and the *Franklin Papers*, 414

Bellot, H. Hale, on Namier, 279

Beloff, Max, work of, on the causes of the American Revolution, 216

Belsham, William, historiographical essay on, 233–5

Bisset, Robert, historiographical essay on, 237–9

Boorstin, Daniel J., work of, on conservative forces in the American Revolution, 219

Boucher, Rev. Jonathan, historiographical essay on, 326–30

Bowen, Francis: on Bancroft's *History*, 347; on Palfrey's *New England*, 360–1

Boyd, Julian Parks, historiographical essay on, 419–23

Brebner, John Bartlet, historiographical essay on, 295–7

Bridenbaugh, Carl: historiographical essay on, 423–8; on Miller's work, 431; work of, undervalued by the Browns, 452

Bridenbaugh, Jessica, collaboration of, with Carl Bridenbaugh, 425

Brooke, John: Namier's influence on, 280; as a historian, 280 and n, 281

Brougham, Henry Peter, Baron of Brougham and Vaux, historiographical essay on, 253–4

A NOTE ABOUT THE AUTHOR

LAWRENCE HENRY GIPSON is Research Professor of History, Emeritus, at Lehigh University. After receiving a bachelor of arts degree from the University of Idaho, he entered Oxford as the first Rhodes Scholar from the state of Idaho; there he gained a degree in the Oxford Honours School of Modern History. He was later a Bulkley Fellow in the graduate school at Yale, where his doctoral dissertation, *Jared Ingersoll: A Study of American Loyalism in Relation to British Colonial Government,* received the Porter Prize as the best work in literary form presented by a student in any division of the university during the preceding year; it was also awarded the Justin Winsor Prize by the American Historical Association. Since then he has written and published many works relating to colonial history (including thirteen volumes of his *magnum opus;* the bibliography is in preparation). During the academic year 1951–2 he occupied the Harmsworth Chair in American History at Oxford; he also has been a member of the board of editors of the *American Historical Review,* was a founder of the Conference on Early American History, and is a past president of both the Conference on British Studies and the Pennsylvania Historical Association. He is the Honorary Consultant in American Colonial History to the Library of Congress for the period 1965 through 1967. Many prizes and honours have come to him as a result of his writing, including the Loubat, Bancroft, and Pulitzer prizes and, most recently, his election as Honorary Fellow of Lincoln College, Oxford University.

March 1967

A NOTE ON THE TYPE

THE TEXT of this book is set in *Caledonia,* a typeface designed by W(ILLIAM) A(DDISON) DWIGGINS for the Mergenthaler Linotype Company in 1939. Dwiggins chose to call his new typeface Caledonia, the Roman name for Scotland, because it was inspired by the Scotch types cast about 1833 by Alexander Wilson & Son, Glasgow type founders. However, there is a calligraphic quality about this face that is totally lacking in the Wilson types. Dwiggins referred to an even earlier typeface for this "liveliness of action"—one cut around 1790 by William Martin for the printer William Bulmer. Caledonia has more weight than the Martin letters, and the bottom finishing strokes (serifs) of the letters are cut straight across, without brackets, to make sharp angles with the upright stems, thus giving a "modern face" appearance.

W. A. Dwiggins (1880–1956) was born in Martinsville, Ohio, and studied art in Chicago. In 1904 he moved to Hingham, Massachusetts, where he built a solid reputation as a designer of advertisements and as a calligrapher. He began an association with the Mergenthaler Linotype Company in 1929, and over the next twenty-seven years designed a number of book types for that firm. Of especial interest are the Metro series, Electra, Caledonia, Eldorado, and Falcon. In 1930, Dwiggins first became interested in marionettes, and through the years made many important contributions to the art of puppetry and the design of marionettes.

Composed, printed, and bound by
Kingsport Press, Inc., Kingsport, Tenn.

Typography and binding based on designs by
W. A. DWIGGINS